CONTENTS

INTRODUCTION

A welcome to this mighty tome, an explanation of important principles, an introduction to the Most Glorious Empire of His Majesty Emperor Karl-Franz I, and an intercepted communication of curious origin.

CHARACTER

A comprehensive primer on how to create your Character and adventuring party for fun and profit!

CLASS AND CAREERS

The exhilarating opportunities for employment in the Old World. This marvellous chapter also informs you how to apply the experience you earn through your efforts, how your status in society affects you, and how you can attempt to improve your position.

SKILLS AND TALENTS

All the abilities you might choose to become adept with, complete with explanations and ways in which you can put them to good use!

RULES

The accurate naming of this chapter defies florid exposition! The mechanisms of the game, incorporating Tests – the main method of adjudicating the action – and sections covering many different situations that may arise!

BETWEEN ADVENTURES

Those events that take place between your escapades, with a menu of options for you to pursue.

RELIGION AND BELIEF

Descriptions of the gods of the Old World and their cults and worshippers. Also contains the blessings and miracles undertaken by those following the divine. Be warned this chapter also touches on blasphemous knowledge best avoided!

MAGIC

Only sinister and deluded fools will dare explore the pages of this catalogue of the arcane and profane. Unless you're a Wizard from the Colleges of Magic, in which case it's required reading.

THE GAMEMASTER

Advice for those who find themselves in charge of an unruly mob. This section also gives advice on travel in the Empire and rewarding those who perform well in the face of inevitable misfortune.

GLORIOUS REIKLAND

All hail the heartland of the Empire – the Glorious Reikland. Sprawling cities, deep dark forests, and awe-inspiring mountains, the Reikland is yours to explore.

THE CONSUMERS' GUIDE

Money, weapons, armour, goods, and services, all presented for your consideration and purchase, should you be able to afford such luxuries!

BESTIARY

All manner of vile creatures you might encounter on your adventures, and details of their capabilities.

CREDITS

Design and Development: Dominic McDowall and Andy Law
Writing: Dave Allen, Gary Astleford, Graeme Davis, Jude Hornborg,
Andy Law, Lindsay Law, Andrew Leask, TS Luikart, Dominic McDowall, Clive Oldfield
Editing: Andy Law, Lindsay Law, Andrew Leask
Art Direction: Jon Hodgson
Cover: Ralph Horsley
Illustration: Dave Allsop, Michael Franchina, Andrew Hepworth, Jon Hodgson,
Ralph Horsley, Pat Loboyko, Sam Manley, Scott Purdy
Graphic Design and Layout: Paul Bourne
Maps: Andy Law
Proofreading: Jacob Rodgers

Special thanks to the Games Workshop Team.

Further thanks to all the fans who took time to contact us by email, by Facebook,
and on Discord during the preview period. Without all of you, this book would not be the same.

Published by Cubicle 7 Entertainment Ltd,
Unit 6, Block 3, City North Business Campus,
Co. Meath, Ireland. Printed in China.

• INTRODUCTION •

'So, what are you here for? Adventure?
Maybe. Gold? Probably. Justice?

Ha, that's a flexible term! What's that I see in your eye, that pious gleam? Oh, you want to do the right thing. So long as it's well enough paid, entertaining, and fits with your political views. Eh, close enough, you'll do, come inside and I'll tell you about the job.'

Welcome to **Warhammer Fantasy Roleplay**. Marvellous things await you. One of your group will control an entire world, while the rest of you will live in and explore it, uncovering glittering wonders, vile darkness, and everything in between.

You'll meet glorious heroes who grimace disdainfully as they step over the suffering poor, and corrupt villains who set down the wrong path in the service of a more laudable cause. Feared but respected wizards master their arts in the high towers of the Colleges of Magic, while outside those safe halls magic users are feared and reviled — and often with good cause, as many dark sorcerers would gladly sell their souls for power. Virtuous priests strive endlessly to improve the lives of the downtrodden, whilst agents of Chaos Gods work to undermine this good work and bring ruination.

Prepare yourself for the struggle of the gutter, to fight for your survival, and to face corruption on all sides. Prepare yourself for danger, as it is everywhere, and you can't face it alone. And, most of all, prepare yourself for the grim and perilous adventure of **Warhammer Fantasy Roleplay**!

ROLEPLAYING GAMES

Warhammer Fantasy Roleplay (WFRP) is a tabletop roleplaying game (RPG). You might be more familiar with computer or console RPGs, in which case you'll be right at home. One of your group will take the role of Gamemaster (GM) — who describes the world and what is happening — and everyone else will be a Player — one of the game's protagonists, interacting with the world the GM presents. Players tell the GM what their

THROWING BONES

Games of **WFRP** use ten-sided dice whenever a random result is required. Ten-sided dice are typically marked from 0–9, where a roll of 0 counts as a result of 10. These dice are called d10s in the rules, and the number you need to roll will always be marked as follows: 1d10 for 1 die, 2d10 for two dice, 3d10 for three dice, and so on.

If you are requested to roll multiple dice like this, the results are always added together. So, if the rules ask you to roll 2d10, you roll two ten-sided dice and add the result of each together; for example: a roll of 0 and 3 would be a result of 13 (10+3=13).

Sometimes, a die roll will be modified by adding or subtracting a number. So, a roll of 1d10+4 means roll one ten-sided die and add four to the result, and a roll of 2d10−3 indicates you should roll 2 ten-sided dice and subtract 3 from the totalled result.

The rules also use a roll of two ten-sided dice to score a number from 1 to 100 (marked as 1d100). To do this, one ten-sided die is designated as a 'tens' die, and the other as the 'units' die. Now roll the two dice, and read the result as a two-digit number. So a roll of 1 on the tens die and 4 on the units die provides a result of 14, or a roll of 4 and 2 results with 42. If both dice roll 0, the result is 100.

Characters are doing, and the GM interprets the outcomes of those actions, using the game's rules where necessary. The game proceeds in that fashion, with the Players pursuing the plot the GM has prepared for the game, or perhaps going off at wild tangents as the poor GM improvises like crazy. It's all good.

This book is the rulebook and includes all the information and options for running your games of **WFRP**. If you've never played an RPG before, we'd recommend you try the **Warhammer Fantasy Roleplay Starter Set** — which is designed to teach you how to play — or take a look at the 'What is an RPG?' section of our website: www.cubicle7.co.uk.

USING THIS BOOK

Roughly speaking, the Player-focused parts of this book are to the front. New players should start by browsing the double-page spreads and letter that introduce the Empire as this is where the initial adventures that **Cubicle 7** publishes will be set.

Players should then use the next few chapters to learn about their Characters and abilities. Chapter 5, the Rules, are for everyone. Players whose characters have a religious or magical background will want to be familiar with the respective sections later in the book. The GM can communicate to the Players as much or as little of the Reikland and Bestiary chapters as they should appropriately know, but remember not to give away too many spoilers.

Game Text

To help keep the rules clear, this book adopts some standard ways of presenting information:

Game Terms: All game terms are capitalised, so you can tell events from Events, and know when a test should be simple and when you should make a Simple Test.

Individual Items: Some game terms encompass many individual items. For example: the game term Spells includes many individual spells a wizard can cast. Each individual item will be italicised. **Example:** a *Banking* Endeavour; a *Bleeding* Condition; the *Curse* Spell.

Tests: When you are asked to make a Test (see page 149), it will be **bolded** so you can find it easily during play. **Example:** make an **Average (+20) Perception** Test.

Acronyms: The rulebook avoids them as much as possible, but it's important in roleplaying games (RPGs) like **Warhammer Fantasy Roleplay** (**WFRP** — we pronounce it WuffRupp) to explain your acronyms the first time the word is used. The Gamemaster (GM) who runs the game can usually clear up any confusion.

Advice: Our Characters are on hand in box-outs throughout the book to offer advice and options. Each discusses different elements of the game. If you want to know more about the Characters, refer to the **WFRP Starter Set**.

Your Warhammer

Warhammer Fantasy Roleplay and the Old World is a phenomenon over 30 years in the making, and we all have our own take on this rich and vibrant setting. That's something we really want to celebrate, and we want your adventures to take place in your version of Warhammer.

Throughout the book we present as many options as we can so that you can tailor the game to your vision, many of which are marked clearly with '**Options:**'. If anything contradicts how you want to play your game, please feel free to change it.

What's Next?

In addition to this rulebook and the **WFRP Starter Set**, there will be regularly published supplements, sourcebooks, and adventures to support the game and expand its scope. Visit www.cubicle7.co.uk for more information, free resources for the game (including a free adventure), and to sign up to our newsletter.

The borders of the Glorious Empire of His Imperial Majesty Emperor Karl-Franz I are the impenetrable plate armour He has erected to protect His people. The Empire extends to the seas, or until the land ceases to be of worth, such as the wasteland stubbornly clung to by those fools in Marienburg. The Bountiful Empire of His Imperial Majesty Emperor Karl-Franz I is of course the envy of all those who survey it, turning all eyes to covetousness. But fear not, for His Imperial Majesty Emperor Karl-Franz I is resolute in our defence, with unbreachable fortresses full of indefatigable soldiers at every mountain pass, river bridge, and other such strategic locations.

The Empire is beset by enemies to all sides, and the defence of its borders is often compromised by the politicking nobles, from lowly barons to the Elector Counts who rule them. Fortunately, mountain ranges and coastlines form a natural barrier along much of the Empire's borders, all of which provide natural lines of defence. Guard duty overlooking a potential invasion route is often a lonely, mind-numbingly dull affair; and, when it's not, chances are the garrison will be overrun long before the alarm is raised.

Many claim the Court of His Imperial Majesty Emperor Karl-Franz I is the heart of the Empire. The Emperor Himself would strike such lickspittles and point out with wisdom and deep humility that it is instead the countless villages of His mighty Empire that supply His limitless strength. For it is there His people nobly toil to provide food for all, to produce goods and raw materials for trade, and raise doughty warriors for the glorious State Armies that protect us. It is a simple life, satisfyingly full of blessed toil, which is its own reward. In many ways, we desk-bound scholars, while unswerving in our duty to His Imperial Majesty Emperor Karl-Franz I, are truly envious of life in this rural paradise.

Far from the courts, peasants tirelessly work the land, much as they have for longer than any can remember. The village boundary is, for most, the end of their world. Some might travel to neighbouring settlements, but such journeys are viewed with trepidation. This can lead to xenophobia, which is often acutely felt towards nearby settlements, probably due to historic conflict over local resources; so, while a visitor from Altdorf may be treated with suspicion, villagers reserve their real hatred for that wretch from the hamlet a few miles yonder who stole their grandfather's chicken.

By the light of day, villagers may scoff at old tales of monsters, beasts, and daemons, believing in the power of their lords and gods to protect them. But as the sun sets over the forest and fields, all lock their doors securely and, in flickering candlelight, exchange nervous glances at any unexpected sound.

It is said the mighty rivers bear the lifeblood of the Resplendent Empire of His Imperial Majesty Emperor Karl-Franz I, flowing from the mineral-laden mountains to bring wealth and prosperity for all. The masters of robust riverboats and barges keep a lucrative flow of goods moving from the furthest reaches of the Empire of His Imperial Majesty Emperor Karl-Franz I to the bustling cities and ports, bringing riches beyond compare. This is all made possible by the eternal vigilance and unstinting protection offered by His Imperial Majesty Emperor Karl-Franz I's Imperial Navy and Imperial River Patrol, who efficiently guard all of His river-borne citizens allowing them to concentrate on their admirable hard work without pause for fear or doubt.

If the rivers bear the Empire's lifeblood, the arteries and veins they flow through are in dangerously poor condition. The Imperial Navy patrols the wide flows of the primary rivers, and Riverwardens theoretically keep watch everywhere else, but minor waterways can go months without seeing a hint of the Emperor's protection. As a result, wreckers and pirates can be found anywhere outside the immediate scrutiny of the authorities, and as the rivers wind through the forest depths, who knows what cruel or unnatural creatures wait to ambush passing vessels. When travelling lesser trafficked stretches, wise folk should be obviously armed and clearly ready for a fight in the hope of persuading those with ill intent to allow them to pass in favour of easier pickings.

The docks of His Imperial Majesty Emperor Karl-Franz I's ports are engineering marvels established to profit from His shrewd trade policies and diplomatic brilliance. Dealing firmly and authoritatively with lesser realms, yet always with magnanimity, His Imperial Majesty Emperor Karl-Franz I has ensured our extraordinary prosperity through lucrative treaties with a range of diverse peoples including the fading power of the Elves from across the sea, the barbaric Kislevites to the east, and the short-sighted Wastelanders who cannot survive without the food we generously provide. But these fade into inconsequentiality when compared to the profound alliance His Imperial Majesty Emperor Karl-Franz I unstintingly maintains with the redoubtable Dwarfs of the mountains, a wise accord that has stood since it was initiated by Holy Sigmar Himself, First Emperor and God-King of us all!

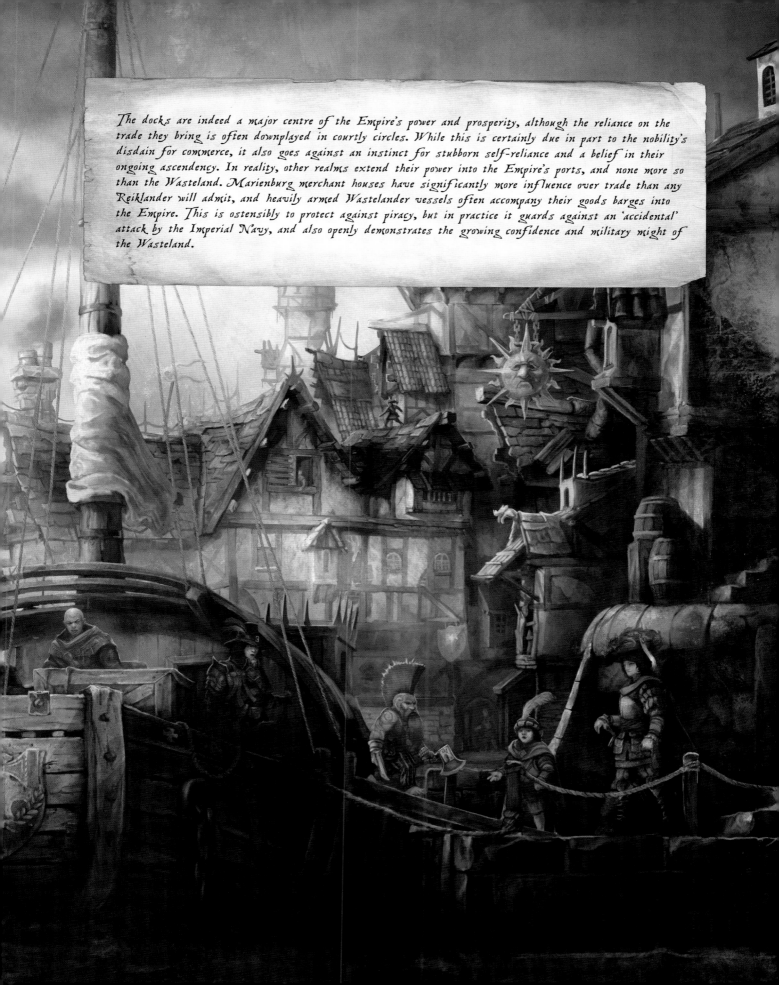

The docks are indeed a major centre of the Empire's power and prosperity, although the reliance on the trade they bring is often downplayed in courtly circles. While this is certainly due in part to the nobility's disdain for commerce, it also goes against an instinct for stubborn self-reliance and a belief in their ongoing ascendency. In reality, other realms extend their power into the Empire's ports, and none more so than the Wasteland. Marienburg merchant houses have significantly more influence over trade than any Reiklander will admit, and heavily armed Wastelander vessels often accompany their goods barges into the Empire. This is ostensibly to protect against piracy, but in practice it guards against an 'accidental' attack by the Imperial Navy, and also openly demonstrates the growing confidence and military might of the Wasteland.

The powerful and awe-inspiring towns and cities of the prosperous Empire are the crown jewels of His Imperial Majesty Emperor Karl-Franz I's realm. Rich, cultured, pious, educated, and thriving, their extraordinary planning and awe-inspiring architecture are the envy of all, and bring wide-eyed travellers from across the world to witness their magnificence. Under the nurturing rule of His Imperial Majesty Emperor Karl-Franz I, each of His multitudinous subjects have opportunities to better themselves and rise to lofty new stations. Even the simple folk of the Empire, despite their lowly and often distasteful appearance, are industrious and optimistic, always seeking new opportunities for the betterment of all.

The major settlements of the Empire may feature some of the most impressive architecture, glorious palaces, and inspirational temples, but these are all surrounded by disgusting filth and squalor, staggering inequality, and incredible levels of crime and disorder. The upper classes are frequently drunk on the power they wield, or corrupted by something much worse, and so the possibility of positive change and improvement in conditions is negligible. This leads to social disorder, agitators brewing discontent, and all-too-many desperate people with little to lose.

The simple, yet glorious inns of His Imperial Majesty Emperor Karl-Franz I's Empire are part of what binds His loyal people together. His Imperial Majesty Emperor Karl-Franz I Himself is said to frequent them in cunning disguises in order to share in the jolly camaraderie and simple pleasures of the thankful common folk, whilst graciously not over-awing these good, honest people with His astonishing Imperial Magnificence. The Empire's finest fare can be found in these palaces of the people, and your humble scribe heartily recommends pickled trotter as a digestive aid.

Inns and taverns are a distraction from the misery of existence for many citizens of the Empire, and an entertaining diversion for many more. They can often be places where political agitators do their work to whip up sentiment against the authorities, or where witch hunters prowl for rumours of the unnatural. Con artists and robbers also ply their trade amongst the inebriated unwary, although there is also some honest respite to be had, and the scribe is right about the pickled trotter.

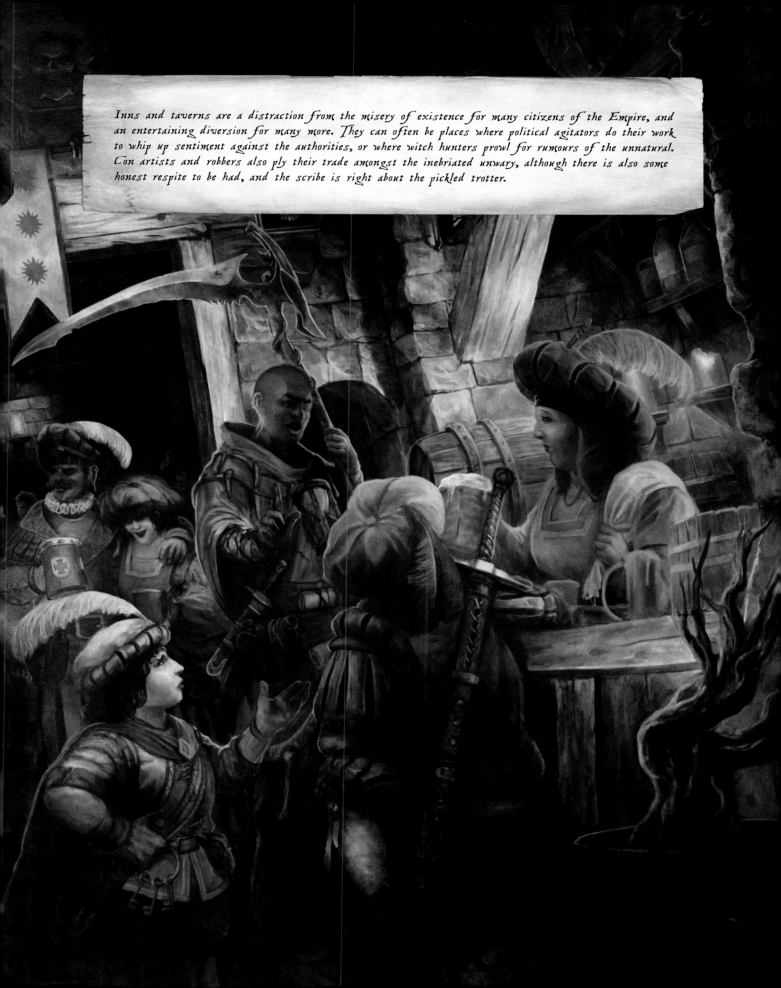

c/o Colonel Reikhardt Mathis Sievers of the Imperial Ostlanders
Wolfenburg's 2nd Regiment of Foot
Stationed in Khypris
The Border Princes

32nd Sigmarzeit, 2511 IC

My Lord Konrad von Siert, Baron of Siert and Castellan of Ostergrootsch,
Greetings and salutations,

Herein find a summons and general information concerning the Empire, your homeland.

I am instructed to inform you that your lord and father, Duke Ottokar von Siert, officially recognises your claim to inherit his land and titles within the Reikland, and orders you to his side. Your exile in the Border Princes is at an end, and you must make immediate preparations for departure.

In his wisdom, your father has employed an armed escort to assist. I am in command, and, Sigmar willing, will arrive sometime near Sonnestill. You will leave with us for the Imperial capital the following morning. Surely, such news will fill your young heart with joy, for you will finally witness the splendour of the greatest city in the Old World: Altdorf the magnificent, seat of Emperor Karl-Franz I and the Grand Theogonist of Sigmar, and current residence of House Siert, where your father holds court not far from the Imperial Zoo on Goellner Hill.

I shall also take your education in hand. Those advising your father believe the present tuition you receive from Colonel Sievers, whilst certainly admirable, is too focussed on southern matters as epitomised by Holy Myrmidia — a goddess without reproach when it comes to the military, I'm sure, but hardly an expert concerning Reiklander rulership. It was decided by your father's advisors that a true devotee of Sigmar — the Empire's patron deity — should promptly take charge of your education. Your father, of course, agreed, for the Cult of Sigmar should always be heeded.

Sadly, I must report poor Sister Bartalin, the nun assigned to this important duty, passed through Morr's Portal when our party was but five days from Altdorf. She was the victim of a most unfortunate accident involving a bedpan, a wilted stick of celery, and a nasty fall. Thus, I humbly take her stead. For, no matter my feelings on the subject, your schooling is imperative; you have yet to set foot in the Empire, and you will be lost without proper instruction.

Before we begin, let us turn to introductions: I am Guardian Alanna Graumann of the Grey Order — and let me pre-empt your assumptions: yes, I am a witch; and, yes, my name is a pseudonym. I have been in the service of your father for over fifteen years, acting as an aide, military advisor, and bodyguard, amongst other things, and am now charged to ensure you, his newly declared heir, reach Altdorf alive. To guarantee this I will, as mentioned, attend to your education, which will start immediately.

Forget What You Know
There are several matters I would have you consider before I arrive in Khypris. You likely think life in the Empire will be much the same as the sunny lifestyle you currently enjoy in the Border Princes — after all, there are the same eight days in the week, the same sun and moons, and the same gods. I regret to inform you such presumptions are incorrect: the Empire is not like the Border Princes, and you are ill-prepared for the threats it hides. Put plainly: you are not safe, and most of what you think you know will lead you to danger.

The Gods

As you know, throughout the Old World folk freely worship many different gods, most commonly those directly impacting their daily lives. So, if someone is hurt, one prays to Shallya, Goddess of Healing and Mercy; when a hunt fails, one prays to Taal, God of Animals and Wild Places; and if crops should wither, one turns to Rhya, Goddess of Life and Fertility.

But in your homeland, one god rises head and shoulders above the others: Sigmar, who founded the Empire when mortal, and now stands as its patron deity. In the grand province where your lands lie, the Reikland, the Cult of Sigmar dominates: every village has a temple, every town has several, and the capital, Altdorf, has more holy sites dedicated to Sigmar than any bother to count. Each Festag (what the locals call the last day of the week – the one you call 'Holiday'), all are expected to attend 'throng' at a local temple, where Sigmar's priests preach lessons concerning the founder of the Empire, he who wielded the Warhammer. Further, many temples require all able bodied folk to train at arms weekly with the local priests or their representatives, forming the core of local militias to support the State Armies. In larger towns and cities, it is only the faithful and the lost that attend these weekly duties, but in rural areas, any not attending are viewed with deep suspicion. Trust me, my lord, this is a cult you will need to understand, for most folk of the Reikland are ingrained with its customs, and you must appear to be, also. You may think you understand Sigmar because there is a shrine in Khypris. You do not.

Witches

One cannot talk of Sigmar without also discussing witches – those able to use magic. Obviously, it's a subject close to my heart, although I prefer to be called a Magister, as I am trained by the Colleges of Magic. The folk of the Empire, like all peoples of the Old World, are solid and practical, and quick to remove dangerous elements from their communities. Given the Cult of Sigmar preaches that Sigmar was tempted and betrayed by evil witches, it will come as no surprise that in areas of strong Sigmar worship, witches are not just viewed with suspicion, they are vilified. Fortunately, the talent for witchery is very rare, but for those born with it any unexpected manifestation of their arcane powers may see them burned at the stake, even if Imperial Law states they should be taken to the Colleges of Magic.

The Colleges of Magic

There is no formal centre of magical learning in the Border Princes. Those able to do magic either work it out independently, accidentally kill themselves, are hunted down, or find a master to teach them. Most such masters practice ancient forms of magic that are certainly dangerous, ranging from supposedly benign hedge witches and seers to those who risk their very souls, including power-blinded fools like necromancers and daemonologists. In the Empire, it's very different. To practice any magic you must have a licence, and the only way to secure one is to be a graduated Wizard of the Colleges of Magic in Altdorf, or be an Elf – they receive special dispensation for their part in founding the Colleges – assuming they register with the Colleges, of course. If you have no licence and cast magic, you are breaking the law and should be either taken to the Colleges for proper training or tried as a criminal. Most commonly, illegal witches are tried by mob and lynched. Which, to be clear, is also illegal, although few are punished for this crime as most would prefer to see a witch dead, regardless of the legality. While murdering suspected witches may sound extreme to your ears, there are good reasons for caution: all witches channel the Winds of Magic, invisible flows of power that course across the world, and many claim these Winds originate from the Ruinous Powers.

The Ruinous Powers

The less I speak of this the better, and might I suggest you never speak of it. There is always something listening. At its simplest, whatever your current tutors pretend, the dark gods *do* exist. They whisper of the ruination of all things, and too many fools listen. But do the Winds of Magic blow from the Ruinous Powers, turning good folk into witches, and twisting minds and flesh in their wake? That's not a question I think I can answer. What I can say is that the dark gods' influence is felt at all levels of society, and those drawing too close are always changed by what they encounter. This is why folk are terrified of mutation: they believe it is a mark of damnation, a sign the dark gods now hold your soul. Even talking in the most general terms about such subjects may well bring you to the attention of the witch hunters, so remain wary for signs of this dark corruption but do not betray that you are even aware of its existence.

The Powers That Be

'In the Borderlands, all may come to power, and all may come to rule! In the Empire, we willingly wrap ourselves in chains!'

Those were the ardent words of a young, idealistic agitator I met in Wissenburg. Consider what she says, for you will soon encounter those who believe it true. In the Empire, you are born to a station, and no amount of cleverness or capability will change what the gods plan, or so those in power repeatedly claim. If you are born noble, you are forever noble; born farming, forever farming. And so it remains. But as you personally know, my lord, the chance offerings of birth can be changed and manipulated by forces far from divine. And even in the Empire, new freedoms are being bought every day.

The Cities and Towns

For all the stratified layers of society are supposedly immutable, the flourishing towns and cities of the Empire, safely wrapped with high walls of stone and patrolled by liveried State Soldiers, have allowed a new class of rich merchants and burghers to rise. The Reikland, as the richest of all the Empire's grand provinces, has a growing 'middle' class of such enormity it frequently rises to prominence, with rich individuals buying their way to freedom and power. An example of this are towns called 'Freiburgs' or 'free towns', meaning they self-govern without significant interference from the nobility in return for services, military support, or, most commonly, large quantities of coin. Although the concept of a Freiburg is old, never have so many been seen in such a small area as increasingly more towns are buying their freedom; although all this seemingly changes nothing for those toiling in the fields.

Rural Life

Where the towns and cities are becoming freer, it could be argued the opposite is the case for many rural communities. Over two hundred years ago, Emperor Magnus the Pious famously enshrined the rights of all to be paid for their labour, but many noble houses did not agree with this attack on their rights and continue to resist to this day.

Enlightened provinces such as the lands ruled by your father, where farmers work land they lease, selling any produce they harvest at local markets for personal profit, paying taxes as determined by the local authorities, are widespread. But in some isolated regions the peasantry are forced to slave on farms they do not own, turning over almost all produce to their lieges, living in total ignorance of the freedoms the Imperial Law grants them. Many folk will put up with a lot so long as horns echo across the land each campaign season as noble lords send the State Army to rid the encroaching forest of whatever foulness has gathered.

And it is there one of the greatest differences between your current home in Khypris and Sigmar's Holy Empire lies: the endless forests. The Empire is blanketed in dense woodlands, and few dare venture into their depths, for their twisted branches hide far worse than simple bandits, beastmen, and forest goblins.

Travel

Bisecting the Border Princes, the Khyprian Road is famous for its relative safety. Its entire six-hundred mile length is cleared on both sides for many miles, ensuring would-be bandits have few places to hide. The opposite circumstances apply in the Empire. Almost all the major roads cut through thick forests with uncounted ambush points, leaving travel by foot extraordinarily dangerous. Thus, wealthy folk travel by river as most major towns are connected by river or canal, and the major waterways of the Empire are often so wide you can barely see the opposite banks — let alone any potential wreckers hiding in the rushes — making them significantly safer than tree-lined highways where bandits lurk around every corner.

Of course, sometimes a road journey is the only option, especially when one is travelling to one of the many highland fortifications or mining towns. In such circumstances, I recommend you travel by coach. These not only provide comfortable travelling conditions between all major destinations, but their routes are patrolled by road wardens, making them relatively safe. The Empire is also significantly more civilised than the Border Princes, so boasts many reliable coaching houses.

Patrols

Recognising the threat posed by highway pillagers, all the major roads of the Reikland are patrolled by mounted squads of road wardens. Most are peacetime State Army cavalrymen put to use by local nobles, but some are privately hired, often by merchant or coaching houses, to better maintain the peace and protect expensive assets. When travelling away from the primary trade routes, the roads are not so well maintained, and some are lucky to ever see a road warden, so I suggest avoiding these dark corners of the Empire, for the local folk are often all too quick to take offense, all your trappings, and perhaps even your life.

The rivers are similarly patrolled, but by strong backed riverwardens in a variety of different vessels ranging from small patrol boats to small warships called Shipswords. These wardens are supported by the Imperial Navy, which is, against all the expectations of outsiders, based in the Reiksport at Altdorf, hundreds of miles upriver from the sea. The navy's large warships patrol the waters to Marienburg, where the river Reik is often many miles wide, and very deep.

The Law

The powers granted to wardens patrolling the rivers and roads, and to the watch patrolling the streets of the Empire's towns and cities, vary significantly from province to province. Small infractions of the law normally result in stern words and spot fines, most of which never leave the pocket of the lawman concerned. In larger towns and cities, it is also common to find petty courts run by watch captains who judge cases brought before them, handing out fines of a shilling or two for most misdeeds, with serious crimes referred to a higher authority. For such crimes, the accused is taken before a local court, most commonly officiated by a judge, noble, magistrate, or a cleric of the Goddess of Justice, Verena. These trials are rarely fair, so it is wise to never let matters proceed so far.

As a lord of the Reikland, you cannot be tried by a normal court, so should you ever find yourself accused, do not be afraid to make your birthright known. Should I not be with you, send word to the Grey College and ask for me by name. I will come. To be sure you understand, only your father, as your lord, has the right to judge you. However, another noble may appeal against your father's judgement; should this occur, only the High Lord Steward of the Reikland has the right to overrule your father in matters of criminal law.

But such almost never happens. The High Lord Steward has not held court for over fifty years, for most nobles are too powerful to bring to task. Instead, deals are made, charges are dropped, and the problems disappear.

Be Careful

So, given the many risks, I hope you can understand why your father sends an escort to ensure your safety. Your inexperience with the folk of the Empire could easily lead to disaster. For all you may think a local watchman is there to help you, or a riverwarden seems a helpful fellow, they may be as corrupt as the folk they are tasked to detain. This is why I come. Let my experience be your teacher, so you need not learn from your own errors, which could prove fatal. There is a reason I use a pseudonym, and why I feel it is important not to say aught openly.

There is, after all, hidden motivations behind all matters. Even this letter.

I look forward to seeing you when you understand. Be careful.

With faith,

A Graumann

Grey Guardian Alanna Graumann
Your servant and guardian.

• CHARACTER •

Players explore the Old World through the eyes of their Character. This chapter shows you how to make your own Character from scratch. Most begin the game as unremarkable inhabitants of the Empire — possibly destined for greatness, but no-one would guess it. That's not to say you can't rise from humble origins, just that you've got a long journey ahead, and that you'll probably need a better pair of boots.

All the information describing your Character's abilities is recorded on a Character Sheet (see page 344). We provide ready-made Characters and sheets in the **WFRP Starter Set**, and online at cubicle7.co.uk. Using ready-made Characters is a great way to start playing and find out how the game works, but sooner or later you'll want to create your own from the ground up. If you are choosing a ready-made Character, it's still worth looking through this chapter, as it will explain what the different parts of the Character Sheet mean (especially the summary on page 44).

When deciding what your Character will be like, discuss the kind of group you want to create with the other players. This makes sure that the group's Characters complement each other and that together you will have a broad and versatile range of abilities. Your GM may also have a particular kind of game in mind, and you'll need to make sure you have the right mix of Characters. Perhaps the GM plans for you to join a group of apprentice wizards who know one another at the Colleges of Magic? Maybe you are part of a unit of soldiers who have all deserted? Or maybe you are one of a disparate band of Reiklanders press-ganged into service by a powerful noble? Knowing this is important to help you build a suitable character which will be more fun to play.

Creating a Character

The first thing you'll need is a blank Character Sheet (see page 344 or the downloads section of cubicle7.co.uk), or a scrap sheet of paper. Once you have that, you'll follow nine steps to create your character. As you move through the nine steps, you'll record the information about your character as you go.

In some sections, you can either choose an option or accept the result of a dice roll to make the choice for you. You may receive bonus Experience Points (XP) for choosing to accept random

outcomes, as if the Dark Gods of Chaos themselves applaud your acceptance of random chance. XP represent learning from experience and are the principal way to improve your abilities — you will be able to spend these points to enhance your character's abilities. XP are covered in more detail in **Advancement** on page 43.

CHARACTER CREATION SUMMARY

1) Species: Page 24
2) Class and Career: Page 30
3) Attributes: Page 33
4) Skills and Talents: Page 35
5) Trappings: Page 37
6) Adding Detail: Page 37
7) Party : Page 41
8) Bringing Your Character To Life: Page 42
9) Advancement: Page 43

---

1) SPECIES

Summary: *Choose one of the five Species.*

Your Character will be a Human, Dwarf, Halfling, High Elf, or Wood Elf. They are described below to help you choose, where you will also find some typical opinions each species has of the others. Alternatively, you can roll 1d100, consult the Random Species Table, and gain +20 XP if you accept the result.

RANDOM SPECIES TABLE

1d100	Species
01–90	Human
91–94	Halfling
95–98	Dwarf
99	High Elf
00	Wood Elf

Humans (Reiklander)

Humans are the most numerous and widespread of the civilised species of the Old World. From the plains of the Estalian Kingdoms to the frozen oblasts of Imperial Kislev, Humans occupy every corner of the continent, and they thrive. The largest, most powerful Human realm is the Empire, a patchwork of powerful provinces blanketed in seemingly endless forests. Standing proud at the heart of this Empire, the Reikland is its richest, most cosmopolitan region.

Many Reiklanders see it as their divine right to rule, for the patron god of the Empire, Sigmar, was himself a Reiklander before he ascended to godhood many centuries ago. Temples and shrines to the god are found everywhere, and the majority of Reiklanders are devout believers in Sigmar's message of Empire and unity. Because of this, they are significantly more friendly, open, and optimistic than other folk, since what could possibly go wrong for a land that birthed a god? By comparison, outsiders often see them as arrogant, over-bearing meddlers who stick their unwanted noses into any affair.

Beyond their affluent lifestyles and pushy personalities, Reiklanders are largely the same as other Humans. They may be shorter-lived than other species, but Humans possess more vigour, versatility, and ambition. They also have a seemingly inextricable relationship with the insidious horrors of the Ruinous Powers, with more Humans falling to corruption than any other species. Perhaps it's no surprise the declining elder species grow increasingly concerned the meteoric rise of Humanity could result in cataclysm.

Opinions

On Dwarfs…
'They've been our allies since Sigmar walked this very city; fought with them meself back in '05. Sure, they're a bit stubborn, seriously vindictive and pretty blunt, but I won't hear a word said against them.'

– Reikäger Jungling, State Soldier from Altdorf

On Halflings…
'If I gets meself the sort wot eats and smokes all day, then I'm happy as Ranald in catnip. It's when I get them without proper manners nicking me crockery or knives and forks: that I just can't abide! They're all smiles and shrugs when the watch come to pick 'em up, like they don't understand what they done wrong.'

– Stefan Krause, Innkeeper from Stirgau

On High Elves…
'Yes, I do trade with them. And, no, don't be ridiculous, I've never been turned to a pillar of salt just by looking at them. Truly, I find them graceful and urbane. Proper civilised, I'd say. But, 'tween you and me, if Verena were to ask, I might also say I find them just… odd. So very intense. Like every deal we make **really matters**.'

– Dorothea Taalenstein, Merchant from Kemperbad

On Wood Elves…
'Elves of the forest you say? Ain't none of 'em around here, mate. You want to be goin' south to Bretonnia. I hear they gots loads of them, and that they're completely horrible!'

– Siggina Gerster, Bawd from Ubersreik

Dwarfs

Dwarfs — or 'Dawi' as they call themselves — are legendarily gruff and stubborn. While the majority reside in vast mountainside fortresses known as Holds, most larger towns and the capital of the Reikland also have Dwarf populations. Given their clannish nature, they tend to band together, forming enclaves or districts wherever they settle. Many of the Dwarfs living in Reikland are the descendants of those driven from Fallen Holds many centuries ago, but most still consider themselves as Dwarfs of the Grey Mountains, although some have never seen a hill, let alone a mountain.

Dwarf culture respects skill in crafting — chiefly stonework, smithing and engineering — and Dwarf Holds are resplendent with impressive feats of artifice. They also covet gold and jewels, mining deep beneath the mountains in the pursuit of precious metals and gemstones. However, more than these material possessions, Dwarfs venerate their elders and ancestors, and have entire religions focussing upon important progenitors. Dwarfs cannot cast spells, although their runesmiths carve artefacts with intricate runes to harness magical power.

However, their prowess as engineers is so impressive that some of their more ingenious clockwork or steam-powered devices are mistaken for magic by simpler folk.

Dwarfs are squat with thick, muscular limbs and stout, broad torsos. Their features are heavy and their hair is thick. Length of hair is a mark of pride and status amongst Dwarfs, with elaborate braids and adornments demonstrating rank: to shave a Dwarf causes terrible shame. Indeed, honour is a fundamental aspect of their character. Given their long memories and proud natures, they bear grudges against those who have slighted or dishonoured them, gripping tight to their grievances for many years, even taking on the grudges borne by their ancestors, knowing their forebears will be watching over them, nursing their bitterness long after death. Whilst it might be hard for others to win a Dwarf's friendship, once given it is absolute. While not as ageless as the near-immortal Elves, Dwarfs can live for many centuries. Indeed, some say that as long as a Dwarf has a purpose, they will not die unless struck down in battle, such is the strength of their conviction.

Opinions

On Reiklander Humans…

'Like my father and my father afore me, I've been living in Reikland all me life. As folk go, they know not to mess with my business, and show the respect I deserve, as is right. Yes, they're unreliable, and as changeable as the wind, but they're also resourceful and shrewd, so I'd recommend them as risky business partners, as they see solutions I'd not even consider.'

– Garral Herraksson, Jeweller from Eilhart

On Halflings…

'They're just not my kind of folk. Always smiling. Always fidgeting. Always talking. Always moving in big groups that just won't shut up! When they come in my store, I like to shoo them off with a broom. Really, what have they got to be so happy about? I just don't trust them.'

– Helgi Galannasniz, Burgher from Schrabwald

On High Elves…

'Don't talk to me about those bloody bastards! Alrug Skycaster, my ultimate granduncle, was bloody betrayed in the bloody War of bloody Vengeance by those… those… ARGH! It's our clan's oldest grudge! Stood for thousands of bloody years! When I find the descendants of bloody Galanthiel Whisperthorn, by Grungni! I'm going to teach them all — every single last one of them — a lesson in manners with my axe!'

– Snorrt Leivvusson, Diplomat from Karak Ziflin

On Wood Elves…

'My great grandfather thought logging forests on t'other side of the Grey Mountains would be lucrative. Ignored all the warnings, he was sure he was onto a winner. What could a bunch of skinny Elves do to him and his lads, after all? A lot, as it turned out. Only my grandfather survived, left alive to spread the message: "Keep away." So, me and my lads are preparing a party to take revenge.'

– Merig Ranvigsdottir, Villager from Azorn-Kalaki

OPTIONS: ANIMOSITY (ELVES)

Given the long memories of Dwarfs and their tendency to bear grudges, many harbour a deep resentment towards Elves for their part in the War of Vengeance. As such, many Dwarfs have the Animosity (Elves) Psychology trait (see page 190). Given some **WFRP** parties contain both Elves and Dwarfs, this may lead to unhelpful tensions. So, you may prefer to ignore this Talent between party members..

HALFLINGS

Halflings are ubiquitous across the Reikland, found working in service industries in all towns, with an entire district of Reikland's capital of Altdorf, known as Haffenstadt, packed tight with hundreds of extended Halfling families supporting restaurants, taverns, pipeweed stores, and an enormous number of street-food hawkers. Halflings are also a common sight in many of Reikland's villages, where it is not uncommon to find them employed to staff an inn or run a farm. They are communal creatures, preferring to live in close-knit family groups, sharing houses, rooms, and even beds with dozens of friends and relatives; everyone contributes and everyone shares. This interdependent lifestyle leaves many Halflings struggling with the concept of private ownership and space.

Halflings are notoriously interested in recording their lineage, and many Halfling clans can trace their ancestry back many centuries to the very founding of the Mootland (their self-governed Grand Province in the Empire). The Elder of the Moot — currently Hisme Stoutheart — is the custodian of the *Haffenlyver*, an ancient embroidered scroll detailing the chief bloodlines of their primary clans, said to be the greatest treasure of the Halflings.

Another peculiar detail is the Halflings' strange affinity for Ogres. Despite their ravenous appetites, and penchant for eating whatever is at hand, Ogres tend to respect Halflings. Indeed, gangs of Ogre labourers are often overseen by Halfling gaffers, and most Ogre mercenary bands have a Halfling cook on staff.

Halflings are short, apple-cheeked and beardless, resembling big-eyed, round-faced (and round bodied) Human children, and their sunny dispositions and curly locks only reinforce this impression. They are known for their enormous appetites in all things and their lack of concern for personal space (they're huggers), social boundaries ('Well me' great aunt's just shacked up with me best mate, and you should hear what they've been up to!'), and property rights ('It's not like he's using it!'); this last has landed more than one Halfling in jail for thievery.

Opinions

On Reiklander Humans…

'Stiff-necked and pious, warlike and jealous… I could go on, but good manners halts me, and, besides, I like them, and they like me pies. As long as you keep away from their temples and the hard-liners, they're an open and pretty welcoming bunch. Good folk, and good for business.'
— 'Tubs' Samworth Rumster XVI, Pie-seller from Kalegan

On Dwarfs…

'My aunt Bessi was the greediest, as were six of her sons. But Bessi has nothing on them Dwarfs. Eyes grow as big as Mannslieb at even a scratch of gold. But, if you tell them that, they'll growl at you like you've taken the last honeycake, and start scribbling notes in one of their damned books about insulting their family honour or whatnot.'
— 'Lilly' Joseppinalina Hayfoot, Pedlar in the Reikland

On High Elves…

'I've seen them on the rivers in their white ships. How do they keep them so clean? And their hair… oh, their hair… it's like sunshine, it is. Snuck on a boat once to see what they do. Same as the rest of us, it seems, just more… earnestly.'
— 'Dainty' Cordelineth Brandysnap IV, Thief from Altdorf

On Wood Elves…

'Elves living in the woods? Don't be bloody ridiculous. Elves live in white towers and pretty boats over in Altdorf-town, you idiot.'
— 'Jammy' Mercimaus Alderflower II, Scholar from Fielbach

HIGH ELVES

High Elves are a relatively common sight on the rivers of Reikland. Both Altdorf and Nuln boast sizeable districts populated by High Elf merchants who ship goods down the Reik through Marienburg to the sea. These merchants are by far the most numerous of the High Elves found in Reikland, alongside diplomatic entourages and support staff. Aloof, alien, and long-lived, they are a passionate, emotional folk widely perceived in the Reikland to be the most beautiful of the species, and also the most arrogant.

Tall and slender with delicately pointed ears, most Elves have long, fine hair and melodious voices. Although they might look frail, their physiology is not only surprisingly strong, but also extraordinarily agile and dextrous. There are very few noticeable gender differences between Elves, which often causes confusion among Humans who interact with them.

The High Elves, who call themselves 'Asur', are native to Ulthuan, a magical island lying to the west of the Old World. A proud species, they boast of being amongst the oldest of the world's civilisations. High Elves show considerable disdain for Dwarfs, with whom they have a long history of conflict. Since their abandonment of the Old World in the aftermath of the War of the Beard, the Asur have been torn apart by civil war, the 'kinstrife', although this isn't something they discuss openly with outsiders. As a result of this millennia-long struggle, Elves from the war-torn north of Ulthuan tend to be hard-bitten, practical, and ruthless.

High Elven society is tightly-bound by ritual and discipline, intended to keep soaring emotions in check and provide focus for their complicated intellects. Seeming contrary to this, some Asur revel in wild adventure. The term 'Sea Elf' is often used by other species to describe the dauntless High Elves who venture beyond Ulthuan's safe shores as mariners, traders, and diplomats, and who stand in stark contrast to any grim Asur accompanying them who follow warrior lifestyles.

Opinions

On Reiklander Humans...
'They are corrupt, jealous, and rapacious in their short-lived hungers. But, when mindful of their petty needs and their fear of what we represent, they are easily shaped.'

– Imryth Emberfell, Ambassador from Caledor

On Dwarfs...
'I suggest avoiding them. They are lost in the past, which blinds them to what's coming. Nod politely, accept the abuse, and move on. There is no point arguing, they will never change their minds.'

– Alathan Crestrider, Seaman from Cothique

On Halflings...
'I find these cheerful creatures genuinely interesting. I lived amongst an extended family group for a while, and found them so open, welcoming, and nurturing it was authentically touching. But, eventually, I had to move on, the smell was simply over-powering, and they have no understanding of personal space, which soon loses its charm.'

– Hoelistor Arceye, Wizard from Saphery

On Wood Elves...
'If the Asrai would bother to look beyond their dirty noses, they would see what we are all up against. Isolationist idiots that deserve everything that's coming to them. I doubt the Eonir are any better.'

– Anaw-Alina Darkstep, Scout from Nagarythe

WOOD ELVES

Wood Elves are a rare sight in the Reikland, and for good reason. During the closing stages of the War of the Beard, most Elves retreated from the Old World, but a few remained and withdrew to the depths of the magical forests they now called home. Over three thousand years of isolation, hardship, and warfare then ensued, leaving 'Wood Elves' culturally very different to their High Elf cousins.

Wood Elf life is entwined with nature, with a society intermixed with spirits of the forest. They are separatists who work hard to hide themselves away, with arboreal outposts cunningly concealed with powerful illusions and misleading magics. On the rare occasions they travel beyond their borders, it is usually for war, as often with their neighbours as with darker forces, leaving other peoples of the Old World deeply unsure of the fae, capricious Elves.

There are two kiths of Wood Elves most commonly seen in Reikland. The 'Asrai' from Athel Loren across the Grey Mountains, and 'Eonir' of the Laurelorn Forest far to the north in Nordland.

The ruthless Asrai of Athel Loren are xenophobic and secretive, and rarely venture beyond their borders. However, a decade ago, Naith the Prophetess foresaw the possible death of Athel Loren. In response, the King and Queen of the Wood, recognising the fate of their forests may lay in the hands of outsiders, sent tattooed kinbands out from Athel Loren to take action, hunting the enemies of the forest at the source.

These ferocious bands are sometimes led by a spellsinger who calls upon the old, magical paths of the Worldroot to transport them between Athel Loren and the depths of other forests long lost to the Elves, but not yet consumed by civilisation or Chaos. Occasionally, these wild hunters perceive some common cause with other Old Worlders and an individual may step from the shadows to join with those fighting a greater evil.

By comparison, the Queen of the Laurelorn takes a very different path to the foretellings given to her and has recently sent a sizeable delegation to make camp in the deep forest of the Amber Hills just south of Altdorf. These Elves observe Human politics concerning the Laurelorn and beyond, and occasionally intervene on matters deemed important. The camp is viewed as a 'temporary' solution by the Elves, but the meaning of that word is very different to the long-lived species. Because of this camp, these Wood Elves are a growing presence in Reikland as they venture from the trees and wander according to their inscrutable purposes, often as hunters or entertainers.

Opinions

On Reiklander Humans…

'I see hateful creatures with darkness in their hearts and a complete disrespect for order. But they are widespread, warlike, and, most importantly, easy to manipulate. Given winter draws near, it is time to use them.'

– Algwyllmyr Twiceseen, Seer from Athel Loren

On Dwarfs…

'More stubborn than the Oak of Ages, they understand one argument only: force. So, use it swiftly and decisively, and be aware they will return for petty vengeance at a later date.'

– Meridrynda Aspengate, Glade Rider from Athel Loren

On Halflings…

'I met one when travelling Middenland during the ninth year of Queen Marrisith. It talked a lot. And I do mean a lot. When we parted ways by a town it told me was named "Delberz", I found it had somehow managed to steal several pouches of herbs from my belt. I was impressed. So, I suggest not trusting the things, but the companionship and local lore they share may be worth the cost!'

– Alafael Harrowlay, Entertainer from the Laurelorn

On High Elves…

'Conceited beyond any sensible measure, don't approach the Asur. They are jaded, arrogant, and likely lost to Atharti. And if they try to look down on you in that superior manner they so prefer, just remind them their Queen in Avelorn lives a life no different to ours.'

– Cynwrawn Fartrack, Hunter from the Laurelorn

SYLVAN COUSINS

The Wood Elves of Athel Loren and the Laurelorn may share a common history and origin in the Old World, but they are culturally different. Unlike the High Elves, neither of the Wood Elven kiths care much for any form of conventional civilisation, seeing it as a threat to their beloved forests and way of life. However, they differ in how they choose to express this.

The Laurelorn Wood Elves proactively engage in politics to protect themselves, mixing with others, and are not above stoking the fires of hatred between other groups to shift focus to their preferred targets. Thus, in character, they are more like the High Elves, whilst still having the Skills and Talents of the Wood Elves.

By comparison, the Athel Loren kinbands prefer to hide in the shadows, shunning contact with all others, instead striking deadly blows designed to cause fear and terror in the hearts of any who would look to the forest with greed.

2) CLASS AND CAREER

Your Class determines your general place in society. Your Career describes your current job and determines your Status, which also influences how much money you earn.

You can simply choose your Class and Career from the options below, write them down on your Character Sheet and move on to step 3. Alternatively, if you are unsure which to choose, or just want to randomly select for bonus XP:

1. Roll 1d100 on the **Random Class and Career** Table. If you don't like the result, move to step 2. If you keep the result, gain +50 XP.
2. Roll twice more on the table, bringing your total to 3 choices. If one of the three now suits you, select one and gain +25 XP. If not, move to Step 3.
3. Choose your Class and Career, or keep rerolling on the table until you get something you like. There is no XP bonus for this.

RANDOM CLASS AND CAREER TABLE

Class	Career/Species	Human	Dwarf	Halfling	High Elf	Wood Elf
ACADEMICS	Apothecary	01	01	01	01–02	–
	Engineer	02	02–04	02	–	–
	Lawyer	03	05–06	03–04	03–06	–
	Nun	04–05	–	–	–	–
	Physician	06	07	05–06	07–08	–
	Priest	07–11	–	–	–	–
	Scholar	12–13	08–09	07–08	09–12	01
	Wizard	14	–	–	13–16	02–05
BURGHERS	Agitator	15	10–11	09–10	–	–
	Artisan	16–17	12–17	11–15	17–19	06–10
	Beggar	18–19	18	16–19	–	–
	Investigator	20	19–20	20–21	20–21	–
	Merchant	21	21–24	22–25	22–26	–
	Rat Catcher	22–23	25	26–28	–	–
	Townsman	24–26	26–31	29–31	27–28	–
	Watchman	27	32–34	32–33	29	–
COURTIERS	Advisor	28	35–36	34	30–31	11–14
	Artist	29	37	35–36	32	15–18
	Duellist	30	38	–	33–34	–
	Envoy	31	39–40	37	35–37	19–25
	Noble	32	41	–	38–40	26–31
	Servant	33–35	42	38–43	–	–
	Spy	36	43	44	41–43	32–35
	Warden	37	44–45	45–46	44–45	–
PEASANTS	Bailiff	38	46–47	47	–	–
	Hedge Witch	39	–	–	–	–
	Herbalist	40	–	48–50	46–47	36–42
	Hunter	41–42	48–49	51–52	48–50	43–52
	Miner	43	50–54	53	–	–
	Mystic	44	–	–	–	53–57
	Scout	45	55	54	51–56	58–68
	Villager	46–50	56	55–57	–	–

CLASS

Summary: *Choose one of the eight Classes.*

Your choice of Class determines from which Careers you can choose. The Careers under each Class are of a broadly equivalent social level that offer similar types of opportunities between adventures.

Academics: Learned people who use their education to make a living. Often, Academics are the only characters who can read and write. They start with low Status but can secure important positions if they advance through the ranks. **Career options:** Apothecary, Engineer, Lawyer, Nun, Physician, Priest, Scholar, Wizard.

Burghers: Generally law-abiding townsfolk who live and work in the many towns and cities of the Empire. Many Burghers are middle class and earn a decent living. **Career options:** Agitator, Artisan, Beggar, Investigator, Merchant, Rat Catcher, Townsman, Watchman.

Courtiers: Those who rule or who provide specialist services to those who rule. Even lowly born Courtiers have higher Status than most, and all have an opportunity to secure positions of significant influence. **Career options:** Advisor, Artist, Duellist, Envoy, Noble, Servant, Spy, Warden.

Peasants: People who live and work in the farms, villages, and countryside. Peasants are all lower class, though it's possible to secure significant influence locally. **Career options:** Bailiff, Hedge Witch, Herbalist, Hunter, Miner, Mystic, Scout, Villager.

Rangers: Roving folk who make a living on the open roads, travelling far beyond their home towns and villages. Most Rangers are lower class, but some can secure positions of high Status if they persevere. **Career options:** Bounty Hunter, Coachman, Entertainer, Flagellant, Messenger, Pedlar, Road Warden, Witch Hunter.

Riverfolk: People who live and work on the rivers and waterways that wind through the Reikland and beyond. Riverfolk all begin

Class	Career/Species	Human	Dwarf	Halfling	High Elf	Wood Elf
RANGERS	Bounty Hunter	51	57–60	58	57–59	69–70
	Coachman	52	61	59-60	–	–
	Entertainer	53–54	62–63	61–63	60–62	71–75
	Flagellant	55–56	–	–	–	–
	Messenger	57	64–65	64–65	63	76–78
	Pedlar	58	66–67	66–67	–	–
	Road Warden	59	–	68	–	–
	Witch Hunter	60	–	–	–	–
RIVERFOLK	Boatman	61–62	68–69	69	64	–
	Huffer	63	70	70	–	–
	Riverwarden	64–65	–	71	–	–
	Riverwoman	66–68	71–72	72–74	–	–
	Seaman	69–70	73	75	65–79	–
	Smuggler	71	74–75	76–79	80	–
	Stevedore	72–73	76–77	80–82	–	–
	Wrecker	74	78	–	–	79
ROGUES	Bawd	75–76	–	83–85	81–82	–
	Charlatan	77	–	86	83–85	–
	Fence	78	79	87	–	–
	Grave Robber	79	–	88	–	–
	Outlaw	80–83	80–82	89	86–88	80–85
	Racketeer	84	83	90	–	–
	Thief	85–87	84	91–94	–	–
	Witch	88	–	–	–	–
WARRIORS	Cavalryman	89–90	–	–	89–92	86–90
	Guard	91–92	85–87	95–96	93–94	91–92
	Knight	93	–	–	95	93–94
	Pit Fighter	94	88–90	97	96–97	95–96
	Protagonist	95	91–93	–	98	–
	Soldier	96–99	94–96	98–100	99–100	97–100
	Slayer	–	97–100	–	–	–
	Warrior Priest	100	–	–	–	–

with low Status, but some have opportunities that can lead to a very comfortable life. **Career options:** Boatman, Huffer, Riverwarden, Riverwoman, Seaman, Smuggler, Stevedore, Wrecker.

Rogues: Mostly town and city folk, these people make a living by acts considered illegal, or at least unsavoury, by most law-abiding citizens. Rogues are usually lower class, but some can make a lot of money, though they may not secure a high Status when doing so. **Career options:** Bawd, Charlatan, Fence, Grave Robber, Outlaw, Thief, Racketeer, Witch.

Warriors: Relying on their physical prowess, these people are all trained fighters, although they are not necessarily from the military. Warriors come from many backgrounds, both high and low Status, and all can carve out a position of influence if they live long enough. **Career options:** Cavalryman, Guard, Knight, Pit Fighter, Protagonist, Soldier, Troll Slayer, Warrior Priest.

CAREER

Summary: *Choose one of your Class's Careers, restricted by your Species.*

Once your Class is established, choose one of the Careers associated with it. There are 8 Careers in each Class, but some

are restricted by Species. Full descriptions of each Career and their restrictions are given in **Chapter 3: Class and Careers**, but for a quick reference, refer to the Random Class and Career Table to see a complete list of every Career and any Species restrictions.

OPTIONS: BUT I WANT TO PLAY A WOOD ELF FLAGELLANT!

You may have a great idea for a character excluded by the rules because normally the species in question doesn't pursue such a career for cultural, religious, or philosophical reasons. That's totally fine! Just take your character concept to your GM and, if you both agree to the unique combination, you're good to go.

3) ATTRIBUTES

Summary: *Determine each of your Attributes by referring to the Attributes Table.*

Attributes describe your character's innate capabilities – how fast or strong you are, how much damage you can sustain, or how well you cope with stressful situations. Attributes include Movement, ten Characteristics, Wounds, Fate, and Resilience.

WAIT! THAT'S NOT FAIR!

You may notice that not all characters are created equal. An Elf has significant Characteristic advantages, for example. Don't be deceived by numbers alone, there are many aspects to character generation and all the Species have advantages and disadvantages at each stage, some of them not always obvious.

CHARACTERISTICS

Your ten Characteristics are used in Tests (see **Chapter 5: Rules**), to determine if you perform an action successfully. The Human average for these Attributes is 30. Those who are gifted, or well-practiced, may achieve scores of over 40; only the most dedicated and experienced will achieve scores over 60. Of course,

other Species have their own strengths and weaknesses, so their averages are different, sometimes significantly so.

Determining Characteristics

When determining your Characteristics:

Step 1) Roll 2d10 for each of the ten Characteristics and make a note of the results. If you feel your Character would be improved if you swapped round some of the dice roll results between Characteristics, move to the next step. If you stick with your random results, add the die rolls to the modifier for each Characteristic from the Attribute Table, write them on your Character Sheet and gain +50 XP.

Step 2) Rearrange the ten numbers rolled under step 1, assigning each to a different Characteristic (and adding its modifier). If you're happy with this new mix, record them on your Character Sheet and gain +25 XP. If not, move to the next step.

Step 3) If you're still not happy with your results, either roll again and swap the rolls around with no XP bonus, or you could ignore the dice completely! Instead, allocate 100 points across the 10 Characteristics as you prefer, with a minimum of 4 and a maximum of 18 allocated to any single Characteristic. Add the modifiers from the Attribute Table and record them on your Character Sheet. Like rolling again, there is no XP bonus for this option.

Weapon Skill (WS)

Your skill at fighting hand-to-hand, your ability to land a measured blow, and effectiveness in the free-for-all of a massed melee. It is also used for unarmed combat, where your body is the weapon!

ATTRIBUTES TABLE

	Human	Dwarf	Halfling	Elf
Weapon Skill	2d10+20	2d10+30	2d10+10	2d10+30
Ballistic Skill	2d10+20	2d10+20	2d10+30	2d10+30
Strength	2d10+20	2d10+20	2d10+10	2d10+20
Toughness	2d10+20	2d10+30	2d10+20	2d10+20
Initiative	2d10+20	2d10+20	2d10+20	2d10+40
Agility	2d10+20	2d10+10	2d10+20	2d10+30
Dexterity	2d10+20	2d10+30	2d10+30	2d10+30
Intelligence	2d10+20	2d10+20	2d10+20	2d10+30
Willpower	2d10+20	2d10+40	2d10+30	2d10+30
Fellowship	2d10+20	2d10+10	2d10+30	2d10+20
Wounds	SB+(2×TB)+WPB	SB+(2×TB)+WPB	(2×TB)+WPB	SB+(2×TB)+WPB
Fate	2	0	0	0
Resilience	1	2	2	0
Extra Points	3	2	3	2
Movement	4	3	3	5

Ballistic Skill (BS)

Your effectiveness at hitting with ranged weapons like bows and throwing knives, and for throwing things generally. It is also used as the basis for other ranged attacks like Trolls vomiting.

Strength (S)

How much damage you do in melee, how much you can lift, and how good you are at things like swimming and climbing.

Toughness (T)

Your physical hardiness. It helps you survive damage in combat but will also help with things like surviving harsh conditions and standing up to poison.

Initiative (I)

Speed of thought and reaction, especially in the heat of battle and when under pressure. It determines combat order, and helps you be the first to react to danger. It also determines your powers of intuition and perception.

Agility (Ag)

Physical coordination and natural athleticism, and the basis for things like running, riding, and hiding. Agility is also used for dodging blows in combat.

Dexterity (Dex)

Your affinity for performing fine and delicate manual tasks like playing a musical instrument or skilled manufacturing. It will also help you with things like sleight of hand and picking pockets.

Intelligence (Int)

Your powers of thought, analysis, and understanding. Useful for healing, evaluating, and general knowledge, and vital for the understanding and casting of magical spells.

Willpower (WP)

General strength of mind, and your ability to shrug off difficulty and plough on with the job in hand. It helps with resisting all sorts of influence and coercion, and guards against fear and terror.

Fellowship (Fel)

Your ability to get on with people and come across as generally pleasant and acceptable. It will help you when chatting to locals or commanding people in battle, charming the guards or attempting to bribe them, and, for pious characters, communicating with your deity.

Characteristic Bonuses

The first or 'tens' digit of each Characteristic is its bonus value. Characteristic Bonuses are used in a variety of different ways throughout the rules, particularly for limiting Talents and defining Spells.

Example: *Strength (S) 39 equates to a Strength Bonus of 3. Willpower (WP) of 51 equals a Willpower Bonus of 5.*

Wounds (W)

Your Wounds show how much Damage you can endure based on your physical power and your force of will to shrug off injury. See **Chapter 5: Rules** for how Wounds are used to track Damage.

Determining Wounds

Unlike other Attributes, Wounds are derived from your Strength Bonus, twice your Toughness Bonus,, and Willpower Bonus (abbreviated to SB, TB, and WPB on the **Attributes Table**). Refer to the Attributes Table to determine the Characteristic Bonuses used to calculate your Wounds. **Note:** Halflings have the *Small* Talent automatically and start with fewer Wounds, (see page 341).

FATE & FORTUNE, RESILIENCE & RESOLVE

Your Fate represents your destiny, and is directly tied to your Fortune, a measure of your luck. Your Resilience is your inner strength, which is directly related to your Resolve, defining your grit. Your Resilience also comes with a Motivation, which is a single word or phrase describing what drives your character forwards. See page 170 for more on all of these.

Determining Fate and Resilience

You start with a base value for Fate and Resilience, and then have a number of Extra Points to spread between these two Attributes as you see fit. The numbers for these are shown in the **Attributes Table**. The more points you allocate to Fate, the luckier you are. By comparison, a higher Resilience shows you can steel through any situation.

Determining Fortune and Resolve

Your initial Fortune is equal to your Fate. Your initial Resolve equals your Resilience. Mark all four values on your sheet.

Determining Motivation

All characters choose a Motivation. It represents your Character's core essence, a word or phrase that sums up what you live for. In addition to the obvious roleplaying benefits for portraying your character, Motivation is used to help you regain Resolve points. When considering your Motivation, think of something that is fundamental to your character's nature. Also try to make your Motivation something fun to roleplay, and something that will work well with the other PCs and their motivations.

Example: *Gustavus, a young Scholar at the University in Altdorf, has 'Thrillseeker' for his Motivation. He lives his life in pursuit of excitement and danger, and Gustavus may regain Resolve points when he actively seeks out risky situations; perhaps he provokes antagonism in taverns, or deliberately breaks the law by stealing the feathers from the caps of State Soldiers.*

Example: *Clotilda, a Reiksguard Knight, has 'Protect the weak' as her Motivation. She is driven to stand up to bullies and braggarts, risking life and limb to save the Reikland's citizenry. Clotilda will regain her Resolve whenever she rescues others, or puts herself in harm's way to protect another.*

Example: *Ebba is a 'Rebellious' apprentice wizard studying at the Light College. She loves to break the rules of the College, flaunting her master's authority, and poking her nose into books best left undisturbed. She regains Resolve whenever she breaks the rules set for her by superiors.*

Other examples of potential motivations include: a 'Perfectionist', who loves to plan meticulously and draws energy from flawless execution of schemes; a 'Nurturer', who gains strength from caring for others, or rescuing them from difficult situations; a 'Penitent Martyr', who revels in hardship to atone for past misdeeds; or a 'Shining Wit', who's ever engaging in witty badinage and banter to lighten the mood. If you can't think of a Motivation don't worry. One may arise as you create more of your character, and the other players and the GM can always help. Even if you do have one, it's possible you may change your mind later. **Step 8) Bringing Your Character To Life** is a good time to reconsider what your Motivation will be.

Movement (M)

Movement is used to determine your Walk and Run speed. Standard Human Movement is 4. If using a grid for movement this indicates how many squares you can move in a Round, or inches across the table top. Over the longer term it indicates how many miles per hour you can comfortably travel on foot. For more on Movement, see page 164

Movement	Walk	Run
3	6	12
4	8	16
5	10	20

ADVANCE CHARACTERISTICS

Turn to your career in **Chapter 3: Class and Careers.** Look to the Advance Scheme and find the three Characteristics marked ✛ without a brass, silver, or gold background. You can allocate a total of 5 Advances across these Characteristics as you choose, and mark them in the Advances box on your Character Sheet.

CHARACTERISTIC ADVANCES

Characteristic Advances show training or experience in your Characteristics. The number of Advances you have in the Characteristic is added to the initial Characteristic to show your current ability. So, if you have an initial Dexterity of 25, and 5 Dexterity Advances, your Dexterity is now 30.

4) SKILLS AND TALENTS

Summary: *Choose your Skills and Talents from those offered by your Species and Career.*

Skills represent areas of trained learning or experience, and Talents describe special abilities your Character can access. A list of all Skills and Talents is provided in **Chapter 4: Skills and Talents**. The Skills and Talents you have available to you at character generation are determined by your Species and Career.

When you learn a Skill, note down the number of Advances you gain in the Advances box of the Skill. If you should learn this skill again, add the extra Advances to the old total to create a new number of Advances. If you learn a Talent, record it in your Talent list on your Character Sheet.

Skills are classified as either *Basic* or *Advanced*. Basic Skills represent common abilities that everyone can perform — you can use these skills without any Advances in them, at a level equal to the governing characteristic. Advanced Skills require specialist knowledge, and you can only use these skills if you have taken at least one Advance in them.

Note: Some Talents can be learned multiple times. If you have an opportunity to learn a Talent a second time, check the Talent entry in **Chapter 4: Skills and Talents** to see if it can be learned multiple times, and mark how many times you've learned it on your Character Sheet.

WHAT ARE SKILL ADVANCES?

Like Characteristic Advances, Skill Advances show specific training in a Skill. All Skills are associated with a Characteristic, and the number of Advances you have in the Skill is added to that Characteristic to show you how skilled you are. So, as Climb is associated with Strength, if you have a Strength of 38, and 8 Climb Advances, your Climb Skill is 46. This is explained in full in **Chapter 4: Skills and Talents**.

SPECIES SKILLS AND TALENTS

Each Species has a variety of Skills and Talents to choose from. You may choose 3 Skills to gain 5 Advances each, and 3 Skills to gain 3 Advances each. If a Talent listing presents a choice, you select one Talent from the choices given. Any Random Talents are determined by the Random Talent table. If you roll a Talent you already have, you may reroll. **Note:** All Characters are assumed to be fluent in Reikspiel,, the language of the Empire, and do not need to take it as a Skill. For more on this, see page 124.

Humans (Reiklander)

Skills: Animal Care, Charm, Cool, Evaluate, Gossip, Haggle, Language (Bretonnian), Language (Wastelander), Leadership, Lore (Reikland), Melee (Basic), Ranged (Bow)
Talents: Doomed, Savvy or Suave, 3 Random Talents

Dwarfs

Skills: Consume Alcohol, Cool, Endurance, Entertain (Storytelling), Evaluate, Intimidate, Language (Khazalid), Lore (Dwarfs), Lore (Geology), Lore (Metallurgy), Melee (Basic), Trade (any one)
Talents: Magic Resistance, Night Vision, Read/Write or Relentless, Resolute or Strong-minded, Sturdy

Halflings

Skills: Charm, Consume Alcohol, Dodge, Gamble, Haggle, Intuition, Language (Mootish), Lore (Reikland), Perception, Sleight of Hand, Stealth (Any), Trade (Cook)
Talents: Acute Sense (Taste), Night Vision, Resistance (Chaos), Small, 2 Random Talents

High Elves

Skills: Cool, Entertain (Sing), Evaluate, Language (Eltharin), Leadership, Melee (Basic), Navigation, Perception, Play (any one), Ranged (Bow), Sail, Swim
Talents: Acute Sense (Sight), Coolheaded or Savvy, Night Vision, Second Sight or Sixth Sense, Read/Write

Wood Elves

Skills: Athletics, Climb, Endurance, Entertain (Sing), Intimidate, Language (Eltharin), Melee (Basic), Outdoor Survival, Perception, Ranged (Bow), Stealth (Rural), Track
Talents: Acute Sense (Sight), Hardy or Second Sight, Night Vision, Read/Write or Very Resilient, Rover

RANDOM TALENTS

Roll	Description	Roll	Description
01–03	Acute Sense (any one)	51–52	Noble Blood
04–06	Ambidextrous	53–55	Orientation
07–09	Animal Affinity	56–58	Perfect Pitch
10–12	Artistic	59–62	Pure Soul
13–15	Attractive	63–65	Read/Write
16–18	Coolheaded	66–68	Resistance (any one)
19–21	Craftsman (any one)	69–71	Savvy
22–24	Flee!	72–74	Sharp
25–28	Hardy	75–78	Sixth Sense
29–31	Lightning Reflexes	79–81	Strong Legs
32–34	Linguistics	82–84	Sturdy
35–38	Luck	85–87	Suave
39–41	Marksman	88–91	Super Numerate
42–44	Mimic	92–94	Very Resilient
45–47	Night Vision	95–97	Very Strong
48–50	Nimble Fingered	98–00	Warrior Born

CAREER SKILLS AND TALENTS

Now turn to your career in **Chapter 3: Class and Careers**. You begin at the first Career level listed in your Career Path. There are 8 Skills and 4 Talents listed with that level, and you can choose which of these you are most proficient at. Allocate 40 Advances to your eight starting Skills, with no more than 10 Advances allocated to any single Skill at this stage. This is enough for you to add 5 Advances to every Career Skill if you wish, which is one of the required steps to complete your Career if you wish to move to a new one (see **Changing Career** on page 48). You may also choose a single Talent to learn.

Example: *Lindsay is creating a Human Noble Scion, which has the following Career Skills: Bribery, Consume Alcohol, Gamble, Intimidate, Leadership, Lore (Heraldry), Melee (Fencing), Play (Any). She decides the character is well-schooled, but naive, so chooses to ignore the Bribery, Consume Alcohol, and Gamble Skills for the moment, and spreads her 40 Advances like so: Intimidate +7, Leadership +10, Lore (Heraldry) +10, Melee (Fencing) +3, and Play (Harpsichord) +10.* **Note:** *Lindsay can do this even if she has already allocated Advances to Leadership for being Human, as the limit of 10 Advances to a single Skill applies only during this allocation of 40 Advances.*

5) TRAPPINGS

Summary: *Determine your initial Trappings from your Class and Career.*

Your Trappings are the equipment, clothes, weapons, and other items your character carries. You begin play with initial Trappings determined by your Class and your Career. If you want to buy more (or sell what you already have!), refer to **Chapter 11: Consumers' Guide.**

All your Trappings should be recorded in the relevant sections of your Character Sheet. Once you've done this, move on to **6) Adding Detail.**

CLASS TRAPPINGS

Your character begins play with general Trappings determined by your Class. Reference your Class in the list below and jot the Trappings into your Character Sheet, rolling dice where required.

Academics: Clothing, Dagger, Pouch, Sling Bag containing Writing Kit and 1d10 sheets of Parchment
Burghers: Cloak, Clothing, Dagger, Hat, Pouch, Sling Bag containing Lunch
Courtiers: Dagger, Fine Clothing, Pouch containing Tweezers, Ear Pick, and a Comb
Peasants: Cloak, Clothing, Dagger, Pouch, Sling Bag containing Rations (1 day)
Rangers: Cloak, Clothing, Dagger, Pouch, Backpack containing Tinderbox, Blanket, Rations (1 day)
Riverfolk: Cloak, Clothing, Dagger, Pouch, Sling Bag containing a Flask of Spirits
Rogues: Clothing, Dagger, Pouch, Sling Bag containing 2 Candles, 1d10 Matches, a Hood *or* Mask
Warriors: Clothing, Hand Weapon, Dagger, Pouch

CAREER TRAPPINGS

Every Career has a list of Trappings for each of its four levels. You begin play with all the Trappings listed in the first level of your Career Path. Find the appropriate Trappings list in **Chapter 3: Class and Careers** and record them on your Character Sheet.

Next, find your character's Status, which is listed beside your Career level's name. It will be marked as either Brass, Silver or Gold, which is you Status Tier, followed by a a number, which is your Standing. Your Status Tier and Standing determine your initial wealth as shown below.

Status Tier	Starting Wealth
Brass	2d10 brass pennies per Status Level
Silver	1d10 silver shillings per Status Level
Gold	1 Gold crown per Status Level

So, if you were Brass 3, you would start with 6d10 Brass pennies; if Silver 3, you would begin with 3d10 silver shillings, and if you were Gold 3, you would have 3 gold crowns.

This money can be used to purchase more Trappings or saved for spending during play. The relative worth of the coins is covered in **Chapter 11: Consumers' Guide.**

6) ADDING DETAIL

Summary: *Choose name, age, hair and eye colour, height, Psychology, and Ambitions.*

The bare bones of your character are in place, so let's add some details, fleshing your character out in your imagination, determining what you look like, how you think, and what drives you.

NAME

While you can choose any name that fits the world, here are some hints and tips to help choose one that's right for you.

Human Reiklander Names
Reiklanders usually have a forename and a surname. Forenames include:

Examples: Adhemar, Anders, Artur, Beatrijs, Clementia, Detlev, Erika, Frauke, Frederich, Gerner, Gertraud, Haletha, Heinrich, Helga, Henryk, Irmina, Jehanne, Karl, Kruger, Lorelay, Marieke, Sebastien, Sigfreda, Talther, Talunda, Ulrich, Ulrika, Werther, Willelma, Wilryn.

HUMAN NAMES AND THEIR ORIGINS

Human names in WFRP are often taken from the real world, making it easy to research fun names online. The Reikland and much of The Empire uses Germanic names, the Wasteland has Dutch and Belgian influences, and Bretonnian names are loosely medieval French.

In the Reikland, Human family surnames passed on from one generation to the next are most common in cities and towns, while in villages Humans are more likely to take on an individual surname when they reach adulthood. It's common to take a surname from where you were born, such as 'Wilhelm of Auerswald'. The nobility often have two surnames, one is the name of their House and the other is preceded by 'von' to indicate where their family holds land, such as Graf Zenechar Trott von Tahme, though individual family traditions vary widely.

The most common surnames are derived from your occupation, or the occupation of a parent or grandparent. Examples include: Bauer (Farmer), Fleischer (Butcher), Schmidt (Smith), and Schuster (Cobbler). If a character has a particularly noticeable physical trait, this might be used as a surname. This can often be passed down from parents to children too, which can become confusing for literal-minded Dwarfs who may not understand a short person claiming to be Lang (Tall). Some other examples include: Augenlos (one eye), Dunn (very thin), Laut (loud voice), Stark (Strong).

Dwarf Names

Dwarf names are comprised of a forename, a surname, and a clan name.

Dwarf Forenames

Dwarf names tend to be short and sturdy like the people they represent, and are most commonly given to celebrate important ancestors, although individual clan traditions vary. Another common practice is to use a birthname to describe a key trait of a newborn in Khazalid, the Dwarf native language.

Examples: Alrik, Bronda, Dimzad, Fenna, Gottri, Gudrun, Snorri.

Khazalid examples: Baragaz (Cannon Mouth), Durak (Hard), Galazil (Golden Haired), Gnoldok (Wise Eyes), Nazril (Shimmering), Okri (Crafter)

Dwarf Surnames

Dwarf surnames are based on who raised the Dwarf, with the following suffixes the most common in use:

-sdottir: Daughter of…
-snev: Nephew of…
-sniz: Niece of…
-sson: Son of…

Examples: Ariksson, Grunnasdottir, Skagnev, Sovrissniz

It's common as Dwarfs age and accrue deeds to their names to adopt a nickname based on physical appearance, prowess, or deed. These are usually bestowed by clan consensus, and it's considered dishonourable to give a name that doesn't represent the true character of a Dwarf. If such a nickname is adopted, it usually replaces the surname completely. So, Gerka Kardadottir would become Gerka Blackhand if she took the nickname 'Blackhand'. Sometimes a nickname is marked in Khazalid, but Dwarfs usually translate such to Reikspiel in order to better explain themselves.

Examples: Axebringer, Finehand, Forkbeard, Ironbraid, Redhammer, Stonefist

Clan Name

Finally, all Dwarfs bear a Clan Name (assuming they have not abandoned Dwarf tradition, which some Dwarfs living in the Empire have, especially rogue engineers). The Clan Name is always derived from the ancestor who founded the Clan, and is often sourced in a Nickname, often expressed in Khazalid. In practice, Dwarfs rarely use their Clan Name outside Dwarf society.

Common Reikland Clans: Ardrungan, Bryntok, Gazani, Gromheld, Harrazlings, Unboki

Common Grey Mountain Clans: Dokkintroll, Ganvalgger, Kvitang, Thrungtak, Wyrgrinti, Zankonk

Elf Names

Elves normally only admit to having names comprising of a forename and an epithet when wandering the Reikland.

Elf Forenames

The Elves use a naming system quite incomprehensible to outsiders. Eltharin (the common language of High Elves and Wood Elves, which has many dialects) is a language that relies on more than simple syllables to convey meaning. The easiest way to create an Elf name is to use the Elf Name Generator.

Elf Epithets

When travelling foreign lands, Elves typically present themselves with a forename and an epithet rather than attempt to explain the deeper concepts of Kindreds, Kinbands, or Houses. These epithets are always translated into Reikspiel as they are much

ELF NAME GENERATOR

If you are finding it difficult to come up with an appropriate name for you Elf character, then roll the tables below. Some Elves only have two elements to their name some have three or more. Keep rolling until you have something you like, or simply choose the elements you think sound best.

1d10	First Component	Second Component	High Elf Ending	Wood Elf Ending
1	Aes	a	andril	arha
2	Ath	ath	anel	anhu
3	Dor	dia	ellion	dda
4	Far	en	fin	han
5	Gal	for	il	loc
6	Im	lor	irian	noc
7	Lin	mar	mor	oth
8	Mal	ol	nil	ryn
9	Mor	sor	ric	stra
10	Ullia	than	wing	wyth

easier for other species to pronounce and understand. Among High Elves, epithets usually describe character traits and physical appearance, but can be more obscure. Wood Elf epithets typically reference the natural world so beloved by the forest kin.

High Elf examples: Emberfell, Fireborn, Foamheart, Goldenhair, Silverspray, Spellsign

Wood Elf examples: Fleetriver, Shadowstalker, Treeshaper, Weavewatcher, Willowlimb, Windrunner

Halfling Names
Halfling names are comprised of a given name and a clan name at a minimum, with middle names included to ensure family trees are not confused.

Halfling Forenames
Halflings proudly bear grand names drawn from their long family trees, but they rarely use these outside official business. Normally, they are known by a cosy-sounding shortened form of their ancestral name. Some Halfling's diminutives are completely unrelated to their formal names and are instead more descriptive, like Rosie or Scrumper.

Halflings place great stock in their achievements and some elders will only answer to nicknames related to their job, such as Gaffer, Guv, or Nan. Halflings also have long had a habit of emulating their neighbours to the point that many grand, formerly-Human names have now become 'traditional' Halfling names.

Examples (with diminutives): Antoniella (Anni), Esmerelda (Esme), Ferdinand (Fred), Heironymus (Hiro), Maximilian (Max), Theodosius (Theo), Thomasina (Tina)

Halfling Clan Names
Halfling clan names are almost exclusively related to food and drink, geographical or natural features, or personal characteristics of the ancestor who first took the name. Halflings who have the same surname are always related and can usually tell you exactly how.

Human's tendency to have the same surname despite being unrelated causes confusion among some Halflings, who will happily pinch pies from a Schmidt on one street because a Schmidt on another street short-changed them.

Common Reikland Clans: Ashfield, Brandysnap, Hayfoot, Rumster, Shortbottom, Thorncobble

PHYSICAL DETAILS
When it comes to cosmetic physical details — those aspects of your appearance that don't influence the game directly — you may either roll them randomly or choose from the range available to your Species.

Age
Average natural lifespans are around 60 for a Human, 120 for Halflings, and over 200 for a Dwarf, while Elves don't appear to age at all and have been known to live for a thousand years or more. Choose your Character's age or use the table below.

Human	Dwarf	Elf	Halfling
15+d10	15+10d10	30+10d10	15+5d10

Eye Colour

While most species roll once on the table below, Elves may roll twice: their innately magical natures mean they often have variegated colours, such as sapphire blue flecked with gold, or a mottled mixture of mossy green and warm chestnut.

Hair Colour

All species barring Elves have hair that slowly turns grey as they move through middle age, then eventually turns white as they reach old age.

By comparison, Elves seem eternally youthful, never showing any signs of age. Humans and Dwarfs may also have significant facial hair, which is usually the same colour as head hair, but not always.

Height

Average heights are: Dwarf (4'8"), Elf (6'5"), Halfling (3'6"), with Humans varying much more widely, averaging somewhere around 5'9" in the Reikland. If you want a truly random upper height for Humans, if either die rolls a 10, roll one more die and add it to the height total.

Human	Dwarf	Elf	Halfling
4'9"+2d10"	4'3"+d10"	5'11"+d10"	3'1"+d10"

AMBITIONS

Ambitions are a Character's goals in life – what they want to achieve. All characters have both a Short-Term and Long-Term Ambition.

Choosing Ambitions

Consult with your GM when choosing your Ambitions. Your GM has final say on the acceptability of an Ambition, and whether it is short-term or long-term. Should you wish to change an Ambition, you may do so between sessions.

Short-term Ambitions

Short-term Ambitions represent your immediate goals. They are outcomes you wish to achieve within days and weeks, possibly

EYE COLOUR TABLE

2d10	Reikland Human	Dwarf	Halfling	High Elf	Wood Elf
2	Free Choice	Coal	Light Grey	Jet	Ivory
3	Green	Lead	Grey	Amethyst	Charcoal
4	Pale Blue	Steel	Pale Blue	Aquamarine	Ivy Green
5–7	Blue	Blue	Blue	Sapphire	Mossy Green
8–11	Pale Grey	Earth Brown	Green	Turquoise	Chestnut
12–14	Grey	Dark Brown	Hazel	Emerald	Chestnut
15–17	Brown	Hazel	Brown	Amber	Dark Brown
18	Hazel	Green	Copper	Copper	Tan
19	Dark Brown	Copper	Dark Brown	Citrine	Sandy Brown
20	Black	Gold	Dark Brown	Gold	Violet

HAIR COLOUR TABLE

2d10	Reikland Human	Dwarf	Halfling	High Elf	Wood Elf
2	White Blond	White	Grey	Silver	Birch Silver
3	Golden Blond	Grey	Flaxen	White	Ash Blond
4	Red Blond	Pale Blond	Russet	Pale Blond	Rose Gold
5-7	Golden Brown	Golden	Honey	Blond	Honey Blond
8–11	Light Brown	Copper	Chestnut	Yellow Blond	Brown
12–14	Dark Brown	Bronze	Ginger	Copper Blond	Mahogany Brown
15–17	Black	Brown	Mustard	Red Blond	Dark brown
18	Auburn	Dark Brown	Almond	Auburn	Sienna
19	Red	Reddish Brown	Chocolate	Red	Ebony
20	Grey	Black	Liquorice	Black	Blue-Black

sooner. Under normal circumstances, a short-term Ambition should take at least two or three sessions to complete.

Example short-term Ambitions include:

- Ruining the reputation of a romantic rival.
- Avenging a fallen comrade.
- Befriending a reclusive scholar.

Long-term Ambitions

Long-term Ambitions are goals you will need to work on for months or years to complete, and may never be achieved at all, perhaps taken more as a description of a primary motivation in your life than a realistic outcome.

Examples of long-term Ambitions include:

- Owning your own coaching inn.
- Building your village into a thriving town.
- Ridding the Colleges of Magic of Elven influence.

OPTIONS: NEFARIOUS PLANS

You may want to keep your Ambitions secret from other players in your party, especially if they are controversial or clandestine. If you want to overthrow the Emperor, or legalise Necromancy in the Reikland, chances are your Witch Hunter ally won't approve!

Achieving Your Ambitions

If you achieve your short-term Ambition, you will receive a bonus of +50 XP, and can choose a new short-term Ambition at the end of the session. If you achieve your long-term Ambition, you may either:

- Receive a bonus of +500 XP and choose a new long-term Ambition at the end of the session.
- Retire your Character — who becomes an NPC under your GM's control — and gain a bonus of half your earned XP of your current character to spend on your next character.

Retired Characters will generally stay in place to take advantage of their achieved ambition. You can build them into the background of your new Character, so that they may continue to help you. If you want to reactivate a retired Character, talk to your GM about how best to bring that into the current story. Retiring Characters allows you to build a network across the Old World, and can be a great source of adventure leads.

7) PARTY

Now you have almost finished making your Character, you need to consider the other players in your party. Everyone will have more fun when your Characters can engage and interact with one another; while some intra-party tension can be enjoyable, it is important you are not constantly at one another's throats.

You will also want to consider how your party know one another. Are you friends? Are you the retainers of a noble, or travelling companions on a river barge? Or is your GM going to have you meet during your first session?

PARTY AMBITIONS

All players in your group should also discuss what your collective goals are, and then choose a short-term and long-term party Ambition. Much like your personal Ambitions, party Ambitions can be changed between sessions.

Short-term Party Ambitions

Short-term party Ambitions have the same scope as your personal short-term Ambitions but are for the whole group. Your personal Ambitions should never be the same as your party Ambitions, but there is no reason they can't complement each other.

Examples of short-term party Ambitions include:

- Outwitting a rival group, securing a job at their loss.
- Hunting down the killer of a lost party member.
- Impressing your patron by completely succeeding in an appointed task.

Long-term Party Ambitions

Much like short-term party Ambitions, long-term Party Ambitions work like your personal Ambitions, and can be just as wide in scope, but are for your entire group.

Examples of long-term Party Ambitions include:

- Eradicate an Empire-wide Chaos Cult.
- Build a castle.
- Become Heroes of the Empire, each earning an Imperial Cross for bravery, pinned on your chests by the Emperor himself!

Achieving your Party Ambitions

If your party achieves its short-term Ambition, each member receives +50 XP, and you can all select a new Ambition for the party at the end of the session.

If your party achieves its long-term Party Ambition:

- All players receive a bonus of +500 XP, and the party chooses a new long-term Ambition at the end of the session.
- As many players as wish to do so can retire their Characters — who become NPCs under the GM's control; those who do gain a bonus of half the XP of their current Character to spend on their next Character.

8) BRINGING YOUR CHARACTER TO LIFE

Fleshing out your Character's personality and history will really help you bring them to life. Some players write detailed backstories for their Character, especially if they are very familiar with the Old World. Others prefer to just decide the basics at the start, and then improvise during the game (discuss this with the GM beforehand so you don't derail any storylines). At the start of the Character creation process we recommended that you talk to the other players and the GM about the kind of group you want to create, and we revisited that while creating Party ambitions. This is the perfect place to complete that process, weaving your Characters' stories together and binding them into a tight-knit group with their own reasons for sticking together.

TEN QUESTIONS

One useful technique for creating an interesting background for your Character is to answer a series of questions about them —

here are ours! If any of these questions make you want to change something about the character you've created so far... do so! For instance, if you add in some detail about your childhood, you may want to revisit the choices you made in **4) Skills and Talents**.

Where are you from?

Do you come from one of Reikland's bustling towns, or a sleepy village? Perhaps your childhood was spent on a remote farmstead, or maybe you called the winding back alleys of Altdorf home? Do you hail from a deep mountain hold, or were your days spent threading the roads and riverways of Reikland, always on the move? See **Chapter 10: Glorious Reikland** for details on the geography and settlements of this corner of the Empire.

What is your family like?

It may take a village to raise a child, but it's your kin who do the heavy lifting. What were your parents' occupations? Are they still alive? Do you have any siblings? Were you close, or were you constantly at one another's throats? Grandparents? Nephews, nieces, cousins? Children, even? Does your family approve of your career choice? Are they proud of you, or are you a stain on your family's honour?

What was your childhood like?

Was your family home full of love, or was it a cold, inhospitable place? Were you coddled, or did you have to fend for yourself? Were you educated, and if so, by whom: a tutor, a family member, a village school, or the local priest? Were you trained in the family business, or were you sent from home, fostered elsewhere or raised in an orphanage?

Why did you leave home?

Do you still live in your childhood home, or did you leave? If so, when? Were you drawn by the promise of excitement of life in the big city? Are you in search of riches, or renown? Are you running from something, or trying to find meaning or purpose in your life?

Who are your best friends?

While you cannot choose your family, your friends are another matter entirely, and you can tell a lot about someone by the friends they keep. Do you have any friends from childhood? Or friends you've made since leaving home? What do you do together? Drink? Gamble? Debate? Are your allies in your party your best friends? Or do you eschew civilised company in favour of a loyal pet?

What is your greatest desire?

What is the fire that burns in your heart? Your Ambitions may be your chief goal, but ambitions are often prosaic or banal. If you could have anything, anything at all, what would it be?

What are your best and worst memories?

We are the sum of our experiences; they shape and mould us, forging us anew. What are your most treasured memories? An afternoon of glorious summer sunshine? A passionate kiss, while huddling from rain, beneath sheltering boughs? A victory scored in a battle of wits or brawn? And what are your less fond recollections? A painful humiliation? A scheme thwarted? The end of a long-term partnership, romantic or business? The hatred, disdain, or, worse, disinterest of your peers?

What are your religious beliefs?

Most folk of the Empire are polytheistic; the existence, and puissance, of the gods is undeniable, and so their veneration is a matter of course. That being said, not all of the gods are favoured equally.

Does your character have a fondness or affinity for one god in particular? Do you cross your fingers for luck, appealing to Ranald? Do you make the sign of the Twin Tailed Comet at your enemy, or mutter an angry prayer to Ulric before battle? See **Chapter 7: Religion and Belief** for details of the gods and their ways.

To whom, or what, are you loyal?

Will you protect your friends above all, or are the ties that bind you to your clan, kinfolk, or partner stronger than iron? Or are you a pious soul, dedicated above all to your god? Or are you loyal to your community, to Reikland, the Empire… or just to yourself?

Why are you adventuring?

And this is the big one: why are you a player character, and not just another citizen of the Empire. Why are you adventuring?

Have you consciously chosen a life of adventure? Are you seeking out the enemies of the Empire, or a big pay day? Or was this life thrust upon you, against your will. Are you seeking justice, or vengeance, or is your adventuring life nothing more than a fight to clear your name, or survive your enemies?

Answer all of those, and you will have a fully fleshed out character, ready to go. But, before you start playing, did you gain any bonus XP during the character creation process? If so, you may wish to spend it before you begin play.

OPTIONS: PSYCHOLOGY

When you are creating your Character's story, you might feel you should have powerful emotions such as Love, Camaraderie, Hatred etc towards family members, situations, enemies or other features of their life. If the GM agrees, you can take a Psychology trait (see page 190).

9) ADVANCEMENT

Experience Points (XP) are used to improve your character. The GM will give you XP after every session of play, and you may be rewarded for doing particularly well. This could include successfully resolving the ongoing adventure, roleplaying your character well or defeating important enemies. Between sessions, you spend your XP to buy new Skills and Talents, to increase Characteristics, and to change Career. The final step in creating your Character is to spend any bonus XP you earned through the Character Creation process. The tables below shows how you can spend these points.

Initially, you can only spend your XP to increase the 3 Characteristics, 8 Skills, and 4 Talents available to your Career level. For more details on spending XP, see page 47.

CHARACTERISTIC AND SKILL IMPROVEMENT XP COSTS

Advances	XP Cost per Advance	
	Characteristics	Skills
0 to 5	25	10
6 to 10	30	15
11 to 15	40	20
16 to 20	50	30
21 to 25	70	40
26 to 30	90	60
31 to 35	120	80
36 to 40	150	110
41 to 45	190	140
46 to 50	230	180

OTHER IMPROVEMENT COSTS

Improvement	XP Cost
+1 Talent	100 XP +100 XP per time the Talent has already been taken
Leave a Complete Career	100 XP
Leave an Incomplete Career	200 XP

FINISHED!

Now your character and party are created, you are ready to play!

CHARACTER SHEET SUMMARY

Personal Details

Here is where you fill in your Character's personal details, such as name, **Species** (see page 24) and **Career** (see page 30), as well as aspects of their physical appearance.

Attributes

Record your Attributes here. Attributes include your **Characteristics** (see page 33), which describe your Character's strengths and weaknesses. As you progress through your game, your Character will gain **Advances** (see page 35), reflecting them getting stronger, tougher or better at different tasks.

Your **Movement** (see page 35) shows how quickly you can move.

Fate and Fortune (see page 170) reflect how lucky your character is, while **Resilience and Resolve** (see page 171) indicate your character's pool of grit and determination to overcome certain obstacles. You will also need to record a **Motivation** (see page 34), which explains what keeps your Character going.

Skills & Talents

Your **Skills** (see page 35) are abilities your character can train or develop. Basic Skills are common or innate and are known by all characters, while Advanced Skills require training. As you acquire new Skills, mark them onto your Character Sheet. As you get gain Advances, your Skills will improve, which increase your chance of succeeding in **Tests** (see page 149).

Talents are additional abilities your character possesses. As many Talents may be taken more than once, keep a tally of how many times you have taken each one.

Experience

As you play WFRP your Gamemaster will award **Experience Points** (see page 43). Keep a record of your current (unspent) Experience, as well as your Spent Experience and a running total.

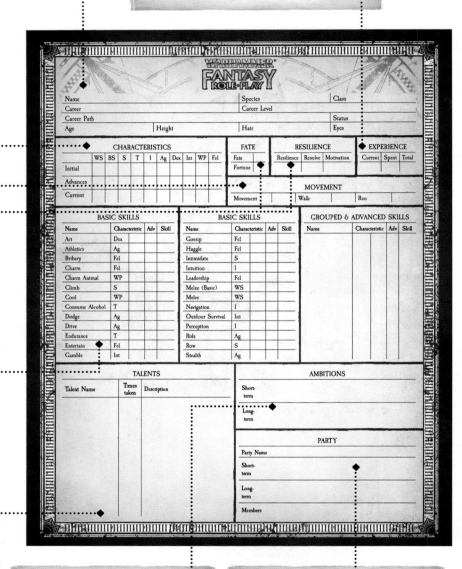

Ambitions

Your **Ambitions** (see page 41) are your Character and party's main goals in life. Short-term Ambitions can be achieved within a few days or weeks, while long-term Ambitions are those that may take years, or may never be achieved at all.

Party

Details about your group goes here: the name your party is known by, and its short-term and long-term **Ambitions** (see pages 41-42). There's also space to note your companions' names as a reminder to use them and help everyone stay in character.

Armour

Record your **Armour** (see page 299) here. Armour is very useful at keeping your character alive, as it reduces incoming Damage, and may save you from **Critical Hits** (see page 159). Record the details of your Armour in the table, and also write the total Armour Points (APs) in each location on the diagram.

Corruption and Mutation

When you face dark horrors, Daemons, and the machinations of the Dark Gods, you may gain **Corruption** Points (see 182). Gathering too many of these can quickly lead to mutation (see page 183).

Psychology

If your character has any **Psychology** (see page 190) record it here. Psychologies include phobias, animosities and strong loyalties. Most starting characters do not begin with any Psychologies.

Trappings, Encumbrance, and Wealth

Your **Trappings** (see page 37) are your belongings. These may include clothing, bags, candles, ropes, or bandages. As your character is limited in how much they can carry, you must also record each item's **Encumbrance** (see page 293). Add up the total Encumbrance of your Armour, Weapons, and Trappings to see how much weight you are carrying.

Your character's Wealth is recorded in brass pennies, silver shillings, and, if you're especially wealthy, gold crowns. Spend it wisely!

Wounds

Record your **Wounds** (see page 34) here. Your Wounds are derived from your Characteristics and Talents. As you are injured in **Combat** (see page 156) your Wounds will go down, while **Healing** (see page 181) will increase them again (though never beyond your maximum). As you gain Advances in your Characteristics and Talents, your Wounds may, in turn, increase.

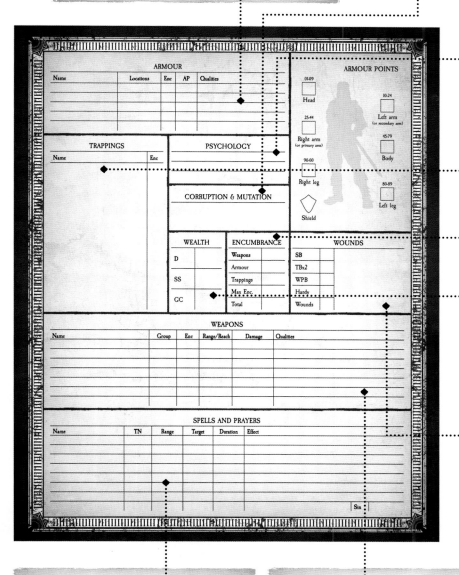

Spells and Prayers

If your character is in a religious or magical Career, you may have access to **Spells** (see page 238) or **Prayers** (see page 217). These represent supernatural abilities, as your characters draws on the winds of magic, or calls on their favoured deity for assistance in times of need.

Weapons

Record details about your **Weapons** (see page 293) here. As well as the type of Weapon, you will also record its Encumbrance (how heavy it is), how much Damage it inflicts, and, if it is a Ranged Weapon, at what Range it can be used.

◆ CLASS AND CAREERS ◆

'Well, I play a character with no class at all who would sell his grandmother for career advancement; you know, exactly the type of fellow frequently encountered in my line of work.'

– Detlef Sierck, Playwright and Actor

Your Career is your job when not off adventuring (or having adventures done to you, as may often be the case). It describes your training, social class, and your future prospects. **WFRP** groups similar Careers into Classes.

CLASSES

A summary of each Class is found in **Chapter 2: Character** on page 30. Classes organise Careers into easily referenced groups. They also impact character development, provide different starting Trappings during Character Creation (see page 37), and influence how you can change Career (see **Changing Career** on page 48). Some Classes have access to different Endeavours — activities you can take between adventures; for more on this, see **Chapter 6: Between Adventures**.

CLASSES

Academics: Page 53.
Burghers: Page 61.
Courtiers: Page 69.
Peasants: Page 77.
Rangers: Page 85.
Riverfolk: Page 93.
Rogues: Page 101.
Warriors: Page 109.

CAREERS

The summary and illustration at the top of the eight Careers in your chosen Class should give you a good idea of which is the one for you. The Careers can be considered to be as broad as possible, so you are encouraged to interpret them imaginatively as part of your Character concept.

CAREER LEVELS

Every Career has four levels, each progressively better than the last. If you take a look at Apothecary, the first Academic Career, you can see the four levels are:

1. *Apprentice Apothecary*
2. *Apothecary*
3. *Master Apothecary*
4. *Apothecary-General*

When choosing a Career for a new character, you always start at the first level of the career — so, if you were an Apothecary, you would start as an *Apprentice Apothecary*.

ADVANCING THROUGH YOUR CAREER

Your Character's Career affects how they will grow through experience. Every Career offers three forms of Advances: *Characteristic Advances, Skill Advances,* and *Talent Advances* — each of which are purchased with Experience Points (XP). You can also use XP to Change Career. Your Career Level determines what Characteristics, Skills, and Talents are available to you.

Characteristic Advances

Every Career has an *Advance Scheme* governing its Characteristic Advances. The Advance Scheme shows your character's 10 Characteristics, 3 marked with ✚, 1 marked with ✖ on a brass background, 1 marked with a ☠ on silver, and the last marked ♛ on gold.

The three marked ✚ are Characteristics you can advance in the first level of the Career. When you enter the second level of a career, the ✖ Characteristic also becomes available. When you enter the third level, the ☠ Characteristic also becomes available. And when you enter the fourth and last level of a Career, the ♛ Characteristic finally becomes available.

The cost in XP of a Characteristic Advance is shown in the *Characteristic and Skill Improvement XP Costs* table, and depends on the number of Characteristic Advances you have already taken in that Characteristic.

Each Characteristic Advance adds +1 to the associated Characteristic. So, if you had purchased 4 Agility Advances, and your Initial Agility was 27, your Current Agility would be 31. The Advances would cost 25 XP per +1 Advance, as at each point the number of Advances previously taken would be in the 0–5 range.

Chapter 5: Rules explains how the Characteristics are used in the game, and **Chapter 2: Character** explains what each Characteristic is. There is no upper limit to the number of Characteristic Advances that can be purchased, although higher levels do become prohibitively expensive. **Note:** While Weapon Skill and Ballistic Skill have the word 'Skill' in them, this is only a historical artefact — they are characteristics and are Advanced as such.

CHARACTERISTIC AND SKILL IMPROVEMENT XP COSTS

Advances	XP Cost per Advance	
	Characteristics	Skills
0 to 5	25	10
6 to 10	30	15
11 to 15	40	20
16 to 20	50	30
21 to 25	70	40
26 to 30	90	60
31 to 35	120	80
36 to 40	150	110
41 to 45	190	140
46 to 50	230	180
51 to 55	280	220
56 to 60	330	270
61 to 65	390	320
66 to 70	450	380
70+	520	440

Skill Advances

You can advance all the Skills listed for your Career level and lower. So, if you were an Apothecary's Apprentice (level 1), you could only access the Skills listed under Apothecary's Apprentice (level 1). But, if you were a Master Apothecary (level 3), you could access all the Skills for Master Apothecary (level 3), Apothecary (level 2), and Apprentice Apothecary (level 1).

The cost in XP of a Skill Advance is shown in the *Characteristic and Skill Improvement XP Costs* table, and depends on the number of Skill Advances you have already taken in that Skill.

Each Skill Advance adds +1 to your Skill level. Therefore, if you had purchased 9 Advances in Stealth and your Agility was 31, your Stealth would be 40. The first 5 Advances would cost 10 XP each, and the 4 remaining Advances would cost 15 XP each.

Note: One of the Skills in the first level of your Career will be marked in italics. This is the Skill you Test when Earning money (see page 51).

The full rules for how to use your Skills can be found in **Chapter 4: Skills and Talents**. Like Characteristic Advances, there is no upper limit to the number of Skill Advances that can be purchased.

NON-CAREER ADVANCES

Characters will inevitably want to advance Characteristics and Skills not listed in their Careers. That's fine, if the GM feels it's appropriate, but it costs double. The GM might want you to find a teacher or otherwise play out this unusual education.

Non-Career Characteristic and Skill Advances cost double the amount of XP listed in the *Characteristic and Skill Improvement XP Costs* table.

Normally, non-Career Talents may not be purchased with XP, although *Training* and *Unusual Learning* Endeavours in **Chapter 6: Between Adventures** provide an opportunity to purchase non-Career Advances as if they were Career Advances, and give the possibility of learning non-Career Talents.

OPTIONS: CUSTOMISE YOUR TRAPPINGS

The Trappings listed in each Career are guidelines only. Feel free to be creative with your Trappings, choosing those that fit your interpretation of your character's Career and how it manifests. So, if you were using the Soldier Career to represent a grizzled Handgunner from Reikland's State Army, you may decide to tweak the required Trappings to include powder and shot.

Trappings are how you are recognised as someone belonging to your career. If you want to go incognito, you might not want to have all your trappings with you. Similarly, if you are trying to use the authority of your Career, not having the trappings of such means people might not take you seriously.

Talent Advances

Talents are only available when you are in the level of the Career that lists them. So, if you are an Apothecary-General, you can only buy Talents listed under Apothecary-General, not those listed under Apprentice Apothecary, Apothecary, or Master Apothecary.

Talents Advances cost 100 XP +100 XP per Advance already taken in that Talent.

The rules for every Talent can be found in **Chapter 4: Skills and Talents**. The first time you purchase a new Talent (for 100 XP) it grants you access to the Talent's special rules. If you purchase a Talent multiple times (second time costs 200 XP, third 300 XP) any additional abilities bestowed are listed in the Talent description.

Note: Not all Talents can be purchased multiple times. Check the Talent listing for any limitations.

Changing Career

When you have taken all the Advances you want in your current Career, it's time to change Career. Changing Career means one of two things:

1) Moving to a different level within your current Career (from *Apothecary* to *Master Apothecary*); or
2) Moving to an entirely new Career (from *Apothecary* to *Scholar*).

In each case, you will have to first determine if you have completed your current Career level. If you have, changing Career costs 100 XP. If you have not, it costs 200 XP.

Completing a Career

Completing a Career represents mastering your current vocation and being ready to move on to something new. To complete a Career, you must have the number of Advances listed below in all your Career level's Characteristics and in eight of your Career level's available Skills. You must also have at least 1 Talent from your current Career level. Skills and Talents you have gained from advancement prior to entering your current Career count towards this..

Level	Advances
1	5
2	10
3	15
4	20

Note: Just because you have completed a Career level does not mean you have to move to a new one. Moving Career is always entirely up to you. If you wish to stay in the first level of Pauper forever, that's completely fine.

Changing to a New Level

If you have completed your current Career level, you can enter the next Career level, or any lower Career level, for 100 XP. So, if you completed Hunter (Hunter level 2), you could exit to Tracker

(Hunter level 3) or Trapper (Hunter level 1) for 100 XP, but not Huntsmaster (Hunter level 4).

With GM permission, you can also skip Career levels. This is normally driven by in-game events. For example: A Scion (Noble level 1) inherits a significant estate during play, so the GM offers Noble Lord (Noble level 4) as a potential change of Career. Like normal, changing to this Career level costs 100 XP if you have completed your current Career level, or 200 XP if you have not.

Changing to a New Career

If you have completed your current Career level, you can enter the first level of any Career from your Class for 100 XP, or for 200 XP if you have not completed your current Career level. If you want to enter the first level of a Career from a different Class, this cost an extra 100 XP. Note: your GM may require in-game justification for such Career changes; after all, not just anyone can enter Noble, even if you are in the Courtier Class.

Further, if you have completed your current Career level, with GM permission, and solid justification, you can enter the same Career level in any Career within your Class. So, if you completed Master Apothecary (Apothecary level 3), you could move to Fellow (Scholar level 3), to show you were taking a teaching position in Altdorf University. This costs 100 XP. However, be aware there are obvious limitations here. Some Careers, such as Wizard, require the basics be learned before the more advanced lore can be understood and the Talents of earlier Career levels will not be open to you at a higher level.

Lastly, between adventures, you can also change Career using the *Change Career* Endeavour (see page 196).

TALENT AND CAREER CHANGE XP COSTS IMPROVEMENT

Improvement	XP Cost
+1 Talent Advance	100 XP + 100 XP per time the Talent is already taken
Leave a Complete Career	100 XP
Leave an Incomplete Career	200 XP
Enter a different Class	+100 XP

ALTERNATIVE CHANGES IN CAREER

Sometimes during play you are offered a job in the most unlikely circumstances. For example: a local Baron may employ you to be his Honour Guard (Guard, Career level 3), or you may escape Altdorf on the run from the city watch, now effectively an Outlaw (Outlaw, Career level 2). In such circumstances, the GM may offer a Career change that lies outside your normal Career Path. That's not only fine, it's recommended, as it's always more fun to tie your Career choices into in-game events.

STATUS

Old World society is highly stratified — common folk are in little doubt as to their place in the society whilst the elite enjoy power and prestige that is brutally enforced and therefore largely unchallenged. Most people in between are acutely aware of their standing, and preoccupied with improving it. This is represented by Status, which can modify the interactions between people of different social classes.

TIERS AND STANDING

Status is expressed as a Tier — from lowest to highest: Brass, Silver, or Gold — and a Standing — which is a number, generally from 1–5, showing how respected the character is within their Tier.

If you have a higher Tier than another character, you have higher Status. If you are in the same Tier as another character, then you are higher Status if you have a higher Standing.

The Three Tiers

The most important distinctions in Status are the three Tiers:

The Gold Tier: Reserved for the rulers of society; those who directly serve them as advisors, protectors, and maintainers of the law; and the independently wealthy. To reach this position requires hard work, success, and not a little luck. All in the Gold tier are rich, respected, and of higher Status than those in the Silver and Brass tiers.

The Silver Tier: Populated by well-to-do townsfolk and those following professions requiring skill and expertise. Tradesmen, craftsmen, and merchants make up most of the upper ranks of the tier, whilst the bottom is filled by those providing services. These folk lead relatively humble lives, but they are still respectable. People of the Silver Tier are of higher Status than those of the Brass Tier.

The Brass Tier: Occupied by peasants and those in the poorest professions which often require no particular skills. The Brass Tier also contains many criminals, ne'er-do-wells, and those who don't make any living at all.

DETERMINING STATUS

Your Status is determined by your Career level. Beside the name of your Career level is your Status, marked as 'Brass 3', 'Silver 1', or similar. This is the Tier and Standing. Should you change Career, check the new Status by the name of your new Career Level, and mark it on your Character Sheet.

CHANGING STATUS

Status changes for the following reasons:

1. You change Career.
2. You gain a Talent that modifies Status.
3. The GM imposes a change in Status due to in-game events.

Whatever causes a change in Status, you should take time to explain what exactly occurred, and the impact this has on your character. If you have changed to a different Career Level, say from a Student to a Scholar, what precipitated this? What subject did you study? And how does your character now feel after graduating? Taking time to explain your changing circumstances makes your character more rounded and believable.

BEYOND THE SOCIAL NORM

Status provides a rough guide to how the folk of the Old World behave when they fit in with acceptable norms. However, some characters will violate this, and that's completely fine. If you wish to randomise how an NPC reacts to Social Status, roll 1d10 on the following table:

1d10	Result
1-2	**Defies Status.** The character defies convention concerning Status and ignores its effects.
3-8	**Standard Reactions.** The character follows the Status rules as normal.
9-10	**Extreme Views.** The character holds extreme views. Modify all Tests influenced by Status by a further +/−10, as appropriate.

THE EFFECTS OF STATUS

Status influences a number of situations that impact your Character. Often these involve making Tests easier or more difficult (see page 153). The GM may expand or limit these influences as they wish.

Charm

Status impacts Charm significantly, with those of higher Status more easily able to get what they want, and those of lower status

finding it harder to secure influence. In most circumstances, those of a higher Tier gain a bonus of +10 to Charm Tests influencing those with a lower tier. Similarly, those of lower Tier suffer a penalty of −10 to influence those of a higher Tier. The GM may also apply these modifiers to those of different Standing in the same Tier, but this is rarer.

If the target of the Charm attempt is atypical, this might not work as usual however. An individual who 'Defies Status' would mean no modifiers apply, and one with 'Extreme Views' might mean that the opposite modifiers apply (−10 rather than +10, for example).

OPTIONS: BEGGING & STATUS

Begging is often most effective when aimed at those who are just above you in the social order.

For example: Most Beggars are Brass Tier and therefore benefit from a +10 bonus when begging from people who are Silver Tier, instead of suffering a −10 penalty.

Entertain

Status does not normally influence Entertain tests. However, a GM ought to consider that some entertainments are thought fitting to particular venues. A peasant playing a hurdy-gurdy is not likely to go down well at an opera house, whilst even a mediocre orchestra is likely to draw a significant audience if it starts performing on the village green.

As such the GM might like to consider the sort of audience a performance is normally aimed at, and the audience that is actually available, and apply suitable modifiers.

Intimidate

If you have a higher Status than the target of your Intimidate, you typically gain a bonus of +10.

Gossip

Gossip tends to be stilted between people of different classes. Any Gossip Test between individuals of different Tiers suffers a penalty of −10.

Leadership

Status plays a very important role in Leadership. Indeed, the State Army normally only grants higher ranks to those of noble birth.

If you are a higher tier than the target of your Leadership Test, you gain a bonus of +10. If you are two tiers higher, the bonus increases to +20.

MAINTAINING STATUS

In order to benefit (or suffer) from Status, you have to act in accordance with your role in society.

It may be that you wish to pass incognito, presenting yourself anonymously. Typically, you will be counted as having a Status of Brass 3 if you do this.

Example: *Hans the noble wears the latest fashions and always buys the best trappings. He rides his lovingly groomed horse into a village, pausing only to let his herald announce his presence to all. He fully benefits from his Gold 2 Status. His brother Heinrich dresses in old clothes, hides all his courtly garb under the bed, and acts like a nameless wanderer. He is treated as having a Status of Brass 3.*

Keeping Up Appearances

Characters need to spend a certain amount of money to maintain their lifestyle. As explained in **The Cost of Living** (see page 289) there are minimum expectations of expenditure for each Tier.

Should a character fail to live up to these levels of expenditure they will begin to be perceived as being of lower Status, losing 1 point of Standing per week.

To stop this decline, the character must resume spending the money expected of them, whereupon they regain 1 point of Standing a week until they recover the lost points.

Should Standing reach 0, your tier drops by one and your Standing is set to 5. If you are already at the lowest tier, then your Status sticks at Brass 0.

Example: *Pietr is a Noble and has been slumming it in the East End of Altdorf for the last two weeks, letting his Standing of Gold 3 drop to Gold 1 as he eats poor food, drinks cheap beer, and hostels in flop houses. Should another week pass and Pietr does not change his ways, his Standing will drop to Gold 0, which immediately becomes Silver 5. Should this occur, Pietr's father will almost certainly step in to curtail the family shame…*

EARNING MONEY WITH STATUS

Your Status is directly linked to the amount of money you earn while working. The higher your Status, the more money you can earn as your good name attracts business. If the GM agrees, during play you can spend a week to work in your Career assuming you are in a place where such is feasible (it's hard to be a Watchman in the middle of a wasteland). This is called Earning.

When Earning, make an **Average (+20) Dramatic Test** (see page 152) against the Earning Skill of your Career (the Skill marked in italics in the Career's first level). If passed, you receive the money marked in the table below. If failed, you receive half the money. If an Astounding Failure (–6) is scored, you have a very bad week, and earn nothing (or have your money stolen, or some similar mishap).

This total is not strictly speaking how much money you earn, it's more a representation of how much money you have left at the end of the week after all your expenses are taken into account.

Tier	Amount Earned per Standing
Brass	2d10 Brass Pennies
Silver	1d10 Silver Shillings
Gold	1 Gold Crown

Note: This is the same amount of coin earned with an *Income* Endeavour (see page 198).

Example: *Gunther the Coachman decides he'll work for the Four Seasons Coaching House for a week while his peers research a library for things he frankly doesn't understand, and secretly thinks may be heretical if he did. The GM agrees to let Gunther enact some Earning, so Gunther rolls against his Drive (Coach) skill (his Earning Skill for Coachman) and passes. Given his Status is Silver 2, he can roll 2d10 and earn that much silver. Unfortunately, he only rolls a 1 and a 2 for a total of 3 silver shillings; clearly Gunther was drinking a lot after his long work shifts, and has little coin remaining…*

GENDERED CAREER NAMES

Although some Careers have masculine or feminine names because of the limitations of language, all careers are intended for any gender; so, no matter how your character identifies, all careers are available.

For example: Anyone may serve any deity. Although some Gods (such as Taal and Ulric, and Rhya and Shallya) are more likely to have servants who identify with the same gender as the God, other deities (such as Verena and Sigmar), have an equal appeal to all.

CAREER FORMAT

The following is a breakdown of the information each Career presents.

- **Name:** The name of the Career.
- **Limitations:** A list of the different Species typically using the Career.
- **Summary:** A one-sentence introduction to the Career.
- **Description:** A paragraph or two describing the career, and alternatives ways it may be used.
- **Advance Scheme:** The Career's Advance Scheme.
- **Career Path:** The Name, Status, Skills, Talents, and Trappings for each of the Career's four levels. Note: if a Talent or Skill is marked '(Any)' it means you can choose **one** of the options for that Talent or Skill when in that Career Level; So, Lore (Any), could be Lore (Geography), Lore (Folklore), Lore (Magick), or any other similar example. Likewise, if one is marked (Local), it means you can choose **one** of the options for the Talent or Skill drawn from the local area; So, Lore (Local), could be Lore (Altdorf), Lore (Riverways), Lore (The Wasteland), or any other similar example.
- **Quotations:** A few in-game quotations about the Career.
- **Adventuring:** Some hints and tips about how those in the Career might find themselves adventuring.

APOTHECARY

Dwarf, Halfling, High Elf, Human

Skilled in chemistry and concoctions, you create and sell medicine of all kinds.

Apothecaries specialise in preparing pharmaceutical medication — commonly pills, draughts, and ointments — for sale to patients and doktors alike. Their workshops are filled with a dazzling array of bubbling alembics, overflowing beakers, worn mortar and pestles, and other physic-making paraphernalia. Some Apothecaries supplement their income selling illicit substances — from stimulants for desperate students, to hallucinogenic weirdroot for bored nobles or shady commissions from even shadier groups. Supplying these is lucrative, but also dangerous. Rare ingredients are expensive, so Apothecaries frequently have cash flow problems, and journey the wilds to collect their own ingredients. Many take temporary employment with expeditions, mercenaries, or the military for extra coin.

'Look for this sigil: white mortar, black pestle. Don't ask for our order without it or you'll be reported to the Watch. And lad, don't ever short our Apothecary; you'll spend the rest of your days wondering if the next drink will be your last.'

– Kathe the Unseen, Assassin

'Human chemistry? As shoddy as their architecture! And just as likely to kill you! I asked for tonic after a hard night's drinking. Had the flux for a week!'

– Thorica Norrasdotr, Dwarf Merchant

Due to Physician Guild pressure, most towns ban Apothecaries from formally practicing medicine, but during play Apothecaries can easily fill the role of a healer. Indeed, they are versatile in this role because they can also identify dangerous and unusual substances the party may encounter, and even turn some into useful medicine.

APOTHECARY ADVANCE SCHEME

WS	BS	S	T	I	Agi	Dex	Int	WP	Fel
			✚	☠		✚	✚	⛊	⚒

CAREER PATH

✚ Apothecary's Apprentice — Brass 3
Skills: Consume Alcohol, Heal, Language (Classical), Lore (Chemistry), Lore (Medicine), Lore (Plants), *Trade (Apothecary),* Trade (Poisoner)
Talents: Concoct, Craftsman (Apothecary), Etiquette (Scholar), Read/Write
Trappings: Book (Blank), Healing Draught, Leather Jerkin, Pestle and Mortar

⚒ Apothecary — Silver 1
Skills: Charm, Haggle, Lore (Science), Gossip, Language (Guilder), Perception
Talents: Criminal, Dealmaker, Etiquette (Guilder), Pharmacist
Trappings: Guild Licence, Trade Tools

☠ Master Apothecary — Silver 3
Skills: Intuition, Leadership, Research, Secret Signs (Guilder)
Talents: Bookish, Master Tradesman (Apothecary), Resistance (Poison), Savvy
Trappings: Book (Apothecary), Apprentice, Workshop

⛊ Apothecary-General — Gold 1
Skills: Intimidate, Ride (Horse)
Talents: Acute Sense (Taste), Coolheaded, Master Tradesman (Poisoner), Savant (Apothecary)
Trappings: Commission Papers, Large Workshop

ENGINEER
Dwarf, Halfling, Human

You create machines and constructions both useful and bizarre, and often downright deadly.

Engineers design and build mechanical devices or structures such as bridges, canals, or fortifications. Most are educated, Dwarfs at the hide-bound Dwarf Engineers Guild, Humans at forward-thinking establishments such as the Imperial Engineers' School at Altdorf, though self-taught prodigies are not unknown. Human Engineers value innovation and discovery, whereas Dwarfs favour traditional, tried-and-tested designs passed down for generations. Mining company engineers are well-paid; less so the State Army Engineers who maintain the Imperial war machines and act as sappers and bridge-builders. Master Engineers often find themselves leading teams on ambitious construction projects. Chartered Engineers are the most trusted in the Empire, called upon to design, test, and build such prestigious Imperial Commissions like the complex Steam Wheel Locks, which have revolutionised the speed of travel in the canals of the Vorbergland.

'What will it do? Well, it's supposed to pluck the chicken, Smallnose. Stand well back!'

– Wolfgang Kugelschrieber, Inventor

'Master Engineer Volker von Meinkopt found inspiration watching students reloading at the Imperial Gunnery School. He had a revelation: more barrels = more shots = more lethality. He soon produced the first repeating handgun, 'Von Meinkopt's Whirling Cavalcade of Death', and pistol, 'Von Meinkopt's Micro-mainspring of Multitudinous Precipitation of Pernicious Lead'. Not content to rest on those laurels, he then created the enormous nine-barrelled cannon, the Helblaster Volley Gun, which is utterly lethal to enemies and, all too often, its crew.'

– 'Great Engineers of the Empire', Lady Theodora Holzenauer, Engineer and Journalist

Some Engineers are drawn to investigate ancient Dwarf Holds, most now abandoned, for entombed within are the secrets of the master builders of old. Those who dare their depths may find millennia-old marvels, many of which are repurposed by Goblins and Skaven for their own nefarious purposes. Equally enticing are the stone sky bridges soaring above the Holds, some stretching for many miles, true wonders of bygone engineering that once connected thriving Dwarf settlements, forts, and farmlands.

ENGINEER ADVANCE SCHEME

WS	BS	S	T	I	Agi	Dex	Int	WP	Fel
+			💀	⚒		+	+	🛡	

CAREER PATH

+ Student Engineer — Brass 4
Skills: Consume Alcohol, Cool, Endurance, Language (Classical), Lore (Engineer), Perception, Ranged (Blackpowder), *Trade (Engineer)*
Talents: Artistic, Gunner, Read/Write, Tinker
Trappings: Book (Engineer), Hammer and Spikes

⚒ Engineer — Silver 2
Skills: Drive, Dodge, Navigation, Ranged (Engineering), Research, Language (Guilder)
Talents: Craftsman (Engineer), Etiquette (Guilder), Marksman, Orientation
Trappings: Guild Licence, Trade Tools

💀 Master Engineer — Silver 4
Skills: Language (Khazalid), Leadership, Ride (Horse), Secret Signs (Guilder)
Talents: Etiquette (Scholar), Master Tradesman (Engineering), Sniper, Super Numerate
Trappings: Workshop

🛡 Chartered Engineer — Gold 2
Skills: Language (Any), Lore (Any)
Talents: Magnum Opus, Rapid Reload, Savant (Engineering), Unshakeable
Trappings: Guild License, Library (Engineer), Quality Trade Tools (Engineer), Large Workshop (Engineer)

LAWYER

Dwarf, Halfling, High Elf, Human

You navigate treacherous legal systems, defending clients and prosecuting the guilty.

Lawyers give legal counsel, interpret the law, and argue on behalf of their clients before the courts. They are often specialists in the laws of the province in which they practice, or in ecclesiastical law. Most are university educated and therefore rich and well-connected, although gifted individuals of low birth are sometimes apprenticed. Cult lawyers learn from their venerable peers, with those trained by the Cults of Verena and Sigmar especially well-regarded. Some Lawyers are hired as mediators, settling informal disputes outside costly courts, a practice favoured by Halflings. Others work for criminal gangs, exploiting legal loopholes to free their always-guilty clients. At the top end of society, Barristers are the only lawyers allowed to address higher appeal courts in the city-states, charging exorbitant prices for their services.

'Sharks! No, worse! Leeches! But not the good kind that suck out bad humours, oh no. They're leeches that drain your coffers and leave you nothing to show for it.'

– Stefan Bachler, Merchant

'It is not what the lawyer says I may do that concerns me, but what is right by reason and justice. Such matters need then be the basis of our new law.'

– Lector Agatha von Böhrn, Supreme Law Lord of the Empire

Lawyers excel at getting people out of trouble, while adventurers excel at getting into it. They can use their knowledge of obscure local laws to avoid problems by suggesting unusual approaches to solve thorny dilemmas. After all, tying up a local thug in court is just as valuable, and arguably much safer, than tying one up in a basement.

LAWYER ADVANCE SCHEME

WS	BS	S	T	I	Agi	Dex	Int	WP	Fel
			●	✝		✝	✝	●	✗

CAREER PATH

✝ Student Lawyer — Brass 4
Skills: Consume Alcohol, Endurance, Haggle, Language (Classical), *Lore (Law)*, Lore (Theology), Perception, Research
Talents: Blather, Etiquette (Scholar), Read/Write, Speedreader
Trappings: Book (Law), Magnifying Glass

✗ Lawyer — Silver 3
Skills: Bribery, Charm, Gossip, Intuition, Language (Guilder), Secret Signs (Guilder)
Talents: Argumentative, Criminal, Etiquette (Guilder), Suave
Trappings: Court Robes, Guild Licence, Writing Kit

● Barrister — Gold 1
Skills: Art (Writing), Entertain (Speeches), Intimidate, Lore (Any)
Talents: Bookish, Cat-tongued, Impassioned Zeal, Savvy
Trappings: Office, Assistant (Student or Servant)

● Judge — Gold 2
Skills: Cool, Lore (Any)
Talents: Commanding Presence, Kingpin, Savant (Law), Wealthy
Trappings: Gavel, Ostentatious Wig

NUN
Human

You are devoted to the service of your deity, having sworn vows for a life of service.

Nuns are members of religious orders, normally cloistered within an abbey, convent, or monastery. Most rise before the sun for morning prayer before toiling in fields, tending to the sick, or preserving important manuscripts. Vows of pilgrimage cause some to travel the Empire, while others take oaths to serve the community, moving amongst the people, tending to their spiritual needs. Devoted hermits and tenders to shrines are also thought of as 'Nuns' or 'Monks' by the folk of the Empire. Many Nuns learn valuable trades such as vintners, brewers or calligraphers. Abbesses use these activities to attract donations and patronage from the local nobility. Leaders of particularly large or martial Orders can gather significant influence both within their own cult and with the ruling classes of a province. For more on religion and the different Orders, see **Chapter 7: Religion and Belief**.

'They came thinking it a simple task to slay a few poor, hapless Brothers and take our relics. I ask Morr not judge too harshly the seven bandits we bury today, as Brother Hild has already inflicted punishment enough.'

– Abbot Ernst Halfhauser

'Quick! Come quick! The Sisters of Faith and Chastity are about to parade through the streets. I want to see if I can get a few coppers caught in their thorns. It brings luck for the whole year!'

– Bengt, Altdorf Street Rat

When a religious order discovers terrible secrets or fragments of prophecy, its leaders may feel they must act, sending brothers and sisters abroad. Abbeys along pilgrimage routes will often also send their members abroad to guard the many pilgrims traversing the lengthy holy roads across the Empire. And there are always itinerant Friars wandering the world, risking adventure with every new land they enter.

NUN ADVANCE SCHEME

WS	BS	S	T	I	Agi	Dex	Int	WP	Fel
			🛡	☠		✚	✚	⚒	✚

Career Path

✚ Novitiate — Brass 1
Skills: Art (Calligraphy), Cool, Endurance, Entertain (Storyteller), Gossip, Heal, *Lore (Theology)*, Pray
Talents: Bless (Any), Stone Soup, Panhandle, Read/Write
Trappings: Religious Symbol, Robes

⚒ Nun — Brass 4
Skills: Charm, Melee (Any), Research, Trade (Brewer), Trade (Herbalist), Trade (Vintner)
Talents: Etiquette (Cultists), Field Dressing, Holy Visions, Invoke (Any)
Trappings: Book (Religion), Religious Relic, Trade Tools (Any)

☠ Abbess — Silver 2
Skills: Leadership, Lore (Local), Lore (Politics), Perception
Talents: Resistance (Any), Robust, Savant (Theology), Stout-hearted
Trappings: Abbey, Library (Theology)

🛡 Prioress General — Silver 5
Skills: Language (Any), Lore (Any)
Talents: Commanding Presence, Iron Will, Pure Soul, Strong-minded
Trappings: Religious Order

PHYSICIAN
Dwarf, Halfling, High Elf, Human

With a strong stomach and steady hand, you practice the art of medicine, striving to save lives.

Physicians study patients' symptoms and prescribe remedies and surgeries. While the healing arts are ancient, many deriving from Elven practices, the formal science of medicine is relatively new and not-entirely-trusted. Due to the Empire's history with necromancy and the safe-guards imposed by the Cult of Morr, studying cadavers is forbidden, making learning of anatomy hard. Medicine's reputation suffered further from swindlers selling 'miracle cure-alls' that do nothing or cause actual harm. Physicians learn their profession at a university or while apprenticed to a Guild Physician. Most cheap surgery is undertaken by back-street physicians known as barber-surgeons whose training is informal. Trained doctors with strong stomachs are in demand for the State Armies. The most famed Physicians almost exclusively tend to wealthy merchants and the nobility.

'Come to Neuber for all your limb removals! I'll 'ave your arm off in seconds! I'll suture it a'fore you even wake up. My work's so fine you'll never miss it!'

– Gotthard Neuber, Barber-Surgeon

'Beware the Brass Doktor.'

– Reikland Proverb warning against cheap Physicians

'They're bastards, all. I can't so much as give you a proper blood-letting without their leave. "Practicing medicine without a license" my arse. I know you can't afford them, deary. Here, luv, take this nice tea. What? Oh no, just tea is all. Just tea. And if you feel better, why, thank Shallya, eh?'

– Jana Palner, Part-time Surgeon

Physician's Guild fees are notoriously expensive, which can cause newer Physicians without steady clientele to seek alternate sources of income. Some Physicians consistently search for more effective treatments and new medicines, which can take them far afield. Others like to expand their knowledge of anatomy by studying grievous wounds first hand, and there are few better ways to do that than by travelling with adventurers.

PHYSICIAN ADVANCE SCHEME

WS	BS	S	T	I	Agi	Dex	Int	WP	Fel
				💀	🛡	✝	✝	✝	⚒

CAREER PATH

✝ Physician's Apprentice — Brass 4
Skills: Bribery, Cool, Drive, Endurance, Gossip, *Heal*, Perception, Sleight of Hand
Talents: Bookish, Field Dressing, Read/Write, Strike to Stun
Trappings: Bandages, Healing Draught

⚒ Physician — Silver 3
Skills: Charm, Haggle, Language (Guilder), Lore (Anatomy), Lore (Medicine), Trade (Barber)
Talents: Coolheaded, Criminal, Etiquette (Guilder), Surgery
Trappings: Book (Medicine), Guild Licence, Trade Tools (Medicine)

💀 Doktor — Silver 5
Skills: Consume Alcohol, Intimidate, Leadership, Research
Talents: Etiquette (Scholars), Resistance (Disease), Savvy, Strike to Injure
Trappings: Apprentice, Workshop (Medicine)

🛡 Court Physician — Gold 1
Skills: Lore (Noble), Perform (Dancing)
Talents: Etiquette (Nobles), Nimble Fingered, Savant (Medicine), Strong-minded
Trappings: Courtly Attire, Letter of Appointment

PRIEST
Human

You carry the word of your god, tending to the spiritual needs of the masses.

Priests tend to congregations of the faithful throughout the Old World. While many are assigned to a specific temple, others choose a wandering life to reach worshippers who cannot, or will not, attend temple. They are expected to exemplify the beliefs of their religion — which vary greatly depending on which deity they serve. High Priests are responsible for a temple and all its Cult and lay members. Alongside Lectors, they will often be called upon to advise the ruling classes, with many active in local politics. Priests have many duties connected to their God, such as Priests of Manann's responsibility to consecrate new ships, or a Shallyan's duty to tend to the sick and wounded, so they touch on most aspects of life in the Empire. For more on religion and the different Orders, see **Chapter 7: Religion and Belief.**

'For sound advice, I seek a Priest of Verena. For everything else, I seek a Priest of Ranald.'

– Wermer Losch, Merchant

'The Shallyan, just a girl she was, stroked my little Anton's forehead and whispered, and the screaming stopped. He smiled at me for the first time in days. I will never forget it. Oh, aye, he died not long after, but not in pain. Not in pain.'

– Sabine Schmidt, Fishmonger

'Listen, there is nothing to fear. Hexensnacht comes every year. We need only call on the Lord of Death to watch over us. So, come the midnight hour, we cry MORR! MORR! MORR!'

– Father Wilhelm Abgott, Priest of Morr

Some temple-bound Priests seek distractions to justify sojourns away. Disturbing matters heard from their congregations can send them on a quest for answers. Some High Priests find their administrative duties so far removed from the life they envisaged when they joined the Cult that they take extended pilgrimages away from their temple.

PRIEST ADVANCE SCHEME

WS	BS	S	T	I	Agi	Dex	Int	WP	Fel
			+	🛡	+		💀	+	⚒

CAREER PATH

+ Initiate — Brass 2
Skills: Athletics, Cool, Endurance, Intuition, Lore (Theology), Perception, *Pray*, Research
Talents: Bless (Any), Holy Visions, Read/Write, Suave
Trappings: Religious Symbol, Robes

⚒ Priest — Silver 1
Skills: Charm, Entertain (Storytelling), Gossip, Heal, Intimidate, Melee (Basic)
Talents: Blather, Bookish, Etiquette (Cultists), Invoke (Any)
Trappings: Book (Religion), Ceremonial Robes

💀 High Priest — Gold 1
Skills: Art (Writing), Entertain (Speeches), Leadership, Lore (Heraldry)
Talents: Acute Sense (Any), Hatred (Any), Impassioned Zeal, Strong-minded
Trappings: Quality Robes, Religious Relic, Subordinate Priests, Temple

🛡 Lector — Gold 2
Skills: Language (Any), Lore (Politics)
Talents: Master Orator, Pure Soul, Resistance (Any), Savant (Theology)
Trappings: Library (Theology), Subordinate High Priests

SCHOLAR

Dwarf, Halfling, High Elf, Human, Wood Elf

You dedicate your life to the pursuit and study of knowledge, wherever that may take you.

Scholars generally study at one of the Old World's learning institutions, foremost amongst them the university in Altdorf. Most specialise in one or two subjects, and many learn just enough to provide a useful career, or give them something to talk about at dinner parties. Poorer Scholars act as scribes, reading and writing notes for others as most of the Empire's citizens are illiterate. Others become tutors educating the wealthy.

The most gifted Masters are invited to join a university, with renowned Professors delivering popular lectures to hundreds of Students. Dwarfs and High Elves are less likely to be employed in an Imperial institution, though they may tour the Empire in search of esoteric knowledge.

'None of us thought much of her. Scrawny thing the Captain dragged out a library in Altdorf, name of Sosber. Kept to herself. Nose in a book. But when we finally faced the Corpse Render, when so-called warriors ran, she stood fast. Her quiet voice rang with steel as she called out where to strike. Not the heads as you'd think, no, but the body. Steel slew the beast that day, but knowledge made it possible.'
– Oskar Reisdorf, Mercenary

Poor Scholars who cannot or will not tutor often need funds to continue their research. A few search the dark corners of the world for lost secrets and ancient tomes. Others are hired to accompany adventuring expeditions where their knowledge can be put to more practical use.

Scholar is a useful Career, with access to rare Lore skills, a good way for the GM to share information with players. Played with common-sense they can counter-balance rash and martially-inclined characters' tendencies to solve every problem with a blade. Scholars can use their knowledge to solve puzzles or come up with unusual strategies and tactics.

SCHOLAR ADVANCE SCHEME

WS	BS	S	T	I	Agi	Dex	Int	WP	Fel
			✚	⚒		🛡	✚	✚	💀

CAREER PATH

✚ Student — Brass 3
Skills: Consume Alcohol, Entertain (Storytelling), Gamble, Gossip, Haggle, Language (Classical), *Lore (Any)*, Research
Talents: Carouser, Read/Write, Savvy, Super Numerate
Trappings: Alcohol, Book, Opinions, Writing Kit

⚒ Scholar — Silver 2
Skills: Art (Writing), Intuition, Language (Any), Lore (Any), Perception, Trade (Any)
Talents: Bookish, Etiquette (Scholars), Speedreader, Suave
Trappings: Access to a Library, Degree

💀 Fellow — Silver 5
Skills: Entertain (Lecture), Intimidate, Language (Any), Lore (Any)
Talents: Linguistics, Public Speaker, Savant (Any), Tower of Memories
Trappings: Mortarboard, Robes

🛡 Professor — Gold 1
Skills: Entertain (Rhetoric), Lore (Any)
Talents: Magnum Opus, Master Orator, Savant (Any), Sharp
Trappings: Study

WIZARD
High Elf, Human, Wood Elf

Feared and distrusted by the citizens of the Empire, you legally wield powerful and dangerous magic.

Wizards channel one of the eight 'Winds of Magic' only spellcasters perceive, to cast potent spells. To legally cast magic in the Empire, a Human must follow the Articles of Imperial Magic and belong to one of the Eight Colleges of Magic in Altdorf — each dedicated to a specific wind, as Wizards can only safely channel one. After graduation, Apprentices become Wizards and serve the Empire. Wizards carefully study and practice their art, which, according to the Articles, they can only use outside their colleges in defence of their own life, or against the enemies of the Empire. Many Wizards are attached to the Empire State Army, and although they are treated with cautious suspicion, none can deny their effectiveness on the battlefield.

'I don't care what promises they make, or what colleges they belong to, they are dangerous abominations. I am continuing to petition for their destruction in the name of Sigmar, for the good of us all.'

– Reikhardt Mair, Witch Hunter

Many Wizards leave the Colleges of Magic in debt for the cost of their tuition. These Wizards may be keen to find immediate employment, or seek out their fortune on land, at sea, or anywhere else they might be able to find relics, artefacts or lost tomes of magical lore. Journeying Wizards, eager to prove themselves, are actively encouraged to test their skills across the Empire by hunting down whatever dangers threaten the local populace.

Wizards are excellent characters to add some firepower to a group, but it can be intimidating for new players to have to learn a whole additional set of rules for spells. Because of this the GM should be aware that they might initially need some extra support to ensure that they are using these rules effectively and to the group's best advantage. You'll choose the colour of magic you study when you take the Arcane Magic Talent. For more on magic see **Chapter 8: Magic.**

WIZARD ADVANCE SCHEME

WS	BS	S	T	I	Agi	Dex	Int	WP	Fel
✛				☠	⚒		✛	✛	🛡

CAREER PATH

✛ Wizard's Apprentice — Brass 3
Skills: Channelling (Any Colour), Dodge, Intuition, *Language (Magick)*, Lore (Magic), Melee (Basic), Melee (Polearm), Perception
Talents: Aethyric Attunement, Petty Magic, Read/Write, Second Sight
Trappings: Grimoire, Quarterstaff

⚒ Wizard — Silver 3
Skills: Charm, Cool, Gossip, Intimidate, Language (Battle), Language (Any)
Talents: Arcane Magic (Any Arcane Lore), Detect Artefact, Fast Hands, Sixth Sense
Trappings: Magical License

☠ Master Wizard — Gold 1
Skills: Animal Care, Evaluate, Lore (Warfare), Ride (Horse)
Talents: Dual Wielder, Instinctive Diction, Magical Sense, Menacing
Trappings: Apprentice, Light Warhorse, Magical Item

🛡 Wizard Lord — Gold 2
Skills: Language (Any), Lore (Any)
Talents: Combat Aware, Frightening, Iron Will, War Wizard
Trappings: Apprentice, Library (Magic), Workshop (Magic)

AGITATOR
Dwarf, Halfling, Human

Charismatic and articulate, you champion your cause in the face of establishment opposition.

Agitators lobby for political causes using print, protest, and public speaking. They muster the down-trodden populace's sympathy and support but must be wary of drawing the attention of Sigmarites or Dwarfs interested in maintaining established traditions. The most dangerous Agitators have destabilised the rule of nobles, towns, and even entire provinces. Pamphleteers nail signs to billboards, or distribute them in market squares, though often those they seek to reach cannot read.

Religious Agitators can make a good living as street preachers, receiving donations from pious devotees and attracting flagellants and zealots as followers. Agitators who survive long enough to become Demagogues are often supported by powerful, hidden allies pursuing change for their own motives.

'ALTDORF FOR ALTDORFERS! MIDDENLANDERS OUT!'
— Pamphlet, Street of a Hundred Taverns, Altdorf

'Mark my words, if you're looking to root out the agents of the Spinner of Fate, follow the clamouring in the streets. They can't resist it. They'll surface, sooner or later.'
— Adrian Hoven, Cleric-Captain, Knights of the Fiery Heart

Agitators often move around, in search of larger crowds or fleeing the authorities. They may become leaders of motley groups of the restless and disaffected, exhorting — or even extorting — them to fight for a greater cause.

Altdorf has a legendary reputation for deep fogs and riots. Perhaps this happens because Altdorf is the Imperial Capital, or maybe its because the Grey College draws swathes of treacherous *Ulgu*, the Grey Wind of Magic, to the city. Whatever the case, it seems that whenever the fog draws in from the Altdorf Flats, mobs rise in the streets, and woe betide any watchmen who try to silence their right to be heard.

AGITATOR ADVANCE SCHEME

WS	BS	S	T	I	Agi	Dex	Int	WP	Fel
☠	✟			🛡	⚒		✟		✟

CAREER PATH

✟ Pamphleteer — Brass 1
Skills: Art (Writing), Bribery, *Charm*, Consume Alcohol, Gossip, Haggle, Lore (Politics), Trade (Printing)
Talents: Blather, Gregarious, Panhandle, Read/Write
Trappings: Writing Kit, Hammer and Nails, Pile of Leaflets

⚒ Agitator — Brass 2
Skills: Cool, Dodge, Entertain (Storytelling), Gamble, Intuition, Leadership
Talents: Alley Cat, Argumentative, Impassioned Zeal, Public Speaker
Trappings: Leather Jack

☠ Rabble Rouser — Brass 3
Skills: Athletics, Intimidate, Melee (Brawling), Perception
Talents: Cat-tongued, Dirty Fighting, Flee!, Step Aside
Trappings: Hand Weapon, Pamphleteer

🛡 Demagogue — Brass 5
Skills: Lore (Heraldry), Ride (Horse)
Talents: Etiquette (Any), Master Orator, Schemer, Suave
Trappings: 3 Pamphleteers, Patron, Printing Press, Impressive Hat

ARTISAN

Dwarf, Halfling, High Elf, Human, Wood Elf

A skilled craftsperson, you take pride in your work, creating products for sale and commission.

Artisans produce goods, ranging from everyday necessities sold by Bakers and Chandlers, to weapons and riverboats crafted by Smiths and Shipwrights. The Empire's larger towns and cities have guilds to protect local Artisans from fraudsters, as an Artisan's entire livelihood can be jeopardised by unskilled competitors hawking cheap low-quality merchandise. Guild Artisans observe strict quality standards, with those failing to meet them blackballed and forbidden to trade locally.

Artisans work at all levels of society not just producing goods, but also repairing them. They are employed by navies to maintain vessels, by armies to manage war machines and siegeworks, and by merchant houses of all sizes to transform raw materials into sellable goods.

'Sorry, mistress, all the shoes are gone! I forgot to put the milk out last night. The Spite must have taken them.'

— Wiebke, Cobbler's Apprentice and Thief

'You must understand, my boy, that Wurtbad's wine has a reputation. This bottle looks like it was blown through a Hochland long rifle. Simply unacceptable.'

— Frau Glasmeister, Glassblowers' Guildmaster

Artisans in training can be sent to practice under other masters. The constant pressure to achieve perfection is so stifling that young Artisans sometimes take a break to pursue more liberating enterprises, sometimes supporting the army or navy.

Dwarf Guilds don't usually admit Humans, and Dwarfs are traditionally allowed to practice their trade in Imperial cities without joining a local Guild. This can cause conflict as the Guilds are rarely pleased with skilled competition. Halflings are not so particular, and most will happily join Human Guilds (if admitted) and allow Humans to join their Guilds. Elves do not have Artisan's Guilds, and though they could join one it is unlikely they would lower themselves to do so.

ARTISAN ADVANCE SCHEME

WS	BS	S	T	I	Agi	Dex	Int	WP	Fel
		✝	✝			✝	🛡	💀	⚒

CAREER PATH

✝ **Apprentice Artisan — Brass 2**
Skills: Athletics, Cool, Consume Alcohol, Dodge, Endurance, Evaluate, Stealth (Urban), *Trade (Any)*
Talents: Artistic, Craftsman (any), Strong Back, Very Strong
Trappings: Chalk, Leather Jerkin, d10 rags

⚒ **Artisan — Silver 1**
Skills: Charm, Haggle, Lore (Local), Gossip, Language (Guilder), Perception
Talents: Dealmaker, Etiquette (Guilder), Nimble Fingered, Sturdy
Trappings: Guild Licence, Trade Tools

💀 **Master Artisan — Silver 3**
Skills: Intuition, Leadership, Research, Secret Signs (Guilder)
Talents: Acute Sense (Taste *or* Touch), Master Tradesman (Any), Read/Write, Tinker
Trappings: Apprentice, Workshop

🛡 **Guildmaster — Gold 1**
Skills: Bribery, Intimidate
Talents: Briber, Magnum Opus, Public Speaker, Schemer
Trappings: Guild, Quality Clothing

BEGGAR
Dwarf, Halfling, Human

Street-smart, you make a living from the charity of others using persuasion and charm.

The countryside rumour that Altdorf's streets are lined with gold is a cruel taunt to its Beggars. They rely upon the generosity of strangers and scraps scavenged from the mud and detritus of city life, though posturing dandies will happily dispose of a few pfennigs to make them go away. The law affords them little protection and the watch has no sympathy for loiterers.

Paupers often land on the streets as orphans and have been in and out of Mercy Houses all their lives. Once the basic skills of scrounging and panhandling are learned, Beggars can advance their techniques using disguises and sympathy ploys. Other Paupers are not destitute but simply employed in some of the worst occupations, on the lowest rung of the social ladder, like Gong Farmers, Bone Pickers, and Rag and Bone Men.

'Please, frau, I beg humbly for enough coppers to buy bread tonight. Even a pfennig would do — Gutbäcker is selling day-olds.'

– Elsie, Halfling Panhandler

'I lost my leg in the Battle of Bögenwasser. Both hands were eaten by a Squig when Goblins ambushed our patrol near Bögenauer. All to protect the Reikland and our Emperor.'

– Klaas, Veteran Soldier

'You can have Königplatz next week — I need you loud and dirty on Luitpoldstrasse today. For why? Best not ask, all you need to know is the Cutters want the Watch distracted. I make it my business not to offend the Cutters, and if you want a prosperous career you'll follow my example.'

– 'The Kaiser', Altdorf Beggar-King

The only direction from rock-bottom is upward. Some Beggars will eagerly leave the gutter behind for adventuring opportunities, so long as they aren't being exploited as battle-fodder. Those unable to afford a porter might hire a Beggar instead, and a Beggar's savvy is useful when penniless and hungry. And, if it all goes wrong, it's easy to return to the begging life.

BEGGAR ADVANCE SCHEME

WS	BS	S	T	I	Agi	Dex	Int	WP	Fel
💀			✚	🛡	✚			⚒	✚

CAREER PATH

✚ Pauper — Brass 0
Skills: Athletics, *Charm*, Consume Alcohol, Cool, Dodge, Endurance, Intuition, Stealth (Urban)
Talents: Panhandle, Resistance (Disease), Stone Soup, Very Resilient
Trappings: Poor Quality Blanket, Cup

⚒ Beggar — Brass 2
Skills: Entertain (Acting), Entertain (Any), Gossip, Haggle, Perception, Sleight of Hand
Talents: Alley Cat, Beneath Notice, Criminal, Etiquette (Criminals)
Trappings: Crutch, Bowl

💀 Master Beggar — Brass 4
Skills: Charm Animal, Leadership, Lore (Local), Secret Signs (Vagabond)
Talents: Blather, Dirty Fighting, Hardy, Step Aside
Trappings: Disguise Kit, Hiding Place, Pauper Follower

🛡 Beggar King — Silver 2
Skills: Bribery, Intimidate
Talents: Cat-tongued, Fearless (Watchmen), Kingpin, Suave
Trappings: Lair, Large Group of Beggar Followers

INVESTIGATOR

Dwarf, Halfling, High Elf, Human

Perceptive and suspicious, you probe deep into the heart of any crime, and find answers.

Most Investigators pursue cases involving stolen property, missing persons, or murders, although some research stories for the emerging newssheets, or even blackmail crime suspects for 'hush money'. Investigative techniques include footprint tracking, cross-examination, deductive reasoning and — if necessary — breaking and entry. Where secular investigators operate on the edge of the law or for an institution like the watch of a Merchant House, religious investigators — most commonly serving Sigmar and Verena — follow stricter ethical codes.

Some experienced Investigators cultivate matter-of-fact airs of sophistication to improve their credibility. While Master Investigators often sell themselves as 'observation specialists' possessing skills they claim cannot be learned. Considerable self-promotion is required to become one of the famous Detectives who receive job offers from across the Old World.

'I regret to inform you that your husband is buried in Frau Kohl's vegetable garden, beneath the turnips. That will be 6 shillings and 4 pence, please.'

– Hemlock Surelight, Elven Sleuth

'We can deduce from this splintered door the thief exited with assistance from a very large creature. But said creature couldn't have descended the narrow stairwell. This leaves only two possible conclusions. Either it materialised from thin air, or else our thief is a shape-changer...'

– Zavant Konniger, 'Sage-Detective'

'As I am sure you know, I am the world's greatest detective. You 'ave 'eard of Alphonse, no?'
– Alphonse Hercules de Gascoigne, Diminutive Bretonnian Detective

Investigators are sometimes hired to solve mysteries far too dangerous to tackle alone, which can be the informal creation of an adventuring party. Of course, the very nature of mysteries can result in each solved case leading to yet another mystery. Investigators may therefore enjoy steady employment, provided they're able to identify willing customers for every new mystery they uncover.

INVESTIGATOR ADVANCE SCHEME

WS	BS	S	T	I	Agi	Dex	Int	WP	Fel
				✝	✝	☠	✝	🛡	⚒

CAREER PATH

✝ Sleuth — Silver 1
Skills: Charm, Climb, Cool, Gossip, Intuition, *Perception*, Stealth (Urban), Track
Talents: Alley Cat, Beneath Notice, Read/Write, Sharp
Trappings: Lantern, Lamp Oil, Journal, Quill and Ink

⚒ Investigator — Silver 2
Skills: Consume Alcohol, Dodge, Lore (Law), Melee (Brawling), Pick Lock, Sleight of Hand
Talents: Etiquette (Any), Savvy, Shadow, Tenacious
Trappings: Leather Jack, Hand Weapon, Magnifying Glass, Lockpick

☠ Master Investigator — Silver 3
Skills: Bribery, Evaluate, Leadership, Lore (Any)
Talents: Bookish, Break and Enter, Sixth Sense, Suave
Trappings: Assistant, Office

🛡 Detective — Silver 5
Skills: Intimidate, Lore (any)
Talents: Acute Sense (Any), Savant (Any), Speedreader, Tower of Memories
Trappings: Network of Informants, Spyglass

MERCHANT
Dwarf, Halfling, High Elf, Human

Shrewd and numerate, you buy low to sell high, making more money than most will ever see.

Most Merchants trade in simple goods such as alcohol, textiles, woodcraft, and pottery. For the ambitious, rare exotic goods such as Dwarf gromril or Eastern spices command higher profits, but risk longer transport routes and require strong foreign contacts. Merchants cannot sell in most towns without approval from (and payments to) a Merchants' Guild, powerful institutions rivalling the noble courts in political influence. Local commerce is managed by Traders who ship goods between backwater villages and nearby towns.

Traders can join guilds by apprenticing under Master Merchants as junior business partners. Powerful Merchant Princes owning warehouses and sales offices in multiple cities enjoy the same status as minor nobles. In addition to trading, some Merchants also branch out into banking, moneylending, and investing.

'If Nuln wants trade wars, so be it, I'll see their river blockaded and raise taxes on guns. After all, the Emperor owes me a few favours...'
– Leo van Haagen, Marienburg Merchant Prince

'How did I become a millionaire? Well, when I was a girl with only a pfennig to my name, I went to the local farmer and bought an apple. Then I walked to the market and sold the apple for two pfennigs. The next day I bought two apples from the farmer and walked to the market again and sold the apples for four pfennigs. And so it went on, every day; I walked to the farm bought some apples, and then walked to the market to sell them at a profit. And by the time I was twenty-five years old, my grandfather died and left me a million crowns.'
– Johanna Sainzburg, Fresh Fruit Magnate

Merchants share a certain kinship with adventurers, often hiring them over professional caravan guards. Adventurers are adaptable and enterprising by nature, making them ideal candidates for partnership in a trading company, bringing Merchants into contact with all manner of colourful characters.

MERCHANT ADVANCE SCHEME

WS	BS	S	T	I	Agi	Dex	Int	WP	Fel
⛊				☠	✚		⚒	✚	✚

CAREER PATH

✚ Trader — Silver 2
Skills: Animal Care, Bribery, Charm, Consume Alcohol, Drive, Gamble, Gossip, *Haggle*
Talents: Blather, Dealmaker, Read/Write, Suave
Trappings: Abacus, Mule and Cart, Canvas Tarpaulin, 3d10 Silver Shillings

⚒ Merchant — Silver 5
Skills: Evaluate, Intuition, Language (Any), Language (Guilder), Lore (Local), Perception
Talents: Briber, Embezzle, Etiquette (Guilder), Savvy
Trappings: Riverboat *or* 2 Wagons, Guild License, 20 GC

☠ Master Merchant — Gold 1
Skills: Cool, Language (Classical), Navigation, Secret Signs (Guilder)
Talents: Cat-tongued, Etiquette (Any), Numismatics, Sharp
Trappings: Town House with Servants, Warehouse, 100 GC

⛊ Merchant Prince — Gold 3
Skills: Lore (Any), Intimidate
Talents: Iron Will, Luck, Schemer, Wealthy
Trappings: 2 Riverboats *or* 4 Wagons, Large Town Estate, 2 Warehouses, 1000 GC, Quality Clothing

RAT CATCHER
Dwarf, Halfling, Human

You spare civilisation from being overrun by vermin with help from your trusty, canine companion.

Rat Catchers patrol every town and city, and for good reason. The Empire's streets are clogged with food scraps and foulness, perfect breeding grounds for vermin. Rat Catchers earn their crusts by killing these rats, clearing their nests from cellars, and by delving the Empire's hopelessly infested sewer systems… provided they're brave enough to face the other things down there. When apprenticed, Rat Catchers usually adopt a stray puppy that they train for ratting. The toughest Rat Catchers are hired by towns as Sewer Jacks to hunt giant rats and other subterranean nasties. On rare occasions, entire towns are overrun and later reclaimed with the aid of Exterminators.

'See there by the midden-heap, Otmar? There's a big one! Make sure it's dead before you pick it up. It'll bite yer hand with its poisonous teeth.'
– Annaliese Rattenfänger, Sewer Jack

'Sorry, mate. The rest of the guild deal with the rats. Me and me mates deal with the bigger ones in the sewers. Tide of them down there, there is…'

– Mårten Stormdal, Ubersreik Exterminator

Rat Catchers move to new towns when the rats become 'too big' or 'too clever', or when competition becomes fierce. When journeying, they may befriend those who welcome help from a streetwise slinger, and Rat Catchers are willing to venture into places normal people won't.

If you want to play a character who may be aware of the 'too big' and 'too clever' Skaven (see page 336), Rat Catcher is for you. However, the Skaven frequently assassinate any who spread rumours of their existence. Because of this, wise Ratcatchers are unlikely to admit what they know, some even using their professional opinion to actively discredit 'tall tales' of 'rat men'.

RAT CATCHER ADVANCE SCHEME

WS	BS	S	T	I	Agi	Dex	Int	WP	Fel
✝	✝	🛡	⚒	💀					✝

CAREER PATH

✝ Rat Hunter — Brass 3
Skills: Athletics, Animal Training (Dog), Charm Animal, Consume Alcohol, Endurance, *Melee (Basic)*, Ranged (Sling), Stealth (Underground *or* Urban)
Talents: Night Vision, Resistance (Disease), Strike Mighty Blow, Strike to Stun
Trappings: Sling with Ammunition, Sack, Small but Vicious Dog

⚒ Rat Catcher — Silver 1
Skills: Animal Care, Gossip, Haggle, Lore (Poison), Perception, Set Trap
Talents: Enclosed Fighter, Etiquette (Guilder), Fearless (Rats), Very Resilient
Trappings: Animal Traps, Pole for Dead Rats

💀 Sewer Jack — Silver 2
Skills: Climb, Cool, Dodge, Ranged (Crossbow Pistol)
Talents: Hardy, Stout-hearted, Strong Legs, Tunnel Rat
Trappings: Davrich Lantern, Hand Weapon, Leather Jack

🖤 Exterminator — Silver 3
Skills: Leadership, Track
Talents: Fearless (Skaven), Menacing, Robust, Strong-minded
Trappings: Assistant, Large and Vicious Dog, Sack of Poisoned Bait (10 doses of Heartkill)

TOWNSMAN
Dwarf, Halfling, High Elf, Human

Ambitious and socially mobile, you are the hardworking glue that holds urban society together.

Townsmen meet these thriving centres of trade and commerce's demand for workers. They fill various roles for private artisans or municipal councils: Bankers, Clerks, Hawkers, Innkeepers, Newspaper Vendors, Ostlers, Shopkeepers, Toll-keepers, Washers, and many more. Pay rates vary; some can haggle for extra commission, whereas civil employees such as lamplighters and toll-keepers are paid fixed salaries. There is little opportunity for promotion, but those with determination, savvy, and luck might eventually own property or a business.

The most successful Townsmen often join local councils overseeing civic matters, with Burgomeisters — the most important municipal leaders — often enjoying the same social status as Merchant Princes and Guildmasters.

'I'm afraid you'll have to remove your backpacks in this shop and leave polearms at the door. The owner deducts broken ceramics from me wage.'

– Frida, Part-time Shopkeeper

Townsmen are part of a growing class of citizen with both time and money at their disposal. Many take one or two days off a week and can easily fit in a life of adventure between shifts or after closing time. Some may wish to go even further afield, and if the Townsman has some money put aside, it should be simple to negotiate some time off with an employer. It's very common for citizens of the Empire to go on pilgrimages for weeks or months at a time. Skilled workers are always in demand, and there will likely be a role waiting when they come home.

TOWNSMAN ADVANCE SCHEME

WS	BS	S	T	I	Agi	Dex	Int	WP	Fel
				⚒	✚	☠	✚	🛡	✚

CAREER PATH

✚ Clerk — Silver 1
Skills: Charm, Climb, Consume Alcohol, Drive, Dodge, Gamble, Gossip, *Haggle*
Talents: Alley Cat, Beneath Notice, Etiquette (Servants), Sturdy
Trappings: Lodgings, Sturdy Boots

⚒ Townsman — Silver 2
Skills: Bribery, Evaluate, Intuition, Lore (Local), Melee (Brawling), Play (Any)
Talents: Dealmaker, Embezzle, Etiquette (Any), Gregarious
Trappings: Modest Townhouse, Servant, Quill and Ink

☠ Town Councillor — Silver 5
Skills: Cool, Lore (Law), Perception, Research
Talents: Briber, Public Speaker, Read/Write, Supportive
Trappings: Coach and Driver, Townhouse

🛡 Burgomeister — Gold 1
Skills: Lore (Politics), Intimidate
Talents: Commanding Presence, Master Orator, Schemer, Suave
Trappings: Chains of Office, Coach and Footman, Quality Clothing, Large Townhouse with Gardens and Servants

WATCHMAN

Dwarf, Halfling, High Elf, Human

You maintain the peace and keep the rabble in line so your town doesn't descend into anarchy.

Watchmen are employed by local authorities to patrol streets throughout the Empire. Most are little more than well-meaning keepers of the peace, and few know the laws they're supposed to enforce. Corruption is rampant, and many Watchmen enlist purely for the authority to hurt people or to support local criminal gangs. Some can earn triple their wages by turning a blind eye.

Only a few towns and cities have professional Watchmen paid to understand and uphold the law; instead, the Emperor's Peace is normally maintained by the local State Army, who man walls, guard gates, and patrol the streets according to the instructions of their superiors.

'So I go up to Middenheim, Ulric's own country, and what did I find? I swear more than half of their City Watch are women! I would have stayed up there for the rest of my career if I could've.'
— Jana Tennisohn, Chief Inspektor (retired), Nuln City Watch

'Sorry, sir, I've got a Halfling killer, a Weirdroot smuggling ring, a gang war, and a noble threatening to have me arrested by my own Station. Your missing cat will have to wait until tomorrow.'
— Sergeant Harri Makkenpieser, Altdorf City Watch

Not every Watchman is crooked, but those with morals are soon jaded by the corruption inherent in the system. By joining adventuring parties, principled Watchmen can champion justice on their own terms. Experience of the street makes Watchmen effective combatants in a small party, and their presence can help legitimise a wandering band of ne'er-do-wells.

WATCHMAN ADVANCE SCHEME

WS	BS	S	T	I	Agi	Dex	Int	WP	Fel
✦		✦		☠			🛡	⚒	✦

CAREER PATH

✦ Watch Recruit — Brass 3
Skills: Athletics, Climb, Consume Alcohol, Dodge, Endurance, Gamble, Melee (Any), *Perception*
Talents: Drilled, Hardy, Strike to Stun, Tenacious
Trappings: Hand Weapon, Leather Jack, Uniform

⚒ Watchman — Silver 1
Skills: Charm, Cool, Gossip, Intimidate, Intuition, Lore (Local)
Talents: Break and Enter, Criminal, Night Vision, Sprinter
Trappings: Lantern and Pole, Lamp Oil, Copper Badge

☠ Watch Sergeant — Silver 3
Skills: Entertain (Storytelling), Haggle, Leadership, Lore (Law)
Talents: Disarm, Etiquette (Soldiers), Fearless (Criminals), Nose for Trouble
Trappings: Breastplate, Helm, Symbol of Rank

🛡 Watch Captain — Gold 1
Skills: Lore (Politics), Ride (Horse)
Talents: Public Speaker, Robust, Kingpin, Schemer
Trappings: Riding Horse with Saddle and Tack, Quality Hat, Quality Hand weapon, Quality Symbol of Rank

ADVISOR

Dwarf, Halfling, High Elf, Human, Wood Elf

Wise and well-informed, you provide advice and guidance so your employer prospers.

Advisors provide counsel to those they serve. Well-versed in the political and social conditions of their employer's domain, they are privy to confidential and sensitive information. While many Advisors are born into their positions, others actively seek noble patronage as a path to wealth and power. Some young royals pick their university or childhood friends as their first Aide, trusting them to say what no-one else will.

Long years at court or in service to a lesser noble pave the way to the loftier heights of their careers. Many Advisors do not serve the nobility at all, instead lending their extensive capabilities to criminals, warlords, merchants, cults, or guilds.

'Sigmar votes with Reikland for three. The dead Emperor, Mootland, and Reikland will vote the same way, taking Reikland to six. As you know, you need seven votes to become emperor. Given Ar'Ulric always votes for Middenheim, it's highly unlikely the Imperial seat will return to Nuln while the House of Third Wilhelm flourishes. Best hope for a daughter, your Grace. A marriageable one.'
– Krammond, Advisor to the Elector Count of Nuln, 2475 IC

If there is something peculiar or dangerous happening within their employer's domain, then an Advisor is well-placed to investigate. At the higher levels of the career, a Counsellor or Chancellor will have their own trusted staff they can rely on to look after matters if they take a short leave of absence. Advisors can approach different classes of people, including the most difficult to access, and they are already in a position where they are expected to ask questions on behalf of their employer.

ADVISOR ADVANCE SCHEME

WS	BS	S	T	I	Agi	Dex	Int	WP	Fel
		✠	✠	✠			💀	🛡	⚒

CAREER PATH

✠ Aide — Silver 2
Skills: Bribery, Consume Alcohol, Endurance, Gossip, Haggle, Language (Classical), *Lore (Politics),* Perception
Talents: Beneath Notice, Etiquette (Any), Gregarious, Read/Write
Trappings: Writing Kit

⚒ Advisor — Silver 4
Skills: Charm, Cool, Evaluate, Gamble, Intuition, Lore (Local)
Talents: Blather, Criminal, Schemer, Supportive
Trappings: Livery

💀 Counsellor — Gold 1
Skills: Entertain (Storytelling), Leadership, Language (Any), Lore (Any)
Talents: Argumentative, Briber, Carouser, Cat-tongued
Trappings: Quality Clothing, Aide

🛡 Chancellor — Gold 3
Skills: Lore (Heraldry), Ride (Horse)
Talents: Commanding Presence, Embezzle, Kingpin, Suave
Trappings: Riding Horse with Saddle and Harness, Quality Courtly Garb, Staff of Advisors and Aides

ARTIST

Dwarf, Halfling, High Elf, Human, Wood Elf

You possess an artistic gift, one that transcends daily life and uplifts the souls of others.

Artists use their talents — for painting, sculpting, writing and similar — to create works of fine art. Often their careers begin as Apprentices to experienced Master Artists, though some are simply prodigies. The best can attract a patron, and some end up teaching, forming their own schools of art and attracting the wealthiest of benefactors to their fashionable salons.

Sadly, most Artists spend their lives in a vain attempt to prove their value to a society that rarely appreciates them. Some make ends meet through different means: satirising nobles and politicians in cartoons for the Altdorf broadsheets, sketching suspects for watch captains, writing social commentary, or even forging the work of more renowned artists.

'Please remain still, my lord. It is rather difficult to capture the majesty of your countenance if you continue to scratch yourself so. Perfect! Now hold that pose for just a few seconds more if you please. And there you've gone and done it again. Might I suggest you pay a visit to the apothecary? He may have several effective remedies for lice, especially if you find your incessant squirming as bothersome as I do...'
– Gottlieb Toman, Painter, prior to his execution

Attracting suitable patrons is not always a simple matter, so Artists of all stripes find themselves traveling abroad in search of one. Even those who have the means to support themselves take to the road in search of new sights to paint, sculpt, or inspire them. Holy frescos and reliefs dedicated to the gods are often commissioned in faraway temples, churches, and abbeys.

ARTIST ADVANCE SCHEME

WS	BS	S	T	I	Agi	Dex	Int	WP	Fel
		✠		✠		✠	🛡	💀	⚒

CAREER PATH

✠ Apprentice Artist — Silver 1
Skills: *Art (Any)*, Cool, Consume Alcohol, Evaluate, Endurance, Gossip, Perception, Stealth (Urban)
Talents: Artistic, Sharp, Strong Back, Tenacious
Trappings: Brush *or* Chisel *or* Quill Pen

⚒ Artist — Silver 3
Skills: Climb, Gamble, Haggle, Intuition, Language (Classical), Trade (Art Supplies)
Talents: Carouser, Criminal, Gregarious, Nimble Fingered
Trappings: Sling Bag containing Trade Tools (Artist)

💀 Master Artist — Silver 5
Skills: Charm, Leadership, Lore (Art), Lore (Heraldry)
Talents: Acute Sense (Any), Dealmaker, Etiquette (any), Nose for Trouble
Trappings: Apprentice, Patron, Workshop (Artist)

🛡 Maestro — Gold 2
Skills: Research, Ride (Horse)
Talents: Ambidextrous, Kingpin, Magnum Opus, Read/Write
Trappings: Large Workshop (Artist), Library (Art), 3 Apprentices

DUELLIST
Dwarf, High Elf, Human

Your blade is an instrument of justice, bound by long tradition and employed with deadly precision.

Duellists fight on behalf of others — settling matters of honour between organisations or individuals — or as surrogates for the law, representing the accused or the accuser in trials by combat. For some Duellists the act of fighting is reward enough for the considerable risks they face. Training is dangerous, leaving some apprentices crippled or scarred for life. Those who live long enough to learn from their mistakes can aspire to the fame of a Blademaster, teaching their techniques to eager students. Judicial Champions duel on behalf of governments and nobles, and their blades can determine the fates of nations. Some modern Duellists, especially hot-headed Altdorf students, favour pistols. This is regarded by the older generation as dishonourable and foolhardy.

'First blood, ye fool! First blood! And here ye've gone 'n run 'im through!'

    - Ortolf Ehardt, Burgher

'In my defence, sir, he was the first to do any sort of bleeding.'

    - Rosabel Viernau, Duellist

'Always make sure you have Doktor Schuller on site. Deniability? Good question. Pay her in advance, treat her with civility, and she'll turn around. Then she sees nothing until the duel is over, one way or another.'

    - Blademaster Aleksandr Amblestadt's advice to his students.

Both inexperienced and esteemed Duellists alike travel the Empire in search of opponents with which to bolster their reputations. For others, the hunt for a veteran instructor drives them to explore the furthest flung of the Old World's locales. Masters of foreign techniques are also sought by Duellists who wish to add unique styles of fighting to their repertoires. As skilled combatants, Duellists often augment their livelihood with mercenary work, even acting as guards for caravans and riverboats in a pinch. Although Dwarfs have no interest in fencing with flimsy swords and the frippery of the duelling scene, they have long traditions of using combat to resolve bitter disputes, and will travel far to enhance their skills.

DUELLIST ADVANCE SCHEME

WS	BS	S	T	I	Agi	Dex	Int	WP	Fel
✠	⚒	💀		✠	✠			🛡	

CAREER PATH

✠ Fencer — Silver 3
Skills: Athletics, Dodge, Endurance, Heal, Intuition, Language (Classical), *Melee (Any)*, Perception
Talents: Beat Blade, Distract, Feint, Step Aside
Trappings: Hand Weapon or Rapier, Sling Bag containing Clothing and 1d10 Bandages

⚒ Duellist — Silver 5
Skills: Charm, Cool, Gamble, Melee (Parry), Ranged (Blackpowder), Trade (Gunsmith)
Talents: Combat Reflexes, Etiquette (Any), Fast Shot, Reversal
Trappings: Main Gauche or Sword-breaker, Pistol with Gunpowder and Ammunition

💀 Duelmaster — Gold 1
Skills: Intimidate, Leadership, Melee (Basic), Perform (Acrobatics)
Talents: Ambidextrous, Disarm, Dual Wielder, Riposte
Trappings: Quality Rapier, Hand Weapon, Trusty Second, 2 Wooden Training Swords

🛡 Judicial Champion — Gold 3
Skills: Lore (Law), Melee (Any)
Talents: Combat Master, Menacing, Reaction Strike, Strike to Injure
Trappings: 2 Quality Weapons

ENVOY

Dwarf, Halfling, High Elf, Human, Wood Elf

An articulate emissary, you travel far and wide, negotiating favourable pacts and treaties.

Experts in negotiation and social interaction, Envoys act as agents serving the interests of the Empire, a regional estate, a foreign entity, or a merchant house. Intrigue abounds in courtly circles, and such a career choice is a risky proposition that only grows more perilous at the highest levels of government. Even when granted some manner of immunity against foreign laws or customs, Ambassadors must tread carefully.

Envoys must first prove their abilities in a lesser capacity as a Herald, assisting Diplomats in hammering out the tedious minutiae of deals, or representing merchants, guilds, or cults, building their reputations with each pact they establish. Some Envoys find employ with Mercenary Companies; the best of these can secure a profit for their employers without shedding a drop of blood.

'Watch that one. She's got a tongue like a snake and nary a scruple. Still, she's got a weakness for Elven wine and handsome young footmen. I'm sure you can arrange something... scandalous.'

– Odmar Horst, Guild Envoy

' My advice to his Imperial Majesty to ensure we maintain our vital trade link with Karak Ziflin: grow a beard and keep your promises.'
– Letter to the High Lord of the Chair, from Ambassador Willemijna von Kotzdam

Envoys travel a great deal, meeting countless individuals from all walks of life, cultivating contacts across the Old World. They are sometimes expected to get their hands dirty to ensure their master's wishes are fulfilled. If failure doesn't lead to their immediate death, they might find themselves on the run from their own employers.

ENVOY ADVANCE SCHEME

WS	BS	S	T	I	Agi	Dex	Int	WP	Fel
			✛	☠	✛		⚒	🛡	✛

CAREER PATH

✛ Herald — Silver 2
Skills: Athletics, *Charm*, Drive, Dodge, Endurance, Intuition, Ride (Horse), Row
Talents: Blather, Etiquette (Nobles), Read/Write, Suave
Trappings: Leather Jack, Livery, Scroll Case

⚒ Envoy — Silver 4
Skills: Art (Writing), Bribery, Cool, Gossip, Haggle, Lore (Politics)
Talents: Attractive, Cat-tongued, Etiquette (any), Seasoned Traveller
Trappings: Quill and Ink, 10 sheets of parchment

☠ Diplomat — Gold 2
Skills: Intimidate, Language (Any), Leadership, Navigation
Talents: Carouser, Dealmaker, Gregarious, Schemer
Trappings: Aide, Quality Clothes, Map

🛡 Ambassador — Gold 5
Skills: Language (Any), Lore (Any)
Talents: Briber, Commanding Presence, Noble Blood, Savvy
Trappings: Aide, Best Quality Courtly Clothes, Staff of Diplomats, Herald

NOBLE

Dwarf, High Elf, Human, Wood Elf

As the scion of a noble bloodline, you stand proudly from the common rabble.

The blood of highborn ancestors courses through the veins of the nobility, granting Nobles the power to rule, make laws, and dispense justice. Nobles often inherit vast wealth and holdings, although only those with a direct line of succession can expect to wield any genuine power. Many spend their lives consolidating this wealth and power through business, politics, and conquest. Those without substantial inheritance must make their own way in the world, joining the State Army or navy as a commissioned officer, or commit to service of one of the gods. It is common to find Nobles working for more powerful noble houses, such as sending their daughters to serve as hand maidens to royalty.

'Everyone thinks that Nobles have it easy, but it's a treacherous life and you're always standing in someone's way. I'd rather take my chances out here with you lot than risk assassins back home. Give me a herd of Beastmen any day.'

– 'Lugner' Rodziner, Tenth of his Line

Many Nobles serve their families abroad in the hopes they can advance their station and earn acclaim amongst their peers. Others, bored by pampered living, search for excitement as adventurers and would-be heroes. Scions with few prospects sometimes seek their fortunes far from courtly intrigue and betrayal, taking up other occupations to expand their options.

The GM should consider carefully whether to allow players to choose the Noble career. It comes with a lot of trappings and temporal power, especially at the higher levels of the career.

NOBLE ADVANCE SCHEME

WS	BS	S	T	I	Agi	Dex	Int	WP	Fel
✚				✚		✚	☠	🛡	⚒

CAREER PATH

✚ Scion — Gold 1
Skills: Bribery, Consume Alcohol, Gamble, Intimidate, *Leadership*, Lore (Heraldry), Melee (Fencing), Play (Any)
Talents: Etiquette (Nobles), Luck, Noble Blood, Read/Write
Trappings: Courtly Garb, Foil *or* Hand Mirror, Jewellery worth 3d10 GC, Personal Servant

⚒ Noble — Gold 3
Skills: Charm, Gossip, Language (Classical), Lore (Local), Ride (Horse), Melee (Parry)
Talents: Attractive, Briber, Carouser, Suave
Trappings: 4 Household Servants, Quality Courtly Garb, Courtly Garb, Riding Horse with Saddle and Harness *or* Coach, Main Gauche *or* Quality Cloak, Jewellery worth 50 GC

☠ Magnate — Gold 5
Skills: Language (Any), Intuition, Lore (Politics), Perception
Talents: Coolheaded, Dealmaker, Public Speaker, Schemer
Trappings: 2 sets of Quality Courtly Garb, 200 GC, Fiefdom, Jewellery worth 200 GC, Signet Ring

🛡 Noble Lord — Gold 7
Skills: Lore (Any), Track
Talents: Commanding Presence, Iron Will, Warleader, Wealthy
Trappings: 4 sets of Best Quality Courtly Garb, Quality Foil *or* Hand Mirror, 500 GC, Jewellery worth 500 GC, Province

SERVANT
Dwarf, Halfling, Human

You serve the great and the good, performing tasks in support of your employer.

Most who serve the nobility come from peasant stock, grateful to escape the beleaguered masses tending the fields. Servants are taught comportment along with the skills necessary to cook, clean, buttle, and groom on behalf of their betters. They are provided with room, board, and a wage, but the quality of a Servant's life depends on how well treated they are. Some Servants dress their employer, cook or serve meals, manage stores of wine and other consumables, or tend to the grounds.

Experienced Servants can aspire to the role of personal Attendant, or even Steward, managing the domestic affairs of their employer and overseeing other Servants. Those directly serving royalty are often drawn from noble stock rather than the peasantry.

'Only a fool mistreats those entrusted to cook food and pour wine. Believe me, there's no end of damage a spiteful servant can wreak upon the unwise.'

– Baron Gerber Jochutzmann

'Why she insists on takin' that blasted cat with her is beyond me. Between her wardrobes, her travelling library, and her damned butterfly collection, I'm at my wit's end! And when it gets lost — oh, it will, believe me — she'll expect me to find her a new one. Sigmar! Where does one find a leopard kitten in Ubersreik?'

– Reynald, Lady Kirstin Gottlieb's Porter

A Servant may be required to accompany their employer, travelling from winter to summer domains, or visiting the great cities. This can provide opportunities for adventures around the Empire. Bored heirs, closeted by over-protective parents, might treat their young Servants more like friends, providing them with encouragement and funds to seek out adventures, living vicariously through them when they report back with tales of derring-do. Favoured Servants are, on occasion, entrusted with duties that take them beyond their familiar surroundings, or even loaned to other family members or peers.

SERVANT ADVANCE SCHEME

WS	BS	S	T	I	Agi	Dex	Int	WP	Fel
		+	+	⚒	+		💀		🛡

CAREER PATH

+ Menial — Silver 1
Skills: Athletics, Climb, Drive, Dodge, *Endurance*, Intuition, Perception, Stealth (Any)
Talents: Beneath Notice, Strong Back, Strong-minded, Sturdy
Trappings: Floor Brush

⚒ Servant — Silver 3
Skills: Animal Care, Consume Alcohol, Evaluate, Gamble, Gossip, Haggle
Talents: Etiquette (Servants), Shadow, Tenacious, Well-prepared
Trappings: Livery

💀 Attendant — Silver 5
Skills: Charm, Cool, Intimidate, Lore (Local)
Talents: Embezzle, Resistance (Poison), Suave, Supportive
Trappings: Quality Livery, Storm Lantern, Tinderbox, Lamp Oil

🛡 Steward — Gold 1
Skills: Leadership, Melee (Basic)
Talents: Etiquette (any), Numismatics, Read/Write, Savvy
Trappings: Hand Weapon, Fine Clothes, Servant

SPY

Dwarf, Halfling, High Elf, Human, Wood Elf

You are the eyes and ears of another, exposing secrets and spreading lies.

Spies are brave (or foolhardy) individuals who secretly gather information for their clients. A well-placed Spy is an asset to anyone desiring knowledge of an opponent's activities. Many take months, even years, cultivating an unremarkable identity with ties to one or more groups or individuals. Their actions are risky. If caught, Spies are rarely executed quickly and often tortured at length. Many Informers are forced into spying via blackmail or other threats. A skilled Spy will earn well, but extrication from such activities can be more perilous than the activities themselves. Given Spies avoid undue attention, they aren't typically known by their reputations unless those reputations are as anonymous as they are.

*'Treason? That's it? For the love of... why didn't I qualify for **high** treason? I've done plenty of other terrible things. Should I list them off for you? What's that? It's not personal? Well, it is now, you prig-powdered gaff'*

– Sieben Dietmund, Accused of Treason and Contempt

Spies are found throughout the Old World and in service to many prominent organisations. During their investigations, Spies are easily embroiled in plots both sinister and benign. They are often forced to flee when their identities or allegiances are exposed. These individuals use their abilities to disguise their true nature and avoid capture. Joining a group of unwitting heroes under false pretences as part of an escape attempt has led more than one Spy to an adventuring career.

SPY ADVANCE SCHEME

WS	BS	S	T	I	Agi	Dex	Int	WP	Fel
⚒				☠	✝		🛡	✝	✝

CAREER PATH

✝ Informer — Brass 3
Skills: Bribery, Charm, Cool, Gamble, *Gossip*, Haggle, Perception, Stealth (Any)
Talents: Blather, Carouser, Gregarious, Shadow
Trappings: Charcoal stick, Sling Bag containing 2 different sets of clothing and Hooded Cloak

⚒ Spy — Silver 3
Skills: Climb, Entertain (Act), Intuition, Melee (Basic), Secret Signs (Any), Sleight of Hand
Talents: Etiquette (Any), Lip Reading, Read/Write, Secret Identity
Trappings: Informer, Hand Weapon, Disguise Kit, Ring of Informers, Telescope

☠ Agent — Gold 1
Skills: Animal Care, Animal Training (Pigeon), Language (Any), Leadership
Talents: Attractive, Cat-tongued, Master of Disguise, Mimic
Trappings: Book (Cryptography), Ring of Spies and Informers, Loft of Homing Pigeons, Quill and Ink

🛡 Spymaster — Gold 4
Skills: Lore (Any), Research
Talents: Briber, Schemer, Suave, Tower of Memories
Trappings: Office and Staff, Large Spy Ring of Agents, Spies, and Informers

WARDEN
Dwarf, Halfling, High Elf, Human

You oversee another's territory, ensuring it is properly maintained and, if necessary, protected.

Wardens see to the care and stewardship of their employer's holdings. Failure to improve — or, at the very least, maintain — an employer's lands or provisions is often met with disfavour. In some instances, multiple wardens work together to keep their employer's estate in correct order.

A Warden's oversight can cover a variety of duties: ensuring the upkeep of a grand estate, overseeing a lord's hunting grounds, or caring for a rarely-visited holidaying home. Wardens might keep watch over forested or agricultural lands, or see to the maintenance of lakes, rivers, or ponds. Those in the employ of the richest and most powerful can rise to immensely powerful positions themselves.

'Yes, m'lord, the duke has been a-bed this last decade. And, yes, m'lord, I am running his estate. No, m'lord, I don't see that changing any time soon. After all, in Penzkirchen, my word is now law… Arrest him!'
— W. Edvart Kurtz, Governor of Penzkirchen

Wardens rarely travel unless their duties call for it. That said, even those assigned to oversee an estate's lands or hunting grounds must make regular patrols to assess the property's condition and to discourage poachers. When between jobs, Wardens often find work as guides or hunters, and such activities can lead to much excitement or terror. Wardens with a grudge against former masters might even be inclined to provide enemies with confidential information regarding their old estates.

WARDEN ADVANCE SCHEME

WS	BS	S	T	I	Agi	Dex	Int	WP	Fel
⚒		+	+				🛡	+	💀

CAREER PATH

+ Custodian — Silver 1
Skills: Athletics, Charm Animal, Consume Alcohol, Cool, Endurance, Intuition, Lore (Local), *Perception*
Talents: Menacing, Night Vision, Sharp, Strike to Stun
Trappings: Keys, Lantern, Lamp Oil, Livery

⚒ Warden — Silver 3
Skills: Animal Care, Melee (Basic), Outdoor Survival, Ranged (Bow), Ride (Horse), Swim
Talents: Animal Affinity, Etiquette (Servants), Strider (any), Rover
Trappings: Hand Weapon *or* Bow with 10 arrows, Riding Horse with Saddle and Harness, Leather Jack

💀 Seneschal — Gold 1
Skills: Bribery, Charm, Gossip, Leadership
Talents: Embezzle, Numismatics, Read/Write, Supportive
Trappings: Breastplate, Ceremonial Staff of Office, Staff of Wardens and Custodians

🛡 Governor — Gold 3
Skills: Evaluate, Language (Any)
Talents: Commanding Presence, Etiquette (any), Savant (local), Suave
Trappings: Aide, Governor's Residence, Servant

BAILIFF

Dwarf, Halfling, Human

You are an official trusted by local rulers to administer their lands efficiently and firmly.

Nobles entrust Bailiffs to gather dues from their lands. Some Bailiffs are respected and upstanding, attending throng at the temple of Sigmar every week. Others are bullies, happy to enforce their lord's rights over property and possessions with threats and violence. Long-serving bailiffs often become trusted servants of the local noble family and enjoy considerable perks. Reeves have a broader reach and greater responsibility. They keep order and maintain the borders of the lord's lands, resolving disputes with neighbouring estates.

Some magistrates are lay-members of the cult of Verena, seeking guidance and wisdom from blind Justice on any difficult cases they judge. However, most provincial magistrates simply find themselves arbitrating a series of petty disputes over livestock and farmland borders.

'Aye, it's been a poor harvest, but dues are dues. I'll take half now and half on Marktag. How's that? It's the best I can offer, can't say fairer than that.'

– Lena Sauer, Bailiff

'I'll go up and have a look at the grazing land in question myself. Until then, I want no trouble from any of your boisterous offspring, do I make myself clear, Bauer, Meier? And you will pay equal shares for the damage to the inn, or you will forfeit any claim you might, or might not have, on the land.'

– Lorenz Schulte, Reeve of Elster Vale

Most Bailiffs have a degree of autonomy, granting them ample opportunity to turn their attention to private matters, or to hire others to do so on their behalf. As many also have broad authority in the areas they influence, they are frequently sent by their employers to resolve problems, which can often lead to unexpected places.

BAILIFF ADVANCE SCHEME

WS	BS	S	T	I	Agi	Dex	Int	WP	Fel
✛				✛	💀		🛡	✛	⚒

CAREER PATH

✛ Tax Collector — Silver 1
Skills: Cool, Dodge, Endurance, Gossip, Haggle, *Intimidate*, Melee (Basic), Perception
Talents: Embezzle, Numismatics, Strong Back, Tenacious
Trappings: Hand weapon, small lock box

⚒ Bailiff — Silver 5
Skills: Bribery, Charm, Evaluate, Intuition, Leadership, Lore (Local)
Talents: Break and Enter, Criminal, Public Speaking, Strike to Stun
Trappings: Leather Jack, 3 Tax Collectors

💀 Reeve — Gold 1
Skills: Animal Care, Lore (Heraldry), Navigation, Ride (Horse)
Talents: Kingpin, Menacing, Nose for Trouble, Read/Write
Trappings: Horse with Saddle and Tack, Breastplate, Bailiff

🛡 Magistrate — Gold 3
Skills: Language (Classical), Lore (Law)
Talents: Commanding Presence, Iron Will, Savvy, Schemer
Trappings: Library (Law), Quality Robes, Seal of Office

HEDGE WITCH
Human

Wise and secretive, you guide your community using ancient magic handed down for generations.

Witch Hunters use the term 'Hedge Witch' for any illegal spellcaster, but this was not always so. Once Hedge Witches were respected members of rural communities, practising magics older than the forests. But decades of persecution since the founding of the Colleges of Magic have left the few surviving Hedge Witches disparate and broken. They hide in the quietest corners of the Old World, their smoky huts and creaking hovels standing astride the boundary between civilisation and the trackless wilds. Most Hedge Witches are solitary to protect themselves from prying strangers, but their talents are often known to locals. Their knowledge of warding evil is usually secret, but their herbalism, midwifery, and healing arts are quickly sought in times of need.

'We tell the folk that the offering o' fish is for Grandfather Reik, 'cause it makes them feel safer than having to explain the river is home to an 'ungry spirit. It keeps the spirit safe, too.'

– Alt Zaunreiter, Hedgewise

A Hedge Witch is often the first to notice supernatural foul play. The subsequent investigations often lead to all sorts of dangers and adventure. When Witch Hunters come to town, Hedge Witches often take a leave of absence, lying low or travelling elsewhere until danger is passed.

The Hedgefolk are known by many names across the Empire, but have one thing in common: the goal of preserving their ancient traditions from destruction. Hedge Witches have little love for the Colleges of Magic, knowing any child taken by them will likely never return to serve their community, instead pressed into service in some far-off war. Whenever possible they hide children they consider 'blessed' from passing wizards, although occasionally one will be sent to the Colleges — as a sacrifice or a spy, who can say?

HEDGE WITCH ADVANCE SCHEME

WS	BS	S	T	I	Agi	Dex	Int	WP	Fel
			✚	✚		✚	⚒	🛡	💀

CAREER PATH

✚ Hedge Apprentice — Brass 1
Skills: Channelling, Endurance, *Intuition*, Language (Magick), Lore (Folklore), Lore (Herbs), Outdoor Survival, Perception
Talents: Fast Hands, Petty Magic, Rover, Strider (Woodlands)
Trappings: 1d10 Lucky Charms, Quarterstaff, Backpack

⚒ Hedge Witch — Brass 2
Skills: Cool, Gossip, Heal, Lore (Local), Trade (Charms), Trade (Herbalist)
Talents: Aethyric Attunement, Animal Affinity, Arcane Magic (Hedgecraft), Sixth Sense
Trappings: Antitoxin Kit, Healing Poultice, Trade Tools (Herbalist)

💀 Hedge Master — Brass 3
Skills: Haggle, Lore (Genealogy), Lore (Magic), Lore (Spirits)
Talents: Craftsman (Herbalist), Magical Sense, Pure Soul, Resistance (Disease)
Trappings: Isolated Hut, Apprentice

🛡 Hedgewise — Brass 5
Skills: Intimidate, Pray
Talents: Acute Sense (Any), Master Craftsman (Herbalist), Night Vision, Strong-minded
Trappings: Assortment of Animal Skulls, Ceremonial Cloak and Garland

HERBALIST
Halfling, High Elf, Human, Wood Elf

Skilled botanists who use Rhya's bounty to create cures for many ailments.

Medicines from apothecaries are expensive and rarely available in the Reikland's hinterlands, so peasants rely on the healing power of plants gathered, doctored, and administered by Herbalists. Most Herbalists' lore is verbally passed down from master to apprentice, so names for illnesses and treatments often vary from village to village. The most experienced Herbwises are sent for in cases of mysterious or stubborn sickness. Herbalists dedicate time to visiting the sick, diagnosing their ailments and searching for herbs to treat them with. Some Herbalists ply a darker trade, sought out by those who can pay a high price for the illicit substances they offer. Although an untrue stereotype, it's a standing joke in the trade that Halfling Herbalists are only interested in pipeweed and wyrdroot.

'This is beyond my skill to heal. The wound's been infected and it's tainting his blood; he needs a doctor, or Shallya's aid. I can give you something to make sure he's comfortable on the journey to town. And something for you, too, to calm your nerves.'
– Kurtis Schwarz, Herbalist

With knowledge of poultices and potions, Herbalists can easily find a place with a band of travellers or mercenaries. When particularly virulent diseases take hold, Herbwises often send their apprentices to far off places in search of rarer herbs, and some find themselves in all manner of unexpected trouble. The Wood Elves' knowledge of plants and herbs is legendary. In the Grey Mountains it is said that The Goddess Shallya wandered Athel Loren to learn their lore when Ranald was dying of an affliction she could not cure. High Elves who study the art of herbalism follow Lileath the Maiden's teachings, and it's rumoured there is an ancient elven library in Marienburg which records the medicinal use of every plant in the Old World, although no Human has yet been granted access.

HERBALIST ADVANCE SCHEME

WS	BS	S	T	I	Agi	Dex	Int	WP	Fel
		+	+	+	⚒	🛡			💀

CAREER PATH

✚ Herb Gatherer — Brass 2
Skills: Charm Animal, Climb, Endurance, Lore (Herbs), Outdoor Survival, Perception, Swim, *Trade (Herbalist)*
Talents: Acute Sense (Taste), Orientation, Rover, Strider (any)
Trappings: Boots, Cloak, Sling Bag containing Assortment of Herbs

⚒ Herbalist — Brass 4
Skills: Consume Alcohol, Cool, Gossip, Haggle, Heal, Lore (Local)
Talents: Dealmaker, Nimble Fingered, Sharp, Sturdy
Trappings: Hand Weapon (Sickle), Healing Poultice, Trade Tools (Herbalist)

💀 Herb Master — Silver 1
Skills: Intuition, Leadership, Lore (Medicine), Trade (Poisons)
Talents: Craftsman (Herbalist), Field Dressing, Hardy, Savvy
Trappings: Herb Gatherer, 3 Healing Poultices, Healing Draught, Workshop (Herbalist)

🛡 Herbwise — Silver 3
Skills: Drive, Navigation
Talents: Concoct, Master Tradesman (Herbalist), Resistance (Poison), Savant (Herbs)
Trappings: Pony and Cart

HUNTER

Dwarf, Halfling, High Elf, Human, Wood Elf

Tough, independent killers who make a living off the fur and flesh of wild creatures.

'Taal's Bounty' is a common greeting in Hochland, where locals proclaim a proud hunting heritage that goes back to the time of Sigmar. Most in the Empire hunt, either as a hobby, a profession, or a necessity, and many Hunters turn to poaching when times are lean.

Particularly skilled Hunters might be engaged as a noble's Huntsmaster, granting access to fine weapons, horses, and falcons. Elves and Dwarfs have little care for the boundaries of men and will occasionally venture deep into Human territory tracking a challenging prize. Stories of the Wood Elves' Wild Hunt petrify children of the Grey Mountains, and not without cause, for if any intruder strays too close to Elven lands, then the hunters quickly become the hunted.

'My lord, those tracks… we're not following a stag. There are Turnskins in these woods.'

– Gundred Maynir, Huntsmaster

'Are you trying to tell me hunting's not a sport because both sides don't know they're playing? Might I suggest you'd been hunting the wrong game.'

– Graf Bernard Leutze von Holthausen

A common punishment for hunter caught poaching is to lose two fingers. Faced with being unable to draw a bow, many will cut and run before the punishment can be administered, preferring to take a chance in the forests. Around the fertile villages of the Suden Vorbergland, Hunters are losing ground to farmers as the trees are cut back and nobles reserve what hunting is left for sport. The Imperial Army is always on the lookout for reliable, local hunters to support their army as they march, acting as support archers or scouts. A life of adventure awaits any Hunter willing to take the Emperor's Shilling.

HUNTER ADVANCE SCHEME

WS	BS	S	T	I	Agi	Dex	Int	WP	Fel
⚒	✚	✚	☠			✚	🛡		

CAREER PATH

✚ Trapper — Brass 2
Skills: Charm Animal, Climb, Endurance, Lore (Beasts), *Outdoor Survival,* Perception, Ranged (Sling), Set Trap
Talents: Hardy, Rover, Strider (any), Trapper
Trappings: Selection of Animal Traps, Hand Weapon, Sling with 10 Stone Bullets, Sturdy Boots and Cloak

⚒ Hunter — Brass 4
Skills: Cool, Intuition, Melee (Basic), Ranged (Bow), Secret Signs (Hunter), Stealth (Rural)
Talents: Accurate Shot, Fast Shot, Hunter's Eye, Marksman
Trappings: Bow with 10 arrows

☠ Tracker — Silver 1
Skills: Navigation, Ride (Horse), Swim, Track
Talents: Acute Sense (any), Deadeye Shot, Fearless (Animals), Sharpshooter
Trappings: Backpack, Bedroll, Tent

🛡 Huntsmaster — Silver 3
Skills: Animal Care, Animal Training (Any)
Talents: Fearless (Monsters), Robust, Sniper, Sure Shot
Trappings: Riding Horse with Saddle and Tack, Kennel of Hunting Dogs

MINER
Dwarf, Halfling, Human

A hewer of stone, you pursue back-breaking work in the darkest depths of the world.

Many prospectors are tempted by stories of gold in the Skaag Hills, but real mining is hard work down dark, dangerous tunnels. Adept at constructing supports and assessing mineral ores for their value, Miners are alert to unexpected dangers from explosive gas to tunnelling Greenskins, and are notoriously tough, both physically and mentally. Prospectors usually work on commission, with a license to prospect in return for sharing finds with the local lord. Some noble houses' fortunes are built on the rich mines in their lands, and often Miners in these pits will be criminals or debtors pressed into service. Quarrymen hewing open-face stone ostensibly have a safer job than those underground, but accidents are common and Beastman attack from the forest is an ever-present danger.

'After your supplies from the store are deducted, and your load of sixteen tons added, you made...let me see... no, you actually owe us two for today. Another day older and deeper in debt, boy.'
– Frederika, Victualler of the Delfgruber Minehead.

Many independent Miners find themselves thrust into peril when set upon by Goblins or other subterranean horrors. Some find the rewards of this life more lucrative, if not less dangerous, than slaving away for a mine owner for a pittance. Prospectors have many opportunities for adventure and can easily pull together a band of like-minded folk eager for riches and glory.

To Dwarfs, mining is not an occupation limited to commoners. Rather, they are considered artisans of great skill and are well-respected amongst the Dawi. Possessed of a keen sense for stone, Dwarfs are drawn to valuable seams and seemingly have a sixth-sense for when to shore up passages. Some Dwarf clans hold such pride in their mining ability that they march to war armed with picks rather than axes.

MINER ADVANCE SCHEME

WS	BS	S	T	I	Agi	Dex	Int	WP	Fel
⚒		+	+	💀				+	🛡

CAREER PATH

+ Prospector — Brass 2
Skills: Cool, Endurance, Intuition, Lore (Local), *Melee (Two-handed)*, Outdoor Survival, Perception, Swim
Talents: Rover, Strider (Rocky), Sturdy, Tenacious
Trappings: Charcoal Stick, Crude Map, Pan, Spade

⚒ Miner — Brass 4
Skills: Climb, Consume Alcohol, Evaluate, Melee (Basic), Secret Signs (Miner), Trade (Explosives)
Talents: Night Vision, Strike Mighty Blow, Strong Back, Very Strong
Trappings: Davrich Lamp, Hand Weapon (Pick), Lamp Oil, Leather Jack

💀 Master Miner — Brass 5
Skills: Gossip, Lore (Geology), Stealth (Underground), Trade (Engineer)
Talents: Careful Strike, Craftsman (Explosives), Tinker, Tunnel Rat
Trappings: Great Weapon (Two-handed Pick), Helmet, Trade Tools (Engineer)

🛡 Mine Foreman — Silver 4
Skills: Charm, Leadership
Talents: Argumentative, Strong-minded, Embezzle, Read/Write
Trappings: Crew of Miners, Writing Kit

MYSTIC
Human, Wood Elf

You have a talent for divining the future, or for convincing others you can…

Searching for meaning in a dangerous world, people turn to Mystics for a glimpse of their future. Wandering caravans of Strigany are a common sight in Reikland, and locals scrape together coin to hear their fortune, and buy charms and love potions. Most Mystics are perceptive and intuitive, able to divine their customers' hopes and fears and give readings just specific enough to be believable. Mystics must be careful, and walk a fine line between accusations of trickery and heretical witchery. Mystics demonstrate their talent in a wide variety of ways: palmists and card readers are common amongst the Strigany, while a Wood Elf is more likely to interpret the signs and symbols to be found around them in nature, or to be inspired by dreams and visions. Many cults also have their own Seers and Sages, each prophesising the future through the paradigm of their beliefs.

'I'll tell you for why we have wheels on our houses: it's because no-one likes to hear the cold truth of Morr a-coming, and if there's one thing for sure, Morr is always a-coming. So, it ain't because we're cheaters, but because we are honest folk!'

– Honest Chupra, Strigany Pedlar

'I never met a Priest who could tell me what the future holds. Well, unless you count the Priest of Morr who Doomed me for thruppence, but don't they say that death and taxes are the only things we can be certain of?'

– Sylvestr Jutzenbach, Ostermarker Noble

Mystics might seek a life of adventure if their insights draw the attention of priests and witch hunters. Dreams and visions also provide an incentive to join a band of adventurers: perhaps the Mystic foresees a terrible future ahead if action is not taken? No matter their motivation, once on the road, Mystics can easily ply their trade wherever they should travel.

MYSTIC ADVANCE SCHEME

WS	BS	S	T	I	Agi	Dex	Int	WP	Fel
				✚	☠	✚	🛡	⚒	✚

CAREER PATH

✚ Fortune Teller — Brass 1
Skills: Charm, Entertain (Fortune Telling), Dodge, Gossip, Haggle, *Intuition*, Perception, Sleight of Hand
Talents: Attractive, Luck, Second Sight, Suave
Trappings: Deck of Cards or Dice, Cheap Jewellery

⚒ Mystic — Brass 2
Skills: Bribery, Cool, Entertain (Prophecy), Evaluate, Intimidate, Lore (Astrology)
Talents: Detect Artefact, Holy Visions, Sixth Sense, Well-prepared
Trappings: Selection of Amulets

☠ Sage — Brass 3
Skills: Art (Writing), Charm Animal, Entertain (Storytelling), Language (Any)
Talents: Nose for Trouble, Petty Magic, Read/Write, Witch!
Trappings: Trade Tools (Writing)

🛡 Seer — Brass 4
Skills: Lore (Prophecy), Channelling (*Azyr*)
Talents: Arcane Magic (Celestial), Magical Sense, Menacing, Strong-minded
Trappings: Trade Tools (Astrology)

SCOUT

Dwarf, Halfling, High Elf, Human, Wood Elf

Intrepid and resourceful, you guide others through the dangerous wilds of the Old World.

Among an illiterate populace where maps are rare, local knowledge can mean the difference between life and death for travellers. Scouts are experts at finding safe paths through the backwoods and muddy roads of the Empire. Local guides will accompany their clients, warning of upcoming dangers, sharing village gossip or showing the best places to forage. Experienced Scouts will barely be seen by their employers as they explore the trails ahead and keep a watchful eye out for hidden dangers. While most Scouts keep to familiar territory, some specialise in safely navigating unmapped terrain. Explorers might venture even further into treacherous and hostile territory, filling in the blank spaces on their maps. Most Scouts do not tackle dangers themselves, preferring to slip away quietly to warn their companions and enable their employers to avoid potential hazards completely.

'You don't want to be going off the road down by the bluff without a guide. There's man-traps in them woods what the reeve put down to catch poachers. Almost 'ad old Billi's leg off last week it did.'

– Gwyn, Scout

Scouts can be invaluable to a group of adventurers, especially those venturing out from a city for the first time to find their fortune. Reliable and knowledgeable Guides may find themselves asked to stay on and act as Scouts, although many still act the loner, slipping in and out of the woods to protect the group from ambush or warn of enemies ahead.

SCOUT ADVANCE SCHEME

WS	BS	S	T	I	Agi	Dex	Int	WP	Fel
	⚒		✝	✝	✝	🛡	💀		

CAREER PATH

✝ Guide — Brass 3
Skills: Charm Animal, Climb, Endurance, Gossip, Lore (Local), Melee (Basic), Outdoor Survival, *Perception*
Talents: Orientation, Rover, Sharp, Strider (any)
Trappings: Hand Weapon, Leather Jack, Sturdy Boots and Cloak, Rope

⚒ Scout — Brass 5
Skills: Athletics, Navigation, Ranged (Bow), Ride (Horse), Stealth (Rural), Track
Talents: Combat Aware, Night Vision, Nose for Trouble, Seasoned Traveller
Trappings: Bow and 10 Arrows, Mail Shirt

💀 Pathfinder — Silver 1
Skills: Animal Care, Haggle, Secret Signs (Hunter), Swim
Talents: Acute Sense (Sight), Sixth Sense, Strong Legs, Very Resilient
Trappings: Map, Riding Horse with Saddle and Tack, Saddlebags with 2 weeks' Rations, Tent

🛡 Explorer — Silver 5
Skills: Language (any), Trade (Cartographer)
Talents: Hardy, Linguistics, Savant (Local), Tenacious
Trappings: Selection of Maps, Trade Tools (Cartographer)

VILLAGER
Dwarf, Halfling, Human

You are the beating heart of rural life, working the countryside to feed civilisation.

Sigmar's bountiful Empire provides an abundant harvest of crops, livestock, and other marketable goods, so there is always plenty of work to be found in the countryside. Villagers make up most of the Empire's population and perform a variety of valuable roles, including Farmers, Charcoal Burners, Woodsmen, Millers, Herders, and many more. Most villages fall under the domain of a noble family, where day-to-day administration of the estate is overseen by a bailiff. Village affairs are usually managed by a village council of local tradesmen and farmers led by an Elder. A village Councillor or Elder can hold significant local influence overseeing many decisions concerning the surrounding land.

'It's a hard life, for sure, but it's a good one. Every year the lady from the manor sends out her guard to clear out the forest and drive off the beastmen and the like. The family keep us safe, we keep their flocks. It's a fair trade most of the time.'

– Gunni Ackermann, Shepherdess

'Look, you can sneer at me all you want, but Konrad the Hero his-bloomin'-self was from a village just like mine, so don't you be talking us down, you hear! Us villagers are good folk!'

– Erika Bauer, Farmer

The pastoral safety of a sheltered village is an unspeakable bore for some young Villagers who listen avidly to the tales of faraway lands. Of course, the stories they hear from wandering Pedlars and Strigany, all fuelling schemes to escape, bear little relation to the harsh reality of Empire life. During winter, when food is short, and the fields do not need tending, young folk venturing to nearby towns and cities for work often never return, soon caught in the net of civilisation's excitement and adventure.

VILLAGER ADVANCE SCHEME

WS	BS	S	T	I	Agi	Dex	Int	WP	Fel
⚒		✠	✠		✠		🛡		💀

CAREER PATH

✠ Peasant — Brass 2
Skills: Animal Care, Athletics, Consume Alcohol, *Endurance*, Gossip, Melee (Brawling), Lore (Local), Outdoor Survival
Talents: Rover, Strong Back, Strong-minded, Stone Soup
Trappings: None

⚒ Villager — Brass 3
Skills: Dodge, Drive, , Entertain (Storytelling), Haggle, Melee (Basic), Trade (Any)
Talents: Animal Affinity, Hardy, Tenacious, Very Strong
Trappings: Leather Jerkin, Hand Weapon (Axe), Trade Tools (as Trade)

💀 Councillor — Brass 4
Skills: Bribery, Charm, Intimidate, Leadership
Talents: Craftsman (Any), Dealmaker, Stout-hearted, Very Resilient
Trappings: Mule and Cart, Village Home and Workshop

🛡 Village Elder — Silver 2
Skills: Intuition, Lore (History)
Talents: Master Tradesman (Any), Nimble Fingered, Public Speaker, Savant (Local)
Trappings: The Respect of the Village

BOUNTY HUNTER

Dwarf, Halfling, High Elf, Human, Wood Elf

Ruthless and determined, you pursue your quarry to the bitter end: for justice, or for money.

Bounty Hunters track down fugitives and outlaws for coin. Most are legally appointed by provincial courts and receive warrant papers granting licence to seize or sometimes kill the target. While some are motivated by Verena's justice, most are more concerned by the rewards, often finding the 'dead' in 'dead or alive' to be the most convenient route to their fortune. Many Bounty Hunters start as Thief-Takers, those hired by crime victims to retrieve stolen goods. Over time, those with an established reputation may find permanent work from a merchant or noble house, guild, or cult, or may build a company of Bounty Hunters, working as a group to collect the largest rewards.

'It's amazing just how many boys will wrap themselves in manacles if you smile sweetly enough. And if that doesn't work, it's out with the knives!'

– Anke Dorflinger, Bounty Hunter

In their pursuit of wanted criminals, Bounty Hunters often stumble into unplanned adventures. As independent operatives, Bounty Hunters are perfectly suited to dropping their day job to pursue whatever business is afoot. Further, given their broad base of skills are always in demand, it is not uncommon to see Bounty Hunters turning their hand to adventuring full-time, hiring their skills out in return for payments. Bounty Hunters are a perfect starting career as they present a solid mixture of social and combat skills allowing you to contribute no matter the circumstances.

BOUNTY HUNTER ADVANCE SCHEME

WS	BS	S	T	I	Agi	Dex	Int	WP	Fel
✢	⚒	💀	✢		✢		🛡		

Career Path

✢ Thief-taker — Silver 1
Skills: Bribery, Charm, Gossip, Haggle, Intuition, *Melee (Basic),* Outdoor Survival, Perception
Talents: Break and Enter, Shadow, Strike to Stun, Suave
Trappings: Hand Weapon, Leather Jerkin, Rope

⚒ Bounty Hunter — Silver 3
Skills: Athletics, Endurance, Intimidate, Ranged (Crossbow), Ranged (Entangling), Track
Talents: Marksman, Relentless, Seasoned Traveller, Strong Back
Trappings: Crossbow and 10 bolts, Leather Skullcap, Manacles, Net, Warrant Papers

💀 Master Bounty Hunter — Silver 5
Skills: Animal Care, Climb, Ride (Horse), Swim
Talents: Accurate Shot, Careful Strike, Dual Wielder, Sprinter
Trappings: Mail Shirt, Riding Horse and Saddle

🛡 Bounty Hunter General — Gold 1
Skills: Drive, Lore (Law)
Talents: Deadeye Shot, Fearless (Bounties), Hardy, Sure Shot
Trappings: Draught Horse and Cart, Mail Shirt, 4 Pairs of Manacles

COACHMAN

Dwarf, Halfling, Human

Determined and rugged, you deliver passengers safely by coach despite the daily dangers you face.

For many, the coach is the only way to get from one town to the next. The wild places between teem with Beastmen, Bandits, and worse, but with just a team of fresh horses and a blunderbuss, brave and hardworking Coachmen make travel possible. To help evade danger, most coaching companies relentlessly pursue speed, and their employees have a reputation for ruthlessness towards other travellers on the roads, never trusting anyone. Coachmen often start as Postilions, riding the lead horse of the team through wind and rain. Instead of transporting passengers, some Coachmen deliver mail, work as chauffeurs for nobles, drive cabs or goods wagons, or the big omnibuses of the great cities, or even become a getaway driver.

'Get 'em fed in a quarter bell. No second portions. We ain't paid for that. Coach Mistress eats last but save 'er the best. One minute longer than the quarter and I take a pfennig off you, the Mistress takes a shilling off me, and Castle Rock Coaches will be in here as quick as silver.'

– Bettina Hoch, Innkeeper

'Three days I was stuck in Weissbruck during the storms. Not a single thing came in and out. Then just when I thought I'd miss my appointment in Bogenhafen there appeared three coaches coming up the frozen track, all together. Bloody typical! You wait days for a coach, and then three come along at once.'

– Stelle Grabbe, Merchant

Good Coachmen are always in demand for unusual, dangerous or illegal jobs. A Coachman looking for a change may find winter is a good time to take a break, as cross-country services are greatly reduced. Coaching companies are always ready to snap up experienced coachmen, so returning to work is usually simple.

COACHMAN ADVANCE SCHEME

WS	BS	S	T	I	Agi	Dex	Int	WP	Fel
☠	✚		✚	🛡	⚒			✚	

CAREER PATH

✚ Postilion — Silver 1
Skills: Animal Care, Charm Animal, Climb, *Drive*, Endurance, Perception, Ranged (Entangling), Ride (Horse)
Talents: Animal Affinity, Seasoned Traveller, Trick-Riding, Tenacious
Trappings: Warm Coat and Gloves, Whip

⚒ Coachman — Silver 2
Skills: Consume Alcohol, Gossip, Intuition, Lore (Local), Navigation, Ranged (Blackpowder)
Talents: Coolheaded, Crack the Whip, Gunner, Strong-minded
Trappings: Blunderbuss with 10 Shots, Coach Horn, Leather Jack, Hat

☠ Coach Master — Silver 3
Skills: Animal Training (Horse), Intimidation, Language (any), Lore (Routes)
Talents: Accurate Shot, Dealmaker, Fearless (Outlaws), Nose for Trouble
Trappings: Mail Shirt, Pistol, Quality Cloak

🛡 Route Master — Silver 5
Skills: Charm, Leadership
Talents: Fearless (Beastmen), Marksman, Orientation, Rapid Reload
Trappings: Fleet of Coaches and Horses, Maps

CLASS AND CAREERS - RANGERS

III

ENTERTAINER
Dwarf, Halfling, High Elf, Human, Wood Elf

Whether high-born or low-brow, you distract people from the harsh realities of life.

Entertainers crop up all over the Old World, and many wander the Reikland's roads, earning their crust. Some stay put at a single theatre, some work as individuals, some as part of a troupe. The worst are little more than itinerant beggars, the best lauded in the company of counts and princes. It is not an easy life and the people will not tolerate poor acts, running them out of town pelted with rotten vegetables.

The most common Entertainers are the perennial crowd-pleasers like jesters, singers, actors, musicians, acrobats, dancers, and jugglers, but the Old World is also home to more obscure and bizarre acts.

A wandering minstrel I,
A thing of shreds and patches,
Of ballads, songs, and snatches,
And dreamy lullaby!
– Libretto from The Emperor of Nippon, by Guillibert and Solomon

'How do you get to the Luitpold Theatre? Practise!'
– Well known Altdorf joke

'Musician and prodigy, Vladimira Tchaikofiev, toured the courts of the Empire performing her compositions for the great and good. On her triumphant return to her native Kislev, during the reign of Bloody Katerin, she premiered her first opera, "The Vampire Counts of Stirland" based on her travels in Sylvania. Unconventionally, she always chose to conduct with a silver baton.'
– 'A Defence Against Necromancy', Patriarch Felip Iyrtu, 2415IC, from the 1st year required reading list, Amethyst College

The open road, a new village every night, the smell of greasepaint and the roar of the crowd — life itself can be an adventure for the Entertainer as they bring excitement to the humdrum, everyday reality of those they captivate. Given their existence on the edge of respectable society, curious Entertainers all-too-often find real adventures of their own.

ENTERTAINER ADVANCE SCHEME

WS	BS	S	T	I	Agi	Dex	Int	WP	Fel
⚒	☠		🛡		✚	✚			✚

CAREER PATH

✚ Busker — Brass 3
Skills: Athletics, Charm, *Entertain (Any)*, Gossip, Haggle, Perform (Any), Play (any), Sleight of Hand
Talents: Attractive, Mimic, Public-Speaking, Suave
Trappings: Bowl, Instrument

⚒ Entertainer — Brass 5
Skills: Entertain (Any), Ride (Any), Melee (Basic), Perform (Any), Play (Any) Ranged (Throwing)
Talents: Contortionist, Jump Up, Sharpshooter, Trick Riding
Trappings: Costume, Instrument, Selection of Scripts (that you can't yet read), Throwing Weapons

☠ Troubadour — Silver 3
Skills: Animal Care, Animal Training (Any), Art (Writing), Language (Any)
Talents: Blather, Master of Disguise, Perfect Pitch, Read/Write
Trappings: Trained Animal, Writing Kit

🛡 Troupe Leader — Gold 1
Skills: Drive, Leadership
Talents: Dealmaker, Etiquette (Any), Seasoned Traveller, Sharp
Trappings: Draught Horses and Wagon (Stage), Wardrobe of Costumes and Props, Troupe of Entertainers

FLAGELLANT
Human

Just when you abandoned all hope, your suffering and the righteousness of Sigmar saved you!

Forgiveness does not come easily, only through struggle, pain, and doing Sigmar's will. Flagellants travel the Empire, flogging themselves in penance for their sins, and the sins of others. They are determined to serve Sigmar until the end of the world, something they believe is imminent. All good folk are expected to welcome, help, and feed them, and to pray with them.

Most Flagellants wander in large groups, guided by a Prophet of Doom who interprets Sigmar's will. Some follow armies, whipping themselves into a frenzy as battle is joined and fighting without any thought for their own safety. Others wander by themselves, believing they best serve Sigmar by righting the wrongs he guides them towards.

'We strike this flesh and spill this blood, for his Empire, in the name of Sigmar!'

– Viktorina Schwefel, Flagellant

'We had some flagellants going through the village a couple of months back. Terrible they were: the agony, the pain, the suffering, and that was just watching them. We knew what to do. We knew we had to open our doors and feed them and pray with them. But in the end, we just hid in the cellar until they'd gone. Scary folk.'

– Wulfrum Barth, villager

'The Ende is Nigh!'

– Common placard carried by Flagellants

It's not hard for Flagellants to stumble upon an adventure, especially involving recognised foes of Sigmar. Flagellants can continue their lifestyle as they adventure, relying on the honest folk of the Empire to offer them food, drink and shelter as they trudge ever onwards to the end of all things.

FLAGELLANT ADVANCE SCHEME

WS	BS	S	T	I	Agi	Dex	Int	WP	Fel
✝		✝	✝	☠				⚒	🛡

CAREER PATH

✝ Zealot — Brass 0
Skills: Dodge, Endurance, Heal, Intimidate, Intuition, Lore (Sigmar), *Melee (Flail)*, Outdoor Survival
Talents: Berserk Charge, Frenzy, Read/Write, Stone Soup
Trappings: Flail, Tattered Robes

⚒ Flagellant — Brass 0
Skills: Art (Icons), Athletics, Cool, Language (Classical), Lore (The Empire), Ranged (Sling)
Talents: Hardy, Hatred (Heretics), Flagellant, Implacable
Trappings: Placard, Religious Symbol, Sling

☠ Penitent — Brass 0
Skills: Charm, Language (any), Lore (Theology), Perception
Talents: Field Dressing, Furious Assault, Menacing, Seasoned Traveller
Trappings: Religious Relic

🛡 Prophet of Doom — Brass 0
Skills: Entertain (Speeches), Leadership
Talents: Battle Rage, Fearless (Heretics), Frightening, Impassioned Zeal
Trappings: Book (Religion), Followers (including Penitents, Flagellants, and Zealots)

MESSENGER

Dwarf, Halfling, High Elf, Human, Wood Elf

Swift and sure-footed, nothing stops you delivering your messages on time.

When the postal service is unsecure or too slow, people send a Messenger. Several courier companies provide express services, competing to show they are the fastest and safest. Most Messengers take their duties very seriously, guarding their packages with their lives. Some courier companies have arrangements with coaching houses allowing their Messengers to swap tired horses for fresh ones, for top-speed delivery.

Runners are employed to carry urgent messages in cities. Many larger settlements host competitions to celebrate the fastest, with the winners taking prizes and lucrative job contracts. Messengers can also be found working for the military, noble houses, large merchant houses, and for criminal gangs seeking to maintain their privacy.

'Are you Herr Schmidt of Hochplatz, Kemperbad? Erm, do you know a Herr Schmidt of Hochplatz, Kemperbad? Erm, do you know a Hochplatz? Kemperbad?'
— Willi Winkle, Messenger on his first day

'It looked like an interesting package, if you know what I mean. I thought I'd just have a quick peek. Thought it was to his girlfriend. Thought it might be a bit, you know, juicy. How was I to know it was all that boring spying stuff. Where's Bretonnia, anyway?'
— Rufus Drucht, Messenger who single-handedly busted the Bloody Bretonnian spy ring, then lost his job.

Messages can contain all sorts of information, and some lead to adventure should they be intercepted. The easiest way for any villain (or innocent party) to get hold of such information will be to waylay a Messenger. If this happens, it will be the Messenger's duty to follow things through until the message is recovered. As Messengers are usually freelance, paid per package delivered, it is simple enough to drop everything then pick-up work when they return.

MESSENGER ADVANCE SCHEME

WS	BS	S	T	I	Agi	Dex	Int	WP	Fel
⚒			+	+	+			☠	🛡

CAREER PATH

✝ Runner — Brass 3
Skills: Athletics, Climb, Dodge, *Endurance*, Gossip, Navigation, Perception, Melee (Brawling)
Talents: Flee!, Fleet Footed, Sprinter, Step Aside
Trappings: Scroll Case

⚒ Messenger — Silver 1
Skills: Animal Care, Charm, Cool, Lore (Local), Melee (Basic), Ride (Horse)
Talents: Crack the Whip, Criminal, Orientation, Seasoned Traveller
Trappings: Hand Weapon, Leather Jack, Riding Horse with Saddle and Tack

☠ Courier — Silver 3
Skills: Charm Animal, Bribery, Consume Alcohol, Outdoor Survival
Talents: Nose for Trouble, Relentless, Tenacious, Trick Rider
Trappings: Backpack, Saddlebags, Shield

🛡 Courier-Captain — Silver 5
Skills: Intimidate, Leadership
Talents: Dealmaker, Hatred (Outlaws), Kingpin, Very Resilient
Trappings: Couriers, Mail Shirt, Writing Kit

PEDLAR
Dwarf, Halfling, Human

Worldly-wise and free of interference, you wander the Empire selling your wares where you will.

Pedlars traipse from village to hamlet, selling goods and services such as knife sharpening, mending, and tinkering. Most carry cheap stock readily available in larger towns, including small luxuries such as ribbons and hair pins. Pedlars are always welcome as even suspicious folk like to treat themselves to baubles and knickknacks.

Some Pedlars also take on messenger work; others act as *de facto* town criers, bringing news and gossip to the quietest corners of the Empire in exchange for bed-and-board. Given the dangers on the road, some Pedlars prefer to keep a stall at a regular town marketplace. It is also common to find them on pilgrim routes making a living selling relics to the devout.

'This here is an absolutely unique, one-of-a-kind, only-one-in-existence, work of art. If you want more, don't worry, I've got another couple of dozen on the back of the cart.'

– Delberz Trötte, Trader

Hearing of profits to be made in far-off lands and listening to the stories of well-travelled merchants is always going to whet the appetite of an ambitious Pedlar. Being self-reliant, they can follow up on any adventure, making a decent profit along the way. They can also gain access to strongholds and settlements without awkward questions.

PEDLAR ADVANCE SCHEME

WS	BS	S	T	I	Agi	Dex	Int	WP	Fel
			✚	💀		✚	🛡	✚	⚒

CAREER PATH

✚ Vagabond — Brass 1
Skills: Charm, Endurance, Entertain (Storytelling), Gossip, *Haggle*, Intuition, Outdoor Survival, Stealth (Rural *or* Urban)
Talents: Fisherman, Flee!, Rover, Tinker
Trappings: Backpack, Bedroll, Goods worth 2d10 Brass, Tent

⚒ Pedlar — Brass 4
Skills: Animal Care, Charm Animal, Consume Alcohol, Evaluate, Ride (Horse), Trade (Tinker)
Talents: Dealmaker, Orientation, Seasoned Traveller, Strong Back
Trappings: Mule and Saddlebags, Goods worth 2d10 Silver, Selection of Pots and Pans, Trade Tools (Tinker)

💀 Master Pedlar — Silver 1
Skills: Drive, Intimidate, Language (any), Perception
Talents: Numismatics, Sturdy, Well-prepared, Very Resilient
Trappings: Cart, Goods worth at least 2d10 Gold

🛡 Wandering Trader — Silver 3
Skills: Lore (Local), Lore (Geography)
Talents: Cat-tongued, Strong-minded, Suave, Tenacious
Trappings: Draught Horse and Wagon, Goods worth at least 5d10 Gold, 50 Silver in Coin

ROAD WARDEN
Halfling, Human

With a wary eye and ready weapon, you tour the highways of the Empire enforcing the law.

Road Wardens protect travellers from the bandits, Greenskins, Beastmen and other dangers that threaten the Empire's highways. The Wardens are supported by a system of tolls, taxes they often collect personally. Successful Road Wardens are well-received and respected, and often have bunks in each inn along their route. Most main-road Road Wardens are part of the State Army, patrolling primary thoroughfares during peace time, so are well-trained and resplendent in neat uniforms. Less-travelled roads make do with local equivalents, some of whom take advantage of their position and lack of supervision for their own gain. Some Wardens prefer sitting in their safe, fortified toll stations to clearing the roads, but travellers often balk at handing over coin when the roads are dangerous and in disrepair.

'What can I say, it's a pfennig a leg. Them's the rules. Nothing I can do about it. Perhaps you should try to find a different route to get your bees to Grünburg.'

– Andreas Muller, jobsworth Toll Keeper

'So, I was stopped by a road warden t'other day. She said I should beware an unscrupulous character out patrolling the roads and charging hapless travellers a thruppence to let them pass. I thanked the warden for the valuable advice. "Taal guide you," she said, "that will be thruppence."'

– Ullrich the Pedlar

Road Wardens frequently find adventure. Anything untoward happening in the countryside is often close to a well-patrolled roadside. When trouble occurs, Road Wardens are summoned to resolve any problems. If they follow up and become involved in an investigation, they are simply doing their job, and might even secure extra pay for their time, even if the resulting adventure takes them far from their regular beat.

ROAD WARDEN ADVANCE SCHEME

WS	BS	S	T	I	Agi	Dex	Int	WP	Fel
⚒	✚		✚	✚			🛡		💀

CAREER PATH

✚ Toll Keeper — Brass 5
Skills: Bribery, Consume Alcohol, Gamble, Gossip, Haggle, Melee (Basic), *Perception*, Ranged (Crossbow)
Talents: Coolheaded, Embezzle, Marksman, Numismatics
Trappings: Crossbow with 10 Bolts, Leather Jack

⚒ Road Warden — Silver 2
Skills: Animal Care, Endurance, Intimidate, Intuition, Outdoor Survival, Ride (Horse)
Talents: Crack the Whip, Criminal, Roughrider, Seasoned Traveller
Trappings: Hand Weapon, Mail Shirt, Riding Horse with Saddle and Harness, Rope

💀 Road Sergeant — Silver 4
Skills: Athletics, Charm, Leadership, Ranged (Blackpowder)
Talents: Etiquette (Soldiers), Fearless (Outlaws), Hatred (any), Nose for Trouble
Trappings: Squad of Road Wardens, Pistol with 10 Shots, Shield, Symbol of Rank

🛡 Road Captain — Gold 1
Skills: Lore (Empire), Navigation
Talents: Combat Aware, Commanding Presence, Kingpin, Public Speaker
Trappings: Light Warhorse, Pistol with 10 Shots, Quality Hat and Cloak, Unit of Road Wardens

WITCH HUNTER
Human

You hunt the illegal witches plaguing the Empire by any and all means necessary.

There are few so feared and respected as the Witch Hunter, and they are given extraordinary leeway in performing their duties. Typically armed with silvered blades and a brace of pistols — for lead is not so easily dispelled — they stalk all corners of the Old World ready to dispense judgement on any witch they find, or any who would harbour them. Most Witch Hunters in the Empire are attached to the Cult of Sigmar. Secular Witch Hunters are sometimes employed by provincial government, though these are little more than specialist bounty hunters. The Colleges of Magic also have Witch Hunters called Wizards Vigilant who pursue rogue wizards, necromancers, and daemonologists — they believe it is wisest to set a witch to catch a witch.

'I ain't met a witch yet that won't catch fire.'
— Father Linken Donatus, Priest of Sigmar,
murdered by a rogue pyromancer

'If you're not a witch, you have nothing to fear.'
— Walter Keller, Witch Hunter Captain,
said the night before the burning of Almshof

A Witch Hunter's existence is one of constant adventure, often ranging the length and breadth of the grand provinces. They are called upon whenever the foul influence of unsanctioned magic emerges, and are expected to hunt it down. The bigger the reputation a Witch Hunter earns, the more dangerous the foes assigned, and the greater the adventures that follow. If you play a Witch Hunter, it is worth while making sure others aren't playing a Hedge Witch or Witch as this may immediately bring the party into conflict.

WITCH HUNTER ADVANCE SCHEME

WS	BS	S	T	I	Agi	Dex	Int	WP	Fel
✛	⚒		✛				🛡	✛	💀

CAREER PATH

✛ Interrogator — Silver 1
Skills: Charm, Consume Alcohol, Heal, *Intimidate*, Intuition, Lore (Torture), Melee (Brawling), Perception
Talents: Coolheaded, Menacing, Read/Write, Resolute
Trappings: Hand Weapon, Instruments of Torture

⚒ Witch Hunter — Silver 3
Skills: Cool, Gossip, Melee (Basic), Lore (Witches), Ranged (Any), Ride (Horse)
Talents: Dual Wielder, Marksman, Seasoned Traveller, Shadow
Trappings: Crossbow Pistol or Pistol, Hat (Henin), Leather Jack, Riding Horse with Saddle and Tack, Rope, Silvered Sword

💀 Inquisitor — Silver 5
Skills: Endurance, Leadership, Lore (Law), Lore (Local)
Talents: Fearless (Witches), Nose for Trouble, Relentless, Strong-minded
Trappings: Quality Clothing, Subordinate Interrogators

🛡 Witchfinder General — Gold 1
Skills: Lore (Chaos), Lore (Politics)
Talents: Frightening, Iron Will, Magical Sense, Pure Soul
Trappings: Best Quality Courtly Garb, Subordinate Witch Hunters

BOATMAN

Dwarf, Halfling, High Elf, Human

You ply the dangerous waters of the Old World, transporting people, goods, and the latest news.

Boats and barges travel the Empire's waterways, bringing goods from the remotest corners of the provinces to the greatest cities. These shallow-drafted vessels can travel much further upriver than larger ships, and a comprehensive network of canals adds to their reach. Barge Masters are expert river sailors and have an exhaustive knowledge of their rivers. A Boat-hand is the dogsbody, but will learn the ropes swiftly. Boatmen crew merchant barges carrying cargo to and from markets, either working for themselves or for a larger Merchant House. Many Boatmen are also ferrymen, taking passengers across rivers, or to and from towns. In large towns, some also crew rivertaxis, sail pleasure vessels, or otherwise pilot boats on the behalf of others.

'Someday a real rain will come. So, don't forget your hat, madam.'
– Travis Binckel, Rivertaxi

'Beware of forking. I say this as an experienced bargeswain. If you approach a dangerous rock or other river hazard be sure to go astarboard and stay astarboard while laying astarboard, or go alarboard and stay alarboard while laying alarboard. Or you will fork, and you might sink. And no-one wants to sink their forking barge.'
– Jacob Walles, Bargeswain who sank his forking barge

A boatman will not need to seek out adventure, for more than likely adventure will come to them. Boats are useful to nearly everyone, and therefore useful to almost any adventure plot; they also make an excellent base of operations. Boatmen will not need to worry about following investigation and adventure if the plot stays on or close to the river. Even if the plot leaves the river, they could still easily allow a talented Boathand to look after their business while they take a break from river life.

BOATMAN ADVANCE SCHEME

WS	BS	S	T	I	Agi	Dex	Int	WP	Fel
		✚	✚	⚒	✚	☠	🛡		

CAREER PATH

✚ Boat-hand — Silver 1
Skills: Consume Alcohol, Dodge, Endurance, Gossip, Melee (Brawling), Row, *Sail*, Swim
Talents: Dirty Fighting, Fisherman, Strong Back, Strong Swimmer
Trappings: Hand Weapon (Boat Hook), Leather Jack, Pole

⚒ Boatman — Silver 2
Skills: Athletics, Entertain (Storytelling), Haggle, Intuition, Lore (Riverways), Perception
Talents: Etiquette (Guilder), Seasoned Traveller, Very Strong, Waterman
Trappings: Rope, Rowboat

☠ Bargeswain — Silver 3
Skills: Climb, Entertain (Singing), Heal, Trade (Boatbuilding)
Talents: Dealmaker, Embezzle, Nose for Trouble, Strike Mighty Blow
Trappings: Backpack, Trade Tools (Carpenter)

🛡 Barge Master — Silver 5
Skills: Leadership, Navigation
Talents: Menacing, Orientation, Pilot, Public Speaker
Trappings: Hat, Riverboat and Crew

HUFFER

Dwarf, Halfling, Human

You pilot ships and boats through the most treacherous waters of the Old World.

Huffers are specialist river guides with expert knowledge of local river systems. They are a common sight near the most dangerous stretches of the Empire's rivers and can command significant wages for what many view as easy work. Others view it as cheap compared to the potential cost of lost cargo.

Many Huffers specialise in a single, notorious stretch of water, while others make their money at certain times of the year when the waters are at their worst. Other Huffers have broader knowledge and will guide vessels for their entire journey, effectively acting as navigators. This is especially true of merchant ships with particularly valuable cargo at difficult times of the year.

'A great big ship came in from Marienburg, low in the water and packed to the gunwales. I said that it would cost them a crown to take them through the Furdienst. Steep, yes, but it was a big ship. The arrogant Wastelander scoffed, said he'd do it himself. But sure enough, they drifted right into the shallows and were holed. They lost a good part of their cargo and it took them a week to repair the damage. Reckon it cost them a bit more than a crown.'

– Ilsa Dasche, Huffer

As an expert for hire, Huffers are often hired by wealthy patrons, frequently brought in as specialists on journeys of discovery. Even when travelling into the unknown, Huffers are useful for their broad range of knowledge concerning river conditions and piloting. Because of the regional and seasonal nature of the work, many Huffers are ready to drop everything and travel to where they're needed. This freedom transfers well to the adventuring lifestyle, and also suits those seeking to return to Huffing should adventuring not supply their needs.

HUFFER ADVANCE SCHEME

WS	BS	S	T	I	Agi	Dex	Int	WP	Fel
+			+	+			☠	⚒	🛡

CAREER PATH

+ Riverguide — Brass 4
Skills: Consume Alcohol, Gossip, Intuition, Lore (Local), *Lore (Riverways)*, Perception, Row, Swim
Talents: Fisherman, Night Vision, Orientation, Waterman
Trappings: Hand Weapon (Boat Hook), Storm Lantern and Oil

⚒ Huffer — Silver 1
Skills: Charm, Cool, Entertain (Storytelling), Language (Any), Melee (Basic), Navigation
Talents: Dealmaker, Etiquette (Guilder), Nose for Trouble, River Guide
Trappings: Leather Jerkin, Rope, Row Boat

☠ Pilot — Silver 3
Skills: Haggle, Intimidate, Lore (Local), Lore (Wrecks)
Talents: Acute Sense (Sight), Pilot, Sea Legs, Very Strong
Trappings: Pole, Storm Lantern and Oil

🛡 Master Pilot — Silver 5
Skills: Leadership, Sail
Talents: Sixth Sense, Sharp, Strong Swimmer, Tenacious
Trappings: Boathand, Small Riverboat

RIVERWARDEN
Halfling, Human

Strong-backed and sure, you patrol the riverways in pursuit of lawbreakers and troublemakers.

A clarion call across the waterways heralds the arrival of the Imperial River Patrol, a river-borne police force known as much for its harassing thugs as for its good work. Most riverside villages and inns set aside moorings for them as, without them, worse criminals would rule the waters. The overworked patrols concentrate on egregious crimes, resolving petty misdemeanours with spot fines. On major trade-routes, the patrols have larger vessels manned by 'Shipswords' trained to tackle larger threats like Greenskins or Trolls.

Some Riverwardens rarely see the water, instead manning remote outposts overlooking strategically important waters. Others crew fast riverboats charged to intercept smugglers in the night. The largest Riverwarden vessels are effectively sea-worthy warships, bristling with cannon and mortars, ready for almost any eventuality.

'So back in the day, when I was a riverwarden, Big Willi came round to tell me I had to leave a certain shipment alone. He said I should just let it through and everything would be alright. Of course, I was young, wasn't I? I told the ship's Master all about it. And was I rewarded for my honesty? Nah, Big Willi came round and beat me up, and the next day I was drummed out of the river patrol. They were all in it together, weren't they?'

– Nikki Schnelling, ex-riverwarden

A diligent Riverwarden, searching vessels and following up leads, might stumble across any sort of nefarious plot or sinister cargo. Riverwardens typically work month-long shifts, but this means they also have months off. This structure is ideal for adventuring: as a Riverwarden need not desert their post to pursue private matters, or even have to persuade their Sergeant that it is their duty to follow up crimes. They can head off, investigate, and be back long before their next cycle begins.

RIVERWARDEN ADVANCE SCHEME

WS	BS	S	T	I	Agi	Dex	Int	WP	Fel
⚒	✚	✚		💀			🛡		✚

CAREER PATH

✚ River Recruit — Silver 1
Skills: Athletics, Dodge, Endurance, *Melee (Basic)*, Perception, Row, Sail, Swim
Talents: Strong Swimmer, Strong Back, Very Strong, Waterman
Trappings: Hand Weapon (Sword), Leather Jack, Uniform

⚒ Riverwarden — Silver 2
Skills: Bribery, Charm, Intimidate, Gossip, Lore (Riverways), Ranged (Blackpowder)
Talents: Criminal, Gunner, Fisherman, Seasoned Traveller
Trappings: Lantern and Oil, Pistol with 10 shot, Shield

💀 Shipsword — Silver 4
Skills: Climb, Cool, Intuition, Leadership
Talents: Fearless (Wreckers), Hatred (Any), Pilot, Sea Legs
Trappings: Grappling Hook, Helmet, Mail Shirt

🛡 Shipsword Master — Gold 1
Skills: Lore (Law), Navigation
Talents: Commanding Presence, Kingpin, Menacing, Orientation
Trappings: Patrol Boats and Crew, Symbol of Rank

RIVERWOMAN
Dwarf, Halfling, Human

Rivers carry most of the Old World's traffic, and you stand in the heart of that excitement.

The fertile banks of the great rivers of the Empire are densely populated, and the folk working day-in, day-out in the nearby waters and marshes provide much of the fresh fish, eels, and crustaceans feeding the towns and cities. Unlike the inland villages, those on the great rivers frequently receive outsiders who trade and restock, meaning Riverwomen are somewhat more open and diverse, and often the first with news from distant lands. There are any number of diverse jobs supported by the river. Many harvest the Reik's bounty: fisherfolk (using rod, spear, or net), eelers (using traps or pots), or diggers for shellfish. Many live in riverside villages labouring, dredging, or lugging, and maintaining the Reik's many thousands of vessels.

'If I drop this branch in the water now, it will eventually get to Marienburg. Unless it sticks in the mud, of course.'

– Jemima the Greenfish

'They say the whole Empire will eventually float by if you sit by the Reik long enough. Well, I've sat here, rod in hand, for twenty years, watching the flow downriver. The things I could tell you. I've seen war and I've seen peace. I've seen good times and bad. I've seen happiness and sorrow. And in all that time, I can honestly say, I've not caught a single bloody fish.'

– Thys Lange, the Reikland's worst Fisherman

A Riverwoman will feel at home on any stretch of water, and their skills ensure they can drop everything, confident that they will be able to find work elsewhere should they need to. A Riverwoman is well-placed to get the lowdown on the more iniquitous side of river life and may have contacts among the river's lowlifes. With their knowledge and experience they can make all the difference to a water-based expedition or investigation.

RIVERWOMAN ADVANCE SCHEME

WS	BS	S	T	I	Agi	Dex	Int	WP	Fel
⚒			✚	☠	✚	✚			🛡

CAREER PATH

✚ Greenfish — Brass 2
Skills: Athletics, Consume Alcohol, Dodge, *Endurance*, Gossip, Outdoor Survival, Row, Swim
Talents: Fisherman, Gregarious, Strider (Marshes), Strong Swimmer
Trappings: Bucket, Fishing Rod and Bait, Leather Leggings

⚒ Riverwoman — Brass 3
Skills: Gamble, Lore (Local), Lore (Riverways), Ranged (Entangling), Ranged (Throwing), Set Trap
Talents: Craftsman (Boatbuilder), Rover, Strong Back, Waterman
Trappings: Eel Trap, Leather Jerkin, Net, Spear

☠ Riverwise — Brass 5
Skills: Charm, Intuition, Melee (Polearm), Perception
Talents: Savant (Riverways), Stout-hearted, Tenacious, Very Strong
Trappings: Row Boat, Storm Lantern and Oil

🛡 River Elder — Silver 2
Skills: Entertain (Storytelling), Lore (Folklore)
Talents: Master Craftsman (Boatbuilder), Public Speaker, Sharp, Strong-minded
Trappings: Hut *or* Riverboat

SEAMAN
Dwarf, Halfling, High Elf, Human

A life on the ocean waves calls to you, though many Reiklander Seamen never see the sea…

Seamen sail the high seas in the Imperial Navy or for one of the Merchant houses. The Reikland may have no coast, but the River Reik from the Wasteland to Altdorf is miles wide and full of ocean-going vessels. The Imperial First Fleet that patrols these waters rarely sees the open sea, because the taxes to pass warships through Marienburg are exorbitantly high.

Seamen can always find work, whether as cabin staff on an Imperial battleship or on the crew of a small trading sloop. Some Seamen travel the world by working to pay their passage. The Reik also houses many 'Missions', buildings provided by the Imperial Navy for their staff, many of which employ Seamen.

'I can see the Sea!'

– Marian Zelman, Optimistic Reiklander Sailor

'Yeah, I've sailed through Marienburg. Bloody Wastelanders made it as difficult as possible for us to get out to sea. I swear the huffer took us three times round the islands just for fun before we even smelled salt water. And they taxed us twice for everything. Even the ship's cat got taxed. Glad to be home, to be honest.'

– Thom Wesserbrug, Boatswain

Beyond Marienburg, the whole world awaits a Seaman: the perilous Sea of Claws, the unfathomable Great Ocean, the exotic Thousand Islands, the Southern Sea, the Black Gulf. And at home, a Seaman can spend a whole life plying the Reik's waters and never have the same day twice.

SEAMAN ADVANCE SCHEME

WS	BS	S	T	I	Agi	Dex	Int	WP	Fel
⚒				☠	✚	✚	🛡		✚

CAREER PATH

✚ Landsman — Silver 1
Skills: Climb, Consume Alcohol, Gamble, Gossip, Row, Melee (Brawling), *Sail*, Swim
Talents: Fisherman, Strider (Coastal), Strong Back, Strong Swimmer
Trappings: Bucket, Brush, Mop

⚒ Seaman — Silver 3
Skills: Athletics, Dodge, Endurance, Entertain (Singing), Language (any), Melee (Basic)
Talents: Catfall, Sea Legs, Seasoned Traveller, Strong Legs
Trappings: Hand Weapon (Boat Hook), Leather Jerkin

☠ Boatswain — Silver 5
Skills: Cool, Leadership, Perception, Trade (Carpenter)
Talents: Old Salt, Strike Mighty Blow, Tenacious, Very Strong
Trappings: Trade Tools (Carpenter)

🛡 Ship's Master — Gold 2
Skills: Charm, Navigation
Talents: Orientation, Pilot, Public Speaking, Savvy
Trappings: Shipping Charts, Sailing Ship and Crew, Sextant, Spyglass

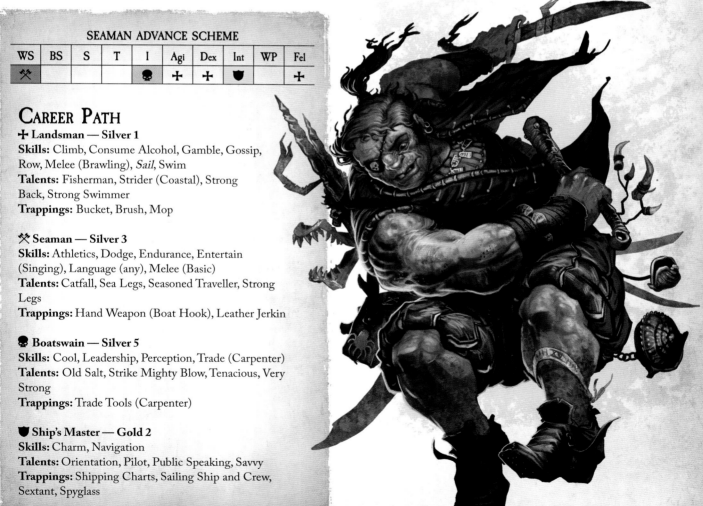

SMUGGLER

Dwarf, Halfling, High Elf, Human

You smuggle cargo, avoiding taxes and risking riverwarden inspections to secure maximum profit.

Most trade is legally taxed by local lords, as well as illegally taxed by bandits and protection rackets. Smugglers see themselves as charitable helpers: merchants make more profit, customers pay less coin, morally flexible Riverwardens take a cut, outlaws are avoided, and more besides. It takes experience and ingenuity to circumvent all the bailiffs, custom officials, excisemen, and busy bodies keen to stop them, but Smugglers dare the risks to support themselves and their families.

Smugglers come in many forms, perhaps transporting tiny, high-value goods for nobles, or large cargoes for shady merchants. Some Smugglers also deal in illicit goods, a crime that will incur significantly more repercussions than a burned finger or smugglers' brand.

'See, this is where the bottle of best Bordeleaux goes. The river wardens will search behind here, and find it, and confiscate it. That's what we want because it means they don't find the twelve bottles we have hidden under here. And if they find those, all is not lost, because they will be so pleased with themselves they won't even bother searching over there where there's twenty-four bottles.'

– Hansel Solomon, Smuggler

Smugglers find adventure, even though they usually want things to stay quiet and uneventful. Any number of things can go wrong on a smuggling mission, and even if things go right, there will always be the lure of the next job, likely bigger and better than the last. Whole adventures can be played out solely on smuggling missions. Similarly, it will be easy for a smuggler to find gainful employment away from their usual work. Someone with a trick up their sleeve, an eye for detail, and a cool head when things get hot is always going to be a desirable companion on dangerous expeditions and adventures.

SMUGGLER ADVANCE SCHEME

WS	BS	S	T	I	Agi	Dex	Int	WP	Fel
				⚒	✛	✛	☠	✛	🛡

CAREER PATH

✛ River Runner — Brass 2
Skills: Athletics, Bribery, Cool, Consume Alcohol, Row, Sail, *Stealth (Rural or Urban)*, Swim
Talents: Criminal, Fisherman, Strider (Marshes), Strong Back
Trappings: Large Sack, Mask *or* Scarves, Tinderbox, Storm Lantern and Oil

⚒ Smuggler — Brass 3
Skills: Haggle, Gossip, Lore (Local), Melee (Basic), Perception, Secret Signs (Smuggler)
Talents: Dealmaker, Etiquette (Criminals), Waterman, Very Strong
Trappings: 2 Barrels, Hand Weapon, Leather Jack, Row Boat

☠ Master Smuggler — Brass 5
Skills: Evaluate, Intimidate, Intuition, Lore (Riverways)
Talents: Briber, Fearless (Riverwardens), Pilot, Strong Swimmer
Trappings: River Runner, Speedy Riverboat

🛡 Smuggler King — Silver 2
Skills: Language (Any), Leadership
Talents: Kingpin, Savvy, Strider (Coastal), Sea Legs
Trappings: Disguise Kit, Small Fleet of Riverboats

STEVEDORE
Dwarf, Halfling, Human

You may officially load cargo for coin, but everyone knows the Stevedores rule the docklands.

With their sole right to load and unload vessels, Stevedore Guilds can slow or even stop trade. This grants power, with many docksides effectively ruled by the guilds. In larger towns, several gangs might violently compete for supremacy. Scowling Foremen deal with guild matters and blow their whistles to summon their gangs from riverside inns, either for fresh work or to defend their territory.

A Stevedore might work alone in a riverside village, or in a large gang on a busy, chaotic city dockside. Sometimes they might be part of a criminal gang that just moves a bit of cargo on the side to cover their tracks. Some Stevedores are enforcers, making sure everyone else is working hard.

'Look, I know we specialise in coal, but don't fence us in, we'll port anything if the coin's good. So, let's do it afore the deal porters arrive; anything goes here, mate.'

– Albert Pförtner, Coal Porter

'Listen, boy. Don't think them dockers have it easy. It's dangerous, claustrophobic work, with heavy goods and high stacks, and if it's done wrong, the cargo may overbalance, perhaps even capsizing the boat. What I'm saying is, pay the Stevedores right — and if you want a boat to sink, pay them extra.'

– Aleida Fuchs, Merchant

Amid the humdrum and repetition of the dockside there are good opportunities for adventure as a Stevedore. Stevedore gangs are virtually a law unto themselves, and they fight for every foot of riverside that they command. Stevedores are useful characters to have around, able to handle themselves, and deal with lowlifes.

STEVEDORE ADVANCE SCHEME

WS	BS	S	T	I	Agi	Dex	Int	WP	Fel
✚		⚒	✚	✚			🛡	💀	

CAREER PATH

✚ Dockhand — Brass 3
Skills: Athletics, Climb, Consume Alcohol, Dodge, *Endurance*, Gossip, Melee (Basic), Swim
Talents: Dirty Fighting, Strong Back, Sturdy, Very Strong
Trappings: Hand Weapon (Boat Hook), Leather Gloves

⚒ Stevedore — Silver 1
Skills: Bribery, Entertain (Storytelling), Gamble, Intimidate, Perception, Stealth (Urban)
Talents: Criminal, Etiquette (Guilders), Strong Legs, Tenacious
Trappings: Guild Licence, Leather Jerkin, Pipe and Tobacco, Porter Cap

💀 Foreman — Silver 3
Skills: Cool, Evaluate, Intuition, Leadership
Talents: Dealmaker, Embezzle, Etiquette (Criminals), Public Speaking
Trappings: Gang of Stevedores, Whistle

🛡 Dock Master — Silver 5
Skills: Charm, Lore (Taxes)
Talents: Kingpin, Menacing, Numismatics, Read/Write
Trappings: Office and Staff, Writing Kit

WRECKER

Dwarf, Human, Wood Elf

You lure vessels to a watery doom and make off with their cargo.

Sometimes the gods send riverfolk an unexpected windfall as goods wash up from an ill-fated vessel. Sometimes the gods need a helping hand: that's where Wreckers come in. Laying devious traps and sending disorienting signals, Wreckers lure unwary river traffic onto sand banks and rocks, then loot the wreck, no matter how any surviving crew may protest.

Some Wreckers pride themselves on their clever traps, making any wreck seem like an accident, and keeping a plausible distance from the actual looters. Some board ships by force and throw its crew overboard, expert at spotting under-armed boats with valuable cargo. These River Pirates are hunted by road and riverwardens, constantly moving to evade the authorities.

'We spied this juicy ripe sloop on its way to Carroburg just as night was falling, and lit some fires on the left bank to make them think the village was a few hundred yards closer. They tacked to starboard just like we planned and hit the sand bank dead on. Sweet as. How were we to know the boat was transporting a company of pistoliers?'
– Greta Lachsmann, shortly before her hanging

'Look, if we let the crew live, they'll tell the wardens where we operate, so the only sensible thing is to kill 'em all.'
– Mandel Stein, Pragmatic River Pirate

A well-planned and executed wrecking is an adventure in itself: avoiding the authorities, disposing of the goods, keeping people's mouths shut, and spending the ill-gotten gains all present their own opportunities and dangers. And who knows what cargo they will find, and who may come pursuing those who stole it. Wreckers who come across such adventure will have no trouble leaving their old lives behind or returning to them again when times are lean.

WRECKER ADVANCE SCHEME

WS	BS	S	T	I	Agi	Dex	Int	WP	Fel
+	☠	+		+				⚒	🛡

CAREER PATH

+ Cargo Scavenger — Brass 2
Skills: Climb, Consume Alcohol, Dodge, Endurance, Row, *Melee (Basic)*, Outdoor Survival, Swim
Talents: Break and Enter, Criminal, Fisherman, Strong Back
Trappings: Crowbar, Large Sack, Leather Gloves

⚒ Wrecker — Brass 3
Skills: Bribery, Cool, Intuition, Navigation, Perception, Set Traps
Talents: Flee!, Rover, Strong Swimmer, Trapper
Trappings: Hand Weapon (Boat Hook), Leather Jack, Storm Lantern and Oil

☠ River Pirate — Brass 5
Skills: Gossip, Intimidate, Ranged (Crossbow), Stealth (Rural)
Talents: Dirty Fighting, Etiquette (Criminals), Menacing, Waterman
Trappings: Crossbow with 10 Bolts, Grappling Hook and Rope, Riverboat

🛡 Wrecker Captain — Silver 2
Skills: Leadership, Lore (Riverways)
Talents: Furious Assault, In-fighter, Pilot, Warrior Born
Trappings: Fleet of Riverboats and Wrecker Crew, Keg of Ale, Manacles

BAWD
Halfling, High Elf, Human

Street-wise and mercenary, you make a living selling illicit goods in the seedier side of town.

Bawds guide folk to establishments offering a variety of illegal and immoral services. Though many Humans and Dwarfs have objections to such activities, most Halflings and High Elves are quite matter-of-fact about drug-dens, brothels, or other houses of vice.

Bawds include drug-dealers, dancers, hustlers and artists' models. Many famous masterpieces of the modern era have been posed for by Bawds plucked from the street. Traveling armies are followed by camp followers, with Bawds among them looking to make coin in any way they can. Ringleaders, proprietors of establishments where Bawds gather, can accrue significant empires providing services to all types of rogues, from fences who need discreet access to rich clients, to providing safe bolt-holes for gang bosses and crime lords.

'Come to the Hammer and Bucket, home of the best music and entertainment in old Altdorf town! You will not be disappointed!'

– Raynald Schmid, Bawd

'Scoff all you like, but those clothes cost money. For a lad born 'neath the dung heap, he lives a life of luxury.'

– Hertel Netzhoch, Innkeep

Bawds living in urban areas sometimes travel to flee plagues and religious persecutions, the latter of which crop up all-to-frequently in areas dominated by Sigmar worship. Others, such as those who rove with entertainers, consider travel as part and parcel of their occupation. Those who secure a patron might have significant lengths of time left to their own devices.

BAWD ADVANCE SCHEME

WS	BS	S	T	I	Agi	Dex	Int	WP	Fel
				⚒	✚	✚	🛡	💀	✚

CAREER PATH

✚ Hustler — Brass 1
Skills: Bribery, *Charm*, Consume Alcohol, Entertain (Any), Gamble, Gossip, Haggle, Intimidate
Talents: Attractive, Alley Cat, Blather, Gregarious
Trappings: Flask of Spirits

⚒ Bawd — Brass 3
Skills: Dodge, Endurance, Intuition, Lore (Local), Melee (Basic), Perception
Talents: Ambidextrous, Carouser, Criminal, Resistant (Disease)
Trappings: Dose of Weirdroot, Quality Clothing

👤 Procurer — Silver 1
Skills: Cool, Evaluate, Language (any), Lore (Law)
Talents: Dealmaker, Embezzle, Etiquette (Any), Suave
Trappings: A Ring of Hustlers

🛡 Ringleader — Silver 3
Skills: Leadership, Lore (Heraldry)
Talents: Briber, Kingpin, Numismatics, Savvy
Trappings: Townhouse with Discreet Back Entrance, a Ring of Bawds

CHARLATAN
Halfling, High Elf, Human

Unscrupulous and charming, you separate fools from their money; thankfully, there is no shortage of fools…

A Charlatan traffics in trust, yet profits from treachery. By preying on emotions and psychological weaknesses, Charlatans offer their 'mark' a prize that is too good to be true. Social privilege provides no protection, and even the loftiest citizens can fall victim to a skilled Charlatan. In addition to a knack for lying, a lack of conscience is also of benefit to Charlatans.

Charlatans include Swindlers, Con Artists, Gamblers, and other Scoundrels seeking to prey on the gullible. Halflings often operate distraction cons in small family groups. Young High Elves, slumming it with Humans, treat their cons as one big game, not motivated by profit, but to prove their superiority. Some experienced Charlatans work with artists, who forge documentation for a cut of any profits.

'I've carried this across countless leagues from the highest towers of the Elves. See how it sparkles in the moonlight? Only magic can cause this inner light! Unbelievable as it may be, I must grudgingly part with it. For such power, any price is but a trifle!'

– Wolmar Rotte, Con Man

'The last living heir of Lord Schwalb, you say? Hogwash! You're the fifth 'heir' to call this afternoon! How much did you pay for that scrap of paper? Better yet, who's the swindler what sold it to you?'

– Gerold Behn, Irritated Butler

To avoid rousing suspicion, Charlatans rarely stay in one area for long. Few Swindlers openly admit to their calling, preferring instead to masquerade as anyone other than themselves. Because of this, there is little stopping Charlatans from pursuing side-matters of interests; equally, afterwards, they can return to grafting anywhere with rich fools willing to part with coin on naught but a promise.

CHARLATAN ADVANCE SCHEME

WS	BS	S	T	I	Agi	Dex	Int	WP	Fel
				✛	☠	✛	🛡	⚒	✛

CAREER PATH

✛ Swindler — Brass 3
Skills: Bribery, Consume Alcohol, *Charm*, Entertain (Storytelling), Gamble, Gossip, Haggle, Sleight of Hand
Talents: Cardsharp, Diceman, Etiquette (Any), Luck
Trappings: Backpack, 2 Sets of Clothing, Deck of Cards, Dice

⚒ Charlatan — Brass 5
Skills: Cool, Dodge, Entertain (Acting), Evaluate, Intuition, Perception
Talents: Blather, Criminal, Fast Hands, Secret Identity
Trappings: 1 Forged Document, 2 Sets of Quality Clothing, Selection of Coloured Powders and Water, Selection of Trinkets and Charms

☠ Con Artist — Silver 2
Skills: Language (Thief), Lore (Heraldry), Pick Lock, Secret Signs (Thief)
Talents: Attractive, Cat-tongued, Dealmaker, Read/Write
Trappings: Disguise Kit, Lock Picks, Multiple Forged Documents

🛡 Scoundrel — Silver 4
Skills: Lore (Genealogy), Research
Talents: Gregarious, Master of Disguise, Nose for Trouble, Suave
Trappings: Forged Seal, Writing Kit

FENCE
Dwarf, Halfling, Human

A shrewd assessor of valuables, you'll buy anything, legal or not, and turn it around for a tidy profit.

A Fence buys thieves' spoils and sells it on for profit, often to those unaware the goods are stolen. Successful Fences sometimes operate as pawn brokers, importers, or other merchants. Others prefer to remain mobile, trafficking only in portable items. Though the average Fence deals in goods and valuables, there are also well-informed specialists who focus on information and forbidden knowledge. Some Fences move stolen items across the Empire. A painting stolen in Altdorf is easier to sell in Talabheim to an audience unaware of the theft. When high profile items vanish, Fences are also the first individuals to be consulted by those looking to acquire them. Some Fences even take commissions from clients, connecting them with those who can steal to order.

'I know it's stolen. You know it's stolen. Even old Sigmar knows it's stolen. So when I ask you if it's stolen, don't insult me by telling me it isn't stolen. Lucky for you, I deal in stolen, so stop panicking.'

– Elene Weslach, Mover

'Why am I called a Fence? Well, it's because I provide you with some de-fence from being caught, innit. So, you go thief, and I'll make sure you don't have to worry about how to shift the merchandise. Think of me like your partner-in-crime.'

– 'Boil' Vakram, Fence

The search for buyers and sellers, or the need to escape a terrible situation, can take a Fence anywhere. They can be found across the Empire and in many regions beyond its borders. Up-and-coming Brokers transport illicit goods between Old World cities in search of buyers. Others, looking to make a name for themselves elsewhere, attempt to make their own niches in existing city underworlds. Given that their interests often collide, Fences and merchants make occasional bedfellows, as well. With all of this criminal activity and movement, trouble often follows.

FENCE ADVANCE SCHEME

WS	BS	S	T	I	Agi	Dex	Int	WP	Fel
				+	+	⚒	💀	🛡	+

CAREER PATH

+ Broker — Silver 1
Skills: Charm, Consume Alcohol, Dodge, *Evaluate*, Gamble, Gossip, Haggle, Melee (Basic)
Talents: Alley Cat, Cardsharp, Dealmaker, Gregarious
Trappings: Hand Weapon, Stolen Goods worth 3d10 Shillings

⚒ Fence — Silver 2
Skills: Cool, Intimidate, Intuition, Perception, Secret Signs (Thief), Trade (Engraver)
Talents: Criminal, Etiquette (Criminals), Numismatics, Savvy
Trappings: Eye-glass, Trade Tools (Engraver), Writing Kit

💀 Master Fence — Silver 3
Skills: Bribery, Entertain (Storytelling), Lore (Art), Lore (Local)
Talents: Kingpin, Strike to Stun, Suave, Super Numerate
Trappings: Pawnbroker's Shop

🛡 Black Marketeer — Silver 4
Skills: Lore (Heraldry), Research
Talents: Dirty Fighting, Iron Will, Menacing, Briber
Trappings: Hired Muscle, Network of Informants, Warehouse

GRAVE ROBBER
Halfling, Human

'You can't take it with you... but I can certainly take it with me.'
– Symon Schreiber, Grave Robber

You brave the threat of necromancy, stealing from the dead to line your own pockets.

Trafficking in bodies and body parts is lucrative, with high demand from universities and physicians for fresh cadavers. As well as the scholarly market, corpses sometimes interred with all manner of valuables can be found beneath the ravenstones in the tombs of Morr's Gardens. Because their labours are obvious, illegal, and sacrilegious, Grave Robbers usually work under cover of darkness. Body Snatchers have been known to cut out the middle man and take beggars or other unfortunates straight off the streets. Tomb Robbers avoid the legal dangers of looting the recently dead, and instead journey to ancient ruins and barrows, risking the restless dead and brigands alike. Peculiarly, some successful Treasure Hunters find themselves celebrated as heroes, their treasures sold to, and displayed by, the aristocracy. It's even rumoured that the great wealth of one of the Knightly Orders came from a group of their members plundering a foreign tomb.

'It's not just the jewels, Herbert. Look at all the bones! There's professors in Altdorf who'd pay good money for these!'
– Tyle 'the Ghoul' Grubsch, Body Snatcher

'The nightmares of Khemri still haunt me. The curses cast by those long-dead tyrants have sealed my fate. I only hope Morr can put a stop to the necromancy that rots my bones and blackens my heart.'
– Lady Estelle Hauptleiter, Treasure Hunter (deceased)

Grave Robbers easily take to the adventuring life, especially if their nocturnal sojourns are discovered by unsympathetic authorities. They may also be sought out by antiquarians who wish to engage their expert services in the excavation of a tomb, or perhaps they will feel compelled to track down a suspected necromancer who is using corpses for nefarious purposes.

GRAVE ROBBER ADVANCE SCHEME

WS	BS	S	T	I	Agi	Dex	Int	WP	Fel
⚒		✚		✚		💀	🛡	✚	

CAREER PATH

✚ Body Snatcher — Brass 2
Skills: Climb, Cool, Dodge, Endurance, Gossip, Intuition, Perception, *Stealth (Any)*
Talents: Alley Cat, Criminal, Flee!, Strong Back
Trappings: Crowbar, Handcart, Hooded Cloak, Tarpaulin

⚒ Grave Robber — Brass 3
Skills: Bribery, Drive, Evaluate, Haggle, Lore (Medicine), Melee (Basic)
Talents: Break and Enter, Night Vision, Resistance (Disease), Very Strong
Trappings: Backpack, Hand Weapon, Spade, Storm Lantern and Oil

💀 Tomb Robber — Silver 1
Skills: Lore (History), Pick Lock, Research, Set Trap
Talents: Read/Write, Strike Mighty Blow, Tenacious, Tunnel Rat
Trappings: Hand Weapon (Pick), Horse and Cart, Leather Jack, Rope, Trade Tools (Thief)

🛡 Treasure Hunter — Silver 5
Skills: Navigation, Trade (Engineer)
Talents: Fearless (Undead), Sixth Sense, Strong-minded, Trapper
Trappings: Bedroll, Maps, Tent, Trade Tools (Engineer), Writing Kit

OUTLAW

Dwarf, Halfling, High Elf, Human, Wood Elf

You prey upon travellers, extracting a toll from the vulnerable and the unsuspecting.

Outlaws ply the roads of the Old World in search of vulnerable travellers and merchant caravans. They lead dangerous and often hardscrabble lives. Many do not see themselves as criminals, but as oppressed groups trying to live their lives free from outside constraints. Many Wood Elf outlaws fit this description, pushing back against the Humans proliferating at the edge of the forests, willing to take more drastic action than others of their kind. Particularly savvy and brutal Outlaws may form bands of their own, sometimes even uniting several bands under a single banner. Such Bandit Kings are feared and reviled by noble and peasant alike. Though few Outlaws discriminate in choosing their prey, some claim to protect the common man. These do-gooders focus their larceny on greedy nobles and, in return, locals may provide them with food, information, and safe harbour.

'They were children, not brigands. Starving, filthy, sickly. They held us under the sight of their arrows and we stood fast… my son's age, they were. Children. Killed six of us…'

– Valentin Behr, Road Warden

'…and he says, "Titus, why d'you carry them shears?" And I says, "These?" And he says, "Aye, those're the only shears I see." So I laughed and answered: "Sometimes they don't want to take off their rings like I ask 'em to. When I show 'em the shears, most of 'em change their tune right quick. And if they don't…". Hehehe.'

– Titus Widmann, Outlaw

Outlaw bands are not all wild mobs, so many can be reasoned with if approached correctly. An Outlaw might be asked to accompany a group of adventurers as a guide or to protect them, especially if the group are trying to stop unholy activity in a Bandit King's domain. Individual Outlaws may find it simple to join an adventuring band, although they may need to disguise themselves if they go anywhere the Outlaw is wanted.

OUTLAW ADVANCE SCHEME

WS	BS	S	T	I	Agi	Dex	Int	WP	Fel
✛	⚒	✛	✛	💀					🛡

CAREER PATH

✛ Brigand — Brass 1
Skills: Athletics, Consume Alcohol, Cool, Endurance, Gamble, *Intimidate*, Melee (Basic), Outdoor Survival
Talents: Combat Aware, Criminal, Rover, Flee!
Trappings: Bedroll, Hand Weapon, Leather Jerkin, Tinderbox

⚒ Outlaw — Brass 2
Skills: Dodge, Heal, Lore (Local), Perception, Ranged (Bow), Stealth (Rural)
Talents: Dirty Fighting, Marksman, Strike to Stun, Trapper
Trappings: Bow with 10 Arrows, Shield, Tent

💀 Outlaw Chief — Brass 4
Skills: Gossip, Intuition, Leadership, Ride (Horse)
Talents: Rapid Reload, Roughrider, Menacing, Very Resilient
Trappings: Helmet, Riding Horse with Saddle and Tack, Sleeved Mail Shirt, Band of Outlaws

🛡 Bandit King — Silver 2
Skills: Charm, Lore (Empire)
Talents: Deadeye Shot, Fearless (Road Wardens), Iron Will, Robust
Trappings: 'Fiefdom' of Outlaw Chiefs, Lair

RACKETEER
Dwarf, Halfling, Human

You are part of an organised criminal gang, collecting debts and extorting money from the weak.

Racketeers extort money from law-abiding citizens and merchants, providing 'protection' or some similar fraudulent 'service'. If the 'fees' are not paid on time, the victims, their families, and their livelihoods are at considerable risk. Large gangs bribe or intimidate local authorities to ignore their activities; their Thugs are always willing to kill — or worse — to keep business running smoothly. Thugs are employed to collect debts of all kind, especially those incurred through gambling losses or high-interest-rate loans. In a world brimming with poverty, the promise of easy wealth is an allure countless fools are unable to ignore. The more organised the graft, the larger and more complex the organisations running them become. While the smallest rackets are run by small gangs with limited territory beyond a building or two, the largest can span cities or even entire provinces, and the Crime Lords who run them can wield extraordinary power.

'I hope you have Hazelmann's money because I really hate the sound of breaking fingers.'
– Claus Betelhof, Well-Mannered Racketeer

'IF YOU CAN'T PAE THE DEBT, DON'T MAKE THE BET.'
– Sign in Bosco's Bones (Altdorf gambling house)

'or bosco wil brake ya legs'
– Bosco's Bones Sign Addendum scrawled in chalk

Thugs and Racketeers are always willing to resort to threats and violence, making them valuable members of any party that expects to face aggressive opposition. Gang Bosses might even take their business on the road, looking to expand their territory or explore new opportunities for intrigue and profit. Given the competitive nature of such rackets, even the most powerful Crime Lords might find themselves deposed by opponents or treachery. Forced to hide or flee, such experienced crooks can seek to use a group of experienced adventurers to their advantage.

RACKETEER ADVANCE SCHEME

WS	BS	S	T	I	Agi	Dex	Int	WP	Fel
✝		✝	✝				🛡	💀	⚒

CAREER PATH

✝ Thug — Brass 3
Skills: Consume Alcohol, Cool, Dodge, Endurance, *Intimidate*, Lore (Local), Melee (Brawling), Stealth (Urban)
Talents: Criminal, Etiquette (Criminals), Menacing, Strike Mighty Blow
Trappings: Knuckledusters, Leather Jack

⚒ Racketeer — Brass 5
Skills: Bribery, Charm, Evaluate, Gossip, Language (Estalian *or* Tilean), Melee (Basic)
Talents: Dirty Fighting, Embezzle, Strike to Stun, Warrior Born
Trappings: Hand Weapon, Hat, Mail Shirt

💀 Gang Boss — Silver 3
Skills: Intuition, Leadership, Perception, Ranged (Crossbow)
Talents: Fearless (Watchmen), Iron Will, Resistance (Poison), Robust
Trappings: Crossbow Pistol with 10 Bolts, Gang of Thugs and Racketeers, Lair

🛡 Crime Lord — Silver 5
Skills: Lore (Law), Lore (Politics)
Talents: Commanding Presence, Kingpin, Frightening, Wealthy
Trappings: Network of Informers, Quality Clothing and Hat, Subordinate Gang Bosses

THIEF
Dwarf, Halfling, Human

You steal from others in order to line your own pockets, and you're rather good at it.

Thieves steal all manner of wealth and goods from their fellow man. From the lowliest footpad to the wiliest burglar, the thought of an honest day's work in return for a respectable wage is little more than a bad joke. Thieves often organize themselves into gangs alongside charlatans, racketeers, and fences to further their mutual wealth. Bitter feuds between such illicit organisations have been known to last for years or even decades. The lowliest Thieves target individuals, picking pockets or waylaying victims in rat-infested alleyways. Burglars avoid confrontation by breaking into businesses and residences, carrying off portable valuables. More ambitious thieves scope out their targets for days or weeks, even going so far as to infiltrate their target locations to get a more precise lay of the land. Working with other professional burglars, such experts can organise heists of which their lesser peers can only dream.

'One creaky floorboard in the whole place and I'm the one to find it…'
– Alette Zimmermann, Thief, Jailed

'What the…? Those aren't dogs… they're bears!'
– Marx the Mauled, Unlucky Thief

'No, the list of charges does not include, "Stealing the magistrate's heart away." You must have me confused with a magistrate who has a heart.'

– Leonora Nithardt, Magistrate

Thieves who run afoul of the law are obliged to hide or flee from justice, putting many would-be inmates on the run. Sometimes the very items stolen by Thieves are of such exorbitant value or supernatural quality they seem to attract trouble like a mouldering corpse draws flies, which can lead them into all sorts of unexpected adventures. Of course, a Burglar's talents are always valuable to adventurers, and reliable examples can expect to be well-compensated for their skills.

THIEF ADVANCE SCHEME

WS	BS	S	T	I	Agi	Dex	Int	WP	Fel
		☠		✛	✛	⚒		✛	🛡

CAREER PATH

✛ Prowler — Brass 1
Skills: Athletics, Climb, Cool, Dodge, Endurance, Intuition, Perception, *Stealth (Urban)*
Talents: Alley Cat, Criminal, Flee!, Strike to Stun
Trappings: Crowbar, Leather Jerkin, Sack

⚒ Thief — Brass 3
Skills: Evaluate, Gossip, Lore (Local), Pick Lock, Secret Signs (Thief), Sleight of Hand
Talents: Break and Enter, Etiquette (Criminals), Fast Hands, Shadow
Trappings: Trade Tools (Thief), Rope

☠ Master Thief — Brass 5
Skills: Bribery, Gamble, Intimidate, Ranged (Crossbow)
Talents: Night Vision, Nimble Fingered, Step Aside, Trapper
Trappings: Crossbow Pistol with 10 Bolts

🛡 Cat Burglar — Silver 3
Skills: Charm, Set Trap
Talents: Catfall, Scale Sheer Surface, Strong Legs, Wealthy
Trappings: Dark Clothing, Grappling Hook, Mask *or* Scarves

WITCH

Human

Wilful and ambitious, you strive to master magic without an officially sanctioned licence to operate.

Any with the rare talent to wield magic must, by law, be trained by wizards of the College of Magic. Not everyone accepts such a fate; some hide their powers or go on the run. Such folk are called Witches. They risk insanity and damnation as magic burns through them without correct tutelage, and rarely understand the nature of the forces in which they dabble. Others embrace their burgeoning powers wholeheartedly, accepting the risks. Witches come in all varieties, with the talent to wield magic playing no favourites. Some are benign figures simply seeking freedom. Others are nobles refusing to accept they are Witches, for to do so is to be disinherited. Yet others are terrified of what they may become, so run away. Whatever the case, few will admit what they are, as all risk burning by over-zealous Sigmarites.

'Do you think only wizards can wield magic? Think again! I, too, have such understanding, and I refuse to become a slave to the so-called Colleges.'

– Apprentice Franz Zimmel of the Gold Order,
3 months before being captured by a Witch Hunter

Witches lead dangerous lives. Though some pose as wizards, such deceptions are easily discerned by anyone with any knowledge of magic. Nevertheless, bands of adventurers — especially those without unwavering faith or moral qualms — rarely care for the specifics of a Witch's education so long as the methods used are effective and have no truck with the Dark Gods. Although unsanctioned witchery is illegal — carrying the death penalty — most wizards have a brief experience as a Witch before entering the Colleges of Magic. This is acknowledged by both the Colleges and the cults, so a Witch, if discovered, should submit to the authorities. Training in the Colleges could be covered as time between adventures, meaning the Witch can return at a later date in the Wizard career, or it could become the focus of a new adventure.

WITCH ADVANCE SCHEME

WS	BS	S	T	I	Agi	Dex	Int	WP	Fel
✚			✚	⚒			🛡	✚	💀

CAREER PATH

✚ Hexer — Brass 1
Skills: Channelling, Cool, Endurance, Gossip, Intimidate, *Language (Magick)*, Sleight of Hand, Stealth (Rural)
Talents: Criminal, Instinctive Diction, Menacing, Petty Magic
Trappings: Candles, Chalk, Doll, Pins

⚒ Witch — Brass 2
Skills: Charm Animal, Dodge, Intuition, Melee (Polearm), Perception, Trade (Herbalist)
Talents: Arcane Magic (Witchery), Attractive, Second Sight, Witch!
Trappings: Quarterstaff, Sack, Selection of Herbs, Trade Tools (Herbalist)

💀 Wyrd — Brass 3
Skills: Bribery, Charm, Haggle, Lore (Dark Magic)
Talents: Animal Affinity, Fast Hands, Frightening, Magical Sense
Trappings: Backpack, Cloak with Several Pockets, Lucky Charm

🛡 Warlock — Brass 5
Skills: Lore (Daemonology), Lore (Magic)
Talents: Aethyric Attunement, Luck, Strong-minded, Very Resilient
Trappings: Robes, Skull

CAVALRYMAN
High Elf, Human, Wood Elf

A dashing and fearless rider, you bring speed, versatility, and skill-at-arms to the battlefield.

Whether it's units of Pistoliers, Outriders, Demilancers, Horse Archers, or similar, Cavalrymen are deployed for maximum strategic advantage. On campaign, that means scouting, raiding, harassing the enemy lines, or defending foragers. On the battlefield, they are also particularly versatile, able to strike quickly and melt away. For speed of movement, scouting, versatility, and sheer élan, Cavalrymen cannot be rivalled. Swift, lightly-armoured cavalry is employed by most armies, including forces of the cults and less formal armed bands including mercenaries or private armies. Bretonnian armies make use of mounted men at arms, while Wood Elf Gladeriders are some of the most feared light cavalry in the Old World.

'Any pistolier not dead by thirty is a scoundrel.'
–General Lasaal, Reikland's 5th Regiment of Cavalry

'An outrider came by yesterday, checking to see if we were safe. Gosh, he was so handsome and dashing, who wouldn't want to go outriding with him? He grabbed my buns and was off like the wind. Never paid for them, mind.'

–Lena Fluffe, Walfenburg baker

A cavalryman currently in the State Army is not just going to drop everything on a whim. Should they have something they wish to personally pursue, they will require permission from senior officers, perhaps buy out their commission if they have one, or go absent without leave. As an alternative, they could be ordered to investigate matters of importance by their superiors? Mercenary cavalrymen have more flexibility to strike out adventuring, being little more than hired swords.

CAVALRYMAN ADVANCE SCHEME

WS	BS	S	T	I	Agi	Dex	Int	WP	Fel
✚	⚒	✚		💀	✚				🛡

CAREER PATH

✚ Horseman — Silver 2
Skills: Animal Care, Charm Animal, Endurance, Language (Battle), Melee (Basic), Outdoor Survival, Perception, *Ride (Horse)*
Talents: Combat Aware, Crack the Whip, Lightning Reflexes, Roughrider
Trappings: Leather Jack, Riding Horse with Saddle and Tack

⚒ Cavalryman — Silver 4
Skills: Charm, Consume Alcohol, Cool, Gossip, Melee (Cavalry), Ranged (Blackpowder)
Talents: Etiquette (Soldiers), Gunner, Seasoned Traveller, Trick Riding
Trappings: Breastplate, Helmet, Light Warhorse with Saddle and Tack, Pistol with 10 Shots, Shield

💀 Cavalry Sergeant — Gold 1
Skills: Intimidate, Intuition, Leadership, Lore (Warfare)
Talents: Combat Reflexes, Fast Shot, Hatred (Any), Warleader
Trappings: Sash

🛡 Cavalry Officer — Gold 2
Skills: Gamble, Lore (Heraldry)
Talents: Accurate Shot, Inspiring, Reaction Strike, Robust
Trappings: Deck of Cards, Quality Clothing

GUARD

Dwarf, Halfling, High Elf, Human, Wood Elf

Your job is simple: keep undesirables out.

The best way to keep something safe is to post a guard. Guarding looks easy enough, it's usually standing around doing very little. Guards live and die, quite literally, by how they behave during that one moment when they are required to spring into action. The best can command high wages and are entrusted with the lives of the Empire's finest personages and most valuable items. Guards are everywhere, from the Imperial palace down to bouncers who stand outside taverns all night, ready to throw drunkards into the street. They also include grave wardens — those who defend Morr's Gardens in the dead of night, watchful for grave robbers — and temple guards who defend holy sites and important priests. Merchants often employ many Guards to defend their valuable stock. Some claim bodyguards have it best because they stay close to their esteemed employers, and often partake of a life far beyond that which their station would normally allow.

'I stood outside the shrine for thirty days and thirty nights, without fail. No-one got in and no-one got out. Of course, it turned out I was stood outside the wrong door.'

– Ernst Bluchard, Ex-Temple Guard of Manann

'If you're not on the list, you're not coming in!'

– Anonymous Altdorf guard to the Grand Theogonist at the coronation of Karl-Franz I, apocryphal

Guards can find adventure when their guardianship is compromised. Any guard worth his salt would wish to follow up and investigate those who have thwarted them, and get whatever they were guarding back to its true owner. This could easily turn into an exciting adventure. Many of those going on expeditions will require guards to accompany them, to adventure, profit or an untimely demise.

GUARD ADVANCE SCHEME

WS	BS	S	T	I	Agi	Dex	Int	WP	Fel
✝		💀	✝	⚒	✝		🛡		

CAREER PATH

✝ Sentry — Silver 1
Skills: Consume Alcohol, Endurance, Entertain (Storytelling), Gamble, Gossip, Intuition, Melee (Basic), *Perception*
Talents: Diceman, Etiquette (Servants), Strike to Stun, Tenacious
Trappings: Buckler, Leather Jerkin, Storm Lantern with Oil

⚒ Guard — Silver 2
Skills: Athletics, Cool, Dodge, Intimidate, Melee (Polearm), Ranged (Bow)
Talents: Relentless, Reversal, Shieldsman, Strike Mighty Blow
Trappings: Bow with 10 Arrows, Sleeved Mail Shirt, Shield, Spear

💀 Honour Guard — Silver 3
Skills: Heal, Language (Battle), Lore (Etiquette), Melee (Two-handed)
Talents: Fearless (Intruders), Jump Up, Stout-hearted, Unshakeable
Trappings: Great Weapon *or* Halberd, Helmet, Uniform

🛡 Guard Officer — Silver 5
Skills: Leadership, Lore (Warfare)
Talents: Combat Master, Furious Assault, Iron Will, Robust
Trappings: Breastplate

KNIGHT

High Elf, Human, Wood Elf

Thundering into battle on a heavy charger, you dominate the field, spreading fear in your wake.

Many believe heavy cavalry are the pre-eminent warriors of the Old World. A massed charge is an awesome sight, but even alone a Knight can stand as a one-person army. There are many Knightly Orders in the Empire, the most famous including the Reiksguard, the White Wolves, the Knights Panther, and the Knights Griffon, each of which have their own gloried history and mighty heroes. Most Empire Knights belong to secular knightly orders, partly because training heavy lancers is too prohibitively expensive for most nobles. The templar orders, those dedicated to the service of a single deity are just as common but are somewhat more independent. Alongside these are an uncounted number of free-lances, mercenary knights, and disgraced knights, most of whom sell their lance to the highest bidder.

'The knight demanded I get out of his way. "Why?" I asked. "I am in the service of the people," he replied. "Well, I'm the people," I said, "so I don't have to get out of your way." He didn't have an answer to that, of course. So he punched me in the face!'

– Holger Kass, 1st Bögenhafen Halberdiers

'Lady Myrmaelia Jaeke is the finest knight in the Order of the Blazing Sun. How can I be so sure? Well, I used to hold that title, and she bested me.'

– Birgitte van der Hoogenband, Abbess-General of the Monastery of the Black Maiden, former Knight of the Blazing Sun.

Knights might be asked to venture out to fulfil a duty on behalf of their Order or be sought out by nobles and employed to accompany a restless heir around the Empire. Similarly, templars will have responsibility to do their god's will. All of these provide perfect opportunities for Knights looking to adventure. By comparison, a free-lance is just that, and a life of adventure is what they follow by default.

KNIGHT ADVANCE SCHEME

WS	BS	S	T	I	Agi	Dex	Int	WP	Fel
⚒		✚		✚	✚			☠	🛡

CAREER PATH

✚ Squire — Silver 3
Skills: Athletics, Animal Care, Charm Animal, Heal, Lore (Heraldry), *Melee (Cavalry)*, Ride (Horse), Trade (Farrier)
Talents: Etiquette (any), Roughrider, Sturdy, Warrior Born
Trappings: Leather Jack, Mail Shirt, Riding Horse with Saddle and Tack, Shield, Trade Tools (Farrier)

⚒ Knight — Silver 5
Skills: Cool, Dodge, Endurance, Intimidate, Language (Battle), Melee (Any)
Talents: Menacing, Seasoned Traveller, Shieldsman, Strike Mighty Blow
Trappings: Destrier with Saddle and Tack, Melee Weapon (Any), Lance, Plate Armour and Helm

☠ First Knight — Gold 2
Skills: Charm, Consume Alcohol, Leadership, Lore (Warfare)
Talents: Fearless (Any), Stout-hearted, Unshakeable, Warleader
Trappings: Barding, Small Unit of Knights

🛡 Knight of the Inner Circle — Gold 4
Skills: Lore (Any), Secret Signs (Knightly Order)
Talents: Disarm, Inspiring, Iron Will, Strike to Injure
Trappings: Plumed Great Helm, Squire, Large Unit of Knights or Several Small Units of Knights

PIT FIGHTER

Dwarf, Halfling, High Elf, Human, Wood Elf

You fight for money, for glory, and for the entertainment of the masses.

Watching fights is a popular pastime. In the cities, organised fights take place every night. There is money to be made charging spectators, and even more in gambling on the result. Winners earn coin and are celebrated as local heroes. Losers are hurt or killed. Because pit fighting is officially frowned upon, the fights are often controlled by criminal gangs, but the rich love to slum it on occasion, especially if it involves a little bloodshed. The gladiators of Tilea are the most renowned pit fighters, though the chain-fighters of Marienburg and bear-wrestlers of Kislev draw a crowd. Pugilists and wrestlers might work a travelling fair, challenging the public to survive three minutes in the ring with them, or they might fight a celebrated opponent in front of cheering crowds. Knives, clubs, chains, boxing, wrestling, there is an almost endless variation of styles and codes a Pit Fighter might adopt.

'It was my big chance. The biggest fight of my life. Then the Hooks came and told me to go down in the fourth or they'd chop off my hand. Well, you know me, of course I went and won anyway. And I've no regrets. After all, there are lots of things you can do with one hand.'
– Sigurda the Bull, Arm Wrestler

'Roll up! Roll up! Dare you face the might of Gosser Papa? Could you last three minutes with Resige Heuhaufer!'
– Raimund Heenan, Ring Announcer

Many Pit Fighters fall into their sport because they have the talent and they simply need the money. Some would jump at the chance to leave their seedy world behind and put their talents to a slightly better use. Fortunately, Pit fighters are generally free to use their time as they will, provided they turn up on time for the next big fight, and even if they don't, there is always another pit…

PIT FIGHTER ADVANCE SCHEME

WS	BS	S	T	I	Agi	Dex	Int	WP	Fel
✝		✝	✝	⚒	💀				🛡

CAREER PATH

✝ Pugilist — Brass 4
Skills: Athletics, Cool, Dodge, Endurance, Gamble, Intimidate, *Melee (Any)*, Melee (Brawling)
Talents: Dirty Fighting, In-fighter, Iron Jaw, Reversal
Trappings: Bandages, Knuckledusters, Leather Jack

⚒ Pit Fighter — Silver 2
Skills: Haggle, Intuition, Melee (Basic), Melee (Flail or Two-handed), Perception, Ranged (Entangling)
Talents: Ambidextrous, Combat Reflexes, Dual Wielder, Shieldsman
Trappings: Flail *or* Great Weapon, Hand Weapon, Net *or* Whip, Shield or Buckler

💀 Pit Champion — Silver 5
Skills: Consume Alcohol, Gossip, Lore (Anatomy), Perform (Fight)
Talents: Combat Master, Disarm, Menacing, Robust
Trappings: Breast Plate, Helmet

🛡 Pit Legend — Gold 2
Skills: Charm, Ranged (Any)
Talents: Frightening, Furious Assault, Implacable, Reaction Strike
Trappings: Quality Helmet

PROTAGONIST
Dwarf, High Elf, Human

A strong-arm for hire, you bully, fight, and maybe even kill for coin.

Protagonists live by their wits and their muscles and are not generally fussy about the sort of work they take on. A merchant might want to frighten their business rival. An employer might decide his workers need a bit of encouragement to get a job done quicker. A noble might want his daughter's no-good suitor to be frightened off. Protagonists are the ones they turn to, and those with the worst reputation get the best jobs. A Protagonist could be the brute in the local bar everyone knows will bully for coin, or with the reputation for unflinching violence. Some Protagonists have their own code of what they will or won't do; others care for nothing but the coin. Some are simple bullies who resort to picking arguments and fights with likely looking targets to see if they can score any money from the situation.

'Remember Thommy Two Knives? I'm not saying he crossed me. I'm just saying you don't see him walking round town no more, do you?'
– Gilly Three Knives, Protagonist

'Yeah, Big Yuri came round and destroyed all my merchandise. Said this town was only big enough for one lotus dealer, and that was that. I completely agreed, so I doubled his pay and sent him back to White Tiger's den. And that was the end of that.'
– Toni Miragliano, Lotus Dealer

On the face of it, Protagonists are always up for an adventure because they're always up for a fight. But they will usually expect to get paid for services rendered. Whether they will join others without a guarantee of payment is a question they will need to ask themselves. Could a hardened protagonist find a cause they will voluntarily pursue? Perhaps they could even turn over a new leaf?

PROTAGONIST ADVANCE SCHEME

WS	BS	S	T	I	Agi	Dex	Int	WP	Fel
✛	☠		✛	⚒	✛				🛡

CAREER PATH

✛ Braggart — Brass 2
Skills: Athletics, Dodge, Endurance, Entertain (Taunt), Gossip, Haggle, Intimidate, *Melee (Any)*
Talents: In-fighter, Dirty Fighting, Menacing, Warrior Born
Trappings: Hood *or* Mask, Knuckledusters, Leather Jack

⚒ Protagonist — Silver 1
Skills: Bribery, Charm, Intuition, Melee (Basic), Perception, Ride (Horse)
Talents: Combat Reflexes, Criminal, Reversal, Strike to Stun
Trappings: Hand Weapon, Mail Shirt, Riding Horse with Saddle and Tack, Shield

☠ Hitman — Silver 4
Skills: Climb, Cool, Navigation, Ranged (Thrown)
Talents: Careful Strike, Disarm, Marksman, Relentless
Trappings: Cloak, Garotte, Poison, Throwing Knives

🛡 Assassin — Gold 1
Skills: Entertain (Acting), Ranged (Crossbow)
Talents: Accurate Shot, Ambidextrous, Furious Assault, Strike to Injure
Trappings: Crossbow with 10 shots, Disguise Kit

SLAYER

Dwarf

You are rage and shame incarnate, seeking a worthy death to reclaim your lost honour.

When Dwarfs suffer an unacceptable shame and lose their honour, they take the Slayer's Oath and walk the path of Grimnir, their ancestral god of warriors. Covering their bodies in tattoos, shaving the sides of their head, dying their remaining hair a brilliant orange, and spiking it with animal grease, they set off into the world, axe in hand, seeking a glorious death.

Slayers wander the Old World hunting deadly beasts, such as Trolls, Giants, or Dragons. Because of the shame they carry, many suffer from bouts of depression, glutting themselves on food, alcohol, or stronger stimulants. The more foes Slayers face and survive, the more dangerous and crazed they become, hunting progressively deadlier creatures in the hopes of finding something that can kill them.

'We avoid them, if given the choice. They are outcasts and have no honour, only the hope of reclaiming such. Still, we'll feed them, and give them a place to rest. They are Grimnir's Chosen, now…'

– Dimrond Zindrisson, Miner

'Herwig didn't mean nothing by it, honest. He just asked why the Dwarf had them strange tattoos. It happened so fast, I didn't even see the Dwarf move, just Herwig hitting the floor.'

– Regimius, Stevedore

'We're all going to die, manling. It's the manner of our going that counts.'

– Gotrek Gurnisson, Slayer

Till they fall in battle, a Slayer's life is one of adventure — they seek out opportunities to face powerful foes in battle. Slayers will occasionally take other odd jobs, for drinking money or to finance their travels, but will seek death along the way. All Slayers previously had a life and a career, so there is more to them than simply being a warrior with a deathwish.

Playing a Slayer is a unique experience because your character wants to die. Embrace this. Seek a mighty doom. Reclaim your honour. **Die well.**

SLAYER ADVANCE SCHEME

WS	BS	S	T	I	Agi	Dex	Int	WP	Fel
✛		✛	⚒	🛡	💀				✛

CAREER PATH

✛ Troll Slayer — Brass 2
Skills: Consume Alcohol, Cool, Dodge, Endurance, Gamble, Heal, Lore (Trolls), *Melee (Basic)*
Talents: Dual Wielder, Fearless (Everything), Frenzy, Slayer
Trappings: Axe, Flask of Spirits, Shame, Tattoos

⚒ Giant Slayer — Brass 2
Skills: Evaluate, Intimidate, Language (Battle), Lore (Giants), Melee (Two-handed), Outdoor Survival
Talents: Hardy, Implacable, Menacing, Reversal
Trappings: Great Axe, Jewellery, Troll's Head

💀 Dragon Slayer — Brass 2
Skills: Entertain (Storytelling), Lore (Dragons), Perception, Ranged (Thrown)
Talents: Ambidextrous, Furious Assault, Relentless, Robust
Trappings: Giant's Head, Throwing Axes

🛡 Daemon Slayer — Brass 2
Skills: Intuition, Lore (Chaos)
Talents: Combat Master, Frightening, Strike Mighty Blow, Very Strong
Trappings: Dragon's Head

SOLDIER

Dwarf, Halfling, High Elf, Human, Wood Elf

You are paid to train, be disciplined, and, when the need comes, go to war.

By the command of Emperor Magnus the Pious after the Great War Against Chaos, all provinces of the Empire had to maintain a standing State Army. Soldiers are the mainstay of these armies, trained to fight as part of a larger group with individual skill supplemented by strength in numbers. Rarely encouraged to think for themselves, Soldiers are famous for their stoic fatalism as they are ordered from pillar to post in the service of their betters. Soldiers could be archers, crossbowmen, halberdiers, handgunners, swordsmen, or spearmen, and that's just in a typical State regiment. Dwarfs employ soldiers like Hammerers and Thunderers, while Elven rank and file are usually archers and spearmen. There are many other Soldiers, such as Mercenaries, local Militias (which are rarely better than Recruits), private armies, cult forces, and more.

'Go down to the bottom of the hill, the captain told us. So we did, and the general told us to go up to the top of the hill and await further orders. Then the captain told us we were wanted at the bottom.'
— Holger Kass, 1st Bögenhafen Halberdiers

'Though Lords and Ladies come and go,
A soldier's life is all I know,
Karl-Franz commands, and we obey,
O'er the hills and far away.'
— Marching Song, Reikland 118th Regiment of Foot,
'The Greenbacks'

Soldiers have little free time, but they still have adventuring opportunities. Outside campaigning season, many receive extended periods of leave. Officers of the State Armies can also command small bands of Soldiers to investigate unusual happenings in their regiment's 'territory' and some officers view this kind of adventuring as excellent training to keep their Soldiers sharp. Non-human Soldiers will often be on missions in the Empire that are adventures by their very nature.

SOLDIER ADVANCE SCHEME									
WS	BS	S	T	I	Agi	Dex	Int	WP	Fel
✚	⚒		✚	☠				✚	🛡

CAREER PATH

✚ Recruit — Silver 1
Skills: Athletics, Climb, Cool, Dodge, Endurance, Language (Battle), *Melee (Basic)*, Play (Drum *or* Fife)
Talents: Diceman, Marksman, Strong Back, Warrior Born
Trappings: Dagger, Leather Breastplate, Uniform

⚒ Soldier — Silver 3
Skills: Consume Alcohol, Gamble, Gossip, Melee (Any), Ranged (Any), Outdoor Survival
Talents: Drilled, Etiquette (Soldiers), Rapid Reload, Shieldsman
Trappings: Breastplate, Helmet, Weapon (Any)

☠ Sergeant — Silver 5
Skills: Heal, Intuition, Leadership, Perception
Talents: Combat Aware, Enclosed Fighter, Unshakeable, Warleader
Trappings: Symbol of Rank, Unit of Troops

🛡 Officer — Gold 1
Skills: Lore (Warfare), Navigation
Talents: Inspiring, Public Speaking, Seasoned Traveller, Stout-hearted
Trappings: Letter of Commission, Light Warhorse with Saddle and Tack, Map, Orders, Unit of Soldiers, Quality Uniform, Symbol of Rank

III

✠ WARRIOR PRIEST
Human

You bring divinity to the thick of battle, slaying the enemies of the Empire with righteous fury.

Some cults of the Empire have clerics trained for war. In the Reikland, the Warrior Priests of Sigmar are the most common example of this, and most armies of the Empire are accompanied by hammer-bearing priests encouraging the soldiers in the name of Sigmar. But other cults, especially those of Myrmidia, Ulric, Taal, and Morr, have Warrior Priests of their own, each with their unique views as to how war should be conducted. Away from the battlefield, Warrior Priests are also expected to administer to soldiers' spiritual wellbeing, as well as making sure morale stays high and discipline is ordered. Some orders of Warrior Priests swear oaths to roam the Empire, seeking heresy wherever it lies, helping where they can. Others prefer not to join armies, but lead them…

'Surrounded, we were, Greenskins on all sides. They knew we were done. Then the priest raises his hammer towards the sky and bellows his prayer. And as the words echoed to silence, the lightning struck. And we were all unharmed, I swear to Sigmar. But the Goblins? All dead.'

– Holger Kass, 1st Bögenhafen Halberdiers

While many Warrior Priests stay with the army, some serve their cult in missionary work, and others wander the Empire as they will. As such, Warrior Priests can be natural adventurers. Of course, to pursue leads to the ends of the Empire they might require the permission of their cult, and perhaps their commanders.

WARRIOR PRIEST ADVANCE SCHEME

WS	BS	S	T	I	Agi	Dex	Int	WP	Fel
✠		⚒	✠	💀				✠	🛡

CAREER PATH

✠ Novitiate — Brass 2
Skills: Cool, Dodge, Endurance, Heal, *Leadership*, Lore (Theology), Melee (Any), Pray
Talents: Bless (Any), Etiquette (Cultists), Read/Write, Strong-minded
Trappings: Book (Religion), Leather Jerkin, Religious Symbol, Robes, Weapon (Any Melee)

⚒ Warrior Priest — Silver 2
Skills: Charm, Entertain (Speeches), Intimidate, Language (battle), Melee (Any), Ranged (Any)
Talents: Dual Wielder, Inspiring, Invoke (Any), Seasoned Traveller
Trappings: Breastplate, Weapon (Any)

💀 Priest Sergeant — Silver 3
Skills: Animal Care, Intuition, Perception, Ride (Horse)
Talents: Combat Aware, Holy Visions, Pure Soul, Stout-hearted
Trappings: Light Warhorse with Saddle and Tack

🛡 Priest Captain — Silver 4
Skills: Consume Alcohol, Lore (Warfare)
Talents: Fearless (Any), Furious Assault, Holy Hatred, Warleader
Trappings: Religious Relic

• SKILLS AND TALENTS •

'Sure, playing Scarlet Empress is 90% luck and 10% skill. But try playing without that 10%, and you'll lose every time.'

– Hermann Graumann, Gambler, Raconteur and Liar

During the game, you'll find yourself in all sorts of situations where the outcome your Character's action is uncertain. Will you jump the ravine or plunge to your death? Will you charm the officious courtier, or will the guards be summoned to deal with you? How well you perform these actions is determined by your Skills and Talents. In general, Skills describe the capabilities of your Character, and Talents are special abilities or tricks you've learned. If you want to know how they all work in practice, refer to **Chapter 5: Rules**.

SKILLS

Where Characteristics represent the raw potential of your body and mind, Skills represent specific areas of training, knowledge, experience. Each Advance you take in a Skill improves the odds of succeeding with appropriate tasks — Characters who are well trained or experienced may be able to best opponents who are more naturally gifted.

DETERMINING YOUR SKILL LEVEL

All Skills are associated with a single Characteristic, noted in the Skill's description. A Skill's rating is determined by taking its associated Characteristic and adding the number of Advances taken in the Skill. Space for recording your Advances for each Skill is provided on your Character Sheet.

Example: *Sigrid has a Fellowship of 41 and has taken 5 Advances in Charm, so her Charm is 46 (41+5=46).*

BASIC AND ADVANCED SKILLS

Skills are classified as either *Basic* or *Advanced*.

Basic Skills represent innate or common abilities that you might practice in day-to-day life. Basic Skills can be Tested even if you have taken no Advances in them. To do this, simply attempt a Test using the Characteristic associated with the Skill as described in **Chapter 5: Rules.**

Example: *Sigrid has no Advances in Athletics. However, as Athletics is a Basic Skill, she can still Test Athletics using the Characteristic associated with it: Agility.*

Advanced Skills require specialist knowledge, training, or first-hand experience to even attempt to use. You may only Test an Advanced Skill if you have taken at least one Advance in it. If you have not, you cannot attempt to Test the Skill. So, no matter how intelligent you are, you will not understand the finer points of law without the Lore (Law) Skill.

Example: *Adhemar has an Intelligence of 36 and no Advances in either the Basic Gamble Skill or the Advanced Heal Skill, both based on Intelligence. He can Test the Gamble Skill at 36% as it is Basic, and anyone can Test Basic Skills. The Heal Skill is an Advanced Skill, so Adhemar has no idea how to patch up wounds beyond screaming loudly for a doctor!*

GROUPED SKILLS AND SPECIALISATION

Some Skills are classified as *Grouped*. This means the Skill is an array of related Skills under one heading. Each related Skill is called a *Specialisation*. When a Specialisation is mentioned in the rules, it is marked in brackets.

Example: *Language is a Grouped Skill, thus represents many related Language Skills under a single Skill heading. Examples of the different Specialisations of Language are: Language (Bretonnian), Language (Magick), or Language (Mootish).*

When you gain an Advance in a Grouped Skill, you must allocate the Advance to an appropriate Specialisation. Sometimes the Specialisation options will be marked clearly in your Career, so you simply select one of the options on offer. In other cases — such as when a Specialisation is marked as 'Any', meaning you can choose one Specialisation — you will need to select a Specialisation yourself; should this be required, either refer to the relevant Skill description and choose from the sample Specialisations found there, or, with GM permission, create a unique Specialisation that fits the Skill and best suits your character.

Example: *Theodora has a choice of Lore (Any) in her career. When she allocates an Advance to that option, she has to decide which Lore Specialisation to take. After some deliberation, she chooses to advance her Lore (Theology), showing she has learned something of the Gods.*

Other than that, Grouped Skills are handled in exactly the same way as normal Skills, with each Specialisation handled like a unique Skill.

Example: *Sigrid has 8 Advances in the Basic Skill, Entertain (Singing), but nothing in Entertain (Acting). This means she Tests her Fellowship of 41 when attempting to act, and Tests 49 when singing (41+8=49). By comparison, Theodora has a single Advance in the Advanced Skill Animal Training (Pigeons), but no Advances in Animal Training (Horses). This means she can use the Skill to train her pigeons to drop bombs on unsuspecting enemies, but she cannot train her horse to do the same, as she has no idea how to train horses.*

COMBAT

Many Skills might also have some application in combat; suggestions for how to do this are marked in each relevant Skill entry. These are not intended to be exhaustive, and if you have some inspired improvisation in mind, talk it through with your GM.

MASTER SKILL LIST

Animal Care (Int) *advanced*

The Animal Care Skill lets you tend and care for animals, and heal them should they fall sick or become wounded.

Having a single Advance in Animal Care means you can keep animals healthy without needing to Test. You can also enact an Animal Care Test to identify and resolve problems with animals, such as:

- Spotting an illness.
- Understanding reasons for fractiousness or discomfort.
- Determining the quality of the animal.
- Heal Intelligence Bonus + SL Wounds (**Note:** an animal can only benefit from one healing roll after each encounter).
- Staunching a *Bleeding* condition.
- Preparing the animal for display.

In combat, you may appraise an enemy animal with an Animal Care Test. If successful, you and all you inform gain +10 to hit when attacking that animal — or anyone using it as a mount — until the end of your next turn, as you point out loose tack, a limp from a niggling wound, or highlight some other weakness or vulnerability. Animal Care may only provide a maximum of +10 to hit per animal, no matter how many Tests are made to spot weaknesses.

ANIMALS

Whether a creature does, or does not come under the auspices of Animal Care and Animal Training is up to your GM. While certain creatures — Dog, Horse, Demigryph — seem obvious, others are less so. You may argue that Dragon should be covered under Animal Training, but try telling that to the Dragon...

Animal Training (Int) *advanced, grouped*
Animal Training represents your understanding of a particular type of animal, and your ability to train them. A successful use of the Skill allows you to identify the Trained abilities possessed by an animal belonging to your Specialisation (see page 118). The Animal Training Skill also allows you to undertake the *Animal Training* Endeavour between adventures (see page 196).

In combat, a successful **Opposed Animal Training/Willpower** Test allows you to intimidate a single animal belonging to your Specialisation; you cause Fear in the animal targeted until the end of your next turn (see page 190). When causing Fear in this way,

you may subsequently use your Animal Training Skill instead of Melee when defending against your target; with your GM's approval you may also use Animal Training to attack your target, issuing specific commands.

Example: *Facing a slavering war-hound, Ilse passes an **Opposed Animal Training (Dog) roll**, in the first round of combat, causing Fear in the beast, and gaining +1 Advantage. In the next round she 'attacks' her target with her Animal Training Skill, beating the dog's defence. Her GM allows her to instruct the beast to flee, which it does, its tail between its legs.*

Specialisations: Demigryph, Dog, Horse, Pegasus, Pigeon

Art (Dex) *basic, grouped*
Create works of art in your chosen medium.

Not having access to appropriate Trade Tools will incur a penalty to your Test. The SL achieved determines the quality of the final piece. For complicated or large works of art, an Extended Test may be required. The Art Skill has little use in combat, but marble busts make marvellous improvised weapons.

Example: *Irina has been commissioned to paint a portrait of a local noble, whose favour her party is currying. Her GM determines this requires a total of 10 SL in an **Extended Art** Test, with each Test representing a week's work.*

Specialisations: Cartography, Engraving, Mosaics, Painting, Sculpture, Tattoo, Weaving

Athletics (Ag) *basic*
Your ability to run, jump and move with speed or grace, and to perform any general physical activity. Refer to **Moving** (see page 164) for details on using Athletics in combat movement.

Bribery (Fel) *basic*

Your ability to judge how likely a person is to accept a bribe, and how best to offer the bribe so they will accept it.

A successful **Bribery Test** tells you if a target may be bribed. If so, your GM will secretly determine the price of their cooperation using the target's Earnings (see page 52), increasing the amount according to their usual honesty and the risk involved in taking the bribe. You then guess that target amount and the GM will tell you if the price is higher, lower, or equal. Each SL from your initial Bribery Test gives you another guess. At the end of this process, you determine how much money to offer, based on what you have gleaned.

Example: *Snorri is trying to bribe his way past a city watchman; a character of the Brass Tier 2, meaning they roll 4d10 Brass for Income. The GM decides the guard can be bribed and secretly rolls 21 on the 4d10, meaning the price for bribing the guard is 21 Brass. Letting Snorri through isn't too risky for the watchman, and he does it often, so the GM doesn't increase the bribe required. Snorri rolls 1 SL on his Bribery Test; so, he knows the watchman is open to a bribe, and has 2 guesses as to his price. Snorri's first guess is 15 Brass, to which his GM replies 'higher'. His second guess is 40, to which his GM replies 'lower'. Snorri now knows he must bribe the watchman between 15 and 40 Brass, so decides to aim high, and offers 30. Smiling, the watchman waves Snorri through.*

In combat, you may use Bribery as above to try to stop the fight, but treat the Test as Hard (–20) owing to the stress of the situation. If your target is not susceptible, you cannot afford the fee, or your foes do not speak your tongue, your pathetic attempts to buy them off will be doomed to fail. Of course, if they have the advantage of numbers, what's to prevent them from taking all of your money?

Channelling (WP) *advanced, grouped*

The Channelling Skill measures your ability to call upon and control the various Winds of Magic, and is solely used by the magic rules. Channelling is a special skill in that it is both Grouped, allowing for Specialisations, and also ungrouped, for those not properly trained to channel magic. See **Chapter 8: Magic** for details concerning this.

Specialisations: *Aqshy, Azyr, Chamon, Dhar, Ghur, Ghyran, Hysh, Shyish, Ulgu* (each is a different Wind of Magic, see **Chapter 8: Magic** for more on this).

Charm (Fel) *basic*

Charm makes people think favourably of you, your opinions, and proposed actions. Passing an **Opposed Charm/Cool** Test allows you to influence the behaviour of one or more targets, up to a maximum number equal to your Fellowship Bonus + SL, affecting those with the lowest Willpower first. If a target is amenable to your Charm, the Test will be uncontested.

Your GM may permit you to use Charm in Combat if they think your foes might be susceptible to you pleading for your life or making persuasive arguments to stop the violence (although good luck charming a Goblin)!

If you use Charm as your Action, calculate the number of targets affected as normal. If you use it to defend, you only affect your attacker. If you succeed, any affected targets will not attack you this round and you gain +1 Advantage as normal. You may do this in successive rounds until you choose to stop or fail a Charm Test, after which your words carry no more weight.

PUBLIC SPEAKING

The Charm Skill can be used to make impressive speeches to sway multiple targets to your way of thinking. Assuming they can hear you and are inclined to listen, you can influence up to your Fellowship Bonus + SL targets with a single Charm Test, influencing targets with the lowest Willpower first. If the crowd is unruly, or not receptive to your words, the Test is Opposed by the crowd's average Willpower (typically 35). A failure shows the crowd is unconvinced.

The *Public Speaking* and *Master Orator* Talents can significantly increase the number of people you affect with public speaking. An Astounding Failure (-6) (see page 152) in a Charm Test means your crowd quickly becomes an angry mob, with you as the target of their ire...

BEGGING

The Charm Skill can be used to beg on the streets. A successful Test will scrounge Fellowship Bonus × SL brass pennies per hour from passers-by, with the Difficulty modified by the pitch chosen for begging, and how much sympathy your appearance can elicit. If you score no SL, but still pass the Skill Test, you only manage to scrounge a single pfennig. An Astounding Failure (-6) means you may have attracted problems from the local Watchmen, found some trouble with other, local beggars, or suffer some other significant set-back.

Note: characters who are caught begging by their peers or associates will likely lose Status unless they are already in the Beggar, or in some other destitute, career.

Charm Animal (WP) *basic*

Your aptitude for befriending, quickly calming, or subjugating animals.

Passing a Charm Animal Test allows you to influence the behaviour of one or more animals, to a maximum of Willpower Bonus + SL. If the target animals are naturally docile, this Test may be uncontested, but it will generally be Opposed by the target's Willpower.

In combat, you may use Charm Animal when facing animals. If you succeed, any affected targets will not attack you this Round and you gain +1 Advantage. You may do this in successive rounds until you choose to stop or fail a Charm Test, after which the creature's instincts take over and you have no further influence.

Climb (S) *basic*

The ability to ascend steep or vertical surfaces.

If time isn't an issue, and a climb is relatively easy, anyone with Climb Skill is automatically assumed to be able to climb any reasonably small height.

For any other climbing, refer to page 165, which also handles Climbing during combat. You may even find yourself climbing large opponents, though whether that is prudent is debatable.

Consume Alcohol (T) *basic*

Your ability to handle alcohol without letting it cloud your judgment or render you senseless.

After each alcoholic drink make a Consume Alcohol Test, modified by the strength of the drink. For each Test you fail, you suffer a −10 penalty to WS, BS, Ag, Dex, and Int, to a maximum of −30 per Characteristic. After you fail a number of Tests equal to your Toughness Bonus, you are Stinking Drunk. Roll on the following table to see what happens:

1d10	Stinking Drunk
1-2	**'Marienburgher's Courage!'**: Gain a bonus of +20 to your Cool Skill.
3-4	**'You're My Besht Mate!'**: Ignore all your existing *Prejudices* and *Animosities* (see page 190).
5-6	**'Why's Everything Wobbling!'**: On your Turn, you can either Move or take an Action, but not both (see page 157).
7-8	**'I'll Take Yer All On!'**: Gain Animosity (Everybody!) (see page 190).
9-10	**'How Did I Get here?'**: You wake up the next day, massively hungover, with little memory of what transpired. The GM and other players with you will fill in the embarrassing gaps if you investigate. Pass a Consume Alcohol Test or also gain a *Poisoned* Condition (see page 169).

After not drinking for an hour, enact a **Challenging (+0) Consume Alcohol** Test. The effects of being drunk will wear off after 10–SL hours, with any Characteristic modifiers for being drunk lost over that time. After all effects wear off, enact another **Challenging (+0) Consume Alcohol** Test. You now gain a hangover, which is an *Fatigued* Condition that cannot be removed for 5–SL hours.

You may expend 1 Resolve point to ignore the negative modifiers of being drunk until the end of the next round (see page 171).

Cool (WP) *basic*

Cool allows you to remain calm under stress, resist fear when faced with horror, and stick to your convictions.

Cool is generally used to resist other Skills — Charm, Intimidate, and similar — but you may also be required to make a Cool Test when faced with anything forcing you to do something you would rather not. Cool is also the primary Skill used to limit Psychology (see page 190).

Dodge (Ag) *basic*

Dodge is your ability to avoid things, through ducking, diving, and moving quickly, and is used extensively to sidestep falling rocks, incoming weapons, unexpected traps, and the like.

In combat, Dodge is generally used to resist attacks or avoid damage. Refer to **Chapter 5: Rules** for more on this.

Drive (Ag) *basic*

Drive lets you guide vehicles — most commonly simple carts and lumbering coaches, not to mention the more 'experimental' creations of the Imperial Engineers — along the roads of the Empire with as little incident as possible.

Under normal circumstances, if you possess the Drive Skill, there is no need to Test. If conditions are less than ideal — perhaps the road is in poor condition, or the weather is terrible — a Drive Test will be required. If you do not possess the Drive Skill, you may be required to make a Test to carry out even basic manoeuvres. An Astounding Failure (-6) on a Drive Test means something bad has happened. Roll on the following table:

1d10	Result
1-2	**Snapped Harness:** One horse (or equivalent) breaks free; reduce speed accordingly.
3-5	**Jolted Carriage:** Passengers suffer 1 Wound and fragile cargos might be damaged.
6-8	**Broken Wheel:** Pass a Drive Test every round to avoid Crashing. Two-wheeled vehicles with a Broken Wheel Crash automatically.
9-10	**Broken Axle:** The vehicle goes out of control and Crashes.

Crashing: Occupants of Crashing vehicles usually suffer 2d10 Wounds modified by Toughness Bonus and Armour Points unless the vehicle was moving slowly (as determined by the GM). Crashed vehicles must be repaired by someone with an appropriate Trade Skill, such as Trade (Carpenter) or Trade (Cartwright). Spare wheels can be installed by anyone with a Drive Test or with an appropriate Trade Test.

In combat, Drive may be used if circumstances allow — for instance, if the party is in a coach being raided by outlaws, and you wish to ram an enemy, or outrun them (see page 165).

Endurance (T) *basic*

The Endurance Skill is called upon when you must endure hardship, withstand deprivation, sit without moving for long periods of time, or survive harsh environments. In particular, Endurance is Tested to resist or recover from various Conditions (see page 167) and helps you recover lost Wounds. Refer to **Chapter 5: Rules** for more on this.

Entertain (Fel) *basic, grouped*

Allows you to delight crowds with the spoken word, perhaps by singing, acting, or attempting a few jokes. A successful use of the Entertain Skill means you have entertained patrons near enough to hear you; the SL indicates how well you have done.

In combat, it is unlikely that Entertain will be of much use, although you may come up with an interesting way to use Entertain (Acting) to confuse or mislead your opponents.

Specialisations: Acting, Comedy, Singing, Storytelling

Evaluate (Int) *advanced*

Lets you determine the value of rare artefacts, unusual trade goods, and works of art. Everybody is assumed to know the relative worth of general items, but a successful use of the Evaluate allows you to identify the value of curious and unique items. A successful Evaluate Test may also alert you if the goods (or coins) you are studying are counterfeit — this Test will usually be Opposed by the forger's SL on their Art or Trade Test. Your GM may apply modifiers based on just how rare or obscure the item is, or on your character's particular expertise or background.

Gamble (Int) *basic*

Allows you to measure the likelihood that a bet will pay off, as well as successfully engage in various games of chance.

To represent a gambling match, all players make a Gamble Test — applying any appropriate modifiers for familiarity with the game — and the player with the highest SL wins. On a tie, any lower scoring players drop out, and those remaining enact another Gamble Test, repeating this process until you have a winner.

If you wish to influence the game through less honest mechanics, see Sleight of Hand.

OPTIONS

Some players prefer to use immersive mini-games at the table, playing real card or dice games to aid the roleplaying experience. If you do this, a successful Gamble Test will allow you to influence the game once — by drawing an extra card, or rerolling a die for example — as the GM dictates. Each SL affords you another opportunity to influence the game.

Gossip (Fel) *basic*

You can quickly ferret out interesting and useful news, and spread rumours of your own. A successful Gossip Test means you have found out one useful piece of information, which your GM can impart to you, about the local area. Each SL either offers you an additional piece of information, or the chance to spread a rumour to a number of individuals equal to your Fellowship Bonus. The time required for a Gossip Test depends on how circumspect the players are being, and how busy the area is, as determined by the GM.

It is unlikely that Gossip will be much use in combat, but if your attacker happens to be local, and you happen to know something really juicy…

HALF-HEARD WHISPERS

While it may be expedient for GMs to quickly share information gleaned from Gossip Tests to all players at once, it is often more fun to share the information only with individual players (either through a note, or through briefly taking them aside). This means the players must relate this information to one another in-character — aiding the immersive roleplaying experience — which allows for mistakes and misunderstandings, sometimes leading to hilarious, or horrific, results.

Haggle (Fel) *basic*

Haggle allows you to secure better deals when negotiating with others. In general, Haggle is used to see whether you do, or do not, make a good deal, most commonly with an **Opposed Haggle** Test. Specifically, it can be used when shopping to secure better prices. For information on this, refer to **Chapter 11: Consumers' Guide.**

Heal (Int) *advanced*

You've been trained to deal with injuries and diseases. A successful Heal Test allows you to do one of the following:

- Diagnose an illness, infection, or disease.
- Treat a disease (see page 188).
- Heal wounds equal to your Intelligence Bonus + SL (**Note:** a patient can only benefit from one Heal roll after each encounter). If sterile liquids or appropriate poultices and dressings are used, no Infection will develop from the injury (see page 181).
- Staunch a *Bleeding* Condition, with each SL removing an extra *Bleeding* Condition.

A Failed Heal Test can potentially cause Wounds if your Intelligence Bonus + SL totals less than 0. On an Astounding Failure, your patient will also contract a Minor Infection (see page 187).

If administering to someone who has a disease, a successful Heal Test ensures that you do not contract the disease for that day. Each SL also prevents one other character encountering the patient that day from catching the disease. For each full day the patient spends resting under your care, the duration of the disease is reduced by one, to a minimum of one. For more information see **Disease and Infection** in **Chapter 5: Rules.**

Certain injuries require Surgery; see the *Surgery* Talent for details. For more information on healing wounds, refer to **Injury** in **Chapter 5: Rules.**

Your GM may apply modifiers to Heal Tests to reflect the virulence of the disease, the suitability of conditions and materials, or the stress of your circumstances. If healing during combat, Tests will likely be **Challenging (+0)** at the very least.

Intimidate (S) *basic*

Allows you to coerce or frighten sentient creatures. The precise manner of initiating an Intimidate Test depends on context: while it is generally accompanied by an overt threat, sometimes a subtle implication or even a look is enough. Intimidate is almost always Opposed by your target's Cool Skill; if successful, you can intimidate a number of targets up to your Strength Bonus + SL. Each will react to Intimidate based on their individual personalities and how successful you were in menacing them, but in all cases, they will back down or move out of the way and will not speak out against you, or they will alternatively accept combat is the only way forward and prepare their weapons.

In combat, you cause Fear (see page 190) in all Intimidated targets. You may also use your Intimidate Skill instead of Melee when defending against those afraid of you, causing the Intimidated parties to back away from the fight with your will and posture alone. Further, with your GM's approval, you may use Intimidate to 'attack' such targets, issuing specific commands, such as 'drop your weapons' or 'get out of here!'. However, if you fail any of these subsequent Intimidate Tests, you no longer Intimidate (or cause Fear) in affected opponents. With your GM's permission you may try to Intimidate them again in a later Round, but this will incur a negative modifier, as they are less likely to fear you having seen through your bravado once already.

Example: *Facing a group of footpads, Svetlana the Strong rolls 4 SL on her Intimidate Test. Combined with her SB of 5, this means she can affect up to 9 targets, more than enough to impact all three footpads who now Fear Svetlana. As she has won by 3 SL, she gains +1 Advantage point until the end of her next turn. In the next round, she 'attacks' the footpads using her Intimidate, intending to scare them into leaving her be. However, she fails the Test, and the footpads realise they outnumber her, and are armed…*

OPTIONS: ALTERNATIVE CHARACTERISTICS FOR INTIMIDATE

While Strength is the default stat for Intimidate Tests, the GM may decree certain situations may allow you to use a different Characteristic: a steely witch hunter may use Willpower to stare down an inquisitive bystander, or an academic may use Intelligence to cow a lowly student with his intimidating knowledge, for instance.

Intuition (I) *basic*

The Intuition Skill allows you to get a feel for your surroundings, leading you to notice when something is wrong, and gives you a sense of when people may be hiding something from you. A successful use of the Intuition Skill gives you subtle or implicit intelligence relating to your environment, determined by your GM. This may be information such as whether someone believes what they are saying, what the general attitude is towards the local noble, or if the helpful local's motives are as pure as they seem. If someone is actively trying to hide their intent, they may resist your Intuition with Cool or Entertain (Acting).

In combat, a successful Intuition Test may be used to give you +1 Advantage as you weigh the environment and your opponents. You may continue building Advantage in subsequent turns providing you are able to observe your targets and are not interrupted (such as being attacked); you may gain a maximum Advantage equal to your Intelligence Bonus in this manner.

Language (Int) *advanced, grouped*

The Language Skill grants you access to extra languages beyond your native tongue. All characters are automatically assumed to be able to speak 'Reikspiel' — the language of the Empire — and their native language (if your character has one different to

Reikspiel), without ever having to Test. If your game is not set in the Empire, replace Reikspiel with the local language.

If you possess a Language Skill, you are generally able to make yourself understood in that language, or to understand simple concepts. You will be asked to Test your Language Skill when a particularly difficult concept must be conveyed, or an obscure dialect or vocabulary is employed.

Note: Language (Magick) is used to cast spells and may occasionally be Tested, with… unpleasant consequences if failed. Refer to **Chapter 8: Magic**, for more on this.

Specialisations: Battle Tongue, Bretonnian, Classical, Guilder, Khazalid, Magick, Thief, Tilean

OPTIONS: BATTLE TONGUE

Battle Tongue represents a series of simple commands and gestures that may be made in the heat of combat. Players with Language (Battle Tongue) may communicate briefly with one another during combat without penalty. Those without the Skill cannot quickly coordinate their attacks or discuss strategy once combat begins.

LANGUAGES OF THE OLD WORLD

Here is a list of the primary languages of the Old World, and who most commonly speaks them. There are an enormous number of other tongues spoken, but these are the most commonly encountered in the Reikland.

Language	Spoken by...
Albion	...the folk of Albion, who hail from a far-off mist-shrouded island-realm and are rarely encountered.
Battle Tongue	...warriors of the Old World. It is very common amongst soldiers and mercenaries and is used for giving orders swiftly during battle. It was supposedly developed by the goddess Myrmidia when she walked the Old World as a mortal.
Bretonnian	...the folk of Bretonnia, who are commonly encountered in the Reikland. Bretonnia is a chivalric realm to the south-west of the Empire.
Classical	...Human academics of all kinds. It is the first recorded Human language of the Old World — over 3,000 years old — used in most scholarly texts of the Empire including wizard grimoires and many holy books.
Elthárin	...the folk of Athel Loren, the Laurelorn, and visiting merchants from Ulthuan. Elthárin is the language of the Elves. The tonal language has many dialects, and is notoriously difficult for non-Elves to learn.
Estalian	...the folk of Estalia, people of the hot, southern-western kingdoms known for their bitter politics and worship of the goddess Myrmidia.
Gospodarinyi	...the folk of Kislev, a hardy people from the frozen oblasts to the east of the Empire. The language is often called 'Kislevarin' or 'Kislevite' by outsiders.
Grumbarth	...Ogres; few others learn this simple tongue, though some mercenary commanders find it useful for communicating with any Ogres they may hire.
Khazalid	...the folk of Karaz Ankor, the Dwarf kingdoms in the mountains. This language is also wide-spread through the Cult of Sigmar, which venerates the strong relationship Sigmar had with the Dwarfs when he was mortal.
Magick	...wizards; a tonal language used to shape the Winds of Magic into material effects. The academic form of the language taught by the Colleges of Magic is called the *Lingua Praestantia*, which is quite different to the debased form of the language used by witches and the untrained. It is not a language used for communication.
Mootish	...the folk of the Mootland; i.e.: the Halfling grand province in the Empire. This language is little known outside the Moot.
Norse	...the folk of Norsca. Norse is commonly spoken across the north of the Empire in Nordland and Ostland, and is well-known in the Wasteland and Kislev, too.
Reikspiel	...the folk of the Empire. Reikspiel is the primary language used in most **WFRP** games. It manifests in uncounted discrete dialects from across the Empire, most of which are mutually intelligible. It is the modern version of the tongue once spoken by the God-King Sigmar when he still walked as a mortal over two thousand five hundred years ago.
Queekish	...the folk of the Under-Empire. Used by the Skaven and their many slaves. Few admit to speaking it, or even being aware of its existence.
Tilean	...the folk of Tilea, who are most commonly encountered in the Empire as traders or mercenaries. The Tilean Princedoms to the south are notorious for their deadly politics and their veneration of Myrmidia.
Thieves Tongue	...street folk of the Old World. Expressions of this language are highly localised and individual to each realm; e.g. Tileans sport a completely different 'Thieves Tongue' to folk of the Empire.
Wastelander	...the rural folk of the Wasteland, a windswept territory to the west of the Reikland. The official language of the Wasteland's capital, Marienburg, is Reikspiel, a reminder that the realm was once part of the Empire.

Leadership (Fel) *basic*

A measure of your ability to lead others and command their respect. While most often associated with martial situations, a resolute leader can quickly direct a fast response to a fire or other such calamity, and nobles use the Skill frequently to command their lessers.

A successful Leadership Test allows you to issue orders to a number of targets equal to your Fellowship Bonus + SL. If the targets are your natural subordinates — a noble commanding serfs, or a sergeant commanding his troops — commands are usually unopposed. If there is no natural hierarchy in place, or the order is particularly challenging — such as ordering your soldiers to charge a Hydra head on — the Test is Opposed by your targets' Cool.

In combat, you may use Leadership to encourage your subordinates. A successful Leadership Test confers a bonus of +10 to all Psychology Tests until the end of the next round (see page 190).

Further, Leadership can be used to transfer Advantage to allies able to hear you; following a successful Leadership Test, you may transfer an Advantage to one ally of your choice, plus a further +1 Advantage per SL scored, which can again go to any allies of your choice within earshot.

Example: *Lord Ludwig von Schemp has been watching his two bodyguards discourse with some ruffians for three Rounds, using his Intuition Skill to build up 3 Advantage. Feeling it is going nowhere, he issues a peremptory order to attack the ringleader; passing his Leadership Test with 5 SL, he gives one bodyguard 2 of his Advantage, and the remaining bodyguard 1 Advantage, hoping this will bring a swift end to proceedings.*

WHO'S THE BOSS?

GMs should be aware that having Players issue orders to other Players may cause friction within the party. If you have Players who are of differing social class, or military ranks, be sure to discuss how this will be reflected in your intraparty dynamics to ensure a smooth and enjoyable game for everyone.

Lore (Int) *advanced, grouped*

Having a Lore Skill means you've been formally taught, or have somehow otherwise learned, a branch of specialist knowledge. Possessing a Lore Skill means you are broadly knowledgeable in the specialisation and don't need to make a Test in order for the

GM to supply you with relevant facts. If you are seeking specific, less well-known information, you will be required to make a Lore Test, modified by how obscure the information is, with the SL indicating how much detail you recall.

In combat, successful Lore Tests may afford you +1 Advantage if appropriate (with your GM's approval). For instance, Lore (Geology) may give you an edge if fighting in a rocky cavern, or Lore (Engineering) may help you if fighting a foe armed with a complex mechanical device. You may continue building Advantage in subsequent turns providing the circumstances are correct (as determined by the GM) and you are not interrupted; you may gain a maximum Advantage equal to your Intelligence Bonus in this manner.

Specialisations: Engineering, Geology, Heraldry, History, Law, Magick, Metallurgy, Science, Theology

Melee (WS) *basic, grouped*

The Melee Skill represents specific training with a single type of close combat weaponry. Each Melee Specialisation indicates training in using a specific class of weapon. If you don't have the correct Specialisation for a weapon you wish to use, refer to **Chapter 11: Consumers' Guide** for the correct weapon entry, and what penalties you will suffer. See **Chapter 5: Rules** for more detail about combat and using the Melee Skill.

Specialisations: Basic, Brawling, Cavalry, Fencing, Flail, Parry, Pole-Arm, Two-Handed

Navigation (I) *basic*

Navigation allows you to find your way in the wilderness using landmarks, stellar bodies or maps. Possessing the Navigation Skill means you know roughly where you are, and can find your way between well-known landmarks without a Test. A Test is only required if you are disoriented or travelling far from the beaten path, with success showing you the correct direction, or allowing you to avoid mishap.

If you are navigating a long journey, your GM may ask for an extended Navigation Test, modified by conditions, visible landmarks, and access to reliable geographical information. The SL required to succeed depends on how far the destination is, with each Test representing between an hour and a day's travel, depending on the nature of the journey.

Outdoor Survival (Int) *basic*

The Outdoor Survival Skill is used to survive in the wild, including the ability to fish, hunt, forage, and build fires and shelters. Experienced travellers are skilled at reading the signs of incoming inclement weather and finding the spoor of various dangerous beasts.

When camping, make an Outdoor Survival Test, modified by the harshness of conditions — for instance, a Test is **Challenging (+0)** if it is raining, **Hard (−20)** in a storm. A successful Test indicates you can provide yourself sustenance and shelter for the night. Each SL allows you to provide for one more character. If the Test is failed, you must make a **Challenging (+0) Endurance** Test or receive the *Fatigued* Condition. If you suffer an Astounding Failure, something untoward has happened, as determined by the GM; perhaps your camp is attacked in the night?

When fighting in the wilderness, you may make an Outdoor Survival Test to receive +1 Advantage, in the same way as Intuition, to a maximum number of Advantage equal to your Intelligence Bonus, as you spy out treacherous and advantageous terrain that you can best use to your advantage.

OPTIONS: GATHERING FOOD AND HERBS

Gathering food or herbs normally takes around 2 hours. Hunting and foraging parties make one Assisted Outdoor Survival Test for the group, with the Difficulty determined by the circumstances.

- **Foraging**: A success grants enough food for one character. Every SL yields sufficient extra food for one more person.
- **Hunting and Fishing**: If you have appropriate bows, spears, fishing rods, or nets, a successful Test feeds two people, and an extra two people per SL.
- **Trapping**: Use the Set Trap Skill to place Animal traps (see page 303). Feeds the same number of people as *Hunting and Fishing*.
- **Lore (Herbs)**: If you are instead gathering herbs using Lore (Herbs), a success gathers enough for a dose of the sought herb (see page 307), with each SL adding an extra dose. Gathering tests are modified by herb Availability: Common (0), Scarce (–10), Rare (–20), or Exotic (–30).

Perception (I) *basic*

Your ability to notice things with your senses — sight, smell, hearing, touch, and taste, and any other senses you may possess, such as magical or non-Human senses. Your GM may ask for a Perception Test to detect something, like movement behind the treeline, the presence of a trap, or someone following you, modified by how easy it is to notice. Perception is also used to resist attempts to hide things through Skills such as Sleight of Hand or Stealth.

Perception has multiple uses in combat, most commonly to notice important details beyond the immediately obvious about the surrounding environment and your opponents, as determined by the GM.

Perform (Ag) *advanced, grouped*

You've learned a physically demanding art, perhaps as a way of making a living, maybe as a street entertainer or as part of a travelling carnival. A successful use of the Perform Skill allows you to entertain all patrons close enough to see and hear you; the SL indicate how well you have done.

In combat, certain physical Perform specialisations may give you an edge. With your GM's permission, Perform (Acrobatics) may be used in lieu of Dodge. Other Perform Skills may be useful in distracting foes, perhaps gaining you an Advantage if you can come up with a creative way to do so. And some Perform skills can be directly used as a weapon if you have the correct trappings, such as Perform (Firebreathing)!

Specialisations: Acrobatics, Clowning, Dancing, Firebreathing, Juggling, Miming, Rope Walking

Pick Lock (Dex) *advanced*

You know the mechanisms of locks and how to open them without their proper keys. Picking a lock is often an Extended Test, with the number of SL required to open the lock dependent on the complexity of the lock.

LOCKS AND LOCK PICKS

Lock Difficulty ratings assume the use of lock picks. Improvised picks such as hairpins and nails can be used at –10 penalty. Each Test normally takes a Round to complete, though the GM may determine some locks are particularity stiff or rusted, and take longer. If the GM deems a lock is sufficiently simple, unskilled characters can attempt a single **Very Hard (–30) Dexterity** Test to pick the lock. The following provides some standard difficulties for locks typically encountered in the Old World.

Lock Type	Difficulty	SL
Latch	Average (+20)	0
Normal Door	Challenging (+0)	2
Secure Door	Difficult (–10)	2
Treasure Chest	Hard (–20)	5
Vault Door	Very Hard (–30)	10

Play (Dex) *advanced, grouped*
Your ability to make music with an instrument, hopefully well enough to impress others. A successful Play Test lets you entertain those near enough to see and hear you; the SL indicates the quality of the piece played.

Specialties: Bagpipe, Lute, Harpsichord, Horn, Violin

THE OLD WORLD'S A STAGE...

While there is some overlap between the Skills of Entertain, Perform, and Play, each reflects a distinct group of Skills.

Entertain is a Basic Skill using Fellowship. It represents those Skills of entertainment that anyone can attempt, even without training, such as singing or telling stories.
Perform is an Advanced Skill using Agility. Perform Specialisations require training to attempt, and rely on physical speed and coordination.
Play is also an Advanced Skill, this time using Dexterity. It represents training in specific musical instruments, all of which need teaching and practice to perform well.

You should choose carefully when determining whether your chosen Specialisation belongs to Entertain, Perform, or Play; consider how the character will physically enact the Skill, and whether an untrained beginner could do so with any success. After all, someone without any musical training could feasibly sing beautifully, but hand them a set of bagpipes...

Pray (Fel) *advanced*
Your ability to invoke, or otherwise commune with, a deity. For more information on using the Pray Skill to seek divine intervention, see **Chapter 7: Religion & Belief.**

In combat, if your GM deems it appropriate considering your circumstances and faith, you may use Pray to meditate and focus your mind. Each round you spend praying in combat — and making a successful Pray Test — gives you +1 Advantage. You can gain additional Advantage this way, up to a maximum of your Fellowship Bonus.

Further, if your enemies understand your language and recognise (and fear) your deity, the GM may allow you to use Pray in lieu of the Intimidate Skill.

Ranged (BS) *advanced, grouped*
Whilst anyone can throw a rock simply using their Ballistic Skill, it takes training and practice to use weapons like bows and pistols. Each Ranged Specialisation is specific to a group of ranged weapons. If you don't have the Ranged Specialisation for a weapon you wish to use, refer to **Chapter 11: Consumers' Guide** to see what penalties you will suffer when using the weapon. See **Chapter 5: Rules** for full detail about ranged combat.

Specialisations: Blackpowder, Bow, Crossbow, Engineering, Entangling, Explosives, Sling, Throwing

Research (Int) *advanced*
How adept you are at pulling useful and frequently obscure knowledge from libraries and other such storehouses of information. Research requires you have the *Read/Write* Talent (see page 142).

Simply possessing the Research Skill indicates you can find straightforward information from a clearly indexed library without a Test given enough time. If you are seeking specific,

less well-known information, or you are in a rush, you will be required to make an Extended Research Test, with the Difficulty modified by the library size, and the target SL depending upon the obscurity of the topic.

Research has no use in combat beyond perhaps finding you a useful manual on sword-fighting techniques.

RESEARCH AND LIBRARIES

Libraries of the Old World vary from small personal libraries of a few dozen books to vast archives found in the universities and temples of the towns and cities.

Using a Research Test in a small library, perhaps to find a specific book, only takes about 5 minutes. By comparison, Research Tests in large libraries can easily takes an hour or more per Test, but are far more likely to find esoteric lore.

Ride (Ag) *basic, grouped*
How proficient you are at riding a particular group of animals; Ride (Horse), for example, will let you ride Horses, Mules, Donkeys, and similar. You'll only need to make a Test when doing something out of the ordinary, such as racing, dressage, traversing dangerous terrain, or charging into combat. Otherwise, if you have at least one Advance in the Skill, you are presumed to be able to ride around without need of a Test.

If mounted on a steed, you move using the steed's Movement statistic; if you wish to run, jump, or leap, you use your Ride Skill, not Athletics. An extended Ride Test may be needed if you are racing somewhere, the target SL depending on the length of the journey, the number of Tests indicating how long you take to arrive. A Ride Test may be modified by environmental conditions, and the temperament of your mount. For more information on mounts, see **Chapter 12: Bestiary.**

The Ride skill can be used extensively in combat. See **Chapter 5: Rules,** for more on mounted combat.

Specialisations: Demigryph, Great Wolf, Griffon, Horse, Pegasus

Row (S) *basic*
Your prowess at pulling an oar and moving a boat through the water. The Row Skill is typically only used when racing, navigating rapids, desperately avoiding Bog Octopuses, or similar unusual or dangerous feats. Anyone with the Skill is automatically presumed

to be able to scull about a pond, or over a gentle river, without a Test. Those without the skill may have to make a Test for anything but the most basic manoeuvres.

Sail (Ag) *advanced, grouped*
Your ability to operate and manoeuvre a sailing vessel — including knotwork, steering, gauging the wind, and more. Assuming you have enough trained crew for your vessel, you only use the Sail Skill when you must push your vessel to perform, either by racing, navigating particularly dangerous shoals, struggling against bad weather, or similar difficulties. Simply sailing with a gentle wind, or guiding a ship downriver, doesn't require a Test for those with Sail. The skill can also be used for sailing-related activities like tying knots, or tying others up in knots.

As sailing one ship is not so different to sailing another, having any Sail Speciality makes all other Sail Specialities Basic Skills for you.

Specialisations: Barge, Caravel, Cog, Frigate, Wolfship

Secret Signs (Int) *advanced, grouped*
You've been taught how to use clandestine markings only intelligible to members of a select group. There are all manner of reasons why someone may want to leave a secret message: vagabonds might indicate which homeowners are likely to offer alms, thieves may want to indicate weaknesses, or likely marks, while scouts may want to warn one another about a dangerous monster's lair nearby.

This Skill does not usually need to be Tested — you can decipher any appropriate signs you can see if you have this Skill. But if the signs have been disturbed, worn away, or if you are pressed for time, then a Test will likely be required. Most messages are very simple, no more than three words.

Specialisations: Grey Order, Guild (any one), Ranger, Scout, Thief, Vagabond

I SAW THE SIGN...

This is a list of the primary secret signs of the Old World, and those who use them. This is only a tiny sample of those most commonly used in the Reikland; there are many more than this short list suggests, and you are encouraged to create those best fitting your game.

Secret Signs	Used by...
Grey Order	...Grey Wizards. The secretive Greys use a complex array of signs, many only perceptible to wizards. They mark the land for their wandering wizards, highlighting safe houses, places of danger, areas where wizards are unwelcome, and much more besides.
Guilder	...guilders. Many of the larger guilds, from masons to stevedores, have an array of marks and signs used to identify matters of importance to their members.
Ranger	...woodsmen and other rural folk. Ranger signs are mostly used to mark territory, point out areas of importance or danger, and indicate safe paths.
Scout	...scouts, particularly those employed by armies and mercenary companies. The signs are mostly used to point out foraging areas, routes for supply trains, and significant dangers ahead.
Thief	...thieves and rogues. The various gangs and criminal outfits of the towns and cities use a variety of marks to point out bolt holes, easy marks, well-patrolled areas, and more.
Vagabond	...wandering vagabonds and pedlars. Vagabond signs are mostly used to identify safe places to sleep, villages to avoid, and sources of food and water.

Set Trap (Dex) *advanced*

From a simple snare, or bear-trap, to more spectacular devices like Von Grizzel's Thief-Render, players are unlikely to venture far in the Old World without encountering traps. The Set Trap Skill measures your ability to set and disarm traps of all varieties. Anyone with the skill is automatically assumed to be able to activate and disarm traps given enough time. A Test is normally only required if attempting to use the Skill swiftly or if otherwise under pressure, or if the trap is especially complex. A selection of simple traps can be found in **Chapter 11: Consumers' Guide.**

Setting or disarming most traps requires an **Average (+20%) Set Trap** Test, but more complex devices may require an extended Test, needing several SL over multiple rounds to set.

Sleight of Hand (Dex) *advanced*

Lets you pick pockets, palm objects, and perform minor tricks of prestidigitation, as well as cheating with games of chance. This Skill is typically Opposed by the Perception Skill of your target; success means you have palmed the object, picked the pocket, or swapped the cards, while a Marginal Success (+0 to +1) may suggest that your nefarious misdeeds have left your opponent suspicious.

You can also use Sleight of Hand to 'help' your Gamble Skill when playing appropriate games of chance. Before any round (or similar, depending upon the game at hand) you can attempt a Sleight of Hand Test (which will be opposed if others suspect). If successful, you may reverse your Gamble Test for the round if this will score a Success. If failed, your opponents may not be best pleased...

Sleight of Hand and combat rarely mix, though inventive players may be able to conjure an impressive distraction with GM approval, perhaps even gaining Advantage by making a Dagger seemingly appear from nowhere, surprising a superstitious foe.

Stealth (Ag) *basic, grouped*

Allows you to creep quietly and conceal yourself in shadows more readily than most. Stealth is generally Opposed by an opponent's Perception Skill, and Tests will be modified by how dark or well concealed your route is, as well as how circumspectly you are dressed. An Impressive or Astounding Failure on a Stealth Test will likely draw the immediate attention of the enemies you were trying to avoid in the first place.

Stealth has many potential applications in combat, most usefully to hide oneself in preparation for an Ambush, or to creep around an opponent in order to attack from behind. See **Chapter 5: Rules** for the implications of this. Of course, you can also use the Skill to escape a conflict unseen...

Specialisations: Rural, Underground, Urban

OPTIONS: SHADOWING

Shadowing is following someone secretly. To do this requires a Combined Perception and Stealth Test (see page 155). If the target is actively trying to lose a tail, it is Opposed with the target's Stealth Skill.

If you pass the Perception Test, and fail the Stealth Test you follow your target, but are spotted. If you fail the Perception Test, yet pass the Stealth Test, you lose your target, but go unnoticed.

Swim (S) *advanced*

Your ability to swim in water without drowning. If you have the Swim Skill, you are automatically presumed to be able to swim freely without a Test. But if you find yourself in difficult currents, racing, or fleeing from an oversized shark sent by Stromfels, the God of Drowning, a Test will be required. This may be modified by the condition of the water, or how encumbered you are by clothes, armour, and other trappings.

Swim is only used in combat if you happen to be fighting in the water, where it replaces Skills like Athletics to govern Movement. If exact speeds are required, you swim at half your Movement rate, using the normal rules for moving found on page 164.

Track (I) *advanced*

Your ability to follow subtle trails left by others. Track is used to follow difficult trails across the wilderness. This is not a skill for following a set of footprints in the snow — a simple Perception test covers that — Track involves deeper knowledge and awareness used to recognise the subtle signs of a quarry's passage. You can also attempt to hide your trail, in which case use your Track skill to oppose your pursuer's Track Test.

Often an Extended Track Test is required to follow a trail, with the Difficulty modified by how fresh the tracks are, and how suitable the ground is: damp earth betrays passage better than stony ground. The GM may also use the Pursuit rules to determine if you manage to track down a fleeing quarry (see page 166).

Trade (Dex) *advanced, grouped*

Most folk of the Reikland follow a trade; even adventurers often have a more reliable, or respectable career to fall back on, between bouts of hair-raising, bowel-loosening excitement.

The Trade Skill represents your ability to create something or provide a service, as well as your knowledge of the relevant lore surrounding your trade.

Having the Skill is enough to automatically perform the tasks associated with your trade, assuming you have the correct resources and tools. You need only Test your Trade Skill if you are seeking to create something quickly, conditions are adverse, or you are seeking to invent or create a high-quality item.

Often Trade Tests of this type are extended Test, with the SL and time required depending upon the scope or scale of what is being produced; a quick meal with Trade (Cook) to impress a local lord will take far less time than constructing a warship with Trade (Shipwright).

You may also make a Trade Test as a Lore Skill, to determine information relevant to the trade in question. In such circumstances, the GM may prefer to use Int over Dex as the base Characteristic, though often this is ignored to keep play simple.

While most Trade Skills have little function in combat, there are as many Trade Skills as there are trades, and some may be of use depending upon the circumstances. For example, a successful Trade (Apothecary) Test may be useful if fighting in an Apothecary's shop as you identify some astringent chemicals to hurl at your foes.

The Trade Skill is also used for enacting a *Crafting* Endeavour (see page 197).

Specialisations: Apothecary, Calligrapher, Chandler, Carpenter, Cook, Embalmer, Smith, Tanner

TALENTS

Where Characteristics represent your raw potential, and Skills are your training and experience, Talents represent all the tricks, quirks, and special abilities you have learned throughout life.

GAINING TALENTS

During character creation you will automatically receive a selection of Talents (see **Chapter 2: Character**). After this, you can use Experience Points (XP) to purchase new Talents, or take existing ones multiple times, if allowed, from the advance scheme of your Career (see page 48).

If you can take a Talent multiple times, it may have a special rule for what this means written into its description. Further, it may have an associated Skill marked under 'Tests' (see Talent Format): if so, for each time you have the Talent, you gain +1 SL on any successful use of a Skill tied to the Talent.

> ## TALENT FORMAT
>
> The following explains how each Talent is presented.
>
> - **Talent Name (situation):** The name of the Talent. If there are parentheses, the word within describes a situation the Talent influences.
> - **Max:** The maximum number of times the Talent may be taken, which is normally 1 or an associated Characteristic Bonus.
> - **Tests:** If the Talent is tied to one or more Tests your character can make, the affected Tests are listed here. Talents tied to a Test come with an extra rule: For each time you have taken the Talent, you gain +1 SL on any successful use of the Skill tied to the Talent.
> - **Description (not titled):** A description of what the Talent does.

MASTER TALENT LIST

Accurate Shot
Max: Ballistic Skill Bonus
You are an exceptional shot and know where to shoot an enemy in order to inflict maximum damage. You deal your Accurate Shot level in extra Damage with all ranged weapons.

Acute Sense (Sense)
Max: Initiative Bonus
Test: Perception (Sense)
One of your primary five senses is highly developed, allowing you to spot what others miss. You may take Perception Tests to detect normally imperceptible details with the associated sense, as

dictated by the GM. This could include: seeing an eagle beyond everyone else's eyeshot, smelling an almost odourless poison, hearing the breath of an unmoving mouse within a wall, feeling a worn away letter in a carving, or tasting that two beers from the same brewer have been drawn from two different barrels.

Aethyric Attunement
Max: Initiative Bonus
Test: Channelling (Any)
Your experience, talent or training lets you more safely manipulate the Winds of Magic. You do not suffer a Miscast if you roll a double on a successful Channel Test.

Alley Cat
Max: Initiative Bonus
Test: Stealth (Urban)
You are at home in shadowy backstreets. When using Stealth (Urban), you may reverse the dice of any failed Test if this will score a Success.

Ambidextrous
Max: 2
You can use your off-hand far better than most folk, either by training or innate talent. You only suffer a penalty of −10 to Tests relying solely on your secondary hand, not −20. If you have this Talent twice, you suffer no penalty at all.

Animal Affinity

Max: Willpower Bonus

Tests: Charm Animal

Wild animals feel comfortable in your presence, and often follow your lead. All creatures with the Bestial Trait not trained to be belligerent will automatically be calm in your presence unless they have a reason not to be, such as pain, an attack, being naturally hyper-aggressive, or having nearby young.

Arcane Magic (Lore)

Max: 1

You either study one of the 8 Arcane Lores of Magic — Beasts, Death, Fire, Heavens, Metal, Shadow, Light, or Life — or practice a lesser known Lore, such as Hedgecraft or Necromancy. You may now memorise spells from your chosen Lore for the following cost in XP.

Number of Spells Currently Known	XP Cost for a new spell
Up to Intelligence Bonus × 1	100 XP
Up to Intelligence Bonus × 2	200 XP
Up to Intelligence Bonus × 3	300 XP
Up to Intelligence Bonus × 4	400 XP

...and so on.

So, if your Intelligence Bonus is 4, it will cost you 100 XP for the first spell, and the next 4, then 200 XP for the next 4, and so on. Full rules for learning new spells are provided in **Chapter 8: Magic.** Under normal circumstances, you may not learn more than one *Arcane Magic (Lore)* Talent. Further, you may not learn the *Bless* or *Invoke* Talents when you have the *Arcane Magic* Talent. You can unlearn this Talent for 100 XP, but will immediately lose all of your spells if you do so.

Argumentative

Max: Fellowship Bonus

Tests: Charm Tests when arguing and debating

You are used to arguing your points and winning. If you roll a successful Charm Test to debate with an opponent, you can choose to either use your rolled SL, or the number rolled on your units die. So, a successful roll of 24 could be used for +4 SL.

Artistic

Max: Dexterity Bonus

Tests: Art (Any)

You have a natural talent for art, able to produce precise sketches with nothing but time and appropriate media. This ability has several in-game uses, ranging from creating Wanted Posters to sketching accurate journals, and has spot benefits as determined by the GM. Further to this, add Art (Any) to any Career you enter; if it is already in Career, you may instead purchase the Skill for 5 XP fewer per Advance.

Attractive

Max: Fellowship Bonus

Tests: Charm Tests to influence those attracted to you

Whether it's your piercing eyes, your strong frame, or maybe the way you flash your perfect teeth, you know how to make the best use of what the gods gave you. When you successfully use Charm to influence those attracted to you, you can choose to either use your rolled SL, or the number rolled on your units die. So, a successful roll of 38 could be used for +8 SL.

Battle Rage

Max: Willpower Bonus

Tests: Melee Tests when Frenzied

You are better able to control your Frenzy in combat. You can end your Frenzy with a successful Cool Test at the end of the round.

Beat Blade

Max: Weapon Skill Bonus

Tests: Melee for a Beat Blade

You are trained to make sharp controlled blows to your opponent's weapon, creating an opening for an attack or simply impeding an incoming attack. For your Action, you can choose to Beat Blade before rolling. Perform a Melee Test; if successful, your opponent loses −1 Advantage, and loses a further −1 per SL you score. This Test is not Opposed. This Talent is of no use if your opponent has no weapon, or has a larger Size than you (see page 341).

Beneath Notice

Max: Fellowship Bonus

Tests: Stealth when in plain sight

The high and mighty pay no attention to your presence, knowing you are well beneath their notice. Assuming you are properly attired and not in an incongruous position, those of a higher Status Tier will normally ignore you unless your presence becomes inappropriate, which can make it very easy to listen into conversations you perhaps shouldn't. Further, characters with a higher Status Tier than you gain no Advantage for striking or wounding you in combat, as there is nothing to be gained for defeating such a lowly cur.

Berserk Charge

Max: Strength Bonus

Tests: Melee on a Round when you Charge

You hurl yourself at your enemies with reckless abandon, using the force of your charge to add weight to your strikes. When you Charge, you gain +1 Damage to all Melee attacks per level in this Talent.

Blather

Max: Fellowship Bonus

Tests: Charm to Blather

Called 'opening your mouth and letting your belly rumble' in Nordland, or simply 'bullshitting' in Ostland, blathering involves talking rapidly and incessantly, or talking volubly and at-length, about inconsequential or nonsense matters, and is used to verbally confuse and confound a target. You use your Charm Skill to Blather. Attempt an **Opposed Charm/Intelligence** Test. Success gives your opponent a *Stunned* Condition. Further, for each level you have in Blather, your opponent gains another *Stunned*

Condition. Targets *Stunned* by Blather may do nothing other than stare at you dumbfounded as they try to catch-up with or understand what you are saying. Once the last *Stunned* Condition comes to an end, the target finally gets a word in, and may not be best pleased with you — after all, you have been talking about nothing or nonsense for some time. Should you stop talking, your opponent immediately loses all *Stunned* Conditions caused by your Blather. Generally, you can only attempt to Blather at a character once per scene, or perhaps longer as determined by the GM, as the target soon wises up to your antics.

Bless (Divine Lore)

Max: 1

You are watched over by one of the Gods and can empower simple prayers. You can now deploy the Blessings of your deity as listed in **Chapter 7: Religion and Belief.** Under normal circumstances, you may only ever know one Divine Lore for the Bless Talent..

Bookish

Max: Intelligence Bonus
Test: Research

You are as at home in a library as a seaman at sea or a farmer a-farming. When using Research, you may reverse the dice of any failed Test if this will score a success.

Break and Enter

Max: Strength Bonus
Tests: Melee when forcing or breaking inanimate objects

You are an expert at quickly breaking down doors and forcing entry. You may add +1 Damage for each level in this Talent when determining damage against inanimate objects such as windows, chests, doors, and similar.

Briber

Max: Fellowship Bonus
Tests: Bribery

You are an exceedingly skilled briber. The GM should reduce the base cost of any required bribe by 10% per level you have in Briber, to a minimum of 10% of the original amount.

Cardsharp

Max: Intelligence Bonus
Tests: Gamble and Sleight of Hand when playing card games

You are used to playing, and winning, at cards, although your methods *may* involve a little cheating. When you successfully use Gamble or Sleight of Hand when playing cards, you can choose to either use your rolled SL, or the number rolled on your units die. So, a successful roll of 28 could be used for +8 SL. If you play a real card game to represent what is happening in-game, you may receive an extra number of cards per deal equal to your level in Cardsharp, then discard down to the appropriate hand-size before each round of play.

Careful Strike

Max: Initiative Bonus

You are skilled at hitting your enemy exactly where you want to, either at range or in melee. You may modify your Hit Location result by up to +/–10 per time you have this Talent. So, if you had this Talent twice and hit location 34, the Right Arm, you could modify this down to 14, the Left Arm, or up to 54, the Body (see page 159).

Carouser

Max: Toughness Bonus
Tests: Charm at Parties, Gossip at Parties, Consume Alcohol

You are a seasoned drinker and know how to party hard. You may reverse the dice of any failed Consume Alcohol Test if this will score a Success.

Catfall

Max: Agility Bonus
Tests: Athletics when falling

You are nimble and balanced like a cat, and are able to fall much greater distances unharmed than others might. Whenever you fall, you attempt an Athletics Test. If successful, reduce the distance fallen by 1 yard, +1 extra yard per +1 SL scored, for the purposes of calculating Damage.

Cat-tongued

Max: Fellowship Bonus
Tests: Charm when lying

Like Ranald the Trickster God, you blend truth and lies as if there were no difference. When using Charm to lie, listeners do not get to oppose your Charm with their Intuition to detect if there is something fishy in what you say.

Chaos Magic (Lore)

Max: Number of Spells available in chosen Chaos Magic Lore

By accident or design you have lost a portion of your soul to one of the Dark Gods, and can now practice the foul magics of Chaos. Your ruinous patron immediately grants you access to a single spell from the chosen Lore (most commonly the Nurgle, Slaanesh, or Tzeentch Lores) and you gain a Corruption point as the spell infiltrates your mind, never to be forgotten.

Each time you take this Talent, which always costs 100 XP per time instead of the normal cost, you learn another spell from your chosen Lore and gain a Corruption point. For more about the available spells, see **Chapter 8: Magic.** Under normal circumstances, you may only ever know one Lore of Chaos Magic.

Combat Aware

Max: Initiative Bonus
Tests: Perception during melee

You are used to scanning the battlefield to make snap decisions informed by the shifting tides of war. You may take a **Challenging (+0) Perception** Test to ignore Surprise, which is modified by circumstance as normal.

Combat Master

Max: Agility Bonus

Your accumulated years of combat experience allow you to keep lesser fighters at bay. For each level in this Talent, you count as one more person for the purposes of determining if one side outnumbers the other. This Talent only comes into play when you are out-numbered. See page 162 for the rules for out-numbering.

Combat Reflexes
Max: Initiative Bonus

You react like a flash of lightning. Add 10 to your Initiative for each level in this Talent when determining Combat Initiative.

Commanding Presence
Max: Fellowship Bonus
Tests: Leadership

Your presence fills others with hushed awe and admiration. Such is your aura of authority, those with a lower Status may not resist your Leadership tests with their Willpower. Of course, enemies are still no more likely to respect or obey you, but the common folk rarely stand against you.

Concoct
Max: Intelligence Bonus
Tests: Lore (Apothecary)

You are skilled at making potions, philtres, and draughts on the go. You may take one free *Crafting* Endeavour to use Lore (Apothecary) without need of a Workshop. Other *Crafting* Endeavours use the normal rules.

Contortionist
Max: Agility Bonus
Tests: Perform and Agility Tests when contorting helps

You can bend and manipulate your body in a myriad of seemingly unnatural ways. This allows you to squeeze through unlikely gaps and bend your body in crazy ways, giving benefits determined by the GM, possibly with a successful Agility test.

Coolheaded
Max: 1

You gain a permanent +5 bonus to your starting Willpower Characteristic this does not count towards your Advances.

Crack the Whip
Max: Dexterity Bonus
Tests: Drive or Ride Tests when Fleeing or Running

You know how to get the most out of your animals. When an animal you control is Fleeing or Running, it gains +1 Movement if you are using a whip.

Craftsman (Trade)
Max: Dexterity Bonus
Tests: Trade (any one)

You have true creative talent. Add the associated Trade Skill to any Career you enter. If the Trade Skill is already in your Career, you may instead purchase the Skill for 5 XP fewer per Advance.

Criminal
Max: None

You are an active criminal making money from illegal sources, and you're not always quiet about it. For the purposes of securing money, either when Earning during play or performing an *Income* Endeavour, refer to the following table:

Career Level	Bonus Money per time the Talent is taken
1	+2d10 brass pennies
2	+1d10 silver shillings
3	+2d10 silver shillings
4	+1 gold crown

Because of your obvious criminal nature, others consider you lower Status than them unless they also have the *Criminal* Talent, where Status is compared as normal — perhaps you have gang tattoos, look shifty, or are just rough around the edges, it's your choice. Because of this, local law enforcers are always suspicious of you and suspect your motivations, which only gets worse the more times you have this Talent, with the exact implications determined by the GM. Lawbreakers without the *Criminal* Talent earn significantly less coin but are not obviously the sort to be breaking the law, so maintain their Status. With GM consent, you may spend XP to remove levels of the *Criminal* Talent for the same XP it cost to buy.

Deadeye Shot
Max: 1

You always hit an opponent right between the eyes… or wherever else you intended to hit. Instead of reversing the dice to determine which Hit Location is struck with your ranged weapons, you may pick a location.

Dealmaker
Max: Fellowship Bonus
Tests: Haggle

You are a skilled businessman who knows how to close a deal. When using the Haggle skill, you reduce or increase the price of the products by an extra 10%.

Note: The GM may put a lower limit on prices here to show a seller refusing to sell below cost.

Detect Artefact
Max: Initiative Bonus
Tests: Intuition tests to detect magical artefacts

You are able to sense when magic lies within an artefact. You may attempt an Intuition Test for any magical artefact touched. If successful, you sense the item is magical; further, each SL also provides a specific special rule the item uses, if it has any. Normally, you may only attempt this Test once per artefact touched.

Diceman
Max: Intelligence Bonus
Tests: Gamble and Sleight of Hand when playing dice games

You are a dicing master, and all claims you cheat are clearly wrong. When you successfully use Gamble or Sleight of Hand when playing with dice, you can choose to either use your rolled SL, or the number rolled on your units die. So, a successful roll of 06 could be used for +6 SL. If you play any real-life dice games to represent in-game dice games, always roll extra dice equal to your Diceman level and choose the best results.

Dirty Fighting

Max: Weapon Skill Bonus
Tests: Melee (Brawling)

You have been taught all the dirty tricks of unarmed combat. You may choose to cause an extra +1 Damage for each level in Dirty Fighting with any successful Melee (Brawling) hit.

Note: using this Talent will be seen as cheating in any formal bout.

Disarm

Max: Initiative Bonus
Tests: Melee Tests concerning this Talent

You are able to disarm an opponent with a careful flick of the wrist or a well-aimed blow to the hand. For your Action, you may attempt an **Opposed Melee/Melee** test. If you win, your opponent loses a held weapon, which flies 1d10 feet in a random direction (with further effects as determined by the GM). If you win by 2 SL, you can determine how far the weapon is flung instead of rolling randomly; if you win by 4 SL, you can also choose the direction the weapon goes in; if you win by 6 SL or more, you can take your opponent's weapon if you have a free hand, plucking it from the air with a flourish. This Talent is of no use if your opponent has no weapon, or is a larger Size than you (see page 341).

WE'RE DOOMED!

The following are examples of Doomings to inspire your own creations for the *Doomed* Talent:

- From darkness cometh the raven.
- Beasts of the field hath eyes for thee.
- Plague and dark disease shall bring thee to thy knees.
- Absence makes thy heart grow weaker.
- The sword shalt bring no justice, only thine end.
- The bun! The pastry! The pie! Lo, they are Morr's dishes!
- The drummer beats out thine end.
- Thine end is not thine end!
- Though shalt sup deep of the cup of corruption.
- High places bring a low end.

Distract

Max: Agility Bonus
Tests: Athletics to Distract

You are trained in simple movements to distract or startle your opponent, drawing eyes from your true intent. You may use your Move to perform a Distraction. This is resolved by an **Opposed Athletics/Cool** Test. If you win, your opponent can gain no Advantage until the end of the next Round.

Doomed

Max: 1

At the age of 10, a Priest of Morr called a Doomsayer took you aside to foretell your death in an incense-laden, coming-of-age ritual called the Dooming. In conjunction with your GM, come up with a suitable Dooming. Should your character die in a fashion that matches your Dooming, your next character gains a bonus of half the total XP your dead character accrued during play.

Drilled

Max: Weapon Skill Bonus
Tests: Melee Tests when beside an ally with Drilled

You have been trained to fight shoulder-to-shoulder with other soldiers. If an enemy causes you to lose Advantage when standing beside an active ally with the *Drilled* Talent, you may keep 1 lost Advantage for each time you've taken the *Drilled* Talent.

Dual Wielder

Max: Agility Bonus
Tests: Melee or Ranged when attacking with two weapons

When armed with two weapons, you may attack with both for your Action. Roll to hit with the weapon held in your primary hand. If you hit, determine Damage as normal, but remember to keep your dice roll, as you will use it again. If the first strike hits, once it is resolved, the weapon in your secondary hand can then target an available opponent of your choice using the same dice roll for the first strike, but reversed. So, if you rolled 34 to hit with the first weapon, you use 43 to hit with the second. Remember to modify this second roll by your off-hand penalty (−20 unless you have the *Ambidextrous* Talent). This second attack is Opposed with a new defending roll, and damage for this second strike is calculated as normal. The only exception to this is if you roll a Critical for your first strike. If this happens, use the roll on the Critical Table to also act as the roll for the second attack. So, if you scored a critical to the head and rolled 56 on the Critical table for a Major Eye Wound, your second attack would then strike out with a to-hit value of 56. If you choose to attack with both weapons, all your defensive rolls until the start of your next Turn suffer a penalty of −10. You do not gain an Advantage when you successfully strike or Wound an opponent when Dual Wielding unless both attacks hit.

Embezzle

Max: Intelligence Bonus
Tests: Intelligence (Embezzling)

You are skilled at skimming money from your employers without being detected. Whenever you secure money when Earning (during play or performing an *Income* Endeavour), you may attempt an **Opposed Intelligence** Test with your employer (assuming you have one). If you win, you skim 2d10 + SL brass pennies, 1d10 + SL silver shillings, or 1 + SL gold crowns (depending upon the size of the business in question, as determined by the GM) without being detected. If your employer wins by 6+ SL, you gain the money, but your embezzling is detected; what then happens is left to the GM. Any other result means you have failed to embezzle any money.

Enclosed Fighter

Max: Agility Bonus
Tests: Dodge in enclosed environments
You have learned to make the most benefit out of fighting in enclosed spaces. You ignore penalties to Melee caused by confined spaces such as tunnels, the frontline, small fighting pits, and similar, and can use the Dodge Skill, even if it would normally be disallowed due to lack of space.

Etiquette (Social Group)

Max: Fellowship Bonus
Tests: Charm and Gossip (Social Group)
You can blend in socially with the chosen group so long as you are dressed and acting appropriately. Example social groups for this Talent are: Criminals, Cultists, Guilders, Nobles, Scholars, Servants, and Soldiers. If you do not have the Talent, those with it will note your discomfort in the unfamiliar environment. This is primarily a matter for roleplaying, but may confer a bonus to Fellowship Tests at the GM's discretion.

Fast Hands

Max: Dexterity Bonus
Tests: Sleight of Hand, Melee (Brawling) to touch an opponent
You can move your hands with surprising dexterity. Bystanders get no passive Perception Tests to spot your use of the Sleight of Hand Skill, instead they only get to Oppose your Sleight of Hand Tests if they actively suspect and are looking for your movements.

Further, attempts to use Melee (Brawling) to simply touch an opponent gain a bonus of +10 × your level in Fast Hands.

Fast Shot

Max: Agility Bonus
Tests: Ranged when making a Fast Shot
If you have a loaded ranged weapon, you can fire it outside the normal Initiative Order before any other combatant reacts in the following Round. You roll to hit using all the normal modifiers. Employing *Fast Shot* requires both your Action and Move for your upcoming turn, and these will count as having been spent when your next turn arrives. If two or more characters use Fast Shot, the character who has taken this Talent most goes first. If any characters have taken *Fast Shot* an equal number of times, both shots are fired simultaneously, and should both be handled at the same time.

Fearless (Enemy)

Max: Willpower Bonus
Tests: Cool to oppose your Enemy's Intimidate, Fear, and Terror
You are either brave enough or crazy enough that fear of certain enemies has become a distant memory. With a single **Average (+20%) Cool** Test, you may ignore any Intimidate, Fear, or Terror effects from the specified enemy when encountered. Typical enemies include Beastmen, Greenskins, Outlaws, Vampires, Watchmen, and Witches.

Feint

Max: Weapon Skill Bonus
Tests: Melee (Fencing) for Feints
You have trained how to make false attacks in close combat to fool your opponent. You may now make a Feint for your Action against any opponent using a weapon. This is resolved with an **Opposed Melee (Fencing)/Melee** Test. If you win, and you attack the same opponent before the end of the next Round, you may add the SL of your Feint to your attack roll.

Field Dressing

Max: Intelligence Bonus

Tests: Heal during combat Rounds

You are used to treating wounds quickly. If you fail a Heal Test when using Bandages, you may reverse the result if this will score a success; however, if you do so, you may not score more than +1 SL as you focus on speed over accuracy.

Fisherman

Max: Initiative Bonus

Tests: Any Test involving fishing

You are a very capable fisherman and know all the best ways to land fish. Assuming a large enough body of water is available, you are automatically assumed to be able to fish enough to feed yourself and a number of others equal to your level in Fisherman, assuming you choose to spend at least an hour or so with a line and bait. You may secure more fish in addition to this using the normal rules for foraging (see page 127).

Flagellant

Max: Toughness Bonus

Tests: Any for resisting the Ruinous Powers

You have dedicated your pain to the service of your God. Each day, you must spend half a bell (half an hour) praying as you maintain a number of Wounds suffered equal to your level in Flagellent. Until you next sleep, if you have the *Frenzy* Talent you may enter Frenzy immediately without testing.

The *Frenzy* Talent is added to the Talent list of any career you are in. Should you fail to flagellate yourself on any given day, or allow your castigated flesh to be healed, you may not spend any Resilience or Resolve until you flagellate yourself again.

Flee!

Max: Agility Bonus

Tests: Athletics when Fleeing

When your life is on the line you are capable of impressive bursts of speed. Your Movement Attribute counts as 1 higher when Fleeing (see page 165).

Fleet Footed

Max: 1

You gain +1 to your Movement Attribute.

Frenzy

Max: 1

You can Frenzy as described on page 190.

Frightening

Max: Strength Bonus

Anyone sane thinks twice before approaching you. If you wish, you have a Fear Rating of 1 (see page 190). Add +1 to this number per extra time you have this Talent.

Furious Assault

Max: Agility Bonus

Tests: Melee when making extra attacks

Your blows follow one another in quick succession, raining down on your opponents with the fury of Ulric. Once per Round, if you hit an opponent in close combat, you may immediately spend an Advantage or your Move to make an extra attack (assuming you have your Move remaining).

Gregarious

Max: Fellowship Bonus

Tests: Gossip Tests with travellers

You just like talking to other folk and it seems they like talking to you. You may reverse any failed Gossip Test if this allows the Test to succeed.

Gunner

Max: Dexterity Bonus

You can reload blackpowder weapons with practiced ease. Add SL equal to your level in Gunner to any Extended Test to reload a Blackpowder weapon.

Hardy

Max: Toughness Bonus

You gain a permanent addition to your Wounds, equal to your Toughness Bonus. If your Toughness Bonus should increase, then the number of Wounds Hardy provides also increases.

Hatred (Group)

Max: Willpower Bonus

Tests: Willpower (Resist Group)

You are consumed with hatred for something in the Old World, as described on page 190. Each time you take this Talent you develop hatred for a new group. Examples you could take include: Beastmen, Greenskins, Monsters, Outlaws, Sigmarites, Undead, Witches.

Holy Hatred

Max: Fellowship Bonus

Your prayers drip with the hatred you feel for your blasphemous enemies. You deal +1 Damage with Miracles for each level in this Talent.

Holy Visions

Max: Initiative Bonus

Tests: Intuition Tests when on holy ground

You clearly see the great works of the Gods all around you. You automatically know when you enter Holy Ground, and may take an Intuition Test to receive visions (often obscure, and seen through the paradigm of your cult or individual belief-system) regarding the local area if significant events have occurred there in the past.

Hunter's Eye

Max: Initiative Bonus

Tests: Any Test to trail or capture game

You are a skilled hunter and know all the best techniques to find game. When travelling through well-stocked lands, you are automatically assumed to be able to hunt down enough game to feed yourself and a number of others equal to your level in Hunter's Eye, so long as you have time and the correct equipment. You may secure more food in addition to this using the normal rules for foraging (see page 127).

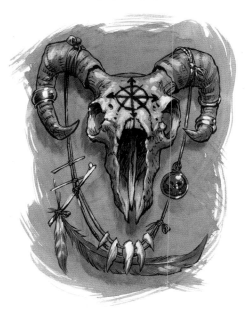

Impassioned Zeal

Max: Fellowship Bonus
Tests: Charm when speaking about your cause
When you talk about your cause, case, or religion, your words fill with passion and fervent zeal. You may double your Fellowship for the purposes of determining the number of people influenced by your Public Speaking (see page 142) when talking about your cause.

Implacable

Max: Toughness Bonus
It takes a lot to finish you off. You can ignore the Wound loss from a *Bleeding* Condition. Each level in this Talent lets you ignore the Wound loss from an extra *Bleeding* Condition.

In-fighter

Max: Dexterity Bonus
Tests: Melee when in-fighting, or to enter in-fighting
You are skilled at drawing in close to an opponent. You suffer no penalties for fighting against an opponent with a longer weapon than you. Further, if you use the optional rules for In-fighting (see page 297), gain a bonus of +10 to hit your opponent.

Inspiring

Max: Fellowship Bonus
Tests: Leadership during war
Your rousing words and pleas can turn the tide of a battle. Refer to the following table to see how many people you can now influence with your Leadership Skill (see page 126) when at war.

Talent Taken	Number of soldiers influenced
1	As normal × 5
2	As normal × 10
3	As normal × 20
4	As normal × 50
5	As normal × 100
6	As normal × 200
7	As normal × 500
8	As normal × 1000
9	All who can hear your inspiring voice

Example: *Abbess Birgitte van der Hoogenband's monastery is under attack by Greenskins, and things are going badly. So, she decides to bolster her soldiers' spirits with a Leadership Test, granting them +10 to all Psychology Tests. Her Leadership Test scores 3 SL. Given she has a Fellowship Bonus of 6, and she can influence her Fellowship Bonus + SL of her soldiers using Leadership, she bolsters 9 soldiers. However, as she has Inspiring 3, that number is multiplied by 20, meaning 180 of her soldiers take heart from her screamed encouragement to, 'HOLD THE LINE!'*

Instinctive Diction

Maximum: Initiative Bonus
Tests: Language (Magick) when casting
You instinctively understand the language of Magick, and are capable of articulating the most complex phrases rapidly without error. You do not suffer a Miscast if you roll a double on a successful Language (Magick) Test.

Invoke (Divine Lore)

Max: 1
You are blessed by one of the Gods and can empower one of your Cult's Miracles. Further, you may purchase extra miracles for 100 XP per miracle you currently know. So, if you already know 3 miracles, your next miracle costs 300 XP to purchase. Full rules for learning new miracles are provided in **Chapter 7: Religion and Belief**. Under normal circumstances, you may not learn more than one *Invoke (Divine Lore)* Talent. Further, you may not learn the *Petty Magic* or *Arcane Magic* Talents when you have the *Invoke* Talent. You can unlearn this Talent for 100 XP, but will lose all of your miracles if you do so, and will also garner the extreme disfavour of your God, with effects determined by your GM.

Iron Jaw

Max: Toughness Bonus
Tests: Endurance tests to resist *Stunned*
You are made of sturdy stuff and can weather even the strongest blows. Whenever you gain one or more *Stunned* Conditions, you may make an immediate **Challenging (+0) Endurance** Test to not take one of them, with each SL removing an extra *Stunned* Condition.

Iron Will

Max: Willpower Bonus

Tests: Cool Tests to oppose Intimidate

You have an indomitable will of iron, and will never willingly bow down before another. Use of the Intimidate skill does not cause Fear in you, and will not stop you speaking out against the intimidating party.

Jump Up

Max: 1

You are hard to keep down. You may perform a **Challenging (+0) Athletics** Test to immediately regain your feet whenever you gain a *Prone* Condition. This Athletics Test is often modified by the Strength behind the blow that knocks you down: for every +10 Strength the blow has over your Toughness, you suffer a penalty of −10 to the Athletics Test, and *vice versa*.

Kingpin

Max: 1

You have earned an air of respectability despite your nefarious ways. You may ignore the Status loss of the *Criminal* Talent.

Lightning Reflexes

Max: 1

You gain a permanent +5 bonus to your starting Agility Characteristic (this does not count towards your Advances).

Linguistics

Max: Intelligence Bonus

Tests: Language (All)

You have a natural affinity for languages. Given a month's exposure to any Language, you count the associated Language Skill as a Basic Skill with a successful Intelligence Test (which can be attempted once per month). **Note:** Linguistics only works for languages used to frequently communicate with others, so does not work with Language (Magick).

Lip Reading

Max: Initiative Bonus

Tests: Perception Tests concerning this Talent

You can tell what people are saying by simply watching their lips; you do not need to hear what they are saying. If you have an unobstructed view of the speaker's lower face, you can attempt a Perception Test to understand what they are saying.

Luck

Max: Fellowship Bonus

They say when you were born, Ranald smiled. Your maximum Fortune Points now equal your current Fate points plus the number of times you've taken Luck.

Magical Sense

Max: Initiative Bonus

Tests: Intuition Tests to detect Wizards

You are able to sense the Winds of Magic in others. You may attempt an **Average (+20) Intuition** Test whenever you encounter a spellcaster. If you pass, you sense the target is a witch. Further,

if you score an Astounding Success (+6), can also determine the target's highest Channelling Specialisation.

Magic Resistance

Max: Toughness Bonus

You are resistant to magic. The SL of any spell affecting you is reduced by 2 per point you have in this Talent. The SL of a spell is only modified by the highest Magic Resistance Talent within its target area. Further, you may never learn the *Arcane Magic, Bless, Invoke, Petty Magic,* or *Witch!* Talents.

Magnum Opus

Max: None

You are an undisputed master in your field, able to create work of such incredible complexity others can but sit back and marvel at your genius. Each time you take this Talent you may create a single, extraordinary work of art with one of your Art or Trade Skills. This work is unrivalled in your field, a unique piece that will always impress, giving bonuses as determined by the GM, most commonly to Fellowship Tests from those who have witnessed your astounding work. Selling the piece will net you at least ten times its normal value, and sometimes significantly more than this.

Marksman

Max: 1

You gain a permanent +5 bonus to your starting Ballistic Skill (this does not count towards your Advances).

Master of Disguise

Max: Fellowship Bonus

Tests: Entertain (Acting) when being someone else

You are an expert at taking on the appearance and mannerisms of others. With nothing but posture changes, face twisting, and careful use of appropriate clothing, you no longer look like yourself without having to use a Disguise Kit.

Master Orator

Max: Fellowship Bonus

You are skilled at firing up crowds. You gain a gain a SL bonus equal to your levels of Master Orator to any Charm Test when Public Speaking before a crowd.

Master Tradesman (Trade)

Max: Dexterity Bonus

Tests: Any appropriate Extended Trade Tests

You are exceptionally skilled at your specified Trade skill. You reduce the required SL of any Extended Test using your Trade Skill by the level of your *Master Tradesman* Talent.

Menacing

Max: Strength Bonus

Tests: Intimidate

You have an imposing presence. When using the Intimidate Skill, gain a SL bonus equal to your levels of Menacing.

Mimic

Max: Initiative Bonus

Tests: Entertain (Acting) Tests where accents are important

You have a good ear for accents and dialects, and can reproduce them accurately. You may replicate any accent you are exposed to for at least a day with an Initiative Test; this Test may be attempted once per day. Once passed, you may always mimic the accent, and locals will believe you to be one of their own.

Night Vision

Max: Initiative Bonus

Tests: Perception tests in low-light conditions

You can see very well in natural darkness. Assuming you have at least a faint source of light (such as starlight, moonlight, or bioluminescence) you can see clearly for 20 yards per level of Night Vision. Further, you can extend the effective illumination distance of any light sources by 20 yards per level of Night Vision.

Nimble Fingered

Max: 1

You gain a permanent +5 bonus to your starting Dexterity (this does not count towards your Advances).

Noble Blood

Max: 1

Tests: Any Test influenced by your Status

You are either born into the nobility, or otherwise elevated to it by in-game events. Assuming you are dressed appropriately, you are always considered of higher Status than others unless they also have the *Noble Blood* Talent, where Status is compared as normal.

Nose for Trouble

Max: Initiative Bonus

Tests: Any Test to spot Troublemakers

You are used to getting into, and preferably out of, trouble. You may attempt an Intuition Test to spot those seeking to cause trouble or seeking to cause you harm, even if normally you would not be allowed a Test (because of Talents or a Spell, for example). This Test will likely be Opposed if others are hiding, and the GM may prefer to take this Test on your behalf in secret so you do not know the results should you fail. If any troublemakers you spot start combat, you may ignore any *Surprised* Condition they would normally inflict.

Numismatics

Max: Initiative Bonus

Tests: Evaluate to establish the worth of coins

You are well versed with the different coinage of the Old World, and are adept at determining their value. You can judge the true value of a coin by experience alone, not even requiring a Test. Further, you can identify forged coins with a Simple Evaluate Test; it is never Opposed by the SL of the Forger.

Old Salt

Max: Agility Bonus

Tests: Sail (any Sea-worthy Vessels)

You are an experienced seaman, and are very used to sea life. You can ignore all negative modifiers to Tests at sea derived from poor weather, rolling ships, and similar. Further, you count as two seamen towards the minimum number of crew to pilot a sea-going vessel.

Orientation

Max: Initiative Bonus

Tests: Navigation

You have an instinctual feel for direction. You automatically know which direction is north with a glimpse at the stars, trees, or whatever other signs you are familiar with.

Panhandle

Max: Fellowship Bonus

Tests: Charm (Begging)

You are a skilled beggar, able to get even the most jaded individual to contribute to your cause. You can perform a Charm Test every half hour when Begging, not every hour (see page 120).

Perfect Pitch

Max: Initiative Bonus

Tests: Entertain (Sing), Language (Tonal Languages, such as Elthárin, Cathayan, and Magick)

You have perfect pitch, able to replicate notes perfectly and identify them without even making a Test. Further, add Entertain (Sing) to any Career you enter; if it is already in your Career, you may instead purchase the Skill for 5 XP fewer per Advance.

Petty Magic

Max: 1

You have the spark to cast magic within you and have mastered techniques to control it at a basic level. When you take this Talent, you manifest, and permanently memorise, a number of spells equal to your Willpower Bonus. You can learn extra Petty spells for the following cost in XP.

No. of Petty Spells Currently Known	XP Cost for a new spell
Up to Willpower Bonus × 1	50 XP
Up to Willpower Bonus × 2	100 XP
Up to Willpower Bonus × 3	150 XP
Up to Willpower Bonus × 4	200 XP
...and so on.	

So, if your Willpower Bonus is 3 and you had 3 Petty spells, it will cost you 50XP for the first learned spell, then 100 XP for the next three, and so on. Full rules for learning new spells are provided in **Chapter 8: Magic.**

Pharmacist

Max: Intelligence Bonus

Tests: Trade (Apothecary)

You are highly skilled at pharmacy, better able than most to make pills, ointments, unguents, oils, creams, and more. You may reverse any failed Trade (Apothecary) test if this allows the Test to succeed.

Pilot

Max: Initiative Bonus

Tests: Row or Sail Tests while navigating unsure waters

You are skilled at leading vessels through dangerous waters. If you fail a Test to pass through dangerous waters, you may reverse the result if it will score a success; however, if you do so, you may not score more than +1 SL as you catch the incoming danger at the last moment.

Public Speaker

Max: Fellowship Bonus

You are a skilled orator and know how to work large groups of people. Refer to the following table to see how many people you can now influence with your Charm Skill (see page 120) when Public Speaking.

Talent Taken	Number influenced
1	As normal × 5
2	As normal × 10
3	As normal × 20
4	As normal × 50
5	As normal × 100
6	As normal × 200
7	As normal × 500
8	As normal × 1000
9	All who can hear your golden voice

Pure Soul

Max: Willpower Bonus

Your soul is pure, quite resistant to the depredations of Chaos. You may gain extra Corruption points equal to your level of Pure Soul before having to Test to see if you become corrupt.

Rapid Reload

Max: Dexterity Bonus

You can reload ranged weapons with practiced ease. You add SL equal to your level in Rapid Reload to any Test to reload a ranged weapon.

Reaction Strike

Max: Initiative Bonus

Tests: Initiative Tests concerning this Talent

Your fast reactions have allowed you to fell many opponents before they have even swung their blades. When you are Charged, you may attempt a **Challenging (+0) Initiative** Test to gain an immediate Free Attack outside the normal turn sequence. This attack is resolved with whatever weapon you are carrying in your primary hand. You may make as many Reaction Strikes in a Round as you have levels in this Talent, but can only attack each individual charger once each.

Read/Write

Max: 1

You are one of the rare literate individuals in the Old World. You are assumed to be able to read and write (if appropriate) all of the Languages you can speak.

Relentless

Max: Agility Bonus

When you have your mind set on a target, there is nothing anyone can do to stop you reaching them. If you use Advantage when Disengaging, you may keep a number of Advantage equal to your level of Relentless. Further, you may use Advantage to Disengage even if you have lower Advantage than your opponents.

Resistance (Threat)

Max: Toughness Bonus

Tests: All those to resist the associated Threat

Your strong constitution allows you to more readily survive a specific threat. You may automatically pass the first Test to resist the specified threat, such as Magic, Poison, Disease, Mutation, every session. If SL is important, use your Toughness Bonus as SL for the Test.

Resolute

Max: Strength Bonus

You launch into attacks with grim determination. Add your level of Resolute to your Strength Bonus when you Charge.

Reversal

Max: Weapon Skill Bonus

Tests: Melee when defending

You are used to desperate combats, able to turn even the direst circumstances to your Advantage. If you win an **Opposed Melee** Test, instead of gaining +1 Advantage, you may take all your opponent's Current Advantage. If you do this, you do not cause any Damage, even if it is your Turn in the Round.

Riposte

Max: Agility Bonus

Tests: Melee when defending

Conforming to 'the best defence is offence', you respond to an incoming attack with a lightning-fast counterstrike of your own. If your weapon has the Fast quality, you may cause Damage when you are attacked, just as if it was your Action. You can Riposte a number of attacks per round equal to your Riposte level.

River Guide

Max: Initiative Bonus

Tests: Any Lore Test concerning river matters

You know all the tricks for navigating dangerous rivers. You don't need to Test for passing through dangerous stretches of water until the Difficulty for doing so is −10 or lower — you automatically pass all Tests easier than this. Further, if you have the appropriate Lore (Local) Skill, you need never Test for navigating dangerous waters — you are assumed to know the route through.

Robust

Max: Toughness Bonus

You are as tough as old boots and just soak up damage. You reduce all incoming Damage by an extra +1 per time you have taken the *Robust* Talent, even if the Damage cannot normally be reduced, but still suffer a minimum of 1 Wound from any Damage source.

Roughrider

Max: Agility Bonus

Tests: Ride (Horse) when in combat

You are at home in the saddle in even the most difficult of circumstances, and know how to get the best out of your mount during conflict. Assuming you have the Ride skill, you can direct your mount to take an Action, not just a Move, without a Ride test.

Rover

Max: Agility Bonus

Tests: Stealth Tests in a Rural environment

You are at home roaming the wild places. When using Stealth in a rural environment, bystanders do not get passive Perception Tests to detect you; they can only spot you if they are specifically on look-out, or watching for hidden spies.

Savant (Lore)

Max: Intelligence Bonus

Tests: Lore (chosen Lore)

You are exceptionally learned, and have a significant degree of specialised knowledge in a single field of study. You automatically know a number of pieces of correct information equal to you Savant (Lore) level about a relevant issue without having to test your Lore Skill. Testing, as always, will provide yet more information as normal as determined by the GM.

Savvy

Max: 1

You gain a permanent +5 bonus to your starting Intelligence Characteristic (this does not count towards your Advances).

Scale Sheer Surface

Max: Strength Bonus

Tests: Climb

You are an exceptional climber. You can attempt to climb even seemingly impossible surfaces such as sheer fortifications, ice shelves, plastered walls, and similar, and you ignore any penalties to Climb Tests derived from the difficulty of the surface climbed.

Schemer

Max: Intelligence Bonus

Tests: Intelligence Tests concerning this Talent

You are a master of politics and see conspiracy around every corner. Once per session, you may ask the GM one question regarding a political situation or entangled web of social connections; the GM will perform a secret Intelligence Test and provide you some observations regarding the situation based upon your SL.

Sea Legs

Max: Toughness Bonus

Tests: All those taken to resist Sea Sickness

You are used to the rolling motion of the oceans, and are very unlikely to get sea sick, even in the worst storms. Under normal conditions at sea, you need never Test to see if you become Sea Sick. At other times (such as a storm, or a magically induced bout of Sea Sickness), you can ignore any penalties to Tests to avoid Sea Sickness.

Seasoned Traveller

Max: Intelligence Bonus

Tests: Any Lore Test concerning local detail

You are an inquisitive soul who has travelled far and wide, learning all manner of local information. Add Lore (Local) to any Career you enter; if it is already in Career, you may purchase the Skill, both times — a different Speciality each time, such as Altdorf, Vorbergland, or Ubersreik — for 5 XP fewer per Advance.

Second Sight

Max: Initiative Bonus

Tests: Any Test to detect the Winds of Magic

You can perceive the shifting Winds of Magic that course from the Chaos Gates at the poles of the world. You now have the Sight (see page 233).

Secret Identity

Max: Intelligence Bonus

Tests: Entertain (Acting) Tests to support your secret identities

You maintain a secret identity that allows you to appear richer, or perhaps poorer, than you actually are. With GM permission, choose any one Career. As long as you are dressed appropriately, you may use the Social Status of the chosen Career you masquerade as rather than your own for modifying Fellowship Tests, and can even ignore the *Criminal* Talent. However, maintaining this identity will require Entertain (Acting) rolls when you encounter those who may recognise your falsehood. You may create a new Secret Identity for each level you have in this Talent.

Shadow

Max: Agility Bonus

Tests: Any Test involving Shadowing

You are skilled at following people without being spotted. You may use the Shadowing rules on page 130 without doing a Combined Test. Instead you test against just your Perception or your Stealth Skill, whichever is higher.

Sharp

Max: 1

You gain a permanent +5 bonus to your starting Initiative Characteristic (this does not count towards your Advances).

Sharpshooter
Max: 1

You can make aimed shots of exceptional accuracy. You ignore any negative Difficulty modifiers to Ranged Tests due to the size of your target.

Shieldsman
Max: Strength Bonus

Tests: Any Test to defend with a shield

You are skilled at using your shield to manoeuvre others in combat so you can take advantage of a desperate situation. When using a Shield to defend, you gain Advantage equal to the number of levels you have in Shieldsman if you lose the Opposed Test.

Sixth Sense
Max: Initiative Bonus

Tests: Intuition Tests involving your Sixth Sense

You get a strange feeling when you are threatened, and can react accordingly. The GM may warn you if you are walking into danger; this will normally come after a secret Intuition Test on your behalf. Further, you may ignore Surprise if you pass an Intuition Test.

Slayer
Max: 1

When determining Damage use your opponent's Toughness Bonus as your Strength Bonus if it is higher; always determine this before any other rules modify your Strength or Strength Bonus. Further, if your target is larger than you, and your score a Critical (see page 159), multiply all melee Damage you cause by the number of steps larger your target is (so, 2 steps = ×2, 3 steps = ×3, and so on); this multiplication is calculated after all modifiers are applied. See page 341 for more about *Size*.

Small
Max: 1

You are much shorter than most folk in the Old World. The full rules for different Sizes are found in **Chapter 12: Bestiary** on page 341.

Sniper
Max: 4

Tests: Ranged (Long–Extreme Range)

Distance is of no import to your shooting skills, and you are just as adept at picking off far away targets as those nearby. You suffer no penalties for shooting at Long range, and half the penalties for Extreme range.

Speedreader
Max: Intelligence Bonus

Tests: Research and Language Tests where speed of reading is important

You read books at a voracious pace. You may reverse a failed Research Test if this will grant success. If the speed at which you read is important during combat, a successful Language Test lets you read and fully comprehend a number of pages per Round equal to your SL plus Speedreader level (minimum of 1, even if you fail the Test).

Sprinter
Max: Strength Bonus

Tests: Athletics Tests concerning Running

You are a swift runner. Your Movement Attribute counts as 1 higher when Running.

Step Aside
Max: Agility Bonus

Tests: Dodge Tests to activate this Talent

You are skilled at being where enemy weapons are not. If you use Dodge to defend against an incoming attack and win the Opposed Test, you may move up to 2 yards as you dive away, and no longer count as Engaged. None of your opponents will gain a Free Attack when you do this.

Stone Soup
Max: Toughness Bonus

Tests: Endurance Tests to resist hunger

You are used to getting by with less, and know how to survive lean times. You can subsist on half the amount of food required without any negative penalties (bar feeling *really* hungry), and need only test for Starvation every 3 days, not 2 (see page 181).

Stout-hearted
Max: Willpower Bonus

Tests: Cool Tests to remove *Broken* Conditions

No matter how bad things get, you always seem to come back for more. You may attempt a Cool Test to remove a *Broken* Condition at the end of each of your Turns as well as at the end of the Round (see page 168 for more on this).

Strider (Terrain)
Max: Agility Bonus

Tests: Athletics Tests to traverse the Terrain

You are experienced in traversing difficult ground. You ignore all movement penalties when crossing over or through a specified terrain. Typical specialities include: Coastal, Deserts, Marshes, Rocky, Tundra, Woodlands.

Strike Mighty Blow
Max: Strength Bonus

You know how to hit *hard!* You deal your level of Strike Mighty Blow in extra Damage with melee weapons.

Strike to Injure

Max: Initiative Bonus

You are an expert at striking your enemies most vulnerable areas. You inflict your level of Strike to Injure in additional Wounds when you cause a Critical Wound.

Strike to Stun

Max: Weapon Skill Bonus

Tests: Melee Tests when Striking to Stun

You know where to hit an opponent to bring him down fast. You ignore the 'Called Shot' penalty to strike the Head Hit Location when using a melee weapon with the *Pummel* Quality (see page 298). Further, you count all improvised weapons as having the *Pummel* Quality.

Strong Back

Max: Strength Bonus

Tests: Row and Swim

You have a strong back that is used to hard work. You may add your levels in Strong Back to your SL in any Opposed Strength Tests, and can carry additional Encumbrance points of trappings (see page 293) equal to your level of Strong Back.

Strong Legs

Max: Strength Bonus

You have strong legs able to carry you great distances when you jump. Add your Strong Legs level to your SL in any Athletics Tests involving Leaping (see page 166).

Strong-minded

Max: Willpower Bonus

You are the epitome of determination and resolve. Add your level in Strong Minded to your maximum Resolve pool.

Strong Swimmer

Max: Strength Bonus

Tests: Swim

You are an especially strong swimmer and used to holding your breath for a long time underwater. Gain a bonus of your level in Strong Swimmer to your Toughness Bonus for the purposes of holding your breath.

Sturdy

Max: Strength Bonus

Tests: Strength Tests when lifting

You have a brawny physique, or are very used to carrying things. Increase the number of Encumbrance Points you can carry by your Sturdy level x 2.

Suave

Max: 1

You gain a permanent +5 bonus to your starting Fellowship Characteristic (this does not count towards your Advances).

Super Numerate

Max: Intelligence Bonus

Tests: Evaluate, Gamble

You have a gift for calculation and can work out the solution to most mathematical problems with ease. You may use a simple calculator to represent what your PC is capable of mentally computing.

Supportive

Max: Fellowship Bonus

Tests: Social Tests to influence a superior

You know what to say and when to make the most impact upon your superiors. When you successfully use a social Skill to influence those with a higher Status tier, you can choose to either use your rolled SL, or the number rolled on your units die. So, a successful roll of 46 could be used for +6 SL.

Sure Shot

Max: Initiative Bonus

You know how to find the weak spots in a target's armour. When you hit a target with a Ranged weapon, you may ignore Armour Points equal to your Sure Shot level.

Surgery

Max: Intelligence Bonus

Tests: Heal Tests outside combat rounds; i.e. when you have time to do it 'properly'

You are a surgeon, able to open and close the flesh in order to heal others. You can treat any Critical Wound marked as needing Surgery. You can also perform surgery to resolve internal issues with an **Extended Challenging (+0) Heal** Test with a target SL determined by the GM (usually 5–10) depending upon the difficulty of the procedure at hand. This will cause 1d10 Wounds and 1 *Bleeding* Condition per Test, meaning surgery has a high chance of killing a patient if the surgeon is not careful. After surgery, the patient must pass an **Average (+20) Endurance** Test or gain a *Minor Infection* (see page 187).

Tenacious

Max: Toughness Bonus

Tests: Endurance Tests for enduring hardships

You never give up, no matter how impossible your travails appear. You can double the length of time successful Endurance Tests allow you to endure a hardship. This includes enduring prolonged riding, exposure, rituals, and similar adversities.

Tinker

Max: Dexterity Bonus

Tests: Trade Tests to repair broken items

You are somewhat of a Johann-of-all-trades, able to repair almost anything. You count all non-magical Trade Skills as Basic when repairing broken items.

Tower of Memories

Max: Intelligence Bonus

A recollection technique first instigated by the Cult of Verena, reputedly from Elven practices taught by the Loremasters of Hoeth, Tower of Memories allows you to perfectly recall a sequence of facts by storing them in an imaginary spire. You can recall a sequence as long as your Intelligence without having to make a Test. For every 10 more items you attempt to memorise, you must make an increasingly difficult Intelligence Test to recall the list correctly, starting at **Very Easy (+60)** for +10, **Easy (+40)** for +20, **Average (+20)** for +30, and so on. Beyond it's obvious utility for Gamble Tests, where having this Talent adds a bonus of +20 to +60 depending upon how useful recalling sequences is to the game at hand, the GM can apply bonuses to other Tests as appropriate. Each time you take this Talent you may recall an extra sequence without having to forget a previously stored one.

Trapper

Max: Initiative Bonus
Tests: Perception Tests to spot traps, Set Trap

You are skilled at spotting and using traps. You may take a Perception Test to spot traps automatically without having to tell the GM of your intention; the GM may prefer to make some of these Tests on your behalf in private.

Trick Riding

Max: Agility Bonus
Tests: Dodge Tests on Horseback, Ride (Horse)

You are capable of amazing feats of agility on horseback. You can use any of your Performer Skills and unmodified Dodge skill when on horseback. Further, when mounted, you can make your Move at the start of the Round instead of on your Turn.

Tunnel Rat

Max: Agility Bonus
Tests: Stealth Tests when underground

You are at home in tunnels, sewers, and other underground environments. When using Stealth in an underground environment, bystanders do not get passive Perception Tests to detect you; they can only spot you if they are specifically on look-out, or watching for hidden others.

Unshakable

Max: Willpower Bonus
Tests: Cool Tests to resist Blackpowder panic

You are a jaded veteran who has survived more than one hail of shots from Blackpowder weapons. You need only take a Cool Test to resist a *Broken* Condition if you are successfully wounded by a Blackpowder weapon, not just if you are shot at.

Very Resilient

Max: 1

You gain a permanent +5 bonus to your starting Toughness Characteristic (this does not count towards your Advances).

Very Strong

Max: 1

You gain a permanent +5 bonus to your starting Strength Characteristic (this does not count towards your Advances).

War Leader

Max: Fellowship Bonus
Skills: Leadership Tests during War

Your stern gaze and inspiring words motivate your soldiers to fight on to the end. All subordinates able to see you may add your level in War Leader to their SL in one Willpower Test per Round. This bonus does not stack.

War Wizard

Max: 1

You are trained to cast magic while in the thick of combat. On your Turn, you may cast one Spell with a Casting Number of 5 or less for free without using your Action. However, if you do this, you may not cast another spell this Turn.

Warrior Born

Max: 1

You gain a permanent +5 bonus to your starting Weapon Skill Characteristic (doesn't count as Advances).

Waterman

Max: Agility Bonus
Tests: Sail Tests for river-going vessels

You are an experienced freshwater sailor and are well-versed with river vessels. You can ignore all negatives to your Tests when onboard a barge derived from rolling waters, swaying vessels, unsure footing, and similar. Further, you count as two boatmen towards the minimum number of crew to pilot a river vessel.

Wealthy

Max: None

You are fabulously wealthy, and are rarely ever short of coin. When Earning (including *Income* Endeavours) you secure +1 GC per time you have this Talent.

Well-prepared

Max: Initiative Bonus

You are used to anticipating the needs of others, and yourself. A number of times per session equal to your level of Well-Prepared, you may pull the trapping required for the current situation from your backpack (or similar) as long as it is Encumbrance 0, could feasibly been bought recently, and doesn't stretch credibility too far. This could be anything from a flask of spirits to fortify a wounded comrade to a pfennig-whistle needed by a passing entertainer. Whenever you do this, you must deduct the cost for the prepared item from your purse, representing the coin you spent earlier.

Witch!

Max: Willpower Bonus

You have learned magic through trial and error. Add Language (Magick) to any Career you enter; if it is already in your Career, you may purchase the Skill for 5 XP fewer per Advance. Further, you may spend 1 Resilience point to immediately cast any spell as if it were one of your Arcane Lore spells; you also instantly memorise that spell as one of your Arcane Lore spells for 0 XP. You can do this a number of times equal to your level in this Talent.

• RULES •

The game is afoot; grim and perilous. The players lean forward in their seats, listening intently to the GM describing the plot as it unfolds, excitedly explaining their characters' actions in response and breathlessly waiting to hear what happens next…

Roleplaying games often work best with minimal interruptions to this narrative flow — the smoother the game proceeds, the more involved everyone will be. However, as the adventure develops, situations will arise where the outcome of a character's action is uncertain. Maybe a character leaps from a wall to hack down a pillaging Goblin — will they land poised for action or flat on their face?

Sometimes, especially with events that don't affect the players too much, the GM can simply decide the outcome and relate it to the group. However, if the success or failure of the action has significant impact on the players, it is more tense and dramatic to roll some dice and let the fates and a character's capabilities determine whether they succeed or fail. Using the game rules also lets players assess their chances and make decisions accordingly — it's a fair and transparent way to resolve things.

At the core of the rules are Tests — rolls of the dice that determine outcomes. There are also additional rules for more complex or unusual tasks – see the box for a handy list with page references. The GM should be familiar with these, but as a player you'll be fine so long as you know the basics of the different kinds of Test.

RULES REFERENCE

Simple Tests – page 149
Dramatic Tests – page 152
Opposed Tests – page 153
Extended Tests – page 154
Combat – page 156
Conditions – page 167
Fate and Resilience – page 170
Injury – page 172
Corruption – page 182
Diseases and Infection – page 186
Psychology – page 190

THE GOLDEN RULE

The rules exist to help you enjoy epic stories in the Warhammer world, so they should never be a barrier to having fun. Arguably, the most important rule in this book is:

If a rule negatively impacts fun for your group, change it or ignore it.

This rule is so important, you will find alternative and optional rules throughout this book to support building a ruleset that best suits your group and your style of play. If it's your first game, ignore these until you become more familiar with how it all works, and you can experiment with some of the variants as the mood takes you.

Be careful not to confuse 'fun' with 'always succeeding' — a sense of risk and the real possibility of failure is an important part of drama. Things going wrong provides players with the challenge of recovering from setbacks, a central part of any hero's journey.

TESTS

'Aye, there are times when things just go wrong. Really, badly wrong. Like that time half way up the Bögen when Olaf jumped into a tree but missed and hit that jagged branch square on. I think he's there still, although there's probably not much of him left after the animals had a season's grazing. By Sigmar's grace, sit yourself down and have some cheese, there's nothing good for you out there!'

– Dieter Käsegeier, Cheesemonger, ex-Adventurer

When your character takes an action, the GM will let you know what happens next. Sometimes, the GM will make a call based on your abilities and any other factors and decide that you achieved what you were attempting, or that you didn't. If the GM isn't sure of the outcome, or if the situation is significant or dangerous, they can resolve the action using the rules. There are a few options, as the **Using Tests** box shows. Tests compare a dice roll to one of the characteristics or skills on your character sheet and provide an outcome.

SIMPLE TESTS

Simple Tests are used when you need to determine if your character succeeds or fails at a simple task. Does Molli leap the

churning stream? Can Wilhelm charm a lower price from the truculent merchant? Often, a quick yes or no answer to these questions allows your adventure to progress swiftly. The exception to this is when a failure would significantly impact the progress of the adventure, in which case you should use a Dramatic Test (see page 152) instead.

To perform a Simple Test, you roll d100 (see Throwing Bones on page 6) and compare the result rolled to the Skill or Characteristic best suited to the action you are attempting.

Note this test may be modified by the GM if it is notably easy or hard to complete (see Difficulty on page 153).

If you roll lower or equal to the Skill or Characteristic, the Test's outcome is a success, and your Character performs the task.

If you roll higher than the Skill or Characteristic, the Test's outcome is a failure, and your Character does not perform the task.

Whatever the outcome of the Test, after testing, the GM should describe what just happened so everyone understands how the Test has impacted the story.

Example: *Molli runs across Altdorf's Königsplatz on a cold, winter's night. The cobbles are blanketed in thick snow hiding treacherous ice beneath, but with a gang of thugs in eager pursuit Molli is not about to slacken her pace. The GM calls for a Simple Athletics Test to see if Molli can cross the slippery platz safely. Molli's Athletics is 42, and her player rolls d100 scoring a 17. As 17 is below Molli's Athletics of 42, the result is a success, so the answer is yes, Molli can cross without mishap. The GM says that Molli crosses the open snow and darts into the relative safety of one of the many dark alleyways at the other side. If her player had rolled over 42, Molli would have slipped, and the thugs would have been upon her!*

TALENTS AND TESTS

Some Talents can improve a Test's chances of success, or grant you access to unique Tests allowing you to attempt extraordinary feats. For more details regarding this, refer to Talents on page 132.

AUTOMATIC FAILURE AND SUCCESS

No matter how skilled or talented a character is, there is always a chance of failure. Equally, there is always a chance of success in **WFRP**, no matter the odds stacked against you.

If you roll 96–00 on any Test, it is *always* a failure. A failure occurs even if your modified characteristic or skill is 96 or higher. Similarly, if you roll 01–05 on a Test, it is *always* a success. A success occurs even if your modified characteristic or skill is less than 01–05.

OPTIONS: AUTOSUCCESS? NOT AT MY TABLE!

Not everybody likes a 5% chance of auto-success on any Test. Similarly, not everyone likes the same chance of auto-failures. If this describes you, then simply change the numbers to your taste. The most common alternative is 96–00 always fails, and 01 always succeeds.

VON MEINKOPF'S PREEMINENT PROBABILITY PARAPHERNALIA

The rules use a selection of mechanics to modify or manipulate percentile rolls. The following explains these in detail:

Rolling a Double: Rolling a double means both the tens and the units die of a percentile test have rolled the same number. For example: 11, 22, 33, 44 and so on.

Reroll: A reroll is when you disregard the result of a dice roll, and roll it again. Once a Test has been rerolled, it cannot be rerolled again under normal circumstances.

Reverse: To reverse a percentile roll, you swap the tens result with the units result. So, a roll of 58 becomes 85, or a roll of 51 becomes 15. Obviously, if you roll a double, it will have the same result when reversed, so 77 reverses to 77.

Modifiers: These numbers are added or subtracted to the one of your Skill to make the Test easier or more difficult. This is most often referred to as the Difficulty of the roll (see page 153).

If you want to introduce some test-specific outcomes for particularly dramatic moments, you can use the methods above as a toolkit.

RESOLVING ACTIONS

An Event or Action with uncertain outcome takes place

Is success or failure going to be particularly important, exciting or dramatic?

YES → Do you need to find out how well the Test succeeds or fails?
- **YES** → Make a Dramatic Test → How well did you do? Roll d100 and find out. See page 152.
- **NO** → Make a Simple Test → Do you succeed? Roll d100 to score a yes or no answer. See page 149.

NO → Does the decision about success or failure need to be made randomly?
- **YES** → Make a Simple Test
- **NO** → GM decides on success or failure based on character's relevant abilities

GREAT GAME RULES

Game rules establish a mutually agreed and understood foundation for how **WFRP** works. They are important as they keep things fair and demonstrate the setting's internal logic. But having the best game experiences depends on your interactions with the other players, too. Here are some points to consider to help make your games the best they can be:

Everyone's invited to the fun: Be welcoming to new or inexperienced players.

Off-limits: Respect people who don't want sex/violence/horror or other uncomfortable topics in the game, and accept they don't have to justify why. There are many very good (potentially traumatic) reasons.

Consideration: Nobody's fun should come at another's expense.

Table manners: Discuss what's OK and not OK at the game table. Eating, use of electronic devices, drinking alcohol, texting, using social media? All of these and more are all worth discussing before play.

Involve others: Don't try to hog every scene, give everyone time in the spotlight.

Teamwork: Don't be needlessly awkward or make your character wander off alone without good reason, (splitting the group slows down play).

Respect your GM: Let the GM worry about the rules — rules arguments are a fun killer (and you can always discuss it with the GM *after* the game).

Contribute: Your actions should help progress the story and develop your character.

Play the game: It's not always about winning, it's about the stories you tell and the fun you have. Sometimes your Character might die, accept that, and, if it happens, make it memorable and fun. Also remember, sometimes, it's just better to run away!

Good mentors: If you have younger players in your group, it is everyone's responsibility to welcome, help, and maintain age-appropriate behaviour.

OPTIONS: TESTS ABOVE 100%

Having exceptional abilities makes it quite possible that a modified Characteristic or Skill may be 100% or higher when tested. If this occurs in your game, you may wish to use the following optional rule to help represent such an awesome figure.

A successful Test gains a bonus of +1 SL for each full 10% a tested Characteristic or Skill exceeds 100%.

Example: *Countess Emmanuelle von Liebwitz has a Charm Skill of 115%: her Fellowship characteristic of 80% plus her Charm advances of +35% (see **Advances** on page 47 for more on this); thus, if she succeeds at a Charm Test, she gains a bonus of +1 SL over an above what she earns by rolling or from any applicable Talents.*

DRAMATIC TESTS

Simply knowing if you pass or fail is not always enough; sometimes, it is useful to know how well you succeed or how badly you fail a Test. This is especially the case when pitching your Skills against another (see Opposed Tests), which is often the case for magic and combat. So, when you want to know exactly how well or badly you have performed a Test, use a Dramatic Test. Another reason for choosing a Dramatic Test is when the progress of the adventure could depend on the Test. Dramatic Tests provide outcomes rather than straight success or failure, which means that even if the test is 'failed' the adventure continues, albeit in a more challenging way than if you had achieved a success. Dramatic Tests are handled in the same way as Simple Tests, and still provide success or failure as outcomes, but the results have more detail. This detail is governed by Success Levels.

Success Levels

Success Levels (shortened to SL) are used to describe the effectiveness of a Test. To determine the SL of a Test, subtract the 10s number of the rolled dice from the 10s number of the Characteristic or Skill being tested, including any modifiers (see Difficulty for more on modifiers). The higher the SL, the better the outcome; the lower it is, the worse things have gone. Marginal results, where you succeed or fail a Test with +0 or –0 SL, could either be interpreted as succeeding or failing by a whisker, with minimal consequences either good or bad, or could give inconclusive results allowing you try again.

Example: *Eichengard is careering across muddy fields atop his stallion, desperately fleeing the lands of a disgruntled noble when a wall blocks his passage. He decides to push his mount to jump, and the GM calls for a **Dramatic Ride (Horse)** test. Eichengard rolls 29 against his Ride (Horse) skill of 41. The 10s number of the Skill being tested is 4, and the 10s number rolled was 2, so the test succeeds with +2 SL (4–2=2) and he clears the wall with space to spare. Buoyed by his success, Eichengard twists around in his saddle and makes the sign of the twin-tailed comet at the horsemen pursuing him. Unfortunately, this means he's not paying attention to where he's going. The GM calls for a **Dramatic Perception** Test, and Eichengard's player rolls 82, significantly higher than Eichengard's Perception skill of 39. The 10s number of the roll is 8, and the 10s number of the skill being tested is 3, so the test has failed with –5 SL (3–8=–5). He has failed rather badly. As Eichengard laughs at the increasingly distant guards sent to capture him, a low-lying branch slams hard into his side, knocking him flying.*

OPTIONS: FAST SL

Determining your SL involves some simple mathematics, so calculating it can slow play during fraught scenes. Fortunately, there is a fast way to calculate SL for those looking to keep their games as fast as possible. When you pass a Test, use the result of the tens die as your SL. So, if you passed a Test with a roll of 36, you score +3 SL. With this optional rule, the closer you roll to your tested Skill, the better, rather than rolling low being best. If a Test fails, you calculate SL as normal, taking your rolled tens die from your tested Skill to determine your negative SL.

OUTCOMES TABLE

SL	Result	Have You Succeeded?
+6 or more	Astounding Success	**Yes, perfectly!:** The result is as good as it can be, perhaps with extra luck and fortunate coincidences thrown in!
+4 to +5	Impressive Success	**Yes, and…:** You achieve your goal with style, exceeding your expectations.
+2 to +3	Success	**Yes:** You achieve a solid success.
+0 to +1	Marginal Success	**Yes, but…:** You more or less achieve what you intend, but imperfectly, and perhaps with an unpredictable side effect.
–1 to –0	Marginal Failure	**No, but…:** You marginally fail, perhaps accomplishing a portion of what you intended.
–2 to –3	Failure	**No:** You just plain do it wrong.
–4 to –5	Impressive Failure	**No, and…:** Not only do you mess up, but you also cause additional things to go wrong.
-6 or less	Astounding Failure	**No, not in any way!:** Everything goes wrong in the worst possible way. The GM will likely add to your woes with unanticipated consequences of your actions. Surely no-one is this unlucky; you have clearly offended the gods.

25

Exactly how well you succeed or fail is shown in the Outcomes Table, which can be used to inspire descriptions of what just happened. Much like simple tests offer a yes or no in answer to 'do I succeed at this test?', dramatic tests also provide answers, just more of them.

If you automatically succeed due to rolling 01–05 (see page 150), you score +1 SL or the SL you rolled, whichever is higher.

If you automatically fail due to rolling 96–00 (see page 150), you score –1 SL or the SL you rolled, whichever is lower.

OPTIONS: CRITICALS & FUMBLES

We introduce some extra rules for Criticals and Fumbles in Combat later in this chapter. They can also be used to add drama for *all* Tests, creating a game that feels epic in scope as extreme results become commonplace. If that describes your group, you could use the following optional rule.

Any Test scoring a success that also rolls a double is called a *Critical*, meaning you've scored an Astounding Success from the Outcome Table; and any failure including a double is a *Fumble*, resulting in an Astounding Failure from the Outcome Table. This optional rule works well with Simple Tests, providing a fun addition to the yes or no results offered there.

CHARACTERISTIC TESTS

Sometimes you may want to do something that is not covered by one of the Skills. In these rare cases, you make a Characteristic Test instead of a Skill Test. The GM determines the most appropriate Characteristic for what you are attempting, and you Test it as normal.

DIFFICULTY

Not all Tests are equal. Climbing a fence is laughably easy but ascending the face of a sheer cliff is incredibly tough. To represent this, the GM assigns bonuses or penalties to Tests called the *Difficulty*. While published adventures define the difficulty for

the GM — for example: calling for a **Hard (−20) Research** test — there are many instances where the GM has to determine them on the fly. Making judgments like this is one of the most common functions of the GM. For each Test, whether simple or dramatic, the GM should decide the Difficulty and then consult the Difficulty Table to determine the appropriate modifier. GMs may choose to assign even greater bonuses or penalties than those shown on the table, but such modifiers should only be used in extreme situations.

Example: *Valentyn, a Jade Wizard, tries to find the tracks of an unruly stag he is hunting. Under normal circumstances, he would perform an* **Average (+20) Track** *Test with his skill of 41, thus test against 61; however, the GM decides that as the rain last night washed away most of the tracks the task is Very Hard and imposes a −30 penalty. Therefore, Valentyn has to roll 11 or under (41−30=11) to succeed. He rolls a 35, which would have been a success under normal circumstances, but in this circumstance is a failure, indicating the rain has foiled the Jade Wizard's attempt.*

DIFFICULTY TABLE

Difficulty	Test Modifier
Very Easy	+60
Easy	+40
Average	+20
Challenging	no modifier
Difficult	−10
Hard	−20
Very Hard	−30

Opposed Tests

Sometimes you match your capabilities directly against those of an opponent. The rules represent this with a special Dramatic Test called an Opposed Test. Opposed Tests are an important part of **WFRP**'s combat rules later in this chapter, but are used in many other situations, as well.

An Opposed Test is handled just like any other Dramatic Test, but both parties make a Test. The party with the highest SL wins the Test. If both participants score the same SL, the party with the higher tested Skill or Characteristic wins. In the unlikely event there is still a tie, then one of two things, as determined by the GM, occurs: 1) there is a stalemate, and nothing happens; 2) both parties re-roll until there is a clear winner.

Example: *Having floored an important Reiklander baron at a party, Salundra makes to leave the ballroom; however, some uneasy guardsmen block her passage, knowing they really should detain the noble captain. Salundra scowls as she approaches.*

The GM calls for an Intimidate Test and opposes it with the guardsmen's commanding officer's Leadership Test. Both the player and the GM roll. Salundra's Intimidate is 47. The officer's Leadership is 46. Salundra rolls a 04, scoring +4 SL (4–0=4), while the GM rolls 16, scoring +3 SL (4–1=3). As Salundra's SL is higher (4 to the officer's 3), she successfully intimidates the guards, who let her pass with barely a grumble.

Like any other Tests, some Opposed Tests are easier or harder than others, so the GM may decide modifiers are required. In most cases, these modifiers are applied equally to both sides, but not always. If no Difficulty is marked for an Opposed Test, it is assumed to be **Challenging (+0)**.

If it is important to know how well the winner of the Opposed Test won, use the difference between the two results to determine a final SL.

Example: *It's Pie Week, an annual week-long festival for everyone's favourite baked goods, and Salundra has entered a pie-eating contest. She's reached the final, and it's her versus Fat Tom Brandysnap, the Ubersreik Pie Eating Champion for the last 5 years running, and a Halfling wider than he is tall.*

*The GM calls for an **Opposed Endurance** Test. Salundra has an Endurance of 45 and Fat Tom has 63. Salundra is possibly in trouble! Dice roll, and Salundra rolls 51, scoring −1 SL. Sali's looking a little green! But Fat Tom's looking worse! He rolls 91 for −3 SL. So, even though she's failed her Endurance roll, she still wins the Opposed Test by 2 SL, though she'll probably be bringing up most of those pies later!*

Extended Tests

Sometimes the adventure will call for a specific number of Success Levels be achieved to fully succeed at a time-consuming or especially taxing task. Doing this requires a special Dramatic Test called an Extended Test. Extended Tests are handled in the same fashion as any other Dramatic Test, but the SL scored from multiple rolls are added together to reach a specified target. If the total SL scored ever falls below 0, you can start again from scratch with the next roll.

Example: *On the run again, Molli is attempting to pick an unexpectedly complex lock before she is discovered. The GM states the lock requires 5 Success Levels with a **Challenging (+0) Pick Lock** Test to pry open, and that she only has three Rounds before the guard arrives. Molli's Pick Lock skill is 58, so she has a good chance of managing it, but time isn't on her side. Unfortunately for her, her first Test scores 63: −1 SL and a terrible start, she's made no progress and will start from scratch next round. Cursing under her breath as footsteps draw closer, Molli tries again, this time scoring 11, for +4 SL! She feels tension in her picks as the lock almost springs, but she also hears the approaching guard is even closer.*

The GM explains the next Test is the last one before the guard arrives, so Molli can either abandon her attempt and avoid the guard or make a desperate effort to secure the last SL she needs

to pick the lock. Knowing she needs to escape, Molli risks the last Test and rolls, scoring… 42! That's +1 SL, taking her to a total of 5. The lock opens with a click! Triumphant, Molli slips through the door and closes it behind her just before the guard arrives.

OPTIONS: EXTENDED TESTS AND 0 SL

Rolling 0 SL in an Extended Test does not benefit or hinder the running SL total, which can feel a little odd given you either passed or failed the Test, and that should perhaps come with some advantage or penalty. If this is an issue for you, use the following optional rule. A successful Test adds a minimum of +1 SL to the cumulative total, and a failed Test removes a minimum of –1 SL from the total.

ASSISTANCE

In some situations, multiple Characters working together have a better chance of completing a task than a Character attempting it alone. With the GM's permission, a Character can assist another Character who is about to take a Test. When doing so, the Character with the best chance to succeed rolls the dice.

Each Character assisting provides a bonus of +10 to the Test. Other than that, the Test is rolled as normal.

Limits on Assistance

Characters can assist each other in most tasks; however, there are limits.

- To assist you require at least 1 Advance in the Skill being tested.

- Assisting Characters must normally be adjacent to the Character taking the Test.

- You may not assist on Tests made to resist disease, poison, fear, hazards, or anything else the GM deems inappropriate.

- You may not be assisted by more Characters than you have in the appropriate Characteristic Bonus (see page 33).

Example: *Adhemar, Perdita, and Valentyn hastily search a room when its owner, an aging merchant, leaves to find some records. The GM declares a* **Difficult (–10) Perception** *Test is required. Since Perdita and Valentyn both have the Perception Skill and are helping, Adhemar (who has the highest Perception Skill, at 59) gains a bonus of +20 to his Perception Test, for a combined total*

of 69 (59–10+20=69). However, he rolls 74, and fails, meaning all three characters have failed to find anything useful before the hobbling merchant returns.

OPTIONS: COMBINING SKILLS

Sometimes, you may be in a situation where you feel two Skills should be tested by the same character for a single task, so it may be appropriate to combine those Skills for a single Test. There are generally two reasons to do this: 1) is faster and limits the number of dice rolls required to press on with the game; 2) having to pass two Tests in a row to perform a single task significantly reduces your chance of passing overall.

The simplest way to do this is to attempt both Skills with one Test, comparing a single percentile roll to each Skill number. If both pass, you succeed at the Test. If only one passes, you partially pass as appropriate. And, obviously, if both fail, you have failed the Test.

Example: *After a string of unlikely events, Salundra finds herself on-stage in yellow and red tights, singing and dancing in the Vargr Breughel Memorial Playhouse's inaugural production of 'Tell Me On A Festag'. The GM calls for a* **Challenging Combined Perform (Dance) and Entertain (Sing)** *Test, thinking it unfair Salundra should have to enact each Test in turn as that would significantly reduce her overall chance of success. Salundra has Perform (Dance) at 53 from her time in court, but doesn't have Entertain (Sing), so must use her Fellowship of 43. She then rolls 46, meaning she managed the dance (succeeded with +1 SL), but hit a few off-notes with her singing (failed at -0 SL) – not perfect, but good enough for the gathered crowds; though Kym Neumann, the Altdorf Spieler's theatre critic, may not be writing a favourable review…*

COMBAT

Sooner or later you will need to stop someone in their tracks, or someone will try to stop you. When diplomacy fails, is not attempted, or is not understood as a basic concept, Combat begins!

In Combat, lots of individuals take actions in a short space of time, many of them in direct opposition to each other. You will still be taking Tests to resolve these actions, but timing and a host of other factors become more important, so we have some rules to make everything work.

TIMING

In Combat, the exact timing of actions matters more, so time is organised into:

- **Rounds**: A Round is enough time for all characters to attempt a Test and move into position. It's normally a just few seconds, the GM can decide exactly how long if necessary.
- **Turns**: During a Round, each combatant has a Turn to perform an Action and a Move.
- **Initiative Order**: Each combatant usually takes their Turn in order of their Initiative Characteristic, from highest to lowest.

COMBAT SUMMARY

Combat follows these steps until one side flees or is defeated:

1. **Determine Surprise**: The GM determines if any characters are *Surprised*. This normally only happens on the first round of combat. See the section below.

2. **Round Begins**: If the rules call for something to happen at the *start of the Round*, it happens now.

3. **Characters Take Turns**: Each combatant takes a Turn in Initiative order, starting with the highest Initiative. Each Character can normally perform a Move and an Action on their Turn (see page 157).

4. **Round Ends**: The Round ends when all combatants have taken a Turn. If the rules call for something to happen at the *end of the Round,* it happens now.

5. **Repeat Steps 2–5 As Required**: Continue to play through Rounds until the combat is resolved.

INITIATIVE ORDER

Combatants act in Initiative order during the Round, with the highest Initiative acting first, until all involved have taken a Turn. If you want this to work quickly at the table, have the players sit in Initiative order. If multiple combatants have the same Initiative,

they act in order from the highest Agility to the lowest. If they also have the same Agility, then roll an **Opposed Agility** Test, with the winner choosing who goes first for the combat. Some Talents impact combat order (see **Chapter 4: Skills and Talents**). **Example:** *Tollich, with an Initiative of 38, always acts ahead of his companion, Perdita who has an Initiative of 33. If they attack a coven of cultists, each with Initiative 35, the combat order would be: Tollich (38), the Cultists (35), Perdita (33).*

ROLL FOR INITIATIVE!

Some groups prefer to randomise Initiative. There are several ways to do this, choose your favourite:

- Each character rolls an Initiative Test to determine a SL.
- Each character rolls 1d10 and adds it to their Initiative.
- Each character rolls 1d10 and adds it to their Agility Bonus + Initiative Bonus.

The GM notes the results in decreasing numerical order and uses this as the Initiative Order. You could use this order for every Round (quickest option) or roll each Round (gives some variety to the order; slow characters have the chance to not always go last).

ROUNDS OUTSIDE COMBAT

Out of combat, the exact timing of those actions is usually flexible. Sometimes it is helpful to use Rounds outside of Combat to help organise everyone's contributions; for example, Extended Tests happen over several rounds, with one Test taken each Round. (see page 154).

SURPRISE

Taking your enemy by surprise gives you a big advantage. If one side is planning an attack, they can attempt to harness the element of surprise by:

- **Hiding**: Make a successful Stealth Test in appropriate cover. Characters may oppose this with a Perception Test if they are wary, or if the GM is feeling generous.

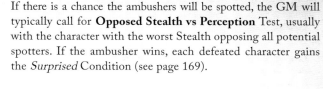

- **Sneaky Tactics:** Attack from behind, in the dark, through heavy fog, or from above! The GM may allow a Perception Test to spot the incoming attackers if appropriate.
- **Distractions:** Loud bangs, milling crowds and an especially engaging sermon are just some of the distractions that could harbour a surprise attack!
- **Unprepared Defenders:** If the enemy are particularly unwary, the attackers automatically surprise their victims.
- **Something Else:** Other sneaky and ingenious plans concocted by cunning players — the GM has the final call on the possibility of surprise.

SURPRISE TALENTS!

Even in situations where the GM states there is no chance of spotting incoming ambushers, some Talents allow Surprise to be avoided. See **Chapter 4: Skill and Talents** for more on this.

Example: Tollich and Perdita fall foul of an ambush by goresmeared Cultists of the Blood God. The combat begins when the Cultists storm from their hiding places, revealing their positions. The GM decides Tollich and Perdita are surprised as they were having a vigorous debate, and neither was at all prepared for an ambush. However, Tollich has the Combat Aware Talent, which grants a Challenging (+0) Perception *Test to avoid Surprise; for Tollich, this is 41. He rolls 23, showing his well-honed instincts have spotted something is wrong. So, for the first round, only Perdita takes the Surprised Condition; Tollich and the Cultists act as normal.*

If there is a chance the ambushers will be spotted, the GM will typically call for **Opposed Stealth vs Perception** Test, usually with the character with the worst Stealth opposing all potential spotters. If the ambusher wins, each defeated character gains the *Surprised* Condition (see page 169).

If no-one is surprised, proceed with the combat as normal.

If anyone is surprised, they can use a Resolve point to remove the *Surprised* Condition (see page 169).

TAKING YOUR TURN

Combat is a dynamic, disorientating experience, with friend and foe desperately weaving around each other, blades flashing as thrust follows parry follows gunshot.

The GM describes the situation — where everyone is, what your surroundings are like — and you can ask for more details to flesh things out and help plan your action. 'How thick is the chandelier rope? Could an arrow cut it?', for example. When it's your Turn, you'll make your Move and take Action!

On your Turn you have a Move and an Action, you can take these in any order — it's presumed you are probably doing both at the same time, and you can freely describe them as one combined manoeuvre. You can also skip taking an Action or Move, though you won't get another opportunity until the next Round!

Vivid descriptions of what you do will bring the Combat to life. Rather than declare your action is, 'hit the Goblin', it's much more fun to say, 'I Kick the chair in front of me towards the Goblins and lunge with my sword at the closest one's throat'. You never know, the GM might reward you with the odd bonus for great roleplaying. This goes for the resolution of your Action too — the GM will describe the outcome, but you can certainly embellish it!

Move

In most circumstances, exact distances don't matter too much. Use your Movement Characteristic as a guide to the ground you can cover, and the GM will let you know if the move will take more than one Turn. Reaching difficult places, perhaps by climbing or jumping, will also use your Action if you need to Test a Skill to get there (perhaps with a Climb or Athletics Test).

If you are not already fighting someone, you can also use your Move to Charge into close combat, gaining +1 Advantage (see page 164). For more on this, and for a detailed breakdown of movement speeds, leaping distances, and more, see **Moving** on page 164.

Action

In combat, your Action is used to do something. Whether that's swing a sword at a Mutant, jump from rooftop to rooftop, or take a moment to gauge the situation, that's up to you. Your Action is only limited by your imagination, the physical constraints of the fight location and the capabilities of your Character.

Describe what you want your Character to do. The GM will then tell you if you need to make a Test to succeed at your planned Action. The results will then be narrated by you and the GM, ending your Action.

For a detailed breakdown of how to use your Action to attack another Character, refer to **Attacking**. If you would like to use prayers or magic, refer to either **Chapter 7: Religion and Belief** or **Chapter 8: Magic. Chapter 4: Skills and Talents** also contains many examples of how to use your Skills during combat.

Example: *Molli looks on nervously from behind a barrel as Salundra is beset by the flying fists of three pub brawlers keen to put the young captain in her place. On her Turn, Molli's player asks if the pub has an upper floor. The GM confirms it does, and that it has a balcony overlooking the fight. Smiling, the player declares Molli will sprint upstairs and push a table down on the fight to help break it up using both her Move and Action. Given the upper floor isn't far away, the GM decides Molli can get there in a single Round but pushing the small table there will take a little effort.*

*The GM calls for an **Average (+20) Athletics** Test to heft the table over the balcony. Molli's Athletics is 34, so she needs to roll 54 or under. She rolls 21, for +3 SL, and the table flies! Molli shouts out as the table tips: 'Stop fighting!' The GM states all combatants below must perform an **Opposed Dodge** Test against the +3 SL*

or be hit by the table. Unfortunately, only Salundra fails this, and the table lands squarely on her head…

Free Actions

Some things you'll want your Character to do won't count as your Action for the round — such as shouting a warning, drawing your weapon, or drinking a potion. It's the GM's decision on what takes up your Action, and what you can do in a Round. A good general guide is that if an act requires you to make a Test, it is an Action rather than a Free Action.

OPTIONS: ON THE DEFENSIVE

What if you want to prepare to dodge or parry incoming blows, to hold a defensive position in a doorway, or use Language (Magick) to deploy an array of dispels? As your Action, choose a Skill to use defensively and you will get +20 to defensive Tests using the Skill until the start of your next Turn.

ATTACKING

One of the most common Actions is to attack an opponent. To make a ranged attack, your weapon must be in range (see **Chapter 11: Consumers' Guide** for weapon ranges) and your target visible in line-of-sight. For melee attacks, you must be adjacent your target with a weapon ready (see **Engaged**).

DEFAULT COMBAT DIFFICULTY

During combat, all Difficulty is assumed to be **Challenging** (+0). So, if no Difficulty is expressly mentioned in the rules, use Challenging.

1: Roll to Hit

Melee: To attack, perform an **Opposed Melee** Test with your Opponent (both you and your opponent Test your Melee Skill — see page 126). Whoever scores the highest SL wins. If you win the Test, you hit your opponent and gain +1 Advantage. If you lose the Opposed Test, your opponent gains +1 Advantage and your Action is finished.

Ranged: Roll a **Ranged** Test for the weapon you're using. If you are successful, you hit your opponent and gain +1 Advantage. If you fail, your Action is over. Your opponent doesn't gain Advantage in ranged combat.

In both melee and ranged Combat, it's possible to score an impressive hit called a Critical, or to make a mistake, called a Fumble. See Criticals and Fumbles in the section below.

Summary: *Test to hit your opponent with your weapon. This Test is Opposed in melee. Any winner gains +1 Advantage.*

2: Determine Hit Location

If you successfully hit, find out where — reverse the roll to hit and compare this number to the Hit Locations table. So, a roll of 23 to hit would become 32 on the table, a hit on the Right Arm.

Creatures with different body shapes may use different hit location tables. Refer to **Chapter 12: Bestiary** for more on the different Hit Location tables.

HIT LOCATIONS

Roll	Location
01–09	Head
10–24	Left Arm (or Secondary Arm)
25–44	Right Arm (or Primary Arm)
45–79	Body
80–89	Left Leg
90–00	Right Leg

Summary: *Reverse your 'Roll to hit' Test result to determine a Hit Location.*

3: Determine Damage

Once you have determined the hit location, it is time to work out how much Damage you deal. Each weapon has a Weapon Damage characteristic (see page 293). This is usually your modified Strength Bonus for melee weapons, or a fixed number for ranged weapons. Take the SL of your Opposed Test and add it to the Weapon Damage of the weapon you're using. This final number is your Damage.

Summary: *Damage = Weapon Damage + SL*

4: Apply Damage

Using the Damage and the Hit Location you struck, you now see how many Wounds your opponent loses from your attack. Subtract your opponent's Toughness Bonus and any Armour Points protecting the Hit Location from your Damage. The remaining Damage is suffered as Wounds by your opponent. If this is 1 or less, your opponent has shrugged off the worst of the attack and only loses 1 Wound. Should the Wounds lost exceed your opponent's remaining Wounds total, your opponent takes a Critical Wound (see page 172) and gains the *Prone* Condition (see page 169).

Summary: *Wounds Suffered = Damage – opponent's (Toughness Bonus + Armour Points)*

OPPOSING A MELEE ATTACK

You can Oppose an incoming melee attack with more than just your Melee Skill. The most obvious choice is Dodge, which allows you to avoid incoming blows, but **Chapter 4: Skills and Talents** lists many other Skills that just might be useful in combat, including Intimidate, Charm, Leadership, and more. If your GM thinks it's appropriate for the situation, and you're happy missing out on the opportunity to score a Critical Hit against your opponent, then why not give it a go.

Engaged

Whenever you attack an opponent, or are attacked, in melee combat, you count as Engaged. This means you are tussling with each other in a fight, and others rules (due to Talents, Spells, etc.) for being Engaged might apply. If you don't attack each other for a full Round, you are no longer Engaged.

SUCCESS LEVELS IN COMBAT

In combat, SL is used to determine damage, rather than getting a result from the Outcome Table. To mix this up a little, Tests in combat also use Criticals and Fumbles.

CRITICALS AND FUMBLES

During the cut and thrust of combat, accidents, mistakes, and moments of extraordinary skill can happen in quick succession. To represent the unpredictable extremes of a life-or-death skirmish, there are Criticals — extraordinarily good hits — and Fumbles — egregious errors.

Criticals

Any successful Melee or Ranged Test that also rolls a double causes a Critical. This means you have dealt a significant blow, and it even happens when you are the defender in an opposed Test.

If you score a Critical, your opponent receives an immediate Critical Wound as your weapon strikes true. See page 172 for more on what this means. Beyond that, SL is calculated as normal, as is who wins any Opposed Tests.

OPTIONS: DEATHBLOW

Some players like a heroic approach to combat, with characters able to wade through lesser foes. If this suits your style of play, use the following rule:

If you kill a melee opponent in a single blow, you may move into the space the character occupied and attack another opponent if there is one available. You may keep doing this a number of times equal to your Weapon Skill Bonus, and may not attack the same Character more than once on the same Turn. Some creatures (see **Chapter 12: Bestiary**) are so big they can activate this rule without killing any opponents.

OPPOSED TESTS AND FUMBLES

During an Opposed Test, it is possible to Fumble and still win if you score a higher SL than your opponent. This is fine, and not a little hilarious, as you ineffectually tussle with your even worse opponent, potentially injuring yourself in the process.

Example: *Molli swipes her dagger at her opponent and rolls 66 for a fumble with -3 SL, but her opponent rolls 92 for -5 SL. So, Molli wins with +2 SL over her opponent, gaining +1 Advantage, which she may quickly lose as she also has to roll on the Oops! Table to see what unfortunate accident will befall her.*

Fumbles

The converse of Criticals, any failed combat Test that also rolls a double is a Fumble, which means something very unfortunate has occurred. To determine what happens, roll on the **Oops! Table**.

OOPS! TABLE

Roll	Result
01–20	You catch a part of your anatomy (we recommend you play this for laughs) — lose 1 Wound, ignoring Toughness Bonus or Armour Points.
21–40	Your melee weapon jars badly, or ranged weapon malfunctions or slightly breaks – your weapon suffers 1 Damage. Next round, you will act last regardless of Initiative order, Talents, or special rules as you recover (see page 156).
41–60	Your manoeuvre was misjudged, leaving you out of position, or you lose grip of a ranged weapon. Next round, your Action suffers a penalty of −10.
61–70	You stumble badly, finding it hard to right yourself. Lose your next Move.
71–80	You mishandle your weapon, or you drop your ammunition. Miss your next Action.
81–90	You overextend yourself or stumble and twist your ankle. Suffer a *Torn Muscle (Minor)* injury (see page 179). This counts as a Critical Wound.
91–00	You completely mess up, hitting 1 random ally in range using your rolled units die to determine the SL of the hit. If that's not possible, you somehow hit yourself in the face and gain a *Stunned* Condition (see page 169).

MISFIRES!

If you are using a Blackpowder, Engineering, or Explosive weapon, and roll a Fumble that is also an even number – 00, 88, and so on – your weapon Misfires, exploding in your hand. You take full Damage to your Primary Arm location using the units die as an effective SL for the hit, and your weapon is destroyed.

RANGED COMBAT

There are some extra considerations that apply to ranged attacks:

- Ranged attacks cannot be opposed with Melee Skills unless you have a large enough shield (see page 298), or if they are at Point Blank range (see page 297), where it is also allowable to Dodge.

- You cannot make ranged attacks whilst Engaged, unless you are armed with a ranged weapon that has the Pistol Quality (see **Chapter 11: Consumers' Guide**).

- If you use your Ranged Skill when you are Engaged with your target, the target may Oppose your attack with any Melee Skill.

COMBAT DIFFICULTY

Combat Tests can be modified in the same manner as other Tests. These modifiers can be used to reflect the effects of terrain, the weather, and a variety of other factors. The following are some of the most common modifiers encountered in combat. For situations not covered here, use these as a guide. Remember, the GM has final say about the difficulty of any particular Test.

COMBAT DIFFICULTY

Difficulty	Modifier	Example
Very Easy	+60	Shooting a Monstrous target (Giant size).
		Shooting into a crowd (13+ targets)
Easy	+40	Shooting a target at Point Blank Range (see page 297).
		Shooting an Enormous target (Griffon size).
		Attacking an opponent you outnumber 3 to 1.
		Shooting at a Large group (7–12 targets).
Average	+20	Shooting a Large target (Ogre size).
		Shooting at Short Range: less than half weapon range.
		Shooting at a small group (3–6 targets)
		Shooting when you spent your last Action aiming (no Test to aim required).
		Attacking an Engaged opponent in the sides or rear.
		Attacking an opponent you outnumber 2 to 1.
		Attacking a target with the *Prone* Condition (see page 169).
Challenging	+0	A standard attack.
		Shooting an Average target (Human size).
Difficult	−10	Attacking whilst you have the *Prone* Condition (see page 169), or otherwise beneath your target.
		Attacking whilst in the mud, heavy rain or difficult terrain.
		Shooting at Long Range: up to double weapon range.
		Shooting on a Round where you also use your Move.
		Shooting a small target (Child size).
		Target in soft cover (behind a hedge for example).
Hard	−20	A called shot to a specific Hit Location. If you succeed you hit that location.
		Fighting in an enclosed space with a weapon with a Length longer than Average.
		Shooting targets concealed by fog, mist or shadow.
		Attacking in a monsoon, hurricane, thick blizzard, or other extreme weather.
		Dodging when you have the *Prone* Condition, or are mounted (see page 163).
		Close combat in darkness.
		Shooting a Little target (Cat size).
		Using a weapon in your off hand.
		Target in medium cover (wooden fence for example).
Very Hard	−30	Attacking or dodging in the deep snow, water or other arduous terrain.
		Shooting a tiny target (Mouse size).
		Shooting at Extreme range, up to three times weapon range.
		Shooting in darkness.
		Target in hard cover (behind stone wall, for example)

COMBINING DIFFICULTIES

There will be instances where multiple factors make taking a particular action more difficult than normal. Lurking in a gloomy forest as you attempt to shoot at a distant opponent through the trees is harder than shooting at the same opponent on a bright day in an open field. When combining multiple difficulties, use the following guidelines:

- If the situation would apply two or more penalties, simply add the modifiers together to a maximum of –30 or Very Hard. For example, fog and aiming for a specific body part both make Weapon Skill Tests **Hard (–20)**. When combined, the Test would simply be **Very Hard (–30)**, rather than suffer a –40 modifier. Similarly, if the situation would apply two or more bonuses, add the modifiers together to a maximum of +60 or Very Easy.

- If the situation would apply a penalty and a bonus, add them together to find the new difficulty. Attacking an opponent while standing in deep snow normally requires a **Very Hard (–30)** Test. But attacking an opponent who is *Prone* requires an **Easy (+20)** Test. In a situation where both apply, the Test would be **Difficult (–10)** since –30 plus +20 equals –10.

Helpless Targets
Melee Tests made to hit a sleeping, unconscious, or otherwise helpless target automatically succeed. Check the *Unconscious* Condition for more on this (on page 169).

Shooting into a Group
Ranged Tests made to hit a group of targets are **Average (+20)** if there is 3-6 of them, **Easy (+40)** if there are 7-12 of them, and **Very Easy (+60)** if there is 13 or more of them. Any successful hits are randomised between all likely targets as the GM prefers. If this modifier allows you to hit when the Test would otherwise have failed, you succeed with +0 SL.

Outnumbering
If you out-number an opponent 2 to 1, you gain a bonus of +20 to hit your opponent in melee combat. If you outnumber an enemy by 3 to 1, you get an even larger bonus of +40 to hit. Further, at the end of every Round, all outnumbered opponents lose 1 Advantage. Outnumbering is generally determined by how many Characters are Engaged with each other; if there is any doubt, the GM decides who is outnumbering whom.

OPTIONS: SHOOTING INTO MELEE

For most, simply choosing a target and rolling to hit is enough of a complication. However, some prefer the rules be more precise when firing at an Engaged target. If this is you, use the following rules:

Ballistic Skill Tests against Engaged opponents are resolved as normal, but suffer a penalty of –20 as you try your best to hit your specified target. If this modifier causes you to fail when the Test would otherwise have succeeded, you instead hit one of the target's Engaged opponents, as determined randomly by the GM. If you do not care whom you hit, you may gain a bonus of +20 to +60 to hit, see **Shooting into a Group**.

Size

Size is an important factor when shooting at a target: it is far easier to hit a barn door than an apple. For more on Size, refer to **Traits** in **Chapter 12: Bestiary**. If this modifier allows you to hit when the Test would otherwise have failed, you succeed with +0 SL.

SIZE

Size	Height or Length	Examples	Modifier
Tiny	Less than a foot	Butterfly, Mouse, Pigeon	–30
Little	Up to 2 feet	Cat, Hawk, Human Baby	–20
Small	Up to 4 feet	Giant Rat, Halfling, Human Child	–10
Average	Up to 7 feet	Dwarf, Elf, Human	0
Large	Up to 12 feet	Horse, Ogre, Troll	+20
Enormous	Up to 20 feet	Griffon, Wyvern, Manticore	+40
Monstrous	20 feet+	Dragon, Giant, Daemon Prince	+60

TWO-WEAPON FIGHTING

Some warriors prefer to fight with a weapon in each hand — such as using a sword and sword-breaker, or a sword and a shield. The following applies when you are fighting with two weapons.

- You may use any one-handed close combat weapon or any pistol when fighting with two weapons.
- You may use either hand to make an attack. Attacks made using your secondary hand suffer a −20 penalty to any applicable Test.
- If you have the *Dual Wielder* Talent you may be able to attack with both weapons. See **Chapter 4: Skills and Talents** for more on this.

SCATTER

On a failed **Ranged (Throwing)** Test, roll 1d10 and consults the following diagram to see where your weapon lands. 'T' marks the target.

1	2	3
4	T	5
6	7	8

A roll of 1-8 provides a direction: roll 2d10 to determine the distance the weapon scatters in yards — it scatters no more than half the distance between you and the target. A roll of 9 and the weapon lands at your feet. A 10, and it lands at your target's feet. Scatter can be used whenever a random direction is required.

UNARMED COMBAT

Not every fight in **WFRP** involves guns or swords. Many conflicts are settled with good, old-fashioned fisticuffs. A successful Melee (Brawling) Test for unarmed combat is handled in the same way as any other combat Test, but you have one extra option: you may enter a Grapple!

Grappling

Instead of inflicting damage with an unarmed attack, you can attempt to Grapple and immobilise your opponent. You must declare this is your intent before rolling to hit your opponent. If you win the Opposed Test, you and your opponent are Grappling, and your opponent gains the *Entangled* Condition. If you begin your turn Grappling, you may break the Grapple if you have a higher Advantage than your opponent, and do not count as being Engaged for your Move; otherwise, you must make an **Opposed Strength** Test for your Action. If you win, you can do one of the following:

- Deal SB + SL Damage using your Strength roll to determine the Hit Location affected. You ignore any Armour Points as you wrench arms and pull muscles.
- Either: 1) Give your opponent an *Entangled* Condition, or 2) Remove an *Entangled* Condition from yourself, plus lose an extra one for each SL by which you win.

If you lose the Opposed Test, you can do nothing but struggle as your opponent gains +1 Advantage.

Those outside the Grapple gain a +20 bonus to hit the grapplers with the lowest Advantage, and a +10 bonus to hit to the grappler with the highest Advantage.

OPTIONS: GRAPPLING WITH SKILLS

If you are Grappling, your GM may allow you to perform a Test other than an **Opposed Strength** Test according to the situation. Perhaps Language (Magick) to cast a spell, or Charm to wheedle your way free, or Leadership to order your grappler to stand down? As long as your GM is happy with this, roll those dice and see what happens. But if you fail, note that you will not be concentrating on the Grapple, so the GM may rule you gain an extra *Entangled* Condition, which could make things very tricky!

MOUNTED COMBAT

Riding into Combat, sword swinging, guns blazing, is not only terrifying for those on the receiving end, it also brings bonuses to the rider. Mounted Combat uses the same rules as any other Combat, with the following additions:

- For the purposes of your Move, riders count as having the Movement Attribute of their mount. Further, riders take Ride Tests for any tests to Run, Jump or similar, and use their mount's Movement Attribute.
- Any melee attack from a Rider on a target smaller than their Mount gains a bonus of +20 to hit.
- If you are rolling to hit a mounted character, you choose whether to hit the rider or the mount. If you are in close combat, you also suffer a penalty of −10 to your Melee Test if you target the rider and are smaller than the mount (see Size on page 162).
- A Mount without the *Skittish* Trait (see page 342) is effectively another combatant, and may use its own Action to attack Engaged targets.
- When Charging, you may use the Strength and Size rules of your mount for the purposes of calculating Damage.
- When riding, you suffer a penalty of −20 to any attempts to use the Dodge Skill unless you have the *Trick Riding* Talent.

Note: Most mounts are bigger than Characters, meaning they may cause Fear or Terror, and gain other combat advantages as explained on page 341.

ADVANTAGE

Advantage represents your momentum in combat, and is gained when you outwit, defeat, or otherwise dominate your opponents. It is recorded with tokens — be these coins, cards, chits, counters, or specially designed Advantage tokens — or by a tally sheet on scrap paper.

OPTIONS: LIMITING ADVANTAGE

Some GMs prefer a more controlled combat environment that isn't so influenced by the whimsy of dice and luck. As Advantage can swing wildly during the course of a battle, and can have a significant impact, consider using one of the following optional rules if you wish to contain this:

- Advantage has an upper level equal to each Character's Initiative Bonus.
- Cap Advantage at a pre-arranged limit, such as 2, 4, or more. 10 also works well as you can easily track it with 1d10.

Gaining Advantage

Advantage is secured each time you win an Opposed Test in combat, you assess the battlefield using your Skills, or when your spirits are lifted. The following provides some examples of this, but is far from exhaustive, and the GM is encouraged to hand out Advantage tokens as suits the circumstances.

- **Surprise:** Attacking Surprised enemies brings +1 Advantage. See page 169.
- **Charging:** Charging headlong into combat grants +1 Advantage. See page 165.
- **Assess:** If you use one of your Skills to secure a tactical advantage, gain +1 Advantage. See individual Skill descriptions in **Chapter 4: Skills and Talents** for more details concerning this.
- **Victory:** Whenever you defeat an important NPC, gain +1 Advantage. Subduing a party nemesis may grant +2 Advantage.
- **Winning:** If you win an Opposed Test during combat gain +1 Advantage.
- **Outmanouevre:** If you wound an opponent without engaging in an Opposed Test, gain +1 Advantage.

There is also an array of Talents that secure Advantage. Refer to **Chapter 4: Skills and Talents** for more on this.

Benefits of Advantage

Each Advantage you secure adds +10 to any appropriate combat Test or Psychology Test (see **Psychology** on page 190). Thus, if you have 5 Advantage tokens, you have an impressive +50 bonus to hit, defend, and resist the influence of others.

Losing Advantage

If you lose an Opposed Test during combat, suffer any Conditions (see page 167), or lose any Wounds, you automatically lose all Advantage. Further, should the combat end, all Advantage you've gained is lost. Lastly, if you have accrued no Advantage for the Round, or end the Round outnumbered, you lose 1 point. Advantage can also be used to Disengage from combat (see page 165). There are also Skills and Talents that cause you to lose Advantage, or transfer Advantage to another character. For more on these, read **Chapter 4: Skills and Talents.**

MOVING

The amount of detail needed for movement depends on how you track where everyone is. Many prefer to use the 'theatre of the mind' method, where you describe relative positions and distance, and the GM adjudicates if it's possible to undertake the Move or Action each player describes. Even during tightly controlled combat Rounds, it is usually enough to narrate how your character negotiates the frenetic action, leaping barrels, sprinting for cover, or dancing around opponents as required.

Other groups use floorplans, grids, tokens, and Citadel Miniatures to represent where the combatants are standing, and this method needs a bit more specific information on distance and movement. If you do this, we recommend a 1-inch grid, with each square representing a distance of 2 yards in the game world. This means if you have Movement 4, you can normally move 4 squares. Humans, Mutants, and other similarly-sized creatures occupy a single square on the map. Larger creatures can take up 2, 4, or even more squares, according to their Size trait (see page 341). If you prefer to go gridless, keep the 1 Movement = 2 yards scale.

MOVING DURING COMBAT

The Movement Table shows how many yards you can normally move in a single Turn, either Walking or Running, without having to make an Athletics Test to sprint. Doing this will use your Move for your Turn.

MOVEMENT TABLE

Movement	Walk (yards)	Run (yards)
0	0	0
1	2	4
2	4	8
3	6	12
4	8	16
5	10	20
6	12	24
7	14	28
8	16	32
9	18	36
10	20	40

Charging

If you are not Engaged in combat already, you can use your Move to Charge. If you Charge, your Action must be a Melee Test to attack an opponent. If your opponent is at least your Move characteristic in yards away before you Charge, but within your Run range (see the Run entry in the Movement Table for how far you can move when Charging), you will also gain +1 Advantage as you barrel into your opponent.

Disengaging

If you are Engaged in combat (see page 159), and no longer wish to be trading blows with your opponent, you have the following two options for leaving combat safely.

Use Advantage: If you have more Advantage than your opponents, you are in a superior position and can easily

manoeuvre yourself beyond reach. If you choose to drop your Advantage to 0, you can move away from your opponents without penalty, perhaps choosing to Charge a new target, run away as fast as possible, or backstep a little and fire a pistol in an opponent's face!

Use Dodge: If you have lower or equal Advantage to your opponents or do not wish to spend your Advantage, you are pinned in place. If you wish to escape, you will need to use your Action to make an **Opposed Dodge/Melee** Test. If you succeed, you gain +1 Advantage, and can use your Move to go anywhere you wish using the normal rules. If you fail, each opponent defeating you gains +1 Advantage and makes it impossible for you to escape without a blow to your back.

Fleeing

If you cannot escape otherwise, you can turn your back and flee as your Move. Often, Fleeing is involuntary, caused by Terror (see page 191) or magic.

If you flee, your opponent immediately gains 1 Advantage and may attempt 1 free attack. The free attack is an unopposed Melee Test using whatever weapon is currently held, using the SL scored to Damage you as normal. As you are throwing caution to the wind, your opponent gains +20 to hit you. If you are hit, your opponent gains +1 Advantage, and you must enact a **Challenging (+0) Cool** Test: if failed, gain a *Broken* Condition, and a further +1 Broken condition per SL below 0. Once the free attack is concluded, you may move up to your Run Movement (see the Movement Table) directly away from your opponent, assuming you still can.

Running

On your turn, you can use your Action to sprint. This requires an **Average (+20) Athletics** Test, and the distance covered is in addition to your Move this round. You sprint your Run movement + SL in yards (see the Movement Table for your Run movement). So, a character with Move 4 who rolled −2 SL would sprint an additional 14 yards (16−2=14).

Climbing

Most climb moves won't need Tests. Climbing rules are only required when the Climb is difficult or if knowing exactly how long you take to ascend is important.

Climbing a ladder or similarly easy-to-climb surface does not require a Test but does slow you down. You move at half rate up or down ladders or other easily climbed surfaces. So, it would cost 4 yards of your Movement to climb a 2-yard ladder. If you want to climb more quickly, spend your Action to make an **Average (+20) Climb** Test. You will Climb an extra Movement + SL yards. So, a character with Movement 4 who rolled +2 SL will climb an additional 6 yards (4+2=6).

If both hands are free, you can climb a surface with suitable handholds with a Climb Test using your Action for the turn. You ascend or descend at a rate of ½ Movement + SL in yards.

Climbing difficulty is set by the GM and varies with the nature of the climbed surface. Some climbs will be beyond the ability of most characters without the *Scale Sheer Surface* Talent (see page 144).

LEAPING, AND FALLING

Jumping to reach high ledges, leaping from rooftop to rooftop, or failing both and plummeting to your death are all essential parts of the **WFRP** experience.

Simple Athletics Tests, or perhaps a Perform (Acrobatics) Test, will be enough to determine the outcome on most occasions, but sometimes knowing exactly how high you jump, how far you leap, or what happens when you fall is useful.

Leaping

You can leap your Movement in feet without having to make a Test. If you want to jump farther, this takes an **Average (+20) Athletics** Test if you have a run up of at least your Movement in yards; if you do not, the Test is **Challenging (+0)**. On a success, each SL adds an extra foot to the leap. If you succeeded with +0 SL, you manage an extra 6 inches with your jump.

Falling

When falling, you suffer 1d10 Damage, plus 3 Damage for every yard you fall. Any suffered Damage is reduced by your Toughness Bonus, but not any Armour Points you may be wearing.

If you are purposefully falling — or, if you prefer, jumping downwards — you can attempt an **Average (+20) Athletics** Test to lessen the damage you may sustain. If successful, you count as having fallen 1 less yard, plus an extra yard less per SL scored.

If you reduce the distance you count as having fallen to 0 or less, you will suffer no Damage from the fall.

If more Wounds are suffered from a fall than your Toughness Bonus, you also gain the *Prone* Condition.

PURSUIT

Desperate chase scenes through busy markets and high-speed pursuits hanging from the back of careening coaches are the centrepiece of many exciting adventures. Here's how to run a pursuit:

1: Determine Distance — The GM decides how far ahead the pursued are from the pursuers, and assigns a number to represent the size of the head start, called the Distance. Typically, this will range from 1 for those almost in reach, to 4 for those with a good lead, to 8 for those almost beyond reach when the pursuit begins.

2: Test — Everyone actively moving in the pursuit rolls a Test for their movement — typically this will be a Drive, Ride, or Athletics Test depending upon the circumstances.

3: Update Distance — The lowest SL of the pursued and the highest SL of the pursuers is compared, the difference between these is added to the Distance if the pursued won, and subtracted from the Distance number if the pursuers won.

4: Determine Outcome — If the Distance falls to 0 or less, the pursuers have caught their quarry! The pursued can then sacrifice their slowest member that Round to delay the pursuers as the rest continue to flee, or they can stop and confront their pursuers. If the slowest of the pursued is abandoned, the pursuers decide who stops to confront the unfortunate and who continues in pursuit. If the poor abandoned runner is not a priority target it's quite likely the pursuers will continue their pursuit of their target. If Distance reaches 10+, the pursuers have lost their quarry and the pursuit is over… for now! If the Distance is still 1–9, the pursuit continues, return to step 2.

As each Round passes, it's important to describe what just happened in a fun and exciting fashion. If you score a large SL, describe people getting out of the way, giving you an opportunity to make ground. If you score a negative SL, describe tripping over crates, running into people, or slamming your coach against a wall, slowing you down.

Example: *Eichengard and Sigrid are chasing three cultists through the streets of Altdorf. The cultists got a decent head start, so the GM gives him a lead of Distance 2. Each character rolls an Athletics Test to start the pursuit. Sigrid scores +3 SL; the cultists score +0, +2, and +2 SL; and Eichengard scores +2 SL.*

So, after the first round, the difference between the slowest cultist (0) and the fastest pursuing character (Sigrid with 3) is 3, meaning that the characters catch up with the cultists. The cowardly cultists abandon their slowest member in the hope of saving their hides, and Sigrid stops to subdue the abandoned aberrant.

Next round the cultists start at a Distance of 1 (the difference between the next slowest cultist and Sigrid last round) so Eichengard just needs to beat them by +1 SL to catch up again.

Movement Modifiers

If some of the characters in the pursuit have a higher Movement, they gain a bonus SL equal to the difference in Movement. So, if you had Move 5 and you were chasing a Move 4 character, you would gain +1 SL on your pursuit roll.

Example: *Perdita is urging her horse forwards, trying to chase down two Bandits. Her horse has Movement 8, where the Bandits are on Movement 7 and Movement 9 horses. Thus, the first Bandit has an unmodified Test, Perdita gains a bonus of +1 SL, and the second Bandit gains a bonus of +2 SL when they all roll their Ride (Horse) Tests.*

OPTIONS: CHASE COMPLICATION

The Pursuit rules are more than enough for a fast, fun chase scene. However, for those looking to add more detail, consider the following two options, and embellish them as required.

Dodge that!: Each round, the character who rolled the highest SL can create an Obstacle. An Obstacle could be pulling a pile of barrels into the path of a pursuer, or perhaps calling out for help to catch someone running away. The winner chooses one Character: that Character suffers a penalty of –1 SL next round as they have to deal with the Obstacle. Make sure to take time to describe exactly what has happened to keep the chase entertaining.

Consider the Environment: Perhaps there is a bridge coming up? Or a gap to jump? Or a fence to leap over? Or a city gate to pass through? The GM can throw in different Tests as the Rounds progress, mixing up the requirement each round. So, Round 1 may need an Athletics Test as everyone runs, Round 2 may require a Leadership or Intimidate Test to pass through a guarded gate, Round 3 may need another Athletics Test to jump a small stream, and Round 4 may be sprint across an open field (modified by Movement again).

CONDITIONS

Conditions represent the effects of things that can happen to you in the course of your adventures. The Conditions you suffer from can be recorded on a scrap sheet of paper, or you can use chits or counters to represent them. Each Condition explains how long any effects usually last in its description; however, it's possible the cause of a Condition — such as a spell or critical wound — may override this. **Note:** If you suffer any Conditions, you immediately lose all Advantage (see page 164).

MULTIPLE CONDITIONS

You can be subject to the same Condition more than once; indeed, sometimes you will receive multiples of the same Condition from a single event. If this occurs, any penalties suffered are stacked. So, if you have three *Bleeding* Conditions, you're losing a worrying 3 Wounds per Round; or if you have 3 *Fatigued* Conditions, you suffer –30 to all Tests. You can also be subject to multiple, different Conditions at once. When this occurs, the effects *do not* stack; you suffer the highest of the

two penalties and apply it. So, if you had the *Fatigued* and *Prone* Conditions, you would suffer a –20 penalty to all active Tests, not –30.

COMPLETE CONDITION LIST

Ablaze, Bleeding, Blinded, Broken, Deafened, Entangled, Fatigued, Poison, Prone, Stunned, Surprised, Unconscious

CONDITIONS AND RESOLVE

A Condition can be removed with Resolve points so, while many are debilitating, if you are careful they can be relatively easily managed (see page 171).

MASTER CONDITION LIST

The following are the conditions used in **WFRP**.

Ablaze

You are on fire! This Condition is normally only applied if you are flammable — for example: wearing clothes that can be set alight — but some magical and divine effects can set you alight even if you are not normally combustible!

At the end of every Round, you suffer 1d10 Wounds, modified by Toughness Bonus and the Armour Points on the least protected Hit Location, with a minimum of 1 Wound suffered. Each extra *Ablaze* Condition you have adds +1 to the Damage suffered; so, three *Ablaze* Conditions result in 1d10+2 Damage suffered.

One *Ablaze* Condition can be removed with a successful Athletics Test, with each SL removing an extra *Ablaze* Condition. The Difficulty for this Test is modified by circumstances: it's much easier to put out a fire rolling around on sand than it is in the middle of an oil-soaked kitchen.

Bleeding

You are bleeding badly. Lose 1 Wound at the end of every Round, ignoring all modifiers. Further, suffer a penalty of −10 to any Tests to resist Festering Wounds, Minor Infection, or Blood Rot (see page 186). If you reach 0 Wounds, you no longer lose Wounds and instead fall immediately unconscious (gain the *Unconscious* Condition). At the end of Round, you have a 10% chance of dying per *Bleeding* Condition you have; so, if you had 3 *Bleeding* Conditions, you would die from blood loss on a roll of 0–30. If a double is scored on this roll, your wound clots a little: lose 1 *Bleeding* Condition. You cannot regain consciousness until all *Bleeding* Conditions are removed (see **Injury** on page 172).

A *Bleeding* Condition can be removed with: a successful Heal Test, with each SL removing an extra *Bleeding* Condition; or with any spell or prayer that heals Wounds, with one Condition removed per Wound healed.

Once all *Bleeding* Conditions are removed, gain one *Fatigued* Condition.

Blinded

Perhaps because of a flash of light, or because of liquid sprayed in your face, you are unable to see properly. You suffer a −10 penalty to all Tests involving sight, and any opponent attacking you in close combat gains a bonus of +10 to hit you.

One *Blinded* Condition is removed at the end of every other Round.

Broken

You are terrified, defeated, panicked, or otherwise convinced you are going to die. On your turn, your Move and Action must be used to run away as fast as possible until you are in a good hiding place beyond the sight of any enemy; then you can use your Action on a Skill that allows you to hide more effectively. You also receive a penalty of −10 to all Tests not involving running and hiding.

You cannot Test to rally from being Broken if you are Engaged with an enemy (see page 159). If you are unengaged, at the end of each Round, you may attempt a Cool Test to remove a *Broken* Condition, with each SL removing an extra *Broken* Condition, and the Difficulty determined by the circumstances you currently find yourself: it is much easier to rally when hiding behind a barrel down an alleyway far from danger (Average +20) than it is when three steps from a slavering Daemon screaming for your blood (Very Hard −30).

If you spend a full Round in hiding out of line-of-sight of any enemy, you remove 1 *Broken* Condition.

Once all *Broken* Conditions are removed, gain 1 *Fatigued* Condition.

Deafened

Whether caused by a loud noise or a blow to the head, you are unable to hear properly. You suffer a −10 penalty to all Tests involving hearing, and any opponent attacking you in close combat from the flank or rear gains an extra bonus of +10 to hit you (this bonus does not increase with multiple *Deafened* Conditions). One *Deafened* condition is removed at the end of every other Round and is often replaced with tinnitus.

Entangled

You are wrapped in something restricting your movement; it could be ropes, spider's webbing, or an opponent's bulging biceps. On your turn, you may not Move, and all your actions involving movement of any kind suffer a penalty of −10 (including Grappling; see page 163). For your Action, you can remove an *Entangled* Condition if you win an **Opposed Strength** Test against the source of the entanglement, with each SL removing an extra *Entangled* Condition.

OPTIONS: GETTING TIRED...

For GMs keen to have characters tiring as they undertake strenuous activity, use the following rule: Gain 1 *Fatigued* Condition if you fail an Endurance Test after a number of Rounds of continued exertion equal to your Toughness Bonus. Each SL extends how many rounds pass before you need Test again.

Fatigued

You are exhausted or stressed, and certainly in need of rest. You suffer a −10 penalty to all Tests. Removing a *Fatigued* Condition normally requires rest, a spell, or a divine effect, though in some instances, such as when a *Fatigued* Condition is caused by carrying too much (see **Encumbrance** on page 293), simply changing your circumstances (carrying fewer trappings, for example) can remove a Condition.

HOW MUCH REST?

How much rest is required to remove a *Fatigued* condition is up to the GM and the style of game you are playing. Some groups prefer a relatively realistic approach and remove a *Fatigue* condition after a prolonged rest. Others require only an hour or so of rest for each *Fatigue* condition, preferring to press on with the adventure rather than worry about tired characters. And some remove a *Fatigue* condition per round of rest, keeping things fast and simple. It's up to you and your group to decide how much rest you need.

Poisoned

You have been poisoned or injected with venom. All Tests to remove poison have their difficulty determined by the poison or venom suffered. At the end of each Round, lose 1 Wound, ignoring all modifiers. Also, suffer a penalty of −10 to all Tests.

If you reach 0 Wounds when *Poisoned*, you cannot heal any Wounds until all *Poisoned* conditions are removed. If you fall Unconscious when *Poisoned*, make an **Endurance** Test after a number of Rounds equal to your Toughness Bonus or die horribly. See Injury on page 172 for more on this.

At the end of each Round, you may attempt an **Endurance** Test. If successful, remove a *Poisoned* Condition, with each SL removing an extra *Poisoned* Condition. A **Heal** Test provides the same results. Once all *Poisoned* Conditions are removed, gain 1 *Fatigued* Condition.

Prone

You have fallen to the ground, possibly because you have run out of Wounds, you've tripped, or because you've been hit by something rather large. On your turn, your Move can only be used to stand up or crawl at half your Movement in yards (note: if you have 0 Wounds remaining, you can only crawl). You suffer a −20 penalty to all Tests involving movement of any kind, and any opponent trying to strike you in Melee Combat gains +20 to hit you.

Unlike most other conditions, *Prone* does not stack — you are either *Prone*, or you are not. You lose the *Prone* Condition when you stand up.

Stunned

You have been struck about the head or otherwise disorientated or confused; your ears are likely ringing, and little makes sense.

You are incapable of taking an Action on your turn but are capable of half your normal movement. You can defend yourself in opposed Tests — but not with Language (Magick). You also suffer a −10 penalty to all Tests. If you have any *Stunned* Conditions, any opponent trying to strike you in Melee Combat gains +1 Advantage before rolling the attack.

At the end of each Round, you may attempt a **Challenging (+0) Endurance** Test. If successful, remove a *Stunned* Condition, with each SL removing an extra *Stunned* Condition.

Once all *Stunned* Conditions are removed, gain 1 *Fatigued* Condition if you don't already have one.

Surprised

You have been caught unawares and you aren't at all ready for what's about to hit you. You can take no Action or Move on your turn and cannot defend yourself in opposed Tests. Any opponent trying to strike you in Melee Combat gains a bonus of +20 to hit.

The *Surprised* Condition does not stack, so you do not collect multiple *Surprised* Conditions, even should you be technically surprised multiple times in a Round.

At the end of each Round, or after the first attempt to attack you, you lose the *Surprised* Condition.

Unconscious

You are knocked out, asleep, or otherwise insensible. You can do nothing on your turn and are completely unaware of your surroundings. An attacker targeting you gains the benefit of the I Will Not Fail rule on page 171 without having to spend a Resilience point. Or, if the GM prefers, any close combat hit simply kills you. Any ranged combat hit automatically does the same if the shooter is at Point Blank range.

The *Unconscious* Condition does not stack — you are either *Unconscious*, or you are not — so you do not collect multiple *Unconscious* Conditions.

Recovering from unconsciousness requires different circumstances depending upon why you fell unconscious. Refer to Injury on page 172 for more on this. If you spend a Resolve point to remove an Unconscious condition, but have not resolved the cause of the incapacitation, you gain another *Unconscious* Condition at the end of the round. When you lose the *Unconscious* Condition, you gain the *Prone* and *Fatigued* Conditions.

FATE & RESILIENCE

Whether it's guts, luck or the favour of the gods, there is something special about you. Fate and Resilience represent the different ways you stand out from the masses.

Characters gain their starting Fate and Resilience in Character Generation (see page 34). Both are related to pools of points: Fate to Fortune, Resilience to Resolve. You may spend your points to achieve small benefits, and these pools will refill over the course of play. You spend your Fate or Resilience points for a significant benefit during play but this permanently reduces them and also reduces the associated pool of Fortune or Resolve points. While Fate and Resilience points may be regained, this occurs only rarely, so spend them carefully.

Although they are very rare and normally reserved for PCs, the GM may also want to apply Fate and Resilience to noteworthy NPCs, like a necromantic nemesis, a local luminary of significance, or a recurring cult leader.

FATE AND FORTUNE

Player characters have destiny. While their ultimate future is a mystery and there is no guarantee it will be glorious, heroic, or even pleasant, they are seemingly fated for something important.

To represent this, you begin play with a number of Fate Points. Fate points mark you out from the rest of the denizens of the Old World. They allow you to survive against impossible odds and prevail where ordinary folk fail.

Fate is directly related to your Fortune points. Fortune points are spent to receive minor bonuses, including the ability to reroll failed Tests or gain an edge as luck favours you, and the number you have will likely fluctuate wildly during play. Fate determines how many Fortune points you can have, and be permanently spent in the direst of circumstances to avoid death.

Spending Fortune

You may spend a Fortune point from your pool to turn luck to your advantage: hitting with that difficult crossbow shot when you would have otherwise missed; or perhaps an opponent slips, granting you a chance to land a blow. Your three options are:

- Reroll a failed Test.
- Add +1 SL to a Test after it is rolled.
- At the start of the Round, choose when to act in that Round disregarding Initiative order.

Spending Fate

You may spend a permanent Fate point to avoid death and survive even the most unlikely situations. When you do this, choose one of the following two options:

- **Die Another Day:** Instead of dying, your character is knocked out, left for dead, swept away by a river, or otherwise taken out of action; your character will survive, no matter the fatal incident's circumstances, but takes no further part in the current encounter.

- **How Did That Miss?:** Your character completely avoids the incoming damage by some extraordinary fluke, such as slipping just as a blow is about to connect, a weapon mysteriously jamming, or an unexpected source of light blinding an opponent; your character can continue on without penalty, but has no guarantee of survival in later rounds.

The first option takes you out of play, but allows you to fight another day, for all your character may be battered, bloody, bruised, and perhaps even captured in the process! The second option allows you to continue fighting side-by-side with your companions, but leaves you in significant danger, meaning you may need to spend more Fate points in later Rounds to ensure survival. Each option has advantages and disadvantages, depending upon the context of the situation, and it is up to you to decide which is the best choice to take.

The GM describes how you survive a given situation after spending a Fate rating point.

Regaining Fate and Fortune

You regain all Fortune points at the start of every gaming session, up to the maximum of your current Fate. In addition, certain in-game encounters may also replenish (or remove!) Fortune points.

Your GM may grant you a Fate point for an act of extreme heroism, bravery, or significance. Normally this only happens at the successful end of an important adventure, so make sure to spend them carefully as they rarely replenish.

LONG GAMING SESSIONS

Some players prefer short sessions of a few hours, others prefer day-long marathons. If your group prefers longer sessions, replenish Fortune points at narratively appropriate moments, roughly every four hours.

RESILIENCE AND RESOLVE

While Fate points represent your destiny, perhaps chosen by some distant, uncaring deity, Resilience is an indication of your personal drive and determination to endure, and overcome, no matter the obstacles you face.

Like Fate, Resilience is directly linked to a pool of points, this time called Resolve. Resolve points are spent to push through minor obstacles, such as ignoring the negative effects of critical wounds for a Round or removing Conditions. Resilience determines your upper limit of Resolve points and can be permanently spent to push yourself through seemingly impossible situations.

Spending Resolve

You may spend a Resolve point to draw upon your inner reserves: maybe confronting a terrifying Ogre without flinching; or ignoring the effects of even the most powerful of blows. Your choices are:

- Become immune to Psychology until the end of the next round. See Psychology on page 190.
- Ignore all modifiers from all Critical Wounds until the beginning of the next round.
- Remove one Condition; if you removed the *Prone* Condition, regain 1 Wound as you surge to your feet.

Spending Resilience

You may also choose to spend Resilience point to defy the corruption curling within, or to succeed where it would seem certain you should fail. Here, you have the following two options:

- **I Deny You!:** You may choose not to develop a rolled mutation. Because you do not mutate, you do not lose any Corruption points. See Corruption on page 182 for more on this.

- **I Will Not Fail!:** Rather than roll the result of a Test, you choose the number instead, allowing you to succeed in even the direst of situations. In an Opposed Test, you always win by at least 1 SL. If you cause a Critical, you can choose the Hit Location struck rather than randomising it. You can even choose to do this on a Test already failed.

Example: *A bandit leader is on the rampage, having built up 10 Advantage while evading the party's blows. Things are about to get messy! Salundra decides to attack the bandit, but loses the Opposed Test by 7 SL, which is going to hurt a lot. So, she spends a permanent Resilience point to invoke 'I Will Not Fail'. This means she automatically wins the Opposed Test by +1 SL. She also chooses the result of the roll to be 11, causing a Critical. The bandit leader will take some Wounds and a Critical Wound. More importantly, his rampage comes to an end as he also loses all 10 Advantage as the fight turns in the heroes favour.*

Saving permanent Resilience to rebuff the influence of Chaos is wise, but it does not remove your Corruption points, meaning mutation is still perilously close. By comparison, using permanent Resilience to succeed in any Test can allow you to land a blow on an otherwise impossible-to-hit target, create an artefact that astounds all who see it with a Trade skill, or even perfectly manifest a spell you would normally find impossible to cast.

When you spend a Resilience point, take time to describe the enormous feat of will your character has undertaken, and how this manifests in play.

Regaining Resilience and Resolve

Resolve is regained whenever you act according to your Motivation (see Motivation on page 34). During play, whenever you feel you have done this, you may ask the GM if you can recover one or more Resolve points.

Example: *Griselda is a nun with the Motivation 'Sigmar'. While her allies gossip in a tavern seeking clues, she elects to visit the local temple to make a donation and offer prayers to her deity. As this fits her Motivation, her GM decides to replenish one of her Resolve points but tells Griselda's player that she will need to pray and donate in a different temple to receive that benefit again this week.*

The GM may grant a Resilience point for an act of extreme importance to your Motivation, permanently nourishing your soul, but such an event will be very rare.

Example: *After many adventures, Griselda finally finances a new temple to Sigmar in her home village of Velten not far from Nuln. The GM recognises the importance of this to Griselda's faith and grants her a permanent Resilience point.*

INJURY

Almost all characters will suffer injuries during the course of play. The injury rules show you how to deal with them and how to heal them, when possible.

WOUNDS, CRITICAL WOUNDS, AND DEATH

Wound loss represents minor cuts and abrasions, bruises and bashes, and even the depletion of spiritual and mental energy reserves. By comparison, Critical Wounds are much more severe, expressing serious injuries, broken bones, torn muscles, and ripped flesh. Gain too many Critical Wounds, and you risk death.

Wounds

Wounds are lost by sustaining Damage. Each time you suffer a point of Damage, you lose 1 Wound. So, if you suffer 8 points of Damage, you lose 8 Wounds. Often, especially in combat, your Toughness Bonus or Armour Points may reduce suffered Damage.

So, if you were hit in the arm for 10 Damage and your Toughness Bonus was 3, and you had leather armour on that arm for 1 Armour Point, you would suffer 6 Wounds (10–3–1=6). The rules will tell you when you can or cannot reduce Damage with Toughness and Armour Points.

If you lose all of your Wounds, your collected injuries overwhelm you, and you gain the *Prone* Condition. Until you heal at least 1 Wound, you cannot lose the *Prone* Condition; worse, if you're not healed within a number of Rounds equal to your Toughness Bonus, you will pass out, gaining the *Unconscious* Condition. You will not regain consciousness until you heal back at least 1 Wound (see **Healing** on page 181).

If you take enough Damage that you would be taken to negative Wounds — say you suffered 5 Damage when you only had 2 Wounds left — you suffer a Critical Wound. If you suffer fewer negative Wounds than your Toughness Bonus (so, fewer than –4 Wounds if your Toughness Bonus is 4), you subtract –20 from your Critical Table result, with a minimum result of 01 (see page 174). **Note:** You never actually go into negative Wounds. The lowest number of Wounds you can ever have is 0.

Critical Wounds

Critical Wounds are most commonly suffered in combat when something *really* wants to hurt you. The two most frequent sources of Critical Wounds are when a Critical Hit is scored, or when you lose more Wounds than you have (see **Combat** on page 159 for more on how Critical Hits happens).

Each Critical Wound you receive will impact your ability to function in a different way. To determine what effects a Critical Wound has, refer to the Critical Tables (see page 174).

PULLING YOUR BLOWS

The rules assume you wish to inflict every possible Critical Wound you can. However, it's also possible you may just want to subdue, not kill, your opponents. Or you may be sparring. With that in mind, you may ignore any Critical Hit you should inflict upon your opponents if you declare you are 'pulling your blow' *before you roll to hit*. If you do this, make sure you describe the situation appropriately, making it clear you're using the flat of your blade or otherwise doing what you can to avoid properly hurting your opponent.

Death

If you take the *Unconscious* Condition and have 0 Wounds, compare the total number of Critical Wounds you currently suffer with your Toughness Bonus. If you have more Critical Wounds than your Toughness Bonus, you succumb to your horrific wounds and will die at the end of the round unless, by some miracle, someone heals one of your Critical Wounds.

Also, if you have the *Unconscious* Condition, anyone attacking you with suitable weapons can kill you, should they wish.

Though, in the thick of combat, those lying apparently dead on the floor are almost always ignored in favour of combatants still standing.

Lastly, a few results sourced from the Critical Tables can result in death. Should any of these occur, it is time to permanently spend a Fate point if you have one (see page 170).

OPTIONS: SUDDEN DEATH

Rather than worrying about Critical Wounds and protracted deaths, you may simply wish to know if someone is dead or not. The GM can do this by using the Sudden Death rules, which significantly accelerates play. When your targets suffer more damage than they have Wounds, they simply die in a suitably dramatic fashion or immediately gain the *Unconscious* Condition. Your choice.

Sudden Death is especially useful for quickly dealing with minor foes such as Brigands, Cultists, or Wild Animals, although it should not be used for PCs or important NPCs.

CRITICAL TABLES

When you receive a Critical Wound by losing more Wounds than you have, roll 1d100 and refer to the appropriate Critical Table to determine what has happened. When you receive a Critical Hit (see page 159), you do not determine the struck location by reversing your roll as normal. Instead, you roll 1d100 again and refer to **Determine Hit Location** (see page 159), then roll another 1d100 and refer to the appropriate Critical Table to determine what has happened. You suffer the number of Wounds indicated, not modified by Toughness Bonus or Armour Points, though these will never trigger a second Critical Wound. Further, you suffer any Additional Effects noted. If your Character suffers from the *Unconscious* Condition, you remain unconscious until the end of the encounter, or until you receive Medical Attention (see Healing on page 181), unless otherwise stated. If a result says you have broken bones, torn muscles, or an amputated body part, refer to **Broken Bones** on page 179, **Torn Muscles** on page 179, or **Amputated Parts** on page 180, for what happens. When you resume resolving the non-Critical Damage of the attack, use any new Hit Location determined by the Critical Wound.

HEAD CRITICAL WOUNDS

Roll	Description	Wounds	Additional Effects
01–10	*Dramatic Injury*	1	A fine wound across the forehead and cheek. Gain 1 *Bleeding* Condition. Once the wound is healed, the impressive scar it leaves provides a bonus of +1 SL to appropriate social Tests. You can only gain this benefit once.
11–20	*Minor Cut*	1	The strike opens your cheek and blood flies. Gain 1 *Bleeding* Condition.
21–25	*Poked Eye*	1	The blow glances across your eye socket. Gain 1 *Blinded* condition.
26–30	*Ear Bash*	1	After a sickening impact, your ear is left ringing. Gain 1 *Deafened* Condition.
31–35	*Rattling Blow*	2	The blow floods your vision with flashing lights. Gain 1 *Stunned* Condition.
36–40	*Black Eye*	2	A solid blow hits your eye, leaving tears and pain. Gain 2 *Blinded* Conditions.
41–45	*Sliced Ear*	2	Your side of your head takes a hard blow, cutting deep into your ear. Gain 2 *Deafened* and 1 *Bleeding* Condition.
46–50	*Struck Forehead*	2	A solid blow hits your forehead. Gain 2 *Bleeding* Conditions and a *Blinded* Condition that cannot be removed until all *Bleeding* Conditions are removed.
51–55	*Fractured Jaw*	3	With a sickening crunch, pain fills your face as the blow fractures your jaw. Gain 2 *Stunned* Conditions. Suffer a **Broken Bone (Minor)** injury.
56–60	*Major Eye Wound*	3	The blow cracks across your eye socket. Gain 1 *Bleeding* Condition. Also gain 1 *Blinded* Condition that cannot be removed until you receive Medical Attention.
61–65	*Major Ear Wound*	3	The blow strikes deep into one ear. Suffer a permanent –20 penalty on all Tests relating to hearing. If you suffer this result again, your hearing is permanently lost as the second ear falls quiet. Only magic can heal this.
66–70	*Broken Nose*	3	A solid blow to the centre of your face causing blood to pour. Gain 2 *Bleeding* Conditions. Make a **Challenging (+0) Endurance** Test, or also gain a *Stunned* Condition. After this wound has healed, gain +1/–1 SL on social rolls, depending on context, unless **Surgery** is used to reset the nose.
71–75	*Broken Jaw*	4	The crack is sickening as the blow hits you under the chin, breaking your jaw. Gain 3 *Stunned* Conditions. Make a **Challenging (+0) Endurance** Test or gain an *Unconscious* Condition. Suffer a **Broken Bone (Major)** injury.
76–80	*Concussive Blow*	4	Your brain rattles in your skull as blood spurts from your nose and ears. Take 1 *Deafened*, 2 *Bleeding*, and 1d10 *Stunned* Conditions. Gain a *Fatigued* Condition that lasts for 1d10 days. If you receive another Critical Wound to your head while suffering this *Fatigued* Condition, make an **Average (+20) Endurance Test** or also gain an *Unconscious* Condition.

81–85	*Smashed Mouth*	4	With a sickening crunch, your mouth is suddenly filled with broken teeth and blood. Gain 2 *Bleeding* Conditions. Lose 1d10 teeth — **Amputation (Easy)**.
86–90	*Mangled Ear*	4	Little is left of your ear as the blow tears it apart. You gain 3 *Deafened* and 2 *Bleeding* Conditions. Lose your ear —**Amputation (Average)**.
91–93	*Devastated Eye*	5	A strike to your eye completely bursts it, causing extraordinary pain. Gain 3 *Blinded*, 2 *Bleeding*, and 1 *Stunned* Condition. Lose your eye — **Amputation (Difficult)**.
94–96	*Disfiguring Blow*	5	The blow smashes your entire face, destroying your eye and nose in a cloud of blood. Gain 3 *Bleeding*, 3 *Blinded* and 2 *Stunned* Conditions. Lose your eye and nose — **Amputation (Hard)**.
97–99	*Mangled Jaw*	5	The blow almost removes your jaw as it utterly destroys your tongue, sending teeth flying in a shower of blood. Gain 4 *Bleeding* and 3 *Stunned* Conditions. Make a **Very Hard (–30) Endurance** Test or gain an *Unconscious* Condition. Suffer a **Broken Bone (Major)** injury and lose your tongue and 1d10 teeth — **Amputation (Hard)**.
00	*Decapitated*	Death	Your head is entirely severed from your neck and soars through the air, landing 1d10 feet away in a random direction (see **Scatter**). Your body collapses, instantly dead.

ARM CRITICAL WOUNDS

Roll	Description	Wounds	Additional Effects
01–10	*Jarred Arm*	1	Your arm is jarred in the attack. Drop whatever was held in that hand.
11–20	*Minor cut*	1	Gain a *Bleeding* Condition as your upper arm is cut badly.
21–25	*Sprain*	1	You sprain your arm, suffering a **Torn Muscle (Minor)** injury.
26–30	*Badly Jarred Arm*	2	Your arm is badly jarred in the attack. Drop whatever was held in that hand, which is useless for 1d10 – Toughness Bonus Rounds (minimum 1). For this time, treat the hand as lost (see **Amputated Parts**).
31–35	*Torn Muscles*	2	The blow slams into your forearm. Gain a *Bleeding* Condition and a **Torn Muscle (Minor)** injury.
36–40	*Bleeding Hand*	2	Your hand is cut badly, making your grip slippery. Take 1 *Bleeding* Condition. While suffering from that *Bleeding* Condition, make an **Average (+20) Dexterity** Test before taking any Action that requires something being held in that hand; if you fail, the item slips from your grip.
41–45	*Wrenched Arm*	2	Your arm is almost pulled from its socket. Drop whatever is held in the associated hand; the arm is useless for 1d10 Rounds (see **Amputated Parts**).
46–50	*Gaping Wound*	3	The blow opens a deep, gaping wound. Gain 2 *Bleeding* Conditions. Until you receive **Surgery** to stitch up the cut, any associated Arm Damage you receive will also inflict 1 *Bleeding* Condition as the wound reopens.
51–55	*Clean Break*	3	An audible crack resounds as the blow strikes your arm. Drop whatever was held in the associated hand and gain a **Broken Bone (Minor)** injury. Pass a **Difficult (–10) Endurance** Test or gain a *Stunned* Condition.
56–60	*Ruptured Ligament*	3	You immediately drop whatever was held in that hand. Suffer a **Torn Muscle (Major)** injury.

61–65	*Deep Cut*	3	Gain 2 *Bleeding* Conditions as your arm is mangled. Gain 1 *Stunned* Condition and suffer a **Torn Muscle (Minor)** injury. Take a **Hard (–20) Endurance** Test or gain the *Unconscious* Condition.
66–70	*Damaged Artery*	4	Gain 4 *Bleeding* Conditions. Until you receive **Surgery**, every time you take Damage to this Arm Hit Location gain 2 *Bleeding* Conditions.
71–75	*Crushed Elbow*	4	The blow crushes your elbow, splintering bone and cartilage. You immediately drop whatever was held in that hand and gain a **Broken Bone (Major)** injury.
76–80	*Dislocated Shoulder*	4	Your arm is wrenched out of its socket. Pass a **Hard (–20) Endurance** Test or gain the *Stunned* and *Prone* Condition. Drop whatever is held in that hand: the arm is useless and counts as lost (see **Amputated Part**). Gain 1 *Stunned* Condition until you receive Medical Attention. After this initial Medical Attention, an **Extended Average (+20) Heal** Test needing 6 SL is required to reset the arm, at which point you regain its use. Tests made using this arm suffer a –10 penalty for 1d10 days.
81–85	*Severed Finger*	4	You gape in horror as a finger flies — **Amputation (Average)**. Gain a *Bleeding* condition.
86–90	*Cleft Hand*	5	Your hand splays open from the blow. Lose 1 finger —**Amputation (Difficult)**. Gain 2 *Bleeding* and 1 *Stunned* Condition. For every succeeding Round in which you don't receive Medical Attention, you lose another finger as the wound tears; if you run out of fingers, you lose the hand — **Amputation (Difficult)**.
91–93	*Mauled Bicep*	5	The blow almost separates bicep and tendon from bone, leaving an ugly wound that sprays blood over you and your opponent. You automatically drop anything held in the associated hand and suffers a **Torn Muscle (Major)** injury and 2 *Bleeding* and 1 *Stunned* Condition.
94–96	*Mangled Hand*	5	Your hand is left a mauled, bleeding mess. You lose your hand —**Amputation (Hard)**. Gain 2 *Bleeding* Condition. Take a **Hard (–20) Endurance** Test or gain the *Stunned* and *Prone* Conditions.
97–99	*Sliced Tendons*	5	Your tendons are cut by the blow, leaving your arm hanging useless — Amputation (Very Hard). Gain 3 *Bleeding*, 1 *Prone*, and 1 *Stunned* Condition. Pass a **Hard (–20) Endurance** Test or gain the *Unconscious* Condition.
00	*Brutal Dismemberment*	Death	Your arm is severed, spraying arterial blood 1d10 feet in a random direction (see **Scatter**), before the blow follows through to your chest.

BODY CRITICAL WOUNDS

Roll	Description	Wounds	Additional Effects
01–10	*'Tis But A Scratch!*	1	Gain 1 *Bleeding* Condition.
11–20	*Gut Blow*	1	Gain 1 *Stunned* Condition. Pass an **Easy (+40) Endurance** Test, or vomit, gaining the *Prone* Condition.
21–25	*Low Blow!*	1	Make a **Hard (-20) Endurance** Test or gain 3 *Stunned* Condition.
26–30	*Twisted Back*	1	Suffer a **Torn Muscle (Minor)** injury.
31–35	*Winded*	2	Gain a *Stunned* Condition. Make an **Average (+20) Endurance** Test, or gain the *Prone* Condition. Movement is halved for 1d10 rounds as you get your breath back.
36–40	*Bruised Ribs*	2	All Agility-based Tests suffer a –10 penalty for 1d10 days.

41–45	Wrenched Collar Bone	2	Randomly select one arm. Drop whatever is held in that hand; the arm is useless for 1d10 rounds (see **Amputated Parts**).
46–50	Ragged Wound	2	Take 2 *Bleeding* Conditions.
51–55	Cracked Ribs	3	The hit cracks one or more ribs. Gain a *Stunned* Condition. Gain a **Broken Bone (Minor)** injury.
56–60	Gaping Wound	3	Take 3 *Bleeding* Conditions. Until you receive **Surgery**, any Wounds you receive to the Body Hit Location will inflict an additional *Bleeding* Condition as the cut reopens.
61–65	Painful Cut	3	Gain 2 *Bleeding* Conditions and a *Stunned* Condition. Take a **Hard (−20) Endurance** Test or gain the *Unconscious* Condition as you black out from the pain. Unless you achieve 4+ SL, you also scream out in agony.
66–70	Arterial Damage	3	Gain 4 *Bleeding* Conditions. Until you receive **Surgery**, every time you receive Damage to the Body Hit Location, gain 2 *Bleeding* Conditions.
71–75	Pulled Back	4	Your back turns to white pain as you pull a muscle. Suffer a **Torn Muscle (Major)** injury.
76–80	Fractured Hip	4	Gain a *Stunned* Condition. Take a **Challenging (+0) Endurance** Test or also gain the *Prone* Condition. Suffer a **Broken Bone (Minor)** injury.
81–85	Major Chest Wound	4	You take a significant wound to your chest, flensing skin from muscle and sinew. Take 4 *Bleeding* Conditions. Until you receive **Surgery**, to stitch the wound together, any Wounds you receive to the Body Hit Location will also inflict 2 *Bleeding* Conditions as the tears reopen.
86–90	Gut Wound	4	Contract a Festering Wound (see **Disease and Infection**) and gain 2 *Bleeding* Conditions.
91–93	Smashed Rib Cage	5	Gain a *Stunned* Condition that can only be removed through Medical Attention, and suffer a **Broken Bone (Major)** injury.
94–96	Broken Collar Bone	5	Gain the *Unconscious* Condition until you receive Medical Attention, and suffer a **Broken Bone (Major)** injury.
97–99	Internal bleeding	5	Gain a *Bleeding* Condition that can only be removed through **Surgery**. Contract Blood Rot (see **Disease and Infection**).
00	Torn Apart	Death	You are hacked in two. The top half lands in a random direction, and all characters within 2 yards are showered in blood.

LEG CRITICAL WOUNDS

Roll	Description	Wounds	Additional Effects
01–10	Stubbed Toe	1	In the scuffle, you stub your toe. Pass a **Routine (+20) Endurance** Test or suffer −10 on Agility Tests until the end of the next turn.
11–20	Twisted Ankle	1	You go over your ankle, hurting it. Agility Tests suffer a −10 penalty for 1d10 rounds.
21–25	Minor Cut	1	Gain 1 *Bleeding* Condition.
26–30	Lost Footing	1	In the scuffle you lose your footing. Pass a **Challenging (+0) Endurance** Test or gain the *Prone* Condition.
31–35	Thigh Strike	2	A painful blow slams into your upper thigh. Gain a *Bleeding* Condition and take an **Average (+20) Endurance** Test or stumble, gaining the *Prone* Condition.

36–40	*Sprained Ankle*	2	You sprain your ankle, giving you a **Torn Muscle (Minor)** injury.
41–45	*Twisted Knee*	2	You twist your knee too far. Agility Tests suffer a −20 penalty for 1d10 rounds.
46–50	*Badly Cut Toe*	2	Gain 1 *Bleeding* Condition. After the encounter, make a **Challenging (+0) Endurance** Test. If you fail, lose 1 toe —**Amputation (Average)**.
51–55	*Bad Cut*	3	Gain 2 *Bleeding* conditions as a deep wound opens up your shin. Pass a **Challenging (+0) Endurance** Test or gain the *Prone* Condition.
56–60	*Badly Twisted Knee*	3	You badly twist your knee trying to avoid your opponent. Gain a **Torn Muscle (Major)** injury.
61–65	*Hacked Leg*	3	A cut bites down into the hip. Gain 1 *Prone* and 2 *Bleeding* Conditions, and suffer a **Broken Bone (Minor)** injury. Further, take a **Hard (−20) Endurance** Test or also gain a *Stunned* condition from the pain.
66–70	*Torn Thigh*	3	Gain 3 *Bleeding* Conditions as the weapon opens up your upper thigh. Pass a **Challenging (+0) Endurance** Test or gain the *Prone* Condition. Until you receive **Surgery** to stitch up the wound, each time you receive Damage to this Leg, also receive 1 *Bleeding* Condition.
71–75	*Ruptured Tendon*	4	Gain a *Prone* and *Stunned* Condition as one of your tendons tears badly. Pass a **Hard (−20) Endurance** Test or gain the *Unconscious* Condition. Your leg is useless (see **Amputated Parts**). Suffer a **Torn Muscle (Major)** injury.
76–80	*Carved Shin*	4	The weapon drives clean through your leg by the knee, slicing into bone and through tendons. Gain a *Stunned* and *Prone* Condition. Further, suffer a **Torn Muscle (Major)** and **Broken Bone (Minor)** injury.
81–85	*Broken Knee*	4	The blow hacks into your kneecap, shattering it into several pieces. You gain 1 *Bleeding*, 1 *Prone*, and 1 *Stunned* Condition, and a **Broken Bone (Major)** Injury as you fall to the ground, clutching your ruined leg.
86–90	*Dislocated Knee*	4	Your knee is wrenched out of its socket. Gain the *Prone* Condition. Pass a **Hard (−20) Endurance** Test, or gain the *Stunned* Condition, which is not removed until you receive Medical Attention. After this initial Medical Attention, an **Extended Average (+20) Heal** Test needing 6 SL is required to reset the knee at which point you regain its use. Movement is halved, and Tests made using this leg suffer a −10 penalty for d10 days.
91–93	*Crushed Foot*	5	The blow crushes your foot. Make an **Average (+20) Endurance** Test; if you fail, gain the *Prone* condition and lose 1 toe, plus 1 additional toe for each SL below 0 — **Amputation (Average)**. Gain 2 *Bleeding* Conditions. If you don't receive **Surgery** within 1d10 days, you will lose the foot entirely.
94–96	*Severed Foot*	5	Your foot is severed at the ankle and lands 1d10 feet away in a random direction — **Amputation (Hard)** (see **Scatter**). You gain 3 *Bleeding*, 2 *Stunned*, and 1 *Prone* Condition.
97–99	*Cut Tendon*	5	A major tendon at the back of your leg is cut, causing you to scream out in pain as your leg collapses. Gain 2 *Bleeding*, 2 *Stunned*, and 1 *Prone* Condition and look on in horror as your leg never works again — **Amputation (Very Hard)**.
00	*Shattered Pelvis*	Death	The blow shatters your pelvis, severing one leg then driving through to the next. You die instantly from traumatic shock.

HEALING HANDS

Critical Wounds are frequently nasty, so if you want to survive your journeys through the Old World, it is recommended you wear armour and bring at least one companion with some form of healing skills or spells, and perhaps even one skilled in surgery. If you do not, you may succumb to your wounds or infection long before you reach the next settlement.

BROKEN BONES

Small fractures may heal on their own accord, but severe breaks, with bone protruding at odd angles from the flesh, are a different matter entirely. If you suffer a *Broken Bone,* it will be marked as minor or major.

Minor

You have fractured one of your bones, but it is still aligned, meaning it may heal of its own accord without medical attention. The Hit Location is unusable until the breakage heals. For Arm and Leg hits, you are down to one limb as the other is too painful to use, and may require binding. Use the rules for a Severed Arm or Leg to represent this (see Amputated Parts).

For Head hits you will be down to a liquid diet and will suffer a penalty of −30 to all Language Tests. For Body hits, your strength and mobility will be severely limited: suffer a loss of −30 to your Strength and Agility Characteristics, and half your Move.

Healing: A fractured bone will take 30+1d10 days to heal. At the end of this, a successful **Average (+20) Endurance** Test means the bone has set well, and no long-term effects will be suffered. If the Test is failed, you suffer a permanent loss of −5 to all Agility Tests when using a damaged arm, a permanent loss of −5 to your Agility characteristic for a badly healed Body or Leg hit, or a permanent loss of −5 to spoken Language Tests for a badly healed Head hit.

A successful **Average (+20) Heal** Test within a week of receiving the fracture will negate the need for the Endurance Test, but the affected area must remain bound and held in place for the duration of the healing. If the binding should be undone, another **Average (+20) Heal** Test enacted within a day will need to be passed to avoid the Endurance Test.

Major

One of your bones is badly broken, and is either resting at an odd angle, or has splintered at the point of breakage. It is unlikely to heal properly without medical attention.

The Hit Location is effectively unusable until the breakage heals. Use all the same rules as for Broken Bone (Minor).

Healing: Healing takes 10 days longer. All associated Tests are **Challenging (+0)**. Any penalties for failed Tests increase to −10.

TORN MUSCLES

Sprains or tears to your muscles or ligaments result in significant pain and possible loss of use depending upon the severity, which will be marked as minor or major.

Minor

One of your muscles is sprained or torn, resulting in impaired capabilities and much pain. Suffer a penalty of −10 to all Tests involving the location. If a Leg is hit, also halve your Movement.

Healing: The muscle will partially heal in 30 – your Toughness Bonus days. Use of the Healing skill will reduce the time by 1 day, plus a further day per SL (you can gain this benefit once).

Major

One of your muscles or some important tendons have been severely damaged, resulting in extreme pain and a significant loss in capability of the afflicted limb.

Suffer the same effects as Torn Muscle (Minor), but the penalties are −20 to all Tests.

Healing: The muscle will partially heal in 30 – your Toughness Bonus days, after which the penalty for using the limb reduces to −10 to all relevant Tests. The muscle will completely heal after another 30 – your Toughness Bonus days. Use of the Healing skill does little but inform you not to use the affected Hit Location.

Amputated Parts

Many of the more severe Critical Wounds result in the loss of a body part, such as fingers, hands, feet, or even a whole leg! Should a character suffer more than one severed body part, it is probably time to start looking for an appropriate replacement to mitigate any possible penalties (see **Chapter 11: Consumers' Guide**).

Whenever you suffer a Critical Wound marked **Amputation (difficulty)**, you must pass an **Endurance** Test (the difficulty is marked in the brackets) or gain a *Prone* Condition. On a Failure (−2) or worse, you also gain a *Stunned* Condition; on an Impressive Failure (−4 or worse), gain an *Unconscious* Condition.

All amputations require Surgery to heal properly, meaning 1 Wound cannot be healed until you visit a surgeon. See Surgery on page 181.

Arm

Use the rules for lost hand, but you cannot strap a shield to the arm since you don't have one.

Ear

Losing an ear is painful, but you will soon learn to live without it. Should you have the bad luck to lose both your ears, permanently suffer a penalty of −20 to all hearing-based Perception Tests. Further, you suffer a penalty of −5 to all Fellowship Tests per ear lost when others can see your earless state.

Eye

For all losing an eye is horrendous, but you soon learn to compensate. Should you have the misfortune to lose both eyes, suffer a penalty of −30 to all Tests influenced by sight, such as Weapon Tests, Dodge Tests, Ride Tests, and similar. Further, you suffer a penalty of −5 to all Fellowship Tests per scarred socket others can see.

Fingers

Losing a finger results in lessened grip, causing an increased chance of fumbling Tests using that hand. For the first finger lost, any relevant, failed Test with a 1 on the units die counts as a fumble. For two lost fingers, any relevant, failed Test with a 1 or 2 on the units die counts as a fumble, and so on.

Further, you suffer a penalty of −5 to all Tests using the hand in question per finger lost. Once 4 or more fingers are lost on a hand, use the rules for a severed hand.

Foot

Reduce your Move by half permanently and suffer a −20 penalty to all Tests that rely on mobility, such as Dodge. Losing both feet makes it hard to walk. Perhaps you could hire a henchman to carry you?

Hand

You take a −20 penalty on all Tests that rely on the use of two hands and you cannot wield two-handed weapons; however, a shield can be strapped to the injured arm. Should the lost hand be your primary hand, you take the customary −20 penalty to Melee Tests made with weapons using your secondary hand. For every 100 XP you spend, you can reduce this penalty by 5 as you relearn how to do everything with the other hand. If you lose both hands, it is probably time to master hook fighting.

Leg

Treat this as a lost foot, but you cannot use the Dodge skill at all.

Nose

A loss of a nose leaves one looking freakish in the extreme. Suffer a permanent loss of −20 to your Fellowship and suffer a penalty of −30 to all Tests involving the sense of smell.

Teeth

Loss of teeth may be unsightly and can make eating difficult. For every two teeth you lose you also suffer a permanent loss of 1 from your Fellowship characteristic.

Further, once more than half your teeth (Humans: 16; Elves: 18; Halflings and Dwarfs: 20) are lost, you find consuming solids significantly more difficult than your peers, doubling eating times, and making some foodstuffs nigh-on impossible to eat, which is largely a matter of roleplaying and narrative description of your actions.

Toes

Loss of toes has an adverse effect on your balance. For each toe lost, suffer a permanent loss of −1 to your Agility and Weapon Skill Characteristics.

Tongue

A loss of a tongue leaves you grunting and humming, or relying on make-shift sign language, for communication. You automatically fail all Language Tests involving speaking.

HEALING

In time, most injuries heal. But some are worse than others. The following explains how to heal Wounds and Critical Wounds.

Healing Wounds

You are considered wounded if you have lost any of your Wounds.

Without medical attention, you can attempt an **Average (+20) Endurance** Test after a good sleep once a day. You Heal Wounds equal to the SL + your Toughness Bonus. For each day you spend taking it easy, you also heal an extra number of Wounds equal to your Toughness Bonus.

If you wish to Heal more Wounds than this, then you need to be attended by someone with the Heal skill (see **Chapter 4: Skills and Talents**) or you'll need bandages, a healing poultice, or similar (see **Chapter 11: Consumers' Guide**).

There is no penalty for being wounded. Lost Wounds are considered to be small cuts, bruises, and other easily ignored injuries.

Healing Critical Wounds

If you have received any Critical Wounds, you are said to be Critically Wounded. Critical Wounds can be very serious. Refer to the appropriate Critical Table to see exactly what penalties you suffer for any Critical Wounds sustained. Critical Wounds do not count as healed until all conditions they inflict are removed, and all non-permanent negative modifiers are resolved. When you are Critically Wounded, you may still heal your Wounds using the normal rules.

MEDICAL ATTENTION

Several Critical Wound results and conditions cannot be resolved until you receive medical attention. This includes, but is not limited to, the following:

- Successful use of the Heal skill.
- Application of a bandage, healing poultice, or similar.
- Successful use of a spell or prayer that heals Wounds.

Surgery

Some wounds are beyond simple stitching and foul-smelling poultices. If you suffer a Critical Wound where surgery is required to attend to it (it will be marked: Surgery), you suffer the marked penalties until you visit an appropriately trained doctor or barber-surgeon, or somehow source a magical or divine surgery equivalent.

Further, if you suffer an amputated body part, you cannot heal 1 of the suffered Wounds until a surgeon successfully treats it with a Heal Test. For more information on surgery, refer to the *Surgery* talent in **Chapter 4: Skills and Talents**.

OTHER DAMAGE

The Old World is a dangerous place, hiding countless ways to die. The following covers some of the more common other ways you can receive Damage during play.

Drowning and Suffocation

If prepared, you can hold your breath for Toughness Bonus x 10 seconds without a Test. After that, you may start to suffocate or drown. If you are unprepared and suddenly deprived of air, you will start to suffocate immediately.

Each Round you are being suffocated you lose 1 Wound. Should you reach 0 Wounds, you immediately receive the *Unconscious* Condition. After that, you will die of suffocation or drowning in Toughness Bonus Rounds.

Exposure

Every 4 hours spent in a difficult environment — such as sub-zero temperatures, a hot desert, or a howling storm — requires you take an Endurance Test. Extreme environments require a Test every 2 hours.

Cold: Your first failure causes a penalty of −10 Ballistic Skill, Agility and Dexterity. The second failure reduces all other Characteristics by −10. Third and subsequent failures cause 1d10 Damage not modified by Armour Points, with a minimum of 1 Wound lost. If you reach zero Wounds, you immediately take an Unconscious condition. Certain Trappings provide bonuses and penalties to these Tests. See pages 302 and 309.

Heat: Your first failure causes a penalty of −10 to **Intelligence** and **Willpower**, and adds a *Fatigued* Condition. The second failure reduces all other Characteristics by −10%, and adds another *Fatigued* Condition. Third and subsequent failures cause 1d10 Damage not modified by Armour Points, with a minimum of 1 Wound lost. Stripping off heavy Trappings cancels 1 failed test.

Thirst and Starvation

Running out of provisions can be bad. Running out of water is worse. Endurance Tests to withstand thirst and hunger become increasingly difficult (cumulative −10 for every test). Characters without food and water cannot heal Wounds or recover Fatigue naturally.

Water: Every day without water requires you make an Endurance test. The first failed Test causes a penalty of −10 **Intelligence**, **Willpower**, and **Fellowship**. Second and subsequent failures reduce all Characteristics by −10 and cause 1d10 Damage not modified by Armour Points, with a minimum of 1 Wound lost.

Food: Every 2 days without food require an Endurance Test. The first failed Tests causes a penalty of −10 Strength and Toughness. Second and subsequent failures reduce all other Characteristics by −10 and cause 1d10 Damage not modified by Armour Points, with a minimum of 1 Wound lost.

CORRUPTION

Every Festag, Sigmarite priests preach from high pulpits about the dangers of the Ruinous Powers, about how good folk must avoid the temptations of daemons whispering from every shadow. They declare all souls are in perpetual peril, mere footsteps from falling to corruption and mutation. And they might be right.

Corruption points are used to show the slow, gradual slip of your soul to the Dark Gods of Chaos. Whenever you are exposed to a potential source of corruption, you may accrue Corruption points. The more you have, the closer you are drawing to Chaos, and the darker your soul becomes until, eventually, you change…

Gaining Corruption Points

During play, there are two primary routes to gaining corruption: *dark deals* and *corrupting influences*.

Dark Deals

Sometimes, you just have to succeed. Most commonly this means passing an important Test. Should such a Test fail, you can use a Fortune point to reroll the Test, hopefully passing the second time. But what if it fails again? Or you have no Fortune points remaining? Then it's time for a dark deal.

You can purposefully choose to take a Corruption point to reroll a Test, even if it has been rerolled already. This is always a choice for you, not the GM — although there is nothing wrong with the GM gently reminding you that you could try again. After all, what's the worst that could happen?

OPTIONS: ENCROACHING DARKNESS…

Some inventive players prefer to embellish their dark deals with disturbing events happening in-game. If you like the sound of this, it's up to you how such events should manifest, but tailoring them to the story of the character involved is always a good idea. Perhaps taint subtly influences the local area causing animals to flee or plants to gently rot?

Perhaps you could roll on the Miscast table from **Chapter 8: Magic** to create a random event (especially appropriate for wizards and witches)? Think of the Test tied to the dark deed, and then consider soul-staining events that could occur to ensure your success.

Corrupting Influences

Corruption points are usually gained by exposure to a place, person, or object tainted by Chaos, or to a situation especially beloved to one of the Dark Gods.

If you encounter a corrupting influence, attempt a **Challenging (+0) Endurance** Test, or **Challenging (+0) Cool** Test, as determined by the GM — usually physical influences are resisted with Endurance, spiritual corruption is resisted with Cool.

The stronger the corrupting influence, the more SL you will need to avoid it. The following provides some examples of corrupting influences with the number of SL needed to completely avoid Corruption points.

Minor Exposure

These corrupting influences, although relatively trivial, still endanger a weak soul. If a Test is failed to resist such a minor exposure, gain 1 Corruption point.

- Witness a Lesser Daemon.
- Contact with a Mutant, refined Warpstone, or Chaos-tainted artefact.
- Giving in to despair, rage, excess, or the need to change your lot.
- Being near Warpstone.
- Prolonged exposure to Chaos worshippers, Chaos Cult Temples, Skaven, Mutant Lairs, and similar.

Moderate Exposure

Moderate corrupting influences are a danger to every soul and should be avoided under all circumstances. If a Test is failed, gain 2 Corruption points. On a Marginal Success (0–1), gain 1 Corruption point. On a Success (2+), you gain no Corruption points.

- Witness multiple Daemons.
- Contact with a Daemon, Warpstone, or profane artefact.
- Embracing despair, rage, excess, or the desire to become someone new.
- Prolonged exposure to refined Warpstone.
- Brief exposure to an environment steeped with *Dhar,* dark magic used by Necromancers and Chaos Sorcerers.

Major Exposure

If you find yourself confronted with a major corrupting influence, flee. Stay for too long, and you may never be the same again. For each failed Test to resist a major exposure, gain 3 Corruption points. If you pass with a Marginal Success (0–1), gain 2 Corruption points. On a Success (2–3), you gain 1 Corruption point. Only if you score an Impressive Success (4+), do you gain no Corruption points.

- Witness a Greater Daemon.
- Prolonged contact with a Daemon, Warpstone, or profane artefact.
- Making a deal with a Daemon.
- Consuming refined Warpstone.
- Prolonged exposure to an environment steeped with *dhar* (see **Magic** for more on this).

CORRUPTING

No-one is left unscathed by exposure to the Ruinous Powers. Eventually, even the strongest fall, their mind and bodies twisting into new unrecognisable forms.

Should you ever gain more Corruption points than your Willpower Bonus plus your Toughness Bonus, immediately attempt a **Challenging (+0) Endurance** Test. If passed, you have managed to hold off your corruption for now but will have to Test again next time you gain Corruption Points. If you fail, then either your body or mind is about to mutate.

Dissolution of Body and Mind

As corruption ravages your soul, the warping breath of Chaos whispers within, either fanning your flesh into a fresh, new form, or fracturing your psyche with exquisite knowledge it can never unlearn.

First, lose Corruption points equal to your Willpower Bonus as you mutate. Next, roll percentile dice and refer to the following table to determine whether it's your body or your mind that blossoms anew.

	Elf	Halfling	Human	Dwarf
Body	–	01–10	01–50	01–05
Mind	01–100	11–100	51–100	06–100

Now roll on either the **Physical Corruption Table** (page 184) or the **Mental Corruption Table** (page 185) to see what happens.

Corruption Limits

A soul can only withstand so much corruption before it collapses upon itself, leaving a mutated, gibbering mess. Should you survive long enough to gain more mutations than your Toughness Bonus, or more mental corruptions than your Willpower Bonus, you have fallen to Chaos, your soul completely lost to the uncaring Chaos Gods. At this point, it's time to create a new character. Your current one is now damned, becoming an NPC controlled by the GM, meaning you may well see the wretched creature again…

LOSING CORRUPTION POINTS

Once the claws of the Dark Gods have sunk into your soul, removing their vile stain is difficult, but not impossible. Beyond the less-than-desirable option of losing Corruption points by gaining mutations, there are two other methods of losing Corruption points: *dark whispers* and *absolution*.

Dark Whispers

Even considering the inscrutable plans of the Dark Gods is enough to break a pious man's sanity, so trying to fathom their intent, and why they reach out to twist one mortal soul or another, is not just foolish, it's extraordinarily dangerous. But reach out they do.

The GM may ask to spend one of your Corruption points to use the darkness building in your soul to twist your actions. The choice to do this or not is *always* in your hands, but if you agree, you lose 1 Corruption Point. Examples of what may be asked include:

- Letting an enemy escape.
- 'Accidentally' shooting an ally.
- Falling asleep on watch.

Of course, if you deny the GM and choose to do none of those potentially terrible things, you keep your Corruption point, but the Ruinous Powers still hold a portion of your soul.

BE VERY CAREFUL

Used sparingly, Corruption Points are great fun as Faustian deals are made for rerolls and traded back for memorable roleplaying moments as minor betrayals spread, but if you're playing with a group that doesn't readily understand the Old World, the points can accrue very quickly, sending characters into a spiral of mutation and madness. This should probably be avoided. Mutation is effectively a death sentence if discovered, so it's important new players are cautioned when their actions may lead to corruption. Just like every child in the Empire is warned of the dangers posed by the Ruinous Powers, players should be warned that Warpstone should not be touched or even approached, that tainted artefacts are dangerous, and the Cultists of Chaos should be avoided at all costs. Of course, the circumstances of the adventure at hand may force your group into the most horrendous situations with corruption around every corner, but that's **WFRP**.

PHYSICAL CORRUPTION TABLE

Use the descriptions below to help create a unique version of your mutation. Take time to describe how it manifests, adding as many gruesome details as you dare. In all cases, if your mutation is obvious, you not only suffer significant penalties to Fellowship Tests as determined by the circumstance, but people will likely flee from your presence, the Watch will be called, Witch Hunters will descend, and life will swiftly become very difficult.

D100	Description	Effect
01–05	Animalistic Legs	+1 Movement
06–10	Corpulent	−1 Movement, +5 Strength, +5 Toughness
11–15	Distended Digits	+10 Dexterity
16–20	Emaciated	−10 Strength, +5 Agility
21–25	Enormous Eye	+10 on Perception Tests involving sight
26–30	Extra Leg Joints	+5 Agility
31–35	Extra Mouth	Roll on the Hit Location table to see where
36–40	Fleshy Tentacle	Gain the Tentacles Creature Trait. See page 342
41–45	Glowing Skin	Effective light of a candle
46–50	Inhuman Beauty	+10 Fellowship; you do not scar
51–55	Inverted Face	−20 to all Fellowship Tests
56–60	Iron Skin	+2 Armour Points to all locations, −10 Agility
61–65	Lolling Tongue	−10 to all Language Tests when speaking
66–70	Patchy Feathers	Roll on the Hit Location table twice to see where
71–75	Short Legs	−1 Movement
76–80	Thorny Scales	+1 Armour Points to all locations
81–85	Uneven Horns	+1 Armour Points to the Head; counts as a Creature Weapon of Damage equal to your SB (see page 343)
86–90	Weeping Pus	Roll on the Hit Location Table to see from where
91–95	Whiskered Snout	+10 Track
96–00	GM's Choice	The GM chooses a Mutation or Creature Trait. See page 338

MENTAL CORRUPTION TABLE

A corrupted mind may be less obvious than a sprouting tentacle, but it can be just as devastating to your life. Use the description you roll to build a unique mental mutation that fits your character, taking a little time to create a believable new mindset. This as an opening to portray your character in a new, potentially horrific way, so you can also use your mental mutation as an opportunity to change your Motivation.

D100	Description	Effect
01–05	Awful Cravings	−5 Fellowship, −5 Willpower
06–10	Beast Within	+10 Willpower, −5 Fellowship, −5 Intelligence
11–15	Chaotic Dreams	Gain the *Fatigued* Condition for the first two hours of every day
16–20	Crawling Skin	−5 Initiative, −5 Dexterity
21–25	Erratic Fantasist	−5 Initiative, −5 Willpower
26–30	Fearful Concern	−10 Willpower
31–35	Hateful Impulses	Subject to Animosity (see **Psychology**) to all not of your species
36–40	Hollow Heart	+10 Willpower, −10 Fellowship
41–45	Jealous Thoughts	−10 Fellowship
46–50	Lonely Spirit	−10 to any Test when alone
51–55	Mental Blocks	−10 Intelligence
56–60	Profane Urgency	−10 Willpower, +10 Agility
61–65	Shaky Morale	Gain the *Broken* condition if you fail a Test derived from Willpower
66–70	Suspicious Mind	−5 I, −5 Int
71–75	Thrill Hunter	+10 Willpower, −10 Initiative
76–80	Tortured Visions	−10 Initiative
81–85	Totally Unhinged	−20 Fellowship, +10 Willpower
86–90	Unending Malice	−10 to any Test not hurting another; +10 on Tests to hurt
91–95	Unholy Rage	Subject to Frenzy (see **Psychology**), +10 Weapon Skill
96–00	Worried Jitters	+5 Agility, −5 Fellowship

Absolution

As Corruption points build, and you feel the oppressive fist of the Dark Gods curling around your beleaguered soul, your dread may lead you to seek absolution. But simply asking forgiveness from a local preacher won't be enough. The stain of the Dark Gods' touch isn't so easily scrubbed clean. The exact limits of what is required to remove Corruption is left in the hands of the GM, but it is rarely, if ever, simple.

Printed adventures may include situations where Corruption can be removed, but if you wish to seek your own route to absolution, consider the following.

- Cleanse a profane temple to the Dark Gods. Though the very act may expose you to more corruption…
- Complete a holy pilgrimage and receive a blessing from a high priest at the end of the long, dangerous journey.

- Destroy an unholy artefact, or otherwise render it safe, foiling the schemes of the Dark Gods.
- Join a holy order and dedicate your life to one of the Gods opposed to Chaos.

OPTIONS: SLOW MANIFESTATIONS

Manifesting a mutation of the body or mind can come quickly, but normally it's a slow process, perhaps starting as an itch, patch of flaky skin, or a new tic, and only later developing into a new eye, unexpected feathers, or an entirely new mindset. If you would prefer to draw the mutation process out, perhaps to play upon the horror of the inevitable mutations to come, you are encouraged to do so. This is left in the hands of the GM to detail according to individual taste and preference.

DISEASE AND INFECTION

Plague and pestilence — the purview of Nurgle, the Chaos God of Disease and Despair — are an everyday fact of Old World life. Yearly outbreaks of disease plague all levels of society, although the common folk usually fare the worst. To ward against these terrible infections, most turn to the welcoming arms of Nurgle's sworn enemy, Shallya, the Goddess of Mercy and Healing, but those actually suffering a disease will often turn to any possible cure, ensuring wise women, herbalists, and travelling doktors are never out of business, even when most peddle quackery rather than true remedies.

DISEASE FORMAT

- **Name:** The name of the disease.
- A description of the disease
- **Contraction:** How the disease is contracted.
- **Incubation:** How long before the victim demonstrates any symptoms.
- **Duration:** How long the symptoms of the disease last if untreated. At the end of the duration, the disease will come to an end.
- **Symptoms:** The effects of the disease on the victim. See **Symptoms** (page 188) for a list of all the symptoms, and how they affect a character.
- **Permanent:** Some diseases are so horrendous they carry permanent consequences. This section is only included if the affliction has such long-term effects.

THE LITANY OF PESTILENCE

The following offers a tiny sample of the infections, poxes, and plagues festering in dark corners of the Old World and are presented as inspiration for creating your own diseases.

The Black Plague

Historians claim that centuries ago rats swarmed the Empire and the Black Plague followed, wiping out nine in every ten souls. Unexplained flare-ups of the horrendous disease still occur today, and when they do, it always brings no-nonsense white nuns. The Cult of Shallya has sworn to do everything in its power to eradicate the foul disease, so, using ancient laws and rights granted to them, white-roped *cordon sanitaires* are erected wherever they encounter the Plague, ensuring none can leave or enter the quarantined area until the outbreak is contained, and all bodies correctly disposed.

Contraction: Enact an **Average (+20) Endurance** Test for each hour, or part thereof, spent in an area infested with infected fleas, or when exposed to infected fluids.
Incubation: 1d10 minutes
Duration: 3d10 days
Symptoms: Buboes, Blight (Moderate), Fever, Gangrene, Malaise

Blood Rot

Your very blood is diseased, and your heart now pumps sickness through your body. Leeching the rot is the accepted cure, but some doktors instead cut careful incisions near the neck to free the contaminated blood, demanding the patient ingest of vast quantities of healthy blood to replace what is lost. Whether the patient accepts such remedies or not, without treatment, Blood Rot is deadly, and will likely end in a visit from the Mourners' Guild and the Cult of Morr.

Contraction: As a development of another disease or a Critical Wound.
Incubation: Instant
Duration: 1d10 days
Symptoms: Blight, Fever (Severe), Malaise

The Bloody Flux

The Bloody Flux is a persistent problem in the Empire, and widely viewed to be a curse upon the impious by the Gods. The foul disease causes its unfortunate victim to evacuate the bowels forcibly and frequently. The Bloody Flux is endemic in the State Armies, where it is commonly claimed to kill more soldiers than any enemy. Typical cures include eating blood pudding to replace lost humours, 'corking', and rubbing fats into the afflicted area to lessen the sting.

Contraction: If you fail an **Easy (+40) Toughness** Test after an infected source enters the mouth.
Incubation: 2d10 days
Duration: 1d10 days
Symptoms: Flux (Severe), Lingering (Challenging), Fever, Malaise, Nausea

USING DISEASES

Some groups love diseases as they add a grim and gritty feel to their **WFRP** adventures, and provide medical characters in careers like Apothecary, Hedge Witch, Herbalist, and Physician — not to mention Priests and Wizards — extra utility. Others find diseases useful in specific circumstances, perhaps deployed for dramatic effect to stories including Skaven or Nurgle Chaos Cultists. And some **WFRP** gamers find diseases to be an easily forgotten nuisance.

It's up to you and your group to find the best way to include diseases in your game, but be aware some can be very nasty, and it's never fun to have a PC stuck in bed recovering as the rest of the group goes adventuring, so be careful how they're deployed.

Festering Wound

Infected cuts and abrasions are commonplace, meaning many superstitions exist explaining how best to treat them. Poultices fashioned from wrapped leaves and dung, the skin of toads, and dove-feathers are common, as is rubbing the wound in Sigmar's Good Soil. Most physicians rubbish such talk, and prefer more scientific curatives, such as mixing the gall of a black ox with three spoonfuls of the patient's urine and half a spoon of sea salt, which is then rubbed into the festering, pus-filled wound. The screams this elicits prove just how effective the remedy is.

Contraction: If you fail an **Easy (+40) Endurance Test** after a combat with a creature with the Infected trait (see **Bestiary**). You can also develop a *Festering Wound* from a *Minor Infection*.
Incubation: 1d10 days, or instantly if developed from another symptom.
Duration: 1d10 days
Symptoms: Fever, Lingering (Challenging), Malaise, Wounded

Galloping Trots

It is said Halfling food won't give you *Galloping Trots*, a messy affliction all too common in the Empire given just how little care is given to the proper preparation of food, but those suffering 'Rumster's Revenge' from the cheap, Halfling pies on sale across Altdorf, would disagree, assuming they could escape the privy for long enough…

Contraction: If you fail an **Easy (+40) Toughness** Test after an infected source enters the mouth.
Incubation: 1d10 hours
Duration: 1d10 days
Symptoms: Flux (Moderate), Malaise, Nausea

Itching Pox

Annual outbreaks of Itching Pox afflict most towns and cities of the Empire. The disease, which causes body-wide itchy blisters, is relatively mild, and very rarely has lasting complications, so it concerns few outside worried parents or vain nobles. So common is it, that most temples of Shallya have vials of white paste on hand to relieve the itching of the afflicted.

Contraction: If you fail an **Average (+20) Endurance** Test when contact is made with an infected individual or fail the same Test when an infected individual coughs or sneezes in your immediate vicinity (at a rate of about one Test per hour of exposure).
Incubation: 1d10 days
Duration: 1d10+7 days
Symptoms: Coughs and Sneezes, Pox
Permanent: Once the disease is contracted, you become immune to catching it again.

Minor Infection

Minor infections — slow-healing wounds with a modicum of swelling and heat — are extremely common. Most heal of their own accord in time, so few worry about them until it's too late, and Morr's Portal opens.

Contraction: If you fail a **Very Easy (+60) Endurance** Test after a combat where you suffered a Critical Wound.
Incubation: 1d10 days
Duration: 1d10 days
Symptoms: Lingering (Easy), Malaise, Wounded

Packer's Pox

A common infection amongst hunters, furriers, and traders, Packer's Pox is contracted from infected cattle and sheep, including their hides and wool, and from the bodies of those killed by the disease. It starts as a small itchy rash, but soon pink, depressed blisters spread across the whole body, concentrating on the torso and arms. Not the worst of the various poxes plaguing the Empire, but it does linger for a very long time, and can occasionally turn deadly.

Contraction: If you fail an **Easy (+40) Endurance** Test after any contact with infected animals, hides, or bodies.
Incubation: 1d10 days
Duration: 5d10 days
Symptoms: Lingering (Challenging), Pox

Ratte Fever

Contracted from infected rodents, dreaded Ratte Fever brings inflamed rashes and ulcerations before a fever rises and the body begins to spasm. Though rarely fatal, it's a debilitating disease, and it takes a long time to recover, so most are willing to try anything to lessen the symptoms. Common remedies include self-flagellation in Altdorf — which reputedly does bring some relief to the skin infections — and smearing oneself in goat-cheese mixed with imported Kislevite ice-peppers in Talabheim. In the bigger towns and cities, Ratte Fever is also known as Pie Fever given just how many savoury pasties contain tainted rat in place of more expensive meat.

Contraction: If you fail an **Average (+20) Endurance** Test after any combat when wounded by rodents (including Skaven) with the Infected Trait, or you fail an **Easy (+40) Endurance** Test after an infected source enters your mouth.

Incubation: 3d10+5 days
Duration: 3d10+10 days
Symptoms: Convulsions, Fever, Lingering (Average), Malaise, Pox, Wounded

SYMPTOMS

This section explains how the symptoms for each infection manifests. Use them to create your own disgusting diseases.

STIRRING NURGLE'S CAULDRON

Nurgle, the Chaos God of Pestilence and Decay, keeps a bubbling cauldron in the foulest corner of its rotting garden, within which is brewed every plague that ever was, or ever will be. And there is no reason you can't do the same! The twelve symptoms provided here are a perfect start for creating your own foul diseases. All you need do is think of a nasty infection, figure out how it's contracted, decide how long it lasts, then assign a few symptoms.

Say you wanted to create a disease called *Weevil Cough*. You first decide how it's contracted (from exposure to those already infected, or to mites in hay, wheat, and flour, requiring an **Average (+20) Endurance** Test to avoid), then how long its Incubation and Duration is (say, 1d10 days for each), then assign Symptoms (Coughs and Sneezes, and Malaise). Done!

Blight

You are seriously ill and perhaps close to Morr's Portal as deadly poisons flood your body.

Pass a **Very Easy (+60) Endurance** daily (normally when you sleep) or die, passing away, perhaps in your sleep, perhaps lost in a fever, perhaps in agony. If Blight is marked as (Moderate), this Test is **Easy (+40)**; if marked as (Severe), this Test is **Average (+20)**.

Treatment: None that work.

Buboes

You have huge swellings of the lymph nodes, possibly in the groin, neck or armpits. These are enormously painful and may bleed or seep pus. They are disgusting, smelly, and some would argue a sure sign of the Lord of Pestilence's favour, believing they hide tiny, growing Daemons. Common practice is to lance these terrible expressions of taint to remove whatever nestles within, though doing so often results in *Festering Wounds*.

Suffer a penalty of −10 to all physical Tests, and to all Fellowship Tests if the buboes can be seen (or smelled!).

Treatment: A successful Heal Test with Surgery can lance your buboes, removing the penalty. If the Test is failed, gain a *Festering Wound*. If your Buboes are lanced, make a **Difficult (−10) Endurance** Test once per day or more swell into place.

Convulsions

Your body periodically spasms or shakes as the infection seemingly uses you like a puppet.

Suffer a penalty of −10 to all physical Tests as your body convulses beyond your control. If this symptom is marked as (Moderate), the penalty increases to −20. If it is marked as (Severe), you need to be tied down in order not to hurt yourself, leaving you effectively incapacitated.

Treatment: Rare herbs and alchemical mixes can lessen this symptom for a day, bringing Severe down to Moderate, and Moderate down to standard convulsions. These can be created by any with the Trade (Apothecary) skill and access to the appropriate ingredients (which can cost upwards of 10 shillings or more per dose). The final medicine is Rare and usually genuine (80%), and can be bought for around 1 GC per dose from Apothecaries, putting it beyond the reach of most citizens of the Empire.

Coughs and Sneezes

You intermittently cough or sneeze, spreading your disease to all around you. Any characters in your environment are exposed to the disease you carry, and need Test for Contraction once per hour, or part thereof, of exposure.

Treatment: None that work.

Fever

Your temperature is high, you're likely sweating, and you really don't look at all well. Suffer a penalty of −10 to all physical and Fellowship Tests. If your Fever is marked as (Severe), it has completely incapacitated you, leaving you bed-ridden. Take the *Unconscious* Condition, though expenditure of a Resolve point can bring consciousness for a few minutes.

Treatment: There are many common, often disgusting, remedies for a fever, most of which don't work (only 10% of commercial cures are genuine). A successful Heal Test does little more that inform you how long the fever will likely last. The cures range from a few pennies to many shillings in cost. If genuine, they will remove the symptoms of a Fever (not a severe one) if you pass a **Challenging (+0) Endurance** Test.

Flux

There's a rumble and a grumble, then you're off for yet another sprint to the splattered outhouse. Pale and weary, you've had better days. Any given situation may be the moment you just have to go to the privy. You are expected to take every opportunity you can to pop off for an essential stop, and this is largely left in your hands. In addition, the GM can choose any point during the session's play to claim you need to go. You have a number of rounds equal to your Toughness Bonus to get to an appropriate place to relieve yourself; whether you get there in time or not, your body will empty itself in a spectacular fashion. If the Flux is marked as (Moderate), the GM can make you go twice a session. If it is marked as (Severe), the GM can do it three times, and you will also lose 1 Wound per visit, as the bloody flux leaves you utterly drained.

Treatment: Real cures for the Flux are rare (10% of commercial remedies are genuine), but many apothecaries and herbalists swear theirs work every time. Costs vary widely according to where you buy the cures, from a few brass coins to small bag of silver. If genuine, the Flux can be held off for your Toughness Bonus in hours by taking a remedy.

Gangrene

Your flesh is turning black, dying, infected with something awful, and it isn't going to get better. Roll percentile dice to determine a Hit Location (see **Combat**). If you roll Body, luckily the Gangrene did not settle in during this infection. If you roll Head, your nose is affected. If you roll Arms, it's your fingers. If you roll Leg, it's your feet. Each day, roll an **Average (+20) Endurance** Test. If you pass, you hold off the Gangrene; if you fail, it grows worse. If you ever fail more times than you have Toughness Bonus, you completely lose all capability with the affected location. If this occurs, use the same rules as Amputation (see **Critical Wounds**). For as long as you have Gangrene, suffer a penalty −10 to all Fellowship Tests, and suffer the Wounded symptom. Further, if not already suffering it, you also suffer from Blight until the affected tissue is amputated; this remains even if you are cured of the disease that started the Gangrene.

Treatment: Amputation of the gangrenous location is the only effective treatment.

Lingering

You have an infection that just refuses to go away. Indeed, you fear it may be getting worse… After your disease reaches the end of its duration, attempt an **Endurance** Test with the Difficulty marked on the symptom like so: Lingering (Average) or Lingering (Easy). If this scores a Marginal Failure (0), the duration extends for an extra 1d10 days. If it scores a Failure (−2), develop a Festering Wound. On an Astounding Failure (−6), you instead develop *Blood Rot*.

Treatment: Cures for lingering infections are commonplace and usually relatively cheap, rarely costing more than a shilling. However, almost all are fake or based on faulty lore. Any bought cure has only a 10% chance of being genuine, but if so will negate the need to roll the Endurance Test if taken on the correct day (which will require a successful Heal Test to determine).

Malaise

You don't feel at all well. You are tired, find it hard to concentrate, and just generally ill. Take a *Fatigued* Condition that you can only remove when you have recovered from your illness.

Treatment: Medicine treating *Malaise*, costing anything from a few pence to a handful of silver, is usually genuine (75% chance); and, if so, pass a **Challenging (+0) Endurance** Test to ignore the symptom for the day.

Nausea

You feel very sick and are prone to vomiting if you move around too quickly. Whenever you fail a Test involving physical movement, your nausea overwhelms you and you vomit. You gain the Stunned condition, which represents you being sick repeatedly or dry heaving, depending upon your current circumstances.

Treatment: Remedies for *Nausea* are Common and usually genuine (60% chance), and typically cost around thirty pennies; if genuine, pass a **Challenging (+0) Endurance** Test, and the Nausea can be ignored for a number of hours equal to your Toughness Bonus.

Pox

You are covered in pustules, inflamed swellings, disgusting rashes, or itchy spots, which are unlikely to be your most attractive feature. *Pox* are largely a cosmetic issue, resulting in a penalty of −10 to Fellowship Tests. Additionally, remember to roleplay and describe all the scratching; if you want to withhold from this for a while, pass an **Average (+20) Cool** Test. When the Pox ends, attempt an **Average (+20) Cool** Test. If this fails, reverse the Test dice and apply permanent scarring to that Hit Location, showing an area where you scratched and the pox there healed badly. If the Hit Location is the head, permanently lose 1 in Fellowship. See **Combat** for more on Hit Locations.

Treatment: Poxes are exceedingly common, and so are remedies, which are usually creams or oils. Larger temples of Shallya often keep a stock of the cream for free (though donations are expected) and apothecaries and herbalists of all kinds sell similar products for relatively low prices (rarely more than six or seven pence for a week's worth of treatment, with a 90% chance of being genuine medicine). Using a cream increases all Cool Tests to resist scratching to Very Easy (+60), but is usually unsightly.

Wounded

You have a wound or open sore that does not heal properly because of an infection. For each Wounded symptom you have, you cannot heal one of your Wounds, which stays open and sore, possibly seeping foul-smelling pus. Every day, take an **Easy (+20) Endurance** Test or gain a Festering Wound if you do not already have one.

Treatment: A daily successful Heal Test ensures the Wound is clean and does not require an Endurance Test to be further infected.

PSYCHOLOGY

Our emotions and instincts have a powerful impact on how we react in certain circumstances. These rules bring another level of drama to your game and help bring the Old World's inhabitants to life.

PSYCHOLOGY TEST

If you are exposed to one of the following Psychological traits, you may resist its effects by passing a Cool Test at the beginning of the Round, with the Difficulty set by the GM. A successful Test lasts until the end of the current encounter, although additional Tests may be required if circumstances change.

Example: *Brokk has* Animosity (Elves). *When the Dwarf encounters some haughty Elves quaffing wine and laughing loudly in a tavern, he Tests his Cool to control himself; he passes, so is not subject to* Animosity, *though he does choose to spit on the ground as he passes the sneering things. Later, when one of the Elves jostles his arm, spilling his ale, his GM asks Brokk to Test again. This time he fails. So, setting down his tankard, he turns around to 'have a word' with the offending Elf, unable to stop himself from launching into a tirade about exactly what he thinks of their so-called nimbleness!*

PSYCHOLOGICAL TRAITS

The following are the most common Psychology traits in **WFRP**.

Animosity (Target)

You harbour an enmity for the *Target*, which will normally be a group of people or creatures, such as 'Nordlanders', 'Beastmen', or 'Nobles'. You must attempt a Psychology Test whenever you encounter the group. If you pass, you may grumble and spit, but only suffer a penalty of −20 to all Fellowship Tests towards that group. Should you fail you are subject to *Animosity*.

At the end of every subsequent Round, you may attempt another Psychology test to bring the *Animosity* to an end. If you do not, the effects of *Animosity* naturally come to an end when all members of the specified group in your line of sight are utterly pacified or gone, or you gain the *Stunned* or *Unconscious* Condition, or you become subject to another Psychology.

When subject to *Animosity*, you must immediately attack the disagreeable creatures, either socially (insults, jibes, and similar) or physically (most commonly with fists), as appropriate. You also gain a bonus of +1 SL on any attempts to socially or mentally attack the group. *Animosity* is over-ridden by *Fear* and *Terror*.

Fear (Rating)

The Fear trait represents an extreme aversion to something. Creatures that cause *Fear* have a Fear Rating; this value reflects the SL you are required to pass on an Extended Cool Test to overcome your Fear. You may continue to Test at the end of every round until your SL equals or surpasses the creature's Fear rating. Until you do this, you are subject to Fear.

When subject to *Fear*, you suffer −1 SL on all Tests to affect the source of your fear. You may not move closer to whatever is causing *Fear* without passing a **Challenging (+0) Cool** Test. If it comes closer to you, you must pass a **Challenging (+0) Cool** Test, or gain a *Broken* Condition.

Frenzy

With a Willpower Test, you can work yourself into a state of frenzy by psyching yourself up, howling, biting your shield, or similar. If you succeed, you become subject to *Frenzy*.

While subject to *Frenzy* you are immune to all other psychology, and will not flee or retreat for any reason; indeed you must always move at full rate towards the closest enemy you can see in order to attack. Generally, the only Action you may take is a Weapon Skill Test or an Athletics Test to reach an enemy more quickly. Further, you may take a Free Action Melee Test each Round as you are throwing everything you have into your attacks. Lastly, you gain a bonus of +1 Strength Bonus, such is your ferocity. You remain in *Frenzy* until all enemies in your line of sight are pacified, or you receive the *Stunned* or *Unconscious* condition. After your *Frenzy* is over you immediately receive a *Fatigued* condition.

Hatred (Target)

You are consumed with *Hatred* for the *Target,* which is normally a group of people or creatures, such as 'Hochlanders', 'Bog Octopuses', or 'Slavers'. You will never socially interact with someone or something you hate in this manner. On encountering the object of your *Hatred*, you must attempt a Psychology Test. If failed, you are subject to *Hatred*. At the end of every subsequent Round, you *may* attempt another Psychology Test to bring the *Hatred* to an end. If you do or not, the effects of *Hatred* naturally come to an end when all members of the specified group in your line of sight are dead or gone, or you gain the *Unconscious* condition. While subject to *Hatred*, you must immediately attempt to destroy the hated group by the fastest and most deadly means possible. You gain a bonus of +1 SL on all combat Tests against the specified group, and are immune to *Fear* and *Intimidate* (but not *Terror*) caused by your hated foe.

Prejudice (Target)

You really dislike the *Target*, which is normally a group of people or creatures such as 'Ostlanders', 'Elves', or 'Wizards'. You must attempt a Psychology Test whenever you encounter the group against which you are prejudiced. If you pass, you may frown a lot, but will otherwise act normally, only suffering a penalty of −10 to all Fellowship Tests towards that group. Should you fail you are subject to *Prejudice*. At the end of every subsequent Round, you *may* attempt another Psychology test to bring the Prejudice to an end. If you do not, the effects of *Prejudice* naturally come to an end when all members of the specified group in your line of sight are gone, or you gain the *Stunned* or *Unconscious* Condition, or you become subject to another Psychology.

When subject to *Prejudice*, you must immediately insult the target of your prejudice. Loudly.

Terror (Rating)

Some creatures are so profoundly unsettling as to provoke a dire, bone-chilling terror in their foes. When you first encounter a creature causing *Terror*, make a Cool Test. If you pass, you suffer no further effects of *Terror*; if you fail, you receive a number of *Broken* conditions equal to the creature's *Terror* Rating, plus the number of SL below 0.

After resolving the Psychology Test, the creature causes *Fear*, with a *Fear* Rating equal to its Terror Rating.

CUSTOM PSYCHOLOGY

You can create your own psychological traits to reflect the events of your game. This is something that will vary depending on your group, and the style of game you choose to play. It is also an area that should be treated sensitively, and if in any doubt avoid anything that could upset a member of the group.

In addition to the mechanical effects of these custom traits, they are a wonderful opportunity for roleplaying; taking on custom psychological traits allows you to show off or practice your roleplaying skills, and maybe earn some extra XP. See **Advances** in **Chapter 2: Character** for more about this.

When making custom traits, you should consider both what provokes the trait to manifest, and what the effect will be. Will it make the character immune to some, or all other psychology traits? Will it offer a bonus in some situations? A penalty in others? As always, your GM is the ultimate arbiter in this situation. Sample bonuses or penalties a Psychological trait may offer include:

- +1/−1 SL to specified Tests
- Immunity to specified psychological traits
- Prescribed or Proscribed Actions and Moves
- Gaining Conditions

The following are some examples of custom traits to inspire your own.

Example: Camaraderie

Camaraderie reflects positive feelings towards a group of individuals.

You must come to their aid if the group is threatened physically or socially, and you gain a bonus of +1 SL to any Tests to defend or support the group.

Example: *Amhold had a difficult childhood, growing up on the streets without a family. Despite his gruff demeanour, he has* Camaraderie (Orphans).

Example: Love

Poets write endlessly of love, and every minstrel of the Reikland knows dozens of songs praising the power of love. If your character has the Love trait towards one or more individuals, this reflects a deep and enduring emotional connection. This may be the intense romantic love for a wife, husband, or lover, a strong familial love for a sibling, parent, or child, or an especially strong friendship.

You must come to the aid of someone you love if they are threatened physically or socially. You are immune to *Fear* and Intimidation while defending your loved ones, and you gain a bonus +1 SL to all related Tests.

Example: *Rilla is a riverwoman and travels the Reik with her close-knit family. She has* Love (Son), Love (Brother) *and* Love (Parents). *You mess with Rilla's family, you mess with Rilla!*

Example: Phobia

A phobia reflects a specific fear; it may be towards a type of creature, or towards a particular object or circumstance, such as *Phobia (Insects)*, *Phobia (Books)*, or *Phobia (Confined Spaces)*. Treat the object of the *Phobia* as causing Fear 1. You may want to increase the Fear rating if the Phobia is especially powerful.

Example: *Doktor Johannsen is a renowned antiquarian. Despite his many adventures and tales of derring-do, he suffers from* Phobia (Snakes); *no matter this aversion, he seems to encounter them with alarming regularity.*

Example: Trauma

The life of most Reiklanders is nasty, brutish and short: that goes double for adventurers, whose lives are often especially traumatic. Everyone processes trauma differently, and you may choose to reflect that in a range of different ways: nightmares, substance abuse, flashbacks, *Animosity* or *Hatred* towards a particular group, or a *Phobia*. A character who has suffered a traumatic experience may manifest that in a range of different ways over time.

Example: *Horst's village was destroyed in a terrible fire – he can still hear their screams at night. If Horst sees any characters — friend or foe — with the* Ablaze *Condition, he must make a* **Challenging (+0) Cool** *Test. If he fails, he receives a Stunned Condition, plus one additional Stunned Condition for each SL below 0. Additionally, every night Horst makes an* **Easy (+40) Cool** *Test; if he fails, he suffers nightmares and gains the* Fatigued *Condition.*

• BETWEEN ADVENTURES •

'Of course there is something wrong with us. This world has more than enough sorrow and pain to go about. So, what do we do? We seek out things that even the courageous fear and confront them in the dark. Truly, we are the favoured pawns of the Gods. So: what do I do with my time when I'm not on some foolish quest? I drink.'

– Lieselotte Aderhold, Adventurer

It may take many game sessions, but eventually all adventures come to an end. When this happens, you may have weeks where your character has nothing to do before the next adventure begins. This chapter provides tools to quickly detail what happens in this downtime.

To begin, you will randomise an Event. You will then spend any money you acquired on your last escapade, and engage in a variety of activities called Endeavours, ranging from commonplace tasks — such as working a trade, or managing their affairs — to more specialised undertakings — such as consulting a sage or attempting to learn a new skill. Once this is concluded, you'll resolve any matters that arise from your choices, and are then ready to start your next adventure.

OPTIONS: IT'S ALL OPTIONAL

Every rule in this chapter is optional. Some will love the quick rules it offers to explain events between adventures, others will prefer to detail this time fully with roleplay, seeing it as as an opportunity to give depth to characters or to pursue leads and ideas that could become adventures in their own right. There is no right or wrong way. Treat this chapter as a source of inspiration and do your own thing!

EVENTS

Before selecting your Endeavours, you first roll 1d100 on the Events table opposite. Some Events will only affect you, others may affect the whole party.

EVENTS TABLE

01–03: Accused Ally

One of your allies (GM's choice) is implicated in a terrible crime. A character with a Law Guild Licence can spend an Endeavour to free the ally with a successful **Average (+20) Lore (Law)** test. Otherwise, 3 Endeavours spent by the party will exonerate their ally (or, if guilty, manufacture an alibi). If the ally is freed, gain a *Major Favour* (see *Do Me a Favour* Endeavour on page 198) for future use. If not, their ally hangs!

04–06: Arcane Auction

The belongings of a recently deceased neighbour are auctioned, including a dusty, old book of unknown origin. If you are able to pay the 10 GC asking price, the book is yours! Beyond any other advantage the book may bring as determined by the GM, any Academic characters attempting the *Research Lore* Endeavour gains +20 on the Test.

07–10: Betrayed!

A friend, family member, or ally turns on you, the ramifications of which will impact your next adventure. If you have no friends, family, or allies, your time between adventures is blissfully uneventful though somewhat dull.

11–14: Bolt from the Blue

A lazy ostler didn't lock the stable door, and your mount bolted! If you succeed at an **Average (+20) Animal Training (Horse)** Test, your well-trained beast returns to the hand that feeds it. If you fail, your steed is gone, unlikely to be ever seen again. If you don't have a mount, you have developed a painful new blister on your foot.

15–18: Oi! You spilled my pint!

A petty argument in the local area has developed into a feud – the GM decides who you offended and how. This person will not pass up an opportunity for petty revenge, probably during the next adventure...

19–21: Crime Crackdown

The Watch is cracking down on crime hard. Rogues can get no funds from the *Income* Endeavour, and if Rogues undertake a *Banking* Endeavour, they may only select a *High-risk* deposit, as legitimate banking houses won't handle dirty money.

22–25: The Exciseman Cometh

An unexpected visit by the tax collector (with several soldiers in tow) sweeps through your local settlement. All characters lose 30% of their funds before any can be spent on Endeavours.

26–29: False Silver

To the horror of the merchants, a run of counterfeit coins plagues the characters' locale. A fifth of all coins are affected. Characters who undertake the *Banking* Endeavour will lose 20% of money banked, and characters undertaking the *Income* Endeavour similarly reduce any money earned by 20%.

30–33: Flowing Profit

Business is particularly good for folk involved in river trade. All Riverfolk make an additional 50% from any *Income* Endeavour pursued during the next batch of Endeavours.

34–36: Forewarned is Forearmed

You are given a cryptic omen by a dream, Strigany mystic, or Celestial wizard you encounter on the street. During your next adventure, your maximum Fortune points are increased by 1.

37–40: Festivities

A celebration is called! Decide the nature of the event with the GM. Possibilities include a local wedding, a bountiful harvest, or a public execution! You are caught up in the event (and its aftermath) and lose an Endeavour.

41–44: Inclement Weather

Particularly bad weather arrives. For the next adventure, all social Skill Tests suffer a penalty of –10 (everyone is in a foul mood) and food prices increase by 20% (due to spoiling of stored provender).

45–48: Glorious Weather

Beautiful conditions inspire you and give you cheer. You can add a new Short-term Ambition. When it's concluded, you do not replace it with a new one.

49–52: Local Crop Failure

Food becomes exceedingly scarce and many folk suffer terribly. Characters from the Peasant class cannot undertake the *Income* Endeavour, and food prices are doubled in the area for the duration of the next adventure.

53–56: Malicious Malady

The Bloody Flux sweeps through town. Make an **Easy (+40) Toughness** Test. On a success, the Flux passes by. On a failure, you and the Washers Guild are soon to know each other very well. Contract the Bloody Flux see page 186.

57–60: Monstrous Complications

A monster (chosen by the GM from **Chapter 12: Bestiary**) is causing panic among the locals. The *Income* Endeavour provides no funds until the beast is dealt with. The characters can choose to each sacrifice one Endeavour to deal with the menace (and this encounter should be roleplayed). If you succeed, you gain a free *Income* Endeavour to represent their individual rewards, and a feast is held in their honour. If not, or if the party chooses to ignore the creature, it will move on or be killed by a local rival.

61–63: Morr's Embrace

One of the character's relatives, friends, or allies dies. It could be of natural causes, an accident, or the beginning of something sinister…

64–65: New Moon

The nights are particularly dark. All Rogue characters undertaking the *Income* Endeavour receive a +20% bonus to their monies earned.

66–67: Old Debts

You have a *Major* or *Significant Favour* called in. Dealing with the favour will be part of your next adventure and you lose one Endeavour in preparation for what is to come.

68–69: Opportunity Saunters Through

Passing soldiers, well-heeled merchants, or vacationing nobles pass through the area, and characters willing to suck up reap the benefits. Burgher and Peasant Class characters gain +50% money from the *Income* Endeavour.

70–71: Peace and Quiet

It's times like these that remind you what life is all about: good sleep and fine cheese. Be smugly content at the start of your next adventure.

72–73: Pedlar

A wizened, well-travelled pedlar who likes a gossip passes through. For the price of a flagon of ale — 3d — you receive a +10 bonus to any *Latest News* Endeavours you attempt.

74–76: Pestilential Pet

One of your animals falls ill; make a **Challenging (+0) Animal Care** Test. If successful, your beast pulls through. If not, the unfortunate creature dies. If you have no animals, you are troubled by ill omens of the GM's creation.

77–79: Ransacked

Before you can undertake a *Banking* Endeavour, your stash is raided, and all your money is taken. If your money amounts to less than 1 GC, the thieves also steal your most highly-valued trapping.

80–82: Riots

The common folk are furious at the high and mighty!

Characters of the Courtier Class cannot take the *Income* Endeavour as, no matter how many bodyguards they hire, it isn't even vaguely safe for them to be abroad on business. Further, any deposits at reputable banks (see page 196) must immediately check to see if the violence and disruption has caused their bank to go out of business. However, players attempting a *Foment Dissent* Endeavour receive +10 bonus to all related Tests.

83–85: Sticky Fingers

Your purse is cut! You lose half of the money you ended the last adventure with.

86–88: Suspicion of Heresy

You fall foul of a Witch Hunter who suspects you have been consorting with Mutants, Cultists, or worse on your so-called 'adventures'. It takes a **Very Hard (-30) Charm** Test to convince the hunter you are innocent. Failure to do this means you have earned an implacable nemesis who is certain to cause trouble in the future…

89–91: Under Suspicion

The party's irregular movements and sudden wealth has drawn suspicion. All characters must forfeit one Endeavour laying low or proving their innocence. Characters in the Rogue class cannot use the *Income* Endeavour until after their next adventure.

92–94: Uneventful

Little of interest occurs, perhaps leaving you with a boredom-inspired appetite for taking risks!

95–97: Unexpected Esteem

Someone you helped in the past has a chance to repay your efforts. The precise nature of the reward should be appropriate to your past deeds, and the NPCs you have assisted during play or in your back story. The tokens of gratitude may vary from a single high-quality item, to a purse of silver (which will be available at the start of the next adventure). Of course, all that glitters is not gold, and not all gifts are what they appear…

98–00: Unusual Mercenaries

One or more rare mercenaries turn up in a nearby settlement looking for work: a Tilean Duellist of great repute, the so-called Birdmen of Catrazza, unemployed Ogres under the command of a Halfling captain, or other unlikely bands. The mercenaries will gladly train any character in any martial Skills or Talents, at a 20% reduction in costs, should the characters undertake a *Training* or *Unusual Learning* Endeavour. Additionally, any characters undertaking a *Combat Training* Endeavour gain a +20 bonus to any relevant Test.

ENDEAVOURS

In-between adventures, you have a selection of activities you can undertake — these are known as Endeavours. You may undertake a maximum of one Endeavour per week you are not adventuring, and you may attempt a *maximum of three Endeavours* in total, regardless of how long the gap between adventures may be. The rest of your time, whether it be weeks, months, or years, is taken up with living your life in relative peace — whatever that may to look like to your character.

While most of these Endeavours can be attempted by anyone, some are better suited to a particular Class or Career.

YEAR IN, YEAR OUT

If the period between adventures is particularly long, you can discuss with the GM how to lengthen the narrative scope of your Endeavours. For instance, if you want to commission a new sword with the *Commission* Endeavour, you may first have to find a skilled smith, then the correct materials, then wait for other commissions to be completed, then maybe your sword is stolen, and so it goes on.

MONEY TO BURN

After you've rolled on the Event Table, you can spend the money earned during your last adventures using the normal rules. Then, after completing your Endeavours, all money held by your character is considered spent. All of it. The silver lifted from a Burgher's purse? Gone. The booty liberated from pirates? Also gone. That Troll hoard you raided? Gone, too. All of it.

What happened to it? It was spent, stolen, drunk, gambled, used for repairs, to pay off debts or taxes, given as a charitable donations or votive offerings, spent on bribes, or used in whatever other way you prefer. You should concoct the best story for what happens to those funds, as it explains a lot about your character.

If you want to keep some of your hard-won coin to use in the future, you should undertake the *Banking* Endeavour on page 196. If you want money at the beginning of the next adventure — honestly, or otherwise, depending on your Career — you should undertake the *Income* Endeavour on page 198.

DUTIES & RESPONSIBILITIES

You may lose one or more of your Endeavours due to your Career or Species.

With Great Power...

'The common folk will never understand my burdens. The sheer weight of the duties I bear. The guilty will not judge themselves and there are always so many villages to cleanse, for our enemies are legion.'

– Lothar Metzger, Witch Hunter

As you climb the ranks of your career, you accrue expectations and responsibilities that cannot be avoided. Noble Lords must see to the affairs of their estates, Guildmasters must oversee their guild's work, and Watch Captains must watch their watchmen. If you neglect your responsibilities, you will soon lose status amongst your peers.

If you have attained one of the top two tiers of your Career Path and do not undertake the *Income* Endeavour, which reflects taking care of your obligations, you drop one level within your Career; reverting from the fourth level to the third, or the third to the second. This costs no Experience Points, acting as a free Career change, albeit downwards.

With this step backwards in your Career Path, you will now have a lower Status, and will earn less money should you perform future *Income* Endeavours. See **Chapter 3: Class and Careers** for more about Status. The loss in status does not remove any Advances acquired while you were in your previous Career.

If you wish to reclaim your lost Career level, you must once again pay the XP cost to re-enter the higher level of your Career and retake your 'proper' place in society.

Elf Improvement

'There are times when I can barely stand Altdorf. It is not the stench — though that is abhorrent — it is not the noise, either — it is just that you are all so very ugly to look upon, I feel that I must gaze at something beautiful for a time or I know that I shall start screaming, and never stop.'

– Irlianmaris Ellarel, Asur Envoy

Elves, even those resident within the borders of Empire, do not consider themselves citizens of the Empire. There are High Elves with diplomatic positions in Karl-Franz I's court, as well as traders and merchant princes in many of the great cities of the Empire, but the majority of the Asur avoid entanglements with Humans (not to mention Dwarfs) and few would call a Reiklander 'friend'.

The Wood Elves are even more removed; nearly mythical, rarely seen, and when they do appear they always have their own concerns that they rarely share with others.

ELF ESTEEM

You will note high-ranking Elven characters who do not wish to lose Career status will only be able to undertake a single 'free' Endeavour. This is intentional, designed to offset some of the innate advantages Elven Characters receive, as well as reflecting the prolonged time it takes the long-lived Elves to adapt to change. Of course, if you feel this is unfairly penalising an Elf character, or making the game less fun, ignore one or both restrictions.

Between adventures, all Elven characters must undertake one Endeavour maintaining contact with their own kind, seeing to their responsibilities to their people. High Elves commonly give reports on interesting things they've learned to agents of Ulthuan in either Altdorf or Marienburg, whereas Asrai do the same with the spies from their arboreal homes. This Endeavour offers no advantage beyond the inherent advantage of being an Elf. **Note:** Elves only lose an Endeavour if the Between Adventures section is at least 3 weeks long, thus the Elves have at least 3 Endeavours to complete.

GENERAL ENDEAVOURS

Below you will find details of the Endeavours any character may undertake between adventures.

FLYING SOLO

Endeavours are designed to be undertaken by individual characters, but if there are reasons for more members of the group to be involved, do roleplay these situations. Equally, some of the Endeavours may present natural starting points for new adventures. For instance, if a player loses all their funds in a *Banking* Endeavour, where did the money go? And did the thieves leave any clues...?

Animal Training

You spend time training one of your animals. Make an **Average (+20) Animal Training** Test. If successful, add one skill to your animal from the *Trained* Creature Trait (see page 342).

Banking

This Endeavour allows you to store funds for future use. As noted in Money to Burn, all coin remaining at the end of your 'Between Adventures' phase is lost before the next adventure begins unless it is saved with this Endeavour. So, if you have a lot of money spare it may be worth a trip to the bank. If you are using a *Banking* Endeavour to retain your money, you must first decide whether to save your money by investing it with a reputable banking institution, or to stash it somewhere less secure.

Investing: You must be of the Gold and Silver social tiers to save with a banking house. Your money will be reasonably safe and it should accrue interest. When undertaking a *Banking* Endeavour to deposit money in a bank, determine the interest rate of your account, by choosing a number between 1 and 10 (alternatively you may simply roll 1d10). This is the rate of interest you will accrue, and also how risky the investment is. Withdrawing funds requires another *Banking* Endeavour. This may take place immediately after the initial Endeavour, or after subsequent adventures have occurred. Roll 1d100: if you roll equal to or less than your rate of interest, the venture has gone bankrupt and you have lost all of your money. If you roll over the interest rate, you receive your initial funds, plus the interest accrued.

Stashing: All characters may choose to stash their loot. This is a risky strategy, involving hiding it on your person, in your mattress, or burying it somewhere. Stashed money never accrues any interest. Players may withdraw money from a stash before the start of an adventure, without undertaking an Endeavour. Roll 1d100: if you roll 10 or lower, your stash has been found and you have lost all your money, otherwise you recieve your initial funds.

If you successfully withdraw your funds they will be available for you when you start your next adventure, in addition to any funds secured via an *Income* Endeavour.

Example: *Gerhard and Ulli's courage in the face of a Greenskin horde (not to mention some judicious looting) has earned them a haul worth 10 gold crowns each. The ever-prudent Gerhard decides to place his money with the esteemed banking house Bent, Crooke & Scarper. The GM rolls 1d10 with a result of 6. Gerhard will earn 6% interest on his deposit (12 silver shillings, see page 288), and the bank will fail if he rolls 6 or less on d100 when he tries to make a withdrawal.*

Ulli — a gambler at heart — buries his money near a mile-marker on the road to Ubersreik. He doesn't need to make an Endeavour to get access to his loot, but tragically he rolls 07 when he tries to recover it, and finds nothing but freshly disturbed earth, an empty chest, and whole heap of regret.

Changing Career

In a society as rigidly hierarchical as the Empire, changing Careers may require grit and perseverance. Taking time to forge the right connections, and learn what is expected of you, can help, significantly. Assuming you GM agrees, and you have completed you current Career, you can move to any Career Level that fits the story of your Character for free. If you have not completed your current Career, the change costs 100 XP. The time spent on this Endeavour represents making the appropriate introductions, doling out bribes, acquiring permits and licences, advertising, and similar activities.

Commission

So, you wish to own one of Von Meinkopt's legendary repeating pistols? Or a custom helm, with a personalised crest representing your epic victories? The *Commission* Endeavour allows you to acquire unusual or highly specialized items that are never simply 'stocked' in the shops of the Empire. It also allows for you to arrange for the creation of unique items. Such things take time, though…

If you are seeking an item with an Exotic rarity and know a source capable of acquiring or manufacturing it, then undertake this Endeavour, spend the necessary funds, and place your order. The item will then be ready for collection after your next adventure. A character can only commission a single Exotic item per Endeavour; acquiring further items, will require undertaking further *Commission* Endeavours. If you are unaware of an appropriate source for their item, you will first have to undertake the *Consult an Expert* Endeavour.

Consult an Expert

The Old World is replete with ancient and arcane knowledge, yet this information is not readily available on some magical box in your pocket. If you want to seek out some piece of obscure arcana, you must first seek out an expert. You may undertake the *Consult an Expert* Endeavour either to facilitate another Endeavour for example: *Commission, Training*, or *Unusual Learning* Endeavours), or to secure a piece of specific knowledge.

There are two stages to this Endeavour: locating the expert, then consulting.

First, you must locate your expert (this stage may be skipped with the GM's permission if you have already identified an appropriate expert during your adventures). Attempt a **Challenging (+0) Gossip** Test (the Difficulty of this Test will vary according to the size of the settlement where your character is currently living). If you succeed, you have located your expert. If you fail, you have located the loudest self-proclaimed specialist in your location, and the GM is given free rein to vary the quality or accuracy of the advice procured. You can of course refuse to deal with this somewhat suspect source, but you never know if you might have found a diamond in the rough. GMs are contrary like that sometimes.

Once successfully locate an expert, you then need to convince them to talk with you. Depending on what you wish to know, this may require no more than a **Simple Charm** Test or a modest donation to the local Temple of Verena. In more extreme cases, you may have to commit to performing one or more Favours

(see *Do Me A Favour!*) which may be called in during a future adventure, or 'bought off' by spending Endeavours between future adventures. The level of Favour owed depends on the complexity — and danger — of the information you want as determined by the GM.

The precise nature of the information gleaned depends on the expert consulted and what you seek to know. Academics will know the origins and full history on a subject with which they are familiar; wizards of the Colleges of Magic in Altdorf understand the history of magic and various mystical objects, particularly aspects relevant to their own order; an Apothecary General can identify even the rarest poison; a Verenan scholar may have information relating to any number of historical incidents. In short, the expert's background will influence how the knowledge is presented, and with which biases.

In addition to any specific information the GM imparts to their player, a successful *Consult an Expert* Endeavour used to seek out knowledge (and not to facilitate another Endeavour) gives you an Expert Reroll (mark this on your character sheet under Notes). This reroll may *only* be used on a Test specifically relating to the lore revealed and must be used before the end of your next adventure.

Crafting

Rather than browse shops or commissioning someone else to do the hard work, you can fashion your own trappings. *Crafting* allows you to make any trapping from **Chapter 11: Consumers' Guide** (or anything else the GM allows) if you have the correct Trade Skills. To do this, you require appropriate Trade Tools, raw materials, and access to an appropriate workshop. In general, the raw materials to create the trapping of your choice will cost a quarter of the trapping's list price, and must be purchased before *Crafting* begins (with an Availability as determined by the GM); the GM may rule the raw materials are cheaper or more expensive according to the trapping to be created, and the nature of the raw materials required.

CUSTOM GEAR

With a GM's permission, a character may undertake two (or more) consecutive Commission Endeavours to acquire even more unusual items: personal commissions from the Engineering Guild, a rare and virulent poison, or a magically ensorcelled item. The prices for such things generally range from 'very high' to 'staggering' and may well involve a Favour or two (see *Do Me a Favour!*) or even an entire adventure to acquire raw materials.

DO ME A FAVOUR!

A Favour is a future burden you take on in return for immediate assistance of some sort. In the Old World, breaking one's sworn word is considered bad form and carries significant social ramifications. No-one trusts oath breakers, meaning your Status is reduced by 1 (see page 49). Powerful and dangerous folks tend to take it very, *very* poorly if someone refuses a Favour owed them, so bloody consequences may follow.

The powerful often find it is far more useful to have various individuals owing them Favours than merely soliciting money in return for their help. What's more, it can be an investment: help a student today, call in a favour from a successful Lawyer years later. Favours may be referred to as 'boons', 'services', or 'obligations' by different folk, but in the end, they all amount to the same.

Favours come in three levels: Minor, Major, and Significant. Regardless of a Favour's level, in almost all cases, the person owed the Favour will take into account the capabilities and sensibilities of the person they're asking. There's no point in demanding that a Priestess of Shallya assassinate a merchant, for example, even if she does owe you a Significant Favour. That being said, Favours are ripe for NPCs to exploit in order to put pressure on your moral compass.

- **A Minor Favour** represents a simple task that can be completed in no more than a few hours. Perhaps you need volunteer at a Shallyan mercy-house or put in a good word for someone. With the GM's permission, you may undertake an Endeavour to pay off this favour.
- **A Major Favour** is a more time-consuming or risky undertaking. It could take up to several weeks to achieve and may involve travel. Perhaps you are needed to act as lookout on a string of burglaries, to convince the Stevedores' and Teamsters' Guild to back down from a guild war, or to transport a package to a different city. With the GM's permission, you may undertake two or more consecutive Endeavours to pay off this favour.
- **A Significant Favour** is relatively rare and will almost certainly involve risking life and limb. Months of travel may be involved, and major violence is likely. Perhaps you will be asked to eliminate a rival gang boss, wipe out a Goblin encampment, or instigate a riot. Significant Favours cannot be paid off via Endeavours; they are roleplayed out as full adventures.

To craft the trapping, attempt an Extended Trade Test, with a Difficulty set by the GM, typically using the Trapping's Availability as a loose guide.

Availability	Difficulty
Common	Average (+20)
Scarce	Challenging (+0)
Rare	Difficult (−10)
Exotic	Very Hard (−30)

The number of SL required to succeed at the Test is also set by the GM, using the listed price for the trapping in the Consumers' Guide as a reference.

The SL required is further modified by the Qualities or Flaws you work into the trapping. Each Flaw halves the SL required, and each Quality adds +5 (worked out after halving for Flaws).

Each Endeavour you spend *Crafting* allows you to make one roll towards your Extended Test. Unfinished work can be kept in whatever you have that amounts to lodgings, or carried around with you as you adventure, should that be possible.

List Price	SL
Brass	5
Silver	10
Gold	15+

Income

This Endeavour covers the many ways you can make money between your bouts of adventuring. The majority will most likely work in a recognized profession — bounty hunters hunt bounties, riverwardens ward rivers, troll slayers slay Trolls — others may rely on a lucrative skill. Wealthier characters, such as Nobles and Merchants, might collect a stipend by (briefly) indulging their family, or collecting interest on their investments and business ventures. Roguish types have any number of means to acquire funds, though it's best not to ask for any details.

You should briefly narrate exactly how your character makes money. This is intended more for fun background detail than to have any direct consequences, though GMs may well gather useful or sinister ideas for future use depending on what you describe. You then acquire the income you'll start your next adventure with, which is your standard income determined by your Status (see page 51). Certain results on the *Events Table* on page 193 may directly affect your income. The money you get from an *Income* Endeavour is given to you after your money from the last adventure is spent (see *Money to Burn*).

In addition to acquiring funds for later use, if you are in the third or fourth level of a Career and undertake this Endeavour, you automatically maintain your standing in your career. See *With Great Power…* on page 195 for details.

Invent!

Invent allows you to invent new trappings. This is done in two stages: Plan and Build. To Plan your new trapping, you first decide the trappings you wish to combine to create your invention. As examples, Pistols have been combined with other Pistols to create Repeating Pistols, and Pigeons and been combined with Bombs to create Pigeon Bombs. Let your imagination go wild. Once you have your plan, it's time to make the blueprints, which costs 1 Endeavour to attempt. Take a **Trade (Engineer)** Test, with a Difficulty set by how outlandish your proposed trapping combination is as determined by the GM. If you succeed, you are ready to start Building. Each SL scored adds +1 SL to the attempt to build your invention, as the plans are well laid out and easy to follow.

To Build the invention, you must either undertake a *Crafting* or *Commission* Endeavour. If it's *Crafting*, you are building the item yourself, and you must have the appropriate Skills to do so for the trappings being combined; so, if you were combining Pigeons with Bombs, you would need Animal Training and Trade (Explosives). The Difficulty to craft the invention is always Very Hard (−30), and the SL is set as normal. The raw materials needed to build the invention cost twice the listed price for the trappings being combined, and have an Availability rating equal to the most scarce of the trappings used in your invention. If you *Commission* the invention, you will likely need to undertake a *Consult an Expert* Endeavour first to find someone with the required Skills. That done, follow the *Commission* Endeavour as normal; it costs six times the listed price for the trappings to be combined to commission the work. The exact rules for your new invention are left to your GM to finalise.

Training

The *Training* Endeavour allows you to train in a Skill or Characteristic outside of your Career, treating it as if it were in-Career. In addition to the normal XP cost, you must also pay money to the tutor. Training for Basic Skills and all Characteristics costs XP+1d10 brass pennies , where XP is the number of XP it costs to buy the Advance. Tutoring in all Advanced Skills costs double that amount. For more, see Advances, see page 43.

You should be able to find a tutor for most skills, certainly in a city-state like Altdorf, but some particularly unusual skills may require you seek out the right instructor, likely by using the *Consult an Expert* Endeavour — 'Professionals' who can teach you how to properly pick a lock generally don't advertise, after all. Other skills, especially Lore Skills, often require an institution of learning, and some are flat out forbidden in the Empire. Finding a tutor capable (and willing) to instruct someone in proscribed matters — such as those relating to the Ruinous Powers or Necromancy — may be particularly dangerous, and perhaps an adventure to even source such an individual. Such tutors will also ask for far more than the 'going rate' for tutoring and will likely require a Significant Favour (see *Do Me A Favour!*).

Unusual Learning

It is one thing to pick up a Skill that can be readily practised, quite another to learn something for which one may have no aptitude at all. This Endeavour allows you to attempt to learn a Talent outside of your Career. There is no guarantee this attempt will be successful, meaning there is a good chance you will fail to learn the Talent you hope to acquire, expending XP and money to no avail.

You can only learn a Talent if you have an appropriate tutor. In most big cities, this will not be a problem, but if the Talent is particularly obscure, or you are far from a large city, the GM may require you complete a *Consult an Expert* Endeavour first.

Once you have acquired a tutor, the fee to train the Talent is 2d10 shillings per 100 XP it costs to purchase the Talent. If you pay this fee, attempt a **Hard (-20)** Test using the Characteristic or Skill most relevant to the Talent as determined by the GM. If you succeed, you have learned the Talent. If not, you have failed this time but can try again with a future Endeavour and gain a +10 modifier for each failed attempt.

CLASS ENDEAVOURS

Class Endeavours tend to be simpler than General Endeavours and often offer benefits more suited to characters in specific Classes. Any character can undertake any Class Endeavour, but if you don't currently belong to the Classes specified under the Endeavour, any Tests you take are one Difficulty Level harder — so, Hard (−20) instead of Difficult (−10), for example.

Combat Training
Rangers, Warriors

Warriors too long from the field can find their fighting skills lose their edge. Hard regular training not only mitigates this, it can add an extra advantage when the time comes. If you undertake this Endeavour, you spend your days training with the weapons you know, honing your skills for the day when it matters most.

After undertaking this Endeavour, attempt a **Challenging (+0)** Test using either a Melee or Ranged Skill. If you succeed, you may reverse a Test with the associated Skill once during your next adventure. Note this on your character sheet. You can enact this Endeavour multiple times if you wish.

Foment Dissent
Burghers, Peasants

If you are looking to sow civil unrest, undertake the *Foment Dissent* Endeavour. By talking with local citizens, leading meetings, and involving yourself, you can direct conversations to slowly feed anger and resentment towards a specific individual, group, or institution. But this takes time, so *Fomenting Dissent* takes two Endeavours to attempt (and will also count as an *Income* Endeavour if you are in the Agitator career).

To undertake the Endeavour, you must first attempt an **Average (+20) Gossip** Test to understand the local movers and shakers. If you succeed, attempt a **Charm** Test with the Difficulty determined by how unpopular the target may be. Rousing anger against an oppressive noble may be an **Easy (+40)** test, while raising a mob to protest the good work of a Shallyan hospice may be **Hard (−20)**. If you fail either of these tests, the Endeavour fails.

If successful, you will find it easier to invoke the wrath of crowds upon your chosen target. During your next adventure, you can attempt a **Charm** Test to gather a rioting mob to accost the target, with the difficulty determined by the GM according to how well-planned the mob-to-be is.

A single success means you gather enough angered townsfolk to confront the target, shouting insults, demanding justice, throwing rotting vegetables, and generally accosting the focus of their ire. An Impressive or Astounding Success may lead to uncontrollable lynch mobs, or even attempted burnings!

Failure means folk have no stomach for wrath; failing by several SL may mean the target, or their sympathisers, become aware of your actions...

Once you have the ear of a mob (successfully undertaking this Endeavour), you can attempt to rally the mob against a different target during an adventure, although this is more difficult, and the Difficulty of the **Charm** Test is two levels higher.

The Latest News
Rangers, Riverfolk

This Endeavour allows you to learn the latest news from afar. Attempt a **Challenging (+0) Gossip** Test. If you succeed, you learn an interesting rumour; each SL adds another rumour, and they may even be connected to your upcoming adventure. If you fail particularly badly (an Impressive Failure) you learn something false you are convinced is true; to allow this, the GM may make this roll in secret on your behalf.

Reputation
Academics, Burghers, Courtiers

Money talks, as they say. If you are looking to exert your influence and elevate your Status, you had best be willing to spread your wealth around. Any boost to your reputation will fade once the coins stop flowing, so you should exploit this advantage while it lasts.

Characters can spend money to increase their Standing by +1 for the next adventure, after which the bonus fades. This costs your maximum Earning income (see page 52) — so, if you would normally earn 4d10 pennies, it costs 40d — and requires a **Challenging (+0) Career Skill** Test. If you succeed, your Standing increases by +1. If you score an Astounding Success (+6), it increases by +2. If you fail, you have just wasted your money. If you score an Astounding Failure (–6), your toadying has so infuriated your peers, your standing decreases by -1 (to a minimum of 0) for the entire duration of your next adventure.

Research Lore
Academics

This Endeavour allows you to seek greater knowledge concerning a specific subject, such as the site of a battle, a famed historical event, or an individual. The character must have access to an appropriate storehouse of lore, such as a library, the annals of a Dwarf Hold, the records of a Guild, or a Temple of Verena.

Attempt an **Average (+20) Lore** Test, using the appropriate Lore Specialisation for the knowledge you seek. If you do not have the correct Lore Specialisation and are literate, you can still attempt to learn something, but it will take a **Difficult (–10) Intelligence** Test. If you succeed, you learn one piece of interesting, useful, or hidden knowledge about the subject researched; each SL adds another piece of relevant information. If you fail particularly badly (an Impressive or Astounding Failure)) you learn something false that you are convinced is true; to facilitate this, the GM may want to make this role in secret on your behalf.

Study a Mark
Rogues

You use this Endeavour to observe a potential target and gain advantages during future criminal enterprises. A Charlatan may study a merchant in order to better impersonate them during a future scam, or a Grave Robber may linger about a Temple of Morr, watching the coming and going of the priests to get an idea of their practices and their Garden of Morr's layout.

Attempt a **Challenging (+0) Perception** Test, though the difficulty may be modified for especially easy or difficult marks. If you succeed, you may reverse a Test concerning your mark once during your next adventure. Note this on your character sheet. You can enact this Endeavour multiple times if you wish. Further, the GM should provide information (or disinformation!) concerning your mark according to the SL you scored.

• RELIGION AND BELIEF •

Signs of religion are everywhere in the Old World, from the magnificent temples in the great cities to the humble wayside shrines and household altars. Old Worlders do their best to stay on the right side of their gods.

High-ranking clerics are wealthy and powerful, wielding as much influence and prestige as the greatest nobles. At the other end of the scale, village priests tend to the spiritual needs of rural communities, preaching the tenets of their faith and interceding with their patron deities on behalf of their flocks. Several faiths also support templar orders: these private armies of priest-soldiers answer to the head of their faith rather than to any noble or elector count, which can cause significant political friction.

THE GODS

The people of the Old World recognise many deities. Some are worshipped across the whole of the Old World; some are restricted to one nation or region; and some are patrons of just a single town or occupation.

GODS OF THE EMPIRE

In the Empire, the pantheon of gods is split into three broad categories: the Old Gods, the Classical Gods, and the Provincial Gods. Standing apart from these is Sigmar, the first Emperor, and patron deity of the Empire as a whole.

The Old Gods

The Old Gods refer to the pantheon of deities worshipped when the Empire was unbroken forest populated by wandering tribes of barbarians. Many Old Gods stood as patrons to one of the tribes, and to this day some are still associated with the old geographical hunting grounds of those ancient peoples. Although few say so out loud, many citizens of the Empire regard the Old Gods as the true deities of the Empire, and the Classical Gods as relative newcomers.

As time passed, five gods rose to prominence amongst the Old Gods, worshipped by dominant cults spread from one end of the Empire to the other: Ulric, Taal, Rhya, Manaan, and Morr, representing the primal spheres of war, nature, fertility, seas, and death.

The Classical Gods

The Classical Gods spread from the southern lands of Tilea, Estalia, and the Border Princes through trade and diplomatic contact. Today, their worship is popular in the cosmopolitan towns and cities, and some nobles and townsfolk secretly regard them as more sophisticated than the Old Gods — though few would risk voicing such opinions aloud!

The most widespread cults of Classical Gods in the Empire are dedicated to Verena, Myrmidia, Shallya, and Ranald, patrons of wisdom, strategy, mercy, and trickery. Hiding behind these, there is also Khaine, the God of Murder, though his cult is outlawed in most places.

The Provincial Gods

The Empire hosts a wide variety of deities — patrons of provinces, towns, forests, lakes, rivers, crafts, and much more besides. Formed into complicated pantheons by local legends and myths, the Provincial Gods often have small cults dedicated to them, but few have much influence. However, there are exceptions: standing high above other Provincial Gods, worship of Handrich, the God of Trade, has spread significantly with commerce and now boasts a significant cult-presence amongst the Empire's rising merchant class.

Sigmar

Sigmar founded the Empire over two-thousand years ago, and his legend recounts how he conquered unthinkable foes and overcame impossible odds. Reigning for fifty years, he eventually abdicated and turned east to return his magical warhammer, *Ghal-Maraz,* to its forgers: his old allies, the Dwarfs. He was never seen again. Not long after, oracles and prophets claimed Sigmar had ascended to godhood, invested by Ulric before the entire pantheon of old gods and new.

Today, many centuries later, the cult of Sigmar, patron of the Empire, has spread to such an extent that its leader, the Grand Theogonist, is arguably more powerful than the emperor himself.

OTHER PANTHEONS

The different countries and species of the Old World all have deities of their own. Some, according to theologians, are aspects of other deities worshipped under different names. Others are

GODS OF REIKLAND

Like all of the grand provinces, Reikland has a wide array of Provincial Gods, some even boasting small, sophisticated cults. The following provides an example of some of these.

God	Spheres	Worshippers	Offerings	Notes
Bögenauer	River Bögen	Boatmen, Merchants, and Bögenhafeners	Coins, sheaves of reeds, rolled stones	A single temple in Bögenhafen with no full-time clerics; shrines line the river.
Borchbach	Rhetoric	Agitators, politicians, lawyers	Written speeches, acorns, quills	Several shrines and two temples to Borchbach are found in Altdorf.
Clio	History	Scholars	Ancient artefacts, peaches, carvings	A significant temple to the Classical God Clio is attached to Altdorf University.
Dyrath	Women	Womenfolk	Fruit, honey, menses	Dyrath has no temples; instead, a secretive cult is spread through the villages and hamlets of the Hägercrybs.
Grandfather Reik	River Reik	Merchants, bargees, fishermen	Beer, eels, silver	Shrines dot the length of the river Reik, but there is no formal cult.
Katya	Disarming Beauty	Bawds, lovers, the lonely	Coins, jewellery, clothing	Temples to Katya double as brothels in the towns of the Vorbergland.

particularly revered by a particular species: examples include Grungni, the Dwarfen God of Mining and Dwarf Pride; Isha, a Goddess of Fertility and Nature who is seen as the mother of all Elves; and Esmerelda, the Halfling Goddess of Hearth, Home, and Family.

THE CHAOS GODS

The Daemonic gods of the Realms of Chaos are the greatest threat to the Old World, each determined to bring absolute ruin to the mortal realm. Their worship by lost and damned souls is pervasive and clandestine, with uncounted dark cultists infiltrating all levels of society. Khorne, Nurgle, Tzeentch, and Slaanesh: Gods of Rage, Despair, Ambition, and Excess. Few dare whisper their twisting names, for they harbour malevolent power, and leave mutation and horror in their wake.

THE CULTS

The Old World has many cults dedicated to appeasing or appealing to deities and promoting the ideals they embody. Leaders of these cults are frequently influential in local politics. They not only stand as representatives of their gods, but also command hundreds or perhaps thousands of clerics and templars: temporal power that cannot be ignored.

To manage their numerous members, most of the larger cults are split into orders, many of which operate from significant holy sites or temples.

Orders

Most Old World cults are split into orders, with each order focussing on different aspects of their god's concerns. Orders come in many different forms, including monastic orders of monks or nuns, templar orders of knights, priestly orders that attend to holy needs in the community, and mendicant orders of friars that wander the Old World, usually subsisting from alms. Each order is organised differently according to individual cult law and tradition, but in all cases they swear allegiance to the head of their cult, not the local nobility.

Holy Sites

The cults maintain holy sites across the Old World, many of them associated with legendary deeds of the gods from mythical times. Most are protected by buildings such as temples, abbeys, chapterhouses, or monasteries. Some older sites, or those not so well known, may only be marked by a shrine or unattended chapel. Cult buildings are usually decorated beautifully inside and out with scenes from the religion's mythology. They vary widely in size and layout and often follow regional styles of architecture. Some hold extreme wealth, especially in the towns and cities where a more affluent population provides greater tithes. Larger cult buildings support dozens of people, including lay craftspeople, guards, and servants, while smaller sites are run by a handful of staff aided by volunteers from the community. In villages, a single priest is the norm, supported by the faithful.

Shrines and chapels are more modest affairs, the size of a one-room house or smaller. They do not normally have a full-time priest, although they may come under the charge of a nearby temple or — especially in rural areas — a wandering priest who travels from one village and shrine to another. In a priest's absence, local villagers pray unsupervised, leave small offerings, and keep the shrine in good repair.

OPTIONS: LITTLE PRAYERS

Prayers to the gods are rarely answered by those not Blessed (see page 134), but the gods do listen sometimes. Prayers offered in holy sites have a chance of receiving divine attention. If the offering, circumstances, and motivation are appropriate, the GM may secretly roll d100 to see if your prayers are heeded. On a roll of 01, they are. If you have the Pray Skill, the GM may increase that chance. When such prayers are answered, the results may not be exactly what you expect — the gods of the Old World do not simply grant wishes — but it will almost always be something that will help you achieve a goal that is important to the deity. This might be a bonus to a dice roll, or a one-shot use of a Skill or Prayer that is otherwise unavailable, or some other advantage.

PRIMARY CULTS OF THE EMPIRE

Although many hundreds of gods are worshipped across the Empire, ten are of particular importance, each worshipped by cults spanning the grand provinces and granted a special position by Magnus the Pious over two-hundred years ago.

THE GRAND CONCLAVE

When Emperor Magnus the Pious rebuilt the Empire after the Great War Against Chaos, he realised previous schisms and civil wars besetting his realm were often sourced in religious unrest.

To help prevent this happening again, Magnus created the Grand Conclave, a meeting of the primary cults in the Empire held every five years to air grievances and discuss resolutions, with the emperor sitting as chair.

Though enormously controversial at the time, the Grand Conclave is now fully accepted, and is held alongside great celebrations and festivities, with the representatives of the following gods required to attend: Manann, Morr, Myrmidia, Ranald, Rhya, Shallya, Sigmar, Taal, Ulric, and Verena. Although other influential cults exist — such as the Cult of Handrich, which is currently lobbying for a seat on the Conclave — the ten currently sitting are widely perceived as the most important in the Empire.

PRIMARY GODS OF THE EMPIRE

God	Spheres	Worshippers	Offerings
Manann	The seas, oceans, the Wasteland	Sailors, fishermen, merchants	Fish, gems, gold
Morr	Death and dreams, Ostermark	Undertakers, the bereaved, undead hunters, mystics	Silver coins, incense, candles
Myrmidia	Strategic warfare, Tilea, Estalia	Estalians, strategists, Tileans	Spears, shields, vows of duty, trophies
Ranald	Trickery, thieves, luck, the poor	Rogues, gamblers, and the poor	Cards, coins, dice, food
Rhya	Fertility, life, summer	Farmers, herbalists, midwives	First reapings, wheat, fruit
Shallya	Mercy and healing	The poor, physicians, the sick, abused women	Food, medicine, coins
Sigmar	The Empire, Reikland	Folk of the Empire	Hammers, coins, food
Taal	The wilds, spring, Talabecland	Herders, foresters, and other rural folk	Land left wild, first kill from a hunt, animals
Ulric	War, winter, wolves, Middenland	Warriors, Middenlanders	Weapons, trophies, ale, wolf skins
Verena	Learning, justice, wisdom	Scribes, lawyers, scholars	Books, knowledge, just acts

THE CULT OF MANANN, GOD OF THE SEA

Seat of Power: Marienburg, the Wasteland
Head of the Cult: Matriarch of the Sea
Primary Orders: Order of the Albatross, Order of the Mariner
Major Festivals: Spring Equinox, Autumn Equinox
Popular Holy Books: *The 1000 Shanties, Tales of the Albatross, Liber Manaan*
Common Holy Symbols: Five-tined Crown, Waves, Anchors

Volatile Manann, the son of Taal and Rhya, is the capricious King of the Sea, Master of the Maelstroms, and Summoner of Storms. Known for his black moods and erratic temper, folk claim his cult is needed more than any other, for if ever there is a god that must be appeased, it's Manaan. He's depicted as an enormous, black-bearded man with seaweed in his hair and a great, five-pointed crown of black iron upon his troubled brow. He's said to dwell at the bottom of the ocean, the rise and fall of his massive chest forming the waves and tides as the greatest monsters of the deep gather in his court.

WORSHIPPERS

Manann is worshipped along coasts throughout the Old World, wherever people make their living from the sea or live close enough for storms and floods to threaten their homes. Even those who know little of Manann will throw a coin or other small treasure into the water before beginning a sea voyage in the hope of a smooth crossing.

The cult has a significant number of orders, mostly monastic, tasked to guard isolated, sacred islands. The Order of the Albatross is largest, comprised of priests who maintain temples across the Old World and bless merchant or naval vessels with their presence. Often accompanying them, the Order of the Mariner is the military arm of Manann, the cult's templar-marines, sworn protectors of Marienburg.

Manann's clerics usually wear robes of dark greenish-blue or blue-grey, trimmed with a white wave-pattern.

HOLY SITES

Manann's temples are found in all coastal towns and cities, and in most river ports where seagoing vessels berth. The high temple is in the great port-city of Marienburg: a huge, lavishly decorated complex open to the tides. The Matriarch of the Sea, head of the Order of the Albatross, is based there, a woman who ostensibly leads the entire cult of Manann, although in practice the sea-god's clerics are as mercurial as their god, and as likely to be stubborn as to serve. The cult also maintains many monasteries and abbeys on small isolated islands, most dedicated to one of Manann's many saints.

PENANCES

Penances from Manann often involve hazardous, maritime pilgrimages, tests of sailing skills, or expeditions against the sea-god's enemies, especially followers of the heretical cult of Stromfels, God of Pirates, Wreckers, and Sharks.

STRICTURES

- No whistling or swearing when at sea or on holy ground.
- Never harm an albatross.
- First catch to Manann.
- A silver and fish to every Manannite temple and shrine approached.
- Hunt down the servants of Stromfels wherever they may hide.

THE CULT OF MORR, GOD OF DEATH

Seat of Power: Luccini, Tilea
Head of the Cult: Custode del Portale
Primary Orders: Order of the Shroud, Order of the Black Guard, Order of the Augurs
Major Festivals: Hexensnacht, Geheimisnacht
Popular Holy Books: *The Book of Doorways, Libro Dei Morti, Thernodies of the Raven*
Common Holy Symbols: Portals, Ravens, Black Roses

Urbane Morr, God of Death and King of the Underworld, is husband to Verena, brother to murderous Khaine, and father of Myrmidia and Shallya. He sends divine ravens to guide dead souls to the Portal, the pillared gateway between the mortal realms and the realm of the gods. He then leads each soul from there to its final resting place: either Morr's Underworld, or the afterlife of another god. He is commonly portrayed as a tall, dark-haired man of aristocratic bearing, with a brooding, intense air.

WORSHIPPERS

Outside Ostermark, where Morr has special importance, few wish to attract the God of Death's attention, so normally only the bereaved pray to him. However, those desperate or brave enough may pray for dreams of what the future may bring, though it is said he rarely divulges anything not associated with dying.

The Order of the Shroud dominates the cult, directly controlling all other orders and the Mourners' Guild, those responsible for overseeing burials and burial grounds. Supporting them, the Black Guard are the cult's largest templar order, tasked to guard temples and hunt down the Undead. The Order of Augurs may be small, but it guides the leadership with its foretellings, and organises the Order of Doomsayers: these wandering priests of Morr tour the land performing Doomings for all Human children on their tenth year. Bringing them all together, every decade a grand convocation of the priesthood of Morr is held at Luccini in Tilea, where the future for the cult is discussed around city-wide festivities.

All Morr's clerics wear plain, black, hooded robes without adornment or trimming.

HOLY SITES

Temples of Morr are within Gardens of Morr: great graveyards wrapped with black roses that bloom all year, and are rarely used for anything other than funeral services. Most are plain structures of dark stone, distinguished by a broad doorway with a heavy lintel-stone — representing Morr's Portal. The doors are always open, like the doors to the Kingdom of Death. Inside, the temples are bare. Any necessary furniture and other equipment is kept in storage until it is needed for a funeral service. Shrines to Morr also take the form of a gateway, usually consisting of two plain pillars and a lintel. In some cases, one pillar is white marble and the other black basalt.

PENANCES

Morr's penances typically involve hunting Necromancers and destroying Undead, or finding and restoring burial places and holy sites fallen to disuse and disrepair. He also occasionally requires servants of Khaine be stopped from fulfilling their dark deeds.

STRICTURES

- Respect and protect the dead.
- Hunt down Necromancers and the Undead wherever they may gather.
- Pay heed to your dreams.
- Never refuse to conduct a funeral service.
- At no time be a party to raising the dead, unless allowed by Morr.

THE CULT OF MYRMIDIA, GODDESS OF STRATEGY

Seat of Power: Magritta, Estalia
Head of the Cult: La Aguila Ultima
Primary Orders: Order of the Eagle, Order of the Righteous Spear, Order of the Blazing Sun
Major Festivals: None in the Empire
Popular Holy Books: *Bellona Myrmidia, Bellum Strategia, The Book of War*
Common Holy Symbols: Spear behind a shield, eagles, suns

In the Empire, bronzed Myrmidia, daughter of Verena and Morr, sister of Shallya, is the Goddess of Strategy and Scientific Warfare. However, in the sun-drenched south, Myrmidia is much more than this: she acts as the patron deity of both the Estalian Kingdoms and the Tilean City States, and is fanatically worshipped in both realms. Because of this, her cult is the largest in the Old World, for all it has a limited presence in the Empire. She is commonly portrayed as a tall, muscular, young woman armed and equipped in archaic, southern stylings. She is known for her calm, honourable approach to all matters, and her clerics do what they can to emulate this.

WORSHIPPERS

Myrmidia grants generals the insight to win battles with minimal losses, and soldiers the skill-at-arms to defeat enemies quickly and without significant losses. Because of this, her cult is steadily growing among the armies and garrisons of the Empire, especially in the Reikland, Averland, and Wissenland. In the Empire, the cult has three orders of significance. The Order of the Eagle tends to the temples and their surrounding communities, and is led from Nuln by the 'Eagle of the North', the most powerful Myrmidian north of the Vaults. The templar Order of the Righteous Spear has a chapterhouse attached to each of these temples, each commanded by the local high priest. A second templar order, the Order of the Blazing Sun, is the oldest Myrmidian order in the Empire, and works independently of the Order of the Eagle.

Myrmidia's clerics in the Empire normally wear blue cowls over white robes with red edging, with her symbol either sewn onto the left breast or worn as a cloak-clasp.

HOLY SITES

Most of Myrmidia's holy sites are found in Estalia and Tilea, and are associated with the goddess's campaigns across those realms when she manifested as a mortal over two-thousand years ago. In the Empire, the goddess has much less of a presence, with temples only in major towns and cities, and only a single monastic order cloistered in the Monastery of the Black Maiden in Wissenland. Temples to Myrmidia tend to follow the architectural styles of Tilea and Estalia, with domed roofs covering square or rectangular halls. Their exteriors are often carved with low reliefs showing battle scenes or tableaux of weapons and shields. Shrines may take the form of miniature temples, statues of the goddess, or free-standing sculptures of stacked weapons, shields, and armour. Myrmidia's holy sites are also known for their scandalous depictions of the goddess and her saints, who are often presented wearing little more than scarves about their waists, which many Sigmarites find completely unacceptable.

PENANCES

Penances from Myrmidia are usually military in nature. A cultist may be ordered to defeat an enemy champion in single combat, or to train a group of peasants and lead them in the defence of their village. Protecting pilgrimage routes to sites of importance to Myrmidia are also not uncommon.

STRICTURES

- Act with honour and dignity in all matters.
- Respect prisoners of war, and never kill an enemy who surrenders.
- Show no mercy to the unrepentant enemies of Humanity.
- Obey all honourable orders.
- Preserve the weak from the horrors of war.

THE CULT OF RANALD, GOD OF TRICKERY

Seat of Power: None officially
Head of the Cult: None officially, though rumours persist of a cult leader marked with ten crosses
Primary Orders: The Crosses, the Brotherhood, the Crooked Fingers
Major Festivals: The Day of Folly
Popular Holy Books: *The Riddles Ten, Midnight and the Black Cat, The Great Joke*
Common Holy Symbols: Crossed fingers, Cats, Magpies

According to myth, Ranald was once mortal, a gentle bandit who robbed from the rich and gave to the poor. This so charmed Shallya that the goddess fell in love. One fateful day, she found Ranald dying, fatally touched by the plagues of the Fly Lord. Unable to accept this, she let Ranald drink from her holy chalice, granting the rogue eternal life. But it was all a trick — Ranald had faked it all — and, laughing, the new god gleefully danced into the heavens. While generally portrayed as a dapper Human wearing a perpetual smile, there is little consistency to the height, weight, skin colour, or even gender of Ranald, though the god is more commonly portrayed as male in the Empire. More a cheerful trickster than outright criminal, Ranald is said to have a love of deflating pride with clever tricks and ruses.

WORSHIPPERS

Ranald most commonly stands as a patron to thieves and rogues, but the cult also attracts gamblers, liars, merchants, tricksters, and the poor and downtrodden.

The cult of Ranald is, by general perception, a disorganised rabble of charlatans, thieves, and ne'er-do-wells. However, it is more co-ordinated than it appears, and split into three primary orders. The Crosses are the most accepted — a priesthood overseeing the cult's gambling-dens, typically using the proceeds to administer to the poor. The Brotherhood is less open, and is somewhat akin to a secret society of merchants — they use business to bring the pompous and greedy to their knees. Lastly, and most widespread, is the publicly disavowed Crooked Fingers, the thieves, rogues, and liars of Ranald, a group that is roundly distrusted.

Cultists of Ranald have no conventional garb to identify them, but always work cross symbols into their clothing somewhere, perhaps as a repeating pattern.

HOLY SITES

Ranald has no formal temple organisation, although the cult maintains seemingly unconnected gambling dens in most towns and cities. Small shrines are found in the headquarters of many criminal gangs and merchant houses, and the poorer quarters of many cities have street-corner shrines dedicated to the God of Luck. The latter are often maintained by local 'shrine clubs' which operate as both social and religious bodies, and are usually led by one of the Crooked Fingers. Shrines are almost never elaborate, often just a simple, smiling statue with crossed fingers behind the back, or a crudely depicted cat or magpie, often fashioned as if smiling.

PENANCES

Ranald's penances usually involve stealing into locked and guarded locations to recover precious items or leave a token of their presence. Humiliating oppressors of the poor is also common — perhaps by framing a brutal Watch captain for a ludicrous crime, for example, or locking him in his own cells. Ranald often sends favoured and disfavoured cultists alike on a 'Pilgrimage of Fingers', a set of tasks proving capability and loyalty.

STRICTURES

- One coin in ten belongs to Ranald.
- Never betray another to the authorities; there is no greater sin than informing.
- Violence is prohibited except in self-defence.
- It is better to live free and die than live under oppression.
- There is no honour among thieves, but there is amongst Ranaldans.

THE CULT OF RHYA, GODDESS OF FERTILITY

Seat of Power: None officially
Head of the Cult: None
Primary Orders: None
Major Festivals: Summer Solstice, with equinoxes also celebrated
Popular Holy Books: None, though many oral traditions exist
Common Holy Symbols: Sheaf of wheat, fruit, spirals

Bountiful Rhya is the Goddess of Fertility and Summer, widely known as the Earth Mother and She Who Sustains Life. Though typically depicted as the wife of Taal, myths connect her to many gods, and she has children from many of those relationships. Most commonly portrayed as a tall, beautiful women wreathed in leaves and bedecked in fruit, Rhya's statues are normally nude, pregnant, and surrounded by her children. Many theologians tie Rhya to the Old Faith, a prehistoric cult comprised of ancient farmers and hunters who wrested a living from the land before the Empire was born, and one still found in secluded communities to this day.

WORSHIPPERS

Rural folk across the Old World venerate Rhya, relying on her to provide the crops upon which their lives depends. Womanfolk comprise the main body of the cult, and most midwives pay at least lip-service to Rhya's Wisdom, a set of oral traditions surrounding childbirth. Although she is not openly worshipped in the towns and cities — townsfolk often turning to Shallya in her stead — her name is frequently tied with Taal's, so she is still well known amongst such people.

Because the cult has no great temples and protects no holy books or relics of significance, many scholars believe her worship to be declining, and possibly already dead. Her many cultists do nothing to contradict such talk.

Rhya's cultists have no fixed vestment or preferred garb, though greens are very common, as is using plants, flowers, or herbs to accessorise any clothing. They often dress in a fashion considered far too revealing by Sigmarite doctrine, which can cause friction as the Rhyans believe giving in to such prudishness is tantamount to encouraging the Prince of Excess into your lives, as it builds forbidden desires. Devotees of Sigmar invariably disagree, believing abstinence and restricting temptation is a better response to such dangers than indulgence.

HOLY SITES

Rhya has no large temples, though many ancient sites constructed from oghams (standing stones) are centres of worship for her cult, and some still echo each equinox with the cries of fevered celebrants.

Shrines to Rhya are usually simple statues of the goddess, often piled high with offerings of food and drink. Older shrines are often made of small standing stones marked with worn, spiralled patterns.

PENANCES

Rhyan penances may involve replanting devastated areas, helping broken households, and maintaining sacred groves. It is also common to find Rhyans tasked to protect helpless families, which can often put them at odds with local bailiffs and law enforcement.

STRICTURES

- Defend families, children, and crops from all harm.
- Never feel shame for the flesh Rhya gave you.
- Life is sacred, do no harm lest another life is in danger.
- Never judge whom another loves.
- Interrupt the work of the Prince of Excess wherever it may thirst.

THE CULT OF SHALLYA, GODDESS OF MERCY

Seat of Power: Couronne, Bretonnia
Head of the Cult: Grande Matriarch
Primary Orders: Order of the Bleeding Heart, Order of the Chalice
Major Festivals: None
Popular Holy Books: *The Book of Suffering, Livre des Larmes, The Testament of Pergunda*
Common Holy Symbols: White doves, keys, heart with a drop of blood

Shallya is the Goddess of Healing, Mercy, and Compassion. She is the daughter of Verena and Morr, and the sister of Myrmidia. Shallya is normally portrayed as a young, beautiful maiden whose eyes are perpetually welling with tears as she weeps for the world's pain. It is said Shallya's compassion knows no bounds, and in some myths — such as the stories of Ranald tricking her into granting him immortality, or Manaan trapping her at the bottom of the sea — she seems trusting to the point of foolishness. However, her cultists maintain her mercy is available to all, without judgment. True foolishness consists of presuming to judge who is worthy of Shallya's grace and who is not.

WORSHIPPERS

Most Old Worlders think of Shallya's cult as composed of healers and physicians, but her worshippers also include many who work to help alleviate suffering of other kinds: charitable souls who help the poor; workers in orphanages, asylums, and refuges; and even brave folk who go in search of lost and missing people on behalf of their loved ones. The cult is ruled by the far-reaching Order of the Bleeding Heart, which maintains all the temples, hospices, mercyhouses, and other holy sites. The significantly smaller Order of the Chalice tasks its mendicants to cleanse the Fly Lord's influence, tackling the worst diseases and plagues wherever they may fester.

Shallya's cultists all wear white robes, often hooded, with a bleeding heart symbol embroidered on the left breast.

HOLY SITES

The high temple of all Shallya's cult is in Couronne, Bretonnia, built over a famous healing spring. Locals claim the magical waters were once poured there from the same chalice Shallya used to grant Ranald immortality, which they claim is the holy grail of the Lady, the patron Goddess of Bretonnia. Whatever the truth, it is a popular destination for pilgrims, many of whom travel there to be healed from intractable disease. Elsewhere, every town or city of any size has a temple to Shallya, and most smaller settlements have at least a shrine dedicated to her. Temples of Shallya normally consist of a courtyard with a temple on one side and an infirmary on the other, all constructed in southern styles. Larger temples have smaller subsidiary chapels, commonly endowed by local families, and are often connected to hospitals. Shrines are usually simple, often with the dove or heart of Shallya carved into stone, or with small fountains gushing eternal tears from simple statues.

PENANCES

Penances set by Shallya always involve helping the sick, poor, or downtrodden. A cultist might be sent to a village struck by a plague to tend the sick until the disease has passed. Shallya often tasks her servants to help the wounded at war, or patrol popular pilgrimage routes for those unable to complete their journeys due to ill health.

STRICTURES

- Always render assistance without judgement, based only on a person's need.
- Never kill except in self-defence or when facing followers of the Fly Lord.
- Hunt down servants of the Fly Lord wherever they may fester.
- Shallya's work is never done, so turn not to self-indulgence.
- Never take up arms; a walking stick and courage will suffice.

THE CULT OF SIGMAR, GOD OF THE EMPIRE

Seat of Power: Altdorf, Reikland
Head of the Cult: The Grand Theogonist
Primary Orders: Order of the Anvil, Order of the Cleansing Flame, Order of the Silver Hammer, Order of the Torch
Major Festivals: Sigmarday (28th Sigmarzeit)
Popular Holy Books: *The Book of Sigmar, Deus Sigmar, The Geistbuch*
Common Holy Symbols: *Ghal-maraz* (Sigmar's Warhammer), twin-tailed comets, griffons

Sigmar is the Empire's patron, and his cult dominates the realm. Because Sigmar was once the emperor, his worship is inextricably interwoven with politics, and three of the cult's highest-ranking members are directly involved with electing new emperors. According to legend, 2,500 years ago Sigmar's birth was heralded by a twin-tailed comet, and he was born the first son of the chief of the Unberogen tribe. When older, he received the magical warhammer *Ghal-maraz* ('Skull-splitter') as a gift from the Dwarf king Kurgan Ironbeard for saving his life from Greenskins. Sigmar later allied with the Dwarfs and their combined forces defeated the Greenskins. He was then crowned as the first emperor of the Human tribes he'd united. After fifty years of extraordinary rule, Sigmar mysteriously vanished, only to later ascend to divinity, crowned as a god by Ulric, Sigmar's patron in life.

WORSHIPPERS

Most folk of the Empire pay at least lip-service to their patron deity. In the most devout provinces, like Reikland, Sigmar worship is an unquestioned part of daily life. Folk attend weekly 'throngs' where the lessons of Sigmar are preached. Many also attend temple to train as local militia, confess sins and purify the soul, or receive advice on how to be more like the God-King of old. Sigmar's cult is comprised of an uncounted number of different orders. The largest is the Order of the Torch: Sigmar's priests who lead their local communities. Other orders of importance include: the Order of the Cleansing Flame, comprised of inquisitors and witch hunters; the Order of the Silver Hammer, which includes warrior priests and yet more witch hunters; and the Order of the Anvil, a monastic order concerned with preserving Sigmar's deeds and laws. The cult also has many templar orders. The most famous are the proud Knights of Sigmar's Blood, the fanatical Knights of the Fiery Heart, and the militaristic Knights Griffon. Given the cult is so large, there are many different uniforms, vestments, and robes worn, all of which have different colours, cuts, and accessories according to local tradition and requirement.

HOLY SITES

Every city, town, and village in the Empire has at least one temple to Sigmar. The Grand Cathedral in Altdorf is staffed by hundreds of priests and lay workers, and guarded by at least two orders of templars; at the other end of the scale, a village chapel may be visited just once every week by a travelling priest, who serves the needs of several small settlements. Shrines can be found in most homes, and wayshrines dot every major highway, mostly marked with hammers or comets.

PENANCES

Sigmarite cultists may be ordered to destroy a cell of Chaos-worshippers, or expose a corrupt official who is secretly in league with the Ruinous Powers or a foreign power. It is also common to be tasked with building, or rebuilding, local communities to better promote unity and strength in the Empire.

STRICTURES

- Obey your orders.
- Aid Dwarf-folk, never do them harm.
- Promote the unity of the Empire.
- Bear true allegiance to the imperial throne.
- Root out Greenskins, Chaos worshippers, and foul witches without mercy.

THE CULT OF TAAL, GOD OF THE WILD

Seat of Power: Talabheim, Talabecland
Head of the Cult: The Hierarch
Primary Orders: Order of the Antler, The Longshanks
Major Festivals: Spring Equinox, with other equinoxes also celebrated
Popular Holy Books: *The Book of Green, Rites of the Ancient Grove, Tome of Summer's Path*
Common Holy Symbols: Antlers, oaks, stone axes

Taal is the God of Wild Places and Animals, and the King of Nature. He is the husband to Rhya, and father to Manaan, and is perceived by Taalites to be the king of the gods, though other cults dispute this. All nature is under his purview, from the snaking rivers to the tallest mountains, from the smallest insect to the greatest beast. He is normally portrayed as a powerfully built, virile man with long, wild hair and great spreading antlers, and is known for his volatile moods and his need to hunt.

WORSHIPPERS

Rural folk across the Old World venerate Taal, and any who make their living in wild places take care not to offend him. Taal is the patron deity of Talabecland in the Empire, where his cult holds significant sway, influencing all levels of society.

Taal's cult has a variety of smaller orders dedicated to holy sites and groves throughout the Old World, but two orders drive the cult forwards. The Order of the Antler are the priests of the cult, who are tasked to teach Taal's ways and protect the wild places from intrusion.

These Taalites are particularly widespread in Talabecland, and their forest temples are hubs of activity for rural folk. The Longshanks are a mix of warrior-priest and templar who typically wander as individuals, cleansing Taal's wild places of corruption and ensuring rural communities do nothing to upset Father Taal.

HOLY SITES

Normally, temples to Taal are small, rustic affairs, built of wood and rough stone in a manner unchanged for countless centuries. They are usually sited close to natural features of wonder such as waterfalls, swirling pools, and mountains, and often have small sweat lodges attached. The high temple of Taal in Talabheim is something of an anomaly when compared to this. It appears more a well-maintained, albeit wild, noble garden than a temple, and huge services are held there under the spreading rowan trees weekly.

Officially, the Hierarch leads the cult from there, though he spends most of his time in the wild groves of the nearby Taalgrunhaar Forest. Shrines to Taal are barely structures at all. Some old trees are regarded as sacred, and offerings pile up at their bases. Caves,

forest groves, and other natural places are also used as shrines, and usually only a local or a devout follower of Taal can find them.

PENANCES

Taal's penances usually involve clearing diseased or mutated monsters from wild areas, replanting sacred trees, and maintaining groves important to the cult. A cultist might also be ordered to climb a high mountain and leave a stone on a cairn at the top, or clear an obstruction at the top of a waterfall. Whatever the specific task that must be undertaken, Taal's penances almost always challenge the cultist to survive in the wild.

STRICTURES

- Offer a prayer of thanks for every animal taken.
- Spend a week alone communing with the wilderness every year.
- Eschew metal armour; clad yourself in the hides of Taal.
- Rely on your own skill, not the advances of gunpowder or cold technology.
- Never harm an animal except in self-defence or for food or sacrifice.

THE CULT OF ULRIC, GOD OF WAR

Seat of Power: Middenheim, Middenland
Head of the Cult: Ar-Ulric
Primary Orders: Order of the Howling Wolf, Order of the Knights of the White Wolf
Major Festivals: Campaign Start, Hochwinter, Campaign End
Popular Holy Books: *Liber Lupus, Teutognengeschichte, The Ulric Creed*
Common Holy Symbols: White Wolves, stylised 'U's, claws

Ulric is the ferocious God of Wolves, Winter, and Warfare. He is the brother of Taal and, according to Ulrican lore, the king of the gods, although other cults dispute this. He is normally portrayed as a massive, heavily bearded barbarian wearing a white wolf-pelt cloak, and bearing a mighty war-axe named Blitzbeil. He's a distant, harsh, and unforgiving god who expects his cultists to rely on individual strength and prowess. He despises weakness, cowardice, and trickery, and favours the direct approach in all matters.

WORSHIPPERS

Ulric's cult is strongest in the north of the Empire. The city-state of Middenheim, with its enormous high temple to Ulric, is the heart of his cult, and the god is regarded as the city's patron. Elsewhere, he is worshipped mainly by warriors and soldiers. Devout Ulricans can usually be spotted by their long hair and beards, for most choose not to cut it, imitating their wild deity. Ulric's cult is split into just two orders: the priestly Howling Wolves, and the templar White Wolves. The Howling Wolves are not very popular outside Middenland and Nordland, viewed by most folk to be too coarse for this enlightened era. By comparison, the Knights of the White Wolf are enormously popular, easily the largest knightly order in the Empire, and the oldest templar order in the Old World. Ulric's priests wear black robes with a howling white wolf emblem on the chest. A wolf pelt across the shoulders is also common, as is fur trimmings.

HOLY SITES

Ulric's high temple is in Middenheim, and the cult's leader, Ar-Ulric (which means the son of Ulric), has enormous temporal and spiritual sway. At the back of the high temple lies the Flame of Ulric, a huge, ever-burning, argent fire granted by the winter god to guide his people. This miracle is the focus of several pilgrimage routes, and all Ulricans of Middenland are expected to bathe in its cold light at least once in their lives. Smaller temples are found in every city and town of any size, but are grander and more numerous in the north than in the south. Chapels and shrines can be found in barracks and forts throughout the Old World.

Temples resemble fortified keeps and are normally square. The interior of the main hall is lit by small windows high in the walls, and by an ever-stocked fire in a circular hearth tended by the priesthood. Behind the fire, usually against a rear wall, stands a statue of Ulric enthroned, often flanked by a pair of enormous wolves. Shrines are similar but smaller, with a lamp in place of a fire and small statues just a foot or two tall.

PENANCES

Penances set by Ulric are almost always tests of strength, courage, and martial skill. Slaying a powerful monster, or clearing out a nest of Beastmen or outlaws, are typical tasks.

STRICTURES

- Obey your betters.
- Defend your honour in all matters, and never refuse a challenge.
- Stand honest and true; outside an ambush, trickery and deception are forbidden.
- Only wear pelts from wolves killed by weapons crafted of your own hands.
- Blackpowder, helmets, crossbows, and technology are not Ulric's way.

THE CULT OF VERENA, GODDESS OF WISDOM

Seat of Power: None
Head of the Cult: None
Primary Orders: The Order of Scalebearers, the Order of Lorekeepers, the Order of Mysteries, the Order of Everlasting Light
Major Festivals: Year Blessing
Popular Holy Books: *Canticum Verena, Eulogium Verena, The Book of Swords*
Common Holy Symbols: Scales of justice, owls, downward-pointing swords

Wise Verena, the Goddess of Learning and Justice, is the wife of dark Morr and the mother of Myrmidia and Shallya. She is generally depicted as a tall, classically beautiful woman, and usually carries a sword and a set of scales. As the patron of justice she is concerned with fairness rather than the letter of the law: she opposes tyranny and oppression as much as crime.

WORSHIPPERS

Verena is worshipped throughout the Old World, especially in the south. Her devout followers include scholars, lawyers, and magistrates, as well as some wizards of the Colleges of Magic, particularly of the Grey and Light orders.

The cult of Verena has no rigid hierarchy: it is said that Verena alone heads the cult, and no mortal intermediary is needed because truth is self-evident and requires no interpretation. Temple priests from the Order of Lorekeepers are tasked to preserve knowledge and communicate it to the community. They keep up a voluminous correspondence with each other, exchanging information and news.

Priests from the equally influential Order of Scalebearers are much sought after to act as judges, arbitrators, and go-betweens, because of their famed impartiality and mastery of the law. The Order of Mysteries is much smaller and less well-known, and contains warrior-priests who seek lost and forgotten lore, wherever it may lie. The last major order is the Knights of the Everlasting Light, templars famed for their sword skills, sense of fairness, and legendary bad luck. Verena's cultists usually wear plain white robes, symbolic of pure truth and impartiality.

HOLY SITES

Temples to Verena can be found in most cities and larger towns, generally situated in the administrative or university quarters. Most libraries and court-houses include a shrine to the goddess, and smaller shrines can be found in the homes of many scholars and lawyers. Temples usually have colonnaded facades, with symbols of the goddess and allegorical figures of learning presented in low relief. Inside is a large statue of Verena, normally seated with a book in her lap, a pair of scales in her left hand, and her right hand resting on the hilt of a sword. Smaller rooms lead off from the main temple, including a library and chambers for the attendant priests. Each temple has at least one meeting room where negotiations can take place under the eyes of the goddess.

PENANCES

Penances set by Verena normally involve the recovery or preservation of knowledge, the righting of an injustice, or the resolution of a dispute. Cultists may also be sent to recover a long-forgotten book of lore, or to mediate in a difficult quarrel. This could be anything from a farmers' boundary dispute to unpicking the complicated politics of two realms on the brink of war.

STRICTURES

- Never refuse to arbitrate a dispute when asked.
- Always tell the truth without fear or favour.
- Protect knowledge at all costs.
- Combat must be a last resort when all alternative routes are fruitless.
- Never become a tool of injustice or heresy.

DWARVEN ANCESTOR GODS

The Dwarfs venerate their ancient ancestors, valuing tradition above all else. Though the Time of the Ancestor Gods was many thousands of years ago, the Dwarfs still hold records of that time in their oldest Holds. Many names echo from that era, creating a broad, inter-related pantheon, but three Ancestor Gods are of especial importance and are known by all Dwarfs: Grimnir, Grungni, and Valaya, each a progenitor of the species as a whole. In addition to the oldest Ancestor Gods, Dwarfs also revere the founders of local clans as guardian deities.

DWARF PRIESTS

Those dedicating themselves to the cults of the Ancestor Gods do not use the Priest, Nun, or Warrior Priest Careers, as Dwarfs have a very different relationship with their gods, seeking to emulate them rather than worship or appease them.

Because of this, if you wish to play a Dwarf dedicated to one of the Ancestor Gods, simply choose an appropriate career to best act like that god. So, if you wanted to emulate Grimnir, effectively becoming a priest of Grimnir, perhaps play a Slayer and join the Cult of the Slayer, or maybe become a Soldier.

ELVEN GODS

The Elves worshipped their own gods long before Humans and most other species existed in their current forms. Their pantheon is extensive, with different groups of deities being held as important by Wood Elves and High Elves.

Loosely, there are two groups of gods, the Cadai and the Cytharai. The Cadai rule the heavens, and have strong connections to their Elven worshippers, directly helping where they can. The selfish Cytharai rule the underworld, and care little for the Elves. Standing apart from both these courts are a loose group of unaligned gods, the most prominent being Morai-Heg the Crone, Goddess of Fate and Death.

The High Elves especially revere the Cadai, and have sophisticated priesthoods dedicated to their teachings. They appease the Cytharai when necessary, but it is unlawful to worship any but Mathlann, whose aid is sought by mariners. According to their myths, Asuryan, the God of Creation, is king of all the gods, able to pronounce judgement upon them all.

The Wood Elves take a much more balanced approach and have temples and shrines to all the gods impacting their lives, be they Cadai or Cytharai. Because of their close association with the woods and forests, they revere Isha the Mother and Kurnous the Hunter above all others, and rumours persist that both gods take a direct hand in Wood Elf affairs.

According to some theologians — mostly Elven — the deities of this pantheon are the true gods, and those worshipped by other species are simply different aspects of the Elven originals.

ELVEN PRIESTS

Both High Elves and Wood Elves have priesthoods for the gods, but they do not have blessings and miracles. The Elves don't believe the gods manifest in this fashion, and instead see magic as a gift from the gods. Because of this, if you wish to be an Elven priest, use the Wizard career, and chose from an appropriate Lore to represent the magic your god has gifted. So, a 'priest' of Kurnous would use the Lore of Beasts, a worshipper of Isha, the Lore of Life, and devotees of Asuryan use the Lores of Light or Fire.

HALFLING GODS

Some say that Halflings are superstitious rather than religious, and the bulk of their deities support this impression. Most Halfling gods and goddesses have to do with hearth and home, cooking, herb lore, earthy matters, and general day-to-day concerns. Halfling gods are practical rather than philosophical: as the saying goes: 'Deep thoughts butter no parsnips'. Halflings also show respect to certain Human deities — Sigmar, Taal, and Rhya in particular — but this is more from a desire to avoid conflict than from any sincere devotion.

HALFLING PRIESTS

Halflings don't really have priests, and they certainly don't build temples (though Humans seem happy to do it for them, especially Sigmarites). There are better things to do than warble on about someone else's business. Of course, they respect the gods, and have shrines on-hand should they need to have a quick natter, but none make a career exclusively talking to just one god — why make yourself so exclusive? Should a particular god need to be appeased, it is usually left up to a local elder to do what's required on behalf of the community, often after a great deal of talking with relevant experts and peers.

PRIMARY DWARF GODS

God	Sphere	Worshippers	Offerings	Notes
Grimnir	Warriors, Courage	Soldiers, slayers	Axes, gold jewellery, resolved grudges	High temple in Karaz-a-Karak; largest Slayer temple in Karak Kadrin. Husband to Valaya; brother to Grungni
Grungni	Mining, Metalworking, Stoneworking	Artisans, miners	Fine stone or metal work, mail armour	High temple in Karak Azul. Husband to Valaya; brother to Grimnir.
Valaya	Brewing, Hearth, Healing	Artisans, scholars, physicians	Beer, shields, food	High temple in Karaz-a-Karak. Wife to Grimnir and Grungni.

PRIMARY ELVEN GODS

	Sphere	Worshippers	Offerings	Notes
Cadai				
Asuryan	All Creation, the Heavens, Phoenixes	Rulers, judges, lawyers in general	White feathers, masks, white crystals	The Creator and king of all the gods. Asuryan created the mortal and divine realms, and separated them.
Isha	Fertility, life	Rural folk of all kinds	Food, tears, green crystals	The Mother. Wife of Kurnous. Isha created the Elves.
Kurnous	Animals, wild places, hunting	Hunters, woodsmen, and those working with animals	Animals, enemy blood, amber crystals	The King of the Wild Hunt, Lord of Beasts, and husband of Isha. Kurnous created all animals.
Hoeth	Wisdom, knowledge, teaching	Scholars, mages, perfectionists	Tomes, swords, yellow crystals	The Lord of Wisdom. Hoeth elevated the Elves to sentience.
Cytharai				
Atharti	Pleasure, seduction, snakes, the mind	Hedonists, bawds, and those lost to their emotions	Snakes, gems, pale pink crystals	The Lady of Desire. Atharti unlocked Elven emotions after their creation. The High Elves largely forbid her worship.
Khaine	War, blood-shed, violence	Warriors and soldiers of all kinds	Blood, weapons, red crystals	The Bloody-Handed.
Mathlann	Oceans	Seafolk of all kinds	Gold, fish, turquoise crystals	The Lord of the Deeps. Has little love for anything land-bound, including Elves.
Unaligned				
Morai-Heg	Death, fate, crows	The bereaved	Bones, black feathers, black crystals	The Crone. Worship is generally shunned as it is seen as unwise to attract her attention.

PRIMARY HALFLING GODS

God	Sphere	Worshippers	Offerings	Notes
Esmerelda	Hearth, home, hospitality	All Halflings try to emulate Esmerelda	Food, fire, comfort	The Many-Times-Grandmother
Hyacinth	Childbirth, Fertility, Sex	Midwives, pregnant women, revellers	Boiled water, palliative herbs	Has a fondness for twins and triplets.
Josias	Farming, domesticated animals	Farmers, herders, gardeners	Crops, food, thick soups	The Faithful. Josias is known for working hard and resting hard.
Quinsberry	Knowledge, ancestry, tradition	Scholars	Books, tapestries, gold	Has a library detailing the complete history and bloodline of every Halfling

CHAOS GODS

The Ruinous Powers of Chaos are the foremost existential threat to the Old World, but much about them remains a mystery. Merely seeking such knowledge is punishable by death without permission from the Cult of Sigmar. And seeking such permission attracts intense scrutiny of your person and motives, and is seldom granted.

The Ruinous Powers are seen by the common folk as the punishing manifestation of sin, and the reason that all must behave within socially acceptable boundaries as espoused by the cults. Indulging in violence, lust, slovenliness or unseemly curiosity has direct repercussions for the individual (as they are corrupted and come to a sticky end) and for their community, as their deviant behaviour attracts the destructive attention of these evil forces.

The average person will know of the most powerful of these forces through euphemistic names, such as the Blood God, the Plague Lord, the Lord of Change, and the Prince of Pain. Even the most learned scholars of this forbidden lore can only guess at what motivates these obscene powers, or if they even have an agenda beyond their primal impulses.

It seems there are competing factions dedicated to different aspects of ruin, and they are as much enemies to each other as to the rest of the Old World. On the rare occasions when they co-operate, much like they did during the Great War Against Chaos over two-hundred years ago, the world trembles. Some claim cults dedicated to the Chaos Gods have infiltrated the Empire. Most dismiss this as nonsense, for no right-thinking individual would be so foolish as to worship one of the Ruinous Powers.

PRAYERS

A small number of the faithful stand apart from their peers, seemingly able to appeal for their deity's direct intervention in the form of miracles. Those who perform such feats are known by many names in different parts of the Old World — including: Living Saints, Gods' Servants, The Hallowed, Divine Wills, Anointed Ones — but, in the Empire, they are most commonly referred to as 'Blessed', which is often used as a title. So, if Sister Anna where to be Blessed by Sigmar — i.e. granted Sigmar's grace, able to have her prayers answered — she would become 'Blessed Anna', or, in full, 'Blessed Anna, Sister of Sigmar'.

THE BLESSED

There are two Talents that specifically mark out those Blessed by the gods: *Bless* and *Invoke*. Characters with the *Bless* Talent may enact Blessings, which are minor manifestations of divine will, while the *Invoke* Talent allows the Blessed to call on their gods for more powerful Miracles. For more on these Talents, see **Chapter 4: Skills and Talents.**

BLESSINGS AND MIRACLES

Blessing and Miracles are prayers spoken by one of the Blessed, and then empowered by a god. To enact a Blessing or Miracle, make a **Challenging (+0) Pray** Test. If you score a Success, your Blessing or Miracle manifests according to its rules, and a high SL will give you bonus effects. If you score a Failure, your words are spoken, but your god, for whatever reason, refuses to listen. If you Fumble the Pray Test, you have offended your god and must roll on the Wrath of the Gods table.

Limitations

You must be able to speak to intone the required prayer, rite, chant, or song to enact a Blessing or Miracle. Each of your Blessings or Miracles can only be in effect once, meaning you have to wait for an existing one to come to an end before using the same prayer again.

Multiple invocations of the same prayer by different individuals do not offer cumulative bonuses. Thus, intoning two *Blessings of Finesse* will only provide a bonus of +10 to Dexterity.

SIN POINTS

The Blessed are watched closely by the gods, and risk gaining the disfavour of their deities if they should act contrary to their gods' will. In game, this is represented with Sin points.

If you violate any of the Cult Strictures listed under your god, the GM will award one or more Sin Points. Every time you receive a Sin point, it is added it to your running total. There is no maximum to the number of Sin points you can earn. The more points you have, the more upset your god is likely to be should you call upon divine aid.

IT'S A SIN!

There are many different ways Blessed Priests can break their strictures; GMs should consider the scale of the infraction when awarding Sin Points, and allocate them proportionately, normally scoring 1 to 3. For instance, one of the strictures of the cult of Myrmidia is to respect prisoners of war. If a Myrmidian priest were to deny a thirsty prisoner of war a drink of water, this may earn a single Sin point. Beating a prisoner would be a great infraction, securing maybe 2 Sin points. Torturing or killing a helpless prisoner is unacceptable to Myrmidia, easily earning 3 or maybe more Sin points.

Kind GMs may wish to warn players before they commit infractions, especially if they are new to WFRP.

Sin and Wrath

Appealing to your deity when you have been acting contrary to the god's wishes is risky. Whenever you make a Pray Test, if the units die of the result is equal to or less than your current Sin point total, then you will suffer the Wrath of the Gods, even if the Pray Test is successful.

WRATH OF THE GODS

The Wrath of Gods table is referenced whenever you Fumble a Pray Test, or when the units die of a Pray Test is equal or lower than your current Sin points. The GM may also use it, or pluck results from it, whenever you foolishly insult any of the gods. When rolling on the Wrath of the Gods table, add +10 to the roll for each Sin Point you have accrued. After rolling and applying the result, reduce your Sin points by 1, to a minimum of 0.

OPTIONS: PREACH IT, SISTER!

Each of the gods have different styles of prayers, designed to be intoned in different ways. Whether these are the warcries of Ulric, the shanties of Manaan, or the threnodies of Morr, each requires the words be spoken (or sung) firmly, and with conviction.

To represent this, the GM may require that any Pray Tests that are intoned quietly or without confidence have a higher Difficulty.

YOU'VE GOT TO PRAY!

If a character behaves in a particularly pious manner, such as completing an arduous pilgrimage, or making a significant donation to their cult, the GM may wish to remove one or more Sin Points with a successful Pray Test, used to show you are begging for absolution. This, of course, also risks the chance of Wrath of the Gods. Otherwise, the only way to remove Sin Points is by rolling on the Wrath of the Gods table.

THE WRATH OF THE GODS TABLE

Percentile Roll	Result
01-05	**Holy Visions:** Visions of your god plague your senses. Attempt an **Average (+20) Endurance** Test. If you fail gain one *Stunned* Condition. The GM determines what the visions may be.
06-10	**Think Over Your Deeds:** Any successful Pray test cannot achieve more than +0 SL for the next week.
11-15	**Heed My Lessons:** You suffer a penalty of −10 to your Pray Skill for the next 1d10+Sin points Rounds.
16-20	**Prove Your Devotion:** Gain the *Prone* Condition. This Condition is not removed until you score a Success with an **Average (+20) Pray** Test.
21-25	**You Try My Patience:** You cannot enact any Pray Tests for 1d10 Rounds.
26-30	**You Do Not Understand My Intent:** You suffer a penalty of −10 to any Skills associated with your deity (as determined by the GM) for the next 1d10+Sin points hours.
31-35	**I Find Your Lack Of Faith Disturbing:** You cannot enact any Pray Tests for 1d10+Sin points Rounds.
36-40	**Share My Pain:** You suffer 1+Sin points Wounds, ignoring Toughness Bonus and APs. Also attempt an **Average (+20) Endurance** Test. If you fail gain one *Stunned* Condition.
41-45	**Your Cause Is Unworthy:** Your targets gain the *Prone* condition. Any Blessings or Miracles of your deity targeting them automatically fail for the next 1d10+Sin points days.
46-50	**Cease Your Prattling:** You cannot enact any Pray Tests for the next 2d10+Sin points rounds.
51-55	**Feel My Wrath:** You suffer 1d10+Sin points Wounds. Also attempt a **Challenging (+0) Endurance** Test. If you fail gain one *Stunned* Condition.

56-60	**I Shall Not Aid You:** You suffer a penalty of −10 to a Skill associated with your deity (as determined by the GM) for the next 1d10+Sin Points days.
61-65	**Divine Wounds:** Gain 1+Sin points *Bleeding* conditions.
66-70	**Struck Blind:** Gain the *Prone* Condition. Gain 1+Sin point *Blinded* Conditions, which can only be removed by passing a **Challenging (+0) Pray** Test, with Success removing 1 + SL *Blinded* Conditions.
71-75	**What Will You Sacrifice?:** You suffer 1d10+Sin points Wounds, ignoring Toughness Bonus and APs. Also attempt a **Difficult (−10) Endurance** Test. If you fail gain one *Stunned* Condition.
76-80	**You Have Sinned Against Me:** Your god is extremely annoyed and forces you to you enact Pray Tests as your Action for the next 1d10+Sin Points Rounds as a penance.
81-87	**Purge the Flesh:** You suffer 2d10+Sin points Wounds, ignoring Toughness Bonus and APs. Also attempt a **Hard (−20) Endurance** Test. If you fail gain one *Stunned* Condition. If you fail with −4 SL or fewer, gain an *Unconscious* Condition that lasts a minimum of 1d10 Rounds.
88	**Daemonic Interference:** The Dark Gods answer your pleas instead of your patron. 1d10 Lesser Daemons appear within 2d10 yards of your position, and attack the nearest targets.
89-95	**Fear my Wrath:** Gain 1+Sin points *Broken* Conditions.
96-100	**Go On Penance:** You must go on a Penance.
101-105	**Castigation:** You are reduced to 0 Wounds (if you are not there already) then gain an *Unconscious* Condition, which cannot be removed until you regain at least 1 Wound.
106-110	**Do Not Use My Name In Vain:** You lose the *Bless* and *Invoke* Talents for the next 1d10+Sin points days.
111-115	**Rely Not Upon Your Vanities:** You have all of your trappings removed, leaving you naked. For each Penance you complete, you will have one taken Magical Item returned to you, should you have any.
116-120	**You Abuse My Mercy:** You lose the *Invoke* and *Bless* Talents for the next 2d10+Sin points days.
121-125	**Behold Your Wickedness:** You suffer excruciating visions of all your failures, which seem to take an eternity, but are over in a moment. Discuss with your GM to build a custom Psychology (see page 190) to reflect your character dealing with the traumatic experience.
126-130	**Thunderbolts and Lightning:** Your god smites you. You are reduced to 0 Wounds (if you are not there already) and gain the *Ablaze* condition.
131-135	**Suffer As I Suffer:** You gain 1+Sin points *Bleeding* conditions every morning, until you have performed a Penance.
136-140	**Excommunication:** You lose the *Invoke* and *Bless* Talents until you perform 2 Penances; the first Penance returns the *Bless* Talent, and the second returns the *Invoke* Talent. All cultists of your god are automatically aware of your circumstance; all Tests to interact with them are automatically Very Hard (−30), and may not be positively modified above this.
141-145	**Prove Your Worth:** A Divine Servant of your deity appears within d100 yards and attacks, intervenes, berates, or similar according to the nature of the offended god.
146-150	**I Cast You Out:** You are abandoned by your god. You permanently lose the *Bless* and *Invoke* Talents, and lose all Pray Advances. Further, all cultists of your god are automatically aware of your circumstance; all Tests to interact with them are automatically Very Hard (−30), and may not be positively modified above this.
151+	**Called To Account:** You are summoned before your god to face final judgement. Unless you have a Fate Point, you never return. If you spend a Fate Point, you are returned at a point of the GM's choosing, and also suffer the effects of **I Cast You Out**.

DIVINE SERVANTS

Divine servants are supernatural minions of the gods in the material realm, in the same way that Daemons serve the Dark Gods. They tend to take the form either of a favoured animal — such as a white wolf for Ulric or a golden eagle for Myrmidia — or a departed devotee of the god, such as a legendary priest or templar. To construct Divine Servants appropriate to the god at hand, use the rules in **Chapter 12: Bestiary**, modifying an animal, Human, or Daemon as you see fit.

Penance

Some Wrath of the Gods results require penance. The GM can decide upon a suitable penance depending on your misdeed, or they may prefer you to choose your own penance, with further punishment awaiting if you are insufficiently penitent. Examples of typical penances are listed in each cult description. Penances may come in the form of a vision, divine inspiration or, very rarely, by direct communication from your deity. If you are not worthy of such contact, a penance may be conveyed through another member of your cult. Alternatively, a Divine Servant of the cult could manifest — this could be a dead teacher, a figure of legend, or an appropriate animal — and inform you what is required. The GM should consider the sins involved, and how the god in question would likely react to these.

BLESSINGS

Blessings are minor manifestations of divine will; a character with the *Bless* Talent receives all six Blessings for their cult as listed in **Blessings by Cult.**

BLESSING AND MIRACLE FORMAT

- The Name of the Blessing or Miracle
- **Range:** A range in yards, or marked as 'touch', showing you need touch your target.
- **Target:** The number of targets affected; it may just be you.
- **Duration:** The duration of the Blessing, usually expressed as 'Instant' or as a number of Rounds.
- The description of what the Blessing does.

OPTIONS: PETTY CONCERNS

The gods grow irritated when the Blessed abuse their privileges. If the GM wishes, multiple uses of Blessings and Miracles in the same scene, on the same injury, on the same target, or similar can anger the gods, and result in Sin Points, typically ranging from 1 to 3.

SUCCESS LEVELS

For every +2 SL you score in a Pray Test when attempting a Blessing, you may choose one of the following benefits:

- **Range:** +6 yards
- **Targets:** +1
- **Duration:** +6 Rounds

If the Blessing in question has a Duration of 'Instant', you may not extend the Duration. You may choose the same option more than once. For instance, if you rolled +4 SL on a Blessing of Healing, you could heal three targets you were touching, two targets up to 6 yards away, or one target up to 12 yards away.

BLESSINGS BY CULT

Manann	Battle	Breath	Courage	Hardiness	Savagery	Tenacity
Morr	Breath	Courage	Fortune	Righteousness	Tenacity	Wisdom
Myrmidia	Battle	Conscience	Courage	Fortune	Protection	Righteousness
Ranald	Charisma	Conscience	Finesse	Fortune	Protection	Wit
Rhya	Breath	Conscience	Grace	Healing	Protection	Recuperation
Shallya	Breath	Conscience	Healing	Protection	Recuperation	Tenacity
Sigmar	Battle	Courage	Hardiness	Might	Protection	Righteousness
Taal	Battle	Breath	Conscience	Hardiness	The Hunt	Savagery
Ulric	Battle	Courage	Hardiness	Might	Savagery	Tenacity
Verena	Conscience	Courage	Fortune	Righteousness	Wisdom	Wit

DIVINE MANIFESTATIONS

Blessings are subtle, completely imperceptible to those without the *Holy Visions* Talent, their manifestation usually indistinguishable to good fortune. In this way, Clerics of the Old World without the *Blessing* Talent often appear to be as effective as those with it.

By comparison, Miracles are overtly manifest, always accompanied by holy signs and portents, which should reflect the circumstances and relevant deity. For instance, an Ulrican Miracle may be accompanied by a chill wind and the spectral howl of wolves, while those receiving a Miracle of Manann may find themselves drenched in saltwater.

Blessing of Battle
Range: 6 yards
Target: 1
Duration: 6 rounds
Your target gains +10 WS.

Blessing of Breath
Range: 6 yards
Target: 1
Duration: 6 rounds
Your target does not need to breathe and ignores rules for suffocation.

Blessing of Charisma
Range: 6 yards
Target: 1
Duration: 6 rounds
Your target gains +10 Fellowship.

Blessing of Conscience
Range: 6 yards
Target: 1
Duration: 6 rounds
Your target must pass a **Average (+20) Willpower** Test to break any of the Strictures of your deity. If they fail, they are overcome with Shame and do not take the action.

Blessing of Courage
Range: 6 yards
Target: 1
Duration: 6 rounds
Your target gains +10 Willpower.

Blessing of Finesse
Range: 6 yards
Target: 1
Duration: 6 rounds
Your target gains +10 Dexterity.

Blessing of Fortune
Range: 6 yards
Target: 1
Duration: 6 rounds
Your target's next failed test may be rerolled. The reroll must stand.

Blessing of Grace
Range: 6 yards
Target: 1
Duration: 6 rounds
Your target gains +10 Agility.

Blessing of Hardiness
Range: 6 yards
Target: 1
Duration: 6 rounds
Your target gains +10 Toughness.

Blessing of Healing
Range: Touch
Target: 1
Duration: Instant
Your target heals +1 Wound.

Blessing of The Hunt
Range: 6 yards
Target: 1
Duration: 6 rounds
Your target gains +10 Ballistic Skill.

Blessing of Might
Range: 6 yards
Target: 1
Duration: 6 rounds
Your target gains +10 Strength.

Blessing of Protection
Range: 6 yards
Target: 1
Duration: 6 rounds
Enemies must make a **Average (+20) Willpower** Test to attack your target as shame wells within for considering violence. If they fail, they must choose a different target, or a different Action.

Blessing of Recuperation
Range: Touch
Target: 1
Duration: Instant
Your target may reduce the duration of 1 disease with which they are afflicted by 1 day. This prayer may only be attempted once per instance of a disease per person.

Blessing of Righteousness
Range: 6 yards
Target: 1
Duration: 6 rounds
Your target's weapon counts as Magical.

Blessing of Savagery
Range: 6 yards
Target: 1
Duration: 6 rounds
When your target next inflicts a Critical Wound, roll twice and choose the best result.

Blessing of Tenacity
Range: 6 yards
Target: 1
Duration: Instant
Your target may remove 1 condition.

Blessing of Wisdom
Range: 6 yards
Target: 1
Duration: 6 rounds
Your target gains +10 Intelligence.

Blessing of Wit
Range: 6 yards
Target: 1
Duration: 6 rounds
Your target gains +10 Initiative.

NAMES

Each Cult has unique names for every Blessing and Miracle – sometimes more than one name. For instance, the Cult of Sigmar may refer to the *Blessing of Battle* as 'The Litany of Sigmar's Wrath', while the Cult of Ulric may call it 'The Sharp Bite of Winter'. The words spoken will be different, but the end effect will be the same.

MIRACLES

Miracles are major manifestations of a god's will, awe-inspiring events everyone will notice; a character with the *Invoke* Talent can empower one of the Miracles for their cult from the following lists.

SUCCESS LEVELS

For every 2 Success Levels you achieve in a Miracle Pray test, you may add additional range, duration or targets equal to the initial value listed in the Miracle. So, a Miracle with a range of 50 yards could be increased by an extra +50 yards for every +2 SL scored.

Miracles with a Range and Target of 'You' may only target the Blessed Priest making the Pray Test, and can never have the range or targets increased. Similarly, if the Miracle has no duration, there is no benefit in choosing to extend its duration.

Certain Miracles may have additional, optional, benefits for additional SL written into their descriptions.

MIRACLES OF MANANN

Becalm

Range: Initiative Bonus Miles
Target: 1 sailing vessel within Line of Sight
Duration: 1 Hour
You steal the wind from the sails of a ship or boat. It is completely becalmed. Even in stormy weather an area of eerie calm and smooth waters surrounds the vessel while gales, lashing rains and towering crests surge and crash around it. This area of calm extends for Initiative yards from the vessel, and if the ship is propelled by some other method, such as oars, the area of calm travels with it.

Drowned Man's Face

Range: Fellowship yards
Target: 1
Duration: Fellowship Bonus Rounds
You implore Manann to drown your foes. Your targets' lungs continuously fill with saltwater while the Miracle is active, and their hair floats around their head as if submerged. Your targets gains a *Fatigued* Condition, and are subject to the rules for Drowning and Suffocation (page 181) while the Miracle is in effect. When the Miracle ends, your targets must attempt a **Challenging (–20) Endurance** Test. If a Failure is scored, also inflict a *Prone* Condition.

Fair Winds

Range: Initiative Bonus Miles
Target: 1 sailing vessel within Line of Sight
Duration: 1 Hour
The target vessels' sails fill with favourable winds, speeding them safely towards their destination. While this Miracle is active, the sailing vessel moves at top speed, no matter the prevailing wind, tide, or current, and all Tests made to steer the vessel gain a bonus of +10.

Manann's Bounty

Range: Touch
Target: 1
Duration: Instant
You implore Manann to provide you with sustenance. Reaching into a body of water you catch enough fish to feed 1 person; if you reach into the sea, you provide enough fish for 2 people. For every +2 SL, you may feed another person.

Sea Legs

Range: Fellowship yards
Target: 1
Duration: Fellowship Bonus Rounds

Your targets are immediately drenched in saltwater, and reel as if on the rolling deck of a tempest-tossed vessel. Their hair is whipped by spectral winds, and a torrent of spray lashes their skin. They gain one each of the *Blinded, Deafened,* and *Fatigued* Conditions, and must attempt an **Average (+20) Agility** Test to use their Move. If they fail, they also gain a *Prone* Condition.

Waterwalk

Range: You
Target: You
Duration: Fellowship Bonus minutes

You call on Manann to allow you to cross a stretch of open water as if it were solid ground. This only works on larger bodies of water that are at least 10 yards wide. Anything smaller is too far removed from Manann's domain for it to be noticed.

MIRACLES OF MORR

Death Mask

Range: You
Target: You
Duration: Fellowship Bonus Rounds

Morr works through you, piercing the Portal to make his presence known to your foes. Your visage takes on a cadaverous mien, and you gain Fear 1.

Destroy Undead

Range: You
Target: Area of Effect
Duration: Instant

You call the power of Morr to smite all Undead. A black fire ripples forth from your body in a perfect circle for Fellowship Bonus yards. All potential targets with the *Undead* Creature Trait lose 1d10 Wounds, ignoring Toughness Bonus and AP. Any Undead destroyed by this Miracle can never be raised with Necromancy again under normal conditions. For every +2 SL, you may increase the area of effect by +Fellowship Bonus yards.

Dooming

Range: Touch
Target: 1
Duration: Instant

Gazing deeply into your target's eyes while muttering a threnody to Morr, you are granted a vision of the target's Doom, a glimpse of what the future holds. This is almost always related to the target's death. This Miracle may only be performed on a character once, after which the *Doomed* Talent may be purchased with XP as if it were in the target's Career.

Last Rites

Range: 1 yard
Target: 1
Duration: Instant

You chant a solemn requiem over a corpse. This miracle ensures that the soul is sent through the portal to Morr's realm, and guarantees the cadaver may not be targeted by any Necromantic spells. If the Miracle targets a foe with the *Undead* **and** *Construct* Creature Traits, it will be destroyed.

Portal's Threshold

Range: Touch
Target: Area of Effect
Duration: Special

You draw a line up to 8 yards long on the ground while incanting a dirge to Morr. Upon enacting the Miracle, an indistinct, shadowy portal seems to manifest to the hoarse croaking of ravens. Creatures with the *Undead* Creature Trait must pass a **Challenging (+0) Willpower** Test to cross the line. Creatures with both *Undead* and *Construct* simply cannot cross the line. The Miracle remains in effect until dawn.

Stay Morr's Hand

Range: Touch
Target: 1
Duration: Fellowship Bonus Hours (Special)

You touch the eyes of someone close to death and request Morr guide the soul within, but not take it. The target must have 0 Wounds and be willing. For the duration of the Miracle, the target gains the *Unconscious* Condition and will not deteriorate until the Miracle ends, staving off disease, ignoring critical wounds and poisons, and similar. This miracle comes to an end should appropriate healing be provided, or should you perform the last rights. If you do this, which takes about a minute, the target's soul will pass through Morr's portal upon death, and the resulting corpse may never be targeted by Necromancy.

MIRACLES OF MYRMIDIA

Blazing Sun

Range: You
Target: Area of Effect
Duration: Instant

You call on Myrmidia to scour the battlefield of dishonourable foes, and a blinding flash of golden light bursts forth. All non-Myrmidians looking in your direction receive 1 *Blinded* Condition. For every +2 SL, they receive +1 *Blinded* Condition.

Eagle's Eye

Range: Fellowship yards
Target: You
Duration: Fellowship Bonus Rounds

You call on Myrmidia to send a Divine Servant to grant you knowledge of your enemies. A spectral Eagle manifests, soaring into the sky above. The eagle looks like and has the capabilities of a normal eagle, but cannot physically affect the world, or be harmed in any way. While the Miracle is in effect, you can see through the eagle's eyes and control its flight, surveying the battlefield and spying upon your enemies. Your vision is acute, but you do not have access to any of your own sense-enhancing Talents such as Night Vision. While looking through the eagle's eyes, you cannot see through your own eyes, leaving you potentially vulnerable.

Fury's Call
Range: Fellowship yards
Target: Intelligence Bonus allies
Duration: Fellowship Bonus Rounds
Your passionate prayers instil your allies with a furious disdain for their foes. All allies affected receive the *Hatred* Psychology towards any engaging them in combat.

Inspiring
Range: Fellowship yards
Target: Intelligence Bonus allies
Duration: Fellowship Bonus Rounds
Your rousing prayers inspire discipline and coordination within the ranks. Affected targets gain the +1 *Drilled* Talent.

Shield of Myrmidia
Range: Fellowship yards
Target: Intelligence Bonus allies
Duration: Fellowship Bonus Rounds
Your stalwart prayers incite Myrmidia to shield your allies in glittering, gossamer strands of light, warding enemy blows. All those affected gain +1 AP on all locations.

Spear of Myrmidia
Range: You
Target: You
Duration: Fellowship Bonus Rounds
If wielding a spear, it gains the *Impact* Quality, and counts as Magical.

MIRACLES OF RANALD

An Invitation
Range: 1 yard
Target: 1
Duration: Instant
You spin one of Ranald's riddles concerning portals, and whether they exist if closed. A door, window, or hatch you target has one method of securing it undone — a lock unlocks, a latch unlatches, a rope unties. For every +2 SL you may target another method of securing the door, window, or hatch.

Cat's Eyes
Range: Fellowship yards
Target: You
Duration: Fellowship Bonus Rounds
Does anything exist that cannot be seen? You riddle with Ranald, who sends a Divine Servant in the form of a cat as an answer. The cat looks like and has the capabilities of a normal cat, but cannot be harmed in any way. While the Miracle is in effect, you perceive

everything the cat perceives — sight, sound, touch — and control its movement. Your senses are as sharp as a cat's, but you do not have access to any of your own sense-enhancing Talents such as Night Vision. While the Miracle is in effect, you cannot perceive anything through your own senses, leaving you vulnerable.

Ranald's Grace
Range: Touch
Target: 1
Duration: Agility Bonus Rounds
You call on Ranald to let your target negotiate the riddles of reality. Your target gains +10 Agility, +10 Stealth, and +1 *Catfall* Talent for the duration of the Miracle.

Rich Man, Poor Man, Beggar Man, Thief
Range: 1 yard
Target: 1
Duration: Fellowship Bonus Minutes
You smile at Ranald as you cheekily ask others what, exactly, is wealth? For each target affected, choose one option:

- the target's purse appears empty
- the target's purse appears full
- the target's attire appears cheap and unremarkable
- the target's attire appears rich and finely crafted
- a single valuable item is impossible to perceive

For every +2 SL you may select an additional effect for one of your targets.

Stay Lucky
Range: You
Target: You
Duration: Special
Crossing your fingers, you pose Ranald's enigma and ask what, exactly, is luck? Gain +1 Fortune point. For every +2 SL you may gain an extra +1 Fortune point, which may take you beyond your normal maximum. You may not invoke this Miracle again until you reach 0 Fortune points.

You Ain't Seen Me, Right?

Range: Fellowship yards
Target: 1
Duration: Fellowship Bonus Rounds

You spin a complex conundrum concerning the reality of that which is unperceived. Targets affected by this Miracle may pass unnoticed and remarked, providing they do nothing to draw attention to themselves, such as touching, attacking, calling out to someone, casting a spell, or making a loud noise. You may only invoke this Miracle if no-one is looking directly at you.

MIRACLES OF RHYA

Rhya's Children

Range: You
Target: Area of Effect
Duration: Fellowship Bonus Rounds

Laying hands on the earth, you chant a prayer to Rhya appealing for her aid in understanding her Realm. This Miracle may only be invoked outdoors, outside settlements. You sense the presence and passing of all sentient creatures within Fellowship yards. Each +2 SL extents the area of effect by +Fellowship yards.

Rhya's Harvest

Range: Touch
Target: You
Duration: 1 Round

You chant to Rhya, and life springs forth. Edible fruit, vegetables, and fungi grow at the point where you touch. For each round in which the Miracle is in effect, you cause enough food to feed 1 person to grow. The type of food depends on your location: in a cavern you may grow mushrooms, while outdoors you may cause many different fruits and vegetables to spring forth.

Rhya's Shelter

Range: You
Target: You
Duration: Special

You sing one of Rhya's hymns concerning shelter and safety. You may only invoke this Miracle outdoors and outside settlements. You discover a perfect natural shelter. Some combination of earth, and trees has formed a perfect location to camp for the night. The spot is protected from all naturally occurring wind and rain, and lasts as long as you remain camped there. The shelter is large enough for 1 person. For every +2 SL it fits another individual. When you break camp, the shelter cannot be rediscovered, as though it only existed through your goddess's will.

Rhya's Succour

Range: Fellowship yards
Target: Fellowship Bonus allies
Duration: Instant

You chant Rhya's song of revitalisation. All affected targets have 1 Condition removed. If this removes all suffered Conditions, the targets feel as refreshed as if they had just awoken from a good night's sleep, and gain a bonus of +10 to any tests on their next Turn.

Rhya's Touch

Range: Touch
Target: 1
Duration: Special

You lay hands upon an injured or diseased target as you sing your prayers. Choose one of the following effects:

* Heal Fellowship Bonus wounds
* Cure 1 naturally occurring disease

For every + 2 SL, you may choose another effect, and may choose the same effect repeatedly. This Miracle is slow, with the effects taking at least 10 minutes to manifest. If interrupted, the Miracle will need to be attempted again.

Rhya's Union

Range: Touch
Target: Special
Duration: Fellowship Bonus Hours

You bless and consecrate the union between two souls. While the Miracle is in effect, if biologically possible, the couple will conceive a child.

MIRACLES OF SHALLYA

Anchorite's Endurance

Range: Fellowship yards
Target: 1
Duration: Fellowship Bonus Rounds

Your earnest prayers appeal to Shallya to grant the target the strength to endure. The target feels no pain, and suffers no penalties caused by Conditions.

Balm to a Wounded Mind

Range: Touch
Target: 1
Duration: Fellowship Bonus Minutes

You call on Shallya to calm the troubled mind of your targets. All Psychology traits are removed for the duration, and afterwards the targets enter deep and restful slumbers that last until next sunrise, assuming they are not disturbed. Unwilling targets may make a **Challenging (+0) Cool** Test to resist sleeping.

Bitter Catharsis

Range: Touch
Target: 1
Duration: Instant

In answer to your heartfelt prayers, Shallya draws a poison or disease into you and purges it, completely removing it from your target's system. For every +2 SL you may purge another disease or poison. For each poison removed or disease cured in this manner, you suffer Wounds equal to 1d10 – your Fellowship Bonus, not modified for Toughness Bonus or Armour Points.

Martyr

Range: Fellowship yards
Target: 1
Duration: Fellowship Bonus Rounds

You intone prayers concerning Shallya's need to take on the world's pain. Any Damage taken by your targets are instead suffered by you. If you suffer any Damage because of this Miracle, your Toughness Bonus is doubled for the purposes of calculating the Wounds suffered from that Damage.

Shallya's Tears

Range: Touch
Target: 1
Duration: Special

You passionately appeal to Shallya to spare a poor, wounded soul as tears flow freely down your cheeks. You pray for 10 – your Fellowship Bonus Rounds, at which point you heal the target of 1 Critical Wound. For every +2 SL you may heal another Critical Wound. If your prayer is interrupted, the target receives no benefit. This Miracle cannot reattach amputated body parts.

Unblemished Innocence

Range: Touch
Target: 1
Duration: Instant

Laying hands on the afflicted, you beg Shallya to rid them of recently acquired corruption. The target loses 1 Corruption point, and can lose another per +2 SL scored. However, the Chaos Gods do not like to be so directly opposed. Should an attempt to invoke the Miracle Fumble, you and the target both gain 1d10 Corruption points on top of any other effects. This Miracle must be enacted within an hour of the target gaining a Corruption point.

MIRACLES OF SIGMAR

Beacon of Righteous Virtue

Range: You
Target: Area of Effect
Duration: Fellowship Bonus Rounds

As you bellow prayers in Sigmar's name, you become infused with holy fire of righteousness. All allies with Line of Sight to you instantaneously remove all *Broken* Conditions, and gain the *Fearless* Talent while the Miracle is in effect and they remain in your Line of Sight. Any Greenskins with Line of Sight to you are subject to Fear 1.

Heed Not the Witch

Range: You
Target: Area of Effect
Duration: Fellowship Bonus Rounds

You call on Sigmar to protect those close to you from the fell influence of Chaos. Any spells that target anyone or anywhere within Fellowship Bonus yards suffer a penalty of −20 to Language (Magick) Tests, in addition to any other penalties. For every +2 SL, you may increase the area of effect by your Fellowship Bonus in yards.

Sigmar's Fiery Hammer

Range: You
Target: You
Duration: Fellowship Bonus Rounds

You chant benedictions of Sigmar's might. If wielding a warhammer, it counts as Magical, deals +Fellowship Bonus Damage, and any target struck receives the *Ablaze* and *Prone* Conditions.

Soulfire

Range: You
Target: Area of Effect
Duration: Instant

You call the power of Sigmar to smite the enemies of the Empire. A holy fire explodes from your body blasting outwards for Fellowship Bonus yards. All targets within range take 1d10 Wounds ignoring Toughness Bonus and APs. Targets with the Undead and Daemon Creature Traits also gain the *Ablaze* Condition. For every +2 SL, you may increase the area of effect by +Fellowship Bonus yards, or cause an extra +2 Damage to any Greenskins, Undead, or servants of the Ruinous Powers affected.

Twin-tailed Comet

Range: Fellowship yards
Target: Area of Effect
Duration: Instant

You invoke litanies to Sigmar, calling on him to smite his foes. A twin-tailed comet, blazing a trail of fire in its wake, plummets from the heavens to strike a point within Line of Sight and range. Everything within Fellowship Bonus yards of the point of impact suffers 1d10 + SL Damage, ignoring Toughness Bonus and Armour Points, and gains the *Ablaze* condition. The target location must be outdoors, and may only target those Sigmar would deem an enemy.

Vanquish the Unrighteous

Range: Fellowship yards
Target: Fellowship Bonus allies
Duration: Fellowship Bonus Rounds

Your prayers instil your chosen allies with a furious disdain for the enemies of Sigmar. All allies affected receive the *Hatred* Psychology towards Greenskins, Undead, and any associated with Chaos.

MIRACLES OF TAAL

Animal Instincts

Range: Touch
Target: 1
Duration: Fellowship Bonus Hours

You intone chants describing Taal's extraordinary senses, and calling upon him for aid. While the Miracle is in effect, you gain +1 *Acute Sense (choose one)* Talent and, if you rest, you will automatically awaken should any threats come within Initiative yards.

King of the Wild

Range: Fellowship yards
Target: 1
Duration: Fellowship Bonus Rounds

You chant a low prayer, and Taal answers with a wild animal appropriate for the surrounding area, which will act according to your wishes for the duration of the Miracle. See **The Beasts of the Reikland** on page 314 for sample animals that may be summoned.

Leaping Stag

Range: You
Target: You
Duration: Fellowship Bonus Rounds

You chant to Father Taal, and he grants you his favour, imbuing you with speed and agility. You gain +1 Movement and +1 *Strong Legs* Talent. Further, you automatically pass all **Athletics** Tests to jump with at least +0 SL; should you score lower, increase the SL to 0.

Lord of the Hunt

Range: You
Target: You
Duration: Fellowship Bonus Hours

You call on Taal to guide you in the hunt for your quarry, which must be an animal you have seen, or an individual you know (as limited by the GM). While the Miracle is in effect, you cannot lose your quarry's trail save by supernatural means. Should your quarry enter a settlement, the trail ends there. You also receive +10 bonus to all Tests regarding your quarry while under the influence of the Miracle.

Tooth and Claw

Range: You
Target: You
Duration: Fellowship Bonus Rounds

You call on Taal to grant you the ferocious might of his kingdom. Gain the *Bite* (Strength Bonus+3) and *Weapon* (Strength Bonus+4) Creature Traits. These attacks are Magical.

Tanglefoot

Range: Fellowship yards
Target: Area of Effect
Duration: Instant

You call on Taal, chanting prayers to protect his wild places. Roots, vines, and creepers wrap themselves around your foes. All targets within Fellowship Bonus yards of the target point gain an *Entangled* Condition. For every +2 SL you may increase the area of effect by your Fellowship Bonus in yards, or inflict an extra *Entangled* Condition. *Tanglefoot* has a Strength equal to your Willpower for the purposes of breaking free.

MIRACLES OF ULRIC

Hoarfrost's Chill

Range: You
Target: Area of Effect
Duration: Fellowship Bonus Rounds

You scream angry prayers, and cold Ulric answers. Your eyes gain a steely blue glint and the air around you grows unnaturally cold. You cause *Fear (1)* (see page 190) in all enemies, and all within your Fellowship yards range lose −1 Advantage at the start of each Round, as they are chilled to the bone.

Howl of the Wolf

Range: Fellowship yards
Target: Special
Duration: Fellowship Bonus Rounds

You howl for Ulric's aid, and he sends a minor Divine Servant in the form of a White Wolf. The wolf fights your enemies for the duration of the Miracle, before vanishing to Ulric's Hunting Grounds with a spectral, blood-chilling howl. The White Wolves have the statistics of a Wolf (see page 317) with the *Frenzy, Magical,* and *Size (Large)* Creature Traits.

Ulric's Fury

Range: Fellowship yards
Target: 1
Duration: Fellowship Bonus Rounds

You chant furious prayers, and Ulric's ferocity spreads. Targets gain the Frenzy psychology.

Pelt of the Winter Wolf

Range: Touch
Target: 1
Duration: Fellowship Bonus Hours

Your bellowed prayers bring Ulric's attention, allowing your targets to survive the bite of his realm. While targets still feel the pain and discomfort caused by cold and wintry weather, they suffer no mechanical penalties.

The Snow King's Judgement

Range: Fellowship yards
Target: 1
Duration: Instant

You call on Ulric to make manifest his disdain for the weak, the cowardly and the deceitful. The target suffers 1d10 wounds ignoring Toughness Bonus and Armour Points. If the GM rules that the target is neither weak, cowardly, or deceitful, you suffer the effects instead.

Winter's Bite
Range: You
Target: You
Duration: Fellowship Bonus Rounds
You roar prayers concerning Blitzbeil, Ulric's ever-thirsty axe. If wielding an axe, it counts as Magical, causes an additional + SL Damage, and any living targets struck must make a **Challenging (+0) Endurance** Test or gain a *Stunned* Condition. Further, struck targets lose any *Bleeding* Conditions as their blood freezes; similarly, attacks from your axe cannot cause any *Bleeding* Conditions.

MIRACLES OF VERENA

As Verena Is My Witness
Range: You
Target: You
Duration: Fellowship Bonus Rounds
By calling Verena as your witness, the truth of your words shines out for all to see. For the duration of the Miracle, providing you speak only the truth, all listeners will believe you speak truly. This does not necessarily mean they will agree with your conclusions, of course.

Blind Justice
Range: You
Target: You
Duration: Fellowship Bonus Rounds
You articulate prayers concerning Verena's acute perceptions, able pierce through to the truth of all things. You may make a **Simple Challenging (+0) Perception** Test to see through spells and Miracles of involving illusion or misdirection. You may also make a **Average (+20) Intuition** Test to tell whether a character speaking to you is lying. **Note:** this will only tell you if the character believes they speak the truth, it will not alert you if they are mistaken.

Shackles of Truth
Range: Fellowship yards
Target: 1
Duration: Fellowship Bonus Rounds
Your appeal to Verena, requesting her judgement concerning a suspected criminal. If your target committed a crime and claims they did not, while affected by this miracle they gain an *Entangled* Condition that cannot be removed for the duration. If you have falsely accused the target, Verena is displeased with your lack of wisdom: you gain +1 Sin point and must immediately roll on **The Wrath of the Gods** table.

Sword of Justice
Range: You
Target: You
Duration: Fellowship Bonus Rounds
You pray to Verena to guide your blade to strike down the unjust. If wielding a sword, it ignores APs, and counts as Magical. Further, if struck opponents are criminals (as determined by the GM), they must make an **Average (+20) Endurance** or suffer an *Unconscious* Condition that lasts for at least Fellowship Bonus Rounds. If any crime is perpetrated on the unconscious opponents, you suffer +1 Sin point per crime.

Truth Will Out
Range: Fellowship Bonus yards
Target: 1
Duration: Instant
You intone prayers of Verena's ability to find any truth. You may ask the targets a single question. It will be immediately answered truthfully and fully. If desired, targets may attempt to resist, by contesting your SL with a **Average (+20) Cool** Test. If successful, they may stubbornly refuse to answer. If they achieve +2 SL they may withhold minor information. +4 SL allows them to withhold significant information while +6 SL allows them to lie outright. You will know if they resist successfully, though you will lack specific knowledge about their deceit, or proof of their dishonesty.

Wisdom of the Owl
Range: You
Target: You
Duration: Fellowship Bonus Rounds
You call on Verena to instil you with her wisdom and knowledge. You gain a bonus of +20 on all Intelligence Tests while this Miracle is in effect. Further, your pupils dilate widely, and your gaze becomes piercing and unsettling: gain +1 *Menacing* and *Acute Sense (Sight)* Talent.

◆ MAGIC ◆

'Keep your cannons, you Nulner idiot! We don't need them.'

– Thyrus Gorman, Patriarch of the Bright Order

Magical abilities mark you as a figure of terror and awe in the Empire. Prior to the establishment of the Colleges of Magic in Altdorf, those able to wield magic were reviled outlaws. Nowadays being a witch is not illegal, but casting magic without a licence is. Spellcasters within the Empire must either study at the Colleges of Magic, refrain from casting spells, or hope no-one notices their illicit activity. Even licenced wizards are generally feared and avoided — legal status has done nothing to reduce the superstitious dread of the common folk.

Magic is seen as unnatural and is notorious for its darker elements: the crippling hexes of witchcraft, the raising of the dead, and the summoning of Daemonic entities. Even when practiced according to the teaching of the Colleges, magic can be the cause of trouble. The very source of magic is unstable, and even the most experienced spellcaster can lose focus, resulting in dangerous accidents and unexpected side-effects.

THE AETHYR

Scholars of magic derive their learning from the Elves, who explained the source of all magical power is the Aethyr. This infinite dimension, said to be the spawning ground of daemons and spirits, exists beyond the physical world. The Elves taught that far to the north of the Empire, a great ragged wound was torn through the fabric of the world to the Aethyr, and it bleeds raw magic. These roiling energies — known as the Winds of Magic — blow throughout the world, gathering and eddying in great heavenly whorls, only to rain down and permeate the land and the creatures dwelling upon it. It is these powerful winds that wizards and witches use to fuel their spells.

THE WINDS OF MAGIC

As magical power bursts into the mortal realm and sweeps down from the north, it splinters and separates, like light splitting through a prism. The Colleges of Magic state this creates eight discrete Winds referred to by colour, each with its own character and strengths. The Elves support this, teaching the same eight winds to their apprentices before moving on to more powerful magics.

Only a small minority of Humans can perceive the Winds, and even fewer can bend them to their will. Most Elves are sensitive to them, and many possess the ability to see the Winds clearly — commonly known as Second Sight, or just the Sight — with many also able to learn how to cast magic. Dwarfs disdain magic, perhaps because they are partially immune to it, and no Dwarf wizards are known. Halflings are largely indifferent towards magic: except when it delivers impressive or entertaining spectacles.

The Elves directed (as a condition of their tuition) that Human spellcasters should each only use a single Wind of Magic. They

WHAT IS THE AETHYR?

There is much heated debate between 'experts' on the nature of magic. The lecture halls of the Empire's most learned institutions often see ambitious scholars expound on their latest theories. Some liken magic to the backstage of a theatre, a mass of mechanisms, props, and hidden pulleys responsible for the drama viewed by the audience. Others resort to mathematical metaphors, complete with incomprehensible esoteric diagrams. Although such may end with an air of confident finality, it will only be met with polite coughs, raised hands, and a litany of objections and exceptions.

argued that while it is possible to cast spells by drawing from multiple winds, doing so is a risky proposition for the feeble, corruptible Human mind. This wisdom has been adopted by the Colleges, and each specialises in a single colour.

Some witches outside the College system consider these restrictions ludicrous, an attempt by the Elves to keep the most powerful magics to themselves. Drawing on multiple winds is a quick route to power, but also to damnation. Many an unlicensed witch has proved unable to resist this temptation, a practice usually called Dark Magic, only to be brought low by Witch Hunters.

Others believe magical energies are not so easily categorised. Many different types of 'wizard' and 'witch' can be found throughout the Old World, with some practicing magic that seems to lie outside colour magic, such as the cold-hearted Ice Witches of Kislev, or the shamans and sorcerers found amongst some of the other species besetting the Empire, such as the Greenskins.

THE LANGUAGE OF MAGICK

The Winds of Magic may blow through all things incessantly, but they are relatively harmless until harnessed by the Language of Magick. For reasons not fully understood, when certain sounds are uttered by those attuned to magic, the Winds answer. The Colleges of Magic teach a complex language called the *lingua praestantia* which form the basis of their spells, originally taught to Humanity by the Elves. Although extraordinarily difficult to correctly annunciate, it is a significant simplification of the Elven tongue *Anoqeyån*, the language used by the Elves to shape their own, more powerful magics. Wizards of the Colleges and the Elves are not alone in their knowledge of the Language of Magick. Its complex forms are also spoken by many magical creatures found across the Old World, including Spirits and Daemons. Many witches seem to instinctively understand the language, almost as if it somehow wormed inside them, begging to be spoken as a spell.

THE EIGHT LORES

Each of the eight Winds of Magic has an associated Lore, a body of spells and knowledge its adepts use. Each of the eight Colleges of Magic is dedicated to the study of a single Lore, and their buildings are constructed to focus their Wind to facilitate relatively safe tuition.

 ### The Lore of Light

The Lore of Light relates to *Hysh*, the white wind. *Hysh* is considered the most difficult Wind to perceive and manipulate, appearing diffuse even to those skilled with the Sight. This makes it tricky to manipulate but less unpredictable than other Winds. *Hysh* is associated with patience, intelligence, and purity. The Hierophants of the Light Order are acclaimed for their discipline, knowledge, and devoted opposition to Chaos.

Spells from the Lore of Light are some of the most powerful, including piercing rays of blinding light, and those that banish Daemons and Undead creatures from the mortal plane. There are also more gentle applications of *Hysh* used to heal comrades or clarify thought.

The Lore of Metal

The Lore of Metal relates to *Chamon*, the gold wind. *Chamon* appears dense and heavy to Second Sight, sinking into the earth and coalescing within dense metals such as lead and gold. The Alchemists of the Gold Order have a reputation for being unusually prosaic in their attitudes for wizards, and many are as interested in learning the facts of physics and chemistry as they are in the working of magic.

Spells from the Lore of Metal often involve the transmutation or alteration of metal. On the battlefield, alchemists have been known to cause fine steel armour and weaponry to corrode or melt, to weigh their foes down with suddenly dense armour, or to enchant their allies' weaponry with uncanny power.

The Lore of Life

The Lore of Life relates to *Ghyran*, the jade wind. Free flowing *Ghyran* is associated with growth, fertility and nourishment. To those with The Sight, *Ghyran* appears much like a light rain, falling to the ground and pooling in eddying swirls. It sinks into the soil and is drawn up into the roots of plants from where it goes on to nourish all living things. The Druids of the Jade Order often prefer life away from the cities, attuned to the seasons and the natural world.

Spells from the Lore of Life commonly involve healing and rejuvenation, from healing wounds to causing a barren field to burst with life. They can have offensive applications, too. The enemies of a Druid may find themselves suddenly tangled up in wickedly sharp brambles and vines.

The Lore of Heavens

The Lore of Heavens relates to *Azyr*, the blue wind. It cascades through the skies over the Old World, crackling through the heavens, like a great charged cloud. Astromancers of the Celestial Order, known for their calm and contemplative manners, use the wind to scry the future, the lens of *Azyr* influencing what they can see in the stars.

Spells from the Lore of Heavens involve the manipulation of fate, throwing up protective barriers, or cursing a foe with an unnatural run of bad luck. On the battlefield, Astromancers also control elemental forces, blasting their enemies with bolts of lightning, or even drawing down shooting stars from the heavens.

The Lore of Shadows

The Lore of Shadows relates to *Ulgu*, the grey wind. To the Sight it appears a thick fog, gathering in pools wherever intrigue and deceit are practiced, rising into great storms and tempests when conflict breaks out. Wizards of the Grey Order, known as Grey Guardians, are secretive in their ways and given to uncertain loyalties. Despite this, the Grey Order is renowned for its wisdom and skill in negotiations, and is often called upon for diplomatic missions.

Spells from the Lore of Shadows can be used to mask or obfuscate, confusing and disorienting their foes. In battle, the shadowy, insubstantial tendrils of *Ulgu* they wield can pierce to the heart of their foes, eviscerating the most well-protected troops, yet leaving armour eerily intact.

The Lore of Death

The Lore of Death relates to *Shyish*, the purple wind. It is attracted to places of death, such as battlefields, Gardens of Morr, and sites of execution. The wind is said to blow strongest during times of transition, so wizards of the Amethyst Order tend to work their greatest rites during the twilight before dawn, or during sunset. While *Shyish* is related to time and mortality, it is distinct from Necromancy, the illegal practice of raising and binding the dead, which uses the dark magic of *Dhar* in lieu of *Shyish*. Indeed, the Amethyst Order, much like the Cult of Morr, works tirelessly to combat the threat of Necromancy.

Nevertheless, spells from the Lore of Death resemble Necromancy to the untrained eye. They can drain their targets of life force, spread fear among their enemies, and contact the spirits of the departed.

The Lore of Fire

The Lore of Fire relates to *Aqshy*, the red wind. *Aqshy* is a hot and searing wind associated with brashness, courage, and zeal and is drawn to empirical heat. The Pyromancers of the Bright Order are bold and hot-tempered and make for impressively destructive Battle Wizards.

Many of the spells from the Lore of Fire are offensive in nature, enabling the caster to conjure up great balls of fire, or cause the blades of their allies to burst into flame. Even their non-offensive spells, such as crude healing magics, are still destructive in nature.

Bright wizards are also adept at inspiring their allies, rallying their courage and inspiring bravery and loyalty in the troops with which they serve.

The Lore of Beasts

The Lore of Beasts relates to *Ghur*, the amber wind, a cold, primal force associated with the savage wilds and the beasts living there. To those with the Sight *Ghur* seems to blow weakly in areas where the wilderness has been tamed and settlements constructed. This may explain why the Shamans of the Amber Order often take up a hermitic existence and shun their fellow men.

The spells of the Lore of Beasts allow a Shaman to communicate with animals, request their aid, and even summon them to battle. Shapeshifting magic may also be used by the wizard to adopt animal forms.

ELVEN MAGIC

Elves are long lived beings whose minds are more attuned to the workings of magic than those of humanity. High Elven mages usually train in several, sometimes all, of the eight winds as part of their apprenticeships, before the most promising move on to study High Magic: *Qhaysh*. This is the blending of multiple winds of magic together into a blinding, coruscating energy. This magic is impressive and difficult, and Elves claim it is beyond the capacity of humankind.

The Wood Elves, too, make use of the eight Winds of Magic, though their Spellsingers usually focus upon the Jade and Amber Winds. The most powerful usually go on to study either High Magic like High Elves, or dread Dark Magic – a foul mixing of the eight winds that can create tremendously destructive effects.

DARK MAGIC

While difficult to master *Qhaysh* is the safe blending of multiple Winds of Magic, *Dhar*, known commonly as Dark Magic, is much more dangerous method of casting spells using multiple winds. It is usually only practiced by evil sorcerers, Necromancers, and powerful witches, offering them a seductive source of raw power, yet one laced with terrible side-effects. Few can channel Dhar for long, without succumbing to the corrupting influence of the malevolent wind, their bodies and minds being warped into unnatural states.

Dhar resembles a stagnant mire to those with the Sight, pooling in places saturated with evil, or corruption: the herdstones of Beastmen, the dark idols of chaos cultists, and places where great workings of several of the Winds of Magic took place. *Dhar* is so dense and potent that it can independently coalesce or crystalize into physical matter, eventually forming the widely feared substance called warpstone.

Warpstone

Warpstone is a lump of pure magic in the material plane. Its unnatural provenance is immediately obvious to all who see it, as it hurts the eyes and mutates anything drawing close for too long. Although its form varies, it often holds hard facets like flint, and radiates a queasy green glow.

Close examination of the substance is not to be undertaken lightly. Warpstone is the stuff of Chaos made manifest and its presence is deeply corrupting. Those who have direct contact with warpstone risk illness, madness and mutation, and anyone who ingests so much as a pinch of the stuff dooms themselves to catastrophic warping of body and mind. Nonetheless, the world is full of reckless, ambitious fools who know that the volatile and dangerous substance is a tremendous source of energy for spells and rituals.

The followers of Chaos and the Skaven do not hesitate to use it. To them, warpstone is a literal gift from the gods to be valued above gold and jewels, and to be used against their enemies.

OTHER LORES

In less frequented corners of the Empire, in villages and rural communities far from the influence of the Colleges of Magic, older forms of magic are still practiced even though they are outlawed and punishable by death. There are uncounted varieties of these, but two of the more common Lores still practised by Humans are Hedgecraft and Witchcraft.

The Lore of Hedgecraft

Practitioners of Hedgecraft generally live quiet lives on the fringes of smaller human settlements, in service to local communities. Just as they live their lives in the 'hedge' between civilisation and the wilds of nature, so much of their magic concerns itself with the liminal space between the material world and the realm of the spirits. Their magic tends to focus on folklore, spirits and the natural world, as well as means to aid the rural communities which shelter them. Once a relatively common sight in the Empire, over two centuries of persecution since the founding of the Colleges of Magic has all but wiped them out.

The Lore of Witchcraft

While the Lore of Witchcraft is not inherently malicious, or tied to the gods of Chaos, it has a justly earned reputation for evil and unpleasantness. Often self-taught and using multiple Winds of Magic, those practising the Lore of Witchcraft lack the discipline or knowledge of College wizards and are at a significant risk of corruption. The combination of the corrosive effects of Dhar and being shunned by right-minded folk of the Empire often makes these Witches bitter, spiteful souls, their hearts hard and flinty, their gaze baleful and ill-omened.

MAGIC RULES

SECOND SIGHT

The *Second Sight* Talent (see page 144) allows you to perceive the Winds of Magic, and how magic influences the world around you. Second Sight affects all your senses, and how it manifests is dependent on individual experience and training: So, where *Aqshy* may have a hot, cinnamon odour to one pyromancer, it could feel like searing ear itches to another.

If you have Second Sight, you may use any appropriate Skills with your aethyric senses, most commonly your Intuition, Perception, and Track Skills. For example, a wizard following the trail of a fleeing witch could make a Track test, following the faint traces of *Dhar* in the witch's path, rather than their literal footsteps. Or a Witch looking to see what kind of magic had gathered locally could use Perception to examine the Winds more closely. Like the mundane senses, Second Sight does not simply switch off, which is a source of great discomfort to those who would rather have no truck with the Winds of Magic but cannot help what they perceive. This means the GM may request Tests, or take Tests on your behalf, to see if you spot subtle magical details in your surrounding environment, even if you're not looking for them.

Spells

There are four types of spell: Petty, Arcane, Lore, and Chaos spells. Petty spells are simple tricks that use negligible amounts of magic. Arcane Spells are generic spells open to those studying any Lore of Magic or Chaos Magic. Lore spells are those you can only learn if you know that Lore; i.e. to learn spells from the Lore of Fire, you need the *Arcane Magic (Fire)* Talent. Chaos spells are those practiced by those who've lost their souls to Chaos.

Memorising Spells

Holding the complex linguistic structures of Language (Magick) in mind is a challenging task, so simply transcribing a spell into your grimoire does not allow you learn a spell.

To memorise a spell — and therefore be able to cast it without access to your grimoire — you typically need to spend the amount of XP noted in your spellcasting Talent (see **Chapter 4: Skills and Talents**). Once a spell has been memorised, a spellcaster knows it permanently, barring special circumstances.

Casting Test

To cast a spell, make a **Language (Magick)** Test. If you succeed, match your SL to the Casting Number (CN) of the spell (listed in the individual spell description). If your SL is equal to or higher than the CN of the spell, it is cast as explained in the spell's description. If failed, the spell attempt fails, and nothing else happens.

Critical Casting

If the casting roll is a Critical (see page 159), the Winds of Magic have flared dangerously high, granting you extra power, but at a cost. Unless you have the *Instinctive Diction* Talent, you roll on the Minor Miscast Table as the power moves beyond your control, but you may also choose one of the following effects:

- **Critical Cast:** If the spell causes Damage, it also inflicts a Critical Wound. See page 172 for details.
- **Total Power:** The spell is cast, no matter its CN and your rolled SL, but can be Dispelled.
- **Unstoppable Force:** If you scored enough SL to cast your spell, it cannot be Dispelled.

Minor Miscast Table

01-05	**Witchsign:** the next living creature born within 1 mile is mutated.
06-10	**Soured Milk:** All milk within 1d100 yards goes sour instantly.
11-15	**Blight:** Willpower Bonus fields within Willpower Bonus miles suffer a blight, and all crops rot overnight.
16-20	**Soulwax:** Your ears clog instantly with a thick wax. Gain 1 *Deafened* Condition, which is not removed until someone cleans them for you (with a successful use of the Heal Skill).
21-25	**Witchlight:** You glow with an eerie light related to your Lore, emitting as much light as a large bonfire, which lasts for 1d10 Rounds.
26-30	**Fell Whispers:** Pass a **Routine (+20) Willpower** Test or gain 1 Corruption point.
31-35	**Rupture:** Your nose, eyes, and ears bleed profusely. Gain 1d10 *Bleeding* Conditions.
36-40	**Soulquake:** Gain the *Prone* Condition.
41-45	**Unfasten:** On your person, every buckle unfastens, and every lace unties, which may cause belts to fall, pouches to open, bags to fall, and armour to slip.
46-50	**Wayward Garb:** your clothes seem to writhe with a mind of their own. Receive 1 *Entangled* Condition with a Strength of 1d10×5 to resist.
51-55	**Curse of Temperance:** All alcohol within 1d100 yards goes bad, tasting bitter and foul.
56-60	**Souldrain:** Gain 1 *Fatigued* Condition, which remains for 1d10 hours.
61-65	**Driven to Distraction:** If engaged in combat, gain the *Surprised* Condition. Otherwise, you are completely startled, your heart racing, and unable to concentrate for a few moments.
66-70	**Unholy Visions:** Fleeting visions of profane and unholy acts harass you. Receive a *Blinded* Condition; pass a **Challenging (+0) Cool** Test or gain another.
71-75	**Cloying Tongue:** All Language Tests (including Casting Tests) suffer a −10 penalty for 1d10 Rounds.
76-80	**The Horror!:** Pass a **Hard (−20) Cool** Test or gain 1 *Broken* Condition.
81-85	**Curse of Corruption:** Gain 1 Corruption point.
86-90	**Double Trouble:** The effect of the spell you cast occurs elsewhere within 1d10 miles. At the GM's discretion, where possible it should have consequences.
91-95	**Multiplying Misfortune:** Roll twice on this table, rerolling any results between 91-00.
96-00	**Cascading Chaos:** Roll again on the **Major Miscast Table**.

MAJOR MISCAST TABLE

01-05	**Ghostly Voices:** Everyone within Willpower yards hears darkly seductive whispering of voices emanating from the Realm of Chaos. All sentient creatures must pass an **Average (+20) Cool** Test or gain 1 Corruption point.
06-10	**Hexeyes:** Your eyes turn an unnatural colour associated with your Lore for 1d10 hours. While your eyes are discoloured, you have 1 *Blinded* Condition that cannot be resolved by *any* means.
11-15	**Aethyric Shock:** you suffer 1d10 wounds, ignoring your Toughness Bonus and Armour Points. Pass an **Average (+20) Endurance** Test, or also gain a *Stunned* Condition.
16-20	**Death Walker:** Your footsteps leave death in their wake. For the next 1d10 hours, any plant life near you withers and dies.
21-25	**Intestinal Rebellion:** Your bowels move uncontrollably, and you soil yourself. Gain 1 *Fatigued* Condition, which cannot be removed until you can change your clothes and clean yourself up.
26-30	**Soulfire:** Gain an *Ablaze* Condition, as you are wreathed in unholy flames with a colour associated with your Lore.
31-35	**Speak in Tongues:** You gabble unintelligibly for 1d10 rounds. During this time, you cannot communicate verbally, or make any Casting Tests, although you may otherwise act normally.
36-40	**Swarmed:** You are engaged by a swarm of aethyric Rats, Giant Spiders, Snakes, or similar (GM's choice). Use the standard profiles for the relevant creature type, adding the *Swarm* Creature Trait. After 1d10 rounds, if not yet destroyed, the swarm retreats.
41-45	**Ragdoll:** You are flung 1d10 yards through the air in a random direction, taking 1d10 wounds on landing, ignoring Armour Points, and receiving the *Prone* Condition.
46-50	**Limb frozen:** One limb (randomly determined) is frozen in place for 1d10 hours. The limb is useless, as if it had been Amputated (see page 180).
51-55	**Darkling Sight:** You lose the benefit of the *Second Sight* Talent for 1d10 hours. Channelling Tests also suffer a penalty of −20 for the duration.
56-60	**Chaotic Foresight:** Gain a bonus pool of 1d10 Fortune points (this may take you beyond your natural limit). Every time you spend one of these points, gain 1 Corruption point. Any of these points remaining at the end of the session are lost.
61-65	**Levitation:** You are borne aloft on the Winds of Magic, floating 1d10 yards above the ground for 1d10 minutes. Other characters may forcibly move you, and you may move using spells, wings or similar, but will continually return to your levitating position if otherwise left alone. Refer to the Falling rules (see page 166) for what happens when Levitation ends.
66-70	**Regurgitation:** You spew uncontrollably, throwing up far more foul-smelling vomitus than your body can possibly contain. Gain the *Stunned* Condition, which lasts for 1d10 Rounds.
71-75	**Chaos Quake:** All creatures within 1d100 yards must pass an **Average (+20) Athletics** Test or gain the *Prone* Condition.
76-80	**Traitor's Heart:** The Dark Gods entice you to commit horrendous perfidy. Should you attack or otherwise betray an ally to the full extent of your capabilities, regain all Fortune points. If you cause another character to lose a Fate Point, gain +1 Fate Point.
81-85	**Foul Enfeeblement:** Gain 1 Corruption point, the *Prone* Condition, and a *Fatigued* Condition
86-90	**Hellish Stench:** You now smell really bad! You gain the *Distracting* Creature Trait (see page 339), and probably the enmity of anyone with a sense of smell. This lasts for 1d10 hours.
91-95	**Power Drain:** You are unable to use the Talent used to cast the spell (usually *Arcane Magic*, though it could be *Chaos Magic*, or a similar Talent), for 1d10 minutes.
96-00	**Aethyric Feedback:** Everyone within a number of yards equal to your Willpower Bonus — friend and foe alike — suffers 1d10 wounds, ignoring Toughness Bonus and Armour Points, and receives the *Prone* Condition. If there are no targets in range, the magic has nowhere to vent, so your head explodes, killing you instantly.

Fumbled Casting

If you lose control of the magical energy you are channelling, things invariably go awry. If you Fumble your Casting Test, you suffer a Miscast. Roll 1d100 and consult the Minor Miscast Table.

MALIGNANT INFLUENCES

Casting close to sources of Corruption makes controlling the Winds of Magic much more difficult. When attempting a Language (Magick) or Channelling Test in the vicinity of a Corrupting Influence (see page 182), any roll of an 8 (representing the eight-pointed symbol of Chaos) on the units die results in a Minor Miscast as the Magic goes wild. If you already have a Minor Miscast on the Test for another reason, the Miscast escalates to a Major Miscast.

Duration

If a spell is successfully cast, it remains in effect for its Duration unless it is dispelled. You may not simply end your spells already in play, but you may attempt to Dispel them.

Grimoires

Some spellcasters own a spellbook, or grimoire, in which they transcribe their spells. Apprentices copy spells from their master, while experienced wizards will actively seek out new spells from other wizards, often trading spells for favours. A spellcaster may cast a spell directly from a grimoire if the spell belongs to a Lore they possess. Doing so doubles the Casting Number.

Magic Missiles

Some spells are marked as *magic missiles*; these are damage-causing spells that all follow the same rules. When a *magic missile* is successfully cast and targets another character, the Hit Location struck is determined by reversing the dice rolled on the Language (Magick) Test and referring to the Hit Location Table (see page 159). The SL of the Language (Magick) Test is added to the spell's listed Damage and your Willpower Bonus to determine the total inflicted Damage. This Damage is reduced by the target's Toughness and Armour Points as normal.

Touch Spells in Combat

Certain spells require you to touch the target. If in combat, or if the target is unwilling to be touched, you must make an **Opposed Melee (Brawling)** Test (generally opposed by the Melee or Dodge Skill) after completing the Casting Test. If you do this and your spell was a *magic missile*, the Melee (Brawling) Test is used to determine Hit Location struck, not the Language (Magick) Test.

Ingredients

Spellcasters may channel their magic through an appropriate ingredient before unleashing their spells. Doing this offers protection against Miscasts as the attuned ingredient absorbs the worst of any magical backlash.

If you use an ingredient when casting, any suffered Major Miscast becomes a Minor Miscast, and any Minor Miscast has no effect. If used in this way, the ingredient is consumed or destroyed by the process, even if no Miscast was rolled.

Ingredients cost the CN in silver shillings for Arcane and Lore spells. Whenever you purchase a new ingredient, mark on your character sheet which spell it supports; ingredients only work for specific spells, not for all spells in your Lore. For those looking to add character to their ingredients, sample ingredients for each of the primary Lores of Magic are provided by the individual spell lists.

Limitations

As spells are spoken, you must be able to speak — not gagged, strangled, or underwater — to cast. If your voice is inhibited, the Difficulty of your Language (Magick) Test to cast a spell should be increased by the GM. Further, the Language of Magick needs to be spoken (or sung, for those using the Lore of Light) clearly, and often loudly, to ensure spells work; magic is anything but subtle. As a loose guide, the higher the CN of a spell, the louder the spell is chanted.

Each of your spells can only be in effect once, meaning you have to wait for a cast spell to come to an end, or be dispelled, before using the same spell again. Further, spells providing bonuses or penalties do not stack. Instead, the best bonus and worst penalty is applied from every spell cast upon you. So, if you had a spell providing a bonus of +20 Willpower, and another providing +10 Willpower, you gain a bonus of +20 Willpower, not +30.

Lastly, unless otherwise specified, you always need to be able to see — i.e. have Line of Sight — to your target.

ADVANTAGE AND MAGIC

Advantage in combat applies to Casting Tests, not Channelling Tests. When casting magic, you can also gain Advantage in the following way: If the target has already had a spell from the same Lore cast upon it in that Round, gain +1 Advantage as you cast, as the upswelling of your Wind aids channelling magic. See page 164 for Advantage rules.

CHANNELLING TEST

Some magical spells require far more magic than can normally be found ambiently flowing through the world. To power such spells, it is possible to draw the Winds of Magic and concentrate them into a more powerful form by using the Channelling Skill. Channelling the Winds of Magic can be a dangerous procedure, but it is the only sure way to cast some powerful spells. To channel magic for a spell, make an Extended Channelling Test.

When your SL reaches the CN of your selected spell, you have channelled enough magic to cast it. On the next Round, you can cast your spell using the normal Casting rules, but count the chosen spell's Casting Number as 0. If the casting Test fails, you also lose all your channelled magical energy, and suffer a Minor Miscast as it all writhes free from your Aethyric grasp.

Critical Channelling

If you roll a Critical when Channelling, you have channelled a mighty flow of magic and can cast your spell next Round regardless of the SL you've scored in the Extended Test so far; however, so much magic so quickly concentrated in one place results in some magical backlash: roll 1d100 on the Minor Miscast Table unless you have the *Aethyric Attunement* Talent (see page 132).

Fumble

Channelling the Winds of Magic in a large flow is dangerous. You count any double or any roll ending in a 0 over your Skill as a Fumble, so, 00, 99, 90, 88, and so on. If you fumble a Channelling Test, you suffer a Miscast. Roll 1d100 and consult the Major Miscast Table.

Interruptions

Concentration is vital when channelling. If you are distracted by anything — loud noises, suffering damage, flashing lights, or similar — you must pass a **Hard (–20) Cool** Test, or suffer a Minor Miscast and lose all SL you have accrued in the Extended Channelling Test so far.

REPELLING THE WINDS

Wearing colours appropriate to the Wind of Magic you are manipulating helps attract the magic to you. This is the reason most wizards choose to dress in the traditional garb of their order.

All Casting and Channelling Tests suffer a –1 SL penalty if you are dressed inappropriately for the Wind of Magic you are trying to attract, as determined by the GM. Specifically, metal and leather armour repel most of the Winds: metal is laden with the golden wind *Chamon*, while leather retains traces of the amber *Ghur*. As such, spellcasters wearing armour suffer –1 SL penalty to all Casting and Channelling Tests for every Armour Point on the location with the most armour. Casters with the *Arcane Magic (Metal)* Talent may wear metal armour without penalty; those with *Arcane Magic (Beasts)* Talent may ignore penalties from leather armour.

DISPELLING

If a spell targets you, or a point you can see within Willpower yards, you may oppose the Casting Test with Language (Magick) as you chant a counterspell. Make an **Opposed Language (Magick)** Test. If you win the Opposed Test, you dispel the incoming spell; if you lose, the spell uses the SL of the Opposed Test to determine whether the casting was successful as normal. You may only attempt to dispel a single spell every Round.

Dispelling Persistent Spells

If a spell has a lasting effect, you may attempt to dispel that spell for your Action. This is done by making an **Extended Language (Magick)** Test. When your SL reaches the CN of the ongoing spell, you successfully dispel it.

Multiple spellcasters attempting to dispel the same spell each roll separately. If they cast using the same Lore, they may decide to make an Assisted Test instead.

USING WARPSTONE

Officially the use of warpstone is precluded by the powers that be. Unofficially, I can say that it is officially never used within this college. Officially, I cannot say what unofficial uses it might have. But unofficially, I might be able to say it has certain unofficial uses. But certainly it is officially unofficial.

–Wilhelm Holswig-Schliestein, Grey Guardian, Raconteur, and Liar

Warpstone is such a rich source of power that even a small fragment of the stuff will offer enough magic to power any spell in short order. Of course, the wisdom of powering any spell with Warpstone, and the wisdom of carrying Warpstone upon your person, is debateable.

A wizard using Warpstone when Casting and Channelling doubles their SL for the appropriate tests. In addition, Casting or Channelling with Warpstone is a corrupting influence. See page 182 for details of Corruption, and page 236 for casting near Malignant Influences.

MULTIPLE ARCANE LORES

If you're an Elf, you can learn a number of Arcane Lores equal to your Willpower Bonus. If you have Willpower 65, you can learn 6 of the 8 Arcane Lores. However, doing this takes time and effort. You can't purchase a new *Arcane Magic* Talent until you have mastered your previous one by taking at least 20 Advances in the Channelling Skill of, and learning at least 8 spells from, your Lore. Alternatively, any wizard can learn a single Dark Lore in addition to another Lore, assuming they are foolish enough and can find a teacher or forbidden grimoire to study.

OPTIONS: THE SWIRLING WINDS

The Winds of Magic swirl in unfathomable patterns and unpredictable gusts. Before every scene — or even every round in magically turbulent areas — the GM can roll for the strength of the Winds relevant to the scene, to see whether they are blowing strongly or weakly. The modifier can be added to your Casting and Channelling Tests. The GM could decide to do this only in areas where the Winds of Magic are particularly wild, for example in the aftermath of powerful spells, at magical loci, near Chaotic portals, and when Morrslieb is at its fullest. If you have the *Second Sight* Talent, an **Easy (+40)** Perception Test will spot such disturbances.

1d10	Modifier
1	−30
2-3	−10
4-7	−
8-9	+10
10	+30

SPELL LISTS

Petty spells are listed first, followed by Arcane spells, then the 8 Elemental Lores (Colour Magic), then 2 Witch Lores, followed by 2 Dark Lores, and finally 1 spell for each of the 3 Chaos Lores. The Dark Lores and Chaos Lores are much shorter than the others given they are presented for NPC characters. Any special rules for each Lore are presented before the spell listings.

OVERCASTING

For every +2 SL you achieve in a Casting Test, you may add additional Range, Area of Effect, Duration, or Targets equal to the initial value listed in the spell. Spells with a Range and Target of 'You' may only ever target the spellcaster making the Casting Test. Spells with a Range of 'Touch' may not be extended. If the Spell has no Duration, you cannot extend it.

You may choose the same option more than once. For instance, if you achieved + 4 SL above your Casting Number on a spell with a Target of 1, you may now Target 3 individuals. Certain Spells may have additional, optional benefits for additional SL noted in their description.

GRIMOIRES

If you start play with a Grimoire, it is up to the GM to determine how many spells your master has recorded within it. Some Masters are more generous than others, but most provide at least four new spells to study, and few provide more than eight. If you have a spell Memorised, you do not need access to your Grimoire to cast it. If you have not yet memorised a spell, you may use your Grimoire to cast it using both your hands. This doubles the CN of the spell and exposes your Grimoire to possible damage or theft.

SPELL FORMAT

- **CN:** This is the Casting Number of the spell.
- **Range:** This is the range of the spell, generally indicated in yards. If the range is 'you', it can only be cast on the spellcaster. If the range is 'touch', the target must be touched by the caster.
- **Target:** This describes what can be targeted by the spell. Often this will be 1 or more individuals. Spells marked AoE (Area of Effect) affect all individuals within that diameter. If the target is noted as 'Special', this will be clarified in the description. Spells with 'Special' for Target cannot use Success Levels to affect additional targets.
- **Duration:** How long the effect lasts. Instant means the spell effect occurs instantaneously then is finished. Duration expressed as related to a Characteristic Bonus Rounds/minutes/hours etc means a number of that unit of time equal to the Characteristic Bonus of the caster.
- **Description:** The effect of the spell is described here.

THE COLLEGES OF MAGIC AND PETTY SPELLS

Petty spells, or cantrips as the Colleges often prefer to call them, use miniscule amounts of whatever winds are around, and are often learned instinctively by spellcasters as their talent first manifests. As such, once their training within the Colleges has begun, Wizards rarely learn new Petty spells. Technically, they are classed as Witchcraft, and are thus illegal in the Empire.

While the Colleges of Magic generally turn a blind eye to their use given they are so minor, Witch Hunters are not always so understanding.

Petty Spells

For the few Humans blessed — or cursed, depending upon your point of view — with the spark of magic, it generally manifests around puberty, and almost always before 25 summers have passed. The first indications of impending witchery are often little tricks, knacks, cantrips, or similar, showing the wizard-to-be should probably be trained for everyone else's safety.

For Elves, this is just a part of growing up, and those with interest in magic are schooled to develop their burgeoning talents. For Humans, assuming they avoid being lynched, it likely means years of training as an apprentice to a wizard from one of the Eight Colleges of Magic, after which they should never use the little tricks they learned when young again. But most do.

As Petty spells are not formally codified, they have many different names. Players are encouraged to devise their own, more characterful names, reflecting their personality.

Animal Friend

CN: 0
Range: 1 yard
Target: 1
Duration: 1 hour

You make friends with a creature that is smaller than you and possesses the *Bestial* Creature Trait. The animal trusts you completely and regards you as a friend.

Bearings

CN: 0
Range: You
Target: You
Duration: Instant

You sense the influx of the Winds of Magic from their source. You know which direction North is.

Dazzle

CN: 0
Range: Touch
Target: 1
Duration: Willpower Bonus Rounds

The target gains 1 *Blinded* Condition, and gains 1 *Blinded* Condition at the start of each round for the duration of the spell.

Careful Step

CN: 0
Range: You
Target: You
Duration: WP minutes

The magic flowing through your feet ensures any organic matter you tread upon remains undamaged: twigs do not break, grass springs back to its original position, and even delicate flowers are unharmed. Those seeking to use the Track skill to pursue you through rural terrain suffer a −30 penalty to their Tests.

Conserve

CN: 0
Range: 1 yard
Target: 1
Duration: Willpower Bonus days

You preserve up to a day's worth of rations. During this time they will not rot, develop mould, or go stale, although they can still be harmed by external factors, such as getting wet or being burned or poisoned.

Dart

CN: 0
Range: Willpower yards
Target: 1
Duration: Instant

You cause a small dart of magical energy to fly from your fingers. This is a *magic missile* with a Damage of +0.

Drain

CN: 0
Range: Touch
Target: 1
Duration: Instant

You touch your targets, draining their life. This counts as a *magic missile* with Damage +0 that ignores Armour Points. You then Heal 1 Wound.

Eavesdrop

CN: 0
Range: Willpower yards
Target: 1
Duration: Initiative Bonus minutes

You can hear what your targets say as if you were standing right next to them.

Gust

CN: 0
Range: Willpower yards
Target: Special
Duration: Instant

You create a brief gust of wind, strong enough to blow out a candle, cause an open door to slam, or blow a few pages to the floor.

Light

CN: 0
Range: You
Target: You
Duration: Willpower minutes

You create a small light, roughly equivalent to a torch, which glows from your hand, staff or some other part of your person. While the spell is active, you may choose to increase the illumination to that of a lantern, or decrease it to that of a candle, if you pass a **Average (+20) Channelling** Test.

Magic Flame

CN: 0
Range: You
Target: You
Duration: Willpower Bonus Rounds

You kindle a small flame that flickers to life in the palm of your hand. It will not burn you, but will emit heat and set flammable objects alight, like a natural flame.

Marsh Lights

CN: 0
Range: Willpower yards
Target: Special
Duration: Willpower minutes

You create a number of flickering magical lights up to your Intelligence Bonus. They resemble torches or hooded lanterns. Providing they remain within line of sight, for your Action you may control the lights by passing a **Average (+20) Channelling** Test; a success allows you to send the lights moving in any direction. They will move at walking pace in a straight line, passing through any objects (or witnesses) in their path, unless you test again to change their direction.

Murmured Whisper

CN: 0
Range: Willpower yards
Target: Special
Duration: Willpower Bonus Rounds

You cast your voice at a point within Willpower yards, regardless of line of sight. Your voice sounds from this point, and all within earshot will hear it.

Open Lock

CN: 0
Range: Touch
Target: Special
Duration: Instant

One non-magical lock you touch opens.

Produce Small Animal

CN: 0
Range: Touch
Target: Special
Duration: Instant

You reach into a bag, pocket, or hat, or under a rock, bush or burrow, producing a small animal of a type you would expect to find in the vicinity, such as a rabbit, dove, or rat. If there are no appropriate local animals, the spell does nothing. The temperament of the animal is not guaranteed.

Protection from Rain

CN: 0
Range: You
Target: You
Duration: Toughness Bonus hours

You can keep yourself dry whatever the weather, unaffected by precipitation. This affects rain, hail, sleet and snow, and any similar water falling from the heavens, but not standing water.

Purify Water

CN: 0
Range: 1 yard
Target: Special
Duration: Instant

You purify all water within a receptacle, such as a water flask, stein, or jug. All non-magical impurities, such as poison or contaminants are removed, leaving crisp, clear, potable water. If the vessel contained another liquid that is predominantly water – such as ale, or wine – this is also purified, turning into delicious, pure, non-alcoholic water.

Rot

CN: 0
Range: 1 yard
Target: Special
Duration: Instant

You cause a roughly fist-sized volume of organic material to immediately rot. Food stuffs perish, clothes crumble, leathers shrivel (losing 1 Armour Point on 1 hit location), and similar, as dictated by the GM.

Sleep

CN: 0
Range: Touch
Target: 1
Duration: Willpower Bonus Rounds

You touch your opponent, sending them into a deep sleep. If the target has the *Prone* Condition, they gain the *Unconscious* Condition as they fall asleep. They remain unconscious for the duration, although loud noises or being moved or jostled will awaken them instantly. If your targets are standing or sitting when affected, they start themselves awake as they hit the ground, gaining the *Prone* Condition, but remaining conscious.

If your targets are not resisting, and are suitably tired, they will, at the spell's end, pass into a deep and restful sleep.

Spring
CN: 0
Range: Touch
Target: Special
Duration: Willpower Bonus Rounds
You touch the ground and water bubbles forth at the rate of 1 pint per Round, to a total of your Initiative Bonus in pints.

Shock
CN: 0
Range: Touch
Target: 1
Duration: Instant
Your target receives 1 *Stunned* Condition.

Sly Hands
CN: 0
Range: You
Target: You
Duration: Willpower Bonus Rounds
You teleport a small object — no bigger than your fist — from about your person into your hand.

Sounds
CN: 0
Range: Willpower yards
Target: Special
Duration: Willpower Bonus Rounds
You create small noises nearby. You can create quiet, indistinct noises that sound as if they come from a specific location within range, regardless of line of sight. The noises can evoke something specific, such as footsteps, whispers or the howl of an animal, but nothing so distinct that it might convey a message.

While the spell is active, you may control the sounds by passing a **Average (+20) Channelling** Test. A success allows you to move the sounds to another point within range, or to increase or decrease their volume.

Twitch
CN: 0
Range: Willpower Bonus yards
Target: Special
Duration: Instant
You cause a small object to move, slightly. Something may fall from a shelf, or a book may slam its pages shut. If the object is held, the holder must pass an **Average (+20) Dexterity** Test or drop the object.

Warning
CN: 0
Range: 1 yard
Target: Special
Duration: Instant
You channel magic into an object, noticing immediately if it has been poisoned or trapped.

ARCANE SPELLS
The Arcane spells represent common formulations of the *lingua praestantia*. How these spells manifest in practice will depend on your *Arcane Magic* Talent. For instance, a spellcaster with the *Arcane Magic (Fire)* Talent casting Drop may cause the object to overheat, while one with *Arcane Magic (Shadows)* may make it slightly insubstantial, causing the object to literally slip between the target's fingers.

Treat Arcane spells as extra options for *every* Lore of Magic, including Witch, Dark, and Chaos Lores. They are counted as Lore spells in all ways, meaning they get all the benefits of Lore spells, and can only be learned from and taught to those sharing the same *Arcane Magic* Talent.

Note: Any spell marked with a '+' at the end of the Duration gains the following extra text: When the spell should end, you may make a Willpower Test to extend the Duration for +1 round.

Aethyric Armour
CN: 2
Range: You
Target: You
Duration: Willpower Bonus Rounds+
You gain +1 Armour Point to all Hit Locations as you wrap yourself in a protective swathe of magic.

Aethyric Arms
CN: 2
Range: You
Target: You
Duration: Willpower Bonus Rounds+
You create a melee weapon with a Damage equal to your Willpower Bonus. This may take any form, and so use any Melee Skill you may possess. The weapon counts as Magical.

Arrow Shield

CN: 3
Range: You
Target: AoE (Willpower Bonus yards)
Duration: Willpower Bonus Rounds+

Any missiles containing organic matter, such as arrows with wooden shafts, are automatically destroyed if they pass within the Area of Effect, causing no damage to their target. Missiles comprising only inorganic matter, such as throwing knives or pistol shots, are unaffected.

Blast

CN: 4
Range: Willpower yards
Target: AoE (Willpower Bonus yards)
Duration: Instant

You channel magic into an explosive blast. This is a *magic missile* with Damage +3 that targets everyone in the Area of Effect.

Bolt

CN: 4
Range: Willpower yards
Target: 1
Duration: Instant

You channel magic into a damaging bolt. *Bolt* is a magic missile with a Damage of +4.

Breath

CN: 6
Range: 1 yard
Target: Special
Duration: Instant

You immediately make a Breath attack, as if you had spent 2 Advantage to activate the *Breath* Creature Trait (see page 338). *Breath* is a *magic missile* with a Damage equal to your Toughness Bonus. The GM decides which type of Breath attack best suits your *Arcane Magic* Talent.

Bridge

CN: 4
Range: Willpower yards
Target: AoE (see description)
Duration: Willpower Bonus Rounds+

You create a bridge of magical energy, with a maximum length and breadth of your Willpower Bonus in yards. For every +2 SL you may increase length or breadth by your Willpower Bonus in yards.

Chain Attack

CN: 6
Range: Willpower yards
Target: Special
Duration: Instant

You channel a twisting spur of rupturing magic into your target. This is a *magic missile* with a Damage of +4. If *Chain Attack* reduces a target to 0 Wounds, it leaps to another target within the spell's initial range, and within Willpower Bonus yards of the previous target, inflicting the same Damage again. It may leap a maximum number of times equal to your Willpower Bonus. For every +2 SL achieved, it may chain to an additional target.

Corrosive Blood

CN: 4
Range: You
Target: You
Duration: Willpower Bonus Rounds

You infuse yourself with magic, lending your blood a fearsome potency. You gain the *Corrosive Blood* Creature Trait (see page 339).

Dark Vision

CN: 1
Range: You
Target: You
Duration: Willpower Bonus Rounds

You boost your Second Sight to assist your mundane senses. While the spell is active, gain the *Dark Vision* Creature Trait (see page 339).

Distracting

CN: 4
Range: You
Target: You
Duration: Willpower Bonus rounds

You wreathe yourself in magic, which swirls around you, distracting your foes. While the spell is active, gain the *Distracting* Creature Trait (see page 339).

Dome

CN: 7
Range: You
Target: AoE (Willpower Bonus yards)
Duration: Willpower Bonus Rounds

You create a dome of magical energy overhead, blocking incoming attacks. Anyone within the Area of Effect gains the *Ward (6+)* Creature Trait (see page 343) against magical or ranged attacks originating outside the dome. Those within may attack out of the dome as normal, and the dome does not impede movement.

Drop

CN: 1
Range: Willpower yards
Target: 1
Duration: Instant

You channel magic into an object being held by an opponent. This could be a weapon, a rope, or someone's hand. Unless a **Challenging (+0) Dexterity** Test is passed, the item is dropped. For every +2 SL you may impose an additional −10 on the Dexterity Test.

Entangle

CN: 3
Range: Willpower yards
Target: 1
Duration: Special

Using magic, you entrap your target, wrapping them in whatever suits your Lore: vines, shadows, their own clothing… Your target gains one *Entangled* Condition with a Strength equal to your Intelligence. For every +2 SL, you may give the target +1 additional *Entangled* Condition. The spell lasts until all *Entangled* Conditions are removed.

Fearsome

CN: 3
Range: You
Target: You
Duration: Willpower Bonus Rounds

Shrouding yourself in magic, you become fearsome and intimidating. Gain Fear 1. For every +3 SL, you may increase your Fear value by one.

Flight

CN: 8
Range: You
Target: You
Duration: Willpower Bonus Rounds+

You can fly, whether by sprouting wings, ascending on a pillar of magical light, or some other method. Gain the *Flight (Agility)* Creature Trait (see page 339).

Magic Shield

CN: 4
Range: You
Target: You
Duration: Willpower Bonus Rounds

You encase yourself in bands of protective magic. While the spell is active, add +Willpower Bonus SL to any dispel attempts you make.

Move Object

CN: 4
Range: WP yards
Target: 1
Duration: 1 Round

Using magic, you grab hold of an non-sentient object no larger than you, moving it with the sheer force of your will, which is considered to have a Strength equal to your Willpower. You may move the object up to Willpower Bonus yards. If anyone attempts to impede the object's movement, make a **Contested Willpower/Strength** Test. For every +2 SL you may increase the distance the object is moved by Willpower Bonus yards.

Mundane Aura

CN: 4
Range: You
Target: You
Duration: Willpower minutes

You drain all the Winds of Magic from within your body and your possessions, removing any magical aura. For the duration of the spell you appear mundane to the *Magical Sense* Talent and similar. You effectively have no magical ability and your magical nature cannot be detected by any means. While this spell is in effect, you cannot cast any other spells. *Mundane Aura* is immediately dispelled if you make a Channelling Test.

Push

CN: 6
Range: You
Target: You
Duration: Instant

All living creatures within Willpower Bonus yards are pushed back your Willpower Bonus in yards and gain the *Prone* Condition. If this brings them into contact with a wall or other large obstacle, they take Damage equal to the distance travelled in yards. For every +2 SL, you may push creatures back another Willpower Bonus in yards.

Teleport

CN: 5
Range: You
Target: You
Duration: Instant

Using magic, you can teleport up to your Willpower Bonus in yards. This movement allows you to traverse gaps, avoid perils and pitfalls, and ignore obstacles. For every +2 SL you may increase the distance travelled by your Willpower Bonus in yards.

Terrifying

CN: 7
Range: You
Target: You
Duration: Willpower Bonus Rounds

You gain the *Terror (1)* Creature Trait (see page 191).

Ward

CN: 5
Range: You
Target: You
Duration: Willpower Bonus Rounds

You wrap yourself in protective magic, gaining the *Ward (9+)* Creature Trait (see page 343).

COLOUR MAGIC

The following provides eight lists of eight spells, with one list for each colour of magic.

THE LORE OF BEASTS

The Amber wind, *Ghur*, carries with it a chill, primal ferocity, that is unnerving to beasts and sentient creatures alike. Whenever you successfully cast a spell from the Lore of Beasts, you may also gain the *Fear (1)* Creature Trait (see page 190) for the next 1d10 Rounds.

Ingredients: Shamans use animal fur, skin, bone, and pelt, wrapped in sinews and daubed with blood runes to focus the Amber wind. Often claws are scrimshawed, organs dried, and feathers dipped in rare humours, and it's not uncommon to find excrement, urine, and other excretions also used.

Amber Talons

CN: 6
Range: You
Target: You
Duration: Willpower Bonus Rounds
Your nails grow into wickedly sharp talons of crystal amber. Unarmed attacks made using Melee (Brawling) count as magical, have a Damage equal to your Willpower Bonus, and inflict +1 *Bleeding* Condition whenever they cause a loss of Wounds.

Beast Form

CN: 5
Range: You
Target: You
Duration: Willpower minutes
You infuse your very bones and flesh with *Ghur*, warping your body into that of a creature. When cast, select a new form from any of the Beasts of the Reikland section of the Bestiary. Gain all the standard Traits of the creature, except the Bestial Trait. Further, replace your **S, T, Agi,** and **Dex** with those of the creature, then recalculate your Wounds. For every + 2 SL, you may include 1 of the included Optional Creature Trait. While in Beast Form, you look like a normal version of the creature, with amber and brown colouring. You may not speak, which means you cannot cast spells, or attempt to dispel. If you have lost any Wounds when the spell ends, you lose the same number of Wounds when you revert to your true form, to a minimum of 0 Wounds.

Beast Master

CN: 10
Range: Willpower Bonus yards
Target: 1
Duration: Willpower Bonus days
Your breath steams and your eyes take on a shining amber sheen as *Ghur* suffuses you. Your gaze and words convince 1 creature possessing the *Bestial* trait that you are its pack master, and it will fight to the death to protect you. While subject to your mastery it will follow your instructions, instinctively understanding simple instructions. If the creature is released from the spell — through the duration running out, or the spell being dispelled — it will retain enough residual respect and fear not to attack you, unless compelled to. Your allies may not be so fortunate.

Beast Tongue

CN: 3
Range: You
Target: You
Duration: Willpower minutes
You can commune with all creatures possessing the Bestial Trait. *Ghur* clogs your throat, and your language comes out as snarls, hisses, and roars as befits the beasts to whom you talk. While the creatures are not compelled to answer you, or do as you bid, most will be curious enough to hear you out. You gain +20 on all Charm Animal and Animal Training Tests While this spell is active, you may only speak with beasts — you may not speak any civilised tongues, and can only communicate with your party using gestures or Language (Battle). Note, this also means you cannot cast any spells, or dispel, while Beast Tongue is active.

Flock of Doom

CN: 8
Range: Willpower yards
Target: AoE (Willpower Bonus yards)
Duration: Willpower Bonus rounds
You call down a murder of crows or similar local bird to assail your foes.

The flock attacks everyone in the Area of Effect who does not possess the *Arcane Magic (Beasts)* Talent ferociously, inflicting a +7 Damage hit at the end of the Round. The flock remains in play for the duration of the spell. For your Action you may make an **Average (+20) Charm Animal** Test to move the flock to another target within range. While within the Area of Effect, all creatures gain +1 *Blinded* Condition.

Hunter's Hide

CN: 6
Range: You
Target: You
Duration: Willpower Bonus Rounds

You cloak yourself in a shimmering mantle of *Ghur*. While the spell lasts, gain a bonus of +20 Toughness and the Dark Vision and Fear (1) *Creature* Traits (see page 339), as well as the *Acute Sense (Smell)* Talent.

The Amber Spear

CN: 8
Range: Willpower yards
Target: Special
Duration: Instant

You hurl a great spear of pure *Ghur* in a straight line. This is a *magic missile* with a Damage of +12. It strikes the first creature in its path, ignoring APs from armour made of leather and furs. If the target suffers any Wounds, also inflict +1 *Bleeding* Condition, after which the spear continues on its path, striking each target in the same manner, but at −1 Damage each time. If the spear fails to inflict any Wounds, its progress is stopped and the spell comes to an end. *The Amber Spear* only inflicts the minimum 1 Wound (see page 236) on the first target it strikes.

Wyssan's Wildform

CN: 8
Range: You
Target: You
Duration: Willpower Bonus Rounds

You call on the wild power of *Ghur* to infuse you, surrendering to its savage delights. Gain the following Creature Traits (see page 338): *Arboreal, Armour (2), Belligerent, Big, Bite (Strength Bonus +1), Fear (1), Fury, Magical, Weapon (Strength Bonus +2).* While the spell is in place you are incapable of using any Language or Lore skills.

THE LORE OF DEATH

The purple wind of *Shyish* carries with it dry, dusty winds and the insistent rustling of sand passing through Time's hourglass. Targets afflicted by spells from the Lore of Death are drained of life, enervated, and listless. You may assign +1 *Fatigued* Condition to any living target affected by a spell from this lore. A target may only ever have a single *Fatigued* Condition gained in this manner at any one time.

Ingredients: The bones of sentient creatures feature heavily in Amethyst magic, as do the trappings of death, including wood or nails from coffins, embalming fluids, hourglasses, silver coins, and grave dirt, all carefully presented or engraved. Purple gemstones, materials, and flowers (particularly roses) are also common.

Caress of Laniph

CN: 7
Range: Touch
Target: Special
Duration: Instant

As you reach out your hand, it appears withered, even skeletal, drawing *Shyish* from your target's corpus. This counts as a *magic missile* with a Damage of +6 that ignores Toughness Bonus and Armour Points. For every 2 Wounds inflicted, you may recover 1 Wound.

Dying Words

CN: 6
Range: Touch
Target: 1
Duration: Willpower Bonus Rounds

Touching the body of a recently departed soul (one that passed away within the last day), you call its soul back briefly. For the spell's duration, you can communicate with the dead soul, though it cannot take any action other than talking. It is not compelled to answer you, but the dead do not lie.

Purple Pall of *Shyish*

CN: 9
Range: You
Target: You
Duration: Willpower Bonus Rounds

You pull about you a pall fashioned from fine strands of purple magic. Gain +Willpower Bonus Armour Points on all locations, and the *Fear (1)* Creature Trait (see page 339). For every +2 SL you may increase your *Fear* rating by 1.

Sanctify

CN: 10
Range: Touch
Target: AoE (Willpower Bonus yards)
Duration: Willpower minutes

Inscribing a magical circle, you ward it with *Shyish*, forming an impenetrable barrier to the Undead. Creatures with the *Undead* Creature Trait cannot enter or leave the circle.

Scythe of *Shyish*

CN: 6
Range: You
Target: You
Duration: Willpower Bonus Rounds

You conjure a magical scythe, which can be wielded in combat, using the Melee (Polearm) Skill. It acts like a normal scythe with a Damage equal to your Willpower Bonus+3. Enemies with the *Undead* Creature Trait do not receive Advantage when Engaged in combat with you.

Soul Vortex

CN: 8
Range: Willpower yards
Target: AoE (Willpower Bonus yards)
Duration: Instant

You hurl a shimmering ball of *Shyish* which erupts into purple flames, swirling with ghostly faces, mouths agape in silent terror. Targets within the Area of Effect receive +1 *Broken* Condition. Against targets with the *Undead* Creature Trait, *Soul Vortex* is a *magic missile* with a Damage of +10 that ignores Toughness Bonus and Armour Points.

Steal Life

CN: 7
Range: Willpower yards
Target: 1
Duration: Instant

Thin strands of purple mist connect you briefly to your target, who wastes away before your very eyes. This counts as a *magic missile* with a Damage of +6 that ignores Armour Points and inflicts +1 *Fatigued* Condition. Further, you remove all *Fatigued* Conditions you currently suffer, and may heal yourself up to half the Wounds the target suffers, rounding up.

Swift Passing

CN: 6
Range: Touch
Target: Special
Duration: Instant

Your touch brings the release of death to a single mortally wounded target. If you successfully touch a target with 0 wounds remaining and at least 2 Critical Wounds, death swiftly follows. Further, the target cannot be raised as Undead.

THE LORE OF FIRE

The Lore of Fire, and the Bright wind of *Aqshy*, is anything but subtle. Its spells are bellowed with fervour and manifest themselves in bombastic fashion, with bright flame and searing heat. You may inflict +1 *Ablaze* Condition on anyone targeted by spells from the Lore of Fire, unless they also possess the *Arcane Magic (Fire)* Talent. Every *Ablaze* condition within Willpower Bonus yards adds +10 to attempts to Channel or Cast with *Aqshy*.

Ingredients: Pyromancers use a wide selection of flammable materials as ingredients, which are often immolated as the spell is cast, including coal, oils, fats, and ruddy woods. Trappings immune to fire are also common, such as iron keys, carved sections of fire-grate, and small oven stones.

Aqshy's Aegis

CN: 5
Range: You
Target: You
Duration: Willpower Bonus rounds

You wrap yourself in a fiery cloak of *Aqshy*, which channels flame into the Aegis. You are completely immune to damage from non-magical fire, including the breath attacks of monsters, and ignore any *Ablaze* Conditions you receive. You receive the *Ward (9+)* Creature Trait (see page 343) against magical fire attacks including spells from the Lore of Fire.

Cauterise

CN: 4
Range: Touch
Target: 1
Duration: Instant

Channelling *Aqshy* through your hands you lay them on an ally's wounds. Immediately heal 1d10 Wounds and remove all *Bleeding* Conditions. Further, the wounds will not become infected.

Targets without the *Arcane Magic (Fire)* Talent, must pass a **Challenging (+0) Cool** Test or scream in agony.. If Failed by −6 or more SL, the target gains the *Unconscious* Condition and is permanently scarred, waking up 1d10 hours later

Crown of Flame

CN: 8
Range: You
Target: You
Duration: Willpower Bonus Rounds

You channel *Aqshy* into a majestic crown of inspiring fire about your brow. Gain the *Fear (1)* Trait and +1 *War Leader* Talent while the spell is active.

For every +2 SL, you may increase your Fear value by +1, or take *War Leader* Talent again. Furthermore, gain a bonus of +10 on all attempts to Channel and Cast with *Aqshy* while the spell is in effect.

Flaming Hearts

CN: 8
Range: Willpower yards
Target: AoE (Willpower Bonus yards)
Duration: Willpower Bonus Rounds
Your voice takes on a rich resonance, echoing with *Aqshy's* fiery passion. Affected allies lose all *Broken* and *Fatigued* Conditions, and gain +1 *Drilled, Fearless* and *Stout-hearted* Talent while the spell is in effect.

Firewall

CN: 6
Range: Willpower yards
Target: AoE (Special)
Duration: Willpower Bonus Rounds
You channel a fiery streak of *Aqshy*, creating a wall of flame. The Firewall is Willpower Bonus yards wide, and 1 yard deep. For every +2 SL you may extend the length of the Firewall by +Willpower Bonus yards. Anyone crossing the firewall gains 1 *Ablaze* condition and suffers a hit with a Damage equal to your Willpower Bonus, handled like a *magical missile*.

Great Fires of U'Zhul

CN: 10
Range: Willpower yards
Target: AoE (Willpower Bonus yards)
Duration: Willpower Bonus Rounds
You hurl a great, explosive blast of *Aqshy* into an enemy, which erupts into a furious blaze, burning with the heat of a forge. This is a *magical missile* with Damage +10 that ignores Armour Points and inflicts +2 *Ablaze* Conditions and the *Prone* Condition on a target. Everyone within the Area of Effect of that target suffers a Damage +5 hit ignoring Armour Points, and must pass a Dodge Test or also gain +1 *Ablaze* Condition. The spell stops behaving like a *magic missile* as the fire continues to burn in the Area of Effect for the duration. Anyone within the Area of Effect at the start of a round suffers 1d10+6 Damage, ignoring APs, and gains +1 *Ablaze* Condition.

Flaming Sword of Rhuin

CN: 8
Range: Willpower yards
Target: 1
Duration: Willpower Bonus Rounds
You wreathe a sword in magical flames. The weapon has Damage +6 and the Impact Quality (see page 298), and anyone struck by the blade gains +1 *Ablaze* Condition. If wielders do not possess

the *Arcane Magic (Fire)* Talent, and they fumble an attack with the Flaming Sword, they gain +1 *Ablaze* Condition.

Purge

CN: 10
Range: Willpower yards
Target: AoE (Willpower Bonus yards)
Duration: Willpower Bonus Rounds
You funnel intense flame to burn away the taint and corruption in an area. Anything flammable is set alight, and any creatures in the area takes +SL *Ablaze* conditions. If the location contains a Corrupting Influence, such as *Dhar*, warpstone, or a Chaos-tainted object, it too will smoulder and blacken, beginning to burn. This spell may be maintained in subsequent rounds by passing a **Challenging (+0) Channelling** Test. The precise time needed to eliminate the Corrupting Influence will be determined by your GM. As a rough guideline, a small quantity (smaller than an acorn) of warpstone, or a minor Chaos-tainted object may require 10–Willpower Bonus Rounds (minimum of 1 Round). A larger quantity of warpstone — fist-sized — or a more potent Chaos-tainted object may require double this. A powerful Chaos Artefact may take hours, or even longer… See page 182 for detail on Corrupting Influences.

THE LORE OF HEAVENS

Arcane spells cast from the Lore of Heavens are accompanied by the crackling of lightning and the smell of ozone. Spells causing Damage ignore Armour Points from metal armour, and will arc to all other targets within 2 yards, except those with the *Arcane Magic (Heavens)* Talent, inflicting hits with a Damage equal to your Willpower Bonus, handled like a *magical missile*.

Ingredients: Astronomical instruments, charts, lenses, and symbols dominate Celestial magic, as do ingredients associated with augury, such as animal innards, mirrors, glass balls, and bird tongues. Some wind-based spells use wings and feathers, where those involving electricity prefer slivers of carved metal.

SEERS

The Seer Career can gain access to the *Arcane Magic (Heavens)* Talent. Seers who take this Talent can only take these spells (and none other, even Arcane Spells): *Fate's Fickle Fingers, Starcrossed, The First Portent of Amul, The Second Portent of Amul, The Third Portent of Amul.* To gain access to the rest of the *Arcane Magic (Heavens)* spells, they would need to enter the Wizard career.

Cerulean Shield

CN: 7
Range: You
Target: You
Duration: Willpower Bonus Rounds

You encase yourself in a crackling cage of sparking electricity and *Azyr*. For the spell's duration, gain +SL Armour Points to all locations against melee attacks. If attacked by metal weapons — such as daggers, swords, and spears with metal tips — your attacker takes +Willpower Bonus Damage.

Comet of Casandora

CN: 10
Range: Initiative yards
Target: AoE (Initiative Bonus yards)
Duration: Special

You channel all the *Azyr* you can muster and reach out to the skies, calling down a comet to wreak havoc amongst your foes. Select a target point within range. At the end of the next round, make an **Average (+20) Perception** Test. For every +SL you achieve, you may move your point of impact by Initiative Bonus yards.

For every –SL, the GM will move the point of impact by Initiative Bonus yards in a random direction. Comet of Casandora then acts as a *magical missile* with Damage +12 that hits all targets in the Area of Effect, who also gain +1 *Ablaze* and the *Prone* Condition.

Fate's Fickle Fingers

CN: 6
Range: You
Target: AoE (Initiative Bonus yards)
Duration: Willpower Bonus Rounds

All allies within the Area of Effect, excluding those with the *Arcane Magic (Heavens)* Talent, create a single pool for their Fortune Points. All may draw on the pool, first come, first served. When the spell ends, you reallocate any remaining Fortune Points as fairly as possible.

Starcrossed

CN: 7
Range: Willpower yards
Target: 1
Duration: Initiative Bonus Rounds

While this spell is active, you can spend Fortune Points to force an opponent to reroll Tests.

T'Essla's Arc

CN: 7
Range: Willpower yards
Target: 1
Duration: Instant

A crackling bolt of lightning shoots from your fingertips, striking your target. This is a *magic missile* with Damage +10 that inflicts +1 *Blinded* condition.

The First Portent of Amul

CN: 3
Range: You
Target: You
Duration: Initiative Bonus Rounds

Gain +1 Fortune Point. For every +2 SL, gain +1 more. Any of these points unused at the end of the Duration are lost.

The Second Portent of Amul

CN: 6
Range: You
Target: You
Duration: Initiative Bonus Rounds

Gain +SL Fortune Points. For every +2 SL, gain +1 additional Fortune point. Any unused points at the end of the Duration are lost.

The Third Portent of Amul

CN: 12
Range: You
Target: You
Duration: Initiative Bonus Rounds

Gain +1 Fate Point. If the Fate point is not used by the end of the Duration, it is lost.

THE LORE OF METAL

The wind of *Chamon* is very dense, and quickly attaches itself to metallic substances. Spells from this lore are accompanied with golden light and heat, and are especially effective against foes foolish enough to encase themselves in metal. Spells inflicting Damage ignore Armour Points from metal armour, and inflict bonus Damage equal to the number of Armour Points of metal armour being worn on any Hit Location struck. So, if your spell hit an Arm location protected by 2 Armour Points of metal armour, it would cause an additional +2 Damage and ignore the Armour Points.

Ingredients: Heavy metals of all types, esoterically inlaid or carved, comprise the majority of Gold ingredients, though many spells also use trappings associated with a forge, including sections of a bellows marked with mathematical formula, inscribed chunks of an anvil, or fragments of a furnace.

Crucible of *Chamon*

CN: 7
Range: Willpower Bonus yards
Target: 1
Duration: Instant

You channel *Chamon* into a single non-magical, metallic object, such as a weapon or piece of armour. The item melts, dripping to the floor as molten metal, cooling almost immediately. If held, the item is dropped. If worn, the wearer takes a hit like a *magic missile* with Damage equal to your Willpower Bonus that ignores Toughness Bonus. While the object is destroyed, the metal retains its base value, and may be used by a smith as raw material.

Enchant Weapon

CN: 6
Range: Touch
Target: special
Duration: Willpower Bonus rounds

You encase a single non-magical weapon with heavy bands of *Chamon*, enhancing its potency. For the duration of the spell it counts as magical, gains a bonus to Damage equal to your Willpower Bonus, and gains the *Unbreakable* Quality (see page 298). For every +3 SL you may also add 1 Quality or remove 1 Flaw from the weapon, while the spell is in effect.

Feather of Lead

CN: 5
Range: Willpower yards
Target: Area of Effect (Willpower Bonus yards)
Duration: Willpower Bonus Rounds

Calling on the golden wind, you alter the density of your target's belongings, raising or lowering their weight. For the duration of the spell, choose one effect for everyone within the area of effect:

- Count as two steps more Overburdened
- Do not count as Overburdened

See page 293 for details on Encumbrance.

Fool's Gold

CN: 4
Range: Touch
Target: 1
Duration: Willpower minutes

You weave *Chamon* into a non-magical object made of metal, fundamentally altering its alchemical nature. For the duration of the spell, all metal in the object becomes gold. This is not an illusion: it has actually transformed into gold. When the spell ends, the item reverts to its original metal. This spell can ruin good weapons, make armour too heavy to wear, and turn lead coins into something much more appealing. Spot effects arising from this spell are left in the hands of the GM.

Forge of *Chamon*

CN: 9
Range: Willpower Bonus yards
Target: Special
Duration: Willpower minutes

You alter the quality of a single item made of metal. You may add 1 Quality or remove 1 Flaw. For every +2 SL, you may add another Quality or remove another Flaw.

Glittering Robe

CN: 5
Range: You
Target: You
Duration: Toughness Bonus Rounds

Wild flurries of *Chamon* whirl around you, deflecting blows and intercepting missiles and magical attacks. Gain the *Ward* *(9+)* Creature Trait (see page 343) against all attacks and spells targeting you. Each hit successfully saved increases the *Ward's* effectiveness by 1, to a maximum of *Ward (3+)*.

Mutable Metal

CN: 5
Range: Touch
Target: 1
Duration: Willpower Bonus Rounds

You touch a non-magical object made of metal, which instantly becomes warm to the touch as you squeeze *Chamon* into it. You may bend and mangle the object with an **Average (+20) Strength** Test. If you wish to make a more complex alteration, you may attempt an **Average (+20) Trade (Smith, or similar)** Test instead.

Transmutation of *Chamon*

CN: 12
Range: Willpower yards
Target: AoE (Willpower Bonus yards)
Duration: Willpower Bonus Rounds

You wrench *Chamon* from the metals worn by your foes, and the earth itself, briefly transforming the flesh of your enemies into metal. This is a *magic missile* affecting all in the Area of Effect, with a Damage equal to your Willpower Bonus; the spell ignores Toughness Bonus and inflicts +1 *Blinded, Deafened,* and *Stunned* Condition, all of which last for the duration of the spell. All affected targets gain +1 Armour Point from the gold wrapped about their bodies, but also suffer from Suffocation (see page 181). If targets die while the spell is in effect, they are permanently encased in a shell of base metals, a macabre reminder of the risks of sorcery.

THE LORE OF LIFE

Spells cast with *Ghyran*, the Jade Wind, are suffuse with life, tending to manifest with a vibrant green light, and are often accompanied by natural phenomena given supernatural qualities. Vines, undergrowth, trees, and rivers all bend to the Druids' wills.

Receive a +10 bonus to Casting and Channelling rolls when in a rural or wilderness environment. Living creatures — e.g. those without the *Daemonic* or *Undead* Creature Traits — targeted by Arcane Spells from the Lore of Life have all *Fatigued* and *Bleeding* Conditions removed after any other effects have been applied as life magic floods through them. Creatures with the Undead Creature Trait, on the other hand, suffer additional Damage equal to your Willpower Bonus, ignoring Toughness Bonus and Armour Points, if affected by any spell cast with the Lore of Life.

Ingredients: Druids use a wide variety of naturally occurring ingredients, ranging from rare seeds and nuts, humours gathered from sentient creatures in the flush of life, uncommon tree saps, fertile loam, spring waters, and a variety of living ingredients, including plants and smaller animals.

Barkskin
CN: 3
Range: Touch
Target: 1
Duration: Willpower Bonus Rounds
You cause the target's skin to become hard and rough like the bark of a tree. While affected by the spell, add +2 to the target's Toughness Bonus, but suffer a penalty of −10 to Agility and Dexterity.

Earthblood
CN: 6
Range: You
Target: AoE (Willpower Bonus yards)
Duration: Willpower Bonus Rounds
To cast this spell, you must be in direct contact with the earth. Standing barefoot counts. For the duration of the spell, any creatures in direct contact with the earth within AoE heal Wounds equal to your Willpower Bonus at the start of every Round.

Earthpool
CN: 8
Range: You
Target: You
Duration: Instant
On casting the spell, you immediately disappear into the ground in a wild torrent of *Ghyran*. You appear at the start of the next Round at any point within your Willpower in yards, erupting from the earth violently. For every +2 SL you may increase the distance travelled by your Willpower in yards. Any enemies engaged by you on your appearance gain the *Surprised* Condition. This spell will not allow you to move through stone but will allow you to move through water.

Fat of the Land
CN: 4
Range: Touch
Target: 1
Duration: Willpower Bonus days
You flood the target's body with nourishing *Ghyran*. The target need not eat or drink, but will still excrete as normal, though any leavings will be verdant green.

Forest of Thorns
CN: 6
Range: Willpower yards
Target: AoE (Willpower Bonus yards)
Duration: Willpower Bonus Rounds
This spell may only target a patch of earth (though the patch can be very small). You cause a dense knot of wickedly spiked brambles and tangled vines to burst upwards, covering the Area of Effect.

While the spell is active, anyone attempting to traverse the area on foot without the *Arcane Magic (Life)* Talent must make a **Hard (−20) Agility** Test. Failure means they gain 1 *Bleeding* Condition, and 1 *Entangled* Condition, with your Willpower used for its Strength. After the spell concludes, the growth remains, but loses its preternatural properties.

Lie of the Land
CN: 5
Range: Initiative Bonus miles
Target: You
Duration: Special
Touching the earth, your senses flow through the *Ghyran* tracing the nearby area. After communing for 1 minute, you receive a detailed mental map of all-natural features — land, forests, rivers, but not settlements — within range. Settlements may be alluded to — areas of clear terrain, or dug trenches, for example. Each time you increase the range with SL increases the time taken communing with the land by +1 minute.

Lifebloom

CN: 8
Range: Willpower Bonus yards
Target: Special
Duration: Special

You cause *Ghyran* to flood an area that is blighted or desolate. You may target either a dry riverbed, well, field, or a domestic animal. If you successfully cast the spell, the target bursts to life:

- A dry river begins to flow once again
- A dry or polluted well becomes clean and fresh
- A planted field, vineyard or orchard bursts into life, with all crops immediately reaching full ripeness
- A sick or unproductive animal becomes healthy. The affected beast is now healthily productive (cows produce milk, hens lay eggs, coats and hides of sheep and cows are healthy and lustrous) and any diseases are cured.

Regenerate

CN: 6
Range: Touch
Target: 1
Duration: Willpower Bonus Rounds

Your target gains the *Regenerate* Creature Trait (see page 341).

THE LORE OF LIGHT

Arcane Spells sung from the Lore of Light tend to emit dazzling rays of blinding white light, or shroud the caster in shimmering waves of radiant purity. You may inflict one *Blinded* Condition on those targeted by Lore of Light spells, unless they possess the *Arcane Magic (Light)* Talent.

If a target has the *Daemonic* or *Undead* Creature Traits, spells also inflict an additional hit with Damage equal to your Intelligence Bonus that ignores Toughness Bonus and Armour Points.

Ingredients: Hierophants of the Lore of Light use many artefacts associated with holiness and holy places, supplemented by crystals, glass, pyramidions, and small statues, all carved with sacred symbols, twisting snakes, and moral tales. White candles, silver carvings, and bleached paper are also common.

Banishment

CN: 12
Range: You
Target: AoE (Willpower Bonus yards)
Duration: Instant

You send a cleansing halo of *Hysh* out from hands, affecting all creatures within the Area of Effect whose Toughness is lower than your Willpower. Targets with the *Undead* and *Daemonic* Creature Traits gain the *Unstable* Creature Trait (see page 343). If they already have the *Unstable* Trait, they are reduced to 0 Wounds.

Blinding Light

CN: 5
Range: Willpower yards
Target: You
Duration: Instant

You emit a bright, blinding flash of light from your hand or staff. Everyone looking at you, unless they possess the *Arcane Magic (Light)* Talent, receives +SL *Blinded* Conditions.

Clarity of Thought

CN: 6
Range: Touch
Target: 1
Duration: Intelligence minutes

You calm your target's mind, allowing them to think clearly. All negative modifiers on their thinking processes — from Conditions, Mental Mutations, Psychologies, or any other source — are ignored while the spell is in effect.

Daemonbane

CN: 10
Range: Willpower Bonus yards
Target: 1
Duration: Instant

You summon a blast of *Hysh* that passes through the border between the Realm of Chaos and the material world. The Casting Test is Opposed by the target making a Willpower Test. If you win, you obliterate a target with the *Daemonic* Creature Trait with a blinding white light, sending it back whence it came. If the spell successfully banishes a Daemon, everyone looking at your target, unless they possess the *Arcane Magic (Light)* Talent, receives +SL *Blinded* Conditions.

Healing Light

CN: 9
Range: Willpower Bonus yards
Target: 1
Duration: Instant

Your target glows with a bright, cleansing light (equivalent light to a campfire), healing Intelligence Bonus + Willpower Bonus Wounds. If the Target passes a **Very Hard (–20) Endurance** Test, 1 Corruption point gained in the last hour is also lost.

Net of Amyntok

CN: 8
Range: Intelligence Bonus yards
Target: 1
Duration: Target's Intelligence Bonus Rounds

You cast a delicate net woven from strands of *Hysh* over your targets, whose minds are overcome with conundrums and puzzles, leaving them paralysed with indecision. Targets gain +1 *Stunned* Condition, which they cannot lose while the spell is in effect. When recovering from the Condition, targets test their Intelligence instead of the Endurance Skill. Targets with the *Bestial* Creature Trait are immune to this spell.

Phâ's Protection

CN: 10
Range: You
Target: AoE (Willpower Bonus yards)
Duration: Willpower Bonus Rounds

You summon a protective aura of pure, holy light. Profane creatures — those with the *Undead* or *Daemonic* Creature Trait, those with mutations, and those with more Corruption than their Willpower Bonus and Toughness Bonus combined — cannot enter the Area of Effect. Any already within the Area gain the *Broken* Condition until they leave. Creatures within the Area cannot gain any Corruption points while the spell is active.

Speed of Thought

CN: 8
Range: You
Target: You
Duration: Willpower Bonus Rounds

A lattice of *Hysh* overlays your mind, allowing you to think rapidly. Gain a bonus of +20 to Intelligence and Initiative.

THE LORE OF SHADOWS

Spells cast from the Lore of Shadows are surreptitious and sly, and so the *lingua praestantia* may be muttered stealthily. Any protective spells you may cast wreath you in shadows and billow smoke, making your body insubstantial, possibly even allowing blades to pass through you seemingly without harm. Further, all spells cast from the Lore of Shadows inflicting Damage ignore all non-magical Armour Points.

Ingredients: Anything used to hide, shroud, or conceal is repurposed as Grey ingredients, including cosmetics, scents, scarfs, spectacles, mirrors, and wigs. Items drawn from professions steeped in intrigue and wisdom are also common, with diplomatic artefacts, symbols of rank, and the ultimate expression of power — a blade — prevalent.

Choking Shadows

CN: 6
Range: Willpower Bonus yards
Target: 1
Duration: Willpower Bonus Rounds

You wrap shadowy tendrils of *Ulgu* around your foes' necks. Assuming they need to breathe, they gain +1 *Fatigued* Condition, cannot talk, and are subject to rules for Suffocation (see page 181).

Doppelganger

CN: 10
Range: You
Target: You
Duration: Intelligence Bonus minutes

You weave a mask and cloak of *Ulgu* around your form, assuming the likeness of another humanoid creature with whom you are familiar (as determined by the GM). Your appearance will automatically fool anyone without the *Second Sight* Talent, though some may note if any of your mannerisms are incorrect. Those with that Talent must pass a **Difficult (–10) Perception** Test to notice you are disguising your form. This does not let them see through the spell. They must dispel it to do so.

Illusion

CN: 8
Range: Willpower yards
Target: AoE (Initiative Bonus yards)
Duration: Willpower minutes

You spin a web of intricate strands of *Ulgu*, obfuscating the Area of Effect with an illusory image of your choosing. You will automatically fool anyone without the *Second Sight* Talent. Those with that Talent must pass a **Difficult (–10) Perception** Test to notice the illusion. This does not let them see through the spell. They must dispel it to do so.

The illusion is, by default, static. For your Action, you may make a **Hard (–20) Channelling** Test to make the illusion move for that Round.

Mindslip

CN: 6
Range: 1 yard
Target: 1
Duration: Willpower minutes

You conjure delicate threads of *Ulgu* in your Target's mind, causing all prior memory of you to disappear for the spell's duration. Once the spell is over, the Target must pass an **Average (+20) Intelligence** Test, or the memory loss becomes permanent until dispelled.

Mystifying Miasma

CN: 6
Range: Willpower yards
Target: AoE (Willpower Bonus yards)
Duration: Willpower Bonus Rounds

You conjure forth a swirling mass of mist shot through with roiling shadow that flits and confounds the senses. Anyone within the mist who does not possess the *Arcane Magic (Shadows)* Talent is affected by the Miasma, gaining +1 *Blinded*, *Deafened*, and *Fatigued* Condition, which remain for the spell's duration. Anyone affected attempting to move must pass a **Challenging (+0) Perception** Test, or gain the *Prone* Condition. If the spell is dispelled once in play, anyone affected by the spell must make a **Routine (+40) Initiative** Test, or gain the *Stunned* Condition.

Shadowsteed

CN: 6
Range: Willpower Bonus yards
Target: 1
Duration: Until the next sunrise

You summon forth a shadowy steed. The creature's unnatural flesh is black as midnight, and at times it appears to be both solid and insubstantial. Use the rules for a riding horse. When the Shadowsteed is out of sunlight, it also gains the following Creature Traits: *Dark Vision, Ethereal, Magical, Painless, Stealthy, Stride, Fear (1) and Ward (+9).*

Even when insubstantial, Shadowsteeds may be ridden. Riders with the *Arcane Magic (Shadow)* Talent do so with a bonus of +20 to Ride Tests. Those without suffer a penalty of −20 to Ride Tests. Shadowsteeds are tireless, so need no rest (though their unsettled riders might!). As the first rays of dawn break over the horizon the steeds melt into insubstantial mist. If still being ridden when the spell ends, or when dispelled, the rider will suffer Falling Damage (see page 166).

Shadowstep

CN: 8
Range: Willpower yards
Target: You
Duration: Instant

You create a shadowy portal of *Ulgu* through the aethyr. You disappear from your current location and immediately appear up to your Willpower yards away. Any enemies Engaged by you on your disappearance or reappearance gain the *Surprised* Condition.

Shroud of Invisibility

CN: 8
Range: Touch
Target: 1
Duration: Willpower Bonus Rounds

You wrap the target in a shroud of *Ulgu*. The Target becomes invisible and cannot be perceived by mundane senses. The spell will automatically fool anyone without the *Second Sight* Talent. Those with the Talent must pass a **Challenging (+0) Perception** Test to notice that someone is nearby, though they will not be able to pin down the precise location. They must dispel the *Shroud of Invisibility* to do so . You are still perceptible to the other senses, and the spell will come to an end if you bring attention to yourself by making large noises or attacking someone.

WITCH MAGIC

The following provides two lists of six spells for spellcasters nor yet absorbed into the Colleges of Magic, who are almost always on the run from Witch Hunters and Sigmarites.

THE LORE OF HEDGECRAFT

The Hedgefolk believe their Lore is a gift from the Gods, referring to their spellcasters as the Blessed Few. Due to their ancient traditions and ingrained belief, their spells cannot be cast without ingredients, which are an integral part of their spellcasting process.

Fortunately, the ingredients they use are easily found on the fringes of settlements and are usually herbs or plants. You receive

1 + SL ingredients on a successful foraging roll, using Lore (Herbalism), as described under Gathering Food and Herbs on page 127, or you can buy them for 5 brass pennies each.

Ingredients: Hedgefolk use easily sourced local materials prepared to exacting standards using special tools. So, ingredients may include things such as the wings of a dragonfly killed with a silver pin, rods of poplar polished with beeswax on Sonnstill, or bones buried beneath a hedgerow for a winter's month.

Goodwill

CN: 0
Range: You
Target: AoE (Fellowship Bonus yards)
Duration: Willpower Bonus Rounds

You create an atmosphere conducive to friendliness and good spirits. All Fellowship Tests within the Area of Effect receive a bonus of +10, and *Animosity* and *Hatred* Psychologies have no effect.

Mirkride

CN: 0
Range: You
Target: You
Duration: Willpower Bonus minutes

Speaking ancient words of magic, your spirit leaves your body, stepping into the Hedge, the dark space between the material world and the spirit realm. For the duration, your stand apart from the world, able to witness it invisibly, but not affect it in any way. Physical barriers are no impediment to you, and you may walk through non-magical obstacles at will. Your body remains in place, immobile and insensate.

At the end of the spell you will be pulled suddenly back to your body. If your body is killed while you are walking the Hedge, your spirit will wander aimlessly for eternity.

Nepenthe

CN: 0
Range: Touch
Target: Special
Duration: Willpower Bonus Rounds

You mutter words of power over a premade potion of herbs, magically transforming it into a potent philtre. If drunk while the spell is in effect, the target may choose to completely forget one individual, permanently.

Nostrum

CN: 0
Range: Touch
Target: Special
Duration: Willpower Bonus Rounds

You incant a spell over an already prepared draught, imbuing it with magical power. If drunk while the spell is in effect, the target immediately heals your Willpower Bonus in Wounds and is cured of one disease. For every +2 SL you may cure an extra disease.

Part the Branches

CN: 0
Range: You
Target: You
Duration: Willpower minutes

Your pupils dilate as you complete your incantation, and you are able to see into the Spirit world. This allows you to perceive invisible creatures, spirits, and Daemons, even those marked as impossible to see.

Protective Charm

CN: 0
Range: Touch
Target: Special
Duration: Willpower Bonus days

You imbue a protective charm with a spell of protection. Those bearing the charm gain the *Magic Resistance* Talent. If they already have that Talent, the charm does nothing more.

THE LORE OF WITCHCRAFT

Spells from the Lore of Witchcraft draw on whichever winds of magic are available, without care or concern for mingling the winds and the potentially horrific results. Each time practitioners of Witchcraft roll on a Miscast table, they also gain 1 Corruption point. Further, you may inflict one Bleeding Condition on anyone targeted by spells from the Lore of Witchcraft. Lastly, channelling or casting spells from this Lore automatically require a roll on the Minor Miscast table unless cast with an ingredient , where the ingredient provides no further protection should you roll a Miscast. Fortunately, ingredients for the Lore of Witchcraft are cheap and readily available: body parts of small animals for the most part. Ingredients cost a spell's CN in brass pennies, instead of silver shillings, to purchase. Alternatively, a Witch may forage for parts, using the Outdoor Survival skill: a successful foraging roll receives 1 + SL ingredients, as described under Gathering Food and Herbs on page 127.

Ingredients: Witches use a horrific mixture of animal body parts, often harvested when a creature is still alive. It is not uncommon to find them clutching lizard eyes, dog toes, donkey gizzard, or much, much worse in their bloody hands as they cast their foul magics.

Blight

CN: 14
Range: Willpower Bonus yards
Target: Special
Duration: Special

You may target either a well, a field, or a domestic animal. If you successfully cast the spell, the target suffers from a blight:

- A blighted well becomes instantly brackish and stagnant
- Any crops currently planted in a Blighted field rot overnight
- A blighted animal sickens. The afflicted beast no longer produces anything (cows produce no milk, hens produce no eggs, coats and hides grow mangy and unusable) and will die in 10–SL days

Creeping Menace

CN: 6
Range: Willpower yards
Target: 1
Duration: Willpower Bonus Rounds

You summon a swarm of creeping, slithering creatures to harass your foes. Each target affected is immediately engaged by a swarm of Giant Rats, Giant Spiders, or Snakes. Use the standard profiles for the relevant creature type, adding the *Swarm* Trait. For your Action you may make a **Challenging (+0) Charm Animal** Test to direct 1 or more swarms to attack a different target.

When the spell ends, any remaining swarms disappear into the shadows.

Curse of Crippling Pain

CN: 10
Range: Willpower yards
Target: 1
Duration: Willpower Bonus Rounds

Stabbing a crude representation of your target — a doll or puppet — you inflict crippling pain. When successfully cast, choose which hit location to stab:

- **Leg** – Leg becomes useless, as if it was Amputated (see page 180). If running, the target also gains the *Prone* Condition and takes falling Damage.

- **Arm** – Arm becomes useless, as if it was Amputated (see page 180). If target was holding anything in that hand, it is automatically dropped.

- **Body** – Target doubles up in agony, gaining +1 *Fatigued* Condition, and must pass a **Hard (–20) Endurance** Test or gain the *Prone* Condition.

- **Head** – Target gains the *Stunned* Condition, and must pass an **Average (+20) Endurance** Test or gain the *Unconscious* Condition for the Duration.

While the spell is in effect, for your Action you may make a Channelling Test, stabbing the doll again, to affect a different location.

Curse of Ill-Fortune

CN: 8
Range: Willpower Bonus miles
Target: 1
Duration: Willpower Bonus days

The ingredient for this spell is something belonging to the target, either a personal possession or a strand of hair. For the duration, your target suffers bad luck. Laces snap, chairs break, and other minor narrative effects inconvenience them. The target suffers a penalty of –10 to all Tests, in addition to any other modifiers, and may not spend Fortune points.

Haunting Horror

CN: 8
Range: Touch
Target: AoE (a single location)
Duration: Willpower days

You target a single location, such as a house or clearing, and inflict haunting dreams and waking nightmares on any who enter there. Those entering while the spell is in effect are unnerved by eerie sensations, flitting shadows, and whispered voices lurking on the threshold of hearing. Unless they possess the *Arcane Magic (Witchcraft)* Talent, they gain +1 *Fatigued* Condition. Then, unless they pass an **Challenging (+0) Cool** Test, they gain another +1 *Fatigued* Condition and the *Broken* Condition, both of which are only removed upon leaving the location.

The Evil Eye

CN: 6
Range: Willpower yards
Target: Special
Duration: Instant

You lock eyes with a single target, who must be looking at you. Perform an **Opposed Intimidate/Cool** Test, adding any SL from your casting roll to your result. Your opponent gains 1 *Fatigued* Condition per +2 SL by which you win. If you win by 6+ SL, your opponent gains the *Broken* Condition.

DARK MAGIC

The following provides two short lists of four Dark Magic spells.

LORE OF DAEMONOLOGY

The forbidden Lore of Daemonology is concerned with summoning, binding, and controlling Daemons, typically to empower the spellcaster. It is horrifically dangerous, usually leading to the Daemonologist's downfall as their soul is taken by the Ruinous Powers and a new Chaos Sorcerer is born.

Destroy Lesser Daemon

CN: 6
Range: Willpower yards
Target: 1
Duration: Willpower Bonus Rounds

Your spell disrupts the *Dhar* holding a target Daemon together, and draws it back to you. A target with the *Daemonic* Creature Trait and a lower Willpower than you loses Wounds equal to your Willpower Bonus, ignoring Toughness Bonus or Armour Points. In turn, you may increase one of your Characteristic by +10 for the duration as you siphon profane energies.

Detect Daemon

CN: 4
Range: Willpower yards
Target: Special
Duration: Instant

Your spell homes in on the daemonic influences in the surrounding area. You automatically know if there is a manifested

Daemon within range, be it summoned, bound into an artefact, possessing another, or similar.

Manifest Lesser Daemon

CN: 8
Range: Willpower Bonus yards
Target: Special
Duration: Willpower Bonus Rounds

You channel a sickening flow of *Dhar*, briefly forcing a rent into the fabric of reality. A Lesser Daemon immediately manifests through the rent (see page 335 for two examples of this: a Bloodletter or a Daemonette). Perform an **Opposed Channel (*Dhar*)/Willpower** Test with the Daemon. If successful, the Daemon will respond to one command issued by you, quite literally, then vanish (assuming the command is completed before the Duration ends). If failed, the Daemon immediately attacks.

Octagram

CN: 10
Range: Touch
Target: AoE (maximum, Willpower Bonus yards across)
Duration: Willpower minutes

Daubing an octagram to the floor, and marking it with unholy symbols, you ward against all daemonic influence. Those with the *Daemonic* Creature Trait cannot enter or leave the octagram unless their Willpower is more than twice yours.

LORE OF NECROMANCY

Necromancy is an ancient and bloody magic art concerned with mastering death and seeking immortality, often by carving up rotting corpses. Considered one of the foulest and most heretical of magics, few take to studying its fell secrets lightly, for the horrors of the dead, and the undead, cannot be underestimated.

Raise Dead

CN: 8
Range: Willpower yards
Target: AoE (Willpower Bonus yards)
Duration: Until sunrise

You channel a heavy flow of *Dhar* into bare earth, causing old bones to gather and rise. SL+1 Skeletons will claw upwards into the affected area at the end of the Round, which are organised as you prefer within the area of effect. They start with the *Prone* Condition. The summoned undead are entirely under your control and can perform simple orders as you command. If you are killed or gain an *Unconscious* Condition, the spell comes to an end and the summoned Undead collapse. For each +2 SL you score, you may summon an extra SL Skeletons.

Reanimate

CN: 8
Range: Willpower yards
Target: AoE (Willpower Bonus yards)
Duration: Until sunrise

You channel worming strands of thick *Dhar* before you, sinking it into corpses, reanimating that which was once dead. Reanimate Willpower Bonus + SL dead bodies (as Zombies) or skeletons (as Skeletons) within range. They start with the *Prone* Condition. The summoned Undead are entirely under your control and can perform simple orders as you command. If you die or gain an *Unconscious* Condition, the spell comes to an end and the reanimated corpses fall dead again. For each +2 SL you score, you may reanimate an extra Willpower Bonus +SL Skeletons or Zombies.

Screaming Skull

CN: 8
Range: Willpower yards
Target: Special
Duration: Instant

You shriek the high-pitched words of the spell and a large, black skull wreathed with greenish-purple fire forms before you, then flies forwards, screaming and cackling as it goes. The skull moves in a straight line for the spell range, following the contours of the land, passing through any obstacles in its way. *Screaming Skull* is a *magic missile* that only affects targets without the *Undead* Creature Trait, and has a Damage equal to your Willpower Bonus. Any suffering Wounds from the spell must pass a **Challenging (+0) Cool** Test or also take a *Broken* Condition.

Vanhel's Call

CN: 6
Range: Willpower yards
Target: Special
Duration: Instant

You manipulate complicated flows of *Dhar* into your targets, filling them with overwhelming energy. Intelligence Bonus targets with the *Undead* Trait gain a free Move *or* Action — you choose one or the other to affect *all* targets — this is taken the moment the spell is cast. For each +2 SL you score, you may invigorate an extra Intelligence Bonus targets.

CHAOS MAGIC

Three of the four Great Powers of Chaos have a unique Lore of Magic — only Khorne, the Blood God, who abhors treacherous magic and all it stands for, has no Lore of his own. One spell is provided here for each of the primary Chaos Lores, which can be added to provide flavour to your Chaos Cultists in addition to the Arcane Spells and the Lore of Daemonology.

LORE OF NURGLE

The Lore of Nurgle spreads foul disease and filth, mixing bloated excesses of the Jade Wind with whatever corruption comes to hand, then spewing it everywhere.

Stream of Corruption

CN: 9
Range: Special
Target: Special
Duration: Instant

Your maw distends horrifically before you vomit forth a foul stream of diseased filth and horror. Immediately make a Breath attack as if you had spent 2 Advantage to activate the *Breath* Creature Trait (see page 338). It counts as a *magic missile* with a Damage equal to your Toughness Bonus, and it ignores Armour Points. The attack also has the *Corrosive* and *Poison* Traits listed under the *Breath* Creature Trait. Further, should any targets take more than their Toughness Bonus in Wounds, they must pass a **Challenging (+0) Endurance** Test or contract *Blood Rot* (see page 186). For every +2 SL achieved, you may also increase Damage by +2.

LORE OF SLAANESH

The Lore of Slaanesh brings torture and excess, all splayed before the Prince of Pain and Pleasure for its eternal enjoyment, typically pressuring a perverse mix of the Amethyst, Gold, and Jade Winds into something twisted and exotic.

Acquiescence

CN: 5
Range: Willpower yards
Target: 1
Duration: Willpower Bonus Rounds

Your magic pierces deep within your target, flooding the soul with an acute awareness of their broken dreams. The target's Initiative Characteristic drops to 10, if it was not already lower, as the mind turns inwards. On the target's Turn, all movement is randomised as determined by the GM as the character bemoans life, lewdly telling all what should have been as hands are flung in the air. Further, the target can only perform an Action if a **Challenging (+0) Cool** Test is first passed; if failed, the Target is far too busy bemoaning what could have been to do anything else.

LORE OF TZEENTCH

Tzeentch is the Master of Magic, Treachery, and Lies. The Lore of Tzeentch epitomises this, as it boasts a multitude of powerful spells focussing upon change, all drawing heavily from the Grey, Amethyst, and Bright Winds.

Treason of Tzeentch

CN: 6
Range: Willpower yards
Target: 1
Duration: Willpower Bonus Rounds

You channel fine strands of traitorous mergings of the Winds of Magic directly into your target's mind, twisting motivations, undermining desires, and fanning fires of discontent. The target can no longer use Talents, and doesn't add Skill Advances when making Skill Tests, meaning the target only Tests against unmodified Characteristics.

• THE GAMEMASTER •

Being the Gamemaster (GM) is the best thing ever. While the Players are busy with their single, measly Character, you're in charge of the entire world! If you're a new GM this can be a little daunting, but don't worry, you'll get the hang of it quickly, and we'll walk you through the basics here.

The most important responsibility of a GM is to make sure everyone has fun, including you. You'll be juggling roles of storyteller, umpire, and host, but don't lose sight of the fact that the reason everyone is playing the game is to have a good time. Balance your storytelling with allowing Players spotlight time and autonomy in their actions. If a scene isn't working, wrap it up quickly and move on. Balance the game rules with everyone's enjoyment of the game — if something seems counter-intuitive or is taking too long, change it. Always focus on what your group finds fun.

You are the world. Everything the Players interact with comes from you. You provide the world they explore. Your descriptions tell them what they see, hear, touch, smell, and taste. You'll play the role of the people and creatures with which they interact. You describe the outcome of every action they take and determine how the game rules are applied.

You are the rules. Make sure you understand the rules so the game runs smoothly and quickly. Be familiar with the rulebook

so you can find what you need. Choose quickly if you are going to resolve an action with a GM decision or if you want the Player to make a Test. This choice will partly be a matter of personal style — do you and your Players like relying on the Character sheets to define what happens or do you prefer to save dice rolls for only the most important situations? Correctly and openly interpreting the results of Tests demonstrates to your Players that their actions have consequences, and that you are consistent and fair in your application of the rules.

You are the plot. Before the game you'll prepare the adventure, making sure you know what events are planned to take place, and who is involved in them. It is generally a good idea to have some contingency plans in place should the Players leap to the wrong conclusions and go off at a tangent (they will do this more often than you might think!). Make sure you have all the game information for the main characters in the adventure, along with anyone or anything the Characters might have to fight. Be familiar with the adventure's background and the area it takes place in, and you will be able to improvise effectively. You can also prepare some stock events to use in case improvisation is required.

You are the leader. Encourage good playing by making sure that everyone has a chance to participate, and that the game runs smoothly. Remind Players that rules discussions take place

outside the game, and that you need to be able to get on with running the game to achieve maximum fun! Be thoughtful and respectful of your Players. Be aware of content that might be uncomfortable for some people, for instance graphic violence, sex, or horror. Check it's okay before those subjects come up in a game. Justify your authority by being fair to everyone, consistent in how you apply the rules, and running the best Sigmar-blessed game this side of the Worlds Edge Mountains.

GENERAL ADVICE

There's a lot of advice on running games out there. It's a huge subject and requires much more space than we have here, so we're adding a lot of advice to the **Cubicle 7** website – keep checking back as we plan to keep building up that section. The rest of this chapter provides some specific advice for what to do at different stages of a game.

As a starter — or refresher for experienced GMs — here's a condensed list of things to think about:

- Get to know this book well.

- Give the players what they want from the game without ruining your own plans.

- Make sure new groups of Characters have reasons to be adventuring together.

- Consider how to handle or bypass content a player might not find to their taste.

- Bookmark sections you will be returning to often, such as **Chapter 8: Magic** if one of your players is a wizard.

- Be aware of plot devices and how to use them to good effect.

- Ensure the challenges you set your Players are achievable, and that any enemies that need to be defeated can be defeated.

- Intersperse some light relief into horror-heavy games.

- Decide which parts of the adventure should be easy and quickly resolved, and which should be the most dramatic and challenging.

- What parts of the adventure need to be successful to make the story satisfying, and how will you ensure they happen without making your players feel too railroaded?

- When it comes to the results of Tests, be firm but fair.

- Be ready to make a big deal of players using or gaining Fate and Resilience points.

- Make a list of descriptive phrases appropriate for the locations the adventure is taking place in, to help improvised scenes.

- If in doubt, err on the side of having fun.

- Give Characters challenges that require improvisation or creative thinking.

- You can't detail everyone the Characters meet, but a single feature — an accent, catchphrase or tic — helps make everyone memorable!

Rules Notes

As you play more games of **WFRP**, the rules will become increasingly familiar. To give you a head start, these points are worth initially bearing in mind:

- **Tests:** Use of the different methods of resolving actions (see page 150) give you considerable control over the pace of the game — use them!

- **Fortune Points:** Encourage your players to spend these during play or you will find cautious players repeatedly have several at the end of the session unused, and have probably failed some Tests they could have passed.

- **Advantage:** Advantage speeds up combat by adding momentum for winning each round. Remember all Advantage is lost when you lose a round, or if you are hit by ranged or magical attacks — Advantage is not as scary as it first appears, even if it stacks high. Should Characters become overwhelmed, they may wish to consider disengaging, then either fleeing or attacking from afar. Characters can also spend Resilience points to automatically win a round and eliminate any build-up of Advantage their foes might have secured.

- **Opposed Tests:** Almost all combat Tests are Opposed, meaning that someone always wins, even if both combatants effectively fail their individual Tests. Remember, the difference in SL will always secure a winner. This means even very poor combatants will be landing blows right from the outset — just without any skill or finesse.

- **No Opposition:** Should you find opponents who refuse to defend themselves for fear of rolling poorly in an Opposed Test, then clearly their Characters are doing nothing, meaning they count as Helpless (see page 162).

CHARACTER CREATION

Before your first WFRP game begins, the Players will need to create Characters, or choose one of the ready-made characters provided on the **Cubicle 7** website or the **WFRP Starter Set**. The ready-made Characters are already formed into a group and are ready to go, but if your Players are creating their own, you should guide them through the process.

Character Creation can take a while, so it can be worth devoting the first game session to it, so let the Players know this in advance to manage their expectations. You can take Players through each step of character creation, but Players having their own rulebooks can speed things up considerably. Guide new Players through how the different parts of their Character will be used in the game, and encourage Players to coordinate their choices so they can build a broadly capable group. A good spread of Classes gives both you and the Players more options during play. If the group has no spellcasters for example, you can't run adventures that require the Players follow magical clues.

Encourage Players to involve other Characters in their own Character's background and provide suggestions to help. This helps bind the group together and should make it easier for them to choose a Group Ambition. Avoid creating a group of disparate desperadoes who won't work together and never cooperate on anything. That gets old fast and can lead to unsatisfying gaming experiences.

The group should have a reason to stick together, work together, and be motivated to engage with the adventures awaiting them. A good way to make sure the group has this is to simply ask your Players to explain exactly why their Characters work together, and why they will adventure together in future. You may be surprised at just how inventive your Players can be.

Having a good idea of the adventures you have planned means you can weave connections to them into each Character's background. If you've got a smuggler in the group, and you know part of the forthcoming adventures involve a smuggling ring, work your smugglers into that Character's background. If a Chaos Cult is central to the adventure, perhaps decide that an important member of one Character's family will be a secret member of the cult. These personal details will make for a more involving game that really immerses the Players in the game world.

If your group are not cooperating, you can always try external motivations. For example: the promise of an incredible reward the Characters can't resist, or being 'asked' to do work by a powerful patron who won't take refusal kindly.

The Character creation phase is also a great place to discuss the kind of game everyone wants to play. Identifying content to avoid — for instance graphic violence, sex, or horror — is just as important as determining the game your Players will enjoy. Some people might not be comfortable talking about this in front of others, so make sure you give everyone the chance to communicate with you privately about it, and don't ask for the reasons why — the preference is enough. If in any doubt, err on the side of caution, and remember the goal is for everyone to have fun.

AT THE TABLE

During sessions where you are running games of **WFRP** as the GM, here's what you'll be doing:

1. Set the scene

At the start of the game, the GM should give a summary of what has happened in the adventure so far — in the first session of an adventure this will instead be some background to the adventure about to begin. It's the recap part of a TV series: 'Previously on **WFRP**…': keep it short and sweet.

Next, you'll describe where the Characters are and what is happening around them. Provide immediate prompts to action — make sure that the game gets off to an exciting start. End with an event or question that means the Players have to get involved right away — even a simple knock on their door, or thrown jar of ale arcing gently across the taproom towards them immediately leads to action!

2. Listen to the Players

The Players will react to the scene-setting and will interpret what is going on, often in a way that us GMs would describe as 'interesting'. As GM, you already know the plot of the adventure, but the Players will need to puzzle it out, perhaps with a false start or two. Don't panic if they head off in the wrong direction — they'll get there in the end, and you'll have a lot of fun along the way.

So, resolve their immediate actions in the game while listening carefully to how they are going to react to the wider plot to give you thinking time for the next part. Make sure each Player has the opportunity to contribute — actively ask any Player who hasn't yet participated what their Character is going to do.

3. Describe the consequences of the Players' actions

You'll react to the Player's actions depending on what they are doing. If they are talking to one of the character's you've described as being present in the scene, you'll respond to them in the role of that person. If they are taking actions that require Tests to resolve, you'll decide which Skill is being tested, any modifiers on the Test, and interpret the outcome — what happens because of that action. Sometimes this will be the start of a sequence of events, which other Players might join, or it may be a simple action that is quickly resolved. Again, make sure everyone has an opportunity to do something and contribute to the game. Ask quieter Players directly to make sure they get a go.

This Player-directed phase of the game can go on for quite some time, as you all take turns to move the story forward, and the GM is largely in a reactive role. Even experienced GMs can be amazed at the tangents Players can pursue, and some very memorable games come from this improvised style of play.

4. Describe events from the ongoing plot

While the Player-directed phase is going on, the GM will be aware of the adventure plot circling in the Aethyr. At the appropriate times, events from the plot will come crashing in. The Players will now be reacting to events before formulating their new plan and pursuing it in their inevitably haphazard style. These moments can be used as course-corrections, giving additional clues on what is really happening, and helping get Players back on track.

Be careful not to be too blunt or obvious with these events however — no-one likes to feel like they are being forced towards an inevitable conclusion. Allow Players the autonomy to really mess things up, but also don't be afraid to modify your plot on the hoof if it makes for a more enjoyable game.

TRAVEL

Travelling in the Old World can be dangerous. Brigands, mutants, and beasts lurk in the shadows, an ever-present threat, perhaps joined by those specifically out to thwart the Players' actions. Some parts of the Empire have been corrupted by magic, Chaos, Necromancy, or worse, and can easily consume the unwary traveller. Even the weather poses a threat!

It's up to you how you want to represent the dangers of travel in your game. Sometimes you'll just want to get on with the adventure and deal with journeys with a simple description of how long the journey was, and the key points along the way. Most journeys will either be by road or by river, with road the more dangerous, and cheaper, option.

Travel by Road

The roads of the Reikland are often crude but reliable. The routes between major cities are relatively safe and well-maintained. However, far-flung routes can be little more than muddy tracks. Regardless of the quality, all roads need to be maintained, so most are tolled.

There is an extensive network of coach routes throughout the province. The busiest routes have coaches running several times per day. The many Coaching Houses of the Reikland are in fierce competition, so the prices are often reasonable and reliability is good. The Four Seasons is the biggest coach company, and is represented along all the major routes.

Roadside inns are often placed at the convenience of the Coaching Houses. Therefore, journeying by foot, especially away from the major routes, runs the risk of not reaching a safe place to rest before nightfall.

Travel by River

River journeys are often straightforward and perhaps even relaxing. However, this relies on finding a boat going to and from convenient locations. Dedicated passenger barges only travel between the major towns and cities, but can be bribed or persuaded to drop people off along the way. Getting to more obscure locations usually requires hitching a ride with a cargo boat, which can be difficult for large parties.

Travel Prices

The prices listed in Travel Costs do not include meals, lodging, or fodder, although coaches and passenger boats usually charge for the whole package for longer journeys. Package prices can be worked out by combining travel with food and boarding prices. On some ferries, lodging is not required, as passengers sleep on the vessel, either on deck or in a private cabin.

Cargo barge travel-costs should be individually haggled with barge masters. Often, such passage can be secured for a greatly reduced price, or even for free, if the passenger is willing to work and they know what they're doing.

High class travel is available and *de rigueur* among the nobility, and can cost many times the listed price, typically ten times or more. Opulent passenger vessels ply between the great cities of the Empire, like the famous Emperor Luitpold plying the River Talebec between Altdorf and Talabheim.

TRAVEL COSTS

All the costs listed here are per mile travelled, and are loose guides only. Faster coaches and barges generally cost twice as much. Slower examples cost as little as half as much. Increase or decrease speed by +/− 1 for faster or slower examples.

Transport	Movement	Cost	Distance
COACH	6		
Inside		−/2	per mile
Outside		−/1	per mile
BARGE	8		
Cabin		−/5	per mile
Deck		−/2	per mile
CAB	6	−/3	per district
FERRY	4	−/1	per 20 yards

Travel Times

Use Movement to determine travel speed in miles per hour. So, if a party's slowest Movement was 3, it would travel at approximately 3 miles per hour.

Taking into account rests, necessary stops, and a typical topography, a party can travel the equivalent of 6 hours a day without requiring Endurance Tests. If travelling faster or farther, give a *Fatigue* Condition to those failing this Test, with extra *Fatigue* if Encumbered (see page 293).

Barge speed can increase or decrease by up to 30% if going downstream or upstream, as you determine is appropriate.

Travel Events

Whether detailing daily travel or simply choosing to allow the party to pay an appropriate fee and then arrive at their chosen destination, every now and again it's good to throw in some travel events. It's an opportunity to show off a different aspect of the Old World, or to give a change of pace to the adventure.

An intrigue-focused game can sometimes do with a clearly defined 'goodies vs. baddies' Beastmen attack. A tense, bleak session can benefit from a night's entertainment sharing camp with a travelling circus. Further, you can work these encounters into your ongoing narrative if you wish.

Finding the burned-out caravans of the circus later in the journey is a poignant way of making the antagonists' actions personal. Travel events are also great for foreshadowing events to come, or reinforcing the themes of an adventure.

It is up to you how much of an issue you want these travel events to be for your players. Some could simply consist of a brief description, while others could form the basis of an entire session of play. Some GMs prefer to roll 1d10 per day of travel and have an event occur on the roll of an 8 (signifying the 8-pointed symbol of Chaos — something unexpected and random has occurred), others like a single event for each journey of a day or more. This is left for you to determine, though if you are playing a printed adventure by **Cubicle 7** that includes a journey, suggested events and travel times will be included. So, the following table can be used as you prefer, and presumes a single event for the journey travelled.

1d10	Event
1	**Restful Journey:** The journey is blessedly uneventful, the Characters get good rest, the scenery is particularly inspiring, and perhaps they meet an NPC healer or helpful priest. The Characters can heal all Wounds and recover all *Fatigued* Conditions.
2	**How Interesting!:** A chance encounter on the road with other travellers, a particularly good inn or shrine, or an intriguing ancient ruin gives a wonderful story to share.
3	**Now That's Useful!:** The Characters find out something relevant to their adventure — gossip, a lost message, a sight they weren't meant to witness, or similar.
4	**Tiring Journey!:** The route is blocked. A bridge could be down, a river blocked or road flooded, or some other insurmountable obstacle. One Character makes a **Average (+20) Outdoor Survival** Test to find a good alternative route, otherwise everyone arrives a day late, with a *Fatigued* Condition.
5	**Pursued!:** An enemy picks up the Characters' trail and has to be dealt with or put off the scent before they can reach their destination. If they don't have an obvious enemy yet, look to the Characters' backgrounds — there will be something in there somewhere. The confrontation could be violent unless they can talk their way out of it, and losing their tail could add days to their journey.
6	**Thieves!:** Somehow the Characters get robbed. Perhaps it was someone travelling with them, sharing their campfire for the night or just a brief conversation on the road. Do they stop to chase down their belongings or write it off as a risk of the adventurous life?
7	**Not Them Again!:** A rival or other source of annoyance plagues the Characters on their journey. Play this for laughs but make them genuinely annoying and a recurring minor bane of the Character's lives. Never enough to fall to violence, but close. They could be a rival guild member obsessed with 'winning' over a member of the group, or a coach passenger with an especially irritating demeanour.
8	**Bad Influence!:** The Characters encounter someone who appears to help them but has sinister intentions. That bad-smelling guy who knows a shortcut through the Garden of Morr and insists you go first. The charming old aristocrat who invites you to stay for dinner in her ancestral home. The scruffy woman who knows where to find all the 'best' mushrooms. Have fun!
9	**Even Nature Hates You!:** The Characters find themselves in danger from nature. Deadly animals, lightning storms, disease, insects, you name it. This could result in violence, or in them receiving a Condition, or in a small but vicious encounter when they choose the wrong shepherd's hut as a shelter.
10	**Attacked!:** The Characters are attacked on their journey. It could be an unlucky encounter relevant to the area they are travelling through (Beastmen in the deep forest, for instance) or something planned by their opponents (hired thugs to stop the Characters reaching their destination). If they fail a **Routine (+20) Perception** Test, they may even be ambushed!

You might like to give Players the opportunity to avoid nasty events with a successful Perception Test, or Outdoor Survival, or whatever other Test makes sense at the time. If they are travelling in paid-for transportation, you might decide that gives them help in overcoming any adversities.

AFTER THE GAME

Try to end your session in a narratively satisfying way, either with a moment of resolution, revelation, mystery, or the dreaded cliffhanger, leaving your Players waiting until the next session before learning what happens to their Characters.

Awarding XP

At the end of every session you should award your players XP. This is your opportunity to reward your Players for cooperation, good roleplaying and making the experience fun. Remember that it's better to use the carrot than the stick — don't punish players who didn't cooperate, reward those who did. People will soon get the message!

Additional bonuses of 25-50 XP could be awarded for excellent roleplaying, teamwork, or otherwise getting in the spirit of things. If you are playing a published adventure from **Cubicle 7**, it will list suggested XP awards for every session.

Recovering Fate and Resilience

A Player spending a point of Fate or Resilience is a significant event. Characters generally have few of these points, and they are powerful, so they should be spent wisely. After all, spending Fate or Resilience will also reduce the number of Fortune and Resolve points a character has available.

Awarding Players Fate and Resilience points is likewise a rare and special occurrence. The end of a long adventure or campaign of significant importance could be rewarded with a Fate point. Or a Character achieving something of extraordinary personal significance could be awarded a Resilience point. If you are playing printed adventures from **Cubicle 7**, obvious points to award Fate points, and sometimes Resilience points, are included.

AWARDING EXPERIENCE POINTS

Normal Session		End of Adventure		End of Campaign	
Performance	XP award	Performance	XP award	Performance	XP award
Poor	75	Poor	100	Poor	150
Good	100	Good	150	Good	200
Exceptional	125	Exceptional	200	Exceptional	250

• GLORIOUS REIKLAND •

To his Imperial Majesty, Emperor Karl-Franz the First, by the Grace of the Gods, Elector Count and Grand Prince of Reikland, Prince of Altdorf, Count of the West March, Defender of Sigmar's Faith, do I commend this text, an examination of his most illustrious realm, the Grand Princedom of Reikland, heartland of Our Holy Empire. Long may he rule!

Herein learn of the mightiest province of the Empire, and of its hard-working people who are united by the worship of the God-King Sigmar. Admire the Elector Counts of the Reikland who have led the glorious Empire for almost a century, and their generous patronage that enriches our homeland beyond measure. Wonder at the Reikland's impressive canal network, extensive roadworks, sophisticated farming, and its rapidly developing mercantile class, all of which confirm the Reikland as a true jewel of the Empire.

Marvel at this richest, most cosmopolitan of all imperial realms, and see that it is a cultural, magical, and academic powerhouse without par, attracting the most impressive artisans, wizards, and scholars to its many learned institutions, cementing its reputation as the greatest domain of the Old World.

Truly, to be born a Reiklander is to be born blessed by the Gods Themselves. Give thanks to Sigmar and be praised.

– The words of Holy Mother Halma Habermann of Sigmar
– Recorded faithfully by the humble scribe Melistius of the Order of the Anvil in 2510 IC

Standing proud in the heart of the Old World, the Reikland is the richest and most powerful of the Empire's grand provinces. Known for its engineers, wizards, and merchants, and for being the birthplace of the Cult of Sigmar, it is a realm of soaring mountains, snaking rivers, dark forests, and powerful trading centres. From his throne in the city of high-spired Altdorf, Emperor Karl-Franz I rules not only the Reikland, but all the Empire that lies beyond.

THE LIE OF THE LAND

The Reikland lies in the shadow of the forbidding Grey Mountains, and its lowlands are entirely forested save for cleared regions around the grand province's multitude of prosperous towns and villages. It has no coastline, but the Reik — the largest river in the Old World that defines most of the Reikland's twisting eastern and northern borders — is so wide and deep an entire navy of warships and merchant vessels plies its length.

Much of the land near the Reik is waterlogged and marshy, with long stretches of bogs, swamps, and dangerous mud plains, the largest of which is the Grootscher Marsh on the border with the Wasteland to the west. Farther inland, the Reikland climbs upwards to the craggy Skaag Hills and the haunted Hägercrybs, two forested uplands hiding isolated regions nigh-on untouched by human hand. The forests eventually give way as the land rises towards the Grey Mountains, the Reikland's natural border with Bretonnia to the south, and opens up to a wide plain of fertile foothills and open grassland known as the Vorbergland.

THE MOUNTAINS, FOOTHILLS, AND VORBERGLAND

The Reikland is a rugged realm, its undulating forests broken by peaks, crags, and ridges, many topped by ruined castles and watchtowers from previous, war-torn eras. Rising above this multitude of minor ranges are the Hägercrybs and the Skaag Hills, two highland regions in central and northern Reikland, their heavily fortified mines responsible for much of the realm's recent prosperity. Farther south, the trees thin out to the exposed plains and foothills of the fertile Vorbergland that lie between the Reikwald forest and the dangerous Grey Mountains, peaks that offer enormous wealth and danger in equal measure.

The Grey Mountains

The forbidding peaks of the Grey Mountains are riddled with crumbling tunnels and topped with ruined skybridges from the time when Dwarfs ruled the region. But that era has passed, and only a handful of determined clans remain to defend their ancestral holds, with recently reclaimed Karak Azgaraz and towering Karak Ziflin being two of the largest still standing.

The mountains and the tunnels beneath them are now overrun with Orcs and Goblins, Mountain Trolls, Skaven, and worse. While this makes the Grey Mountains especially dangerous, many claim the fallen Dwarf holds hide treasures lost to time, so the foolhardy and desperate are drawn to the ancient halls like moths to a flame. Few survive their greed.

Clinging precariously to the craggy edge of the Grey Mountains, the southern lords of the Reikland have sunk many mines seeking to extract the significant mineral and metal wealth of the range. These are protected by lone watchtowers and high fortresses that stand guard against attack from the mountains, each surrounded by the rubble of older fortifications that failed.

So high is the glacial spine of the Grey Mountains that it is all but impassable, forming a near impenetrable border between the Reikland and the Bretonnian duchies to the south-east. Only two reliable passes pierce the frozen heights: the well-defended Axe-Bite Pass guarded by the fortresses of Helmgart and Monfort, and the winding Grey Lady Pass leading from Ubersreik to Parravon. Both passes are heavily patrolled and taxed, leading some impoverished merchants and smugglers to hire mountain guides to lead them across lesser passes such as the Crooked Corridor or Durak Way, an undertaking few would recommend.

The Hägercrybs

Dominating the centre of the Reikland, the mist-shrouded Hägercrybs extend from the Princedom of Altdorf in the north all the way to the Freiburg of Ubersreik in the south, and are so heavily forested that no road pierces through their heights from east to west, resulting in long journeys for those traveling from one side to the other.

The foothills are mostly populated by sheep and their shepherds, but, antiquarians claim, the Hägercrybs were once the sacred burial ground of the Unberogens, the Human tribe of Sigmar Himself. Supporting this, ancient cairns can be seen rising from clearings on many of the highlands, some of which are also marked by looming menhirs. Perhaps because of these, the Hägercrybs have a foul reputation for being haunted, and few are willing to stray too deep into its forests. It is said those who do encounter thick fogs rising from ancient barrows, with moans of the dead echoing from within. Locally, such talk is nervously dismissed as the ravings of shepherds drunk on too much hard cider, for the alternative is to believe tales of ancient kings hungry for the blood of the living.

Ignoring such talk, lords of the Hägercrybs repeatedly order mines be sunk into the hills in the search of rare metals and minerals. Most fail, their miners never seen again, but a handful are successful, and have brought considerable wealth to the area.

The Skaag Hills

The rocky Skaag Hills lie to the west of the River Bögen and run along the southern bank of the Reik before falling beneath the trees of the Duchy of Gorland. Near the centre, the Reikwald recedes from the stony crags and layers of stratified rock rise to the scree-laden highlands of the Prie Ridge. A single road crosses the gentler slopes of the Skaag Hills to the south, starting at Trosreut in the shadow of Castle Grauenberg and wending its way through to Holthausen, but many minor tracks and trails also cross the region, most of which started as goat tracks.

Once, the hillsides were bustling with small mines boasting rich veins of silver and iron. Down through the centuries most of these played out, leaving many abandoned settlements, many of which the forest reclaimed. Locals now approach such ruins cautiously, for hunters, outlaws, and far more sinister folk are said to make use of what intact buildings remain.

The Vorbergland

Between the threatening peaks of the Grey Mountains and the deep forests of the Reikwald lies the Vorbergland, a hilly region extending the length of the Reikland known for its fertile valleys, rolling grasslands, and windswept plains.

The productive south-eastern provinces around Böhrn, Ubersreik, Stimmigen, and Dunkelberg are known locally as Suden Vorbergland, and are the most heavily cultivated regions of the Reikland. They are peppered with many flourishing towns, villages, farms, and vineyards, and are often referred to as 'Ranald's Garden' for the vast quantities of wine they produce for export.

Further west, the Vorbergland is tormented by frequent Orc and Goblin attacks from the mountains, meaning much of the land is sparsely populated, little more than a hunting ground for wild animals and monsters from the peaks. This makes the local baronies and duchies a popular destination for game hunters and natural historians from the Imperial Zoo seeking to capture rare creatures, though only the unwise travel this region without a heavy guard and knowledgeable guide.

Drachenberg

Soaring high above central Vorbergland, its base wrapped by the shimmering River Bögen, the twisting peak known as the Drachenberg can be seen for miles around. Whenever trouble arises, the nearby townsfolk of Wheburg cast an eye towards the mountain and make the comet sign of Sigmar to ward evil, for Drachenberg has a fell reputation. Its name roughly translates to 'Dragon Peak' and, true to its name, the mountain has long been a favoured haunt of the great beasts, as well as to other monstrous creatures such as Basilisks, Wyverns, and Manticores.

The immense Red Dragon, Caledair — the 'Scythe of Fire' — once made her lair in caves near the peak of the mountain, and hunted across the fields of the Vorbergland for uncounted generations. While she has not been seen for more than a century, none can say for certain if she is truly gone or if she sleeps in the mountain still.

The Drachenberg is treacherous, with steep sides that thwart climbers, and no easy routes to its sheer summit. Though trees clog its foothills, they are sparse along its upper slopes and the top soil is very loose, which has caused more than one imprudent climber to slide free to a broken death. Even so, the brave and the foolish still attempt to climb the Drachenberg, for who knows what treasures may lie hidden within its unknown heights?

The Grim, Dark Forests

The widespread forests of the Reikland are regarded as some of the safest in the Empire, but stray from the busy rivers and tree-lined roads and such impulsive talk is soon forgotten. Uncharted miles of towering oak, pine, elm, and beech hide much more than desperate bandits and wild animals. And the deeper one goes, the more dangerous it is.

The Reikwald

The Reikwald blankets almost all the Reikland outside the Vorbergland, only thinning around the jagged Skaag Hills or where it is cleared by the towns and villages lining the Reik river and its many tributaries. Most travellers through the region prefer the relative safety of river travel to journeying along uncertain roads, and with good reason; the Reikwald is a favoured haunt of outcasts, cut-throats, and other lawless folk. While all major routes are patrolled by road wardens, their numbers are too few and the roads too long, so it's not uncommon to encounter upturned coaches and other signs of banditry. The majority of the open clearings and abandoned ruins from past wars are claimed as camps by outlaws or by one of the herds of Beastmen roaming the deeper wood, and forays to clear these isolated places by regiments of the Reikland State Army are not uncommon.

In most parts, the Reikwald's canopy is not so overgrown as to block sunlight, but its depths are frequently gloomy and heavy fogs are common, especially along the marshier stretches of the river Reik. Scholars claim before the Empire was founded the Unberogen tribe of Humans ranged across this misty forest alongside older tribes whose names are now lost to memory. Concentric rings of carved standing stones called 'oghams' still exist from this era, though many are overgrown and almost impossible to find without a guide. Isolated communities still following ancient ways — old beliefs said to predate the coming of Sigmar — are said to hold such sites sacred. Intellectuals from the Colleges of Magic postulate terrible battles were once fought for these ancient, megalithic sites, and it's not uncommon to find richer wizards funding explorations into the Reikwald's depths to learn more about the magical stones.

Bloodpine Woods

South of Altdorf an outcrop of pine trees grows down the southern face of the magical Amber Hills and spills into the depths of the Reikwald. Called bloodpine for its deep-maroon wood, the lumber here is greatly desired by the artisans of Altdorf, and is most often used to produce exquisite furniture destined for the high-class markets of Marienburg and Nuln. Recently, bloodpine has become hard to source, for the Bloodpine Woods are plagued by Forest Goblins of the Spiderclaw tribe who've managed to tame a handful of swift-moving Giant Spiders. Few dare to work there now, for those attempting to cut the trees simply disappear, their cries echoing from the mists high in the trees before suddenly falling silent. This has, of course, only served to increase the value of bloodpine, which has deeply enraged purchasers, several of whom have taken to hiring mercenaries and private parties to clear the Goblins, figuring it is cheaper to throw bodies at the problem than pay more for their new filing cabinet.

The Grissenwald

The south-easternmost end of the Reikwald branches southwards along the Stirland border and thins out as it heads upriver towards the City-State of Nuln. This wide section of the forest is known locally as the Grissenwald, a tight woodland packed with distorted trees and twisted undergrowth, the depths of which are said to be swarming with Beastmen, Witches, and tribes of feral Mutants. Because of this, most local woodsmen travel in groups and seldom stay outdoors come nightfall, and its commonplace to find fluttering bills posted on roadside trees offering rewards for the retrieval of lost family and friends from the bowels of the forest.

THE RIVERS, CANALS, AND LAKES

The many rivers spilling from the glacial lakes and waterfalls of the Grey Mountains down to the Reik are central to the Reikland's economic success. Barges brimful with merchandise navigate the largest of these rivers, bringing diverse goods to the capital of Altdorf, many of which are then shipped elsewhere in the Empire or sold down the river to Marienburg.

To further support the Reikland's wide-ranging mercantile ambitions, the richer noble and merchant houses invest in extensive canals planned and constructed by Altdorf's famous engineers. The impact of these impressive waterways is undeniable, with trade goods moving faster than ever before, but they require maintenance and protection, both of which are costly. To ensure the wreckers and river pirates the canals attract have minimal impact, road wardens, guards, and riverwardens are employed as required, but frequently these are little better than the criminals they purportedly thwart.

The Reik

The Reik carries more traffic and trade than all the other rivers in the Old World combined. Indeed, so massive is the river that almost half the fresh water of the Old World flows down its length, for it not only drains all the Reikland with its many tributaries, but most of the Empire beyond. By the time the Reik flows into the Reikland, it is already so wide it frequently appears more lake than river, leaving it impossible to bridge using standard engineering methods. As this immense watercourse approaches Altdorf to meet the dark waters of the Talabec, both rivers split into a complex network of channels that spread outwards to form the foggy Altdorf Flats. Many of the thinner distributaries caused by this are bridgeable, ensuring Altdorf is a natural centre for trade as it is the only place where the Reik can be crossed on foot for many hundreds of miles. This single fact has secured Altdorf's dominance of the area, both militarily and fiscally.

Beyond the Altdorf Flats, the boggy channels reconverge and the Reik begins its long journey westwards to the sea. By this point, it is so wide the opposite bank sometimes slips into mist, and is so deep that even the largest sea-faring vessel can navigate without fear. Resultingly, warships of the Imperial Navy, some so large to have crews out-numbering the populations of smaller towns, not only patrol these waters, but are built there, most launching from the Reiksport, a deep-water harbour built on the shores of Altdorf. Rocky islands are common in this last stretch, most of which are secured with ancient fortresses, overridden by river pirates, or abandoned completely, boasting nothing more than a handful of old smugglers' coves.

The Bögen

The people of Bögenhafen claim Bögenauer, their town's patron deity, is responsible for the commerce-blessed state of the Bögen. A relatively placid river with a clear, smooth, but not overly swift flow, the Bögen readily allows traffic to sail upriver nearly as easily as down. Its great depth allows larger river going vessels to navigate safely from the Reik all the way to Bögenhafen. Though its source lies deep in the freezing peaks of the Grey Mountains, the Bögen turns warm as it flows through the hilly Vorberland, which frequently causes heavy mists to gather along its banks. Most evenings, fingers of roiling fog rise from the Bögen, wrapping tendrils about nearby settlements and the surrounding Reikwald. This is frequently thick enough to obscure vision, so thieves, smugglers, and worse use it to conceal their nocturnal activities.

The Grünberg Canal

The Grünberg canal is a recent addition to the waterways of the Reikland. Commissioned by Emperor Luitpold III as part of an extensive dowry paid to the previous Baron of Grünburg, it was completed in 2506IC and has seen heavy use ever since. The canal bypasses the treacherous shallows of the Reiker Marshes overlooked by Castle Reikguard, and it now takes much of the river Teufel's barge traffic heading for Altdorf. Grünburg's walls protect the tollhouse on the south end of the canal, and any barge wishing to pass it must pay a tax based on the length of the vessel entering the canal system. Queues are common at first light and dusk, but otherwise the tollhouse sees infrequent business. At the north end there is a lock-keeper's house on the outskirts of Prieze that doubles as a barracks and stables for the twelve road wardens paid to patrol the canal path and help any barges as required. This help typically comes in the form of impromptu protection taxes, which if not paid leave the offending barge open to bandit attacks. Attacks that inevitably follow for any who refuse to pay.

The Teufel

The Teufel flows down from the mountains to Ubersreik, then northwards to the Reik through Auerswald and Grünburg. Its waters have a distinctly reddish hue caused by iron deposits in the mud and silt, though storytellers suggest it's the unending wars between the Grey Mountain Dwarfs and Goblins that have permanently stained the river red. A great deal of rain feeds into the Teufel and it regularly overflows, especially in spring, frequently flooding its mud-filled waters deep into the surrounding forest. Inns — often built high to avoid floodwater — are common along the Teufel, as are bandits, since much of the river runs through the Reikwald. Road wardens regularly patrol the banks of the Teufel and they are not fond of any that linger without good reason.

The Vorbergland Canals

The Vorbergland Canals are an engineering marvel. Commissioned by the previous Archduke of Upper Teufel in conjunction with merchant houses from Nuln and Marienburg, the canals are the pride of the south, carrying trade from Wissenland across the Vorbergland and back again. Comprised of five canals connecting five major tributaries of the Reik, the system links Nuln through to Carroburg, skipping the high taxes of Altdorf completely.

Recently, the Dwarfs of Karak Azgaraz sent delegations to the lords of Suden Vorbergland demanding the canals be shut, claiming old treaties from centuries past were being broken by an unacceptably large display of shoddy workmanship. This has caused an uproar from graduates of the Imperial Engineers' School who see the steam locks and clever water-pumps as a pinnacle of human engineering.

The Weissbruck Canal

Connecting the Bögen and Reik rivers — bypassing Middenland's Carroburg taxes in the process — the Weissbruck canal sees steady traffic year-round as trade flows to and from Altdorf. A toll to use the canal is paid once at whatever end a vessel enters. The canal is 25-feet wide, with frequent berthing points and numerous places to stay along its length.

Local bargees do not readily discuss it with strangers, but there are many unusual stories whispered about the canal. Supposedly, the Dwarf engineers that designed it unearthed pre-Unberogen artefacts when they first dug the waterway, and things have never been right in the area since. Some even swear that should Morrsleib — the smaller of the two moons — be full, one can sail the canal north to somewhere other than the Reik…

THE CURSED AND FETID MARSHLANDS

Although Middenland to the north claims many famous marshlands — such as the Furdienst, Midden Marshes, and Shadensumpf — the river banks of the Reikland are no less waterlogged, frequently giving way to fens, mires, and dangerous mud plains, especially down the length of mighty River Reik. The largest of these is the Grootscher Marsh on the border with the Wasteland, but many other examples exist, such as the Altdorf Flats, the Reiker Marshes, and the Uhland Bogs.

Grootscher Marsh

The largest wetland of the Reikland, the Grootscher Marsh spreads out on both banks of the Reik. It extends some fifty miles into the Reikland and Middenland from the border with the Wasteland, and is considered by many to be a cursed place, for it is the site of one of the Empire's most famous military defeats of the last century: The Battle of Grootscher Marsh, where the Wasteland secured its independence from imperial rule.

In modern times, the Grootscher Marsh remains the foul-smelling fenland it always was, filled with ill-sounding birds and infested with River Trolls. In leaner years, when meat cannot be found for their rotting larders, the Trolls grow hungry and rumour holds they slip into the Reik to pluck the unwary from passing ships. Being sent to clear out the Grootscher Marsh is considered one of the worst punishment details imaginable by the State Armies of the Reikland; even the hardiest soldiers hesitate when ordered there.

Travellers on the Reik occasionally report the sounds of strange, ominous horns echoing through the thick fogs that frequently coalesce across the marsh, and wise locals note Trolls don't make use of such. Old hands on the Reik agree, and then swiftly change the subject…

SHROOM BOOM

Physicians, apothecaries, and scholars all pay high prices for the multitude of rare mushrooms and unusual plants that only grow in the perilous Cursed Marsh about the city of Marienburg. However, several crops of Daemon's Tand, Rood Puffball, and Dodeshors Polypore, three of the most valuable Wastelander fungi, have recently been discovered growing in the murk of the Grootscher Marsh. Sensing heavy profits, Klaes Adaans, an ever-frowning merchant lodging in the village of Oberseert overlooking the marsh, is hiring mushroom-pickers willing to brave the wetlands. This brings increased activity that not only attracts hungry River Trolls to the area, but also Goblins keen to capture them. Klaes cares little for such trivialities, and certainly won't mention them; all he wants is a steady crop of lucrative fungus. Those with stern hearts and keen eyes can reap real rewards here... or become meat for a Troll's larder.

Altdorf Flats

The rivers Reik and Talabec split around the city of Altdorf into hundreds of shifting channels, black-soiled mudflats, and marshes that spread north and south of the great city. Known as the Altdorf Flats, these wide wetlands are dominated by rushes and reeds, and are notorious for their foul stench and slurping, River-Troll-infested bogs. Some twenty miles west of Altdorf, the snaking channels converge again into the wide River Reik, where the waters flow further westwards to the Princedom of Carroburg.

The flats are crossed by six primary causeways that fan from the fertile farmlands immediately surrounding Altdorf. Each causeway is punctuated by several stone bridges, some of which are Dwarf-wrought and date from the Time of Sigmar. Their roads are ever-busy with coaches and merchant trains coming to and from the capital, so are heavily patrolled by road wardens. Similarly, the marshy waterways are a haven for smugglers looking to circumvent Altdorf's heavy tolls and taxes, so riverwarden and Shipswords are a frequent sight plying the unsure waters, seeking criminals and driving back larger marsh monsters.

Reiker Marshes

Lying between the Reiker Heights and the Hohesesienen Hills at the sluggish confluence of the River Reik and the River Teufel, the Reiker Marshes are notoriously treacherous, and inexperienced captains frequently run aground in its deceptively shallow waters. Tattered flags and corroded signposts mark the most perilous sections, but these are woefully insufficient. River guides locally known as 'huffers' are available to guide boats through the waters for a reasonable price, most of whom gather in the towns of Prieze and Babenborn on the Reik, and in significantly fewer numbers in Buxhead on the Teufel. The waters are at their most dangerous in the five-mile stretch at the end of the Teufel where it meets the Reik. Locally called 'Leopold's Folly' after the emperor who tried, and failed, many times to dredge the red-silted waters in order to make it safe for deep-drafted ships, wise barge captains avoid it completely, preferring to pay tolls to pass through the Grünberg Canal rather than risk their crew and cargo.

Uhland Bogs

A windswept peatland lying to the south of the County of the West March, the mossy Uhland Bogs are pierced through by the Westerfluss, the river that forms the natural border between the Wasteland and the Reikland. Towers of peat cut from the bog can be found stacked in the small villages near the mire, where dried blocks are used to fuel local fires in winter or shipped downriver to be sold along the Reik. In the south-west depths of the bog a number of ancient, carved stones rise from the sodden land, drawing local cultists of Rhya and older deities to worship during important equinoxes. One group of these stones, called the Crowstones, has a particularly foul reputation, and the surrounding bog is permanently blackened. Locals warn never to travel to the stones near the festival days of Geheimistag or Hexenstag, for they claim crows gather in impossible numbers and unspeakable things rise from the bog to wreak terror upon the living.

TIMELINE OF THE REIKLAND

Being a summary of the major events concerning the history of the Grand Province of Reikland.

c. -500 IC

The Unberogen tribe of Humans settle the land where Altdorf now lies, and begin fortifying the area. It will be sacked many times by rival tribes, Beastmen, Orcs, Goblins, and other vile creatures. Nevertheless, the site is strategically important at the confluence of the Reik and Talabec, and a mixture of conquest and trade helps the settlement flourish. Soon, scholars claim, the fortified town is known as the 'rich village', or Reichsdorf. As centuries pass, this becomes Reikdorf, with the surrounding land called the Reikland.

-30 IC

A twin-tailed comet streaks through the sky, heralding the birth of Sigmar to Chief Björn of the Unberogen tribe in Reikdorf. The comet leads a crazed warparty of Orcs to Sigmar's birthplace, and his mother, Griselda, is killed in the attack, leaving Sigmar with a life-long hatred of Greenskins.

-15 IC

A merchant-train from Karaz-a-Karak is ambushed by Orcs, and they capture King Kurgan Ironbeard. Sigmar rescues the king, and in return is named a *dawonger*, Dwarf-friend, and given the king's greatest heirloom, the magical warhammer Ghal-Maraz.

-8 IC

After his father dies, Sigmar becomes chief of the Unberogen tribe.

-7 IC

Sigmar realises the threat the Greenskins pose is far too much for his tribe to tackle alone, so he starts a campaign to bring all the surrounding Human tribes under his rule.

-2 IC

After several years of warfare and diplomacy, Sigmar binds twelve of the human tribes under his rule and allies himself with several more.

-1 IC

The First Battle for Black Fire Pass. The largest horde of Orcs and Goblins the world has seen is defeated by Humans and Dwarfs led by High Chief Sigmar and King Kurgan, ending the centuries-long Goblin Wars.

0 IC

Sigmar is crowned emperor over the chiefs of the twelve tribes and the Empire is born. The Dwarf Runesmith Alaric the Mad is commissioned to create twelve runeswords, one for each of the tribal chiefs, as a symbol of their office and as thanks for their sacrifices to end the Goblin Wars.

1 IC

The First War Against Chaos. The newly founded Empire is attacked by the forces of Morkar the Uniter, Everchosen of Chaos. The war is desperate, short, and devastating. Eventually, Morkar is slain by Sigmar in a day-long battle that was said to have split the earth and rent the sky.

c. 2 IC

Sigmar names the twelve tribal chiefs his 'counts', which modern scholars claim can be sourced in the Classical word *comes*, meaning 'companion', for they were his companions on the battlefield against the Greenskins and against the Chaos tribes from the north.

c. 7 IC

Sigmar kills the Necromancer Morath and takes the Crown of Sorcery. Recognising its evil, Sigmar locks it away beneath Reikdorf.

11 IC

Battle of Drakenmoor. The Great Enchanter, Constant Drachenfels, leads an army of Goblins and Daemons against Sigmar's new capital and suffers the first defeat of his eternal existence. This shocking loss will haunt him long after he reincorporates several centuries later.

15 IC

Battle of the River Reik. Nagash, the Lord of Undeath, gathers a shambling horde of unliving monsters, and attempts to claim the Crown of Sorcery from Sigmar. The Undead almost overwhelm the Reiklanders and their Dwarf allies, but, after an exhausting battle, Sigmar eventually strikes Nagash down, causing the unliving army to crumble to dust.

50 IC

After five decades of extraordinary rule, Sigmar vanishes. To avoid destroying Sigmar's empire, the tribal chiefs eventually agree to vote for a new emperor from their own number, and select Siegrich of the Asoborn tribe. Thus, the counts became 'elector counts', and each swears to be a companion and protector of their elected emperor.

51 IC

Emperor Siegrich I dies in a hunting accident. After a fraught month, Prince Hedrich of the Unberogens is elected Emperor Hedrich I, bringing the seat of the Empire back to Reikdorf.

69 IC

Johann Helstrum arrives in Reikdorf and claims to have holy visions concerning Sigmar. He preaches that he witnessed Sigmar's Ascension to Godhood. Such is the love the Unberogens have for their lost emperor, Helstrum is readily believed.

73 IC

Johann Helstrum builds a temple to Sigmar in Reikdorf. History will forever remember him as the first Grand Theogonist of the Cult of Sigmar, and the first man to recognise Sigmar's divinity.

c. 100 IC

Emperor Hedrich I receives the twelve runeblades from Alaric the Mad that were commissioned 100 years earlier. Each of these 'Runefangs' is a unique weapon of extraordinary power, and they are passed to the tribal chiefs. In time, the Runefangs will become powerful symbols of the Elector Counts.

246 IC

A High Temple to Sigmar is completed in Reikdorf, and it acts as the centre of worship for a cult that now extends throughout the Empire. This rapid expansion leads to open conflict with the cults of Ulric and Taal.

990 IC

Emperor Ludwig I, commonly called Ludwig the Fat, grants the Grand Theogonist a vote to select the next emperor. Though some Elector Counts cry foul, and the other cults are astounded at the blatant favouritism, Emperor Ludwig appears far more interested in the lavish banquets prepared for him by the Cult of Sigmar in Reikdorf.

1000 IC

1000 years after Sigmar was crowned emperor, the Cult of Sigmar completes a new High Temple in Reikdorf. It is the largest temple in all the Empire, and cements Sigmar worship as the primary cult in the Reikland. In celebration, Emperor Ludwig I renames his city Altdorf, demonstrating its age and importance to the Empire as a whole.

1053-1115 IC

The Rule of Boris Goldgather. Emperor Boris I proves to be exceptionally unpopular and corrupt, with his rule known for exorbitant taxes, weak leadership, and a complete neglect of the military.

1106-1110 IC

Rise of the Drakwald: Beastmen and other vile creatures swarm from beneath the twisted bowers of the Drakwald, sacking villages, towns, and fortifications across the Drakwald province. When the last heir to the Drakwald throne is slain in battle with an enormous Bestigor, Emperor Boris I chooses to place the Drakwald Runefang in his Altdorf palace. Publicly, when a suitable heir is found, the Runefang will be passed on. Privately, Boris has no intention of ever giving up the magical blade.

1111-1115 IC

The Black Plague. Disease sweeps through the Reikland, killing nine in every ten people, and debilitating half of those left alive. Skaven then erupt from their under-Empire and attack. When Emperor Boris I dies of the plague in 1115 IC, no-one replaces him in the ensuing anarchy.

1115-1124 IC

The Rat Wars. Skaven move to systematically enslave the remaining population of the Empire, and effectively wipe-out what remains of the Drakwald province. In response, Elector Count Mandred of Middenland rallies a desperate defence, and with the help of Elven allies from the Laurelorn Forest, finally drives the Skaven back below ground. At the end of the war, the victorious Mandred is elected emperor by the three surviving elector bloodlines.

1152-1359 IC

Age of Wars. Emperor Mandred II is assassinated by the Skaven in 1152 IC. The Elector Counts cannot agree on a successor as they are too concerned about rivals invading their devastated grand provinces, so a fraught interregnum ensues for over two centuries. During this time, the Princes of the Reikland rule their Grand Province unfettered as civil war rages across the Empire.

1359-1547 IC

The Time of Two Emperors. In a desperate bid to end the bloodshed, the Electors meet in Altdorf and eventually agree on a choice for emperor, crowning Elector Count Wilhelm of Stirland as emperor by a majority of one. Elector Countess Ottila of Talabecland is outraged at this, and claims the vote is rigged. When she returns to Talabheim she declares herself Empress without a vote, and is supported in her claim by the Cults of Taal and Ulric. She then outlaws the Cult of Sigmar in Talabecland, a decree that stands for almost a thousand years. The civil wars escalate.

1421 IC

Shipbuilding rises to prominence in Altdorf's natural harbour, the Reiksport. Soon, quality vessels built in the Reikland are plying the Reik river system.

1489 IC

The prince of the Reikland formally commissions a navy, worried about the influence of ships sailing from Talabheim, Carroburg, Nuln, and Marienburg. To help limit their influence, Altdorf builds several low bridges across the Reik and Talabec to block larger ships and to control trade.

1547-1979 IC

The Time of Three Emperors. After Sigmarites botch an assassination attempt when Electors refuse to back their choice for the next emperor, the Elector Count of Middenland denounces the imperial elections as a corrupt sham, and declares *himself* the rightful emperor. He has the support of the cult of Ulric, which had recently fallen out with the Talabecland emperors.

The Empire now has three Emperors: The Electoral Emperor supported by the cult of Sigmar, the Ottilian Emperor supported by the Cult of Taal, and the Wolf Emperor supported by the Cult of Ulric. The civil wars intensify.

c. 1450-1550 IC

Knights returning rich from the crusades against Araby found new knightly orders and chapterhouses across the Reikland. They also fund the first temple of Myrmidia in Altdorf, a simple building sponsored by the newly invested Knights of the Blazing Sun.

1681 IC

The Night of the Restless Dead. The dead stir in the Gardens of Morr. Corpses rise, bones rattle, and the dead walk the land, sowing terror and confusion. Entire towns and villages are overrun before dawn brings a reprieve from the rapacious hunger of the deceased.

1707-1712 IC

WAAAGH! Gorbad! and the First Siege of Altdorf. Taking advantage of the divided Empire, the Orc Warboss Gorbad Ironclaw invades with a tide of Greenskins at his back, destroying the Grand Province of Solland, sacking Nuln and much of Wissenland, and eventually sweeping through the Reikland razing almost a third of its settlements before his green wave eventually breaks against the walls of Altdorf; but not before the Prince of Altdorf, and Electoral Emperor, Sigismund IV is killed.

1940 IC

The Poisoned Feast. The Great Enchanter, Constant Drachenfels, in one of his most famous treacheries, invites the Electoral Emperor, Carolus II, and the entire imperial court and its families, to a great feast held in his castle. Drachenfels poisons his guests, paralysing them. He then starves them to death in front of the marvellous banquet he prepared. This wipes out several important noble bloodlines of the Reikland, deeply destabilising the grand province and the Electoral Emperors as a whole.

1979-2303 IC

The Dark Ages. Elector Countess Magritta of Westerland is elected empress, but the Cult of Sigmar refuses to crown her, or indeed any other Elector Count or Countess, leaving the Electoral Emperors without a voted emperor. The entire electoral system collapses, and soon most provinces fight only for themselves. Petty warlords claim titles on a whim as new kingdoms, counties, duchies, princedoms and more rise and fall as terror spreads across the former Empire.

2010-2146 IC

The Vampire Wars. The Empire has collapsed into thousands of competing factions, and the Vampire Lords of Sylvania rise to exploit the turmoil. In total, three major wars result as three different vampire counts attempt to eradicate the fractured Empire. Each time, the Vampires are driven back through a mixture of unlikely alliances, desperate gambits, and clever strategy.

2051 IC

Second Siege of Altdorf. The vampire lord Vlad von Carstein is slain. His wife, Isabella von Carstein, commits suicide, unable to continue unlife without him. Their armies soon splinter into feuding factions, ending the First Vampire Wars.

2100 IC

After the inconclusive Battle of Four Armies ended in multiple assassination attempts by supposed allies on the Empire side, it is decided that it is time to elect an emperor to pull everyone together. Elector Count Helmut is the most popular candidate for this, until its discovered he is actually a zombie in the thrall of Konrad von Carstein, the very vampire lord they are trying to defeat. All plans to elect an emperor are abandoned.

2135 IC

Third Siege of Altdorf. The vampire lord Mannfred von Carstein launches a surprise winter attack on the Reikland capital as it recuperated from a summer of civil conflicts but is eventually driven back when the Grand Theogonist of Sigmar uses a forbidden spell to unbind the vampire's necromancy.

2203 IC

A rift into the Realms of Chaos opens at Castle Drachenfels, resulting in the annihilation of almost every living soul from Bögenhafen to Ubersreik. After more than a week of terror, the rift mysteriously closes.

2302-2304 IC

The Great War Against Chaos. Asavar Kul, Everchosen of Chaos, leads a horde of unimaginable size into Kislev, laying waste to everything in his path. In response, Magnus von Bildhofen, a young Nulner noble claiming to be inspired by Sigmar, rallies the fractured and broken Empire into a mighty army to relieve Kislev. He eventually defeats Asavar Kul at the Gates of Kislev alongside Kislevite, Dwarf, and Elven allies.

2304-2369 IC

The Reign of Magnus the Pious. Magnus von Bildhofen is elected Emperor Magnus I, the first elected emperor representing all Sigmar's Grand Provinces for almost a thousand years. Riding the wave of popularity he secured by winning the Great War Against Chaos, he immediately initiates sweeping reforms to end the corruption that previously brought the Empire to its knees, creating new laws to limit the nobility, cults, guilds and much more. He also oversees the foundation of many new institutions, including the formal creation of the Empire State Armies, Imperial Navy, and, controversially, the Colleges of Magic in Altdorf, making magic legal across all the Empire for the first time.

2308-2310 IC

The Third Parravon War. The Bretonnian duchy of Parravon invades the Reikland across the Grey Lady Pass, claiming the military escalation in Ubersreik caused by the mustering of the new State Army breaks an ancient treaty. They are quickly driven back, and the following year Parravon is besieged. Eventually, after a year of occasional skirmishes outside Parravon's extraordinarily high walls, and a great deal of standing around shouting insults, the King of Bretonnia treats on behalf of Parravon with Emperor Magnus I, ending the war.

2402-2405 IC

The Fourth Parravon War. The Bretonnian duchy of Parravon again invades the Reikland across the Grey Lady Pass. Ubersreik is besieged twice during the war, but doesn't fall. Peace is eventually brokered by the intervention of Emperor Dieter IV who agrees to pay the Parravonese an extortionate sum of money to retreat, drawing much criticism at court.

2415 IC

The Night of a Thousand Arcane Duels. War erupts between the Eight Colleges of Magic in Altdorf, razing large sections of the city and resulting in the death of six of the eight Patriarchs. The Cult of Sigmar pressures the Prince of Altdorf and Emperor Dieter IV to lock the Colleges down, which they do, resulting in the execution of many wizards, and effectively bringing legal magic use to an end in the Empire. Many of the surviving wizards flee the Colleges, never to return.

2420-2424 IC

WAAAGH! Grom! The Goblin Warboss Grom the Paunch leads an enormous horde of Greenskins across the Empire, sacking many Reikland towns and villages, before eventually heading westwards, undefeated, where he then takes to the sea. The lack of wizards from the suspended Colleges of Magic is widely blamed for the repeated military defeats suffered by Reikland's armies.

2429 IC

Westerland buys its independence from the Empire by bribing Emperor Dieter IV, reforming itself as The Wasteland with Marienburg as its capital. Using anti-corruption laws put in place by Magnus the Pious almost a hundred years earlier, the

Elector Counts depose Dieter in the ensuing scandal. He is replaced by Grand Prince Wilhelm of House Holswig-Schliestein of the Reikland, who is named Emperor Wilhelm III, starting the imperial dynasty that rules the Empire to this day.

The Battle for Grootscher Marsh. Emperor Wilhelm III, under pressure from the Elector Counts to respond to the Wasteland's secession from the Empire, gathers the State Armies to invade Marienburg. In late Autumn, the opposing forces meet at the Grootscher Marsh just outside Siert, and the Empire is routed by the advanced Marienburg navy, well-trained mercenaries and militias, and the magics of the Wasteland's High Elven allies. Begrudgingly, Wilhelm verbally recognises the Wasteland's independence, but refuses to ratify it with a treaty. Marienburg accepts this and draws their new border at Siert.

2430 IC

Appalled at the State Army's inability to effectively counteract the Elven mages and Marienburg ships, Emperor Wilhelm III reinstates the Colleges of Magic after their 15-year suspension and invests significant resources into shipbuilding at the Reiksport.

2431 IC

The Great Fire of Altdorf. The newly reinstated Bright College accidentally sets Altdorf alight when a spell misfires, burning many buildings to the ground. Many lobby Emperor Wilhelm III hard to suspend the colleges again, but eventually he decides to keep them open, but with greater oversight from the Cult of Sigmar.

2453 IC

Fourth Siege of Altdorf. The Liche King, Arkhan the Black, invades the Reikland with a seemingly endless swarm of walking corpses that march straight for Altdorf. Once the siege begins, Arkhan slips unnoticed into the High Temple of Sigmar and steals the dreaded Liber Mortis kept within. Minutes after he escapes, his army collapses, leaving thousands of carcasses mouldering outside the city walls as state soldiers look on in confusion and relief.

2480 IC

In Drachenfels Castle, Constant Drachenfels is slain by Crown Prince Oswald von Königswald of Ostland.

2483 IC

Emperor Luitpold III signs treaties with the Wasteland to allow warships of the Imperial Navy to pass through the city-port of Marienburg. For the first time since the secession of the Wasteland, the Reiklander navy is sailing the high seas, although the tolls to do so are extortionate.

2502 IC

Emperor Luitpold III dies in his sleep. In a close vote, Luitpold's son is elected to replace him, and is crowned Emperor Karl-Franz I in the High Temple of Sigmar in Altdorf.

2505 IC

By imperial appointment, the playwright Detlef Seirk attempts to stage an ambitious play in Castle Drachenfels for Emperor Karl-Franz and the gathered nobility of the Empire. It goes disastrously wrong.

2508 IC

Malathrax the Mighty, an enormous Doomfire Dragon, terrorises the Vorbergland, razing villages and taking livestock, before its driven north across the Hägercrybs. After several months of pursuit, and the eradication of the entire Knightly Order of the Ebon Sword, the Dragon is slain by the Imperial Huntsmarshal, Markus Wulfhart, who places three arrows in its heart.

POLITICS

The Reikland perceives itself as a progressive, civilised realm, standing apart from the backward barbarity of the other provinces. It is ruled by an Elector Count bearing the title 'Grand Prince of the Reikland' — the 'grand' appellation indicating the prince is an elector for the next emperor when the current one dies. The grand prince's land is divided into a patchwork of individual fiefs governed by dukes, counts, margraves, high priests, abbots and other rulers. These provinces, whose lords swear directly to the grand prince, are collectively titled the 'Reikland Estates', most of which have been ruled by the same families or institutions for uncounted generations, affording them significant influence. The grand prince's decrees are ratified by the 'Reikland Diet', an assembly comprised of the lords of the Reikland Estates. However, certain powers were reserved for the crown during Magnus the Pious's Imperial Reforms two centuries ago, including: the right to summon and command the State Army of the Reikland, the raising of emergency taxes in times of crisis, the right to authorise new coinage, and the right to call a High Lord Steward's Court should a powerful noble be charged with a crime.

REIKLAND COUNCIL

The day-to-day business of ruling the province is handled by the Reikland Council, which comprises ten 'High Lords'. The council meets weekly in the Wilhelm Chamber of the Volkshalle in Altdorf to discuss matters of import. It is rare for more than six of the high lords to attend simultaneously, and almost unheard of for the prince to attend in person.

The High Lords of the Reikland

The Ten High Lords of the Council of the Reikland, are appointed by the grand prince. Whilst most commoners could never hope to encounter such luminaries, their agents and representatives can be found everywhere.

High Lord of the Chair

A close advisor to the grand prince, the High Lord of the Chair officially leads the Reikland Council in the elector count's stead.

The current High Lord of the Chair, the stoic Graf Archibold von Lilahalle, was granted the influential position after being gravely wounded whilst saving the life of Emperor Luitpold III from an assassin's blade. Lingering, painful injuries confine him to a steam-driven wheelchair; an irony only the unwise note aloud.

High Lord Steward

The High Lord Steward is the only man legally allowed to judge a crime committed by the lord of a Reikland Estate. As a High Lord Stewart's Court is rarely called — most lords being simply too powerful to call to task — the position is largely ceremonial. Nevertheless, the High Lord Steward is arguably the most senior High Lord, and often stands in for the Grand Prince when he is unable — or unwilling — to attend court.

The current High Lord Steward is Archduke Adelbert von Bögenberg, a quiet man with little experience of the law, but a shrewd understanding of people. As much of the grand prince's time is taken up with imperial matters, he is arguably the *de facto* ruler of the Reikland, much to the High Lord of the Chair's chagrin.

High Lord Treasurer

The High Lord Treasurer is responsible for the Reikland's treasury and for raising revenues. The position is extraordinarily important and is almost always held by a close ally of the crown.

The current High Lord Treasurer is the aging genius Grafina Elena von Midwald, a dear friend of the previous grand prince, well known for her outspoken appreciation of fine wine and fine men.

High Lord Ambassador

The High Lord Ambassador organises the Reikland's foreign relations and runs the Altdorf Black Chamber: the infamous spies of the Reikland.

Graf Liepmund Holzkrug, the current High Lord Ambassador, is an intense, fiercely ambitious man, whose family are strong rivals to House Holswig-Schliestein in Altdorf. He is known for his vindictive nature, his ruthless politics, and his love of hunting rare and exotic game.

High Lord Judge

The High Lord Judge is the ultimate voice on all Reiklander Law, which is quite different from Imperial Law.

The current High Lord Judge of the Reikland also serves as Supreme Law Lord of the Empire: Lector Agatha von Böhrn of Verena. She is experienced in all legal matters, and widely regarded as one of the most intelligent people in the Empire, especially by those who have bribed her.

High Lord Chancellor

The High Lord Chancellor is the crown's spiritual advisor, and oversees the Reikland Chancery and the Silver Seal.

The current High Lord Chancellor is High Priestess Halma Habermann of Sigmar, a robust woman with a pale complexion, rosy cheeks, and thick limbs. Though generally charming and approachable, she is zealously out-spoken in her opposition to the Colleges of Magic, and rumours abound regarding the atrocities she witnessed during her service in the Order of the Silver Hammer.

High Lord Chamberlain

The High Lord Chamberlain runs the Palace of Altdorf and the adjoining Volkshall. The position is arguably one of the most influential in the Reikland, as most high-level imperial politics take place within the chamberlain's domain.

The current High Lord Chamberlain is rake-thin Duchess Elze von Skaag, an astute negotiator and careful planner who publicly supports Emperor Karl-Franz in all matters. Elze's husband, Duke Alardus von Skaag, is said to be deeply frustrated at his wife residing in Altdorf and not in Skaggerdorf with him; by comparison, it seems to suit her perfectly as most evenings she can be found carousing through the city with her bodyguards.

High Lord Reiksmarshal

The High Lord Reiksmarshal is responsible for leading the armies of the Reikland, and ensuring each of the Reikland State Regiments is raised, financed, and made available to the crown as required.

The current Reiksmarshal is the veteran general Duke Kurt Helborg, close friend and tutor to the current grand prince — Emperor Karl-Franz — and said to be the finest swordsman in the Empire. Helborg's military commitments ensure that he rarely takes his seat on the council, a circumstance that suits his natural inclination.

High Lord Constable

The High Lord Constable is the ultimate authority on the genealogy and heraldry of the Reikland.

The current High Lord Constable is smiling Grafina Matrella von Achern, a woman with no interest in genealogy, but a voracious appetite for political intrigue. She has made the most of this relatively inconsequential position, by chairing several private councils on the Grand Prince's behalf. It is hard to reconcile the bubbly, maternal demeanour she projects, and her reputation amongst her peers as the most ruthless woman in the Reikland.

High Lord Admiral

The High Lord Admiral is responsible for the Admiralty of the Reik, and thus the entire Reikland navy.

The current High Lord Admiral is the venerable Sea Lord Adalmann von Hopfberg. The Sea Lord — who is now quite senile — took residency in the Great Hospice some fifteen years ago, and the Admiralty has governed the navy without his influence — or interference — since then.

THE REIKLAND DIET

The Reikland Diet, which meets as required in the Holzkrug Chamber of the Volkshall in Altdorf, is responsible for scrutinising decrees issued by the Grand Prince of Reikland, either passing them or returning them to the crown with suggested amendments.

As most lords of the Reikland Estates don't have time to attend the diet themselves, they generally send favoured children, spouses, relatives, or minions in their place, although decrees of significant import will often bring worried lords from across the Reikland to attend in person. Given the number of agents the Grand Prince of Reikland tasks to influence the Reikland Diet, most votes are a formality.

THE REIKLAND ESTATES

The Reikland Estates are ruled by vassals of the Grand Prince of Reikland. Their rulers can do as they will with their lands, parcelling out fiefs to family and friends as they wish — though the creation of new hereditary titles requires the approval of the Prince of Reikland and the Reikland Diet.

Each estate has a range of distinct legal and military obligations to the crown, but all are required to build and maintain at least one regiment for the Reikland State Army, soldiers typically used in peacetime as watchmen, road wardens, or guards. Most Reikland Estates are feudal, comprised of smaller fiefs ruled by vassals, many of whom hold hereditary titles that have existed for centuries.

SAMPLE REIKLAND ESTATE

The Barony of Böhrn is a Reikland Estate of the Vorbergland ruled by House Böhrn for over four centuries. Baroness Agetta holds court in the town of Siedlung and currently has six vassals: three with hereditary titles — Baron Markham of Siebbach, Countess Osterhild of Kaltenwald, and Baron Baltzer of Ettlindal — and three with non-hereditary titles, all of which were appointed by Agetta personally — Warden Fabian of Ort, Warden Luethold of Koff, and Castellan Fronika of Neumarkt. The three hereditary vassals have, in turn, a total of seven vassals of their own.

The Baroness does not attend the Reikland Diet; instead she relies on her influential younger sister, Lector Agatha von Böhrn, to watch over it in her place. Agatha resides in Altdorf serving as a member of the Imperial Council of State and the Reikland Council, as well as tending to her duties as a Lector of Verena.

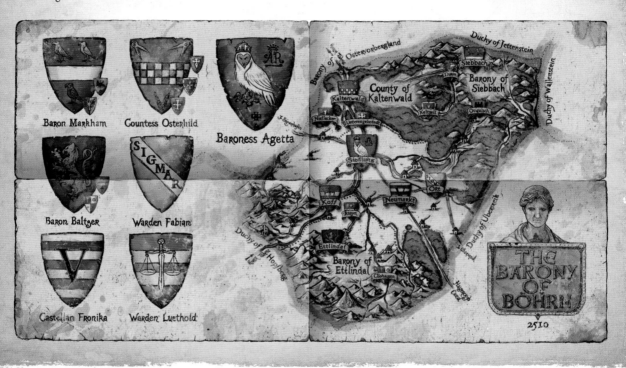

SETTLEMENTS

The Reikland prides itself as one of the most populated and civilised of the Empire's grand provinces. Nevertheless, great swathes of the realm are still wild, blanketed in forest and untouched by Human hand. Though these woodlands are relatively safe when compared to the extraordinary dangers found in the great forests elsewhere in the Empire, the darker corners of the Reikwald are still home to all manner of terrible creatures.

So, even after two thousand five hundred years of expansion, most Reikland settlements are found along the Reik and its many tributaries, connected by river if not always by road. It is only to the south of the Vorbergland, in the breadbasket of the Reikland, that rural settlements spread freely, connected by well-maintained roads and remarkable canals.

ALTDORF AND THE MANIFOLD TOWNS

It is said that all the roads and the rivers lead to Altdorf, the largest, richest city of the Empire, but there are many other interesting places to visit beyond that city's high, white walls. Numerous towns, both large and small, can be found across the Reikland, most acting as centres of trade or manufacture. A growing number of these flourishing centres of commerce also hold the status of 'freistadt', meaning they are 'free towns': granted charters to govern themselves, usually via a council of burgomeisters with little or no interference from the local noble houses.

Altdorf

Emperor Karl-Franz I holds court in Altdorf, the capital of the Reikland and the Empire as a whole. It stands proudly at the confluence of the mighty Reik and Talabec rivers, as well as at the end of many major trade routes, and is easily the wealthiest city in the Empire. This ensures it is always expanding and renewing, with fresh, wide-eyed hopefuls arriving daily, and more commissions for new bridges, buildings, and engineering marvels presented weekly to the city's burgomeisters than most cities consider in a year.

Today, Altdorf is a city of steam-powered bridges, mismatched islands, enormous tenements, and seemingly endless hordes of people: one cannot traverse its crooked streets without becoming intimately familiar with complete strangers. Because it draws merchants and diplomats from across the Known World, it is also surprisingly cosmopolitan; not only do folk of all ranks, species, creeds, and backgrounds rub shoulders freely, but even wizards are a common sight, rarely receiving more hostility than a wary glance or muttered blessing.

Always surprising outsiders, a populous Elf quarter thrives near the Reiksport — Altdorf's deep-water harbour and shipyard — founded by High Elf merchant princes trading up the Reik from Marienburg over a century ago. The old alliance between the Empire and Dwarfs has stood since Sigmar's time and ensures many Dwarf clans also reside there in tight-knit communities, some having toiled on the city's stonework for untold generations, though naturally their stubborn natures preclude them from ever calling Altdorf home. There is even a healthy Halfling population, with most earning their crusts serving fine food and better ales in Altdorf's hostelries, many of which are guarded by the city's sizeable Ogre population. Even odder creatures also call the city home, with none more fantastic than those found in the Imperial Zoo, which boasts myriad monsters and animals including the Abomination of Stirland and the Drakwald Gibberbeast, each caged and displayed for the amusement of all.

This enormous and varied population helps secure one of Altdorf's more notorious traits: it is infamously smelly, known affectionately, and all too accurately, as 'The Great Reek'. During the hot, summer months the stench rolling in from the Altdorf Flats grows so potent that many of the city's wealthiest citizens flee to country estates or the sumptuous, sun-kissed palaces of Grenstadt in Southern Averland.

The ever-present fetor does little to ease Altdorf's citizenry, a mob known for being uniquely vocal and prone to rioting at any imagined slight, especially if it involves new taxes. Even seemingly trivial actions of the local burgomeisters and nobles can earn their ire; but the fact that many of their protests are entirely fair does not lessen the crown's fervour in quashing any rebellious rabbles that may take to the streets.

Altdorf is also a renowned centre for learning. The sons and daughters of wealthy households matriculate at the University of Altdorf, often with little regard to academic ability; those with scholarly potential, but without the financial clout to match it, often find their way to the High Temple of Verena, for the Goddess of Wisdom always has space for those blessed with intellect. The famed Imperial Engineers' School — founded by Tilean genius Leonardo da Miragliano — also lies within Altdorf's walls. Here some of the Empire's bravest, and most reckless, souls devise new and inventive methods for raining fiery death on the enemies of mankind. Perhaps unsurprisingly, the school has been rebuilt over a dozen times since it was founded.

Arguably the most significant educational institution in Altdorf is also its most mysterious: The Colleges of Magic. Founded over two centuries ago at the behest of Emperor Magnus the Pious, the colleges are guided by the principles and precepts of the elven Loremaster Teclis. The colleges are charged with training magically gifted citizens to channel their dangerous talents in the defence of the Empire. Rumours of the warping influence of the potent magical energies gathered by so many wizards living in such close proximity persist; allegedly the very streets of the capital have been twisted, and certain college buildings are believed to be hidden from all but those few blessed — or should that be cursed — with witchsight, but few believe such talk.

Standing in stark contrast to the arcane mysteries of the Colleges of Magic, and as a bulwark against any errant witches or rogue wizards, Altdorf is also the beating heart of the Cult of Sigmar. Over two-thousand five-hundred years ago, Sigmar was born, raised, and eventually crowned as first emperor within the boundaries of modern Altdorf, and fittingly the city now boasts more Sigmarite temples and holy sites than all the other cities of the Empire combined. Indeed, it is often said that one cannot throw a heretic without hitting a temple of Sigmar in the city.

'SPECIAL' DELIVERY

A merchant is offering a ludicrously large fee to whomever will deliver a package. The catch is the package is bound for one of the Colleges of Magic; the merchant claims to be terrified of wizards. To complicate matters, no-one actually knows where the college in question — the Light College — can be found, with some claiming that it exists 'outside of normal space' – whatever *that* means. The package is warm to the touch and seems to vibrate faintly when pressed; just how desperate for cash are the would-be messengers?

Auerswald

The lively town of Auerswald rises by the confluences of the Teufel, Tranig, and Ober rivers, so is on one of the busiest — and thus best patrolled — trade routes of the Reikland. The folk of Auerswald tend to be strong willed and determined, but their easy charm and famous wit ensures no matter how steely their negotiations, they rarely cause offence.

The ruling graf, Ferdinand von Wallenstein, leaves the running of Auerswald to a council of burgomeisters, far preferring his luxurious palaces in Altdorf and Nuln to dirtying his hands with direct rule. His uncle, Lord Adelbert von Wallenstein, is a grizzled but hale, old warhorse who spends most of his days rooting out Goblins and bandits in the Reikwald to the east of the town.

Much of Auerswald is built on thick stilts over the flood-plain of the river Teufel, which is often in spate. Connected by a bewildering labyrinth of ramps, bridges and rope ladders, outsiders can easily become lost. More than one careless carouser has fallen to a muddy death after over-indulging themselves in the local taverns.

In recent years, rumours have sprung up about an organised gang of blackmailers and confidence tricksters operating from the town, though no witnesses have lived long enough to testify to their existence.

Bögenhafen

The largest and most prosperous of all the Vorbergland's market towns, Bögenhafen lies in the very heart of the Reikland and serves as the crossroads of the grand province. Lying equidistant between the capitals of Altdorf and Monfort, it is a crucial stop on the principle trade route between The Empire and Bretonnia. Goods from Bretonnia and the four corners of the Empire are traded here for local lumber, wool, and metals shipped down from the Grey Mountains.

Bögenhafen is located in Graf Wilhelm von Saponatheim's duchy, but he is quite content to let the town be run by a local council — whose membership is dominated by members of the local Merchants' Guild, as well as representatives from the Stevedores and Teamsters' Guild — so long as they keep the money flowing his way. As goods coming north are transferred from wagon to barge in Bögenhafen, the city is always well stocked with warehouses full to the brim of fine wines and expensive, fragrant cheeses.

DIRTY BUSINESS

The citizens of Bögenhafen are justifiably proud of their bustling town for many reasons, not least of which is their extensive sewers that are well-maintained by the town's Masons' Guild. Pleasing local gangs of criminals, the privacy of the sewer system has proven to be something of a boon to smugglers looking to avoid the taxes, tariffs, and fees levied by the guilds and nobles of the unknowing town above.

The town watch regularly hires interested citizens to sweep the sewers for miscreants and ne'er-do-wells; of course, criminal gangs aren't the only danger that might be found lurking beneath Bögenhafen...

Diesdorf

One of many towns lying on the River Reik between Altdorf and Nuln, Diesdorf and its surrounding villages are dedicated to the production of corn, which is mostly traded downriver to the capital. The town's reliance on a single crop does mean that should a blight cause the corn to die off, the town itself may follow. However, those who visit Diesdorf may conclude that its chief export is, in truth, religious fervour. Magnus the Pious once gave a legendarily powerful speech in the town after folk travelled far and wide to hear him.

Ever since, Diesdorf became a major pilgrimage site for devout Sigmarites, and on holy days the town's population is frequently doubled. Despite its relatively small size, Diesdorf has numerous temples and shrines to Sigmar, and most families in the town have at least one member serving in the Sigmarite clergy.

Dunkelberg

Southernmost of the Reikland's major trade centres, the market town of Dunkelberg stretches across several hills along the banks of the River Grissen. The older, richer portions of the town sit high on the hills, giving the nobles, and the rising merchant class wealthy enough to afford the oldest townhouses, a commanding view of the surrounding countryside. Despite its ever-increasing size, travellers note Dunkelberg's 'rustic' feel, with regular markets clogging its winding streets. There shoppers can purchase livestock; local produce; several excellent, fruity wines produced by the surrounding villages; and hand-crafted goods from across the Suden Vorbergland. Wide-ranging 'bleachfields' extend from the town, where local linen is dyed white by the sun around crops.

Dunkelberg's position near the looming Grey Mountains and the wild Graugrissen forest leads to regular raids by Goblin tribes. While the richer portions of the town are well fortified and protected by a high, stone wall, the rest lack any significant defences. As such, the poorer citizenry have learned not to grow too attached to their homes, belongings, or loved ones.

ORPHAN WHITE

Dunkelberg has an excess of orphans, the result of frequent Goblin raids, diseases, and other unpleasant occurrences. Rather than leave them underfoot, the local duke has established a number of orphanages to provide shelter and sustenance for the children; however, to earn their keep, he puts the orphans, clad in their distinctive white uniforms, to work in the bleachfields. Visitors to Dunkelberg may be shocked to see so many urchins deployed as a labour force, though the callous disregard many of the wealthy of the town have developed toward orphan children is perhaps worse. Sister Alella, a local Shallyan priestess, has recently expressed concern over the wellbeing of these urchins, even claiming that a number of the children have vanished under suspicious circumstances, and is looking for help to uncover the truth of what's *really* happening.

Eilhart

Known and celebrated by wine drinkers throughout the Old World, the vineyards around Eilhart produce the succulent grapes, and thus the wine, that shares its name. Eilhart is widely considered one of the Reikland's best white wines, valued not just for its crisp, light flavour, but also for its famously mild hangovers that grow no worse no matter how much of it was quaffed the night before, or so Eilharters claim. Recently, Eilhart has recently also become famed in the Reikland, and as far afield as Marienburg, for its sharp, acidic beers making use of fragrant hops and local grain.

Given the excellent quality of its alcoholic beverages, Eilhart has become a popular destination for riverboat cruises, wherein epicures travel to the town to sample its wares from the many drinking houses, breweries, and vineyards on offer. Some claim the high number of visiting Bretonnians — drawn by the excellent wine — may account for the locals' recent enthusiasm for beer.

Grünburg

Downriver from several major trading towns, Grünburg is no stranger to trade goods bound for the Reik, but it is in riverboat manufacture that Grünburg truly excels. The town's boatyards are in constant operation, churning out the barges that keep the Reikland's trade afloat.

The open fields to the south-east of Grünburg appear verdant and peaceful, but are known locally as the Battle Plains. It was here, long ago, the ruthless advance of the fearsome Orc Warlord Gorbad Ironclaw was finally stalled. Uniquely in Imperial military history, the Battle of Grünburg was almost entirely contested by mounted troops on both sides. This quirk of history has made the Battle Plains a site of interest for archaeologists, antiquarians, and grave robbers, all keen to excavate debris from beneath the blood-soaked earth.

Holthusen

Nestled along the River Schilder, Holthusen is a major point on the trade route between Eilhart and Marienburg. The town primarily deals in wine and beer, and the barrels in which they are stored. The coopers of Holthusen are rightly renowned for their sturdy barrels, most famously the Holthusen Hogshead, allegedly stout enough to withstand direct cannon fire, while leaving the precious drink within unscathed. The majority of the vintners and brewers of the western Vorbergland use Holthusen barrels; indeed, many age their stock here in specialised warehouses sunk deep into the ground to keep them cool.

Holthusen is enclosed in several rings of tall palisades and the folk of the town are frequently on edge, for while few bandits would dare to menace the town, wild Beastmen living deep in the nearby Reikwald regularly attack without warning before melting back into the forest. Many citizens believe that the creatures have an insatiable thirst for wine, though some fear blood is their tipple of choice. Whatever the case, the town has taken to leaving barrels of cheap wine at the outskirts of the surrounding forest in the hopes the beasts will take their offerings and leave in peace. Of course, should any Witch Hunters hear of this appeasement, there will likely be a reckoning…

THE RIME TREE

In a clearing a few miles to the north-east of Holthusen stands a tree unique in all the Reikwald: a magnificent pine locked in ice all year round. The Rime Tree, as it is called, never melts, and sends constant flurries of ice and snow cascading down onto the frosty undergrowth below. The tree is freezing to the touch and even the mightiest axe blows barely crack the thick ice coating its bark.

The site has been claimed by the Cult of Ulric, and is the major terminus for devout Ulricans on pilgrimages south of the Reik. For those of an arcane bent, the perpetually icy bark of the tree has certain useful – and therefore valuable – magical properties. But Ulricans are rarely happy to have wizards poking about their sacred sites, so obtaining some of the bark safely is something of a risky endeavour. Therefore, Lord Pyromancer Schlotter of the Bright Order is willing to pay good coin for brave men to secure what he cannot.

Kemperbad

An ancient town with a long and convoluted history, the Grand Freistadt of Kemperbad is known and celebrated for producing the finest brandy in the Reikland. Though part of the Reikland, Kemperbad lies on the eastern bank of the Reik; historically the town has been fought over, and ruled by, nobles from Talabecland, Stirland, and the Reikland, changing hands time and again through a series of marriages, treaties, and wars. Since gaining a charter affording it the right to self-rule in 1066IC from Boris Goldgather, Kemberbad has been a Freistadt led by a local council.

Its prime location on the river, coupled with the ability to impose and retain its own taxes, has made the town very rich indeed. Because of this, the merchants of Kemperbad are legendarily ostentatious, dressing in outfits so gaudy as to shame a peacock, and costly enough to beggar folk of more modest means. Unsurprisingly, the neighbouring nobility regard Kemperbad's coffers with envious eyes, and some send agents to destabilise the town.

Schädelheim

Sitting near the Grootscher Marsh at the confluence of the River Mos with the Reik, Schädelheim makes the most it can of its lucrative position on the trade route between Marienburg and Altdorf, boasting a high number of inns and berths for passing ships and barges. Ferries here regularly run travellers back and forth over both rivers, and it is a hub for the disparate communities of the nearby marshlands.

Just south of the centre of the town lies an ancient temple dedicated to Morr, the God of Death. The grand, crumbling building has presided over Schädelheim since its infancy, possibly even predating the town's founding. Because of this, many of the locals have an especially strong affinity with Morr, a situation rarely seen in the Empire outside Ostermark, and highly unusual for the strongly Sigmarite Reikland. This is something local Sigmarites are keen to rectify.

Schilderheim

Standing proud at the confluence of the Schilder and Reik rivers, Schilderheim is one of the Reikland's most important trading towns. It is also home to a surprisingly diverse array of wildfowl, particularly wading birds. Most notable is the red crane, a sedentary river bird found predominantly on the Reik that is known for using heavy stones to crack open river clams.

Though already a prosperous town, the Merchants' Guild and burgomeisters of Schilderheim have grander aspirations, eyeing the wealth of Altdorf and Marienburg enviously. Wanting their piece of this pie, the local stevedore guild has recently raised its prices, a highly unpopular move that has brought much dissatisfaction, some of which has spilled into the streets. To avoid this extra fee, a number of merchants have occasionally sought to bypass the stevedores altogether, conducting their business on the river itself, swapping not just stock, but whole barges. Merchant houses connected to this practice have recently found wharves set alight, warehouses raided, and barges sunk; of course, the Stevedores claim it has nothing to do with their honourable members. The Merchants' Guild, in turn, is willing to pay a lot of money to any who can prove it is.

Stimmigen

The major bridge over the River Ober, coupled with access to the Vorbergland canal system, ensures a great deal of trade passes through Stimmigen on its way to Ubersreik, making it one of the busiest market towns in the Suden Vorbergland. It is widely famed for its lush orchards, and is the source of the Reikland's best known apple, the sweet, yet tart, Ernwald. The Ernwald only flourishes in Stimmigen's environs, proving resistant to attempts to cultivate it elsewhere in the Empire. In addition to curious horticulturists and jealous farmers, the Ernwald has attracted a significant Halfling population to the area, whose delicious apple pies, pastries and crumbles — not to mention crisp cider — can be found in most local hostelries all year round, and especially during Pie Week at the start of autumn. This Halfling festival is celebrated by all in Stimmigen, an opportunity for rich and poor alike to enjoy tastings and eating competitions, and generally gorge themselves on all manner of sweet, baked goods.

Ubersreik

The town of Ubersreik is situated near Grey Lady Pass, one of only two major passes over the Grey Mountains into Bretonnia. Because of this, the town regularly sees traders and travellers from across the Old World. The mighty fortress known as the Black Rock is connected to the walls of the town should any less welcome travellers attempt ingress. Ubersreik has had a long association with the nearby Dwarven clans of the Grey Mountains, and in a situation unique to Ubersreik, representatives of the city's Dwarf population sit on the town council. One of Ubersreik's more famous edifices, its spectacular bridge over the River Teufel, was built by Dwarfs during the time of Magnus the Pious. Widely regarded as one of the most impressive feats of engineering to be found in the Reikland, it connects the trade road which runs all the way from Bögenhafen to Dunkelberg then Nuln. Ubersreik deals in trade of all kinds, but is most well-known for ore and the skilled metal-work of the Dwarfs.

For exhaustive details on Ubersreik, see the **WFRP Starter Set**.

Weissbruck

Originally little more than one of many tiny fishing villages along the River Bögen, Weissbruck has in the past century grown rapidly into a bustling port for goods and travellers moving between Bögenhafen and Altdorf. Weissbruck's change in fortune is due to its shrewd rulers, the Grubers, who decided to capitalise on the rich deposits of coal and iron found in the Skaag Hills. This ready supply of much needed resources enabled the Grubers, with the permission and partnership of the Prince of Altdorf, to commission Dwarf engineers to construct a canal in 2462IC, which rapidly accelerated the town's growth, bringing all manner of citizenry with it.

While the output of the mines has slowed in recent years, trade has steadily increased. Despite its rulers' riches, Weissbruck retains something of the character of a typical mining town; burly miners and dockworkers ensure an uneasy peace, and the threat of violence is never far removed. As the mines' output has diminished, more and more miners have descended from the Skaag hills, a growing, agitated, unemployed workforce with little to do but drink cheap rotgut and scowl at strangers.

Wheburg

Wheburg is the first town encountered after leaving the Grey Mountains on the road from Helmgart to Bögenhafen. Its proximity to the fortress of Helmgart ensures troops pass through regularly, and the town offers a sizeable barracks for visiting soldiers. Having survived the mountains' extreme weather — to say nothing of ravaging armies of Orcs and Goblins, and potential monsters roosting on the nearby Drachenberg — most visitors arrive to Wheburg with a powerful desire to celebrate life.

To accommodate that need, Wheburg has become renowned for its hospitality, and its locals are widely regarded as the friendliest in the Reikland — for a price. The streets are lined with taverns, inns, and gambling dens, not to mention some less salubrious establishments where all the pleasures of the flesh are purveyed, and illicit substances may be procured. Though fist-fights and petty crime are common, things rarely get too out of hand given the significant number of soldiers usually on hand to disperse any rowdy revellers (except, of course, when those revellers are, themselves, off-duty soldiers). Spending time in Wheburg prior to marriage has become something of a rite-of-passage for well-heeled Reiklanders, and it's common to hear men and women calling out, 'what happens in Wheburg, stays in Wheburg!' from many a street corner.

THE BASTIONS AND FORTRESSES

The Reikland's southern border is dominated by the Grey Mountains, which are, in turn, dominated by a series of

strongholds, built and rebuilt to defend against raiding Mountain Trolls, Greenskins, and the restless dead, not to mention the neighbouring kingdom of Bretonnia.

The River Reik is similarly littered with bastions to ward attack, but there most are stony relics of the Empire's broken past when the Reikland warred with the other grand provinces and itself. Only strategic fortresses now remain, easily outnumbered by castles fallen to disrepair, their ancient strength and storied past all but forgotten, just as their crumbling stonework is lost to time and decay.

Blackstone Tower

While the Axe Bite and Grey Lady passes are the best-known routes over the Grey Mountains, they are not the only ways through the range. The Crooked Corridor is a narrow gorge through the mountains not far from the border with the Wasteland. It is useless to most merchants, being far too tight for wagons or horses, and dangerous to boot as much of the path is perched precariously on the edge of steep cliffs, meaning the slightest slip of a foot could lead to a painfully inglorious end.

Completely impassable in the winter and perilous at all other times, the Crooked Corridor was known only to goat herders and smugglers until a spate of Greenskin raids brought the pass to the attention of the authorities.

Several decades ago, Emperor Mattheus II ordered the construction of a fortress to watch over the Crooked Corridor after repeated invasion. Nine years later, Blackstone Tower was completed, drawing its name from the locally quarried dark stone that forms its walls, and the slate that tops its towers.

Its position high above the Crooked Corridor offered the Emperor's sharpshooters an excellent perch from which to employ their lethal skills; however, its status as a Reiklander bastion was short-lived. An oversight at the planning stage resulted in the tower being built on lands claimed by the Dwarfs of Karak Ziflin. Not wanting to upset the Dwarfs, the Emperor ceded the tower, much to the annoyance of the Margrave of Geetburg who had helped finance it.

Today, the Dwarfs 'generously' allow a limited garrison to barrack alongside their own troops at Blackstone Tower, a largely rebuilt structure. With the Reiklanders chafing under the Dwarfs' leadership, and the Dwarfs constantly belittling the shoddy human stonework they've yet to replace, the Tower is a powderkeg of grievances and resentment, generating a tense — and some would say unsustainable — atmosphere.

Steirlich Manor

On the southern slopes of the Hägercrybs, in the Duchy of Grauwerk, sits a heavily fortified manor atop a windswept ridge. The manor is ancient, a holding of the von Bruner family, and currently ruled by Graf Steirlich: both the Graf and his imposing manor were named for a famous ancestor who was gifted the land by Emperor Mandred Ratslayer in 1138IC.

The Graf is steely eyed and ambitious, with a ruthless streak as wide as the Reik. He is well thought of amidst the local smallfolk for his determination to root out bandits and hunt down other menaces that would dare impinge upon his property. Indeed, there are whisperings that he may be a little too willing to investigate unnatural occurrences, for dark rumours of corruption swirl around the scions of the von Bruner line.

Certainly, the darkly handsome Graf is always on the lookout for stout hearts, stern wills, and strong sword-arms to help him maintain the peace, so few air their fears aloud.

Helmgart

Set high in the Grey Mountains, the fortress town of Helmgart guards the border with Bretonnia from the eastern side of Axe Bite Pass. The Empire's relations with Bretonnia have not always been civil, and while the ramparts of Helmgart are no longer lined with aging skulls in elaborate helms, they most likely remain in the castle's cellars. These days, the soldiers of Helmgart are more often called upon to patrol the pass, protecting travellers and merchants from Greenskins, bandits, and other menaces.

Helmgart's keep was carved directly out of the mountainside by Dwarfs long ago. Three tiers of stout stone walls buttress a great granite mountain, dominating the surrounding terrain and offering an excellent view of the road below. Adjoining Helmgart proper, is a huge, imposing wall broken only by a single, long tunnel standing between the two, sheer mountainsides: the only route through to Bretonnia. Amongst the troops garrisoning the fortress are a number of storied regiments. Most famously, the gunners of Mackensen's Marauders – a Reiklander State Regiment – are well known for their deadly accuracy, a fearsome reputation perhaps aided by the lack of cover on the road below the high walls. The fortress sits at one end of the great road that leads directly to Bögenhafen, and from there onto Altdorf.

As guardian of the principle trade route into the Empire from Bretonnia, Helmgart is equal parts imposing citadel and bustling trade town. Here, Bretonnian merchants barter brandy, wine, fine fabrics, arms, and armour, while their Reiklander counterparts in turn funnel their province's goods south. The local Dwarf clans, too, trade ingots of silver, lead, and iron, along with precious pieces of Dwarf-smithed metalwork. With so many merchants and traders, the Marketplatz of Helmgart is a bustling place, rife with endless opportunities and uncounted thieves.

The Stone

Towering over one of the many islands in the Reik by Essel, the massive promontory known simply as The Stone can be seen for miles around. A winding path coils up the steep, craggy face from the small, seemingly insignificant jetty at its base to the severe walls of the squat citadel crowning the rocky mount. Captains give it a wide berth when they pass, the more superstitious among them making an offering of salt and steel to Grandfather Reik to safeguard their passage. No pennants fly atop the grim battlements, though the occasional gleam from a guard's helmet attests to the troops patrolling the ramparts.

Unknown to most, the Stone is a secure prison containing dangerous criminals that, for various sensitive, political reasons cannot simply be executed. Some have powerful friends and family, or are themselves nobles whose crimes, if publicly acknowledged would cause scandal and shame to the great and good of the Reikland. Others are political hostages, held to ensure the compliance of wayward relatives. And, of course, a few simply know too much, their precious secrets safeguarded in The Stone against their future need. No-one really knows about the conditions within The Stone's walls; no-one really wants to ask.

THE VILLAGES, HAMLETS, AND HOLY PLACES

Throughout the Reikland, most of the uncounted hundreds of villages and hamlets are clustered close to towns for protection and trade. By comparison, in the open Suden Vorberland, settlements are strewn more freely amongst the farmlands, dotting the landscape every few miles or so, relying on the protection of fortresses in the mountains and the state regiments from the large market towns. Due to a quirk in Reikland law installed by Sigmarites many centuries ago, villages are defined as any small settlement including a temple of Sigmar; hamlets, by comparison, are those without such spiritual support, and are often smaller because of this.

Besides these smaller settlements, the Reikland hosts an uncounted number of isolated monasteries, abbeys, way-temples, and other holy sites. While most are sited in locations not too far from protection, some well-fortified examples can be found in the most unlikely places, often for religious or historical reasons, be that upon the sides of a mountain, the depths of a forest, the centre of a lake, or in an even less likely location.

Monastery of the Holy Word

Deep in the Reikwald west of Altdorf, far from any easily traversed road, lies the Monastery of the Holy Word. This hallowed site is tended by the Sigmarite Order of the Anvil. The Order of the Anvil is responsible for keeping the laws that govern the Cult of Sigmar and maintaining all details of the cult's practices.

The Monastery of the Holy Word houses the order's greatest treasure: the Testaments of Sigmar. Collected not long after Sigmar abdicated, the Testaments are a gathering of the written memories of warriors and citizens who knew Sigmar Heldenhammer before he ascended to godhood. Considered to be the most accurate collection of the things Sigmar actually said and the practices he maintained in life, the Testaments are some of the holiest works in the Reikland.

It is not normally the practice of the Order of the Anvil to accept visitors, but the Monastery of the Holy Word is no normal monastery. Penitents seeking obscure details about the foundations of Sigmar's Law will travel from across the Empire to query the black and green robed monks on doctrine.

Nobles and exceedingly wealthy merchants who have repeatedly shown their devotion to the Cult of Sigmar will occasionally be granted leave to take a pilgrimage to the Monastery of the Holy Word. While none are allowed to read the original Testaments, or even to touch them, leave to gaze upon one or two of the original pages is deemed to be a sacred honour beyond price.

Rottfurt

Scores of settlements line the River Teufel, most easily forgettable, even interchangeable. Not so Rottfurt, whose name is spoken of in hushed, reverential tones by scholars and wizards throughout the Empire. Though primarily a village of shepherds, producing wool and mutton, Rottfurt also produces a famous — and famously pricy — sheepskin parchment: Rottfurt Silver. The parchment possesses a faint sheen, takes ink well, and resists fading far longer than other, lesser parchments.

Because of this, the thick-wooled, pale sheep of Rottfurt are the village's pride and afforded every comfort. They feed on the luscious grass of the nearby Hammastrat Heights and are generally allowed to wander as they will during the day. The shepherds contribute to a rotating militia, tasked with protecting their precious flocks at all costs.

However, of late the livestock have been going missing; intriguingly, those on guard have always found themselves falling asleep, despite their best efforts. On waking, another sheep has vanished. What began as a minor frustration has grown to a full-blown obsession for the locals, with as many wild and spectacular theories flying around as there are stars in the heavens.

Wörlin

The small fishing hamlet of Wörlin is almost impossible to spot from the river. The settlement is surrounded by a number of small, rocky islets and promontories, and sheltered by thousands of bowing trees. These 'Willows of Wörlin' line the banks of the Reik for many miles around, and it seems none have any interest in using their lumber. A great deal of trade passes by Wörlin, but very little actually happens *in* Wörlin as most of the passing goods are bound for more lucrative markets.

THE ROOT OF THE PROBLEM

On the festival day of Sonnstill, the 'hamlet circle' – a council of the hamlet's elders – gather to 'Water the Willows'. This simple ceremony involves singing, dancing, feasting, and the slicing of a virile stranger's throat, splashing blood across the thirsty roots of the Queen Willow, quenching her sanguinary appetites for one more year.

Should the ceremony be completed, the Queen is pleased, and will ensure the hamlet's safety from the children of the forest. Should the ceremony be interrupted, the Queen awakes and summons her children, bringing braying Beastmen by the score to slaughter all in their path. But outsiders rarely consider such consequences when they have a knife to their throat.

Zahnstadt

Isolated Zahnstadt is considered by locals to be the 'last village of the Vorbergland', after which the rolling hills turn barren and cold before reaching upwards to the Greenskin-infested Grey Mountains. In the shadow of those peaks, Zahnstadt skulks along the southern bank of the River Mos, deep in a dark valley with bleak crags rising to all sides. In summer, the sun only shines on the village for an hour or two at midday, hiding behind the surrounding cliffs in the morning, and creeping behind the mountains as the day lengthens.

In the winter, there is no direct sunlight at all, locking the village in a gloomy cycle of twilight and darkness. Despite this, the folk of Zahnstadt are famous for their bright dispositions and perpetual cheerfulness, a trait outsiders often find forced and off-putting. Every house in Zahnstadt is brightly painted in a garish medley of different, often clashing colours. Its homely inn, the Wayward Sun, is famous for its ever-burning hearthfire and for the relentlessly cheerful songs that echo long into the night.

THE SINS OF THE PAST

Zahnstadt has long been in the grip of something far worse than a lack of enriching sunlight: vampires. Near the End of the Third Vampire Wars, Janos von Carstein deserted the vampire lord Mannfred von Carstein's depleted armies. After weeks of evading pursuit from his master's vengeful minions, he chanced upon dark Zahnstadt and realised it was the perfect place to go to ground. Almost three-hundred years later, and he hides there still, and time has made him bold. He now sleeps beneath the Wayward Sun in an ostentatious, velvet-lined coffin, rising each evening to hold 'court' in the inn, forcing enthralled locals to sing happy songs of his homeland Sylvania.

Rumour of this has not only reached the ears of Witch Hunters, but also the pawns of recently resurrected Mannfred von Carstein, who has ordered his traitorous son be brought before him. It would be unfortunate, indeed, should poor, unsuspecting souls happen to hostel in the Wayward Sun on the same night the Witch Hunters arrive to investigate, and the same night that Mannfred's agents choose to extract Janos before the Witch Hunters uncover his true nature...

THE ANCIENT SITES AND TERRIBLE RUINS

The Reikland's long and bloody history stretches back long before the time of Magnus the Pious and the Great War Against Chaos; relics of ancient atrocities litter the realm, and it is a wise and wary traveller that checks for ancient standing stones before erecting their camp of an evening. Some of these sites bear haunting legends of gruesome renown and macabre spectacle, but most towns and villages boast their own local ruins, with accompanying tales of horror and bloodshed.

The Darkstone Ring

The wise do not venture to the Darkstone Ring. The path to this place of terrible and ancient power lies to the north of Blutroch near the Altdorf-Bögenhafen road. When night falls, the six suggestively-carved stones glow green with a wan luminosity, flaring bright as Morrslieb waxes.

At the centre of the Darkstone Ring lies a monolithic slab of unidentifiable rock, permanently stained with the blood of the countless innocents sacrificed there down through the millennia.

Despite the ring's fell reputation, travellers seem drawn to its malevolent environs, lured by legends of mystical potential and lost artefacts of terrible arcane power. Not even frequent sightings of beastmen and cultists — especially around Geheimnisnacht — can deter these brave, some may say foolhardy, souls.

Castle Drachenfels

Like the twisted talon of a malformed claw, the seven towers of Castle Drachenfels clutch at the sky in a gesture of malevolence and spite. Each of its misshapen turrets is festooned with windows, resembling eyes without number, alert to the arrival of any traveller unlucky — or unwise — enough to stumble upon the lair of the Great Enchanter, Constant Drachenfels.

Drachenfels — a mythically powerful sorcerer, necromancer, and daemonologist — has tormented mankind since before the time of the Empire; already ancient when he suffered his first great defeat at the hands of Sigmar Heldenhammer, he has returned time and again to his haunt in the Grey Mountains, like a festering wound that refuses to heal. Rumours abound that the seemingly quiescent ruins, mostly reduced to rubble and long forsaken, are less abandoned than they appear…

Helspire

Looming perilously in the peaks overlooking Axe-Bite Pass, the Helspire is a grim fortress, carved directly out of the living rock of the Grey Mountains and inlaid with the bones of countless fallen. It appears long abandoned and as still as the grave; yet, on rare nights of occult significance, eldritch lights can be seen blazing along its battlements, casting eerie shadows across the pass, even in the blackest of nights. On such nights, the Helspire reveals itself as a citadel of the unquiet dead, and skeletal knights charge forth, scouring the mountainside, terrorising both Reiklanders and Bretonnian alike. Little is known about the castle, and none living claim to have pierced its bleak walls or know who

commands the legions of the undead that lurk therein. Some say a cabal of necromancers call it home, others whisper it is the vault of a vampire, and a few even murmur the fortress is commanded by a powerful Liche, in life a powerful sorcerer, clinging to undeath in the pursuit of bloody vengeance for some centuries-old slight. Perhaps because of this uncertainty, the Helspire is said to be filled with riches looted from across the Old World, but none know the truth, as those who seek such treasures never return or never talk.

The Lorlay

Possessing a breathtaking vista, the Lorlay is an imposing rock formation standing proud in the centre of the Reik some 40 miles downstream of Grissenwald. The channels on either side of the jutting island flow swift and deep, and despite the relative narrowness of the river at this point, no crossing has been successfully constructed.

Romantic legends abound of a beautiful, elven maiden, pale of skin and supple of limb, who swims in the fast-moving waters at dawn and dusk. Because of this, the Lorlay is popular spot for affluent Reiklanders' to hold Taalite stag parties before marriage, and a surprising number of high-class inns can be found nearby. Tales of the singing water maiden are especially rife amongst the Reikland's river-bound sailors, and if their stories are to be believed, she has been spotted by half the seamen of the navy.

The Singing Stones

West of Schädelheim, deep in a wooded valley, stands an ancient dolmen. Its stones are old beyond reckoning, arrayed in a spiralling pattern around a central arrangement of huge pillars capped with an enormous slab, resembling nothing more than a titanic altar. From the ground it is nigh on impossible to discern the intricate pattern of the stones, especially given the trees and bushes that have grown in amongst the menhirs.

When a westerly wind blows up the valley, in from the Wasteland, the stones produce an eerie keening that echoes for miles around. While some locals claim listening to the stones' song can give insight into problems or grant strange wisdom, others declare such nonsense is heresy, knowing nothing but trouble comes from trafficking in such ungodly power, and are more than willing to use violence to save the souls of the foolish.

• THE CONSUMERS' GUIDE •

'After sixty years in the trade, here are the three most important lessons I've learned. One: friendship means nothing. Two: without ambition you're nothing. Three: no matter how fruitless the prospect, you can always squeeze more blood from a stone.'

— Ubel Rikard-Goellner, Merchant Prince

The trappings you receive from your Class and Career (see **Chapter 2: Character**) are enough to get you started, but you may want more equipment. During character creation, additional items can be purchased from the lists in this chapter without restriction. However, once you start to play, the availability of some trappings is limited, so make sure you buy everything you want and can afford before you begin play.

TRAPPING LISTS

Weapons: Page 293
Armour: Page 299
Packs and Containers: Page 301
Clothing and Accessories: Page 302
Food, Drink, and Lodging: Page 302
Tools and Kits: Page 303
Books and Documents: Page 304
Trade Tools and Workshops: Page 305
Animals and Vehicles: Page 306
Drugs and Poisons: Page 306
Herbs and Draughts: Page 307
Prosthetics: Page 308
Miscellaneous Trappings: Page 308
Hirelings: Page 309

MONEY

Before you can buy new trappings, you first need to understand how money works in the Empire.

The Empire's coins are most commonly minted in 3 denominations: *Brass Pennies* (d), *Silver Shillings* (/), and *Gold Crowns* (GC). Coins usually weigh around an ounce and, as their inherent value is determined by weight, even foreign coins can be easily valued with a set of scales, though will likely draw a suspicious eye.

Standard coin values are:
1 gold crown (1GC) = 20 silver shillings (20/–) = 240 brass pennies (240d)

1 silver shilling (1/–) = 12 brass pennies (12d)

This is usually abbreviated to:
1 GC = 20/– = 240d

MONEY, MONEY, MONEY

For those new to **WFRP**, remembering there are 12 pennies in a shilling and 20 shillings in 1 crown, for a total of 240 pennies to 1 crown, can take some getting used to, especially if the money is mixed up a little, such as this: 6/8, or 6 shillings and 8 pence. That number may initially look arbitrary, but if you translate it to pennies, it becomes a far more understandable 80d, or one third of a gold crown. Indeed, an 80d coin is fairly common in the Empire, and is called a noble.

Don't worry too much about fully understanding the coins to begin with. An easy way to keep everything right in your head is to translate all prices to pennies and think of it in your local currency to get a grip of the numbers. So, if British, you could think of a brass penny as £1, a silver coin as worth around £12, and a crown as £240. It's not accurate, but does help keep the money understandable until you are used to it. So, if someone offered you a job for 10 shillings, think of it as £120, which is a fair bit of money. But if someone offered you a job for 10GC, that's a far more tempting £2400!

THE COST OF LIVING

As they wander the Empire, adventurers likely fill their purses with coins of all three denominations, perhaps poor one day, unexpectedly rich the next. However, outside adventuring, most lives centre on a single coin type as determined by Social Status (see page 49).

Those seeking to maintain their Status must also keep up appearances. After all, if you repeatedly appear as poorer than you are, others will unsurprisingly think you're poor. In practice, dressing and eating as expected, and using trappings that are fitting for your station, is enough for most folks to simply accept you at face value. What this requires in practice is left up to the GM to determine, using the following as a guide:

- **Brass Tier:** The poorest members of society are unlikely to see a gold coin in their lifetimes. They live humble lives, subsisting on plain foods and sleeping in shared rooms, and have little appearances to maintain. Indeed, peers are more likely to call them out for having airs and graces for spending too much on fine clothes and food than they are likely to note spending too little.

- **Silver Tier:** The swelling middle-classes may use pennies for ale and gold for major purchases, but shillings are their standard currency. They dine well, sleep in comfortable beds, and wear good quality clothing.

- **Gold Tier:** The wealthiest elites rarely bother themselves with pfennigs. They eat luxury foods, sleep on satin sheets, and always stand out from the crowd due to their expensive garb and trappings.

For GMs preferring hard numbers, spending around half your Status every day is usually enough to maintain appearances, though you may be living a little frugally. So, if you have a Status of Silver 4, spending at least 2 shillings per day will do for food and board, where if you have Brass 2 Status, you need only spend a pfennig a day.

MONEY SLANG

Various slang terms are used for coins across the Empire. Here are some of the more common terms.

- **Gold Crowns:** Marks, Karls, Gelt
- **Silver Shillings:** Bob, Shimmies, Mucks
- **Brass Pennies:** Pfennigs, Clanks, Shrapnel

CRIMINAL COINAGE

Of course, if there is money involved there will be folk looking to take any advantage they can, including criminal options. For the Rogues in your party, two schemes concerning coins are worth knowing.

Counterfeiting

The diversity of coinage circulating the Empire means counterfeiting is rife. Reiklanders may be accustomed to seeing coins from other provinces, but are always wary of being scammed. A successful **Evaluate** Test will detect counterfeit coins, typically by inspecting coins for weight and hardness.

Actually producing counterfeit coins is much harder. It requires an **Art (Engraving)** Test to carve a convincing stamping die, then a **Trade (Blacksmith)** Test to strike the coins, usually with the aid of an assistant. Including a higher precious metal content makes Evaluate Tests to detect counterfeits more difficult; using less than a fifth makes it much easier to spot the fake coins.

Clipping

Embezzlers can trim slivers of precious metal away from the edges of coins. This scam is called 'clipping' or 'shaving' and is practised mainly by shopkeepers or tollkeepers who have access to large quantities of other peoples' money. Gold and silver filings are then melted down and sold to jewellers, counterfeiters, or fences. Clipped coins can be detected with the Evaluate Skill; the more of the coin that's clipped, the easier the Test.

THE NULN STANDARD

Altdorf may be the current capital of Reikland and the Empire, but coinage standards are established in the city-state of Nuln to the south. Historically, Nuln was the Empire's capital until House Holswig-Schliestein restored the throne to Altdorf a century ago, and many imperial institutions still call that city home. The Nuln Standard only governs coin weight and metallurgy, not stamp imagery, which varies significantly across the provinces.

GOING TO MARKET

Once you start play, the availability of rarer goods is restricted. After all, it's hard to find a harpsichord in a five-house hamlet, but not so hard in the shops and markets of imperial capital, Altdorf.

The following rules for buying and selling are all optional. The GM may prefer to roleplay every visit to each market, hawker, or shop, meaning Tests for Availability are unrequired as the GM simply states what is or isn't purchasable. Equally, the GM may prefer you to simply check the trapping lists, roll for Availability and, if the Test succeeds, spend the coin on whatever you want. Possibly without even Haggling!

OPTIONS: TRACKING MONEY

Where some groups like to track every penny closely, perhaps even using chits or fantasy coins to represent in-game coins, others prefer to ignore all fiscal book-keeping. The game rules assume you are counting every coin, but if you wish to simplify money, you can do so using your Status. If an item costs less than your Status level — so if you have a Status of Silver 2, any item costing 2 silver shillings or less — you are assumed to be able to buy as much as needed of that item. Beyond that, you can buy a maximum of one item a day that costs more with a Haggle Test, with the difficulty set by the GM according to the cost of the item and the local markets.

AVAILABILITY

All Trappings have an Availability, either Common, Scarce, Rare, or Exotic.

Common items are found in almost every corner of the Empire and are always assumed to be readily available.

Scarce and Rare items are less common, and you need to pass an Availability Test to find any locally in stock; the chance of passing the Test depends upon the settlement size.

Exotic items are super rare, and only available if the GM says so, or if you commission the item from an appropriate artisan (perhaps with a *Commission* Endeavour, see page 197), or make it yourself (perhaps with a *Crafting* Endeavour see page 197).

Once you know an item's Availability, check it on the following table to see if it is in stock.

	Village	Town	City
Common	In Stock!	In Stock!	In Stock!
Scarce	30%	60%	90%
Rare	15%	30%	45%
Exotic	Not in Stock	Not in Stock	Not in Stock

If you fail an Availability Test for Scarce or Rare items, you can either reroll when you arrive at a new settlement or you can try again next week if the settlement is Town-size or larger.

If an item is in stock, it's up to the GM to determine how many are available. As a general rule-of-thumb, villages have a single item in stock, towns have 1d10 items, and cities have as many

as the GM deems appropriate. These quantities are generally doubled for Common items, and halved for Rare ones (rounding up).

BARGAINING AND TRADING

People of the Empire love a good bargain, and crowds of eager shoppers fill town squares every day looking for the best deals. When buying goods, there are two primary Skills to Test: Evaluate and Haggle.

Evaluate is used by consumers to identify the quality of an item (see Craftsmanship below). Similarly, the vendor can use Evaluate to appraise coins for their exchange value, or spot counterfeits. Anyone can also use Evaluate to estimate the prices of Rare or Exotic items to within +/-10%.

Haggle is used routinely by consumers and vendors alike, typically with Opposed Tests. Haggling is expected and most prices are marked up slightly to account for this. Winning a Haggle Test reduces the price by 10% (or possibly up to 20% with an Astounding Success (6+) or with the *Dealmaker* Talent). Failing a Haggle contest badly usually means the vendor distrusts your coinage.

Roleplaying Shopping Trips

Trips to the market for routine purchases don't need to be roleplayed in detail. The GM might prefer you browse the equipment lists and check for Availability yourself. Major purchases that involve item Craftsmanship, or require extra Haggling, can be fun to roleplay in-character. In certain scenarios, shopkeepers are important NPCs with distinct personalities or story roles, so it's always worth interacting with them. Consider the following when roleplaying shopping:

- The GM may overrule Availability as dictated by local details. For example, basic rowboats are automatically available if the adventure is located in a fishing village that features a renowned boat-builder.

- Availability percentages can be increased by +10% or +20% if a character is especially diligent, belongs to a relevant career such as Merchant or Fence, or spends an entire day shopping and making Gossip Tests.

SELLING

Selling your trappings during desperate times, or simply offloading loot, is handled in exactly the same fashion as Buying, but this time you'll be making money, not spending it. So, you first check for Availability of a buyer in the same fashion as checking for stock. You then bargain and trade, with Evaluate Tests and Haggle Tests as the GM prefers, and finally you set a price. Typically, the base cost when selling is half the item's listed price, meaning, when selling second-hand, you usually make between a quarter to half an item's worth after Haggling.

If you have a Career like fence or merchant, and you put time into Gossip Tests and wandering the local town, you might find someone willing to pay up to 80% of the item's listed value, though that is left in the hands of the GM.

Lowering the Price

If you can't find a buyer, you can try lowering the price. Each time you half the money you are willing to accept, the Availability of a buyer increases by one step.

Example: *Corporal Mauser has fled his State Army regiment with a Hochland Longrifle he stole, and is keen to sell. As it's an Exotic item, there are no immediate buyers he can find on the street. The GM determines the base price Mauser can expect is half the weapon's value (so 50GC, half of the 100GC it's worth), so Mauser decides to drop the price by half two times, saying he will accept 12GC 10/–, which increases the Availability of a Buyer two steps from Exotic to Scarce.*

BARTERING

Rural and mercantile commerce often involves trading one commodity for another without exchanging money. To resolve bartering of this type, compare the Availability of the items being traded against those being acquired. The barter ratio indicates how many 'units' must be traded, and how many 'units' of the other commodity are acquired. 'Units' are defined by checking the equipment list prices of both items and grouping them into packages of roughly equivalent value.

BARTERING RATIOS

Traded Items	Acquired Items			
	Common	Scarce	Rare	Exotic
Common	1:1	2:1	4:1	8:1
Scarce	1:2	1:1	2:1	4:1
Rare	1:4	1:2	1:1	2:1
Exotic	1:8	1:4	1:2	1:1

CRAFTSMANSHIP

The items available in the shops, stalls, and merchant halls of the Empire vary significantly in quality. Not everything is made equal, and the Craftsmanship rules reflect this using Item Qualities, and Item Flaws.

An Item Quality makes the trapping a little better, but harder to find. An Item Flaw makes the trapping a little worse, but easier to find.

ITEM QUALITIES

A Trapping is called a Quality Trapping if it has more Item Qualities than Flaws. For each Item Quality the Trapping has, double its price and make it one step less available. A Trapping with more Qualities than its Encumbrance, and that lacks any Flaws, is called a Best Quality Trapping.

Example: *A spade that has the Fine and Durable Item Qualities costs quadruple the list price, and drops availability from Common to Rare.*

Durable

Laboriously crafted using strong materials, the item can take +Durable Damage points before it suffers any negatives (see Weapon Damage and Armour Damage on pages 296 and 299) and gains a saving throw of 9+ on a 1d10 roll against instant breakage from sources like Trap Blade (see page 298). This Quality can be taken multiple times. Each time it is taken, the saving throw improves by 1 (e.g. From 9+ to 8+).

Example: *Molli owns a high quality sword with Durable 3, meaning it can take 3 Damage before suffering any negatives, and has a saving throw of 7+ against breaking.*

Fine

Meticulously crafted to please the eye. This Quality is a sign of social status and can be taken multiple times. The higher the quality, the more impressive it seems.

Lightweight

Cleverly crafted for ease of carrying. Reduce Encumbrance points by 1.

Practical

Expertly crafted with utility in mind. A failed test using this item receives +1 SL. If the item is a piece of armour, any penalties for wearing it are reduced by one level (for example from –30 to –20).

OPTIONS: CRAFTING GUILDS

Most Artisans in the Empire are members of guilds that protect their rights and ensure appropriate standards of craftsmanship. If a town or city contains a crafting guild, related goods of poor quality are rarely available.

If the GM states you are shopping in a town with relevant crafting guilds, each item Flaw reduces Availability instead of increasing it. Furthermore, the first Item Quality does not reduce Availability. Prices are still modified as per usual.

ITEM FLAWS

A Trapping is called a Flawed Trapping if it has more Item Flaws than Qualities. Each Flaw halves the listed price and improves Availability by one step. Many vendors sell flawed items, but pretend they are anything but. A successful Test with any appropriate skill — such as Evaluate, or Melee for weapons, or Trade for tools — will spot such underhanded activities.

Note: Exotic items do not have their Availability modified by being Flawed — they are always difficult to find, even shoddy examples.

Example: *A suit of chainmail that is both Bulky and Unreliable costs a quarter of the list price, and raises Availability from Rare to Common.*

Ugly

Crafted without any aesthetic awareness whatsoever, Ugly items attract negative attention, and related Fellowship Tests might even suffer a –10 penalty.

Shoddy

Hastily crafted by an amateur or fraudster. The item breaks when used in any failed Test rolling a double. Similarly, *Shoddy* armour breaks if any Critical Hit is sustained to a Hit Location it protects.

Unreliable

Crafted without attention to functionality, a failed test using this item receives −1 SL. Further, penalties for wearing *Unreliable* armour are doubled.

Bulky

An awkward design crafted clumsily. Increase Encumbrance by +1 (small trinkets cannot normally have this flaw). *Bulky* clothing and armour are Enc 1 even when worn, and Fatigue penalties for armour are doubled.

ENCUMBRANCE

Even the doughtiest Dwarf cannot carry a limitless number of trappings. To help you track how much you are carrying, all items are marked as weighing a number of Encumbrance points (sometimes abbreviated to 'Enc'), typically from 0–3, where 0 shows a trifling item that's easily carried, and 3 represents something that's a struggle to heft. The number of Encumbrance points you can carry without penalty is determined by your Strength Bonus + Toughness Bonus. Thus, average humans begin play able to carry around 6 Encumbrance points.

ENCUMBRANCE EXAMPLES

Enc	Example Trappings
0	Knives, Coins, Jewelry
1	Sword, Mandolin, Sling Bag
2	Greatsword, Tent, Backpack
3	Halberd, Cask, Large Sack

SMALL ITEMS

Common sense usually dictates the number of smaller items someone can carry before becoming Encumbered. To provide a rough guide, money weighs 1 Encumbrance point per 200 coins.

OVER-SIZED ITEMS

Certain large items weigh 4 or more Encumbrance points, such as barrels or saddlebags. You may normally only carry one oversized object, and it likely requires both hands.

BEASTS OF BURDEN

Draft animals ignore the standard Strength Bonus + Toughness Bonus formula for Encumbrance points. Encumbrance points for mules, horses, carts and wagons are listed in their descriptions. Each Human-sized passenger is assumed to weigh around 10 Encumbrance points, modified by the GM as necessary.

WORN ITEMS

Worn items such as armour, clothing, and jewellery all have their Encumbrance dropped by 1, which often means they count as Encumbrance 0 when worn.

OVERBURDENED

Characters who exceed their Encumbrance capacity may be slowed, and will become fatigued by travel. Movement reduction and Travel Fatigue incurred from Encumbrance stacks with any Armour penalties. Further, whenever you have to take a *Fatigued* Condition when Overburdened for a reason other than being Overburdened, gain an extra +1.

Enc	Penalty
Up to limit	No penalties
Up to double limit	−1 Movement (min: 3), −10 Agility, +1 Travel Fatigue
Up to triple limit	−2 Movement (min: 2), −20 Agility (min: 10), +2 Travel Fatigue
More than 3×	You're not moving.

Encumbrance and Attributes

Movement penalties for Encumbrance are applied immediately and can only be removed by dropping equipment.

Encumbrance and Travel Fatigue

Fatigued Conditions are accrued at the end of a day's travel and can only be removed with a long rest.

WEAPONS

Weapons used across the Empire vary according to provincial preference, religious requirement, individual inclination, and trusty old tradition. Here you will find a selection of the most commonly wielded melee and ranged weapons, which are presented using the following format.

- **Weapon Group:** Each Weapon is listed by its Weapon Group. If a weapon is two-handed, it is marked (2H)
- **Price:** The price for an average example of the weapon.
- **Enc:** The Encumbrance for the weapon.
- **Availability:** The Availability of the weapon.
- **Reach/Range:** The Weapon's length, or the range of the weapon in yards.
- **Damage:** The weapon's Damage, which is added to your SL to hit.
- **Qualities and Flaws:** Any Weapon Qualities or Flaws the weapon possesses.

Strength Bonus is abbreviated to SB in the weapon tables.

MELEE WEAPONS

Weapon	Price	Enc	Availability	Reach	Damage	Qualities and Flaws
BASIC						
Hand Weapon	1GC	1	Common	Average	+SB+4	–
Improvised Weapon	N/A	Varies	N/A	Varies	+SB+1	Undamaging
Dagger	16/–	0	Common	Very Short	+SB+2	–
Knife	8/–	0	Common	Very Short	+SB+1	Undamaging
Shield (Buckler)	18/2	0	Common	Personal	+SB+1	Shield 1, Defensive, Undamaging
Shield	2GC	1	Common	Very Short	+SB+2	Shield 2, Defensive, Undamaging
Shield (Large)	3GC	3	Common	Very Short	+SB+3	Shield 3, Defensive, Undamaging
CAVALRY						
(2H)Cavalry Hammer	3GC	3	Scarce	Long	+SB+5	Pummel
Lance	1GC	3	Rare	Very Long	+SB+6*	Impact, Impale
FENCING						
Foil	5GC	1	Scarce	Medium	+SB+3	Fast, Impale, Precise, Undamaging
Rapier	5GC	1	Scarce	Long	+SB+4	Fast, Impale
BRAWLING						
Unarmed	N/A	0	–	Personal	+SB+0	Undamaging
Knuckledusters	2/6	0	Common	Personal	+SB+2	–
FLAIL						
Grain Flail	10/–	1	Common	Average	+SB+3	Distract, Imprecise, Wrap
Flail	2GC	1	Scarce	Average	+SB+5	Distract, Wrap
(2H)Military Flail	3GC	2	Rare	Long	+SB+6	Distract, Impact, Tiring, Wrap
PARRY						
Main Gauche	1GC	0	Rare	Very Short	+SB+2	Defensive
Swordbreaker	1GC 2/6	1	Scarce	Short	+SB+3	Defensive, Trap-blade
POLEARM						
(2H)Halberd	2GC	3	Common	Long	+SB+4	Defensive, Hack, Impale
(2H)Spear	15/–	2	Common	Very Long	+SB+4	Impale
(2H)Pike	18/–	4	Rare	Massive	+SB+4	Impale
(2H)Quarter Staff	3/–	2	Common	Long	+SB+4	Defensive, Pummel
TWO-HANDED						
(2H)Bastard Sword	8GC	3	Scarce	Long	+SB+5	Damaging, Defensive
(2H)Great Axe	4GC	3	Scarce	Long	+SB+6	Hack, Impact, Tiring
(2H)Pick	9/–	3	Common	Average	+SB+5	Damaging, Impale, Slow
(2H)Warhammer	3GC	3	Common	Average	+SB+6	Damaging, Pummel, Slow
(2H)Zweihänder	10GC	3	Scarce	Long	+SB+5	Damaging, Hack

* Lances count as Improvised Weapons if used on a round where you have not Charged.

RANGED WEAPONS

Weapon	Price	Enc	Availability	Range	Damage	Qualities and Flaws
BLACKPOWDER*						
(2H)Blunderbuss*	2GC	1	Scarce	20	+8	Blast 3, Dangerous, Reload 2
(2H)Hochland Long Rifle*	100GC	3	Exotic	100	+9	Accurate, Precise, Reload 4
(2H)Handgun*	4GC	2	Scarce	50	+9	Dangerous, Reload 3
Pistol*	8GC	0	Rare	20	+8	Pistol, Reload 1
BOW						
(2H)Elf Bow	10GC	2	Exotic	150	+SB+4	Damaging, Precise
(2H)Longbow	5GC	3	Scarce	100	+SB+4	Damaging
(2H)Bow	4GC	2	Common	50	+SB+3	–
(2H)Shortbow	3GC	1	Common	20	+SB+2	–
CROSSBOW						
Crossbow Pistol	6GC	0	Scarce	10	+7	Pistol
(2H)Heavy Crossbow	7GC	3	Rare	100	+9	Damaging, Reload 2
(2H)Crossbow	5GC	2	Common	60	+9	Reload 1
ENGINEERING*						
(2H)Repeater Handgun*	10GC	3	Rare	30	+9	Dangerous, Reload 5, Repeater 4
Repeater Pistol*	15GC	1	Rare	10	+8	Dangerous, Pistol, Reload 4, Repeater 4
ENTANGLING**						
Lasso	6/–	0	Common	SBx2	–	Entangle
Whip	5/–	0	Common	6	+SB+2	Entangle
EXPLOSIVES						
Bomb	3GC	0	Rare	SB	+12	Blast 5, Dangerous, Impact
Incendiary	1GC	0	Scarce	SB	Special***	Blast 4, Dangerous
SLING						
Sling	1/–	0	Common	60	+6	–
(2H)Staff Sling	4/–	2	Scarce	100	+7	–
THROWING						
Bolas	10/–	0	Rare	SB×3	+SB	Entangle
Dart	2/–	0	Scarce	SB×2	+SB+1	Impale
Javelin	10/6	1	Scarce	SB×3	+SB+3	Impale
Rock	–	0	Common	SB×3	+SB	–
Throwing Axe	1GC	1	Common	SB×2	+SB+3	Hack
Throwing Knife	18/–	0	Common	SB×2	+SB+2	–

* All Blackpowder and Engineering weapons have the Blackpowder and Damaging Qualities.

** Entangling weapons have no range bands, just the listed range.

*** An Incendiary gives every affected target 1+SL *Ablaze* Conditions.

AMMUNITION

Weapon	Price	Enc	Availability	Range	Damage	Qualities and Flaws
BLACKPOWDER AND ENGINEERING						
Bullet and Powder (12)	3/3	0	Common	As weapon	+1	Impale, Penetrating
Improvised Shot and Powder	3d	0	Common	Half weapon	–	–
Small Shot and Powder (12)	3/3	0	Common	As weapon	–	Blast +1
BOW						
Arrow (12)	5/–	0	Common	As weapon	–	Impale
Elf Arrow	6/–	0	Exotic	+50	+1	Accurate, Impale, Penetrating
CROSSBOW						
Bolt (12)	5/–	0	Common	As weapon	–	Impale
SLING						
Lead Bullet (12)	4d	0	Common	–10	+1	Pummel
Stone Bullet (12)	2d	0	Common	As weapon	–	Pummel

HAND WEAPONS

'Hand Weapon' is used to describe any of a number of basic weapons that, though different, are assumed to be effectively the same in-game, including swords, axes, hammers, maces, short spears, and more.

BLACKPOWDER AMMUNITION

Blunderbusses are the only weapons listed that use the Small Shot or Improvised Shot ammunition. All other Blackpowder and Engineering weapons use bullets.

WEAPON DAMAGE

Some Fumble results (see page 160) or spells may damage your weapon. For each point of damage your weapon receives, reduce its Damage by –1. If the Damage is reduced to +0 (or SB +0), the weapon is mangled beyond all recognition, and now counts as an Improvised Weapon. If an Improvised Weapon is Damaged, it is considered useless for melee combat.

Weapons can be fixed by appropriate Artisans for 10% of the weapon's cost per damage point sustained. Weapons reduced to Improvised Weapons cannot be fixed. You can also repair your own weapons if you have the appropriate Trade Skill, Trade Tools and, for more than a single point of Damage, a Workshop.

MELEE WEAPON GROUPS

All melee weapons are assigned to a Weapon Group. Each Weapon Group requires a separate skill to master its use. So, Melee (Flail) allows you to use Flails and is a separate skill from Melee (Polearm), which allows you to use Polearms. If you use a weapon from a Group where you have no Advances, you Test your Weapon Skill to hit with the weapon. While you still suffer all the weapon's Flaws, you cannot use any of its Qualities. Some Melee Weapon Groups also have special rules.

Cavalry

Cavalry weapons are assumed to be used when mounted. When not used from horse-back, all two-handed weapons in the Cavalry Weapon Group also count as Two-Handed weapons. Single-handed Cavalry weapons are not normally used when unmounted.

Flail

Unskilled characters add the Dangerous Weapon Flaw to their Flails, and the other listed Weapon Qualities are not used.

Parry

Any one-handed weapon with the Defensive Quality can be used with Melee (Parry). When using Melee (Parry), a weapon can be used to Oppose an incoming attack without the normal –20 off-hand penalty (see page 161).

WEAPON REACH

The lengths of the weapons are progressively bigger as follows.

- **Personal:** Your legs and fists, perhaps your head, and anything attached to those.
- **Very Short:** Less than a foot in length.
- **Short:** Up to 2 feet in length.
- **Average:** Up to 3 feet long.
- **Long:** Up to 6 foot long.
- **Very Long:** Up to 10 feet in length; can Engage enemies up to 4 yards away, rather than just 2.
- **Massive:** Anything over 10 feet long; can Engage enemies up to 6 yards away, rather than just 2.

OPTIONS: WEAPON LENGTH AND IN-FIGHTING

These are simple rules for those who like to use Weapon length for more than simple description of appearance, and a possible impediment to fitting down dark tunnels.

WEAPON LENGTH

If your weapon is longer than your opponents', they suffer a penalty of –10 to hit you as you find it easier to keep them at bay.

IN-FIGHTING

As your Action, you can perform an **Opposed Melee Test** to attempt to step inside your opponent's weapon length. The winner chooses if combat continues as normal or as 'in-fighting'. During in-fighting, any weapon longer than Short counts as an Improvised weapon.

RANGED WEAPON GROUPS

Ranged weapons are difficult to master. You cannot attempt a Ranged Test for a weapon you do not have the correct speciality for. So, if you know Ranged (Blackpowder), you cannot attempt a Ranged (Bow) Test. However, there are a few exceptions.

Blackpowder and Explosives

Those with Ranged (Engineering) can use Blackpowder and Explosive weapons without penalty.

Crossbows and Throwing

Crossbows and Thrown weapons are relatively simple to use. You can attempt a Ranged (Crossbow) or Ranged (Throwing) Test using your Ballistic Skill, but the weapon loses all Qualities whilst retaining its Flaws.

Engineering

All Engineering weapons can be used by characters with Ranged (Blackpowder), but the weapons lose all Weapon Qualities whilst retaining their flaws.

WEAPON RANGE

A weapon's range is its medium range in yards. **Chapter 5: Rules** presents modifiers if a weapon is at Point Blank, Short, Long, or Extreme range. Calculate ranges as follows:

CALCULATING RANGE BANDS

Point Blank = Range ÷ 10
Short = Range ÷ 2
Long = Range x 2
Extreme = Range x 3

SAMPLE WEAPON RANGES

Weapon	Point Blank	Short	Med	Long	Extreme
Bow	5	25	50	100	150
Heavy Crossbow	10	50	100	200	300
Pistol	2	10	20	40	60
Sling	6	30	60	120	180

WEAPON QUALITIES

Some weapons have specific advantages over others, which are described with Weapon Qualities.

Accurate

The weapon is accurate and easy to hit with. Gain a bonus of +10 to any Test when firing this weapon.

Blackpowder

The crack of gunfire followed by gouts of smoke and confusion can be terrifying. If you are targeted by a Blackpowder weapon, you must pass an **Average (+20) Cool** Test or take a *Broken* Condition, even if the shot misses.

Blast (Rating)

All Characters within (Rating) yards of the struck target point take SL+Weapon Damage, and suffer any Conditions the weapon inflicts.

Damaging

A Damaging weapon can use the higher score from either the units die or the SL to determine the Damage caused from a successful hit. For example, if you roll 34 in your attack Test and the target number was 52 you can choose to use the SL, which in this case is 2, or the units die result, which is 4. An Undamaging weapon can never also be Damaging (Undamaging takes precedent).

Defensive

Defensive weapons are designed to parry incoming attacks. If you are wielding such a weapon, gain a bonus of +1 SL to any Melee Test when you oppose an incoming attack.

Distract

Distracting weapons can be used to drive an opponent back due to their dangerous or whip-like natures. Instead of causing Damage, a successful attack with a Distracting weapon can force an opponent back 1 yard per SL by which you win the Opposed Test.

Entangle

Your weapon wraps around your opponents, entangling them. Any opponent successfully hit by your weapon gains the *Entangled* Condition with a Strength value equal to your Strength Characteristic. When Entangling an opponent, you cannot otherwise use the weapon to hit. You can end the Entangling whenever you wish.

Fast

Fast weapons are designed to strike out with such speed that parrying is not an option, leaving an opponent skewered before they can react. A wielder of a Fast weapon can choose to attack with the Fast weapon outside of the normal Initiative sequence, either striking first, last, or somewhere in between as desired.

Further, all Melee Tests to defend against Fast weapons suffer a penalty of −10 if your opponent is using a weapon without the Fast Quality; other Skills defend as normal. Two opponents with Fast weapons fight in Initiative order (relative to each other) as normal. A Fast weapon may never also be Slow (Slow takes precedent).

Hack

Hacking weapons have heavy blades that can hack through armour with horrific ease. If you hit an opponent, you Damage a struck piece of armour or shield by 1 point as well as wounding the target.

Impact

Some weapons are just huge or cause terrible damage due to their weight or design. On a successful hit, add the result of the units die of the attack roll to any Damage caused by an Impact weapon. An Undamaging weapon can never also have Impact (Undamaging takes precedent).

Impale

Impale weapons can kill with a single clean blow. Impale weapons cause a Critical Hit on any number divisible by 10 (i.e.: 10, 20, 30, etc.) as well as on doubles (i.e.: 11, 22, 33) rolled equal or under an appropriate Test in combat.

If the impale comes from a ranged weapon, the ammunition used has firmly lodged itself in the target's body. Arrows and bolts require a successful **Challenging (+0) Heal** Test to remove — bullets require a surgeon (see the *Surgery* Talent in **Chapter 4: Skills and Talents**). You cannot heal 1 of your Wounds for each unremoved arrow or bullet.

Penetrating

The weapon is highly effective at penetrating armour. Non-metal APs are ignored, and the first point of all other armour is ignored.

Pistol

You can use this weapon to attack in Close Combat.

Precise

The weapon is easy to get on target. Gain a bonus of +1 SL to any successful Test when attacking with this weapon.

Pummel

Pummel weapons are especially good at battering foes into submission. If you score a Head hit with a Pummel weapon, attempt an **Opposed Strength/ Endurance** test against the struck opponent. If you win the test, your opponent gains a *Stunned* Condition.

Repeater (Rating)

Your weapon holds (Rating) shots, automatically reloading after each time you fire. When you use all your shots, you must fully reload the weapon using the normal rules.

Shield (Rating)

If you use this weapon to oppose an incoming attack, you count as having (Rating) Armour Points on all locations of your body. If your weapon has a Shield Rating of 2 or higher (so: Shield 2 or Shield 3), you may also Oppose incoming missile shots in your Line of Sight.

Trap Blade

Some weapons are designed to trap other weapons, and sometimes even break them. If you score a Critical when defending against an attack from a bladed weapon you can choose to trap it instead of causing a Critical Hit.

If you choose to do this, enact an **Opposed Strength** Test, adding your SL from the previous Melee Test. If you succeed, your opponent drops the blade as it is yanked free. If you score an Astounding Success, you not only disarm your opponent, but the force of your maneuver breaks their blade unless it has the Unbreakable quality. If you fail the Test, your opponent frees the blade and may fight on as normal.

Unbreakable

The weapon is exquisitely well-made or constructed from an especially strong material. Under almost all circumstances, this weapon will not break, corrode, or lose its edge.

Wrap

Wrap weapons typically have long chains with weights at the end, making it very difficult to parry them effectively. Melee Tests opposing an attack from a Wrap weapon suffer a penalty of −1 SL, as parried strikes wrap over the top of shields, or around blades.

WEAPON FLAWS

Some weapons are just difficult to use, or simply dangerous, as described with Weapon Flaws.

Dangerous

Some weapons are almost as likely to hurt you as your opponent. Any failed test including an 9 on either 10s or units die results in a Fumble (see **Chapter 5: Rules** for more on Fumbles).

Imprecise

Imprecise weapons are difficult to bring to bear as they are unwieldy or hard to aim. Suffer a penalty of −1 SL when using the weapon to attack. An Imprecise Weapon can never be Precise (Imprecise takes precedent).

Reload (Rating)

The weapon is slow to reload. An unloaded weapon with this flaw requires an **Extended Ranged** Test for the appropriate Weapon Group scoring (Rating) SL to reload. If you are interrupted while reloading, you must start again from scratch.

Slow

Slow weapons are unwieldy and heavy, making them difficult to use properly. Characters using Slow weapons always strike last in a Round, regardless of Initiative order. Further, opponents gain a bonus of +1 SL to any Test to defend against your attacks.

Tiring

The weapon is fatiguing to use or difficult to bring to bear. You only gain the benefit of the *Impact* and *Damaging* Weapon Traits on a Turn you Charge.

Undamaging

Some weapons are not very good at penetrating armour. All APs are doubled against Undamaging weapons. Further, you do not automatically inflict a minimum of 1 Wound on a successful hit in combat.

ARMOUR

First off, avoid all contact. That's yer basic principle. And in case you can't, always wear protection. ... What?'

– Corporal 'Nobbs' Nobbilar, Basic Combat Instructor.

Armour is listed in the following format:

- **Armour Type:** Each armour is listed by the material its constructed from, in order of protective effectiveness.
- **Price:** The price to buy an average piece of the armour.
- **Enc:** The Encumbrance for the armour.
- **Availability:** The Availability of the armour.
- **Penalty:** Any penalty for wearing that specific piece of Armour in addition to Encumbrance (Page 293). **Note:** Some armour brings a penalty if you wear any of it, such as wearing any chain brings a penalty of −10 Stealth.
- **Locations:** The Hit Locations the Armour protects.
- **APs:** The number of Armour Points the armour provides to the protected Hit Locations.
- **Qualities and Flaws:** Any Armour Qualities or Flaws the armour may possess.

ARMOUR DAMAGE

As blows rains down on your armour, it can be damaged, possibly permanently. Whenever you are instructed to damage a piece of armour, the APs in the location damaged are reduced by 1.

If this lowers the APs to 0 in that location, the armour there is rendered useless.

Armour is generally damaged in one of two ways:

1. A special ability triggers, such as a spell or Talent, damaging a piece of armour
2. A Critical Wound is deflected

Critical Deflection

This only occurs should you choose it to. If you suffer a Critical Wound from an incoming attack on a location protected by armour, you can choose to let your armour be damaged by 1AP in order to ignore the Critical Wound.

You still suffer all normal Wounds (and given your APs are now 1 point lower, you probably suffer an extra Wound), but you avoid the Critical Wound effects as the blow is absorbed by your now-damaged armour.

ARMOUR

Armour	Price	Enc	Availability	Penalty	Locations	APs	Qualities and Flaws
SOFT LEATHER*							
Leather Jack	12/–	1	Common	–	Arms, Body	1	–
Leather Jerkin	10/–	1	Common	–	Body	1	–
Leather Leggings	14/–	1	Common	–	Legs	1	–
Leather Skullcap	8/–	0	Common	–	Head	1	Partial
BOILED LEATHER							
Breastplate	18/–	2	Scarce	–	Body	2	Weakpoints
MAIL**							
Mail Chausses	2GC	3	Scarce	–	Legs	2	Flexible
Mail Coat	3GC	3	Common	–	Arms, Body	2	Flexible
Mail Coif	1GC	2	Scarce	–10% Perception	Head	2	Flexible, Partial
Mail Shirt	2GC	2	Scarce	–	Body	2	Flexible
PLATE**							
Breastplate	10GC	3	Scarce	–	Body	2	Impenetrable, Weakpoints
Open Helm	2GC	1	Common	–10% Perception	Head	2	Partial
Bracers	8GC	3	Rare	–	Arms	2	Impenetrable, Weakpoints
Plate Leggings	10GC	3	Rare	–10 Stealth	Legs	2	Impenetrable, Weakpoints
Helm	3GC	2	Rare	–20% Perception	Head	2	Impenetrable, Weakpoints

* Soft Leather can be worn without penalty under any other Armour.

** Wearing any Mail or Plate confers a Penalty of –10 Stealth each.

Repairing Armour

It costs 10% of the armour's base price per AP lost to repair it. So, if you had a Sleeved Chainmail Coat with 1AP of damage on the Body, and 1AP of damage on the Arms, it will cost you 20% of your armour's base cost to fix it, in this case 12/–. If a section of your armour is completely broken, it will cost you 30% of the armour's base cost to fix, and you'll likely be waiting some time before it's completed.

You can also repair your own armour if you have the appropriate Trade Skill, Trade Tools and, for Plate Armour, a Workshop.

ARMOUR QUALITIES

Armour can possess the following Armour Qualities:

Flexible

Flexible armour can be worn under a layer of non-Flexible armour if you wish. If you do so, you gain the benefit of both.

Impenetrable

The armour is especially resilient, meaning most attacks simply cannot penetrate it. All Critical Wounds caused by an odd number to hit you, such as 11 or 33, are ignored.

Armour Flaws

Some armours have points of weakness, as described by Armour Flaws.

Partial

The armour does not cover the entire hit location. An opponent that rolls an even number to hit, or rolls a Critical Hit, ignores the partial armour's APs.

Weakpoints

The armour has small weakpoints where a blade can slip in if your opponent is sufficiently skilled or lucky. If your opponent has a weapon with the Impale Quality and scores a Critical, the APs of your armour are ignored.

OPTIONS: QUICK ARMOUR

For those who want fast, simple rules for armour, use the following. Armour is split into three bands: Light, Medium, and Heavy. Those in Light are wearing mostly leathers, those in medium are wearing mostly chain, and those in heavy are wearing mostly plate.

Armour	Price	Enc	Availability	Penalty	Locations	APs	Qualities and Flaws
Light Armour	2GC	1	Common	–	All	1	Flexible
Medium Armour	5GC	5	Scarce	−10% Perception −10 Stealth	All	2	Flexible
Heavy Armour	30GC	6	Rare	−20% Perception −20 Stealth	All	3	Impenetrable, Weakpoints

PACKS AND CONTAINERS

Trappings can be packed into backpacks, sacks, and pouches, making them easier to carry. The table shows the Encumbrance value for carrying a pack or other container (**Enc**), and the number of Encumbrance the container can carry (**Carries**). You only count the **Enc** value to determine the number of Encumbrance points carried. Common sense dictates whether items can be carried in containers (e.g. halberds cannot be carried in backpacks).

Item	Cost	Enc	Carries	Availability
Backpack	4/10	2	4	Common
Barrel	8/–	6	12	Common
Cask	3/–	2	4	Common
Flask	5/–	0	0	Common
Jug	3/2	1	1	Common
Pewter Stein	4/–	0	0	Common
Pouch	4d	0	1	Common
Sack	1/–	2	4	Common
Sack, Large	1/6	3	6	Common
Saddlebags	18/–	4	8	Common
Sling Bag	1/–	1	2	Common
Scroll Case	16/–	0	0	Scarce
Waterskin	1/8	1	1	Common

Backpack: Counts as 'worn' when strapped to your back.
Barrel: Capacity: 32 gallons of liquid.
Cask: Capacity: 10 gallons of liquid.
Flask: Capacity: 1 pint of liquid.
Jug: Capacity: 1 gallon of liquid.
Sack: Requires 1 hand to carry.
Sack, Large: Requires 1 hand to carry (or 2 hands if full).
Sling Bag: Counts as 'worn' when slung over your shoulder.
Waterskin: Capacity: 1 gallon of liquid.

CLOTHING AND ACCESSORIES

Clothing styles in the Empire vary considerably. As a general guideline, commoners wear simple tunics with breeches or gowns. Middle-class citizens favour puff-and-slash fashions with hats and hosiery or dresses. The elites flaunt capes, furs, and flamboyant hats with extravagantly enormous feathers – the more exotic the better!

Item	Cost	Enc	Availability
Amulet	2d	0	Common
Boots	5/–	1	Common
Cloak	10/–	1	Common
Clothing	6/–	1	Common
Coat	18/–	1	Common
Costume	1GC	1	Scarce
Courtly Garb	12GC	1	Scarce
Face Powder	10/–	0	Common
Gloves	4/–	0	Common
Hat	4/–	0	Common
Hood or Mask	5/–	0	Common
Jewellery	Varies	0	Common
Perfume	10/–	0	Common
Pins (6)	10/–	0	Scarce
Religious Symbol	6/8	0	Common
Robes	2GC	1	Common
Sceptre	8GC	1	Rare
Shoes	5/–	0	Common
Signet Ring	5GC	0	Rare
Tattoo	4/– +	0	Scarce
Uniform	1GC 2/–	1	Scarce
Walking Cane	3GC	1	Common

Cloak: Protects wearer against the elements.

Coat: Protects wearer against the elements and extreme cold; without a good coat or similar, you will receive penalties to resist cold exposure (see page 181).

Courtly Garb: Nobles' garb features embellishments such as lace cuffs & collars, excessive high-quality fabric and pointed shoes. Servants also wear courtly garb to banquets and ceremonies, although their surcoats and corsets are less ostentatious than the nobles' fashions and can therefore be purchased at half price.

Hat: Fine quality hats are status symbols in the Empire's towns and cities. The more flamboyant the hat, the better.

Jewellery: Prices vary by craftsmanship, metal type, and gem value. As a general guideline, common rings without any gemstones cost 10 coins equal to their metal type (i.e. brass, silver or gold) whereas necklaces cost 20 coins of the same metal type.

Sceptre: The highest-ranking legal officials carry sceptres to indicate their status.

Signet Ring: Gold rings with engraved stamps are worn by nobles and guild officials, who use them to imprint heraldry or insignia into sealing wax.

Walking Cane: Polished wooden canes with metal caps are status symbols amongst wealthier townsfolk.

FOOD, DRINK, AND LODGING

Poor quality room and board costs half the listed price, and fine quality costs double the listed price. Consuming poor quality food or drink comes with a 10% risk of exposure to the *Galloping Trots* (see page 187).

Item	Cost	Enc	Availability
Ale, pint	3d	0	Common
Ale, keg	3/–	2	Common
Bugman's XXXXXX Ale, pint	9d	0	Exotic
Food, groceries/day	10d	1	Common
Meal, inn	1/–	0	Common
Rations, 1 day	2/–	0	Common
Room, common/night	10d	–	Common
Room, private/night	10/–	–	Common
Spirits, pint	2/–	0	Common
Stables/night	10d	–	Common
Wine, bottle	10d	0	Common
Wine & Spirits, drink	4d	0	Common

Ale, keg: Capacity 3 gallons. Empty kegs can be refilled for 18d.

Bugman's XXXXXX Ale: Merchants travel across the Old World to purchase this potent Dwarfen ale from the famous brewery founded by Josef Bugman. Bugman's Ale is distributed to most major cities. One mug of Bugman's counts as 4 mugs of normal ale for intoxication purposes (see **Consume Alcohol** on page 121), and grants immunity to Fear Tests for 1d10 hours.

Room, Common: Guests sleeping in common rooms should be wary of thieves.

Room, Inn: Accommodates 2 guests. Large rooms cost double the price and accommodate 4 guests.

TOOLS AND KITS

The majority of tools count as Improvised Weapons when used in combat, however GMs may rule that heavy or sharp tools (e.g. crowbars and sickles) count as Hand Weapons. Many of the individual tools listed here are included in Trade Tool packages and Workshops, and need not be bought separately.

Animal Trap: Used to catch game (see **Gathering Food and Herbs** on page 127).

Antitoxin Kit: Contains a small knife, herbs, and a jar of leeches. A successful Heal Test with an antitoxin kit removes all *Poisoned* Conditions. Treatment takes at least two Rounds.

Disguise Kit: Contains enough props for four disguises (e.g. wigs and make-up) and also materials for changing your appearance used by those with the Entertain (Acting) Skill (e.g. wax, fake blood, and prosthetics).

Fish Hooks: Can be used to catch fish (see **Gathering Food and Herbs** on page 127).

Lock Picks: An assortment of small, variously-shaped tools needed to use the Pick Lock Skill without penalty.

Item	Cost	Enc	Availability	Item	Cost	Enc	Availability
Abacus	3/4	0	Scarce	Lock Picks	15/–	0	Scarce
Animal Trap	2/6	1	Common	Manacles	18/–	0	Scarce
Antitoxin Kit	3GC	0	Scarce	Mop	1/–	2	Common
Boat Hook	5/–	1	Common	Nails (12)	2d	0	Common
Broom	10d	2	Common	Paint Brush	4/–	0	Common
Bucket	2/6	1	Common	Pestle & Mortar	14/–	0	Common
Chisel	4/2	0	Common	Pick	18/–	1	Scarce
Comb	10d	0	Common	Pole (3 yards)	8/–	3	Common
Crowbar	2/6	1	Common	Quill Pen	3/–	0	Common
Crutch	3/–	2	Common	Rake	4/6	2	Common
Disguise Kit	6/6	0	Scarce	Reading Lens	3GC	0	Rare
Ear Pick	2/–	0	Scarce	Saw	6/–	1	Common
Fish Hooks (12)	1/–	0	Common	Sickle	1GC	1	Common
Floor Brush	1/6	0	Common	Spade	8/–	2	Common
Gavel	1GC	0	Scarce	Spike	1/–	0	Common
Hammer	3/–	0	Common	Stamp, engraved	5GC	0	Scarce
Hand Mirror	1GC 1/6	0	Exotic	Tongs, steel	16/–	0	Common
Hoe	4/–	2	Common	Telescope	5GC	0	Rare
Key	1/–	0	Common	Tweezers	1/–	0	Scarce
Knife	8/–	0	Common	Writing Kit	2GC	0	Scarce

Manacles: Prisoners trying to break out of manacles suffer 1 Wound and must pass a **Very Hard (-30) Strength** Test.

Pole: A long pole used for barging; counts as an Improvised Weapon.

Reading Lens: Glass lenses with handles provide a +20 bonus to Read/Write Tests for deciphering tiny or unintelligible writing. Perception Tests to search for fine details such as secret doors or compartments also receive a +20 bonus.

Writing Kit: Contains a quill pen, inkpot, and ink blotter.

BOOKS AND DOCUMENTS

The printing press is a recent invention in the Empire, so most books are still hand-written, some with pages adorned with exquisite illuminations, others little better than scribbled notes. In larger settlements, official documents, newssheets, and leaflets are typically press-printed, as are many poems, romances, and important academic texts. All prices are loose suggestions only, as contents and quality vary significantly.

Item	Cost	Enc	Availability
Book, Apothecary	8GC	1	Scarce
Book, Art	5GC	1	Scarce
Book, Cryptography	8GC	1	Exotic
Book, Engineer	3GC	1	Scarce
Book, Law	15GC	1	Rare
Book, Magic	20GC	1	Exotic
Book, Medicine	15GC	1	Rare
Book, Religion	1GC	1	Common
Guild License	N/A	0	N/A
Leaflet	1/–	0	Common
Legal Document	3/–	0	Common
Map	3GC	0	Scarce
Parchment/sheet	1/–	0	Common

Book, Apothecary: Apothecary books are usually hand-written. A basic apothecary book contains ingredient descriptions and diagrammed instructions for brewing processes. Formulas for Digestive Tonics, Healing Draughts, and Vitality Draughts are usually included (see **Herbs & Draughts**). Advanced texts contain formulas for more exotic draughts.

Book, Art: Plays, poems, and ballads or perhaps musical arrangements scribbled on loose parchment, Art books come in

many forms. They also include treatises on perspective, form, and style, often written by famous painters or sculptors — such as Leonardo da Miragliano — for mass printing.

Book, Cryptography: Where individual ciphers and encryption keys can be written on a single page or two, Cryptography books are often hand-scribed codices dealing with mathematics, numerology, and polyalphabetic encryption.

Book, Engineer: The majority of engineering books are press-printed. Engineering is an advanced science in the Empire, largely due to the Imperial Engineers' School in Altdorf and the Dwarf Engineers' Guild. Because of this, Engineering texts are often authored, co-authored, or edited by Dwarfs.

Book, Law: Laws vary considerably from one region to the next. Cities with printing presses compile legislation in bound volumes, whereas judges in smaller towns often rely on documents hand-written centuries ago. Law books used by travelling lawyers or judges often combine printed and written pages from different towns across the Empire, collated and bound together within the same cover.

Book, Magic: Spell grimoires are usually scribed by wizards, and their covers are often secured with locks. Sometimes grimoires are even protected by magical alarms or wards. Carrying a spell grimoire is punishable as heresy unless the owning wizard is licensed by the Colleges of Magic.

Book, Medicine: Medical texts can either be scribed or press-printed, depending on the authoring physician's prestige. Illuminations are common, and usually include detailed autopsy drawings and procedural diagrams.

Book, Religion: Religions books come in all forms in the Empire, a realm renowned for its religious observances. There is a eager market for the most popular texts, most of which are cheaply produced by printing presses.

Guild License: Guild licenses are usually printed on single sheets of parchment, stamped with an official seal, and signed by the local guild master. Guild licenses are not purchased; instead, they are granted to guild members according to each guild's traditions and laws.

Legal Document: A simple legal document such as a will, IOU or letter of intent.

OPTIONS: GUILDERS

If you have an appropriate guild license, you can use your special contacts to locate rare items. If you fail an Availability Test when trying to buy an item, you can make a **Gossip Test** to talk with your fellow Guilders and see if any of them know where you might find what you need. If you succeed, one of your contacts has a few useful suggestions, and you can reroll the Availability Test.

TRADE TOOLS AND WORKSHOPS

Trade Tools are needed if your wish to take a Trade Test to make or fix something, and the examples below are a sample of the many options available. Workshops are needed for larger projects, such as creating new trappings.

Item	Cost	Enc	Availability
Trade Tools	3GC	1	Rare
Workshop	80GC	N/A	Exotic

Apothecary: Tools include pestle and mortar, spoons, jars, and weights and scales. Workshops also include oil burners and shelves full of ingredients.

Artisan: The potential range of tools used by Artisans is wide. Sample packages include:

- **Carpenter:** Hammer and nails, saw, measuring rod, chalk, and plumb lines. Workshops also include lathes, planes, clamps, and a supply of lumber.

- **Engraver:** Gravers, punches, wax, acid, hammer, and chisels. Workshops also include dies and presses.

- **Smith:** Hammer, tongs, punches, swages, bits, and augers. Workshops also include an anvil, furnace, swage block, sledgehammers, and metal ingots.

Other Artisans include: Armourer, Bowyer, Brewer, Candlemaker, Calligrapher, Cartographer, Cobbler, Cook, Cooper, Embalmer, Gem Cutter, Glassblower, Goldsmith, Gunsmith, Jeweller, Leatherworker, Mason, Painter, Potter, Shipwright, Stoneworker, Tailor, Tanner, Vintner, Weaver, Weaponsmith and Woodcarver.

Artist: Brushes and paints, hammer and chisels, rasps and files, and scrapers. Workshops also include easels or pedestals and supplies of canvas, parchment, vellum, wood, clay or uncut stone.

Engineer: Hourglass, measuring rod, fuse cord, drafting compass, and T-square. Workshops also include pulleys, ropes, and drafting tables.

Herbalist: Pestle and mortar, small knives, pruning shears, and gloves. Workshops also include drying racks, strainers, funnels, bowls, and jars.

Navigator: Quadrant, astrolabe, charts and compasses, hourglass, and sounding line.

Physician: Needles and sutures, bandages, scalpel, vinegar, forceps, and a speculum. Workshops also include anatomical drawings, assorted implements, and a surgery table.

ANIMALS AND VEHICLES

Animals are used at all levels of society in the Empire. See the **Chapter 12: Bestiary** for sample animal profiles. Like **Packs and Containers** (see page 301), all vehicles have an entry for the number of Encumbrance points they can carry (**Carries**).

Item	Cost	Enc	Carries	Availability
Cart	20GC	–	25	Common
Chicken	5d	1	0	Common
Coach	150GC	–	80	Rare
Coracle	2GC	6	10	Scarce
Destrier	230GC	–	20	Scarce
Dog collar and lead	1/7	0	–	Common
Draught Horse	4GC	–	20	Common
Homing Pigeons	3/–	1	0	Scarce
Hunting Dog	2GC	–	0	Rare
Light Warhorse	70GC	–	18	Common
Monkey	10GC	2	1	Rare
Mule	5GC	–	14	Common
Pony	10GC	–	14	Common
Riding Horse	15GC	–	16	Common
River Barge	225GC	–	300	Rare
Row Boat	6GC	–	60	Scarce
Saddle and Harness	6GC	4	–	Common
Wagon	75GC	–	30	Common
Worms (6)	1d	0	–	Common

Cart: One driver and one draft animal required.
Coach: Two drivers and four horses are standard.
Coracle: Coracles are small, lightweight boats that accommodate one person and can be carried easily. They are made from leather or bark stretched over a wood frame, and rowed with a single oar.
Destrier: Horse trained for war.
River Barge: Three crew are standard.
Row Boat: One rower is standard.
Wagon: One driver and two horses are standard.

DRUGS AND POISONS

Recreational drugs, although not illegal in most parts of the Empire, are frequently associated with dubious rituals and cults by the Cult of Sigmar. Attitudes are more liberal in large cities where dens can be found offering spit, weirdroot, or Ranald's Delight. Poison is not illegal either, but owning poison is bound to raise questions about its intended use.

Item	Cost	Enc	Availability
Black Lotus	20GC	0	Exotic
Heartkill	40GC	0	Exotic
Mad Cap Mushrooms	5GC	0	Exotic
Mandrake Root	1GC	0	Rare
Moonflower	5GC	0	Scarce
Ranald's Delight	18/–	0	Scarce
Spit	1GC 5/–	0	Rare
Weirdroot	4/–	0	Rare

Black Lotus: This deadly plant grows in Southland jungles and is used for blade venom. Victims who suffer at least 1 Wound from a sap-coated blade immediately take 2 *Poisoned* Conditions. Resisted with a **Difficult (–10) Endurance** Test.

Heartkill: Combining the venoms from an Amphisbaena (a rare, two-headed serpent) and a Jabberslythe produces an odourless, colourless poison. When ingested, the deadly mixture inflicts 4 *Poisoned* Conditions. Resisted with a **Difficult (–10) Endurance** Test.

Mad Cap Mushrooms: These hallucinogenic mushrooms are eaten by Goblin fanatics before battle. They induce a berserker rage, adding +10 Strength, +4 Wounds, and the *Frenzy* Talent. When the effect wears off, the user loses 1d10 Wounds. Non-Greenskins must also pass a **Challenging (+0) Endurance** Test or contract a Minor Infection. **Duration:** Active when chewed plus an additional 2d10 minutes.

Mandrake Root: This highly-addictive deliriant grows under gallows, and is chewed to keep an unquiet mind still. Users must pass a Willpower Test every Round to perform an Action *or* a Move (choose one); further, Movement is halved. However, Cool Tests receive a bonus of +20. **Duration:** Active when chewed plus an additional 1d10×10 minutes.

Moonflower: This tranquilliser is a dried moss which grows only on leaves in the Laurelorn forest. Elves use Moonflower to treat Black Plague, granting a bonus of +30 to any associated Tests for Elves to resist the disease, otherwise it has no effect on their species. Others can inhale vapours from boiling the moss and if they fail a **Very Hard (–30) Willpower** Test will gain an *Unconscious* Condition; if passed, they receive a bonus of +20 to Cool Tests and gain a *Fatigued* Condition. Moonflower is used by the most expensive Physicians as an anesthetic. **Duration:** 1d10+5 hours.

Ranald's Delight: This highly-addictive stimulant is a synthetic compound made from sulphur, mercury and other elements. Inhaling the powder provides a bonus of +1 to Movement, and +10 to WS, S, T, and Agi. This last for 3 hours, after which the user suffers a penalty of –2 Movement and –20 on Weapon Skill, Strength, Toughness, and Agility. **Duration:** 1 day.

Spit: Extracted from Chameleoleeches found in the marshes of the Empire, this extraordinarily powerful hallucinogen brings visions of something deeply desired, such as a lost lover, a dead friend, or a missing child. Called Spit on the streets, it's popular with those lost to despair. Upon exposure, you must pass a **Very Hard (–30) Toughness** Test or be lost to a fully real fantasy, which is a matter for the GM to handle. **Duration:** 1d10 minutes.

Weirdroot: One of the most common street-drugs in the Empire, Weirdroot is chewed, bringing a sense of euphoria and pleasant hallucinations, which some suggest may be connected to the Winds of Magic. The drug gives a +10 bonus to Toughness and Willpower Tests, but a penalty of –10 to Agility, Initiative, and Intelligence Tests. **Duration:** Active when chewed plus an additional 1d10×10 minutes.

HERBS AND DRAUGHTS

Medicinal herbs can either be purchased or gathered from the wild (see Gathering Food and Herbs on page 127). Preparation with Trade Tools (Herbalist) is usually required to extract the plant's medicinal ingredients and create poultices. Draughts can be brewed using the Trade (Apothecary) Skill.

Item	Cost	Enc	Availability
Digestive Tonic	3/–	0	Common
Earth Root	5GC	0	Scarce
Faxtoryll	15/–	0	Exotic
Healing Draught	10/–	0	Scarce
Healing Poultice	12/–	0	Common
Nightshade	3GC	0	Rare
Salwort	12/–	0	Common
Vitality Draught	18/–	0	Scarce

Digestive Tonic: Provides +20 to recovery Tests from stomach ailments such as the *Galloping Trots* or *Bloody Flux* (see **Disease and Infection** on page 186).

Earth Root: This herb is ingested to negate the effects of Buboes caused by the Black Plague (though the swellings are still significant). Further, gain a bonus of +10 on all Tests concerning the disease. **Dose:** 1 per day.

Faxtoryll: When smeared on a wound, poultices made from this herbal coagulant remove all *Bleeding* Conditions without a Heal Test. **Dose:** 1 per Critical Wound.

Healing Draught: If you have more than 0 Wounds, recover Toughness Bonus Wounds immediately. **Dose:** 1 per encounter.

Healing Poultice: This foul-smelling medicinal wrap is made from animal dung and urine combined with any number of common herbs such as Sigmafoil, Tarrabeth, and Valerian. You do not suffer any Minor Infections from a Critical Wound treated with a Healing Poultice.

Nightshade: Consuming this herb causes the victim to fall into a deep sleep after 2-3 hours, unless an Endurance Test is passed. A Nightshade slumber lasts 1d10+4 hours. **Dose:** 1 per person.

Salwort: When held under someone's nose, the aroma from a crushed sprig of this herb removes 1 *Stunned* Condition. **Dose:** 1 per encounter.

Vitality Draught: Drinking this draught instantly removes all *Fatigued* Conditions.

PROSTHETICS

Whether through disease, warfare, or misfortune, it's a relatively common occurrence in the Empire to lose body parts. For those who do, there are a variety of alternatives on offer. All Prosthetics have an Encumbrance of 0 when worn.

Item	Cost	Enc	Availability
Eye Patch	6d	0	Common
False Eye	1GC	0	Rare
False Leg	16/–	2	Scarce
Gilded Nose	18/–	0	Scarce
Hook	3/4	1	Common
Engineering Marvel	20GC	1	Exotic
Wooden teeth	10/–	0	Rare

Eye Patch: Often decorated, an eye patch is used to cover scarred eye sockets.

False Eye: Particularly popular amongst the rich who prefer not to wear cruder eye-patches, false eyes come in many forms, from wooden to polished glass.

False Leg: A False Leg (or just a False Foot, for half price), allows you to ignore 1 point of Movement loss due to the missing body part. Further, for 100 XP you can regain the last point of Movement Loss as you train yourself to use your new body part, and for 200 XP you relearn how to use Dodge again. This all requires you not to lose your False Leg, though.

Gilded Nose: Though most are made of wood or ceramic, the term gilded nose is widely used regardless. You can ignore the Fellowship loss for having no nose.

Hook: You have a hook strapped where you used to have a hand. A surprisingly nimble tool once you are used to it, you can buy back the −20 penalty on all Tests involving two hands for 100 XP per 5 you subtract from the penalty, removing the penalty completely for 400 XP. **Append:** In Close Combat, Hooks count as Daggers.

Engineering Marvel: Only for the exceedingly rich, you commission a work of art from one of the Engineers' Guilds, allowing you to completely ignore the loss of an ear, hand, arm, or leg, as steam hisses and machinery clicks in place of blood and muscle. Should you ever receive a Critical Wound to the marvel, it automatically breaks down, and needs to be taken back for costly repair (at least 10% of the base cost, depending upon the nature of the Critical Wound received).

Wooden Teeth: False Teeth are often beautifully carved and painted, and sometimes a significant improvement to the originals. You ignore all penalties for loss of teeth.

MISCELLANEOUS TRAPPINGS

If players wish to buy something that isn't included on this list, the GM can reference similar items for price and availability guidelines.

Item	Cost	Enc	Availability
Ball	5d	0	Common
Bandage	4d	0	Common
Baton	1/–	0	Common
Bedroll	6/–	1	Common
Blanket	8d	0	Common
Candle (dozen)	1/–	0	Common
Canvas Tarp	8/–	1	Common
Chalk	10d	0	Common
Charcoal stick	10d	0	Common
Cutlery	3/6	0	Common
Davrich Lamp	2GC	1	Rare
Deck of Cards	1/–	0	Common
Cooking Pot	8/–	1	Common
Cup	8d	0	Common
Dice	10d	0	Common
Doll	2/–	0	Common
Grappling Hook	1GC –/10	1	Scarce
Instrument	2GC	1	Rare
Lamp Oil	2/–	0	Common
Lantern	12/–	1	Common
Storm Lantern	1GC	1	Scarce
Match	1d	0	Common
Pan	7/6	1	Common
Pipe and Tobacco	3/4	0	Scarce
Placard	1/–	2	Common
Plate	1/–	0	Common
Bowl	1/–	0	Common
Rags	1d	0	Common
Rope, 10 yards	8/4	1	Common
Tent	12/–	2	Scarce
Tinderbox	4/2	0	Common

Bandage: A successful Heal or Dexterity Test removes +1 extra Bleeding Status.

Bedroll: Endurance Tests rolled to resist cold exposure (see page 181) gain a bonus of +20 when resting.

Candle: Provides illumination for 10 yards when lit.

Davrich Lamp: A safety lamp emitting the light of a candle, first developed for Reikland's mines by Master Engineer Davrich Stephansson. It flares brightly in 'firedamp' (explosive gasses); after 1d10 rounds of exposure to the lamp the firedamp will explode. It is wise to withdraw before this happens.

Grappling Hook: Coupled with a rope, allows unscalable surfaces to be climbed.

Instrument: Various instruments are included in this category. The standard price and encumbrance reflects medium-sized instruments (e.g. mandolin, coach horn, small drum). Small instruments are half the price and 0 Encumbrance points (e.g. flute, recorder, tambourine). Larger instruments are double the price and 2 Encumbrance points (e.g. harp, lute, large drum).

Lamp Oil: Contains enough fuel for 4 hours of standard use, or 8 hours of low flame equivalent to a candle.

Lantern: Provides illumination for 20 yards.

Storm Lantern: Shutters protect the flame from wind, and also enable the light to be directed in a 90° arc or darkened altogether. Provides illumination for 20 yards, or 30 when targeted.

Tent: A medium-sized tent accommodating four people sleeping in close quarters. Small tents accommodate 2 people for half the price and 1 Encumbrance point. Large tents accommodate 8 people for double the price and 4 Encumbrance points.

HIRELINGS

If you need extra muscle or brains whilst adventuring, you may pay Hireling NPCs to accompany you. You can hire any Career with GM permission, and they are paid an amount of coin equal to their Social Status for a quick job, or paid triple for a full day's work. The GM may increase or decrease this amount according to individual personality and local circumstances.

If the job at hand is unexpectedly dangerous, Hirelings will expect double the normal pay unless a **Leadership** Test is passed. Leadership Tests may also be required when Hirelings are

assigned complex, independent tasks, or if they have good reason to flee from an encounter. Quick Hireling profiles are created by adding 5 Advances to every Career Characteristic and Skill per level of the Career hired, and 1 Talent per level. Hirelings with more experienced than this usually cost more.

SAMPLE HIRELINGS

Hireling	Quick Job	Daily Cost	Weekly Cost	Notes
Local Scout	5d	15d	10/–	Works independently without Leadership Tests
Seasoned Mercenary	3/–	9/–	3GC 12/–	Demands a share of loot in lieu of danger pay
Lawyer	3/–	9/–	3GC 12/–	Drafting a simple legal document costs 2–4 shillings
Porter	1/–	3/–	1GC 4/–	Carries 10 Encumbrance points
Scribe	2/–	6/–	2GC 8/–	Also translates 1–2 other common languages
Doktor	5/–	15/–	5GC	A single visit costs 4–6 shillings for medical attention

HENCHMEN

Henchmen are Hirelings, companions, friends, pets, or other NPCs that are effectively permanent members of your party. Unlike other NPCs, Henchmen should have full character sheets, just like a PC, and are typically attached to one player, either as an employee, friend, owner, or similar. The Henchmen earns half the XP of that player, rounding down, which the player may spend on the Henchman's behalf. Henchmen not only make memorable allies, but should your character die, they can also make marvellous PC replacements instead of creating a new character.

• BESTIARY •

'Adversity with the monster makes the man. Prosperity with the man makes the monster.'

– Albrecht Zweistein, Middenlander Professor

The creatures presented in the Bestiary are generic, typical starter examples of their ilk. You are encouraged to customise them and create your own, using the statistics found here and adding Skills and Talents as you feel are necessary, perhaps even using the full Career system to create terrifying opponents. The quickest way to create fast NPC adversaries is to use Creature Traits; all creatures come with one or more Creature Traits as standard, but additional ones can be added as required, and they can be mixed with Skills and Talents as you see fit.

The **Optional** traits listed alongside each creature presents some of the most commonly found variants of the species. However, you may choose to apply any trait to any creature if it fits what you want to represent in your game.

For Creature Trait rules, refer to page 338.

CREATURE HIT LOCATIONS

At some point you may need to determine a Hit Location for a non-Human-shaped creature. Normally, this is simple. For quadrupeds, simply make arm hits foreleg hits, and leg hits rear-leg hits. Or for birds, make arm hits equate to wing hits. However, some require special attention, such as Snakes and Spiders. For those, use **Alternative Hit Locations**.

For any creature 2 steps larger than you (see **Size** on page 341), choose a location to hit according to what's closest to you (or in Line-of-Sight for shooting).

If an animal has a Hit Location without a Critical Table, such as a tentacle, tail, or wing, roll on the Arm table and describe the results in an appropriate way.

ALTERNATIVE HIT LOCATIONS

Snakes		Spiders	
01–19	Head	01–09	Head
20–00	Body	10–79	Legs
		80–00	Body

GENERIC CREATURE TRAITS

Generic Creature Traits add extra variety to your NPCs. The following traits are appended to the Optional list of all creatures.

Afraid, Animosity, Armour, Big, Brute, Clever, Cunning, Elite, Fast, Hardy, Hatred, Leader, Prejudice, Tough, Weapon

Note: Most creatures have a suggested Weapon included, and maybe Armour too, but that doesn't preclude them from being changed as you see fit.

BESTIARY FORMAT

- **Name:** The creature's name
- The creature's description.
- **Attributes:** The creature's 12 attributes.
- **Traits:** The Creature Traits the creature almost always has.
- **Optional:** Common Creature Traits the creature may have when creating your own.

THE PEOPLES OF THE REIKLAND

Chapter 2: Character presents the primary peoples of the Reikland. This section explains how to create fast NPC equivalents, and also introduces Ogres.

For important characters in your campaign, you may want to use the full character creation rules. However, sometimes you just want a fast NPC. To quickly create an NPC, use one of the following standard profiles and apply Creature Traits as required, with those listed in **Generic Creature Traits** being the best initial choices.

HUMANS

M	WS	BS	S	T	I	Ag	Dex	Int	WP	Fel	W
4	30	30	30	30	30	30	30	30	30	30	12

Traits: Prejudice (choose one), Weapon+7
Optional: Disease, Ranged+8 (50), Spellcaster

DWARFS

M	WS	BS	S	T	I	Ag	Dex	Int	WP	Fel	W
3	40	30	30	40	30	20	40	30	50	20	16

Traits: Animosity (choose one), Hatred (Greenskins), Magic Resistance (2), Night Vision, Prejudice (choose one), Weapon+7
Optional: Fury, Ranged+8 (50)

HALFLINGS

M	WS	BS	S	T	I	Ag	Dex	Int	WP	Fel	W
3	20	40	20	30	30	30	40	30	40	40	10

Traits: Night Vision, Size (Small), Weapon+5
Optional: Ranged+7 (25), Stealthy

ELVES (HIGH AND WOOD)

M	WS	BS	S	T	I	Ag	Dex	Int	WP	Fel	W
5	40	40	30	30	50	40	40	40	40	30	13

Traits: Animosity (choose one), Prejudice (choose two), Night Vision, Weapon+7
Optional: Arboreal, Magical, Magical Resistance, Ranged+9 (150), Stealthy, Spellcaster (any one), Tracker

OGRES

Big, loud, brutish, and extremely violent, Ogres are driven by the need to fill their prodigious, muscled bellies. They lack the wit or intelligence to do this cleverly, defaulting to might is right in most situations. Hailing from lands far to the east, Ogres are a common sight in the Old World for they love to wander, always on the hunt for new meats over the horizon. As they pass through on decades-long food excursions, they work hard to integrate, wearing local clothing and following the local customs they understand, as that's more likely to attract the next meal.

In the Empire, they frequently serve in the State Army, and are an everyday sight in larger towns, contracted as muscle for hire. The Halfling Gaffers Guild (building contractors) has effectively cornered the market in cheap Ogre labour in many towns and cities of the Empire, a source of great annoyance to their rivals.

M	WS	BS	S	T	I	Ag	Dex	Int	WP	Fel	W
6	30	20	45	45	10	25	20	20	30	20	30

Traits: Armour 1, Hungry, Prejudice (Thin People), Night Vision, Size (Large), Weapon+8
Optional: Belligerent, Infected, Tracker

'Yes, I summoned them because I needed reinforcements. Yes, I know they are eating your prize cattle. And, yes, I know Ogres have large appetites. I've put a notice on the local watch-house offering a small payment to anyone with the wherewithal to make them go. That should prove more than sufficient.'

– Augustus von Raushvel, Baron of Raush Vale

HALFLINGS AND OGRES

None know why, but Halflings and Ogres just get on. Most elders of Halfling clans have one or two Ogre bodyguards, and it's said the Elder of the Moot rarely travels without his old friend Zorarth Legbiter, a hoary Ogre who's lived in the Empire for almost a century. In return, many Ogre mercenary bands employ Halfling cooks. However, this relationship doesn't always hold, such as when Golgfag Maneater, mercenary captain of the imaginatively named Golgfag's Maneaters, famously employing a small clan of Halflings to feed him and his regiment after a great victory. Which was fine until Golgfag realised the cooks tasted far better than the food they'd prepared...

DOGS

Dogs are bred for myriad purposes throughout the Old World. While the pampered pooches of the courtiers of Altdorf pose only a threat to an adventurer's dignity, larger breeds, including those bred for war and dogfighting can be a formidable threat.

M	WS	BS	S	T	I	Ag	Dex	Int	WP	Fel	W
4	25	–	20	20	35	30	–	15	10	15	5

Traits: Bestial, Night Vision, Skittish, Size (Small), Stride, Weapon+5
Optional: Armour 1, Frenzy, Infected, Size (Little to Average), Territorial, Tracker, Trained (Broken, Entertain, Fetch, Guard, Magic, War)

GIANT RATS

Rats get everywhere and are especially prevalent in the cities and towns. The more densely people are packed in, the more densely Rats are packed in with them, which is especially bad when the creatures carry disease. Though typically small, they can grow to monstrous proportions, with reports of rats beneath Altdorf the size of a Human and larger. Rat catchers are employed to keep them in check.

M	WS	BS	S	T	I	Ag	Dex	Int	WP	Fel	W
4	25	–	30	25	25	35	–	15	15	–	5

Traits: Bestial, Infected, Night Vision, Size (Small), Skittish, Stride, Weapon+4
Optional: Armour 1, Disease (Ratte Fever or Black Plague), Size (Little to Average), Swarm, Trained (War)

GIANT SPIDERS

Giant Spiders lurk deep within the forests and caves of the Empire, but can live anywhere, including dusty attics and dark cellars. Most trap their prey with strong webs before injecting venom. Though most are the size of a large Rat, some Giant Spider species are terrifyingly large. Forest Goblins often capture larger examples for mounts.

M	WS	BS	S	T	I	Ag	Dex	Int	WP	Fel	W
5	35	25	15	25	10	35	30	5	25	–	2

Traits: Bestial, Night Vision, Size (Little), Wallcrawler, Web 40, Weapon+3
Optional: Armour 1, Arboreal, Bite, Size (Little to Enormous), Swarm, Venom (Average), Trained (Broken, Guard, Magic, Mount, War)

HORSES

Horses are bred for many jobs, including speedy mounts for messengers, sturdy destriers for knights, and mighty drays for farmers. They are so useful, horse trading is almost a competitive sport in the Reikland. Unscrupulous 'Horse Copers' (horse salesmen) are keen to make money at the expense of the ignorant buyer, painting and filing teeth of elderly horses or stuffing rags up noses to soak mucous, so the unknowledgeable buyer should beware.

M	WS	BS	S	T	I	Ag	Dex	Int	WP	Fel	W
7	25	–	45	35	15	30	–	10	10	10	22

Traits: Bestial, Size (Large), Skittish, Stride, Weapon+7
Optional: Armour, Trained (Broken, Drive, Entertain, Magic, Mount, War)

PIGEONS

Pigeons are bred across the Reikland to carry messages of all kinds. Recently, they have become renowned for carrying a deadlier cargo, as the easily accessible bird has become a favourite amongst engineers, used to deploy their 'pigeon bombs' to varying degrees of success.

M	WS	BS	S	T	I	Ag	Dex	Int	WP	Fel	W
2	15	–	5	15	25	40	–	10	20	10	1

Traits: Bestial, Fly 100, Size (Tiny), Skittish, Weapon+0
Optional: Size (Small), Trained (Broken, Home)

SNAKES

Snakes are found throughout the Empire, especially deep within the forests. Most are harmless, but some possess deadly venom or constrict their victims until they die of suffocation. Like many creatures of the Old World, they can grow to gigantic proportions, such as the enormous Fen Worm, posing a real danger to even the strongest mercenary.

M	WS	BS	S	T	I	Ag	Dex	Int	WP	Fel	W
3	40	–	30	25	25	40	–	5	45	–	8

Traits: Armour 1, Bestial, Cold-blooded, Fast, Size (Small), Weapon+5
Optional: Constrictor, Size (Tiny to Enormous), Swamp-strider, Swarm, Venom (Very Easy–Very Hard)

WOLVES

Wolves usually hunt in packs and have a reputation for being tenacious hunters, pursuing their prey over dozens of miles without rest or respite. Several species prowl the Reikland, including the fierce Giant Wolves, which are captured and bred by Goblins to use as guards and mounts.

M	WS	BS	S	T	I	Ag	Dex	Int	WP	Fel	W
4	35	–	35	30	35	30	–	15	15	–	10

Traits: Armour 1, Bestial, Night Vision, Skittish, Stride, Tracker, Weapon+6
Optional: Frenzy, Infected, Size (Large), Territorial, Trained (Broken, Drive, Fetch, Guard, Magic, Mount, War)

THE MONSTROUS BEASTS OF THE REIKLAND

Throughout the Reikland, all manner of large and dangerous monsters hunt, preying on the unwise and the unwary, dragging them back to their bone-lined lairs to be consumed at leisure.

BASILISKS

These eight-legged reptilian creatures are solitary and elusive. Claimed to be one of the most ancient creatures of Chaos, they are said to be filled with such spite and venom the very ground they walk on is poisoned. Their bite, too, is poisonous, but it's their petrifying gaze most fear. Rarely encountered these days, basilisks are a most dangerous foe. Their glands and organs are highly prized by wizards and alchemists, so opportunist hunters often chase rumours of Basilisks in the wild-places of the Vorbergland, though few return.

M	WS	BS	S	T	I	Ag	Dex	Int	WP	Fel	W
4	45	35	55	55	25	15	–	15	15	–	64

Traits: Armour 2, Bestial, Bite+9, Cold-blooded, Immunity (Poison), Infected, Night Vision, Petrifying Gaze, Size (Enormous), Stride, Tail+8, Venom, Weapon+9
Optional: Mutation, Territorial

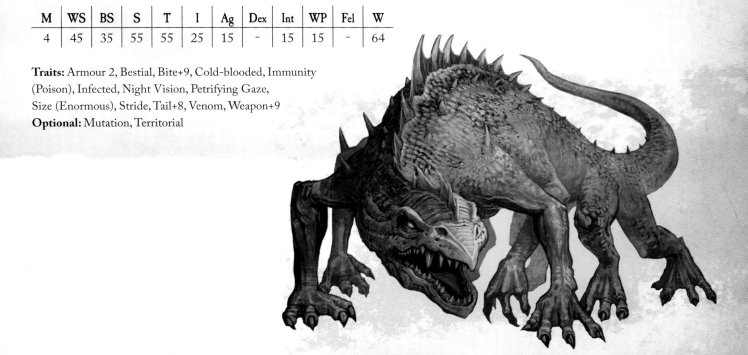

BOG OCTOPUSES

Bog octopuses skulk in shallow waters, usually in marsh and swampland. They await prey in perfect stillness, able to sense the vibrations of approaching creatures, then erupt from the muddy water, seeking to grapple and drown using their strong tentacles. Usually mottled green and brown, Bog Octopuses are perfectly camouflaged for boggy environments, their huge, limpid eyes often the only clue betraying their presence. Most have tentacles of twenty feet or so and a body some six-feet long, but stories claim they grow many times that size, especially if they have a regular supply of meat.

M	WS	BS	S	T	I	Ag	Dex	Int	WP	Fel	W
3	35	–	80	75	15	55	–	5	65	0	56

Traits: Amphibious, Bestial, Constrictor, Size (Large), Stealthy, Swamp-strider, 8×Tentacles+9
Optional: Size (Enormous–Monstrous), Territorial

CAVE SQUIGS

Squigs are large, generally round, fungoid creatures that live deep below ground in the dankest, darkest caves. They possess a gaping maw and large, sharp teeth, and are prized by Goblins for their flesh and their hides, and to act as guards and pets.

M	WS	BS	S	T	I	Ag	Dex	Int	WP	Fel	W
4	45	–	50	30	10	40	–	5	15	–	12

Traits: Bestial, Bounce, Infected, Night Vision, Weapon+9
Optional: Amphibious, Breath (Acid or Gas), Dark Vision, Frenzy, Fury, Horns, Size (Tiny-Enormous)

DEMIGRYPHS

With head of eagle and body of lion, demigryphs are powerful creatures with a noble bearing. They roam the forests and grasslands of the Empire, usually far from human habitation, hunting as individuals. Captive demigryphs are deployed by the Empire's doughtiest knightly orders as war mounts. Unlike larger monstrous mounts, which are generally taken when young or bred in captivity, the capture of a full grown demigryph is a rite of passage among some orders.

M	WS	BS	S	T	I	Ag	Dex	Int	WP	Fel	W
7	35	–	55	40	30	45	–	15	25	–	30

Traits: Armour 1, Bestial, Bite+9, Night Vision, Size (Large), Stride, Weapon+9
Optional: Trained (Broken, Drive, Guard, Mount, War))

DRAGONS

Dragons ruled the skies long before the elder species walked the Known World. While the Dragons of today are mere shadows of their ancient brethren, they remain some of the most powerful creatures known to the Empire. The few surviving elder dragons are terrifyingly immense and rarely rouse from their slumbers. Should a Dragon take umbrage with a small party of adventurers, it's time to run.

M	WS	BS	S	T	I	Ag	Dex	Int	WP	Fel	W
6	65	60	65	65	60	25	15	45	85	25	104

Traits: Armour 5, Bite+10, Breath+15 (various), Flight 80, Night Vision, Size (Enormous), Tail+9, Weapon+10

Optional: Arboreal, Immunity (choose one), Infestation, Magical, Mental Corruption, Mutation, Size (Monstrous), Spellcaster (various), Swamp-strider, Trained (Mount), Undead, Venom

FENBEASTS

Raised by spellcasters from the filth of marshes and bogs, Fenbeasts are seemingly mindless automatons held together by magic. Vaguely humanoid, they are comprised of mud, bones, branches, and slime, and require significant quantities of magic to retain their integrity. Occasionally, they are raised by wizards skilled in Jade magic to act as a bodyguard or to fulfil a specific task requiring brute strength or mindless killing. Sometimes they rise independently, spawned in stagnant festering pools where the flow of magic has been corrupted. The Jade College in Altdorf is said to maintain a score of the creatures as drudges, fetching and carrying for senior wizards, maintained by the ceaseless channelling of dozens of apprentices.

M	WS	BS	S	T	I	Ag	Dex	Int	WP	Fel	W
5	35	-	50	55	10	15	10	-	-	-	40

Traits: Construct, Dark Vision, Die Hard, Infected, Regenerate, Size (Large), Stupid, Swamp-strider, Unstable, Weapon+8

Optional: Frenzy, Hungry, Infestation, Territorial

FIMIR

Fimir are secretive, one-eyed, reptilian creatures that stalk the darkest recesses of the dank swamps and boglands of western Reikland. They shun sunlight, usually only appearing at dawn or dusk, or under the cover of mist and fog to spirit away victims for mysterious, loathsome purposes. Human witches reckless or desperate enough to meddle in the affairs of Daemons have been known to seek out the Fimir to learn their malign mysteries, for it is said they summon and control such entities. Whether the greater risk lies in trafficking with the Ruinous Powers, or treating with the Fimir, is anyone's guess. The Fimir have a matriarchal society. The leader of each clan is a powerful witch called a Meargh, and she's aided by a cadre of lesser spellcasters called Dirach. The majority of the clan members are lowly Shearls, who are protected by a warrior caste, the Fimm, who have bony spikes and knobs on their tails, used to break the bones of unwary opponents.

M	WS	BS	S	T	I	Ag	Dex	Int	WP	Fel	W
6	35	20	45	40	30	20	20	30	30	15	30

Traits: Armour 2, Cold-blooded, Night Vision, Size (Large), Swamp-strider, Weapon+8
Optional: Tail+7, Spellcaster (Daemonology)

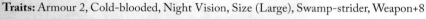

'We spent our honeymoon at the family's summer house by the sea. One morning, when taking the air along the bluffs, the mist closed in. It was suddenly calm and strangely quiet. Then, out of nowhere... Bog Daemons! Huge, one-eyed, barrel-chested brutes. I was sent crashing to the ground with a swipe of a tail. Another bundled Greta up and threw her over its shoulder. Then they just vanished into the mist, as swiftly and as silently as they had appeared. I swear that is Verena's own truth.'

– Oleg Grauhof, Reiklander Merchant, shortly before being hanged for the murder of his wife

GIANTS

Giants are solitary creatures who usually shun civilisation. Most stalk remote and high places surrounding the Empire, holing-up in caves and forgotten ruins far from smaller folk, though they sometimes migrate to the foothills in search of food. They have a reputation for belligerence and ferocity, due in equal parts to their intimidating size, their cattle eating, and their association with marauding Greenskin armies that enslave them. In truth, many giants are gentle souls, prone to raging tantrums and fiercely protective of their privacy, but not necessarily hostile to others. Because they are so long-lived, rumours suggest they hoard ancient lore, though most seem less than lucid, and certainly more interested in alcohol than debates about history.

M	WS	BS	S	T	I	Ag	Dex	Int	WP	Fel	W
6	30	30	65	55	30	20	15	25	25	20	72

Traits: Armour 1, Night Vision, Size (Enormous), Stride, Tough, Weapon+10
Optional: Bestial, Breath (Drunken Vomit), Hungry, Infected, Infestation, Size (Monstrous), Stupid

GRIFFONS

With the forequarters and wings of an eagle and the hindquarters of a great cat, Griffons are elegant beasts with a naturally proud and regal bearing. They nest high in the mountains that surround the Empire and are swift, efficient killers, not prone to the indiscriminate destruction of creatures like Manticores or Hippogryphs. Perhaps because of this seeming nobility, the image of the Griffon is extraordinarily popular in the Empire, used on heraldry, religious iconography, and as a symbol of the Empire itself. Griffons are also one of the most intelligent of beasts. If captured relatively young and subject to correct training, they can be incredibly loyal, able to anticipate and obey a wide variety of commands. They are so highly sought after that hunters regularly die trying to secure Griffon eggs to sell. Perhaps the most renowned Griffon in Reikland is Deathclaw. Housed in the Imperial Zoo in Altdorf, Deathclaw is personally owned by the Crown Prince of Reikland and was reputedly hatched by Emperor Karl-Franz himself — a story that led to all manner of lewd cartoons being printed in seditious pamphlets.

M	WS	BS	S	T	I	Ag	Dex	Int	WP	Fel	W
6	50	–	50	50	45	60	–	20	40	–	76

Traits: Armour 1, Bestial, Bite+9, Flight 80, Night Vision, Size (Enormous), Weapon+9
Optional: Trained (Broken, Guard, Magic, Mount, War)

HIPPOGRYPHS

Extraordinarily ferocious and territorial, Hippogryphs normally have the head, wings, and front quarters of an eagle and the hind quarters of a horse. Hailing most commonly from the Grey Mountains, they attack without provocation, almost reckless in their fury, tearing flesh into ribbons to be devoured later. Such is their rage, entire fields of livestock will be wiped out by a single Hippogryph, which will then make off with its choice of meat, leaving the rest to carrion birds. Having little in the way of intelligence, when Hippogryphs hunt, they tend to kill everything in sight, assuming anything unseen is gone forever, meaning that actual casualties to Hippogryphs are relatively low, given all it takes to avoid them is finding a good hiding place.

M	WS	BS	S	T	I	Ag	Dex	Int	WP	Fel	W
7	45	–	55	50	20	55	–	5	35	–	72

Traits: Animosity (Everything), Belligerent, Bestial, Bite+9, Flight 120, Night Vision, Size (Large), Stride, Territorial, Weapon+9
Optional: Broken, Frenzy, Fury, Hatred (Everything), Trained (Broken, Mount)

Hydra

The many-headed, lizard-like Hydra has a hulking body supporting a maze of necks and heads that breathe smoky fire and bite ferociously. A surprisingly tenacious and stealthy creature, Hydras will stalk prey for miles; however, they all too often lose patience and charge, heads roaring.

M	WS	BS	S	T	I	Ag	Dex	Int	WP	Fel	W
6	45	–	50	55	15	35	–	15	25	–	68

Traits: Armour 3, Bestial, Breath+10 (Fire), Constrictor, Night Vision, Regeneration, Size (Enormous), Stealthy, Stride, Tracker, Weapon+9
Optional: Belligerent, Territorial, Venom

Jabberslythes

The Jabberslythe is an ancient creature of Chaos that lurks beneath the shadowy eaves of the deepest, darkest forests. A maddening creature, the Jabberslythe is a disguisting mixture of Toad, Sludge-drake, and Insect, all filled with corrosive, black blood that spurts free at the slightest wound. Worse, any viewing this horror seem to lose their minds, gibbering and rhyming, clawing at their eyes, and shrieking with manic laughter, which leaves easy prey for the Jabberslythe.

Further, it has a sticky tongue that can lash out and pull its next meal into its gaping maw. As befits its appearance, the creature moves in a lolloping and awkward manner, and even possesses wings, though they're too small to properly lift its bloated torso.

M	WS	BS	S	T	I	Ag	Dex	Int	WP	Fel	W
7	45	40	55	50	20	35	–	10	20	–	68

Traits: Armour 3, Bestial, Bite +9, Bounce, Corrosive Blood, Distracting, Infected, Night Vision, Size (Enormous), Tail +8, Tongue Attack +5 (12), Venom, Weapon +9
Optional: Mutation, Territorial

MANTICORES

Fortunately rare, Manticores are unrelentingly ferocious, driven to clear their territory of predatory rivals with extraordinary brutality. This means you normally know when you're moving into the territory of a Manticore — corpses of other monsters litter the high grounds. The creature has the head and body of a twisted great cat (though sometimes its face appears almost too Human), the wings of a Bat, and a wicked, thrashing, barbed tail.

M	WS	BS	S	T	I	Ag	Dex	Int	WP	Fel	W
6	55	-	55	55	50	65	-	10	35	-	72

Traits: Armour 2, Bestial, Bite+9, Flight 80, Size (Enormous), Tail+8, Territorial, Venom, Weapon+9
Optional: Hatred (Predators), Mutant, Trained (Broken, Magic, Mount)

'When I was travellin' with the Elves to Ulthuan, I seen a great many things as would astound most folks back 'ome. One time I saw a Manticore, only in the centre of its lion-head it had the face of a great Elf! I suppose it was less a Manticore, than an Elf-ticore.'

– Adhemar Fitztancred, Grey Guardian, Raconteur and Liar

PEGASI

Pegasi are handsome white horses with great swan-like wings. They are dogged and inexhaustible flyers that fly in great herds in the high mountains, seemingly taking great delight as they swoop and swirl on the spiralling thermal currents. They are obvious candidates for steeds and many a warrior or scout has tried to catch a Pegasus of their own. They are very intelligent, and some believe they only allow themselves to be captured if they wish to be, which has led to all manner of fancifully romantic legends insisting only those worthy, or virtuous enough may be chosen.

M	WS	BS	S	T	I	Ag	Dex	Int	WP	Fel	W
8	35	-	45	40	30	45	-	20	25	-	28

Traits: Flight 100, Size (Large), Stride, Weapon+7
Optional: Trained (Broken, Drive, Magic, Mount, War)

'Ayup, the fields are lush round these parts, as it 'appens. It's the Pegasi, see. No need to buy manure for fertiliser, it falls from the 'eavens, like a gift from the gods. Mind, you don't wanna be standin' underneath the 'erds when they fly over. Messy. Very messy.'

– Berthold Bruner, Farmer and Pegasus-watcher

TROLLS

Trolls are filthy, foul creatures that infest all corners of the Old World. Quick to adapt to their surroundings they come in a variety of types, but all are huge and imposing. They are dim and led by their instinct for food, but they like to hoard and their lairs can be a trove of useful and valuable treasures… and the grisly remains of their meals. Although there are many species of Troll, they all share some common features: they are usually extremely stupid, which means any quick-witted foe can get an edge over them; they can regenerate, which makes them extremely difficult to kill; and they are able to regurgitate their last meal at will, vomiting acrid bile over a shockingly impressive distance — although they are loathe to do this as it leaves them extremely hungry.

M	WS	BS	S	T	I	Ag	Dex	Int	WP	Fel	W
6	30	15	55	45	10	15	15	10	20	5	30

Traits: Armour 2, Bite+8, Die Hard, Infected, Regenerate, Size (Large), Stupid, Tough, Vomit, Weapon+9
Optional: Amphibious, Bestial, Frenzy, Hungry, Infestation, Magic Resistance, Mutation, Night Vision, Painless, Stealthy, Swamp-strider

'I assure you, sir, we have done extensive surveys on this subject, and have lost some of our bravest taxonomists in this endeavour. There are precisely twenty-three varieties of Troll living in the Empire at this moment — including seventeen sub-varieties and two unverified sightings that are yet to be classified. This level of detail is exactly what the Imperial Society was set up to do; we know our figures are accurate.'

– Ignatius of Nuln, Man of Letters

GOING FOR A TROLL

There are a number of species of Trolls so you should feel free to customise them at will. Some of the Trolls most likely to trouble parties in the Reikland include:

Chaos Trolls: These bear one or more Mutations. These 'gifts' from the Dark Gods of Chaos make them especially dangerous and unpredictable. These unfortunate creatures are often pressed into the service of marauding chaos warbands, or Beastman Warherds — the more severely mutated the Troll, the greater the perceived favour of the Ruinous Powers, and the greater the value of the monster to its herd.

River Trolls: Skulking in the stagnant, foetid marshes of the Reik, River Trolls are an unfortunately common sight. They are opportunistic hunters, using their weed-like hides as they float like clumps of weed or flotsam, or lie in wait in muddy banks waiting for small boats or unwary travellers.

Stone Trolls: Rarely seen outside of the mountain ranges of the Empire, Stone Trolls have exceedingly tough hides that have ossified into rough, stone-like armoured plates, which both protect the troll from damage and help them blend into their surroundings. They make their lairs in caves and are one of the most common hazards encountered by those crossing the Grey Mountains.

WYVERNS

Although the uneducated often mistake them for Dragons, beyond their superficial similarities, foul-smelling Wyverns are nothing like those dignified creatures. Cowardly scavengers with weak eyesight, they tend to sate their rapacious appetites by picking off defenceless creatures — mostly sheep and goats — avoiding outright combat when possible. Unlike other monsters of the Mountains, Wyverns are not especially territorial, and tend to move on when their hunting grounds are invaded.

M	WS	BS	S	T	I	Ag	Dex	Int	WP	Fel	W
4	55	–	60	55	15	45	–	10	50	–	84

Traits: Armour 2, Bestial, Flight 90, Size (Enormous), Venom, Weapon +10
Optional: Breath (Venom), Horns, Mount, Tail+9, Trained (Broken, Guard, Magic, Mount, War)

THE GREENSKIN HORDES

Orcs and Goblins are the scourge of civilisation. They raid ceaselessly from their crude fortifications, most commonly warring amongst themselves, culling the weak and revering the strong. Inevitably, a Greenskin warlord will eventually arise from these internecine skirmishes and bind the neighbouring tribes under one banner. Then the drums of war sound, and the green tide swells once more, ready to wash over every village and town in its path, leaving nothing but blood and ruin in its wake.

ORCS

Orcs are nasty, brutal, belligerent, and almost immune to pain. They have muscular, hulking bodies, wide, powerful shoulders, and won't let a little thing like a lost arm get in the way of a good scrap. They are built for fighting and like nothing more than doing so. When they have no enemies to fight, they take on rival groups of Greenskins. If there is no rival group, they will fight among themselves. Though not as numerous as Goblins, they are bigger and tougher, and they let them know it at every opportunity. Orcs can grow to prodigious size, with larger Orcs stronger, tougher, and more aggressive, and therefore accorded more prestige: for might equals right in their warlike society. Some Orcs ride huge boars into battle, a sight that rarely fails to terrify.

M	WS	BS	S	T	I	Ag	Dex	Int	WP	Fel	W
4	35	30	35	45	20	25	20	25	35	20	14

Traits: Animosity (Greenskins), Armour 3, Belligerent, Die Hard, Infected, Night Vision, Weapon+8
Optional: Painless, Ranged+8 (50), Size (Large)

'We iz the best. We iz not dem weedie Gobbos or stoopid Trollz, we iz well 'ard! An' if anywun sayz we ain't, we iz gunna stomp on der edz.'

– Gurkk Skulltaka, Orc Boss

GOBLINS

Scrawny, spiteful, nimble, and intelligent, a Goblin's instinct for self-preservation should never be underestimated. Though cowardly, Goblins readily band together if this secures an overwhelming advantage in numbers. Goblins frequently join with Orc armies — not always by choice — opportunistically helping themselves to the spoils of war while others do most of the actual fighting.

M	WS	BS	S	T	I	Ag	Dex	Int	WP	Fel	W
4	25	35	30	30	20	35	30	30	20	20	11

Traits: Animosity (Greenskins), Armour 1, Afraid (Elves), Night Vision, Infected, Weapon+7
Optional: Arboreal, Dark Vision, Hatred (Dwarfs), Ranged+7 (25), Venom

'Goblins, sir, thousands of 'em!'
– Lieutenant Bromkopf, Reikland's 24th Regiment Foot

SNOTLINGS

Pea-brained creatures akin to enthusiastic, uncontrolled puppies, Snotlings are scavengers and natural mimics, picking up bones and shiny things wherever they go, or copying the actions of anything they see.

If pushed into conflict by Goblins or Orcs, they fight in stinking swarms, trying to overwhelm their foes through sheer weight of numbers. To do this they find all sorts of disgusting and noxious substances, like poisonous fungus and bodily waste, to hurl at their enemies.

M	WS	BS	S	T	I	Ag	Dex	Int	WP	Fel	W
4	25	15	25	20	20	30	-	15	30	-	7

Traits: Bestial, Dark Vision, Infected, Size (Small), Weapon+4
Optional: Broken, Swarm, Trained (Broken, Fetch, Guard), Venom

THE RESTLESS DEAD

Neither living, nor truly dead, the Undead are the animate corpses of once living beings, granted an unholy parody of life through the fell arcane discipline of Necromancy. The shambling hordes of the restless dead come in many forms, from the reanimated corpses of Zombies and Skeletons, to the shrieking, spectral Ghosts and Banshees, to the brooding, manifest evil of the Vampire Lords.

SKELETONS

Skeletons are the fleshless bones of those long dead, reanimated by dark magic to walk the earth as mockeries of the living. Those who died and were not laid to rest according to the rituals of Morr, the God of Death, may be resurrected in this form by a sufficiently powerful necromancer. Utterly mindless, Skeletons will fight until their bones are smashed to pieces. They have no courage for they have no fear. They cannot be killed because they are not alive.

M	WS	BS	S	T	I	Ag	Dex	Int	WP	Fel	W
4	25	25	30	30	20	20	25	–	–	–	12

Traits: Armour 2, Construct, Dark Vision, Fear 2, Painless, Undead, Unstable, Weapon+7
Optional: Corruption (Minor), Infected, Territorial

IT'S ALIVE! ALIVE!

Necromancers can raise and command the Undead, but they are, themselves, living mortals (albeit creepily morbid ones obsessed with conquering mortality). Use the Human attributes on page 311 and add *Spellcaster* (Necromancy) to create a Necromancer.

OPTIONS: DEM BONES

To reflect the bony nature of Skeletons, you may want to impose a penalty of –1 damage to Wounds inflicted by weapons without the Pummel trait.

'I raised the heavy lid expecting to find the glorious golden death mask of Khetanken. But we had been misinformed. A bony hand flew out and grabbed my neck. Startled, I dropped the lid, and the hand and lower arm were severed, trapping the undead creature within the sarcophagus.
'But it held on tightly, squeezing my neck so I could hardly breathe! I thought I was going to die. But Sister Celestine threw some of her sacred water over the thing, and it became lifeless once more.
'I use it as a back scratcher now.'

– Hubert Karter, Tomb Robber

ZOMBIES

Like Skeletons, Zombies are Undead creatures reanimated and bound together with foul magics. Unlike Skeletons, they are so recently dead that much of their corporeal body still exists, rotting and diseased flesh sagging over their maggoty, swollen organs. As they fight, their flesh and organs slough from their bones, releasing a nauseating, noxious stench, powerful enough to turn the stomachs of all but the most hardened of soldiers.

M	WS	BS	S	T	I	Ag	Dex	Int	WP	Fel	W
4	15	-	30	30	5	10	15	-	-	-	12

Traits: Construct, Dark Vision, Fear 2, Painless, Undead, Unstable, Weapon+7
Optional: Armoured, Corruption (Minor), Diseased, Distracting, Infected, Infestation, Territorial

UNQUIET DEAD

Any Undead creature with the Construct trait is magically bound together with sinews of dark magics. They are either mindless automatons reanimated by a necromancer, or those who came to unlife in a place where *Shyish*, the magical wind of death, or *Dhar*, vile black magic, gathers and stagnates, twisting death into something new.

DIRE WOLVES

When the earth gives up the dead, it is not just humans who rise; macabre parodies of Giant Wolves, with glowing eyes, and tatters of flesh falling from their rotting, festering carcasses, Dire Wolves prowl the night on behalf of their necromantic masters. In the Reikland, they are said to roam the haunted forests of the Hägercrybs when Morrslieb is full, running wild in search of prey to sate their insatiable hunger, cursed with an appetite for flesh and a heightened instinct for the smell of blood.

M	WS	BS	S	T	I	Ag	Dex	Int	WP	Fel	W
9	30	-	35	35	30	30	-	-	-	-	24

Traits: Armour 1, Construct, Dark Vision, Fear 2, Size (Large), Stride, Tracker, Undead, Unstable, Weapon+6
Optional: Corruption (Minor), Distracting, Infected, Painless, Territorial

CRYPT GHOULS

Some of the most pitiable creatures of the Old World, Crypt Ghouls are ugly, stooping creatures with sallow, filthy skin and sharp, yellow teeth capable of tearing flesh from their victims. Ghouls are drawn to the magical energies of *Shyish* and *Dhar*, which in practice means they gravitate to graveyards and crypts, and around battlefields.

M	WS	BS	S	T	I	Ag	Dex	Int	WP	Fel	W
4	30	-	35	30	30	35	25	20	20	5	11

Traits: Bite+5, Infected, Night Vision, Weapon+6
Optional: Bestial, Painless, Venom

VARGHULFS

Most Vampires balance their Undead need for blood with a veneer of civility and decorum, styling themselves as the aristocracy of the Undead. However, some eschew their human façade, embracing the beast within. These Varghulfs are savage and wild, creatures devoid of all sophistry, abandoned entirely to animalistic self-gratification. They manifest as a big, bloated, bat-like beast, basking in their base urge for blood.

M	WS	BS	S	T	I	Ag	Dex	Int	WP	Fel	W
8	55	-	55	55	30	50	20	10	60	-	42

Traits: Armour 1, Bestial, Bite+8, Fear 4, Dark Vision, Hatred (Living), Hungry, Regeneration, Size (Large), Terror 3, Undead, Vampiric, Weapon+9
Optional: Corruption (Minor), Flight, Frenzy, Fury, Territorial, Tracker

CAIRN WRAITHS

Cairn Wraiths are especially potent spirits, the spectral remains of aspiring necromancers who sought to prolong their existence through dark magic. In life they were strong-willed; in death their malevolent will drives them to exact a fearful vengeance on the burning souls of the living. Many such Wraiths haunt the mist-shrouded cairns that dot the landscape of the Empire, such as the fell Hägercrybs.

M	WS	BS	S	T	I	Ag	Dex	Int	WP	Fel	W
6	35	-	35	30	15	30	25	25	50	15	14

Traits: Chill Grasp, Dark Vision, Ethereal, Terror 3, Undead, Unstable, Weapon+9
Optional: Bestial, Champion, Painless, Territorial

TOMB BANSHEES

Tomb Banshees are the spectral remains of once powerful witches whose spirits are steeped in the foetid energy of *dhar*. Their restless afterlife is tormented by loss and bitterness, a yawning void in their souls that drives them to release terrifying, soul-wrenching howls potent enough to drive those hearing it insane, or even to stop their very hearts.

M	WS	BS	S	T	I	Ag	Dex	Int	WP	Fel	W
6	30	-	30	30	20	30	30	25	40	20	13

Traits: Dark Vision, Ethereal, Ghostly Howl, Terror 3, Undead, Unstable, Weapon+7
Optional: Bestial, Flight, Fury, Painless, Territorial

VAMPIRES

Vampires see themselves as the rulers of the night. Many can pass as Human, some even functioning for long periods amongst the living. Despite their outwardly Human appearance, no heart beats beneath their pale skin, and in lieu of mortal hungers they possess an abiding thirst for blood. All Vampires of the Old World are ultimately descended from ancient bloodlines that originated millennia ago far to the south. Many are fiercely proud of their heritage and the traits and traditions that set them apart from others. The Vampires of different bloodlines are often bitter rivals, but they are astute enough to come together when necessary to face greater foes.

M	WS	BS	S	T	I	Ag	Dex	Int	WP	Fel	W
6	60	40	50	40	50	70	40	40	60	40	19

Traits: Bite+8, Night Vision, Undead, Vampiric, Weapon+9
Optional: Bestial, Champion, Corruption (Minor), Dark Vision, Die Hard, Distracting, Fear, Flight, Frenzy, Fury, Hungry, Mental Corruption, Painless, Petrifying Gaze, Regeneration, Spellcaster (Death or Necromancy), Tracker, Wall Crawler

GHOSTS

Ghosts are the sprits of tormented souls who died with unfinished business. Much like Skeletons and Zombies, Ghosts may be summoned by Vampires or Necromancers, or may haunt areas suffused with *Dhar*. In exceptional circumstances, particularly driven spirits may claw their way from the Realm of Morr in pursuit of their own business, though such occurrences quickly draw the attention of the cult of Morr, or the wizards of the Amethyst Order. When summoned through the necromantic arts, Ghosts swarm together, forming great Spirit Hosts that swoop and plunge amongst their foes, spreading fear and disarray in their wake.

M	WS	BS	S	T	I	Ag	Dex	Int	WP	Fel	W
6	30	-	30	30	10	30	20	15	15	-	10

Traits: Dark Vision, Ethereal, Fear 2, Undead, Unstable, Weapon+6
Optional: Bestial, Fury, Hatred, Swarm, Territorial

SLAVES TO DARKNESS

Chaos. The very word is enough to send superstitious smallfolk scurrying for the temple of Sigmar, making the sign of the hammer as they flee. But, for all good citizens of the Empire fear Chaos invasion or Beastmen attack, the true danger lies within the Empire's borders; cultists lurk in basements, corrupt nobles treat with Daemons, and ignorant villagers make offerings of their mutated offspring rather than killing them swiftly, unwittingly swelling the ranks of armies of the damned.

BEASTMEN, THE CHILDREN OF CHAOS

Beastmen are grotesque hybrids of animal and Human. They consider themselves the true children of Chaos, blessed by the Dark Gods before all other species. Their savage herds stalk the forests, gathering numbers and worshipping at profane altars of stone daubed with excrement.

GORS

Gors, the most common Beastmen, haunt almost every forest of the Old World. Their appearance varies widely, but all combine bestial and Human traits, often with the heads and legs of Goats with the torso and arms of Humans. The only feature all Gor universally possess is a large pair of horns — the larger the better, for they denote status amongst Beastmen — a trait that distinguishes them from Ungor and Turnskins. The largest Gors are known as Bestigors.

M	WS	BS	S	T	I	Ag	Dex	Int	WP	Fel	W
4	45	30	35	45	30	35	25	25	30	25	14

Traits: Arboreal, Armour 1, Fury, Horns +6, Night Vision, Weapon+7
Optional: Armour 2, Corruption (Minor), Disease (Packer's Pox), Infected, Infestation, Mutation, Size (Large), Spellcaster (Beasts)

UNGORS

Ungors have vestigial or very short horns and are thus barely considered 'Gor' by the rest of the herd. Some even sport Human-like faces, making them effective infiltrators, but also a target for ridicule. Indeed, Ungors are poorly treated by the Gors, and are often stunted or malnourished in comparison to their larger-horned brethren, leaving them bitter creatures eager to take out their jealousy on others.

M	WS	BS	S	T	I	Ag	Dex	Int	WP	Fel	W
4	35	30	30	35	30	35	25	25	35	25	12

Traits: Arboreal, Night Vision, Weapon+6
Optional: Armour 1, Corruption (Minor), Disease (Packer's Pox), Infected, Infestation, Mutation, Ranged+7 (25), Size (Small)

MINOTAURS

Massive and hulking, bull-like Minotaurs tower above even the greatest Bestigors. Herds with a large contingent of Minotaurs consider themselves especially blessed by the Dark Gods. Beastmen herds congregate around the Minotaurs as their imposing presence gives the lesser beasts courage.

M	WS	BS	S	T	I	Ag	Dex	Int	WP	Fel	W
6	45	25	44	45	20	35	25	20	30	15	30

Traits: Horns+9, Hungry, Night Vision, Size (Large), Weapon+9
Optional: Arboreal, Belligerent, Corruption (Minor), Disease (Packer's Pox), Fury, Infected, Infestation, Mutation

BRAY-SHAMAN

Bray-Shaman are born with the instinctive ability to wield the powers of Chaos, which they deploy with terrifying capability. Uniquely amongst Beastmen, they need never defend themselves from other members of their herd, as none would dare harm a Bray Shaman, as they are believed to speak the will of the Dark Gods themselves.

M	WS	BS	S	T	I	Ag	Dex	Int	WP	Fel	W
4	40	30	30	45	40	35	25	30	50	30	16

Traits: Arboreal, Corruption (Minor), Fury, Horns+6, Night Vision, Spellcaster (Beasts, Any Chaos, Death, or Shadow), Weapon+7
Optional: Disease (Packer's Pox), Infected, Infestation, Mutation, Size (Large)

CULTISTS, THE LOST AND THE DAMNED

Like a rotten beam beneath white-washed walls, a terrible enemy lurks unseen within the Empire. In every province and town, men and women are seduced by the subtle lures of Chaos, tempted by the promise of power, knowledge, strength, or release.

MUTANTS

One of the most tragic fates to befall a Human is to succumb to the mutating influence of Chaos. It can happen without rhyme or reason, and even babies can be born mutated. When such happens, many parents find they cannot summon the will to murder their children, so instead abandon their offspring to the woods, either to die or be taken in by other Mutants or Beastmen. No matter how innocent they may be, all mutants are a source of terror for the common folk, so most fall to the Dark Gods, abandoned and embittered, or end it all before it's too late.

M	WS	BS	S	T	I	Ag	Dex	Int	WP	Fel	W
4	30	30	30	30	30	30	30	30	30	30	12

Traits: Corruption (Minor), Mutation, Weapon+7
Optional: All Creature Traits

OPTIONS: THE ENEMIES WITHIN

Cultists and Mutants tend to hide in plain sight, and most are, or were, ordinary members of society. As such, the **Peoples of the Reikland** guidelines for creating NPCs on page 311 provides an alternative starting point.

CULTISTS

For those untainted by the blight of Chaos, it appears horrifyingly alien, but to those it affects, every step towards damnation, every idea bringing them closer to Chaos, seems not only logical, but inevitable. Some especially devout followers of proscribed cults are granted 'gifts' by their gods; foul mutations that will ensure their deaths should the witch hunters unearth their secret.

M	WS	BS	S	T	I	Ag	Dex	Int	WP	Fel	W
4	30	30	30	30	30	30	30	30	30	30	12

Traits: Weapon+6
Optional: Armour 1, Corruption (Minor), Mutation, Spellcaster (Chaos)

CHAOS WARRIORS

Heavily armoured hulking brutes adorned with ornate spikes and eye-watering symbols of their gods, Chaos Warriors are clearly no longer Human. Nothing is left of their former lives, they exist to serve their dark patron and nothing more. While most Chaos Warriors are exalted marauders from lands far to the north, a select few cultists may be gifted a prize of Chaos Armour by the Dark Gods, affording them great power at the cost of never removing the armour for as long as they live. As few warriors are their better, and no knight better protected, their lives are often very long indeed.

M	WS	BS	S	T	I	Ag	Dex	Int	WP	Fel	W
4	55	30	45	45	45	55	30	35	55	25	17

Traits: Armoured 5, Champion, Corruption (Minor), Weapon+8
Optional: Belligerent, Disease, Distracting, Frenzy, Mental Corruption, Mutation, Spellcaster (Chaos)

'In the dreaded north lies the greatest danger. It is the product of another place, another time, released upon us by the misfortune and mistake of long-dead gods. It hungrily grasps for our world, quivering with expectation, sending forth hordes of the most warlike and jealous people of them all: our own kin, the tribes of Man.'

— Phitzer, Wissenlander Witch

DAEMONS, THE GIBBERING HOSTS

Daemons are blasphemous horrors from the Realms of Chaos, the unholy will of the Chaos Gods made manifest. In the Reikland, Daemons likely only appear if summoned by Cultists of the Ruinous Powers. Though their presence is unlikely to last for long as the material realm abhors their existence, the havoc they wreak is so profound that none who encounter Daemons ever forget the mind-fracturing experience.

While most Daemons owe allegiance to one of the four Chaos Gods, some are simple beasts of the Aethyr, possessing no particular will of their own, spilling forth into the Old World in a frenzy of mindless destructiveness whenever they can. Only four samples of Daemons are given here — two Lesser Daemons and two Daemon Princes — but any other Daemon you require can easily be built using Creature Traits.

BLOODLETTERS OF KHORNE

Khorne's chosen, Bloodletters stalk the battlefields of the Old World, taking skulls and lives in honour of the Blood God. Sharp, needle-like teeth protrude from monstrous, horned visages. Their blood-red skin is hard as brass, forged upon the anvil of ceaseless war. Each Bloodletter bears a Hellblade, a wickedly sharp blade steeped in gore, which it wields with reckless abandon, surrendering itself to the sweet sensation of senseless slaughter.

M	WS	BS	S	T	I	Ag	Dex	Int	WP	Fel	W
5	55	35	45	35	60	40	30	25	70	15	17

Traits: Armour 5, Champion, Claws, Corruption (Moderate), Daemonic 8+, Fear 3, Frenzy, Horns+8, Painless, Unstable, Weapon+9

DAEMONETTES OF SLAANESH

Like all creatures of the Prince of Pain and Pleasure, Daemonettes of Slaanesh are at once beautiful and horrifying. Possessing an unearthly allure that defies all sense and rationality, they render their enemies powerless to resist, so entranced are they by the profane sensuality of their monstrous forms. They have creamy, pale skin and large jet-black eyes. Wild, flowing, unnaturally coloured hair graces their delicate crowns. In lieu of hands their slender arms terminate in sinuous, crab-like claws.

M	WS	BS	S	T	I	Ag	Dex	Int	WP	Fel	W
4	60	50	40	30	65	60	35	30	70	45	17

Traits: Champion, Corruption (Moderate), Daemonic 8+, Distracting, Fear 2, Night Vision, Unstable, Weapon+9

DAEMON PRINCES

The ultimate goal of all champions of Chaos is apotheosis: to ascend to the rank of Daemonhood and serve their master for eternity as a Daemon Prince in the Realms of Chaos. Mighty figures of great power, Daemon Princes are terrible foes that even the greatest heroes of the Empire would balk to face.

Slenderthigh Whiptongue – Daemon Prince of Slaanesh

M	WS	BS	S	T	I	Ag	Dex	Int	WP	Fel	W
6	95	110	115	120	100	95	40	70	85	85	86

Traits: Armour 1, Champion, Corruption (Major), Daemonic 8+, Distracting, Horns+15, Night Vision, Size (Large), Spellcaster (Slaanesh), Terror 3, Unstable, Weapon+16

Fr'hough Mournbreath – Daemon Prince of Nurgle

M	WS	BS	S	T	I	Ag	Dex	Int	WP	Fel	W
4	70	35	120	150	50	20	30	85	120	50	108

Traits: Armour 4, Breath+12 (Corrosion), Corruption (Major), Daemonic 7+, Dark Vision, Disease (Itching Pox), Horns+14, Infected, Infestation, Size (Large), Spellcaster (Nurgle), Terror 3, Unstable, Weapon+15

THE LOATHSOME RATMEN

Skaven are a malevolent species of ratmen living beneath everyone's feet, watching, waiting, and impatient. They eke out a foul existence in the sewers and tunnels beneath the Empire's cities and are so rarely seen that those who do usually dismiss them as mere Beastmen or Mutants. Few ever suspect the sinister truth: an Underempire exists right beneath their feet, its tunnels stretching between every city of the Old World and beyond.

Skaven society is built on the backs of slaves captured from across the Old World. Supporting this, many shady Humans supply slaves and warpstone in exchange for unsavoury favours and secret knowledge: for the Skaven spy network is vast and pervasive.

Aware of the delicate position they inhabit, feasting on the subterranean entrails of other societies, the Skaven protect their secrets by any means necessary. Those foolish enough to talk openly of a complex civilisation of sentient ratmen beneath the Empire's cobbled-streets may find themselves dead in a gutter, an unfortunate victim of an unlikely accident.

'I never seen nothin'. There were no ratmen, you hear? Just bad luck. Wilbur slipped and fell, that's all. He got careless, fell down a ladder onto his own knife. Ten times. Just bad luck.'

– Kristiana Fellger, retired Sewer Jack

CLANRATS

Most Skaven are Clanrats, hailing from one of the many complex Skaven clans that constantly bicker, politic, backstab, and eventually war on each other. They generally act on the orders of higher-status Skaven, but are always looking for a way to secure a better position, most often by betrayal. They usually dress in mouldering leather or filthy cloth, with scraps of rusty and tarnished metal serving as makeshift armour. Clanrats are often sent out as scouts or raiders to scavenge for goods, search for warpstone, or raid for slaves.

M	WS	BS	S	T	I	Ag	Dex	Int	WP	Fel	W
5	30	30	30	30	40	35	30	30	20	20	11

Traits: Armour 2, Infected, Night Vision, Weapon+7
Optional: Disease (Ratte Fever), Mutation, Skittish, Stealthy, Tracker

STORMVERMIN

The elite fighters of the Skaven are the Stormvermin: bigger, stronger, tougher and more disciplined than Clanrats. They will serve as the core of any major assault and comprise the bodyguard of important Skaven. Stormvermin are usually well armed and armoured, sporting weapon combinations favoured by their clan.

M	WS	BS	S	T	I	Ag	Dex	Int	WP	Fel	W
5	45	35	35	35	55	50	30	30	25	20	11

Traits: Armour 4, Infected, Night Vision, Weapon+8
Optional: Disease (Ratte Fever), Mutation, Tracker

RAT OGRES

Rat Ogres are hulking brutes, bred in the dark caverns of the Underempire by the demented ministerings of Clan Molder's packmasters. They are stupid, but when driven by their Skaven masters are fearless and unrelenting in combat. Rarely encountered on their own, they tend to be accompany Grey Seers, or other ranking Skaven, serving as a bodyguard.

M	WS	BS	S	T	I	Ag	Dex	Int	WP	Fel	W
5	35	10	55	45	35	45	25	10	25	15	30

Traits: Armour 1, Infected, Night Vision, Size (Large), Stupid, Weapon+9
Optional: Corruption (Minor), Dark Vision, Disease (Ratte Fever), Infestation, Mutation, Tail+8, Tracker, Trained (Broken, Guard, Mount, War)

CREATURE TRAITS

These are the Creature Traits. Use them to create unique NPCs.

Afraid (Target)
The creature gains Fear (0) to the Target. See page 190 for Fear rules.

Amphibious
The creature is at home in water. It can add its Agility Bonus to the SL of all Swim Tests and move at full Movement through water.

Arboreal
The creature is at home in the forests. In the woodlands, it adds its Agility Bonus to the SL of all Climb and Stealth Tests.

Animosity (Target)
The creature dislikes the Target. See page 190 for Animosity rules.

Armour (Rating)
The creature is protected by armour or thick hide. It has Rating Armour Points on all Hit Locations.

Belligerent
The creature loves to win a fight. As long as it has more Advantage than its opponent, it is Immune to Psychology.

Bestial
The creature has no rational thought or language. It shies away from fire and gains a *Broken* Condition if struck by it. In defence, it only uses the Dodge Skill. If it loses more than half its Wounds, it will attempt to Flee unless protecting its young or cornered, or unless it has the *Territorial* Trait. If so, it enters Frenzy (see page 190). Bestial creatures have no Fellowship characteristic.

Big
The creature is a large example of its species. It receives +10 Strength and Toughness, and −5 Agility.

Bite (Rating)
On its turn, the creature may make a Free Attack by spending 1 Advantage. The Damage of the attack equals Rating and *includes the creature's Strength Bonus already.*

FREE ATTACKS
A Free Attack is a normal Ballistic Skill or Weapon Skill attack that does not use your Action on your Turn.

Blessed (Various)
The creature is Blessed and can enact Blessings; the relevant deity is indicated in brackets.

Bounce
The creature can bounce high, perhaps with powerful limbs, magic, or stubby wings. When Charging or Running, it doubles its Movement Characteristic, and can ignore all intervening terrain and characters as it leap over them.

Breath Rating (Type)
The creature's breath is a powerful weapon. On its turn, for the cost of 2 Advantage, it can activate its *Breath* as a Free Attack. Choose 1 target it can see within 20+Toughness Bonus yards. All characters within Strength Bonus yards of that target are struck, as are all characters between the creature and the target. Perform an **Opposed Ballistic Skill/Dodge** Test against all affected targets (the creature's single roll opposed by each individual target). All targets that fail take Damage equal to the attack's Rating. Further, if the Trait is marked with any of the following types in brackets, apply the associated rules.

- **Cold:** Targets gain a *Stunned* Condition for every full 5 Wounds suffered (minimum of 1).
- **Corrosion:** All Armour and Weapons carried by affected targets suffer 1 Damage.
- **Fire:** Any Wounds caused ignore Armour Points. Targets gain an *Ablaze* Condition.
- **Electricity:** Any Wounds caused ignore Armour Points. Targets gain a *Stunned* Condition.
- **Poison:** Any Wounds caused ignore Armour Points. Targets gain a *Poisoned* Condition.
- **Smoke:** The area fills with smoke, blocking Line of Sight for Toughness Bonus Rounds.

The creature is immune to its own *Breath*. This attack is *Magical*.

Brute
The creature is heavy and brutish. It receives −1 Movement, −10 Agility, and +10 Strength and Toughness.

Champion
The creature is an extraordinarily skilled warrior. If it wins an Opposed Test when defending in melee combat, it can cause Damage just as if it was the attacker.

Chill Grasp
The creature's touch chills its enemy's souls. For the cost of 2 Advantage and its Action, it can attempt an **Opposed Weapon Skill/Melee or Dodge** Test. If it wins, its target loses 1d10 + SL Wounds with no modification for Toughness Bonus or Armour Points. This attack is *Magical*.

Clever
The creature is particularly sharp-minded. It receives +20 Intelligence and +10 Initiative.

Cold-blooded

The creature is cold-blooded and slow to react. It can reverse all failed Willpower Tests.

Constrictor

The creature can squeeze and crush its prey. Any successful roll to hit gives the target an *Entangled* Condition. The creature may then enter a Grapple if it wishes. See page 163.

Construct

The creature is a construct of magic, quite mindless, bound together with magical sinews. It has no Intelligence, Willpower, or Fellowship Characteristics, and need never Test them. If it has no wizard controlling it, or does not possess the *Territorial* Trait, it meanders mindlessly, following flows of ambient magic.

For the purposes of calculating its Wounds, it uses its Strength Bonus whenever Willpower Bonus is required. All its attacks are *Magical*.

Corrosive Blood

The creature's blood is corrosive. Every time its is Wounded, blood splashes free, and all targets Engaged with it take 1d10 Wounds modified by Toughness Bonus and Armour Points, to a minimum of 1.

Corruption (Strength)

The creature is tainted by Chaos, or perhaps suffused with Dark Magics. The Strength of the Corruption is marked in brackets. See page 182.

Cunning

The creature is exceptionally cunning. It receives +10 Fellowship, Intelligence, and Initiative.

Dark Vision

The creature can see in the dark as daylight.

Daemonic (Target)

The creature's essence is raw magic, and unholy ichor pumps through what passes for its veins. Daemonic creatures do not require the normal prerequisites for life: food, water, air…

All its attacks are *Magical*. Roll 1d10 after any blow is received, if the creature rolls the Target number or higher, the blow is ignored, even if it is a critical. Should the creature be reduced to 0 Wounds, its soul returns to the Realms of Chaos immediately, removing it from play.

Die Hard

No matter how hard the creature is hit, it gets back up. All Critical Wounds not resulting in death can be healed; just attach the requisite body parts to the correct places, perhaps with staples or large spikes to hold them in place, and it's good to go. Even 'death' may be 'healed' if the appropriate parts, such as a lost head, are attached to the body. If death occurs and all parts are in place, it may attempt a **Challenging (+0) Endurance** Test requiring an **SL of 6** at the start of every round for Toughness Bonus Rounds after death. If a Test is successful, the creature chokes back to life with 1 Wound.

Disease (Type)

The creature carries the disease listed. Others will have to Test as appropriate for Contraction. See page 186.

Distracting

The creature distracts or confuse foes, possibly exuding a soporific musk or nauseating reek, or maybe its appearance is bizarrely horrifying. All living targets within a number of yards equal to its Toughness Bonus suffer a penalty of −20 to all Tests. A target can only suffer this penalty once, no matter how many Distracting foes there are.

Elite

The creature is a hard-nosed veteran. It receives +20 to Weapon Skill, Ballistic Skill, and Willpower.

Ethereal

The creature's form is insubstantial, allowing it to pass through solid objects. It can only be harmed by Magical attacks.

Fast

The creature moves unexpectedly fast. It receives +1 Movement and +10 Agility.

Fear (Rating)

The creature causes supernatural Fear in other creatures, with a rating equal to its Rating. See page 190.

Flight (Rating)

As the creature's Move, it can fly up to Rating yards. When flying, it ignores all intervening terrain, obstacles, or characters. At the end of the move, it decides whether it has landed or is still flying. It can use this move to Charge. If it starts its turn flying, it must choose to Fly for its Move. If it cannot do this, the GM decides how far the creature falls (see page 166).

When targeting it, measure horizontal distance as normal, then increase range by 1 step. So, a Long Range shot would become Extreme Range, and if it was at Extreme Range it could not be shot at all.

When flying, it suffers a penalty of −20 to all ranged combat attempts as it swoops and wheels in the sky.

Frenzy

The creature can *Frenzy*. See page 190.

Fury

The creature can work itself into an all-consuming rage. It can spend all of its Advantage (minimum of 1) to become subject to *Hatred* to close combat opponents. If the creature has at least 3

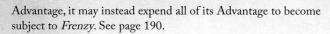

Advantage, it may instead expend all of its Advantage to become subject to *Frenzy*. See page 190.

Ghostly Howl

The creature can emit a chilling howl, capable of killing those who hear it. On its turn the creature can spend all its Advantage (minimum of 2), to unleash a hideous scream as a Free Attack.

All living targets within a number of yards equal to the creature's Initiative immediately gain 3 *Deafened* Conditions and suffer 1d10 Wounds ignoring Toughness Bonus and Armour Points. Those affected must also pass a **Average (+20) Endurance** test or gain a *Broken* Condition.

Hardy

The creature can sustain more damage than most. Increase its Wounds by a number equal to its Toughness Bonus (applied before any *Size* modifiers).

Hatred (Target)

The creature really hates the Target. See Hatred on page 190.

Horns Rating (Feature)

The creature has horns or some other sharp appendage (if its *Horns* Trait represents a different feature it will be noted in brackets). When the creature gains an Advantage for Charging, it may make a Free Attack with its Horns, performed as normal, using Rating to calculate Damage (its Strength Bonus is already included).

Hungry

The creature is always hungry for fresh meat. If it kills or incapacitates a living opponent (or encounters a fresh body), it must pass a **Average (+20) Willpower** Test or feast, losing its next Action and Move.

Immunity (Type)

The creature is completely immune to a certain type of Damage, such as poison, magic, or electricity. All Damage of that type, including from a Critical Wound, is ignored.

Immunity to Psychology

Whether brave, exceedingly stupid, or just caught up in the moment, the creature is utterly fearless. It ignores the Psychology rules. See page 190.

Infected

The creature, or its weapon, carries a nasty infection. If it causes a living opponent to lose Wounds, it must pass an **Easy (+40) Endurance** Test or contract a *Festering Wound* (see page 187).

Infestation

The creature's hide is infested with biting fleas or similar. All opponents suffer a penalty of −10 to hit it in melee combat as the parasites distract and overwhelm them.

Leader

The creature is a practiced leader. It receives a bonus of +10 to Fellowship and Willpower. **Note:** this Trait cannot be taken by creatures with the *Bestial* Trait.

Magical

The creature is wreathed in magic. All its attacks count as Magical, meaning it can harm creatures only susceptible to magical attacks.

Magic Resistance (Rating)

Magic has a reduced effect on the creature. The SL of any spell affecting it is reduced by the Rating given. So, *Magic Resistance 2* would reduce the SL by 2.

Mental Corruption

The creature has Chaos on the mind. Roll on the Mental Corruption Table found on page 185.

Miracles (various)

The creature can enact Miracles; the relevant deity is indicated in brackets.

Mutation

The creature is 'blessed' with a Mutation. Roll on the Physical Corruption Table found on page 184.

Night Vision

The creature has the *Night Vision* Talent. See page 141.

Painless

The creature feels no pain or can ignore it. All non-amputation penalties suffered from Critical Wounds are ignored, although Conditions are suffered as normal.

Petrifying Gaze

The creature's gaze can turn flesh to stone. For its Action, it can spend all its Advantage to unleash its gaze (minimum of 1). The creature performs an **Opposed Ballistic Skill/Initiative** test, adding 1 SL per Advantage spent. Its opponent gains 1 Stunned status per 2 SL by which it wins. If it wins by at least 6 SL, its target is permanently turned to stone.

If the target is a spellcaster, the test can be Opposed with Language (Magick) instead of Initiative as counter spells are cast.

Prejudice (Target)

The creature just doesn't like the Target. See page 190 for rules on Prejudice.

Ranged Rating (Range)

The creature has a ranged weapon. The weapon does Damage equal to the Rating and the range in yards is marked in brackets.

Rear

For its Move, the creature may make a Stomp attack if it is larger than its opponent (see *Size*).

Regenerate

The creature is capable of healing at an extraordinary rate, even regrowing severed parts. At the start of each round, if it has more than 0 Wounds remaining, it will automatically regenerate 1d10 Wounds. If it has 0 Wounds remaining, it will regenerate a single Wound on a 1d10 roll of 8+. If it ever rolls a 10 for regenerating, it also fully regenerates a Critical Wound, losing all penalties and Conditions associated with it. Any Critical Wounds or Wounds caused by Fire may not be regenerated and should be recorded separately.

USING SIZE

If you wish to use *Size* to make a creature bigger — for example converting a Giant Spider to a Gigantic Spider — then increase Strength and Toughness by +10 and reduce Agility by −5 per step of size you increase the creature. Reverse this if you wish to make a creature smaller.

Size (Various)

This trait represents creatures whose size differ from the game standard (i.e. roughly human sized). There are seven steps of *Size*, ranging from Tiny to Monstrous.

Size	Examples
Tiny	Butterfly, Mouse, Pigeon
Little	Cat, Hawk, Human Baby
Small	Giant Rat, Halfling, Human Child
Average	Dwarf, Elf, Human
Large	Horse, Ogre, Troll
Enormous	Griffon, Wyvern, Manticore
Monstrous	Dragon, Giant, Greater Daemon

Size Combat Modifiers

If larger:
- Its weapons gain the Damaging Quality if the creature is one step larger, and Impact if two steps or more larger.
- It multiplies any Damage caused by the number of steps larger it is (so, 2 steps=×2, 3 steps =×3, and so on); this multiplication is calculated after all modifiers are applied.
- All successful strikes against smaller targets activate the Deathblow rule, even if the target survives (see page 160).

If smaller:
- It gains a bonus of +10 to hit.

Defending Against Big Creatures

You suffer a penalty of −2 SL for each step larger your opponent is when using Melee to defend an Opposed Test. It is recommended to dodge a Giant swinging a tree, not parry it!

Fear and Terror

If the creature is perceived to be aggressive, it causes Fear in any creature smaller than it, and Terror in any creature two or more steps smaller. The rating of the Fear or Terror equals the Size step difference. So, if the creature is Large, and its opponent is Small, it will cause Terror 2. See page 191.

Moving in Combat

A creature that is larger ignores the need to Disengage if it wishes to leave melee combat; instead, it brushes smaller combatants out of the way, moving where it wishes.

Opposed Strength

During **Opposed Strength** Tests (and similar), if one creature is 2 or more size steps larger, it wins automatically. If one creature is 1 size step larger, the smaller creature must roll a Critical to contest the roll. If it does, SL are compared as normal. All other results mean the larger creature wins.

Stomp

Creatures that are larger than their opponents may make one Stomp as a Free Attack, by spending 1 Advantage, as they kick downwards or otherwise bash smaller opponents out of the way. This attack has a Damage equal to their Strength Bonus +0 , and uses Melee (Brawling).

Wounds

Larger creatures have more Wounds:

Size	Wounds
Tiny	1
Little	Toughness Bonus
Small	(2×Toughness Bonus) + Willpower Bonus
Average	Strength Bonus+(2×Toughness Bonus) + Willpower Bonus
Large	(Strength Bonus+(2×Toughness Bonus) + Willpower Bonus) ×2
Enormous	(Strength Bonus+(2×Toughness Bonus) + Willpower Bonus) ×4
Monstrous	(Strength Bonus+(2×Toughness Bonus) + Willpower Bonus) ×8

Skittish

The creature is easily scared by magic or loud noises. If such occurs, it receives +3 *Broken* Conditions.

Spellcaster (Various)

The creature can cast spells; the specific Lore of Magic will be indicated in brackets.

Stealthy

The creature is especially stealthy. It adds a number equal to its Agility Bonus to the SL of all Stealth Tests.

Stride

The creature has a long stride, perhaps because it is a quadruped or has especially long legs. Multiply Run Movement by 1.5 when Running.

Stupid

While not entirely devoid of self-awareness (and so lacking the Bestial trait), the creature is stupid. If it is near any allies without the *Stupid* Trait, they guide it and nothing happens. Otherwise, it must pass an **Easy (+40) Intelligence** Test at the start of each round, or become very confused. Should this occur it will drool, perhaps sitting down or picking its nose, doing little of use, losing both its Move and Action for that Turn.

Swamp-strider

The creature is at home in a swamp. It suffers no Movement penalties for moving through boggy ground.

Swarm

Swarms are large numbers of the same creature acting as one. The swarm counts as a single Creature that ignores the Psychology rules (see page 190), and can ignore the Engaged rules when using its Move. If the Swarm successfully strikes an opponent it activates the Deathblow rule (even if it has not killed its opponent — see page 160). All opponents Engaged with a Swarm automatically lose 1 Wound at the end of every Round as the Swarm overwhelms anything close. The Swarm has five times the Wounds of a normal example of the creature and gains +10 Weapon Skill. Any attempts to shoot the Swarm gain a bonus of +40 to hit. Swarms ignore all the *Size* Creature Trait rules.

Tail Attack (Rating)

The creature's tail is capable of sweeping foes from their feet. On its turn, it may make a Free Attack by spending 1 Advantage. The Tail does Rating Damage, *which includes its Strength Bonus already.* Opponents with a smaller *Size* than the creature, that suffer any Wounds from the attack, also gain the *Prone* Condition.

Tentacles (Rating)

The creature has a number of tentacles equal to #. It gains one Free Attack Action per tentacle. Each tentacle's attack does Rating Damage, *which includes its Strength Bonus already.* If it causes Damage, it can also give its opponent an *Entangled* Condition, which will initiate a Grapple between the target and that tentacle. If a tentacle is Grappling, use the tentacle's Free Attack Action to resolve that Grapple, not the creature's Action (see page 338).

Territorial

This creature is protective of a particular area or location. It will fight to the death to protect it and will not normally pursue enemies if they flee this area.

Terror (Rating)

The creature supernaturally causes bone-chilling *Terror* in other creatures, at the Rating given. See page 191.

Trained (Trained Skills)

This trait represents animals that have been trained through the Animal Training Skill. The skills the animal knows is marked in the brackets. Feel free to create your own trained skills.

Broken: The animal is trained to ignore its Bestial trait. It receives 2d10 Fellowship.

Drive: The animal is trained to pull a coach, cart, plough, buggy, or similar.

Entertain: The animal is trained to entertain others. It adds a +10 bonus to appropriate Entertain, Perform, or Play Tests.

Fetch: The animal is trained to fetch. This is normal reserved for Dogs and similar.

Guard: The animal is trained to stay in one place or prowl around as a guard, granting it the Territorial Trait.

Home: The animal is trained to return home if it is released or lost.

Magic: The animal is trained to ignore *Skittish* when it comes to magic, which is required for most horses used by Wizards.

Mount: The animal will accept a rider. Some creatures are especially belligerent, and will not accept a rider without the correct skill. So, to ride a Griffon, you need the Ride (Griffon) skill.

War: The animal is trained for war, gaining +10 Weapon Skill. It can also ignore *Skittish* for loud noises.

Tongue Attack Rating (Range)

The creature's prehensile tongue can wrap itself around prey, dragging it to a grisly end. On its turn, it may make a Free Attack by spending 1 Advantage. This is a ranged attack that does Damage equal to its Rating (the range is in brackets). If the attack hits, the target receives 1 *Entangled* Condition and, if a smaller *Size*, is dragged towards the creature, and is Engaged in melee combat. The creature can then choose whether to release the target, perform a Free Attack using its *Weapon* Trait, or to keep the target wrapped in its tongue, initiating a Grapple (see page 163).

Tough

The creature is more resistant to damage than normal, and unlikely to back down. It receives +10 Toughness and Willpower.

Tracker

Trackers are adept at following their prey, generally through scent or hearing. They add SL equal to their Initiative Bonus to all Track Tests.

Undead

The Undead are neither living, nor dead, meaning they are not reliant on the usual prerequisites for life: air, food, water… This Trait most commonly come into use when spells, miracles, or other abilities affect Undead only.

Unstable

The creature's corpus is maintained by foul magics that are inherently unstable in the material realm. Whenever it ends a Round engaged with any opponents with higher Advantage, the creature is driven back, and the magics holding it together weaken. It loses as many Wounds as the difference between its Advantage, and the highest Advantage engaged with it. So, if the creature had 1 Advantage, and its opponent had 3, the creature would lose 2 Wounds. If the creature ever reach 0 Wounds, the magics holding it in place collapse, and it 'dies'.

Vampiric

The creature feeds on blood and draws great physical strength from this act. Whenever it performs a successful Bite attack against an appropriate opponent, it heals as many Wounds as its opponent loses. Drinking blood in this way is the *only* way it can heal.

Venom (Difficulty)

The creature's attacks are poisoned or envenomed. When it causes Wounds, its opponent gains a *Poisoned* Condition. If no Difficulty is marked to resist the Venom, it is assumed to be Challenging. See page 169.

Vomit

The creature can spew a stream of corrosive corruption, dowsing its opponents in foul, semi-digested filth. On its turn, by spending 3 Advantage, the creature can activate its Vomit as a Free Attack. The creature chooses 1 target it can see within Toughness Bonus yards and lets loose; all targets within two yards are also hit.

The creature performs an **Opposed Ballistic Skill/Dodge Test** against all affected targets (its single roll opposed by each individual target). The Test is typically **Easy (+40)** for the vomiting creature, due to the close range, and **Challenging (+0)** for opponents. All losing targets suffer a hit with a Weapon Damage of the creature's Toughness Bonus +4 and receive a *Stunned* condition.

All Armour and Weapons carried by affected targets suffer 1 Damage as the acidic vomit corrodes it away.

Ward (Rating)

Perhaps because they are magical, wear a special talisman, or are just plain lucky, some blows just seem to miss. Roll 1d10 after any blow is received, if the creature rolls Rating or higher, the blow is ignored, even if it is a critical.

Wallcrawler

The creature can effortlessly scale vertical surfaces and even traverse ceilings, ready to drop on unwary prey. It moves at full Movement across any appropriate surface and automatically passes all Climb tests.

Weapon (Rating)

The creature carries a melee weapon, or uses teeth, claws, or similar in combat.

The weapon causes Damage equal to its Rating which *already includes the creature's Strength Bonus*. Typically it will be 4 + its Strength Bonus (representing a Hand Weapon).

Web (Rating)

The creature can create webbing to trap unwary foes. Whenever it successfully hits, opponents gain 1 *Entangled* status, with a Strength of the Rating given. See page 168.

WARHAMMER FANTASY ROLE·PLAY

Name _____ Species _____ Class _____

Career _____ Career Level _____

Career Path _____ Status _____

Age _____ Height _____ Hair _____ Eyes _____

CHARACTERISTICS

	WS	BS	S	T	I	Ag	Dex	Int	WP	Fel
Initial										
Advances										
Current										

FATE

Fate	
Fortune	

RESILIENCE

Resilience	Resolve	Motivation

EXPERIENCE

Current	Spent	Total

MOVEMENT

Movement		Walk		Run	

BASIC SKILLS

Name	Characteristic	Adv	Skill
Art	Dex		
Athletics	Ag		
Bribery	Fel		
Charm	Fel		
Charm Animal	WP		
Climb	S		
Cool	WP		
Consume Alcohol	T		
Dodge	Ag		
Drive	Ag		
Endurance	T		
Entertain	Fel		
Gamble	Int		

BASIC SKILLS

Name	Characteristic	Adv	Skill
Gossip	Fel		
Haggle	Fel		
Intimidate	S		
Intuition	I		
Leadership	Fel		
Melee (Basic)	WS		
Melee	WS		
Navigation	I		
Outdoor Survival	Int		
Perception	I		
Ride	Ag		
Row	S		
Stealth	Ag		

GROUPED & ADVANCED SKILLS

Name	Characteristic	Adv	Skill

TALENTS

Talent Name	Times taken	Description

AMBITIONS

Short-term _____

Long-term _____

PARTY

Party Name _____

Short-term _____

Long-term _____

Members _____

ARMOUR

Name	Locations	Enc	AP	Qualities

ARMOUR POINTS

01-09
☐
Head

10-24
☐
Left arm
(or secondary arm)

25-44
☐
Right arm
(or primary arm)

45-79
☐
Body

90-00
☐
Right leg

80-89
☐
Left leg

⬠
Shield

TRAPPINGS

Name	Enc

PSYCHOLOGY

CORRUPTION & MUTATION

WEALTH

D	
SS	
GC	

ENCUMBRANCE

Weapons	
Armour	
Trappings	
Max Enc.	
Total	

WOUNDS

SB	
TB×2	
WPB	
Hardy	
Wounds	

WEAPONS

Name	Group	Enc	Range/Reach	Damage	Qualities

SPELLS AND PRAYERS

Name	CN	Range	Target	Duration	Effect

Sin	

CONTINUE YOUR ADVENTURES WITH...

WARHAMMER FANTASY ROLE-PLAY

ROUGH NIGHTS & HARD DAYS

FIVE GRIM AND PERILOUS
SCENARIOS BY GRAEME DAVIS

Find out more about the adventures presented in **Rough Nights and Hard Days** as well as other marvellous game expansions and a host of additional resources at

www.cubicle7.co.uk

CUBICLE 7 SEVEN